THE QUOTABLE

Alexander H. Stephens

ᷰᷰ THE LOCHLAINN SEABROOK COLLECTION ᷱᷱ

SEA RAVEN PRESS

Thought Provoking Books For Smart People

SeaRavenPress.com

THE QUOTABLE

Alexander H. Stephens

Selections From the Writings & Speeches
of the Confederacy's First Vice President

Collected and Edited, with an Introduction and Notes, by

Lochlainn Seabrook

WINNER OF THE JEFFERSON DAVIS HISTORICAL GOLD MEDAL

SEA RAVEN PRESS, FRANKLIN, TENNESSEE, USA

THE QUOTABLE ALEXANDER H. STEPHENS

Published by
Sea Raven Press, PO Box 1054, Franklin, Tennessee 37065-1054 USA
www.searavenpress.com • searavenpress@nii.net

First Sea Raven Press Civil War Sesquicentennial Edition: March 2013
ISBN: 978-0-9858632-4-1
Library of Congress Catalog Number: 2013933443

The Quotable Alexander H. Stephens: Selections From the Writings and
Speeches of the Confederacy's First Vice President / collected and edited,
with an introduction and notes, by Lochlainn Seabrook. Includes
bibliographical references.

Front and back cover design, interior book design and layout, by Lochlainn Seabrook
Typography: Sea Raven Press Book Design
Front cover sketch: Alexander H. Stephens © Chris Rommel
All other images © Lochlainn Seabrook

The views on the American "Civil War" documented in this book are those of the publisher.

The paper used in this book is acid-free and lignin-free. It has been certified by the Sustainable Forestry
Initiative and the Forest Stewardship Council and meets all ANSI standards for archival quality paper.

PRINTED & MANUFACTURED IN OCCUPIED TENNESSEE, FORMER CONFEDERATE STATES OF AMERICA

Dedication

To my kinsman Alexander Hamilton Stephens.
We share the same ancestor—Edwin Stephens
of Lugwardine, Herefordshire, England—and
the same love of the American South and the
U.S. Constitution.

Epigraph

ON THE GOVERNMENT OF THE U.S. FOUNDING FATHERS

"Virtue affords the only foundation for a peaceful and happy government. When the wicked rule, the nation mourns. Not that rulers must necessarily profess religion by being attached to some visible church—but they must venerate it, and be men of the highest moral and political honesty. Disease and corruption affect the body politic and produce dissolution with the same certainty that they prostrate the physical powers of man. If the head is disordered, the whole heart is sick. If the political fountain becomes polluted, its dark and murky waters will eventually impregnate every branch with their contagious miasma. The history of the past proves the truth of these assertions; the passing events of the present day afford too frequent demonstration of the baneful effects of intrigue and peculation. Without virtue our union will become a mere rope of sand, the victim of knaves and the sport of kings. Self-government will become an enigma with monarchs, rational liberty a paradox, and a republic, the scoff of tyrants. Let every freeman look to this matter in time. Let him look back to the sages who wisely conceived, nobly planned, and boldly laid the foundations of the freedom we now enjoy, but which cannot, will not be perpetuated unless we imitate their examples and obey their precepts. They were virtuous, many of them devotedly pious, and all of them politically honest."

Levi Carroll Judson, 1839
(Pennsylvania attorney and Freemason)

Contents

List of Illustrations

Notes to the Reader

🖐 Vice President Stephens' words have been printed here exactly as they appear in the original manuscripts, including typographical and grammatical peculiarities inherent to both Stephens and to 19th-Century American writing and speaking (including long paragraphs). Stephens' quotes are marked with a traditional Victorian "hand" pointer. My explanatory comments appear in italics above Stephens' quotes, and my clarifications are in brackets within his quotes. Where applicable, entries are in chronological order.

🖐 Between his letters, speeches, and books, Stephens left behind a truly voluminous corpus of writings. For this volume, as with my companion work, *The Alexander H. Stephens Reader*, I have selected excerpts from those writings that I feel best represent the Confederate vice president's views, beliefs, and opinions.

Concerning the illustrations of individuals in this particular work, I chose them because they are either mentioned by Stephens in his writings and addresses, or because they had a profound impact on his life in some way. As such, though some are alphabetized, they are not placed in any particular order.

🖐 As always, I have identified unnamed or ambiguous individuals, events, items, and places for my foreign readers, many who may not be familiar with American history.

🖐 Stephens' use of the words *Federal* and *Federation* bear explanation, as they have meant different things at different periods in history. Indeed, there is so much confusion surrounding these words that to this day they continue to be defined differently in different countries. In the U.S. the word federal is a conflation (abbreviation) of the original word confederal, and federation is a conflation of the original word confederation.

Thus, the sense in which the Vice President used these two words is immediately clear: For 19th-Century Americans, "federal" referred to a conservative, even libertarian, form of government. For Stephens then, a federation was identical to a confederation or rather a confederacy: a small weak central government operating under the auspices of strong independent sovereign states—preferred by men like Thomas Jefferson, Patrick Henry, and Jefferson Davis.

Again, in 19th-Century parlance, the opposite of a federation would be a nation (or something akin to an empire): an all-powerful government ruling over weak dependent states—preferred by men like John Adams, Daniel Webster, and Abraham Lincoln. Thus we would call the U.S. Federalists of Stephens' day Conservatives and the U.S. Nationalists of his day Liberals. Stephens himself sometimes also referred to his liberal foes in government as "Centralists" or "Consolidationists," due to their desire to do away with states' rights completely and unify all political power in the central government. (As Stephens himself often complained, the definitions of these words were further confused when Liberals among the Founding generation hijacked the word "Federal" [i.e., Confederal or Confederate] and changed its meaning to "National.")

⛾ In connection with the previous topic, in any study of the "Civil War" it is vitally important to keep in mind that the two major political parties were then the opposite of what they are today. The Democrats of the mid 19th Century were conservatives, akin to the Republican Party of today, while the Republicans of the mid 19th Century were liberals, akin to the Democratic Party of today. Thus the Confederacy's Democratic president, Jefferson Davis, was a conservative (with libertarian leanings); the Union's Republican president, Abraham Lincoln, was a liberal (with socialistic leanings).

⛾ The cause of the "Civil War" (in essence, the South's limited government conservatism vs. the North's big government liberalism—or what Stephens called "Constitutionalism vs. Centralism") continues to this day. Now it is a war of words rather than of weapons. The pro-North movement will stop at nothing to suppress the facts about Lincoln's War and prevent you from learning what really happened between 1861 and 1865. As Stephens himself said: "Our opponents will leave no stone unturned, no lie untold, and no dollar they can raise unspent." As a result of their nefarious efforts, their version of events, the *Northern* version of Lincoln's War, has long been accepted as the final word. However, the pro-South movement is coming to life once again after 150 years of near dormancy, and, as a Southern historian, I am proud to be doing my part to preserve authentic American history for future generations through my literary works. For those interested in the Truth about the War for Southern Independence (that is, the *Southern* version of Lincoln's War on the Constitution and the American people), please visit the online store of my publisher, Sea Raven Press, where you will find a complete list of my titles, along with book descriptions and purchasing information.

SeaRavenPress.com

Introduction

M y cousin Alexander Hamilton Stephens is one of my favorite historical figures. Not merely because I descend from the Stephens family, but because he was an outstanding individual who stood with the Constitution, the Southern people, and the Confederacy against big government liberal Abraham Lincoln and his progressive meddling Yankee constituents.

Stephens is all the more remarkable due to his life story. Born in poverty on February 11, 1812, at Crawfordville, Wilkes (now Taliaferro) County, Georgia, he was an orphan by the age of fourteen, after which his family home was sold and he went to live with relatives. Despite the hardships of his early childhood, his native intelligence, eloquent mannerisms, and spiritually elevated heart drew attention, support, and aid from those around him, even complete strangers.

After attending school, paid for by numerous benefactors, he entered the law profession, blossoming into a successful and prosperous attorney. As his reputation rose, so did his income, with the modern equivalent of $2,250,000 coming from his writings alone. After buying back his childhood home (one of his lifelong dreams), he restructured it, then opened it up to all classes and races of men, including his critics and enemies. All were welcomed. Indeed, it was more like a complimentary bed and breakfast than a true home, which is why he named it "Liberty Hall."

A generous philanthropist who took care of his family members, friends, and servants into old age, he was understandably known as the "stay of the weak and helpless and friend of all the world." Indeed, following the teachings of the Master of Galilee, he gave unstintingly to those in need, even those who had done nothing to earn his charitableness. At one time or another, for example, he paid for the entire college education of over 100 youngsters, giving away most of his fortune to others before he died. According to some accounts, his body servant was wealthier than Stephens at the time of the Confederate vice president's death in 1883.

Stephens' inner life was as fascinating as his outer life. For example, he was obsessed with dogs, the weather, being at home on his estate, the Constitution, and his younger half-brother Linton (the child of his father's second wife). When Linton passed away in 1872, the regal statesman seemingly lost the will to live. Stephens saved himself by returning to politics, an occupation he detested, but which gave his life a sense of purpose and meaning.

Like all of the truly great historical personages, Stephens was a man of contradictions: a passionate, sociable individual who craved companionship and loved family life, he never married and bore no children: believing that he was destined to live a short life as an "invalid," he did not want to burden a wife with either his care or with unnecessary sorrow. Thus, despite having fallen deeply in love with at least two women that I am aware of, he consciously chose to live out his days as a bachelor—no doubt one of the most difficult and heartbreaking decisions he was ever forced to make.

Another contradiction: obsessed with health, the hypochondriac was almost always unwell, for he sabotaged his own efforts by smoking, poor diet, and overwork, often staying up until well after midnight to finish work projects, receive and pamper guests, read newspapers, write letters, and hold political meetings.

A devout Christian and well versed Bible reader, he never promoted any particular Christian denomination, and eschewed the blind paganistic devotion of Jesus that is so common to the orthodox and spiritually immature. As he put it: "I have always had such an aversion to what I consider the cant of religion." Instead, like fellow Southerners Robert E. Lee and Stonewall Jackson, Stephens followed Jesus' simple teachings and strove to be Christ-like. "True religion" is merely "a change of heart from evil to good," Stephens once said.

One of only a tiny minority of Southern leaders who actually defended slavery (in his case, using the Bible), he gained a reputation in the North for being a racist and an anti-abolition "slave-hound." On a personal level, however, the truth is that no white Southern slave owner was ever more kindly disposed toward African-Americans, and certainly none were ever so loved and respected by their own black servants than was Stephens.

Not only did he treat them as literal family members (and they him), when it came to various freedoms he gave them wide latitude, permitting them to come and go as they pleased, marry and bear children, educate themselves, go to church, celebrate holidays, and attend parties and dances both on and off his property. During the months the Southern conservative was away in Richmond or Washington fighting the advocates of Monarchy and Liberalism, he turned over his plantation and his home entirely to his slaves, who ran them both like a well oiled military machine. They did far more than just simple maintenance, however. They also took care of his guests, crop lands, and pets, kept up his paperwork, and in general saw to it that all of his affairs remained in perfect order.

During Lincoln's War—which Stephens commonly referred to as an "unholy crusade" and a "monster evil"—like 95 percent of all Southern blacks, his servants remained loyal to both Stephens and the Southern Cause. After the War, every single one of his slaves chose to stay on with him, despite the fact that they were now free to pursue their own individual lives. In May of 1865, when Stephens was illegally arrested and taken North, his servants wept tears of sadness. Upon his release from prison and return home five months later, they wept tears of joy.

As was the custom in the Old South, he supported all of his former slaves into their dotage, kindly permitting them to live and farm on his property until their deaths. In the postwar world he renounced his earlier biblical defence of the North's "peculiar institution" (both the American slave trade and American slavery got their start in Massachusetts), and campaigned for full civil rights for all races. At his funeral in 1883 thousands of blacks showed up to pay their final tribute to the man they considered the kindest and most charitable in all of Georgia.

So much for the "bigoted fiend" and "racist author of the infamous Cornerstone Speech," as uneducated pro-North writers like to call him.

One more striking contradiction: though he abhorred both politics and politicians, he himself was involved in the running of government for most of his adult life: not only was he put forth as a candidate for both U.S. president and C.S. president (positions which he immediately turned down), he served an astonishing thirteen terms as a U.S. Congressman, one term as vice president of the Confederate States of America (a republic he helped found and whose Constitution he helped write), and a partial term as governor of Georgia. As he said many times, he did not enjoy any of this. He did it out of an innate love for justice, constitutional values, and the American people.

If Stephens' life bore one tragedy, it derived from his views on secession, that great states' right that he called "the Continental Regulator." Though he viewed secession as the foundational principle of the U.S. government, and indeed fervently defended it from the 1830s until his demise in 1883, he did not approve of it as a legitimate reason to break up the Union over the election of Abraham Lincoln in 1860. This caused him to be misunderstood in both the South—where he came to be regarded by many as a "Southern Yankee," and in the North—where he was seen as a "Northern Dixiecrat." As such, he was criticized by portions of both sections. An attempt was even made on his life by a fellow Southerner, who, like many others South of the Mason-Dixon line, believed he had betrayed Dixie.

Though seen as a traitor to the Confederate states by some Southerners and a traitor to the United States by some Northerners, in the end Stephens proved them all wrong when he penned his life's work, *A Constitutional View of the Late War Between the States*—without a doubt the most thoroughly convincing defense of the Founding Fathers' principles ever written.

By the time you reach the last page of this book, it is hoped that you will have come to love this celebrated Georgian as much as I do. While he was indeed a product of his time (as we all are), politically speaking he stood squarely for Truth, which he called "fixed, inflexible, immutable, and eternal; unbending to time, circumstances, and interests"; changeless ideas concerning the Constitution and the natural rights of men and women; rights that are just as important and relevant now as they were in the Victorian Era.

Thank God for individuals like my cousin Alexander Hamilton Stephens. During his seventy-one years he slowed the Northern Liberals' consolidation of governmental power and helped foil their all-out attempt to forge an empire over the grave of what the Founding generation originally intended to be a "Confederate Republic." If only we had more politicians like him today. Fearless, moral, incorruptible men and women who hold the Constitution in higher regard than their popularity at the polls.

Lochlainn Seabrook
Franklin, Williamson County, Tennessee, USA
March 2013, Civil War Sesquicentennial
Luke 17:20-21

Historical Time Line

1812 - Alexander Stephens is born on February 11 at Crawfordville, Wilkes (now Taliaferro) County, Georgia. His parents, Andrew Baskins Stephens and Margaret Grier, name him after his paternal grandfather, Alexander Stephens, a native of England.

1812 - Three months after his birth, Stephens' mother Margaret dies on May 12.

1814 - Stephens' father Andrew remarries to Matilda Lindsay, producing two half-sons and one half sister.

1823 - July 1 Stephens' younger half-brother Linton Stephens is born. It was with Linton that the unmarried Alexander would form the strongest and most enduring relationship he would ever experience.

1823 - In September both Stephens' half-brother Benjamin Bullock Stephens (born 1821) and his half-brother Andrew Baskins Stephens (born 1819) die.

1825 - Stephens only full sister, Mary Stephens (born 1807), dies.

1826 - May 7 Stephens' father Andrew dies.

1826 - May 14 Stephens' step-mother Matilda dies.

1826 - Following the deaths of his parents, the Stephens family home is sold. Stephens, age fourteen, is now a homeless orphan. His uncle, General Aaron W. Grier of nearby Washington, Georgia, takes the boy in. His brother, two stepbrothers, and stepsister are sent to live with other relatives.

1826 - Stephens attends school in the winter and works on his uncle's farm in the summer.

1826 - A local educator, Charles C. Mills, recognizing Stephens' above average faculties, loans the youngster the money to attend the Academy at Washington, Georgia, considered "one of the best classical schools in the state." Here he falls under the tutelage of the esteemed clergyman Reverend Alexander Hamilton Webster. So enamored was Stephens of Webster that he gave himself the middle name "Hamilton."

1828 - Continuing on with his education, Stephens enters college at the State University at Athens, Georgia, in August. (It is today known as Franklin College of Arts and Sciences.)

1832 - Stephens graduates from college with "the highest honors," and begins his teaching career at Madison, Georgia. Miserable, he leaves after only four months.

1833 - Stephens takes up teaching school in Liberty County, Georgia.

1834 - May 26, Stephens embarks on a study of law and is soon working as an attorney at Crawfordville, Georgia. Self-taught, he stations himself at the local sheriff's office, a man to whom he gives legal advice in exchange for a room. While there he clerks for the sheriff as well, gaining much experience in accounting and other detailed administration work.

1834 - July 22, twenty-two year old Stephens is admitted to the bar. His first year as a lawyer he earns $33.00 a month, or about $400.00 a year. He soon finds himself working in the court at Washington, Georgia.

Mid 1830s - Stephens, a book worm, lives alone, is poor, sickly, and friendless. Yet, over time he develops himself into a well respected and influential lawyer.

1836 - The naturally small framed, boyish looking Stephens—who stands five foot, seven and a half inches tall and sports a 20 inch waist—tips the scales at a mere 96 pounds, the most he would ever weigh. For the rest of his life, often mistaken for a teenager, strangers would call the diminutive Georgian "sonny."

1836 - Against his wishes, Stephens' friends nominate him for the lower branch of Georgia's general assembly. To his surprise, he is elected for a four year term. He is now a member of the Georgia House of Representatives and the recently created Whig Party. (Unbeknownst to him, he would serve in the U.S. government, in one capacity or another, from President Andrew Jackson to President Chester A. Arthur, a span of forty-seven years.)

1836 - Despite numerous bouts with pneumonia and "attacks of bilious fever," Stephens rises up the ranks of his profession, and is soon known as a fierce debater, inspirational orator, and an ingenious scholar with a splendid memory.

1837 - Now twenty-five, Stephens becomes the legal guardian of his half-brother Linton Stephens. He sends the youngster through school and serves as his father-figure until Linton's death after a short illness in 1872. (Linton was an accomplished lawyer and legislator himself, one who spent some twenty-five years in Georgia politics. Frail and sickly like Alexander, unlike Alexander, Linton married several times and had three children with his first wife Emmeline Bell. A fellow Southern conservative, Linton served with distinction in the Confederate army, rising to the rank of lieutenant colonel.)

1837 - Stephens is "utterly prostrated by disease" and is confined to bed for months. Unable to move his legs, he must be carried from room to room "like a child."

1837 - During the summer he manages to gain enough strength to travel in the Georgia mountains, where the fresh air and scenic views help build his health back up. However, now a "confirmed dyspeptic," he continues to eat very little, surviving mainly on a diet of bread and milk.

1838 - In April, after another round of ailments, he takes a sea voyage to Boston, Massachusetts, in an effort to recover his health. From Boston he travels to New York, then back south, where he spends time rehabilitating at the Green Briar White Sulphur Springs resort in Virginia—a favorite haunt of numerous other famous Southerners, among them future Confederate General Stonewall Jackson.

1839 - During the summer Stephens is reelected to the Georgia legislature, and, despite his afflicted condition, attends sessions during the winter. This year he appears before the public for the first time to deliver a speech at Charleston, South Carolina. The audience is mesmerized by the contrasts between his tiny emaciated frame, modest dress, attractive melodious high pitched voice, oratorical talents, and great intellectual powers.

1840 - This summer Stephens is once again reelected to the Georgia legislature.

1841 - Stephens declines reelection, resigns from politics, and focuses on his now very successful law practice, which is growing exponentially each year. His health has improved, but he continues to suffer from severe headaches and digestive problems.

1842 - Stephens is elected to the State Senate, but becomes bed ridden for six weeks due to an abscess of the liver.

1843 - In October, without his knowledge or approval, Stephens' friends nominate him, as a Whig, for the first time to the United States House of Representatives. He reluctantly accepts and wins the election after a brilliant debate with his primary opponent, Democratic Senator Walter T. Colquitt. Thus, with the 28th Congress, begins Stephens' nearly lifelong career as a congressman.

1843 - Stephens' only full brother, Aaron Grier Stephens (born in 1810), dies.

1843 - Shortly after his triumphant election, Stephens is taken ill yet again, this time nearly dying. Diagnosed as a hepatic, he is put on nitric acid.

1844 - Though he was not ambitious, by now Stephens has become rather famous, financially secure, and the bearer of numerous friends and admirers.

1844 - December 19 Stephens comes out publicly in favor of the annexation of Texas.

1845- Stephens, a dyed-in-the-wool states' rights advocate, finds he has many differences with his party, the Whigs.

1845 - Stephens has finally saved enough money to achieve his boyhood dream: buying back his childhood home, sold after his father died in 1826. In 1875 he removes part of the main structure and builds "Liberty Hall" in its place, where he lives for the rest of his life. Several thousand acres originally accompanied the large home, which is today a National Historic Landmark near Crawfordville, Georgia.

1845 - Stephens is elected to his second term as a Georgia state representative, this time in the 29th Congress.

1846 - June 16 Stephens publicly voices his opposition to the Mexican-American War, which he believes was started unconstitutionally by then U.S. President James K. Polk, as part of a general American plan of empire building.

1847 - Stephens is elected to his third term as a Georgia state representative, this time in the 30th Congress.

1847 - Around this time Stephens challenges fellow Georgian Herschel V. Johnson to a duel over a dispute concerning the Mexican-American War. Johnson refuses. The pair do not reconcile until 1855, when Johnson is elected governor of Georgia (a position Stephens himself would hold many years later).

1848 - On September 4, at Thompson's Hotel in Atlanta, Georgia, an unarmed Stephens is attacked by a knife-wielding Georgia politician, Judge Francis H. Cone, who accuses Stephens of being "a traitor to the South." Though Stephens manages to keep his assailant at bay for a few moments with an open umbrella, Cone, who is twice the size and weight of Stephens, quickly overpowers him, throws him to the ground, and plunges the knife into his chest, severing an intercostalery artery. As he is about to cut Stephens' throat, Stephens grabs the blade of the knife with his bare hand, and throws Cone off. His right hand badly mangled, the two scuffle until Stephens is rescued by onlookers. Stephens' life is saved only by the "fortunate presence of Dr. Hitchcock of the United States Army." Stephens, ever the exemplary Christian, forgives his attacker and he and Cone later become good friends.

1848 - Stephens' resolutions on the Mexican-American War turn into the Whig platform in the presidential campaign in November.

1848 - Stephens promotes the nomination and election of Whig candidate Zachary Taylor, who becomes America's twelfth president.

1849 - Stephens is elected to his fourth term as a Georgia state representative, this time in the 31st Congress.

1850 - Strongly pro-Union, Stephens, while supporting the right of secession, declares his opposition to the growing secession movement in the Southern states. A supporter of the Clay Compromise, he accurately predicts the coming "Civil War."

1850 - During the Georgia State Convention, December 10-14, Stephens switches his allegiance to the newly formed Constitutional Union Party (also known as the Union Party), which—along with Robert A. Toombs and Howell Cobb—he helped launch. The party's nonpartisan platform is based on strict adherence to the Constitution in the hopes of maintaining the Union.

1851 - Stephens is elected to his fifth term as a Georgia state representative, this time in the 32nd Congress.

1851 - Stephens aids in the election of Constitutional Union Party candidate Howell Cobb to governor of Georgia, a win for the Unionists, a defeat for the Secessionists.

1851 - Stephens becomes gravely ill (possibly due to nephritic calculus) and, for the next three months, is carried gently about his house by his favorite servant, Harry Stephens. Stephens weighs only eighty pounds.

1852 - The Constitutional Union Party, created by Stephens, Toombs, and Howell, dissolves. (Note: the party would resurface in 1859 in an attempt to gain the White House in the 1860 election. Made up of former Whigs and Know-Nothings, it nominated John Bell of Tennessee for president and Edward Everett of Massachusetts for vice president; hence its other name, the Bell-Everett Party. With the election of Lincoln and the secession of the

Southern states, the party broke up in early 1860.)

1852 - Stephens comes up with the idea of a great birthday celebration for George Washington. On February 22, Washington's birthday, Stephens delivers a forceful speech at Baltimore, Maryland. In it he sternly reminds the country of our first president's warning to avoid "entangling alliances" with foreign nations.

1852 - The Whig Party nominates General Winfield Scott as its presidential candidate. But Scott refuses to endorse Henry Clay's Omnibus Bill, which Stephens supports. Faced with choosing between Whig Scott and Democratic candidate Franklin Pierce [a Conservative of the day] that November, Stephens decides to support the Independent Whig Party's nominee, Daniel Webster of Massachusetts. Webster, however, dies shortly before the election is held (Stephens casts his vote for him nonetheless), and Pierce goes on to win the election, becoming America's fourteenth president.

1853 - Though he has never been in complete agreement with the Whig Party, Stephens considers it the lesser of two evils. He switches his allegiance back to it, and for a brief time he and Toombs try to revive the party. But with the emergence of the new Republican Party (the Liberals of the day), the effort fails and Stephens joins the Democratic Party (the Conservatives of the day). (Note: after the Whig party completely disintegrates, many former members join the Know-Nothing Party—which Stephens opposes due to its secretiveness and its intolerant stance toward Catholics and immigrants. When the Know-Nothing Party dissolves, its members join the party of white supremacy at that time: the Republican Party, the Liberals of the day, headed by arch white supremacist and big government Liberal Abraham Lincoln—a man who campaigned for American apartheid his entire life.)

1853 - Democrat Stephens [a conservative] is elected to his sixth term as a Georgia state representative, this time in the 33rd Congress.

1853 - June 9, Stephens is riding in a train near Macon, Georgia, when it derails. He receives numerous injuries, including a broken collarbone, a crushed left elbow, and a "severe gash" on his head. He is bedridden for the entire summer.

1853 - During the Fall Stephens suffers from another attack of liver disease.

1854 - Stephens helps secure the passage of Northern Democrat Stephen A. Douglas' Kansas-Nebraska Act, which opens up new Western lands for development and gives settlers the choice of whether to practice or prohibit slavery in their respective territories and states.

1855 - Stephens, who is more popular than ever and is heralded at numerous public dinners held in his name, is elected to his seventh term as a Georgia state representative, this time in the 34th Congress.

1856 - Stephens votes for Democratic candidate James Buchanan during the presidential election this year, though his support for him is only lukewarm. Buchanan becomes America's fifteenth chief executive.

1856 - June 28 Stephens gives a speech before Congress defending slavery as a biblically sanctioned institution.

1856 - In July Stephens' half-brother John Lindsay Stephens (born 1815) dies.

1856 - An angry Stephens challenges Georgia politician Benjamin H. Hill to a duel over political differences. (After Stephens left the Whig Party for the Democratic Party, Hill accused him of having "betrayed the Whig Party and having acted worse toward it than Judas Iscariot.") Hill declines the challenge and the fight never materializes.

1857 - Stephens is elected to his eighth term as a Georgia state representative, this time in the 35th Congress.

1857 - Stephens' half-sister Catherine Baskins Stephens (born 1816) dies.

1858 - March 10, Stephens makes the famed Lecompton Report.

1859 - On February 12 Stephens gives what he believes will be his last speech before the U.S. Congress.

1859 - In March, with the close of that Congress, homebody Stephens officially retires from politics to once again become a private citizen—with no intention of ever returning to public service. He returns to "Liberty Hall."

1859 - As early as the winter of this year, Stephens' name is brought forward as a Democratic [Conservative] candidate for the following U.S. presidential election in November 1860. He has no interest in the position and discourages his supporters from placing his name on the ballot.

1860 - Near the end of July Stephens is walking out the front door of his home in Crawfordville, Georgia, when the heel of his shoe catches on the carpet strip in the hallway. He trips and falls down eight feet of stairs, landing face first on the "hard gravelled ground." The fall, which Stephens called "frightful," left him with bruises all over his face and injured wrists and hands.

1860 - Stephens comes out against what he considers secessionist extremists at the Charleston Convention, and supports Northern Democrat Stephen A. Douglas (a Conservative of the time) for president in the November election. Unfortunately for America, the victory goes to a little known big government Liberal from Illinois, Abraham Lincoln. Pro-Union Southern conservative Stephens observes the ascension of "Dishonest Abe" and the beginning of the secession of the Southern states on December 20 with horror and dread.

1861 - January 19 Georgia secedes from the Union, and Stephens, who regards his home state as his country, reluctantly leaves with it.

1861 - February 4 Stephens attends the Montgomery Convention (of the Southern states), and is placed on the committee to create the Constitution for the South's newly formed republic: The Confederate States of America, or C.S.A.

1861 - On February 9, after drawing up the rules for the Confederate Congress, Stephens is unanimously elected vice president of the C.S.A. under the provisional Confederate Constitution. (Note: South Carolina delegates had wanted Stephens to be president, but Stephens himself favored Robert A. Toombs. Stephens declined the position, considering it "inappropriate," as he was against secession.)

1861 - February 11, forty-nine year old Stephens is inaugurated vice president of the C.S.A., serving under Democratic President Jefferson Davis.

1861 - March 21 Stephens delivers his "startling" and infamous "Cornerstone Speech" at the Athenaeum in Savannah, Georgia. It is misunderstood by many, as it still is to this day.

1861 - November 6 Stephens is elected vice president of the C.S.A. under the permanent Confederate Constitution.

1861 - Stephens' portrait is engraved on the new Confederate twenty-dollar bill.

1862 - Stephens, a strict constitutionalist who places principle above expediency, finds that he differs greatly in opinion from that of other members of the Davis administration, including President Davis himself. Stephens is particularly disturbed by the Confederacy's erosion of states' rights and personal constitutional rights, as well as issues concerning the military draft, taxes, suspension of the writ of *habeas corpus*, and martial law in the South.

1863 - During the summer Stephens makes numerous diplomatic attempts to put a stop to Lincoln's War. He also seeks to arrange a prisoner exchange program between the C.S. and the U.S. Heartless warmonger Lincoln refuses to see him, or even let him come to Washington, D.C.

1864 - March 16 Stephens gives a speech before the Georgia legislature censuring the administration of Confederate President Jefferson Davis. Stephens increasingly feels that the policies of the Confederacy are at odds not only with the Constitution, but with a successful prosecution of the War. Mistaken as being anti-South, some begin calling him a "Southern Yankee."

1865 - February 3 Stephens, along with two Confederate colleagues, attends the Hampton Roads Conference, in which the three men meet with Lincoln face to face. During the meeting Lincoln admits that he had not wanted to issue the Emancipation Proclamation, and only did so as a "military measure" in an effort to cripple the Southern "rebellion." Lincoln also states that his main goal is to bring the Southern states back into the Union. After reunion, he promises, they can defeat the proposed Thirteenth Amendment and go back to practicing slavery if they so desire. But the Yankee leader demands an "unconditional surrender" from the South, something that Stephens will never agree to. The meeting fails and the War continues for another two months.

1865 - In February, fully aware that the South is about to be beaten, Stephens returns to his home in Georgia to await his fate.

1865 - April 9 Confederate General Robert E. Lee surrenders his army at Appomattox, Virginia. Lincoln's War is over.

1865 - Lincoln is assassinated April 14, and dies the next day.

1865 - May 11 Stephens is illegally arrested at his Georgia home, "Liberty Hall," on a charge of "treason" by U.S. authorities, and shipped northward with President Davis and several other Confederate officials.

1865 - May 25 Stephens is imprisoned at Fort Warren, Boston Harbor, Boston,

Massachusetts. A private citizen who is being held unlawfully in a military prison, the political prisoner is denied *habeas corpus*, a crime under the U.S. Constitution.

1865 - On October 13, without a trial or explanation, Stephens is released from prison on "parole" after a stay of five months, two days.

1865 - Before returning home, he stops in Washington, D.C. to pay his respects to the new U.S. president, Andrew Johnson of Tennessee.

1865 - Upon his arrival in Georgia, Stephens is urged to return to his old job in the U.S. Congress, or accept the governorship of his state. He turns down both offers.

1866 - In January, Stephens, again contrary to his wishes, is elected a U.S. senator from Georgia. Due to the North's cruel and illegal "Reconstruction" policies, however, he is not allowed by the Senate to take his seat (former Confederate officials were forbidden to hold public office at this time).

1866 - February 22 Stephens speaks before the Georgia legislature, promoting "submission, courage, and hope," as well as full civil rights for African-Americans.

1866 - April 16-17 Stephens is summoned to Washington, D.C., where he is ruthlessly interrogated before the U.S. Reconstruction Committee of Congress.

1867 - Stephens begins work on the first volume of his brilliant two-volume pro-South work: *A Constitutional View of the Late War Between the States*—which has been called "the most exhaustive and the most able defense of the secession of the Southern states in existence."

1868 - The first volume of *A Constitutional View* is published, and he begins work on the second volume.

1868 - Stephens is offered a professorship of political science and history by the University of Georgia.

1869 - During an accident in which a heavy gate falls on Stephens, his sciatic nerve is injured, resulting in an "acute attack" of inflammatory rheumatism. Now a cripple, from this time forward he walks on crutches and uses a roller-chair (now known as a wheel chair). The effects of both the accident and the illness keep him confined to his house for the following four years, and cause him to decline the professorship.

1870 - The second volume of *A Constitutional View* is published.

1870 - Late this year Stephens begins work on his book, *School History of the United States*.

1871 - Stephens, now a respected historian, becomes editor and part owner of the *Atlanta Sun* (in some sources it is called the *Southern Sun*).

1872 - July 14 Stephens' beloved half-brother Linton dies in Georgia after a brief illness, leaving behind two wives and three daughters (some sources say one son and two daughters).

1872 - Stephens finishes his book *School History of the United States*, and it is published and distributed throughout the Southern school system.

1873 - December 1 Stephens is elected to his ninth term as a Georgia state representative, this time in the 43rd Congress.

1873 - Stephens is given an honorary degree of LL.D. from Bowdoin College, and is selected to be an associate editor of Johnson's *Encyclopedia*.

1873 - Finding his editorial work at the *Atlanta Sun* ungratifying, he quits the paper, losing some $20,000 of his original investment.

1875 - Stephens is elected to his tenth term as a Georgia state representative, this time in the 44th Congress.

1875 - Stephens begins serving as a trustee of the University of Georgia, declining the offer of another position of professorship at the institution.

1877 - Stephens is elected to his eleventh term as a Georgia state representative, this time in the 45th Congress.

1879 - Stephens is elected to his twelfth term as a Georgia state representative, this time in the 46th Congress.

1881 - Stephens is elected to his thirteenth term as a Georgia state representative, this time in the 47th Congress.

1882 - This Spring Stephens' name is put forth as a candidate for governor of Georgia.

1882 - November 4 Stephens retires from Congress at the end of his thirteenth term.

1882 - November 4 Stephens is elected governor of Georgia by over a 60,000 majority.

1883 - Stephens completes and publishes his last book, *History of the United States*.

1883 - Sunday, March 4, a lifelong bachelor and childless,[1] but by now nationally celebrated, seventy-one year old "Little Alick" (as he was known to friends and family) dies in the governor's mansion at Atlanta, Georgia. His physician attributes his death to "the constant and excessive overtaxing of his brain." He is later buried on his estate, "Liberty Hill," near Crawfordville, Georgia.

South and North

"I think the [Liberals' big government political] system at the North is a failure. But our people [here in the South] are different. We have more virtue, and by far more political intelligence in the masses of our people than they have. The great body of our people are honest, industrious, frugal, pure, and not disposed to look to Government for anything but wise and equal laws. In other words, they look to Government for nothing but justice. At the North the great mass look to Government as a means for living by their wits in some way. Government with them is a license to rob and plunder in some way or other; and to get control of Government for these purposes is the highest object of their ambition. The people there, as well as their rulers, have been corrupted for years,—at least a large portion of them, if not the majority. The same thing is true of a portion of our people, and we have some corrupt leaders. But the great majority are not so. They understand their rights, and all they want of rulers is to give them good government." - A.H.S., 1862

Alexander H. Stephens

1

Personal Letters & Observations

Part One

From Stephens' diary (started in 1836) regarding his last day at the Roman Catholic Locust Grove Academy in 1827. He was fifteen or sixteen years of age at the time:

☛ "I well remember my feelings the last evening I was at that school. I remember how I gathered up all my things,—books, papers, slate-pencils, and ink,—put some in my basket and some under my arm, and then bade all good-bye. I reflected, as I walked along the path homeward, that this was the last time I should ever tread its beaten track, and the last day I should ever go to school. Life, I thought, was just then beginning to open before me. The next week I was to go to Crawfordville, to seek employment in a store."[2]

From a personal letter concerning his college days (1828-1832), Stephens wrote:

☛ "I cannot give either you or any one a full or exact idea of my college-days. They were by far the happiest days of my life. In memory they seem more like a dream than a remembered reality. The sudden change of my feelings after I left college and went out into the world was like the change wrought in tender and luxuriant vegetation by a severe and sudden frost. The very soul of my life seemed nipped and killed. All my days at college were pleasant. Not a word of censure, or even of reproof, was ever addressed to me by professor or tutor. I was on good terms with them all, and indeed seemed to be a favorite with all, from the president down. Dr. [Moses] Waddell, the president, seemed to be favorably impressed toward me from the day of my admission. . . .

"During the four years that I spent at college, I was never absent from roll-call without a good excuse; was never fined; and, to the best of my belief, never had a demerit mark against me in college or in the society—the *Phi Kappa*—to which I belonged. No one in my class, at any examination, ever got a better circular than I did. While I was on good terms with the faculty, I was on quite as good with the boys. I did not have a quarrel while I was there; and if there was one who disliked me, I did not know it. My room, from first to last, was the resort for a large number, more so than that of any other boy in my class. I enjoyed company very much. In my rooms we talked, laughed, told stories, and indulged in fun and good humor more than in any room in college. But there was never any dissipation in it: neither liquor nor cards were ever introduced; nor were indecent stories or jests ever allowed. My intimates and associates were a strange compound. Boys met there who never met nor recognized each other elsewhere; the most dissipated young men in college would come to my room, and there meet the most ascetically pious.

"I was always liberal in my boyish entertainments. I 'treated' as much in the way of fruit, melons, and other nicknacks in season as any other boy in college; and yet my average annual expenses were only two hundred and five dollars. My entertainments were of an inexpensive kind, but they were relished by all. Tobacco was not on my list. What I saved in hats, shoes, and clothes I spent in this way. It was not to gain popularity: I never thought of that; but only to give pleasure and entertainment to those about me; and I endeavored to do this as much by promoting agreeable conversation and cheerful social intercourse as by the little refreshments which were always to be found in my room in the proper season.

"Laughter, even though uproarious, in my room would never bring any of the faculty to look after it; nor were such bursts ever to be heard there at improper hours. Had such peals of merriment as were often heard there proceeded from other rooms, they would have excited suspicion that there was liquor about, and the matter would have been looked into; but I think no such suspicions were ever provoked by any mirthful demonstrations in mine, though there were many such during the four years, which seemed long years to me then, but short—how short! now."[3]

As a youth Stephens wrote these words to his younger brother Linton Stephens:
☛ "Life to me is desolate. For what object should I wish to live? Weak and sickly, I was sent into the world with a constitution barely able to sustain the vital functions. Health I have never known and do not expect to know."[4]

From Stephens' diary, May 2, 1834, as he began studying for the bar:
☛ "The morning of this day I employed profitably on the 10th, 11th, 12th, 13th, and 14th chapters of the 4th vol. of [Sir William] Blackstone. In the evening I did nothing, on account of having company, but read newspapers (for which, by the way, I have a passionate fondness), and conversed on various topics. My feelings and hopes seem ever to be vibrating and vacillating between assurance and despondency. My soul is bent upon success in my profession, and when indulging in brightest anticipations, the most trivial circumstance is frequently sufficient to damp my whole ardor and drive me to despair. This remark is founded on experience. The other day, as I was coming from my boarding-house in a cheerful, brisk walk, in high spirits, I was instantly laid low in the dust by hearing the superintendent of a shoe-shop ask one of his workmen, 'Who is that little fellow that walks so fast by here every day?' with the reply, in a sarcastic tone, 'Why, that's a lawyer!'"[5]

From Stephens' diary, May 3, 1834:
☛ "This day brother came to see me. In the evening we walked down to Mr. Brown's school-house, two miles distant, to attend the meeting of a debating society. Question for discussion: 'Which enjoys the more happiness, a farmer or a merchant?' I took some part in the debate. Spent the night with Major Guise. During the night there was a great fall of rain. However, we set out from his house after breakfast for Crawfordville, but finding the creek full, we had to wind and trapse about through the wet leaves and muddy ground before finding any log upon which we could cross. At this time my feelings were at a low ebb. It being Sunday, cloudy and rainy, and I wandering about on foot, with an old umbrella, trying to cross a creek! How ashamed I should have felt had I met one of my Athenian [school] friends! What conscious remorse I felt at my lowered situation! But my motto is, *Cedendum est fato*. He that exalteth himself shall be abased. The world must be taken as it comes and made the best of, as all other bad bargains. May be it . . ."[6]

From Stephens' diary, May 7, 1834:
☛ "This is the eighth anniversary of my father's death. The day never returns in each revolving year without bringing to my mind many sad reflections. I easily read the scenes, the griefs, the woes of which I keep it in

commemoration. But alas! the course of time is onward. And though at each return of the 7th of May I may seem as if moving in a circular motion, to be nearer the point and period of that memorable event than at other seasons of the year, yet this is only a delusion providentially afforded to soothe the soul with the pleasing hope of paying an annual visit to the shades of affliction and the place of bereavement. This day I finished the review of Blackstone's *Commentaries*. Spent part of the evening with Dr. [Leonidas B.] Mercer, who called on me. We examined some minerals he has. I was upon the whole well pleased with him. I shall cultivate his acquaintance."[7]

From Stephens' diary, May 12, 1834:
☛ "Have been reading to-day, but slowly. Crawfordville is a dry place. I do not feel satisfied. I have a restlessness of spirit and ambition of soul which are urging me on, and I feel that I am not in a situation to favor this inward flame. My desires do not stop short of the highest places of distinction. And yet how can I effect my purpose? . . . Poor and without friends,—no prospect of increasing my means,—time passing with rapid flight, and I effecting nothing! Day is succeeding day, and I do nothing but ponder over a few pages of my law, and mix with kind-hearted but uninformed people, who know very little themselves and can impart little or nothing to others! Oh, that I were able! I would seek society congenial to my feelings; I would converse with those who could entertain and instruct. Such once was my situation, but that day is gone, and its remembrance chokes my utterance!"[8]

From Stephens' diary, May 15, 1834. At the time he was working as an assistant to a town official at Crawfordville, Georgia:
☛ "I was for the first time offered pay for my legal services, but very gentlemanly refused [it]!"[9]

From Stephens' diary, May 17, 1834:
☛ "Brother is still with me. Have done nothing for the last two days. Had an introduction to a man to-day who [due to my appearance] addressed me familiarly as 'my son.' Such has often happened to me. Last fall, when I was in Savannah, I was asked by a youngster-candidate for the Freshman class if I were going to college, and I was more amused at the joke than surprised at the question, considering that my appearance is much more youthful than that of most young men of twenty-one. My weight is ninety-four pounds, my height sixty-seven inches, my waist twenty inches in circumference, and my whole appearance that of a youth of seventeen or eighteen. When I left college, two years ago, my net weight was seventy pounds. If I continue in a proportionate

Alexander Hamilton Stephens

increase I shall reach one hundred in about two years more."[10]

From Stephens' diary, May 18, 1834:
☛ "This is Sunday. Last night I and brother spent at Thomas Ray's. This morning was beautiful. The air was calm, clear, and serene; the sun shone warm and joyously. Brother and myself and Thomas rambled over the scenes of my early days, visited Father's grave, saw all the haunts of my boyhood, the fields in which I have labored, the trees I have planted, the rocks I have piled, the hedges in which I have reclined. Thought much of the past, of which I can

here give no utterance."[11]

From Stephens' diary, May 19, 1834:

☛ "Brother left me this morning. I am quite unwell. Inferior Court sat; no business. One case only, and it dismissed. Starvation to the whole race of lawyers! Read a little in [Thomas] Chitty, and did nothing as usual."[12]

From Stephens' diary, May 23, 1834:

☛ "I do detest vulgarity. Sometimes I almost have a contempt for the whole human race,—the whole appearing like a degenerate herd, beneath the notice of a rational, intellectual being. Sensuality is the moving principle of mankind, and the most brutish are the most honored. I long for a less polluted atmosphere. Of all things to me, an obscene fool is the most intolerable; yet such I am compelled to mix with daily. Will I never find one whose company will please me? No; of this I despair. I have once been so fortunate, but never expect to be again. My notion of merit is what is intellectual in its nature. I honor and long to be associated with the mind that soars above the infirmities and corruptions of human nature; that is far out of the region of passion and prejudice: that lives and moves and has its being in the pure element of Truth. But how revolting, how sickening to my feelings, how disgusting, how killing to my soul, to see beings bearing the majestic form of Man, possessing speech, reason, and all the faculties of an immortal mind, hopping and skipping all night to an old screaking fiddle like drunken apes, or lounging about a grog-shop from morn to eve, or wallowing, swine-like, in the mud and mire! 'O judgment, thou art fled to brutish beasts, and men have lost their reason!' But my feelings are taking me too far. The error is in nature; it must be pitied, not blamed. Perhaps I may appear as objectionable and as odious to others as others to me. But I do wonder if this poor world is thus always to remain! If low, degraded, selfish, lascivious, foolish, besottedly foolish men are always to figure most conspicuously here in it, or if there is any ground on which to rest the consolation of a hope for better things to come?"[13]

From Stephens' diary, May 26, 1834:

☛ "Did nothing to-day. Played chess in the morning. Got some notes to collect for the first time; find it a miserable business collecting money. Have a headache; but withal have this evening been pleased looking at the constant lightning in the east. I like, of a summer eve, when darkness prevails, to get to my window, and look upon the broad bosom of a cloud lighted up with successive coruscations of electricity. As I sit and behold one blaze begin and run from one extremity of the horizon to the other, and then disappear, leaving all in darkness, to be instantly followed by another on the same arena, my thoughts turn to the life of man and the history of nations. A burning genius bursts forth in the darkness of surrounding ignorance, and shines afar, but soon expires and sinks to nought, leaving darkness in his train. One nation, for the moment of a few short years, as our little republic is doing now, may prosper and flourish; but it is like the flash of the lightning, sublime in its passage, yet hastening to its end."[14]

From Stephens' diary, May 30, 1834:
☞ "Have read little or nothing, spending the day very unprofitably in chit-chat on various subjects. Examined some drawings representing the ancient statues, the Apollo Belvidere, Venus de'Medici, the Gladiator, Antinous, etc. With the Gladiator and Venus I am delighted; the muscular energy of the one, and the luxurious grace of the other, stand unrivalled in any specimens I have yet seen in nature or art. I think it a pity, but some of our fashionable [Southern] belles should take a lesson from this elegant form of true grace. If they could, I am persuaded that they would change their present disgusting waspish taste, and adapt their conformation to the lines and curves of natural beauty."[15]

From Stephens' diary, June 2, 1834:
☞ "It appears impossible for me to study. I supposed when I got this room that I should be by myself, retired from all noise and all company, and have an undisturbed time for reading, writing, musing, or doing anything else my inclination might lead to; but to my great disappointment and mortification, I am sometimes interrupted from morn till night, and do nothing the livelong day but jabber with each transient interloper who may be disposed to give me a call. I seem to be constitutionally unfortunate in this respect. When in college I was always pestered more with company and interruptions by incomers than any one student of my acquaintance. Frequently my chums have left the room to me and my company, as they would tell me in private, and sought retreat in some adjoining cloister to prepare their recitations, while I, as Horace on his walk to the gardens of Caesar, could have breathed a fervent prayer to Apollo or any other divinity for aid in obtaining a similar release."[16]

From Stephens' diary, June 3, 1834:
☞ "The railroad is the topic of the day. Some think it will be a profitable investment of capital; others fear to run the risks with their own pockets; while all seem very anxious that it may be effected by some means or other. For my own part, I must confess that my opportunities of gaining information on the subject have been so limited, and my judgment on such matters is so immature,

that I cannot say I have any decided opinion on the great question of interest. If, however, my premises are correct, I think the legitimate conclusion must inevitably follow in favor of the project. Railroads, it is true, are novel things in the history of man; and as yet so little experience has been had on their practicability as leaves the whole subject somewhat a matter of hazard. In my estimation, the greatest obstacle is the greatness of the enterprise. The stupendous thought of seeing steam-engines moving over our hills with the safe and rapid flight of fifteen miles an hour, produces a greater effect in the dissuasion of the undertaking than any discovered defect in the chain of arguments in its favor. Speed to the work. Ripe apples to-day for the first."[17]

From Stephens' diary, June 6, 1834:

☛ "I do wish I had an associate,—a bosom confidant,—an equal in every degree, neither above nor below, whose tastes and views were similar to my own, and whose business and pursuits were the same as mine. With such an one I could live and learn and be happy. But as it is, I sit in my room from morn till night, nor see nor converse with anybody of like tastes with myself. I try to read and advance in information, but having no person to converse with, to create interest, or elicit new thought upon the subject-matter of my studies, I find that I am not only failing to gather up new stores, but even permitting former ones to escape. . . . I have this day read in the *Southern Recorder* (the only paper I take, and devoted to State-rights) a chapter on cats, with which I was pleased, and which I hope long to remember."[18]

From Stephens' diary, June 7, 1834:

☛ "I have done nothing to-day but saunter about, loll on the bed, and chat foolishness. When will my days of folly pass and I be what I wish to be? This day I for the first time drew a plea in answer to a process, etc. It was for a Mr. James Brooker, sued in the Justice' Court. I was under considerable embarrassment; however, finally succeeded; but at this time have a most contemptuous opinion of myself. I believe I shall never be worth anything, and the thought is death to my soul. I am too boyish, childish, unmanful, trifling, simple in my manners and address. I must commence anew. Lethargy is my fatal fault. I am like the kite: I soar only in the rage of the gale. In the calm I sink into inactivity. I am like the flint which emits no spark unless brought into contact with something almost as hard as itself. I was made to figure in a storm, excited by continual collisions. Discussion and argument are my delight; and a place of life and business therefore is my proper element. Crawfordville is too dull. I long to be where I shall have an argument daily."[19]

From Stephens' diary, June 8, 1834:
☛ "Sunday.—In my room all day."[20]

From Stephens' diary, June 9, 1834:
☛ "Monday.—I to-day feel the ragings of ambition like the sudden burst of the long smothered flames of a volcano. My soul is disquieted within me, and there is an aching, aspiring thirst which is as indescribable as insatiable. I must be the most restless, miserable, ambitious soul that ever lived. I can liken myself to nothing more appropriately than to a being thrown into vacant space, gasping for air, finding nothing but emptiness, but denied to die. These are my intolerable feelings."[21]

From Stephens' diary, June 10, 1834:
☛ "The weather continues very warm; and whether it be the effect of external circumstances, or but one among other constitutional defects, I cannot tell, but I do have too contemptuous an opinion of this world to be entitled to the privilege of a resident. And were there any safe known passage to another, I should soon be making preparation for an exit, trusting to the probability of its being a better [world]."[22]

From Stephens' diary, June 17, 1834:
☛ "Tried this morning to borrow a horse to go to Uncle Grier's on business for Thompson, but was so disappointed as to fill me with mortification and a due sense of my humble dependence. Nothing hurts me worse than to ask and be refused. Therefore I had rather (and have often done it) walk than ask for a horse. I finally got O'Leary's, but could not return, on account of a heavy rain in the evening. I recollect that in 1826, on this day, we had a good rain, after a considerable drought."[23]

From Stephens' diary, June 20, 1834:
☛ "Read Blackstone in review. Had a visit from Dr. [Thomas] Foster, and promised him to deliver an oration on the Fourth of July."[24]

From Stephens' diary, June 25, 1834:
☛ "Went to a party at Mr. John Rogers's. Intolerably warm, but time spent very pleasantly. For the first time witnessed the new dance [the waltz, presumably, then of recent introduction] which disgusted me much. Oh, the follies of man, and how foolish are some of his ways! Returned in the evening, with a narrow escape of my life. My borrowed horse, a large and spirited animal, seldom used, having stood some time in the rain, and having been left

by his companions, upon my starting evinced a disposition to run, and I soon found that it would be impossible for me to manage him or hold him in. Off he went at full speed, passed gigs, carriages, and all wheeled vehicles. My umbrella fell, then my hat. Away we went, Gilpin-like, over logs and gullies, hills and valleys, for two miles before I could arrest him, when I was so exhausted as to be hardly able to dismount. During the whole danger I felt composed, and determined to exert myself to the last to keep the saddle,

Andrew Jackson

although I was conscious of my perilous situation, and thought of the instability of human affairs, and how soon I might be hurried from the scenes of mirth in which I had just been into eternity. This was a solemn reflection; and I have reason to be thankful that a kind Providence did not permit this danger to become a fatality."[25]

On July 3, 1834, Stephens, already a strong advocate of states' rights, wrote out his first political speech. The address, meant for a Fourth of July celebration, was not published until thirty years later. Nonetheless, it was as germane in 1864 as it was in 1834—and in 2013. After illustrating the relationship between the Articles of Confederation and the individual states, he goes on to discuss the "new" U.S. Constitution and the Union:

☛ "The Government has not even changed its name. Its powers were enlarged, but its character is the same; and the relations between the States and the Government have been multiplied, but the nature of those relations is unaltered. The new Constitution is a compact between the sovereign States separately, as the old Confederation was; and if this be so, and if the first Article of the Confederation expressly declares that sovereignty or supremacy is retained to the States,—denying the right or power of Congress to coerce or compel the States, the parties to it, to obey its edicts,—where is this right or power derived under the present Constitution? I am constrained to think that it is derived nowhere, and that it has its existence only in the breasts of the parasites of power who wish to overthrow the liberties of the people.

". . . That to some may appear a strange doctrine for the perpetuation of the Union of the States which allows one part to withdraw when under the feeling of oppression. But such err in their opinions on the strength of governments. The strength of all governments, and particularly republics, is in the affections of the people. A republic is a government of opinion,—it wavers and vacillates with opinion,—the popular breath alone is sufficient to extinguish its existence. Such is our Government. It was formed by each party entering it for interested purposes: for greater safety, protection, and tranquillity; and so long as these ends are answered, it will be impregnable without and within. Interest and self-preservation are the ruling motives of human action, and so long as interest shall induce the States to remain united, the Union will have the support and affection of the people. A separation need not be feared. But whenever the General Government adopts the principle that it is the supreme power of the land, that the States are subordinate,—mere provinces,—that it can compel and enforce, and commences to dispense its favors with a partial hand, to tax and oppress a few States to the interest and aggrandizement of the many, or otherwise transcend its powers,—then will the days of our republic be numbered. For it is false philosophy to suppose that these States can be kept together by force. Dangerous elements are not the less to be dreaded by a compression of the sphere of their action; neither are the energies of a people by an infringement of their rights. It is contrary to all observation on the conduct and motives of men. But let it be the established policy of the Government that it has no power over a State withdrawing from the Union when in her deliberate judgment the compact has been broken, and the others will soon cease, or rather never begin to oppress; for the Union should be an advantage to all, but an injury to none."[26]

From Stephens' diary, July 22, 1834:
☛ ". . . [I] was this day admitted an attorney at law, and released from a great burden of anxiety."[27]

From Stephens' diary, July 24, 1834. The twenty-two year old started his new career as a Georgia lawyer with the following prayerful wish:
☛ "Was this day engaged for the first time in my professional line, with a contingent fee of about one hundred and eighty dollars. May a superintendent Providence look propitiously upon me! The little bark of my fortunes and my all is now launched upon a troubled sea, and a better helmsman than I am is needed. And now, in the beginning, I do make a fervent prayer that He who made me and all things, and who rules all things, and who has heretofore abundantly blessed and favored me, and to whom I wish to be grateful for all His mercies, may continue them toward His unworthy servant; that He may, though unseen, direct me in the right path in all things, and in all my intercourse with mankind; that He may make me unassuming and not bold and self-confident; that He may inspire me with a sound mind and quick apprehension, and that He may so overrule all my acts and all my thoughts and my whole course that a useful success may attend all my efforts; that I may not be a useless blank in creation and an injury to men; but that I may be of benefit yet to my fellow-beings, that His name may be glorified in my existence, and most of all that, at least, I may ever be filled with a sense of dependence upon His arm for assistance in all things."[28]

During this period Stephens encountered Robert A. Toombs for the first time, a man with whom he would forge a powerful lifelong friendship. Stephens describes the meeting:
☛ "Toombs was at the court when I was admitted: I was not introduced to him, however. The next week I went over to Wilkes, and there we became personally acquainted; but how I do not recollect. Our acquaintance soon grew to intimacy. We were associated in some cases in 1835; in 1836 we were very friendly, and by this time always occupied the same room when we went on the

circuit. In 1838 be proposed to lend me money to travel for my health. We had been in the Legislature together in 1837. He attended to nearly all the business that my brother could not do while I was gone. Our personal relations have never been interrupted from the first day of our acquaintance."[29]

From Stephens' diary, September 1, 1834:
☛ ". . . made my first address to a court. It was the Court of Ordinary of this county. I spoke for James Farmer, and received two dollars in silver." [He later added: "These four half-dollars I kept a long time. I ought to have charged more for this and for the job of the Ellington papers; but I did not know the value of my services."][30]

From Stephens' diary, September 10, 1834:
☛ "This day I was employed by Mr. [James] Hilsman with the conditional fee of twenty dollars. But of all my business, the most important was the purchase of a horse. What will be the result of my first trade I can not tell."[31]

From Stephens' diary, February 22, 1835:
☛ "Have been for some time in serious thought upon the subject of my future prospects; and feel compelled to leave a place to which I feel so much attached. . . . We have in this village a society for debate in which I take much interest, and in which I feel that I have a formidable competitor in A. R. W., one of my old classmates."[32]

From Stephens' diary, March 19, 1835:
☛ "Cleared off in the night, with high wind from the N.W.: not very cold. To-morrow night, by appointment, I am to take part in our debating society in the discussion of nullification. Have bestowed some thought upon the question, but find the whole involved in much obscurity. I have found what I consider to be a correct definition of Sovereignty. It is a moral attribute, vested with full moral power, natural or adventitious, to do whatever is consistent with right and duty. In its nature it is inalienable: it cannot be transferred. It can be delegated as a trust, but can never be conveyed in fee. It is an *estate tail general* [a legal term] in the male line, secured through Adam to all his posterity, and of which no father can deprive his offspring, nor any government its subjects."[33]

In March and April of 1835, Stephens took a journey on horseback with eight of his friends. What follows are some of his observations of his trip from Georgia "out West":
☛ ". . . There is no uniformity of character among the people of Alabama, the population being composed of immigrants from all parts of the world, and of

all varieties of morals, dispositions, tempers, and conditions of life. The whole presents a heterogeneous mass of irregular and confused material, much needing the hand of time and education to shape and to form into symmetrical order."[34]

During their tour "out West," Stephens and his companions had to pass through the territory of the Creek Indians, one with whom they spent the night:
☞ "We found that our host was a man of authority among his own people, the chief of his town. His name was Witholo-mico. He lives on the banks of the Tallapoosa, near his own ferry, about twelve miles above Autossee battle-ground. It was night when we arrived, and found for our accommodation that there were two cabins upon the premises, about twelve feet square and eight feet high each, and having puncheon floors. One had a small piazza in front, and both had the crevices between the poles of which they were built neatly stopped or daubed with red clay. Into one of these we, nine in number, were conducted, saddles, blankets, bridles, and all except horses, which were turned into a neighboring lot, where the chief gave them corn and fodder. We found but four Indians about,—the chief, his wife, and two others, one a boy. The wife soon arrayed herself in a new clean dress, seeming to think the dirty smock in which we found her not becoming the lady of a chieftain in the presence of white men. She then busied herself in preparing us some supper, which, when it came (in about an hour), consisted of fried bacon, eggs, corn-bread, and coffee,—very good fare for travellers. At table we had all the accommodations of civilized life, such as plates, knives and forks, cups and saucers, etc. But in the sleeping line we were not so fortunate. Two bedsteads were standing in two corners of the house, having, instead of cords, boards laid across their sides, over which were thrown some blankets. All our company were soon extended on one or the other of these hard couches,— all but myself. For my part I felt little like sleeping. The hour, the place, and circumstances allowed no repose to my mind. The lofty look and dignified mien of Witholo-mico (who had retired to the other house), his keen, deep-sunken eye, his strange guttural sounds, which flowed while speaking to his wife in such commanding eloquent tone, were all before me. Then the whole Indian history, the origin of that powerful race which once occupied undisturbed this vast extent of country, their habits as observed by the first settlers and before their contamination by the white man, their virtues, their patriotism,—all these, compared with their present sunk and degraded condition, crowded themselves upon my mind in such a tide of reflection, that I was absorbed in thought until almost the breaking of day.

"In the morning, I was delighted to see the chief arrayed in his national

Daniel Webster

costume, which I supposed he had donned in compliance with a wish I had made to that effect the evening before in his presence, not thinking that he could understand what I was saying. His dress was buckskin leggings, reaching up to the hip, beaded with materials of different colors, but mostly red, on the outer seams; a coat or gown reaching half-way down the thigh, also beaded in various parts; a shirt extending in peaked form in front nearly to the knee; a red band about the waist, which was elegantly beaded; in front a kind of case or sheath for the reception of a large butcher-knife or dirk. This belt hung nearly to the ground, much like the sash of one of our field-officers. And to conclude, his head was bound about with a kind of loose bandage of red color, very full, passing directly around and across the forehead, leaving the top of the head perfectly bare.

"The chief had nothing to say to the whites, which I at first attributed to his want of acquaintance with our language; but afterwards was disposed to think it owing to some other cause, either a sense of his superior dignity, or the fear of appearing to his own people to show too great familiarity towards foreigners, particularly their worst enemies. He kept himself close in his own apartment during the night, and though he was up early in the morning, and appeared very active and diligent in serving us and making us as comfortable as possible, yet all was done in the most dignified, reserved, and unrelaxing taciturnity."[35]

From Stephens' diary, July 16, 1835:

☛ "Business was quite lively to-day. William Jones, a merchant in this place, absconded, and left many creditors to suffer. I have since last night written twelve attachments, and I suppose that as many have been issued elsewhere. It seems to me that the laws providing for the satisfaction of the claims of absconding debtors are, like many others of our system, very defective. For they can be called nothing but a snatch-and-take. The individuals who are nearest the scene of action and can use their fingers the quickest, or have money to secure this end, can always be safe; while those at a distance, or such as are lying under some other disadvantage, are totally losers. Not only so, but our present system of attaching might be used as an instrument of the grossest fraud. For should a man of extensive securities and debts become too much involved to meet the demands upon him, and then communicate this fact to a few of his creditors whom he feels disposed to favor, it is evident that arrangements may be all made ready for the favored creditors to attach and secure themselves instantly upon the departure of the debtor, while others quite as justly entitled to relief are excluded by this snatch law."[36]

From Stephens' diary, November 27, 1835:
☛ "Went to Warrenton for the purpose of aiding McGuire in obtaining his enlargement. He was confined in jail for assault with intent to murder. Rain in the evening. I got three of the court together between nine and ten o'clock P.M. One drunk. Court could not agree upon the amount of the bond, and adjourned until eight o'clock next morning. Succeeded the next day in getting bail for McGuire; felt gratified at the relief afforded the prisoner."[37]

Of this period in his life, Stephens would later write:
☛ "No one can imagine how I worked, how I delved, how I labored over books. Often I spent the whole night over a law-book, and went to bed as the dawn of day was streaking the east. My business increased, and I studied hard to keep up with it and keep the mastery over it. My brother, A. G., who in 1834 taught school in the Asbury settlement, visited me often, and we spent many pleasant evenings together, when there was no preaching in town, in walking over to the old homestead, and running over the hills and up and down the [river] branches. These excursions constituted most of my recreation during these two years, except when I went up to see him, or went on a visit to Uncle Aaron G. Grier and old Aunt Betsey. My time was occupied almost constantly on weekdays in reading, studying, and office business. I never lounged about with village crowds."[38]

From a May 25, 1838, letter to his fourteen year old half-brother Linton Stephens:
☛ "Be true to yourself now, in the days of your youth. Improve your mind;

apply yourself to your books: and when I am silent in the grave you may then be treading the floors now presented to my eye, honored with office of the highest rank. Always look up; think of nothing but objects of the highest ambition which can be compassed by energy, virtue, and strict morality, with a reliance upon a holy, pure, and all-ruling Providence. But never forget your dependence and mortality. Let them be your morning and evening musings; and in all things do nothing on which you could not invoke the divine blessing."[39]

Stephens wrote the following to Linton on June 4, 1838, from Keene, New Hampshire:
☞ "I have a great deal of anxiety of mind about you. No day passes but you are in my mind; and you do not escape from my dreams by night. Sometimes I fear I did not counsel you enough before leaving home. Only one thing I neglected: that was to advise you what to do in case you and [your teacher] Mr. _____ do not agree. In such case, I want you to quit *instanter* ["without delay"] and await my return. I do not intend that you shall be abused or trodden upon by any mortal. . . . In all your dealings give offence to no one, and be you the subject of no man's offence. . . . But if a crisis comes, show that you are a man, and have a spirit that never cowers; and if any wretch pulls your nose or ears, asking 'who are you?' tell him that you are a freeman's son, and be sure you do honor to his blood. But never condescend to notice small offences. Be above them."[40]

Of the 1840 presidential election, Stephens wrote:
☞ "I was opposed to the administration of [Martin] Van Buren and also to the support of [William H.] Harrison. I wanted the State rights party of Georgia to stand by the nomination of George M. Troup which I had considerably contributed in getting the men of that party in the legislature of 1839 to make. But in the summer of 1840 a convention of that party was held at Milledgeville, and withdrew the nomination of Troup and declared for Harrison. I was not in the convention. I acquiesced, though I thought it bad policy. There were but two candidates in the field, Harrison and Van Buren. I preferred Harrison as a choice of evils. Indeed, the greatest objection I had to Harrison's nomination was the political alliances it would bring about. Him I considered sound enough on all political and constitutional questions; but his supporters generally at the North were the old Centralists and Consolidationists, known in 1800 as Federalists [that is, Liberals]."[41]

Young lawyer Stephens, who defended numerous black slaves before Lincoln's War, wrote to his brother Linton on June 2, 1842, with this news:
☞ "I was absent yesterday and the day before at Warrenton attending the trial

of a negro, charged with the offense of assault and battery, with intent to murder, on a white man. I defended him and he was acquitted."[42]

From a February 2, 1840, letter to his brother Linton:
☞ "There is no virtue in the human character nobler than candor,—plain, real, unsophisticated candor. It is the legitimate offspring of truth, and always begets independence."[43]

From a February 28, 1840, letter to his brother Linton:
☞ "In regard to the doctrine of the Universalists you allude to in your letter, and particularly that part wherein you request my opinion, I will only say, without entering fully into the subject, that I do not agree with the belief that 'there is no personal devil or fallen spirit, and that what is commonly called the Devil is no more than the inclination of man to do evil.' What I mean by a personal devil is an evil spirit or a spiritual intelligence apostate and fallen. There are doubtless many spiritual intelligences besides the Deity. Some are pure and holy: others are of opposite nature, being evil, rebellious, and disobedient."[44]

Eli Whitney

From a May 5, 1840, letter to his brother Linton:
☞ "This is true religion: a change of heart from evil to good, a renewal of the soul from low and grovelling desires to an expanded and enlarged love for the universe and an unbounded reverence for its Author. To worship is the natural prompting after regeneration, that process by which, in a mysterious way, the depraved nature of fallen man is exchanged and purified by the exercise of a saving faith in Christ the Redeemer and Mediator.

". . . The subject of religion I have seldom alluded to in my communications with you, either by word or letter. The principle on which I acted required me, I believe, to pursue such a course. Perhaps hereafter I may dwell more at large upon the subject."[45]

From a June 2, 1840, letter to his brother Linton:
☛ "I never like to be a lecturer, or to give advice, because I am so sensible of my own errors and imperfections; and this is why I have said so little to you on subjects of religion, morality, and piety. But I trust you will not think the less of them yourself, or be more remiss in your action. If I have said nothing, it is not because I feel nothing. I do hope, therefore, that you will not even trust yourself to your own judgment or caution, but ask assistance from one who is able to direct you, daily. I believe in a special Providence. Of all Christian virtues, cultivate humility, meekness, and a spirit of dependence upon the great Ruler of the universe for 'every good and perfect gift.'. . . The world is transitory at best, and there is little in it worth living for but the bright prospect it affords of a blessed immortality. Its hopes are delusive, its honors are vain, its pleasures are empty."[46]

From an August 2, 1840, letter to his brother Linton:
☛ "In the beginning of the Government under the new organization, in 1787 and 1788, all who were in favor of ratification of the Constitution, or were friendly to the compact or *Foedus* as it was called, assumed the name of Federalists. Those who opposed took the various names of Anti-Federalists, Democrats, Republicans, etc. At that time [James] Madison and [Thomas] Jefferson were known as Federalists, or friends to the Constitution. Patrick Henry and many other noble sons of Virginia were opposed to it. After the Constitution, however, was ratified, and the Government went into operation, many measures were proposed which some of the friends of the Constitution thought were not authorized by that instrument, and which, if carried out, would centralize all power in the General Government to the subversion of the States. That class of course fell into the ranks of the Republicans [then Conservatives]. Among these were Mr. Jefferson, Mr. Madison, and many others, while Patrick Henry and others fell into the ranks of the Federals [then Liberals], saying that these powers of which the others were complaining were granted in the Constitution, and it was then too late to raise the complaint; that they had warned them of the danger, and foretold these consequences. It was now too late: the Constitution was established, and the country had to abide by it. Many of the measures of the Federalists of that time—say from 1790 to 1800—were no doubt good ones, while others were truly obnoxious, particularly the one against Aliens, and one upon the subject of Sedition. It was those measures which showed a disposition on the part of the Federal party to the grasping of power that caused the overthrow of that party in 1800 by the election of Mr. Jefferson. . . . Considering the merits of even the most obnoxious measures of those days, apart from all party and personal bearing,

just as you would look at the laws of ancient nations, I believe that there is not a great deal more to censure in them than in many of the laws we have had passed in much later times. The patriotism, however, of those men who were called Federalists, even at the election of Mr. Jefferson, no man can doubt. They were among the earliest and most devoted friends and movers of the Revolution, and were the master-spirits that struggled for our independence. They were all no doubt friends to good government; but differed, as men always will, as to the best methods and medium of administering it. It is true that Mr. Jefferson in his *Ana* (some notes in the end of his works) intimates that a large party then existed in the country favorable to a monarchy. But for my own part I do not believe one word of it. His aim was at [Alexander] Hamilton; but he was, in point of intellect, integrity, and patriotism, high above all such suspicions. Jefferson even intimates openly, in one of his letters, that [George] Washington was aspiring to a throne. With Hamilton's notions of government I do not agree; but that he was in favor of changing it to a kingly government, none, I think, would pretend to believe who knows anything of his opinions of the formation of the Constitution. He was truly a great man, but his theories did not suit the genius of our institutions.

"[PS:] I dreamed last night you were dead; and, though no believer in dreams, have nevertheless all day been more or less under the influence of this strange phantom."[47]

From a February 14, 1841, letter to his brother Linton. Stephens' old friend William Le Conte had recently passed away:

☛ "Remember me to Louis and Joseph Le Conte. I much sympathize with them in their late bereavement. Their brother was one of my most beloved and esteemed friends. His departure is another evidence of the fleeting and transient nature of all things connected with this life's hopes and expectations. Little did I think last fall in Milledgeville, when I shook the hand that I had often shaken both in parting and greeting, that it was for the last time, and that our farewell was to be for ever! What a mystery is death—and life!"[48]

From a March 25, 1841, letter to his brother Linton:

☛ "There is a philosophy in life and in the proper way of living that few seem to understand. Hence many who really are rich live worse than some who are seemingly poor. These remarks I think peculiarly applicable to _____ and his family. The whole aim of his life has been to accumulate and save without any regard to proper enjoyment. To accumulate and save are both admirable actions; but they should not be the ruling motives: they should be subservient to the great objects of life,—usefulness, contentment, and happiness. Had he spent more in the education of his only son, the enlightenment of his understanding and the refinement of his manners, and then left him much less of the property, he would have acted a much better part by him. The great difficulty with mankind is in spending,—in knowing how and when to spend their money."[49]

From an April 11, 1841, letter to his brother Linton. U.S. President William H. Harrison had passed away on the 4th, only one month after his inauguration:
☛ "There is no doubt that General Harrison is dead. What effect it will have upon the country time alone can disclose. I look upon it, however, as at this time one of the greatest calamities that could have befallen the nation. Harrison had the confidence of the people of all sections of the Union. There was nothing sectional, partisan, or offensive to any portion of the people in his inaugural. The whole country was calm in quiet expectation of the measures to be proposed by him at the opening of the called session of Congress. [Extra session called for the last day of May.] No other man living could have wielded such influence over public opinion as he could, because he had the confidence of the people. They believed him to be, as he was indeed, a patriot. I fear his death will give rise to dissensions and divisions."[50]

From a March 1842 letter to his brother Linton:
☛ "Rhetoric, properly taught, is one of the easiest and most improving and useful studies of a college course, and to me it was the most interesting. But it requires some training to get in the right way of learning it. It is to be effected by system, method, and generalization. The usefulness of the study depends mostly upon its effect upon the mind in subjecting it to system and method, and the exercises it imposes upon the memory. It should never be taught or learned by questions and answers. You might as well attempt to teach the beauties of a painting to a mind unacquainted with the art of catching the perspective, by a similar system of interrogatories. In the study of rhetoric usefully, the mind must first be taught to put forth its strongest faculties, and survey the entire subject—that is, the lecture for any given recitation. The author's object being thoroughly understood, his manner of treating it, and his various subdivisions, soon occur easily to the mind, which naturally again suggest his ideas, and then the task is performed, and the whole lecture is indelibly impressed upon the mind like a map or chart spread out before you. In mastering a lecture in rhetoric, the author's words should never be studied; if they occur readily to the mind in reciting, they should be used; but in studying, the memory should not be taxed to retain them; the ideas, and the order in which they come in the

Linton Stephens

lecture, should be the task of the student. The ideas he should convey in his own words. For when he understands his author, and knows what his ideas are, the student can always have words at command to make known what they are. But it is a remarkable fact, that with a little practice with this kind of study, so quick does the memory become, and so retentive of an impression, that the student will be enabled to repeat almost the identical words of his author from beginning to end. This strengthens the memory, and imparts vigor to the mind, and enables the faculties to encompass a whole subject at once, and understand the whole and every part at the same time. This is exceedingly necessary for writers and public speakers. When a student, therefore, goes to recite a lesson in rhetoric, or moral philosophy, or any such studies, he should know everything in his recitation, and be able forthwith and without hesitation to repeat, if called upon, every idea in it, just as he would tell, if called upon, what he heard a man say on any particular subject on a given occasion. . . . When once you get in the way of it, you will find it the easiest study learned. The mind will take it readily, and you will be astonished at the amount of learning you can acquire. To me, at first, it appeared very hard, because I had nobody to teach me; but when Dr. Olin became professor and gave us a few lectures, the whole subject assumed a new appearance, and the study became delightful; and when I graduated, there was no subject in Blair, Paley, Say, Evidences of Christianity, Brown's Moral Philosophy, or Hedge's Logic, that I could not have told everything about instantly, or as fast as I could have spoken; and I could have commenced at the beginning of the catalogue above named, and have given substantially everything contained, from the beginning to the end, without interruption or suggestion. The same principles of system, method, and analysis I brought to the study of law; and when I was admitted, I could have rehearsed Blackstone in the same way. The whole I attributed to Olin's method of teaching; and I would not have given the advantages derived from that for all my college course besides. It has been of more use to me. It called forth all the powers of the mind, and taught it to exercise its every faculty. My previous instructions were like keeping a child forever sliding and crawling: Olin made us stand up and walk. A little assistance was at first necessary, while the knees were weak, and before strength and confidence were acquired; but soon we (I mean the whole class, for there was no student in the class that did not understand the studies) began to walk without assistance, and then to run and bound, and become the perfect masters of all our faculties. I wish you to adopt the right method in these studies, and to become perfectly master of them. When a subject is mentioned, be able to give an outline of the whole, and show that you have studied your author, by being able, without assistance, to go on and tell what he says."[51]

Stephens' March 1842 letter to his brother Linton continues:
☛ "In many things that make man truly great, that show the power of his mind, the boldness of his conceptions, and the lofty sentiments of his soul, I think the ancients were greatly our superiors. Look at their works, their temples and other public buildings, which, after withstanding the ravages of centuries, are yet unequalled by anything that man in subsequent times ever erected. Why, even the public roads leading from the city of Rome, constructed before the Julian day, are now better and more substantial than any in the United States, and perhaps in England and France. Part of a bridge is yet standing on the Danube which was built soon after the time of the Caesars. What a people they must have been to leave such vestiges behind them! If this country should be overrun by savages, what have we that would remain one thousand years to tell that such a race as ours ever existed?"[52]

From an August 14, 1842, letter to his brother Linton:
☛ "I have very little hope of ever getting well. This I mention, not from any peculiar feelings of despondency I entertain, but as the deliberate expression of my apprehension. It is true that with great care, prudence, and caution I may recover my former health, nor am I at all disposed to abandon the means. But still, from my constant watchfulness over my state and condition of health for some years, my apprehensions are as above expressed."[53]

From an August 16, 1842, letter to his brother Linton:

☛ "I did not write at all to excite your alarm so as to render you in the least uneasy. That I am in a delicate and precarious condition I feel confident; but then I am not at all apprehensive of any immediate or speedy turn in my disease in any direction. . . . I will keep you advised of my situation; and I want you by all means not to permit yourself to grow uneasy. I do not feel so myself, and do not wish anybody to feel so on my account. Life and death, as well as everything else, should be considered philosophically."[54]

From an April 1843 letter to his brother Linton. Stephens, on his way home from a trip to Florida, was writing from Hamilton, Georgia, where he had stopped at his brother John's home. One of John's children had just died and another was quite ill:

☛ "I do not remember when I approached a family in the midst of so much gloom, or when my own heart has been so much saddened. I came expecting enjoyment and hoping to partake of such pleasures as generally attend the meetings and greetings of kindred and friends after long intervals of absence. Instead of this, I came to a house of mourning, and my office was to comfort the grieved and soothe the afflicted. This is, perhaps, after all, the best way in which to spend our time. Our life is but a chequered scene at best, furnishing much more over which to mourn than to rejoice. Now and then, it is true, it is favored with a ray of sunshine and beauty to warm and gladden the soul, and cause its young hopes to bud and blossom. But no sooner are they fully blown than they are nipped by untimely frosts or blasted by chilling rains, or dashed to pieces by reckless storms. Man's history is a strange mixture of pleasure and pain, joy and sorrow, hope and despair, life and death! A mystery, deep, dark, and unfathomable! To live to-day,—to be warm, to move and think: to-morrow to be silent, cold, and dead,—devoid of mind and sense, fast mouldering into dust.——fit food for worms. To-day with a spirit that can scan the universe and make its own impress upon the world that ages cannot efface,—to-morrow to be nothing but loathsome matter to be hidden away to rot. This is man."[55]

From a May 28, 1843, letter to his brother Linton. It concerns a visit Stephens paid to the "old-fashioned Georgia farm" of his cousin Sabrina Ray:

☛ "They [the Rays] seem peculiarly fitted for taking the world easy and making the most of it as it goes. Tom [Mr. Ray] is really amusing. I hardly know what to make of him. He has no desire to make any more than just enough to live comfortably on, and then to live to enjoy it. They were all hands at work. Cousin was weaving, while William's wife and Granny [both servants] were making the wheels fly. They were all glad to see me. We had a fine supper. Cousin milked her own cows. I went with her to the pen. She has a fine spring-house, and I saw all her jars and pans of milk, butter, etc., fresh and as cool as the fountain. At supper no one had coffee but myself: milk was the only beverage, some taking buttermilk and some sweet milk, and every one having his mug. All seemed contented and cheerful, and full of such happiness as, when weary and tired with a long day's work, night brings to the industrious when in health. No sooner was the evening meal over than preparations were made for bed, and in a few minutes all of this world, its cares and losses, its trials and ambitions, were forgotten in sleep."[56]

From a June 14, 1843, letter to his brother Linton. Here Stephens speaks of Linton's final college exam, and how it reminded him of when he sent Linton off to school four years earlier:

☞ "Well do I remember with what solicitude and intensity of feeling, known only to myself, I fitted you out for your departure to college. And then, when all things were ready, the hour arrived, the last words were spoken, and in a few moments more the whirling car rushed recklessly on in the darkness, and I returned to my room, how I committed you and your fortunes into the hands of that mysterious Providence who guides our destinies. At that time, owing to the great feebleness of my health, I hardly permitted myself to indulge the hope of living to see the time of your graduation. But now your course is nearly ended, and that period has almost arrived. If you shall live a few short weeks longer, you must take your stand among men. Have you ever seriously considered and fully realized how near you are to so important a crisis in life? If not, it is time that the subject, with all its gravity and responsibility, was kept constantly in mind. Would that I had time and space to present it in its various shapes! The past has been pleasant; you have been agreeably entertained in looking at the world at a distance, and as a stranger or disinterested spectator, philosophizing perhaps upon its various characters, its pursuits, its inconsistencies, its passions, its shifts, its struggles, and its treacheries. But your position is now to be changed, and all these are to be encountered. Some liken college life to the world in miniature, and the illustration is not without some aptness. But such a life compared to that of the outer world is more like sailing upon the unruffled surface of the broad river, or the still, widening bay, just before it issues from its restricted channel and the protecting embrace of its banks and capes, into the wide expanse of waters just ahead, compared to the breasting and weathering the mighty waves and raging billows that are ever heaving and rolling and surging on ocean's bosom. Life's passage is over a tempestuous sea, and well built, well manned, well piloted must be the barque that safely makes the voyage. Many spread their sails joyously to the breeze, but few reach the wished-for haven. Be not, then, inattentive. It is an important period of your life. You never did and never will stand in more need of cool thought, sober reflection, and good judgment than now. Especially let not passion control your feelings. Life is just before you; and the part you are to act in it has now soon to be shown, and the character you wish to sustain is now to be formed."[57]

From a July 2, 1843, letter to his brother Linton, who has just passed his final exam:
☛ "I was indeed gratified to learn that you had received the First Honor in your class; not that I attach the least importance to the mere show or *éclat* ["great achievement"] of such a distinction, but I was gratified to have the evidence that you had not misspent your time, and that during the four years of your absence you had not been unmindful of the first of all duties,—your duty to yourself in the cultivation of your morals and your mind, and in fitting yourself for usefulness in those scenes of life into which you are now about to enter. . . . In rendering yourself worthy of this distinction, you have but done what you ought to have done, and deserve the same commendation due to all persons who pursue a similar course of conduct, and nothing more. From want of a correct way of viewing such things many young men, who otherwise would have succeeded well in life, have been utterly ruined by being the favored objects upon whom such distinctions have been once bestowed. The nature of true honor is misunderstood by them."[58]

To his brother Linton Stephens in 1844. Stephens, having unwillingly entered politics in October 1843, is now a Georgia congressman. The letter concerns a "diplomatic dinner" he attended at Washington, hosted by Senator John M. Berrien of Georgia. Numerous foreign ministers and famous Americans were present at the June 11th party:
☛ "The table was decorated with flowers, etc., and filled with glass, but nothing eatable was to be seen except some jellies and strawberries. Everything was handed round by servants. First soup, then fish, then beef, then something else, I know not what; then sweetbreads, then chicken, then birds, then beans and asparagus, then strawberries, then Charlotte de Russe, with jellies, then ice cream, then cherries and apples. A change of plates took place at each of these courses. Six wine glasses were placed near each plate, and in them we first had sherry, immediately after soup, then Madeira, claret, champagne, brandy, etc., with hock and just what each wanted at all times. I forgot to mention Henderson, the late Texas plenipotentiary, as one of the company; and I forgot to say also that the last course was a snuff-box handed all round. The candles were lighted as dark came on, and we left the table at half-past ten, and repaired to the drawing room, where coffee was served in the handing order. The whole passed off very well and nobody got drunk. The whole company was jovial and

the conversation spirited. The servants who handed meats, etc., were called 'waiters,' those who served wine were called 'butlers.' They were all colored but one, a French cook, who figured largely, and all wore silk gloves and had on aprons. . . . But I can say no more; and this I have said to you only in order to write a few moments before going to bed. . . . I don't write such stuff as this for anybody but yourself."[59]

From a January 19, 1845, letter to his brother Linton. Congressman Stephens describes a speech he attended by Henry Clay, who was a member (and later the president) of the American Colonization Society. The racist Yankee organization was formed for the express purpose of "cleansing" the U.S. of its black population via deportation to foreign colonies, mainly in Africa, South America, and the Caribbean. The mission of the ACS, which was fully supported by lifelong member and onetime Illinois chapter leader Abraham Lincoln, was to make America "white from coast to coast":

☛ "Last night Mr. Clay made a show on the Colonization question, and such a show I never saw before. Men came from Baltimore, Philadelphia, and New York, to say nothing of Alexandria and this city. The House and galleries were jammed and crammed before five o'clock. When I came over at half-past six, I found I could not get in at the door below, much less get up the steps leading to the House. The people were wedged in as tight as they could be squeezed, from outside the door all the way up the steps, and the current could neither move up nor down. There were several thousands still outside. I availed myself of my knowledge of the meanderings of an intricate, narrow passage under the rotunda, and round by the Supreme Court room, into the alley from the Clerk's room, into the House at the side-door by the House postoffice; and through this Mr. [Howell] Cobb and I, with Robinson, of Indiana, wound our way, finding it

Thomas Jefferson

unobstructed until we got to the door, where the crowd was as tight as human bodies could be jammed; but we drove through the solid mass and got in, and passed on the space by the fire to the left of the Speaker's chair, where, by looking over the screen, we could see the chair. When we got to this place, what a sight was before our eyes! The great new chandelier, lighted up with gas, was brilliant and splendid indeed; and then, what a sea of heads and faces! Every nook and corner on the floor below, and the galleries above, the aisles, the area, the steps on the Speakers rostrum, were running over. The crowd was pushed over the railing, and men were standing on the outside cornice all around; and they were even hanging on the old clock and the figure of Time. Such a sight you never saw. None in the hall could turn: women fainted and had to be carried out over the solid mass. At about seven Clay came, but could hardly be got in. The crowd, however, after a while was opened, while the dome resounded with uninterrupted hurrahs. . . . After a while order was restored. . . . Dayton, of New Jersey, offered a resolution and began speaking; but one fellow crying 'Clay! Clay!' the cry became general, and soon also became general with, 'Put him down!' 'Put him out!' 'Pitch him out of the window!' but Dayton held out and kept speaking until he was literally drowned with, 'Down! down!' 'Hush!' 'Clay! Clay!' etc., and then the old hero rose. Three more cheers for Henry Clay were suggested, three more! three more! Three More! At length quiet reigned. Clay began speaking, and all were silent. Of his speech I say nothing. He was easy, fluent, bold, commanding; but, in my opinion, not eloquent. At about nine an adjournment was announced. . . . I understand that whole acres of people had to go away without getting in at all. Shepperd, of North Carolina, whom you know as being more Whiggish than Clayish, rather snappishly remarked, when we got to our quarters, that Clay could get more men to run after him to hear him speak, and fewer to vote for him, than any man in America."[60]

From a February 27, 1845, letter to Howell Cobb. Stephens is writing from on board a steamboat traveling from Wilmington, Delaware, to Charleston, South Carolina:
☛ "Dear Cobb, According to promise I drop you a line, though I write on the boat where I am rocked and shaken so I fear you can not read it. I have had a fine and comfortable travel so far, and expect soon to take leave of the sea and its dangers. I never had a smoother passage from Wilmington to Charleston. The wind was perfectly calm and the sea at rest. Touching the stages, I ascertained that there is a daily line from Raleigh to Columbia—two horse, I was told. It leaves Raleigh at 2 P.M., and after being out two nights arrives at Columbia at 8 P.M. the third night. Another line leaves the Wilmington railroad at the breakfast house Warsaw, for Fayetteville and Columbia. That is

the best route, and it gives you an opportunity of judging of the probable state of the weather—as you can pay to that place, and then if the weather threatens to be bad you can take that line. It leaves the railroad 45 miles from Wilmington; is a four horse coach, but did not look to me as if it could carry more than six. It is a small and slender looking North Carolina affair. But I can say no more."[61]

From a March 17, 1845, letter to his brother Linton concerning Stephens' black servants. Contrary to Yankee mythology, we see a typical Southern home in which the "slaves" have both enormous responsibilities and numerous freedoms:
☛ "Since I have been keeping Bachelor's Hall, Bob (who has been running all about town during my absence in Washington) has been kept at home more than his wont. He is now the main man upon the place; attends to the horse and hogs, brings in breakfast, dinner, and supper, pours out the coffee, and waits upon the table. Old Mat cooks, and Bob and Pierce do the rest. Who carries the keys I don't know. I have laid in a supply of sugar, coffee, tea, etc.; but where it is kept and who keeps it I don't know. . . . Bob told me the other day he would have to buy some chickens somewhere before long. I told him to buy them; and we continue to have chicken every day, but I can't tell where they come from. To-day I missed Bob at dinner, and was told he had gone to mill. So I conclude that we are out of meal, or that Bob wanted to take an airing."[62]

From an April 20, 1845, letter to his brother Linton:
☛ "The night is lovely beyond description. The moon shines bright, the air just stirs enough to rustle slightly among the now full-grown leaves. The whippoorwill is heard at a distance, and ever and anon the mockingbird sends forth his sweet notes upon the bosom of the breeze. To sit at my window and look out upon the sleeping earth is like listening to sweet music."[63]

From a July 22, 1845, letter to his brother Linton concerning Stephens' dog "Pup":
☛ "Poor Pup is much worse than he was yesterday. He cannot walk or crawl to-day. I think he has lock-jaw. He looks anxiously at all who go to see him, and wags his tail when called. I have had him put on the back piazza, where he can get water without trouble. I am very fearful that the poor fellow who met me so cordially on my return, when I was so filled with sadness, will himself be numbered with the dead before another similar opportunity occurs. I had become very much attached to the dog, for the reason, I suppose, that he was so much attached to me. When I went away he was always the first to meet me on my return, and was always so glad to see me. If he dies I shall miss him, and

shall again feel the truth of the maxim that all things here below are vain and illusory."[64]

From a July 27, 1845, letter to his brother Linton, again concerning Stephens' dog "Pup":
☛ "Pup is a little better. I have been giving him shocks from the galvanic battery. He walked ten steps this morning. The shower-bath also I have tried upon him, and think that did him most good."[65] [Editor's note: Pup subsequently made a full recovery.]

From an August 24, 1845, letter to his brother Linton. Stephens had planned to spend a peaceful evening alone, when six of his male friends showed up unexpectedly at dinnertime:
☛ "Would you know how I entertained them? I lay in the little shed room most of the time, the company sitting on the back porch, and while they talked, I either snored or read Byron. . . . I do dislike to be bored by company when I wish to be alone; and if I ever was in that humor it was to-day. I longed to be alone, shut out entirely from the world. There comes over me sometimes a kind of depression, a sickening at the heart, and weariness of life. . . . Yet there is a pleasure in these indulgences. Indeed, what state of mind is without pleasure? Even rage, anger, envy, and hate are pleasant while they are felt. And as for sorrow and grief, Solomon says it is better to go to the house of mourning than to the house of mirth. Hence the pleasure of witnessing tragedies, which is so great that we will even pay to be made to weep. But enough of this. Since I commenced writing a little cloud has formed overhead and a little to the northeast."[66]

From a September 22, 1845, letter to his brother Linton. Stephens' good friend "Mr. C. Bristow" had died while he was on his way to visit him:
☛ "I never saw a family more deeply distressed. The effect of their sorrow upon me was overwhelming. It brought to mind the scenes of other days, and the sorrows I have felt. As one and another of the children would come in and gaze upon their dying father, I could fully realize the intensity of the pang that caused such intensity of sorrow, for I too had felt the same. It seemed as fresh in memory as if it had been but yesterday, when I stood by the bedside of a dying father and anxiously watched his heaving breast. I felt his failing pulse. And when the last long breath was drawn with a piteous moan, it seemed as if I too must die. It seemed yet fresher than the incidents of yesterday when I saw my poor [older] brother [Aaron Grier Stephens, who passed away in 1843]—But oh, God!—I cannot write. The slightest thought connected with

him brings right before me, as plainly and distinctly as in real life, all the scenes of that distressing night, and opens afresh all its bleeding wounds. Life seems to me to have in it but little good. It is made up of lying vanities, an empty and cheating train, and hopes which result in nothing but vexation, disappointment, and remorse. . . . But enough. It is nearly the time for the funeral service, and I must away to see the end of one who has done me many favors."[67]

From a January 9, 1846, letter to his brother Linton:
☛ "Whenever I get time, I will give you a long letter upon the Ancients, as I have been closely engaged reading up on that subject lately. Rather, I should say, I have been for some time closely studying Ancient History, which I never did before. And though, as you know, I have always had a high opinion of the men of olden time, you may be surprised when I tell you that my late reading has greatly increased my admiration."[68]

". . . [Concerning the ancient Egyptians and Chaldeans, you] may depend upon it, any people who would do all these things: build monuments to survive the ravages of ages, firm almost as the everlasting mountains; who excavated for themselves a final resting-place in the solid rock, covered with paintings relating their history, which time and the elements can never obliterate; who had even the art of embalming their dead, and almost of arresting nature's first law of dissolution, giving to their mortal clay a kind of immortality,—have no equals on the earth at this time."[69]

From a February 1, 1846, letter to his brother Linton:
☛ "I have just come from a long and lonely walk, thinking and musing over many scenes and events long passed and far off. These solitary walks I am of late much in the habit of indulging in. They afford me the solitude which is congenial to my spirits. The present has but little to engage my thoughts or attention . . ."[70]

From a May 29, 1846, letter to his brother Linton. A week earlier Congressman Stephens had returned to his "old quarters" in Washington, D.C.:
☛ "I am getting tired of this place, and I am beginning to think that Congress is the last place that a man of honor and honorable ambition should aspire to. There is a recklessness of purpose here perfectly disgusting and almost alarming. What will become of our country and institutions I do not know. The signs of the times to me are ominous of evil. I have ceased to take much interest in what is done in the House. All is done by party will and for party effect. . . . [I have concluded that I shall take a short visit to New York with Toombs] for a little airing and to get rid of a fit of the blues."[71]

From a January 1, 1847, letter to his brother Linton:

☞ "Yesterday I wrote you a valedictory for 1846, and to-day it seems right enough that I should present you a salutatory for 1847. For several years, I believe, the first time I have written the new date was in a letter to you. . . . Yesterday was chill, damp, foggy, and gloomy in the extreme: to-day it is clear, bright, and mild as a May day. But I have to be contented with a look from the window and the reflection of the sun which I cannot see. I am still confined to my room, though I believe I feel better than I have done for several days."[72]

From a January 5, 1847, letter to his brother Linton. Stephens predicts, as he often did, the coming "Civil War" between the South and the North:

☞ "To give you political news would be impossible. I can only tell you what we do [here in Washington, D.C.]; but to say anything about what is ahead, or what is coming, would be out of my power. The truth is, nobody here, I believe, knows. The whole Government, I think, is about to break down,—at least, the Administration. There is no concert in any party, and nobody knows what will pass the House. The Treasury is nearly empty, and soon will be quite so. The new Tariff is falling far short of the supposed or estimated receipts. [R. J.] Walker [U.S. Secretary of the Treasury] says he cannot borrow money unless a duty be laid on tea and coffee; and the House say they will not tax the stomachs of their constituents in order to flog the backs of Mexicans. In the mean time quite a storm is brewing about the slavery question. The North is going to stick the Wilmot amendment to every appropriation, and then all the South will vote against any measure thus clogged. Finally, a tremendous struggle will take place; and perhaps [James K.] Polk in starting one war [the Mexican-American War] may find half a dozen on his hands. I tell you the prospect ahead is dark, cloudy, thick, and gloomy. I hope for the best, while I fear the worst."[73]

From a January 13, 1847, letter to his brother Linton, concerning a speech made by his friend Robert A. Toombs:

☞ "It was decidedly one of the best speeches I ever heard Toombs make, and I have heard him make some fine displays. It was even superior to his Oregon speech. He had fully prepared himself, was calm and slow, much more systematic than usual, and in many points was truly eloquent. The House was full, and the galleries crowded, and all ears were open and all eyes upon him. He commanded their entire and close attention from the beginning to the end, and the effort has added full fifteen cubits to his stature as a statesman and a man of talents in the opinion of the House and the great men of the nation. I was better pleased with it than with any speech I have heard this session. . . . He is

Henry Clay

destined to take a very high position here."[74]

From a December 22, 1847, letter to his brother Linton:
☛ "I think injustice has been done me; but, by a law of my nature, I think it will be of advantage to me. I am very much like some chronometers, I need a weight or something bearing down upon me, to keep me in motion. I have felt

it all my life. Without it, I am disposed to be inert and idle; but the greater the weight, the greater the reaction. I therefore report the real state of my feelings to be gratification."[75]

From a December 25, 1847, letter to his brother Linton, concerning Christmas Day:
☛ "It is true we have no great display here: no guns, no [fire] crackers, no great exhibition of spirits of any kind,——though our landlady sent round some [egg] nogg a while ago,——no music, no plays, no visiting, and not even sunshine, for it has been snowing the livelong day, and we are all housed. But nevertheless it is Christmas,——that same good old day which awakens in me many reminiscences much more pleasant than even the Fourth of July. For this is the anniversary of my own individual days of liberty."[76]

From a December 29, 1847, letter to his brother Linton:
☛ "Yet mankind is not so bad after all as we sometimes are disposed to conclude. It is only the lowly inclined, the mean in spirit, the bad by nature, who suffer themselves to be the tools and hacks of the rich. Wealth is good in its proper place, when possessed by those of the right spirit. But it is by no means essential for the truly noble to enter successfully all the honorable contests with which life abounds."[77]

From a December 31, 1847, letter to his brother Linton:
☛ "The business of another day is well-nigh closed, and with it the business of another year. The hour of midnight is near at hand, and all without is as still and quiet as if no great event were expected. The footman is no longer in the streets, the busy hackman and his weary team are alike enjoying nature's sweet repose. No sound of music, dance, or song is heard. In the mansions of the rich, as well as in the hovels of the poor, the inmates are asleep, while I am keeping the vigils of the night, and watching with anxious care the last glimmerings of the year as they fitfully flicker in the socket of time. A few moments more, and it will be gone forever. To me it has been, in many particulars, a good friend; and I feel it a sort of duty to sit by it in its last moments. . . . I believe that I have never passed the same period of time in my life with as few incidents to affect me in body or mind. It is therefore with reluctance I witness the separation."[78]

From a January 11, 1848, letter to his brother Linton:
☛ "We have a great many politicians in this country, but few statesmen."[79]

From a December 31, 1848, letter to his brother Linton:

☛ ". . . Let us indulge in no forebodings of the future, but rest in hope that all, under the guidance of a kind Providence, will eventuate well; and that, whatever the next twelve months shall bring forth, will be the best for the promotion of the general advancement and happiness of this poor, degenerate, and sorely-afflicted world. Who will live to see the close of 1849 is at present beyond human conjecture. Who are to be the victims of violence, or slow disease, or scorching fevers, or racking pains, or raging pestilences, no one now can tell. But every one has his time, known only to the Ruler of the Universe; and all should act upon the principle of being always ready. To do the most good we can in relieving misery, supplying want, allaying strife, establishing peace, promoting happiness, advancing morals, and extending intelligence and virtue, and so to act in all things as to be ready at any time to close our career on earth,—these are the great objects of life. The close of every year fills me with sadness. Perhaps this is the last I shall ever see. In view of such a contingency, keep this letter, and it will always present to your mind a picture of my thoughts and feelings on this thirty-first of December, 1848. Twenty years from this time it will be a fruitful theme of meditation for you."[80]

From a December 2, 1849, letter to his brother Linton:
☛ "To-morrow is the great day for organizing the [U.S.] House [of Representatives]; and the elements without [a fierce snow-storm was raging] are not very unlike the elements of passion which are now beclouding and casting a chilling darkness over coming events. My most serious apprehensions of the difficulties before us will, I fear, be realized; the indications of most boisterous times are looming upon the horizon. I never saw greater sectional feeling exhibited. The North is insolent and unyielding. What is to be the result I cannot imagine. Winthrop will not get the entire Southern vote. I shall not vote for him myself. Last night, in caucus, we wanted the Northern Whigs to agree not to press the [Wilmot] Proviso, and not to favor or vote for the abolition of slavery in the District. This they would not do. I believe they are bent on mischief.

"I quitted the meeting, as did Toombs, Cabell, Morton, Hilliard, Owen, and some others. I told them distinctly and positively that I should hold no connection with a party that did not disconnect itself from these aggressive abolition movements. And I intend to abide by what I have said. I think the Northern Whigs intend to pass some obnoxious measure in reference to slavery, to compel President [Zachary] Taylor either to veto it or to sign it. But enough of this now. I am perhaps under too much excitement. My Southern blood and feelings are up, and I feel as if I am prepared to fight at all hazards and to the last extremity in vindication of our honor and rights . . .

"The Whigs, I understand, after we left, nominated Winthrop, and then refused to nominate a Clerk, because he would have to be taken from the South, and that they did not intend to grant. The North, according to their views, is hereafter to have all the offices. No Southern slaveholder is to have any. But enough. Good-night."[81]

From a December 4, 1849, letter to his brother Linton:

☛ "Few changes in the votes to-day. I am more and more convinced every day that the Slave question is rapidly approaching a crisis. If the South intends really to resist the abolition of slavery in the District and the forts and arsenals, it is time they were making the necessary preparations of men and money, arms and munitions, etc., to meet the emergency. I speak plainly and frankly. It is no time for humbug resolutions or gasconade [empty words]. No step should be taken unless we intend to stick to the constitutional Union at every hazard. For myself, after thinking of this subject as dispassionately as I could for several days under the excitement here, I hesitate not to say that, in my opinion, a maintenance of our honor, to say nothing of vindication of our rights, requires us to resist the aggression. In my course here, while I shall pursue in all things the policy which I shall believe will most likely avert such a result, yet I shall yield nothing to the aggressor. It is becoming bootless now to quarrel with ourselves about who contributed most to the present state of things. I believe the agitators of the South for several years have done more to effect it than all others united. But as Southern men we must look things in the face as we find them. Our fortunes are united, and our destiny must be common.

"It is also bootless to count the chances of success in a struggle with the Federal Government. No people who are not fit for the lowest degradation count the cost or hazard of defending their honor or their rights. It is better to fall in a manly struggle than to live and fatten in inglorious ease. And I would rather to-day see the whole Southern race buried in honorable graves than see them insolently trampled over by such canting, whining, puling hypocrites as are now setting themselves up as their judges and reformers. I would rather see Georgia share the fate of Hungary or Poland than see her truckling to the dictation of Northern hordes of Goths and Vandals who are now threatening her with their power.

"But this is the gloomiest side of the picture. I do not think we should be so easily subdued. We have spirit and energy, and we should have friends also. Let us, then, be firm. These views I give you in the worst aspect of the question. Perhaps all this may be averted. I shall do all in my power to avert it."[82]

From a January 15, 1850, letter to his brother Linton:
☞ "The general signs of the times augur no good, as I read them. Men's minds are unsettled. The temper of the country is fretful. The centrifugal tendency in our system is now decidedly in the ascendant."[83]

From a January 21, 1850, letter to his brother Linton. Here Stephens considers, ten years prior to the secession of South Carolina, a possible Southern Confederacy:
☞ ". . . My deliberate opinion at this time, or the opinion I have formed from the best lights before me, is that it [the Wilmot Proviso and accompanying anti-South policies] will be the beginning of an end which will be the severance of the political bonds that unite the slaveholding and non-slaveholding States of this Union. . . . When I look at the causes of the present discontent, I am persuaded there will never again be harmony between the two great sections of the Union.

Robert Augustus Toombs

When California and New Mexico and Oregon and Nebraska are admitted as States, then the majority in the Senate will be against us [Southern states]. The power will be with them to harass, annoy, and oppress. And it is a law of power to exert itself, as universal as it is a law of nature that nothing shall stand still. Cast your eye, then, a few years into the future, and see what images of strife are seen figuring on the boards! In the halls of Congress, nothing but debates about the crimes and the iniquity of slavery, and the duty of the General Government to withhold all countenance of the unholy institution of human bondage. Can Southern men occupy seats in the halls of a Legislature with this constant reproach? It is not reasonable. It is more than I expect. It is more than human nature can expect. The present crisis may pass; the present adjustment may be made; but the great question of the permanence of slavery in the Southern States will be far from being settled thereby. And, in my opinion, the crisis of that question is not far ahead. The very palliatives now so soothingly administered do but more speedily develop the stealthy disease which is fast approaching the vitals. . . . My opinion is that a dismemberment of this Republic is not among the improbabilities of a few years to come. In all my acts I shall look to that event. I shall do nothing to favor it or hasten, but I now consider it inevitable.

". . . If I were now in the Legislature, I should introduce bills reorganizing the militia, for the establishment of a military school, the encouragement of the formation of volunteer companies, the creation of arsenals, of an armory, and an establishment for making gunpowder. In these lies our defence. I tell you the argument is exhausted; and if the South do not intend to be overrun with anti-slavery doctrines, they must, before no distant day, stand by their arms. My mind is made up; I am for the fight, if the country will back me. And if not, we had better have no Resolutions and no gasconade. They will but add to our degradation.

"In reference to the Legislature, I should prefer that nothing should be done in the way of resolutions, but the expression of the fixed and unanimous determination of our State [Georgia] to support the Union under the Constitution and its compromises, and to resist to the utmost of our means any violation of its letter and spirit by Congress, so far as the institution of slavery is concerned. These are my feelings, and this is the language I should hold. Partisans and demagogues might take care of themselves. To this complexion it will come at last. It is a great mistake to suppose that the South can stave off this question. We have, ultimately, to submit or fight.

". . . I consider the Wilmot Proviso a humbug. In itself it is a dispute about 'goats' wool.' I should regard its passage as a good cause of resistance only so far as it might be considered an insult to the South. The expression to the world of the deliberate opinion of the Federal Government that institutions tolerated in the South deserve public censure and national odium, would be no small offence to the people of fifteen States of the Union.

"One other thought. Could the South maintain a separate political organization? On this I have thought a great deal. It has been the most perplexing question to my mind. The result of my reflections is that she could, if her people be united. She would maintain her position, I think, better than the North. She has great elements of power. But I cannot dwell upon this now."[84]

From a March 6, 1850, letter to his brother Linton, concerning the death of one of Stephens' good friends, Andrew Jones:

☛ "Poor Andy! How often have I thought of him! How often have I sympathized with him! and how often, when furthest removed from him, has my compassion gone out to him! Many of the joyous days of my boyhood were spent with him. In my tender years, when oppressed with real and imaginary trouble, when I had no one to condole with me, I often sought him out and found relief in his innocent and simple diversions. Whole days and nights I have taken refuge from the buffeting world in the sunshine of his mild and gentle spirit. In the hours of bitterest affliction he was always near to administer comfort to the best of his ability. . . . The day father died, when I went out into the old field and threw myself upon the ground almost crushed with anguish, Andy was near me. He lay by my side upon the grass, and lamented as if he too had lost a father. And can it be true that his body was mangled and life extinguished with no kind hand to minister to his sufferings? Oh, Andy, Andy! would I could have been there in your last moments! . . . Life has many changes. I have passed through many, and perhaps many more are in store for me, but I never can forget my early associations with Andy. . . . Poor fellow! Our lots in life have been cast in different places; but it makes my heart bleed to think of the past and to think of him. . . . Well, no marble may mark his grave; but the sod above him shall not be unbedewed with tears, should I ever be permitted to pay such a tribute to his memory. . . . Last Friday night, the night before this accident, I had a dream that filled me with apprehension that some bad news would reach me. In my dream I saw brother [Aaron]. I knew him: I talked to him. But oh how changed from the likeness he used to wear! He seemed to be a messenger from another world, but vanished before announcing the object of his mission. I tried to talk to him of his own last sufferings, but got no reply. . . . Life is full of mutation. We are all but bubbles on the tide of time. There will soon be left but few of my former friends; but as the number grows smaller, my love for them increases. As the hopes of life die out, my spirit turns toward the graves of my departed friends. I have stronger inclinations towards home now than ever. I am utterly sick of this place, of public men and public affairs. . . . But I am grieved and afflicted, and will close this disconsolate strain by bidding you good-night."[85]

From a March 31, 1850, letter to his brother Linton, regarding the death of Southern statesman John C. Calhoun:

☞ "The Angel of Death has just passed by, and his shadow is seen lingering upon the startled countenances of all. A great man has just fallen—Calhoun! His race is ended. His restless and fiery spirit sleeps in that deep and long repose which awaits all the living. He died this morning about seven o'clock. Peace to his ashes! His name will long be remembered in the history of this country. He has closed his career at a most eventful period of that history, and perhaps it is most fortunate for his fame that he died just at this time."[86]

Known for his moderate love of alcoholic spirits, Stephens frequently drank from a "small bottle" of whiskey while delivering his speeches. On one occasion he held his glass aloft to the delighted audience and, with a broad smile, said:

☛ "This is pure Democracy—pure Jeffersonian Democracy."[87]

Another time, after winning one of his many elections, he told the supporters who had gathered at his house:

☛ "Gentlemen, I am charged with being a Bourbon [i.e., a reactionary Southern politician]. If you will come with me to my dining-room I will introduce you to the only Bourbon I know anything about."[88]

From an April 15, 1850, letter to his brother Linton:

☛ "I feel less interest in politics, and particularly in parties, than I ever did. I don't think, if spared many a year to come, that I should ever again feel any deep interest in the success of any ticket upon mere party considerations. The principles at issue, and the men before the country, combined, shall always hereafter control my vote. All parties are corrupt, and all party organizations are kept up by bad men for corrupt purposes. I am out of party. I have been very much pained lately at seeing the course of men that I once thought well of, and for whose elevation to office I strove so hard. My only consolation is the consciousness of the integrity of my own motives. I looked to nothing but the common good and prosperity of the country. I was green enough to suppose that there was such a thing as disinterested patriotism. I find I was mistaken. I feel mortified at my disappointment; but bear my mortification as I do a bruise or a sprain. I shall endeavor to avoid such accidents in future."[89]

From an April 21, 1850, letter to his brother Linton:

☛ "You have no idea of my solicitude on this point. I have never told you how intensely I feel about it. Perhaps it is wrong to indulge such feelings, but all the hopes, desires, and ambitions of my life are now centred in you. I feel as if my race is nearly run. I feel that I am unfit to mix among men. I am inclined to retire, at an early day, from public life, and seek the pleasures of solitude."[90]

From an April 28, 1850, letter to his brother Linton. It is Sunday. Stephens has fallen ill and has decided to stay at home instead of going to church:

☛ "I thought I should feel better in spending my time in writing to you than in turning my attention to the faces and fantastic attire of the fashionable crowd who go up to the house of the Lord in this city of Pharisees. If I knew where there was some humble building in the outskirts of the town where the meek, the lowly in heart, congregate, I might venture out and spend an hour with pleasure and profit to myself; but not knowing any such place, I have resolved to stay in my room and talk a little with you."[91]

From a May 7, 1850, letter to his brother Linton:
☞ "I sat to-day for my portrait. What do you think of that? It is one of the strangest events of my life. I never thought before of having my portrait taken. I was walking by a committee-room,—I saw some portraits,—walked up to look at them. The man of the brush asked me to let him take mine. I told him I might, perhaps, at some other time. He said *then* would do as well as any time: he would not want me to sit longer than ten minutes at a time; so down I sat and to work he went. When all was done, I asked him how much he charged for them. He said 'fifty dollars.' I walked off, thinking I was a fool for once. His pictures are very good, but fifty dollars is too much for mine."[92]

From a May 10, 1850, letter to his brother Linton:
☞ "The portrait I mentioned some days ago is completed, and a most detestable-looking thing it is. The consolation I have is that all my friends say it is no likeness at all. So much for a disposition to encourage the fine arts."[93]

From a May 18, 1850, letter to his brother Linton. During a walk that day attorney Stephens had passed by a prison:
☞ "The house of criminals, the strong place for the lawless; that doubtful evidence of civilization, where the innocent are often crowded with the guilty. . . . This world's justice is a great farce—no, a dark tragedy. I never see a jail that I do not feel sympathy for all the poor inmates, whether guilty or not: and I never see a poor wretch peeping through the iron grates without thinking that if all mankind who have done nothing worse than he were in similar places, there would be, in all probability, but few at large. These poor wretches who are punished, even when guilty, are only the scapegoats: the great villains are at large.

"... A day is very much like a lifetime. Both have their morning, their noon, and their evening. The morning with me was spent in strolling in beautiful grounds, over gravelled walks, amid roses and pansies; the noon in action, exercise, looking for places not found, and hunting for a fountain of lost water that did not exist. And then comes the evening with its meditation and philosophy. After all, if my life shall prove as pleasant on the whole as this day has been, I shall have no cause of complaint. I shall desire no greater blessing than to see the sun of its evening go down as clearly and gently as the sun of this day is now softly and sadly laying his head upon the verge of the western horizon. If this should be my fortunate lot, I shall, without regret, close my career here below, as I do this letter, by saying to the world, as I now say to you, 'Good-by; and may heaven's choicest blessings rest upon you!'"[94]

From a July 10, 1850, letter to his brother Linton, concerning the death of President Zachary Taylor, who had gone to the Better World the day before:
☛ "Thus has passed away General Taylor. I had for him a high respect and sincere regard. I was mortified almost to death at the folly of his Cabinet; but General Taylor was an honest, well-meaning, patriotic man, and if he had obeyed his own impulses instead of being governed by the foolish counsels of his Cabinet, his Administration, if he had lived, would have been eminently pacific and successful. As it was, with such as he had about him, it is perhaps best for him that Providence has removed him. He is fortunate in his death."[95]

From a January 23, 1851, letter to his brother Linton, regarding his beloved dog Rio:
☛ "Oh that I were with you and Rio! I fear you do not feed Rio well enough. . . . I would not give one week at home,—no, not one night with you and Rio, for all the pleasures I enjoy here in a month."[96]

Dog lover Stephens once made the following comment to Judge Kontz:
☛ "The hardest cry I ever had was when one of my dogs died."[97]

From a February 3, 1851, letter to his brother Linton:
☛ "After reading your letter I relapsed more profoundly into a musing mood in which I was indulging when it was handed me, and to break that spell is the only object I have in writing. Thought often settles upon me like a nightmare, and as in the case of nightmare, action is necessary to break it, so in troubles and mental anxieties I have often found relief in nothing but action of some sort. This world is a strange place, and man's life is but a dreamy pilgrimage through an inhospitable clime. His path is over mountains and in deep and dark valleys, through bogs and morasses, beset on all sides not only by brambles and thorns, but by gnats, flies, mosquitoes, stinging insects, and venomous reptiles. Occasionally he comes to an open space where the light of heaven seems to smile with benignant rays upon the prospect around him, and where he may pluck a violet or a rose. But ere the flower withers in his hands, the summons of destiny bids him onward to encounter new dangers and new annoyances.

"Sometimes I have thought that of all men I was most miserable; that I was especially doomed to misfortune, to melancholy, to grief; that my pathway of life not only led over the same mountains, heaths, and deserts with others, but that an evil genius was my inseparable companion, following at my side, forever mocking and grinning, and making those places which in the lives of others are most pleasant, to me most miserable. If on the way I—but no, it is useless. The misery, the deep agony of spirit I have suffered, no mortal knows nor ever will. The torture of body is severe; I have had my share of that,—rheumatism, neuralgia, headache, toothache, fever, and most maladies flesh is heir to. But all these are slight when compared with the pangs of an offended or wounded spirit. The heart alone knoweth its own sorrow. I have borne it these many years. I have borne it all my life. . . .

"I am tempted to tell you a secret. It is the secret of my life. I have

Alexander Hamilton Stephens

never told it to any one. But I will tell it to you, and I fear you will not believe it. But it is true; and if you never suspected it, that shows how true I have been to myself in keeping it.

"The secret of my life has been—revenge reversed. That is, to rise superior to the neglect or contumely of the mean of mankind, by doing them good instead of harm. A determination to war even against fate; to meet the world in all its forces; to master evil with good, and to leave no foe standing in my rear. My greatest courage has been drawn from my deepest despair; and the greatest efforts of my life have been the fruits of a determination, a firm resolve, excited by so slight a thing as a look. This feeling, this principle,—call it what you will,—is the mainspring of my action. When I have looked upon the world and seen it filled with knaves and fools, and have seen in the whole waste not one well of water from which I could draw a drop to slake my thirsting, parched soul, with all hopes blighted: when I have been ready to lie down and die under the weight of that grief which is greater than all other griefs. . . .

"I have often had my whole soul instantly aroused with the fury of a lion and the ambition of a Caesar by, I repeat, as slight a thing as a look! What have I not suffered from a look! what have I not suffered from the tone of a remark, from a sense of neglect, from a supposed injury,—an intended injury! But every such pang was the friction that brought out the latent fires. My spirit of warring against the world, however, never had in it anything of a desire to crush or trample; no, only a desire to get above them, to excel them, to enjoy the gratification of seeing them feel that they were wrong; to compel their admiration. . . . This is the extent of my ambition; this the length, breadth, and depth of my revenge. It has in it nothing low or mean, for it is to triumph over the base that it stimulates me to action. To be really sweet it must be essentially pure,—pure in principle, and pure in exertion.

"But what poor consolation is this! What short-lived pleasures attend victory thus attained! Sometimes my evil genius, like Job's comforters, jeers and taunts my human kindness, casts scorn upon my good nature, bids me turn cynic and man-hater,—an Ishmaelite,—bids me raise my hand against every man as every man's hand is raised against me. Oh, the fiendish genius of the tempting imp! I shall take none of his counsels.

"Now you may think that I am somewhat moody to-night, to be indulging in such a strain. No; not more than usual. It is true, I was musing when I got your letter, thinking over many things that have annoyed and pained me excessively,—small things, it is true; but things that sent their sting to the soul,—to the very quick of life,—and your letter added some fuel to the flame. But still I am not in what I sometimes call a melancholy mood."[98]

From a June 23, 1851, letter to Howell Cobb, concerning Cobb's upcoming campaign:
☞ "I have been extremely ill—but am now better—am able to sit up, that is all. I cannot walk out yet. I see you are going to have a bitter and heated contest. You must be wide awake with all your wits at command from the word go. No time is to be lost. You have an adroit and wily competitor. Take the stump and keep it on all suitable occasions. . . .

"In reference to the calling out of the militia, etc., maintain the right of the President and duty of the President to execute the law against all factious opposition whether in Mass. or S.C. Maintain the power to execute the fugitive slave law at the North and the power to execute the Revenue or any other law against any lawless opposition in S.C. Turn the whole force of this upon the revolutionary movement in S.C., and urge all good citizens who value law and order and the rights of liberty and property to stand by the supremacy of the law. This is the life and soul of a republic. Warn the good people of Georgia to beware of revolution—refer to France—and plant yourself against the factionists of S.C., upon the constitution of the country. The right of secession treat as an abstract question. It is but a right to change the Govt., a right of revolution, and maintain that no just cause for the exercise of such right exists. And keep the main point prominent, that the only question now is whether we should go into revolution or not. S.C. is for it. This is the point to keep prominent. I wish I had strength to write more or to give you my views more at large. Our central committee must be at work soon. There never was a more bitter contest I expect in our state than will be this fall. Our opponents will leave no stone unturned, no lie untold, and no dollar they can raise unspent. You must be up and awake."[99]

From an October 26, 1851, letter to his brother Linton. Stephens here relates a story told to him by his friend William Campbell of Atlanta, Georgia:
☞ "William said that a man got off the [railroad] cars at _____ and ran out on the platform, and cried out, 'Aleck Stephens is on the cars!' whereupon a number of persons came out and gazed about, and looked in. One old man came up and asked him if he knew me. Will said 'yes.' 'Is he on the cars?' 'Yes.' 'Where is he? I want to see him,' said the old man. 'If you want to see him you must be in a hurry, for the cars will start in a moment.' 'Oh, I just want to look at him; I never saw him; point him out to me; that will do.' William then led him forward to the baggage-car, where I was sitting smoking, looking out on the other side. 'That is he,' said William. The old man raised his hands, exclaiming, 'Good Lord!' William told us of several other similar scenes on the [rail]road the same day, how persons got him to point me out. But they all laughed heartily at the exclamation of the old man, so great was his

disappointment.

"I added to their glee by telling them that the old fellow was like a man I met in Cherokee in 1843, who came up to me after I had spoken, and said, 'Well, if I had been put in the road to shoot a smart man, you would have passed safe, sure!' At this—which was strictly true—they all laughed more heartily, I believe, than at William's story. For they then seemed to laugh with a liberty,—I had given them a license to laugh."[100]

The following comments on "energy" are from Stephens' July 21, 1852, address at Emory College, Oxford, Georgia:
☛ "By energy I mean application, attention, activity, perseverance, and untiring industry in that business or pursuit, whatever it may be, which is undertaken. Nothing great or good can ever be accomplished without labor and toil. Motion is the law of living nature. Inaction is the symbol of death, if it is not death itself. The hugest engines, with strength and capacity sufficient to drive the mightiest ships across the stormy deep, are utterly useless without a moving power.

"Energy is the steam-power, the motive-principle of intellectual capacity. A small body driven by a great force will produce a result equal to, or even greater than, that of a much larger body moved by a considerably less force. So it is with our minds. Hence it is that we often see men of comparatively small capacity, by greater energy alone, leave—and justly leave—their superiors in natural gifts far behind them in the race for honors, distinction, and preferment.

"It is this principle in human nature which imparts that quality which we designate by the very expressive term, 'force of character,' which meets, defies, and bears down all opposition. This is, perhaps, the most striking characteristic of those great minds and intellects which never fail to impress their names, ideas, and opinions indelibly upon the history of the times in which they live.

"Men of this class are those pioneers of thought who sometimes, even 'in advance of the age,' are known and marked in history as originators and discoverers, or those who overturn old orders and systems of things and build up new ones. To this class belong Columbus, Watt, Fulton, Franklin, and Washington. It was to this same class that General Jackson belonged; for he not only had a very clear conception of his purpose, but a will and energy to execute it. And it is in the same class, or among the first order of men, that Henry Clay will be assigned a place.

"His aims and objects were high, and worthy of the greatest efforts; they were not to secure the laurels won on the battlefield, but those wreaths which adorn the brow of the wise, the firm, the sagacious, and far-seeking statesman. In his life and character a most striking example is presented of what energy and indomitable perseverance can do even when opposed by most adverse circumstances."[101]

From a December 31, 1852, letter to his brother Linton:
☞ "How time flies, and how the years pass by us! I well remember the first letter I ever wrote. It was in 1826. It was, I think, the second Sunday after I went to my new home upon the breaking-up of our little family-circle on the death of father and ma. Its date therefore, I think, was May 28th, 1826. The letter was written to Uncle James Stephens, of Pennsylvania, giving him an account of our affliction. The day and its incidents I shall never forget. Uncle Aaron had gone to meeting. . . . Brother Aaron Grier and I were both writing letters. The day was clear, calm, and warm. We had a table in the middle of the big room. It was some time before we could get a pen a-piece. I need not tell you that at that time no such thing as a pen of any kind but a goosequill was ever heard of, in those parts, at least. Our inkstand was a little leather-covered phial that Uncle Aaron used to take with him when he went from home: in this phial was some cotton that held the ink; and the pen was filled by pressing it against the saturated cotton. . . . I wish I could see that letter now. I was all day at it. When Uncle Aaron came home, he looked over both letters and made some corrections, and then we had them to write over again. . . . This was my first letter. It was the utterance of the bitterest grief. As children come into the world crying, so my first effort of speech through the medium of writing was to make known by such signs as I could command the almost unutterable emotions of a wounded spirit. The body is better off in this respect than the soul: the body can weep and cry; its pains have a natural outlet. But the afflicted soul has no voice; it cannot cry: it has no tears; it cannot weep. This I have often felt, but never so keenly and oppressively as at the death of father. Could my suffering spirit then have given one shriek, it seemed to me that it would have afforded some relief. . . . But there are no words that can convey any idea of the agonies with which I was tortured. . . . But where am I wandering to? When I began this epistle I had no idea of saying all this about my first letter.

"But an old year never goes out without receiving from me a melancholy farewell. I am in the mood of mind to-day well suited for such a leave-taking. I am confined to my room, half sick, and lonely. I am sitting up, but feel weak and giddy, and should fall or faint if I were to attempt to walk or stand long."[102]

Franklin Pierce

Stephens, whose public speeches would sometimes stretch on for two and half hours in length, was well-known for his forceful denunciation of his political opponents. In the early 1850s, when asked if he thought he was being too harsh in his attacks on the political party called Know-Nothingism, he replied:

☞ "No; it is a disease, not for plasters [band-aids], but for the knife."[103]

From a May 1853 letter to his brother Linton, who has recently married:

☞ "If it were not for you, it seems that this wide world would be a perfect desert to me. Among the millions who inhabit it, no other congenial spirit is found with whom I can hold full communion of thought. . . . Perhaps you may think I am low-spirited. Perhaps it is so. Have I not enough to make me so? But I assure you that I do not feel depressed. I have an elasticity of soul which seems to bear me up even in the midst of the greatest troubles of mind and body."[104]

From a July 6, 1853, letter to his brother Linton, concerning his dog Rio:
☛ "In all my strolls from one room to another I have a constant companion,—it is none other than Rio. The dog never stuck so close to me in his life. He sleeps at my feet in the day, and at night, before I go upstairs to bed. Last week when it was so hot, he got into a way of starting with me, but when I mounted the first step of the stairs he would throw himself at the foot of it with a grunt, and remain there for an hour or so, and then come up and see that I was in bed, when he would return to the cool place. During the night he would repeat his visit several times. He seemed to think that by his sleeping at the foot of the steps I could not get out without his knowing it. . . . But, notwithstanding many praiseworthy traits, he has a good deal of the dog about him. To-day he deliberately took a bone away from Edmund's dog, Watch, and ate it up. That, I thought, was a downright doggish trick. I tried to make him feel mean about it; but he did not seem to comprehend me at all."[105]

From a December 22, 1853, letter to his brother Linton. Stephens is in Washington suffering from a severe illness:
☛ "I have been very sick since I wrote to you last. That night—Monday—I was taken with high fever, ending in an attack which I call colic. Tuesday I suffered greatly, but got easy about three o'clock. Last night I had a return of high, burning fever, which lasted all night, and is not off now, at two P.M. My pulse is 100. I am taking quinine, and am sitting up, though perhaps I ought to be in bed, but I have some letters that I must answer. When I shall write to you again I do not know. I am now getting too sick to proceed. I will keep you advised of my condition by others, if I cannot write myself. I am going to have a serious attack, I feel assured of that. Withal, my lungs are badly affected, though I think only sympathetically."[106]

From a December 25, 1853, Christmas letter to his brother Linton:
☛ "A bright, joyous-looking day without. I am sitting up a little to have my bed made, while enjoying the cheerful light from my window. How delicious is pure light! It falls upon the senses like pure water upon the body. It invigorates and vivifies.

"... There is one thing, however, that I wish to impress upon you, and that is an earnest desire that you shall not permit yourself to become uneasy on my account, or suppose that I suffer from any apprehension. I had more uneasiness when I felt the first touch of the disease than now. I have grown used to confinement, used to my room, feel no restlessness to be out, and am prepared to get along in the best way I can, without any heavy care about it. 'Patience is a great virtue,' some one has said. If this be true, I have at least one great virtue."[107]

From a May 26, 1854, letter to J. W. Duncan of Pennsylvania:
☞ "Dear Duncan, Long before you get this, you will have heard the glorious news of the result of the Nebraska bill and the triumph of the compromise of 1850. The contest in the House was close and hot but we whipped the opposition out and carried the measure by 13 majority. The excitement has nearly all passed away. Nobody says anything now against it but the abolitionists. Let them howl on. "'Tis their vocation."

"We shall soon have another question which will absorb all others. That is our relations with Spain growing out of the state of affairs in Cuba. What is to become of this no one now can tell. The position of the [Pierce] Administration is not known upon it. You need put no reliance on rumours from this city on that point. They are as yet mum. But of one thing I am pretty well persuaded at this time and that is there will be a revolt in Cuba before the late registration edict of the Gov. of Cuba goes into effect in August. By that edict about half of the slaves of the island will be declared free. The planters there will not submit. Will not aid in that struggle go from the United States? I think it will, in spite of proclamations and indictments. My sympathies will be with the revolutionists and so will the sympathies of a majority of our people. But I can say no more now.

"I expect to start home Monday. I am to be at LaGrange at court on the first Monday in June. I wish to get you to do me a favour and that is to look over the files of the Federal Union and copy an editorial of that paper, printed I think on the 7th July, 1844, reviewing a speech I made in Milledgeville on the night of the 4th July 1844. It was the first paper printed after the 4th and I think its date was the 7th. A copy of that editorial I wish you to send me at Crawfordville. I will get it there when I return from LaGrange. Your attention to this will greatly oblige me."[108]

From a June 6, 1854, letter to his brother Linton:
☞ "Yesterday I spent down on the plantation. I walked all over the old place, 'solitary and alone.' With feelings of deep sadness I surveyed many a spot

sacred in memory. . . . Harry [a servant] will take this on to you to-morrow, and will also take Rio. Poor dog! he has stuck to me this time as close as a brother."[109]

From a June 26, 1854, letter to W. W. Burwell:
☛ "Dear Sir: Mr. Toombs a few days ago showed me a letter from you enclosing some editorials from the *Patriot*. It so happened that only one of my papers in which these editorials appeared ever came to hand. That was the one containing the last. How this occurred I do not know. There has been no failure to receive the paper (save in these instances) since I ordered it. I mention the fact that you may if you choose make inquiry to ascertain if a suppression of the issues was general towards the South or Southern subscribers.

"I was highly pleased with the position assumed and the views presented in the articles alluded to—and I will also add that I showed them to a number of Southern Whigs of the House, including Preston of Ky., Zollicoffer of Tenn. and Caruthers of Mo., who were quite as well pleased with them as I was myself. The truth is the Southern Whigs must strike out a lead for themselves. They can not afford either for their own sake or that of the country to fall into the ranks of either of the great nominal parties as they are now organized and constituted. I see the *Columbus Enquirer* of Georgia is advocating the policy of our starting a ticket of Southern men for Pres. and Vice President. This I am decidedly opposed to and have so written to the author of the articles in that paper of this character. What we want is a sound national organization upon broad—national—republican principles. We want no sectional men or sectional issues—at least so long as national men enough can be found to make a party on national issues and principles. If the Southern Whigs will but maintain their position of 1850 and the principles of the Kansas and Nebraska bill just passed, and hold no affiliation with any party North or South which does not make these principles the test of their organization, all will be well and a most glorious triumph in a short time will be the result. Decision, firmness and boldness in the maintenance of this position is all that is wanted. Hundreds and thousands of Northern Whigs when they see that this is our fixed determination will abandon the Seward ranks of Antislavery agitators. There is nothing that will tend so much to a speedy purification of both parties North as a resolute purpose on our part to adhere to this course. I have no time to say more now but to bid you good cheer and to invoke you to keep the flag flying. The *National Intelligencer* has already calmed on the question of repeal, and many more papers worse than that will follow suit when they see that we are in earnest."[110]

From a November 16, 1854, letter to his brother Linton:

☛ "The life of a religious man is beautiful to contemplate, and his end is one that angels might envy."[111]

From a December 23, 1854, letter to his brother Linton:

☛ "I have been so pressed with business, and so unwell withal under my pressure, that I have not been able to write you. It seems to me that my labors here increase with my length of service. I am worn down and nearly worn out, and yet I keep up at work until eleven o'clock every night. I believe I never stood so high in public estimation here as I now do, and this is what puts so much business on me. My position on the Ways and Means makes it necessary for me to see a great many persons and look into a great many matters."[112]

From a December 24, 1854, letter to his brother Linton:

☛ "It is Sunday and Christmas-eve. I am not exactly alone, but lonely in feeling. About me I have company in abundance, but my mind wanders to persons and scenes far distant. The closing year always fills me with sadness. At least it has done so ever since our family was dispersed, when I was but a boy. Before that painful crisis in my life Christmas was a joyous time. Its coming was looked to for weeks as a period of jubilee. Never has it been so with me since I left the old homestead and fireside lighted up with a father's smile. To-day, I know not why, I feel particularly melancholy on the return of that season which to all others is usually the season of festivity. Perhaps the dreariness of the day adds some weight to the depression of my spirits. At any rate, so it is; the very signals of joy that others are firing sound in my ears like minute-guns at sea.

"Shall I ever see another Christmas-eve? Why should I wish it? Life to me is desolate. For what object should I wish to live? As to myself, I assure you I have none. Yet to the world I am by no means misanthropic, while there are cords which bind me to a few as tender as the very nerves of life. But what can my longer stay on this theatre do for them? Will it not be, if such a future is in store for me, but a prolongation of painful anxiety and miserable solicitude for their welfare, without any ability to shape, much less to control, their destiny? These you may look upon as gloomy reflections. They are. I am utterly enveloped in gloom. Shadows surround me and thick darkness seems coming over me. My life is burdened with the discharge of duties heavy and onerous. Among these duties none oppress me more than the ordinary civilities and courtesies of life. I mean the entertainment of those whom I meet, so as to render them as happy as I can without making known to them by word or look the 'aching void' within. This I consider a duty, but it requires a great effort to perform it. It is a legitimate tax to society which every member ought to pay. . . . It is often a matter of thought and reflection to me, when friends have left my room whom I have kept in a roar of laughter, how little do they know of the miserableness of one who appeared to be in such spirits. Then comes the self-inquiry, Am I indeed a hypocrite?—of all characters to me the most detestable. I think not. A man is under no more obligation to expose his griefs than to exhibit his bruises and sores. These should be shown to only the trusted few who have access to the inner shrine of his heart. To this shrine, with me, but one living being upon earth was ever admitted, and that one is yourself. If I had not one at least with whom I thus could communicate, it appears to me that life would become intolerable. Do you ask, then, why I am thus miserable? It is because I meet with little sympathy from the world. Even the praise of those who approve, from whatever motive given, is often, indeed most frequently offered, in a manner which is gall and wormwood to me. My life has been a warfare from the beginning. My strife has been with fate. The contest began in the cradle and will end only in the grave. Weak and sickly, I was sent into the world with a constitution barely able to sustain the vital functions. Health I have never known and do not expect to know. But this I could bear: pain I can endure; I am used to it. Physical sufferings are not the worst ills I am heir to. I find no unison of feelings, tastes, and sentiments with the world. . . . I feel myself to be alone; and feel that my habitation should be in solitude. But do not think that I cower before fate. No; to my destiny I bow, submissively bow to that which is beyond my control. I yield to nothing else. And even in solitude I feel that spirit within me which would enable me, so far from sinking into despair, to drink to the very dregs the bitterest cup that time can measure out, and looking up, ask for more."[113]

From a December 31, 1854, letter to his brother Linton:
☛ "Public sentiment in this country is in a transition state, so far as the principle of party organization is concerned. Old parties, old names, old issues, and old organizations are passing away. A day of new things, new issues, new leaders, and new organizations is at hand. The men now in power, holding their places by the foulest coalition known in our history, seem not to foresee that doom which evidently awaits them. Standing upon no policy but the division of the spoils, their time is taken up in revelry and riotous living out of the public treasury. But like Belshazzar at the feast, they have the handwriting on the wall, whether they can read it or not."[114]

From a January 4, 1855, letter to his brother Linton. Stephens is in Washington, D.C.:
☛ "Mr. and Mrs. Toombs and myself gave [newlyweds] Mr. [William C.] and

Cotton Gin

Mrs. Dawson a sort of bridal or complimentary dinner. We had thirteen persons at table besides ourselves. The company consisted of Mr. and Mrs. Dawson, Governor and Mrs. Pratt, Governor and Mrs. Brown, Mr. and Mrs. Badger, Mr. Hilliard, of Alabama, Dr. Reese, of Georgia, Colonel Hardee, U.S.A., Judge Wayne, and Mr. Pearce, of Maryland. The dinner was a splendid one,—one of the best I ever saw served in Washington.

". . . We had one pass that made a roar of laughter in which all joined. Badger proposed to drink my health. He was at the farther end of the table, so that all heard him. He began by saying that when La Fayette visited this country, he inquired of some one who was presented to him if he was married. The gentleman answered that he was. 'Happy man!' replied the old general. The next one coming up was asked the same question, and the answer was 'No.' 'Lucky dog!' exclaimed La Fayette. Badger then drank to me as the 'lucky dog.' When all had emptied their glasses, I said that La Fayette had shown great tact in getting out of a scrape; greater, I feared, than I should show. But, as I knew nothing of the mysteries of the 'happy man's' case, I could only reply in the language of a Western lawyer I once heard of, who concluded his argument by saying, 'May it please your Honor, I know nothing of the mysteries of the law of this case, and my only reliance is to trust to the sublimity of luck, and float on the surface of the occasion.' All laughed heartily and agreed that I had got off very well."[115]

From a January 8, 1855, letter to his brother Linton:
☞ "It seems to me that but for an effort that no other mortal upon earth would make, I should sink into profound indifference to all things connected with men and their affairs. But with that effort that I daily exert, to the persons about me I appear, I have no doubt, to be one of the most cheerful and happy men upon earth. I dined on Saturday at [William B.] Preston's. There was a large party,—a splendid show, and I went through it just as if I enjoyed it. I thought it my duty to do so, and for that reason I did it. But if I had consulted my own inclinations, I should have spent the time in solitude."[116]

From a January 18, 1855, letter to his brother Linton:
☞ "I have been quite unwell all this week. Monday I spoke. I had an immense audience, and made, I think, a good speech."[117]

From a January 21, 1855, letter to his brother Linton. Note that the Northernization of the South, one of the meddling Yankee's many goals, is already in full swing:
☞ "The Democratic members from the South are generally a good-for-nothing set. They follow the Administration, and the whole Administration policy now is courting the North. They are undisguisedly against Cuba, and against Kansas coming in as a slave State. That is, they want the people there to prohibit it, and hence Southern members do not look with favor upon any argument in favor of Southern institutions. As to the Southern press, what shall I say of it? It does nothing but revamp Northern ideas and Northern news. If I were to illustrate it by a figure, I could draw a very apt one from Ohio, on which my thoughts have lately been mostly occupied. The way of fattening hogs there in some places is to put them in pens or floors in tiers over each other. The corn is first given to the topmost tier. What passes through is fed upon by the next, and so on down to the last, and what stuff they have! Such is just the stuff which descends from the Northern to the Southern press."[118]

From a Spring 1855 letter to his brother Linton:
☞ "I have a presentiment that my career is nearly run. I have a great deal to say to you; but it does seem when we are together that I have no time to talk. Soon we shall be separated, never to meet in this life; and then how strange it will seem to you that we talked so little about those things that you will then think most about!"[119]

From an April 20, 1855, letter to his brother Linton:

☛ "I have determined to have nothing more to do with politics under the new regime. I notified them in conversation at Oglethorpe that I was out of the field. I was not a candidate for re-election, and I should not be as things were now going. The leading ideas now sought to be inculcated upon the Whigs are to proscribe foreigners and Catholics; but I should do neither. . . . The most dangerous enemies to our country are the Free-Soilers and Abolitionists. To crush them out I would join with any honest man, be he Jew or Gentile, American-born or adopted citizen."[120]

From a May 26, 1855, letter to his brother Linton:

☛ "To-morrow night I intend to go to Augusta and declare myself a candidate for Congress. I have heard taunts that I am afraid to run. I will run, let the consequences be what they may. I may be beaten; but I may sow seeds of truth in the canvass that hereafter may save the country. If I can do that, what though I fall? The times are ominous, and every man should do what he can to arrest a monstrous outrage upon the Constitution, though he fall in his work. . . . I feel my blood up. When the preacher's voice is raised for religious persecution, and against the Catholics, I think of the infamous [English perjurer] Titus Oates. Enough! I shall be in the fight, thick and heavy."[121]

In late May 1855 Stephens uttered the following words during his reelection speech at Augusta, Georgia:

☛ "I am again a candidate for Congress from this district. My name is hereby presented——not by any convention but by myself. Do with it as each of you may think proper."[122]

From the same Augusta speech. The first two sentences would later be inscribed on his grave site memorial at his home "Liberty Hall":

☛ "I am afraid of nothing on earth, or above the earth, or under the earth, but to do wrong. The path of duty I shall endeavor to travel, fearing no evil, and dreading no consequences. I would rather be defeated in a good cause than to triumph in a bad one. I would not give a fig for a man who would shrink from the discharge of duty for fear of defeat."[123]

From a June 23, 1855, letter to his brother Linton, who had just been nominated a candidate for Congress in a district adjoining Stephens':

☛ "The ride to me this evening was one of meditation. . . . You were the central figure of my thoughts. Your success, not only in this new step you are about to take, but in the greater future of life before you, just now beginning to open,—this was the engrossing theme of my thoughts. You embody all that is really dear to me in life. In you and about you are centred all my hopes and aspirations of an earthly nature; and whatever affects your welfare and happiness touches me more sensitively, if possible, than anything that affects my own. I could bear almost anything if I knew that all was well with you. And I shall feel and take much more interest in your success in this race than in my own. If you are elected I shall feel content, whatever may be my fate. Arm yourself, therefore, for the fight. The first thing is to get a perfect command of your temper: on all occasions on the stump to be in a good humor. Provide yourself with every document or reference that you may want. Think of the question in all its length and breadth, until your soul shall glow with the ardor of patriotism, which shall seek vent by utterance through the lips. Good-night. My old house looks cheerless tonight."[124]

From a November 30, 1855, letter to his brother Linton:
☛ "I am once more, as you see, in Washington, and I feel badly. If I had my course for the last nine months to go over again, I believe now I should not be a candidate, but should remain at home and attend to my business. In public life the game with me is not worth the candle. I find it is all I can do to live here without going in debt; while my affairs at home are sadly neglected in my absence. At the hotel I could not get comfortable quarters for less than about one hundred and fifty to one hundred and seventy-five dollars per month for myself and servant. I looked about a day or two, and am now settled on the corner of Sixth and D Streets, at Crutchett's."[125]

From a December 11, 1855, letter to his brother Linton:
☛ ". . . Sometimes I have a good will to quit work and take my ease, and go home and attend to my business, letting the people get some one else to do their work. For what does it all amount to? Nothing—absolutely nothing. This world's honor, when the cup of ambition is filled to the brim, is nothing at last but vanity and vexation of spirit."[126]

Yankee slave market

2

Personal Letters & Observations

Part Two

From a January 8, 1856, letter to his brother Linton:
☞ "The snow is still unmelted. The thermometer yesterday morning was 6° below zero, in the city. Mine, hanging at my window, was at 2° above when I got up at seven. It was intensely cold: never since I have been in Washington was it colder."[127]

From a February 5, 1856, letter to his brother Linton:
☞ "[My servant] Harry sends me word that my old white cow is dead. Poor old soul! She went to jump into Billy Bell's field, and encountered a ditch on the other side of the field, into which she fell, and out of which she never came alive. She got her head up-stream, dammed up the water, and, Harry thinks, drowned. Another motherless calf has mourned the loss of an ill-fated dam."[128]

From a March 9, 1856, letter to his brother Linton:

☞ ". . . By the way, I have thought it a little strange that I have never yet but once been invited (and that when I was very ill two months ago) to dine with [U.S. President Franklin] Pierce, nor have I yet dined with a single member of his Cabinet. Whether I have been omitted by intention or from forgetfulness I do not know nor do I care. I only mention the fact as a singular one. It never occurred with any previous President, not excepting [James K.] Polk or his Cabinet."[129]

From a March 11, 1856, letter to his brother Linton:
☞ "I have just come from the House, where I spoke upon the Kansas election, on the motion to empower the Committee to send for persons and papers. I will give you no opinion of the speech, except that I did not disgrace myself, *me judice* ["in my judgement"]. What the audience thought of it I shall be better able to judge when I see the papers. I received many compliments, but they are so cheap here I do not regard them as of much importance. I had a large audience; the largest that has assembled since the House was organized; galleries full and crowded. No other person has drawn anything like such a crowd. . . . I got your letter this morning. It was greeted with pleasure. I was anxious to hear from you. Poor Rio! my heart yearned for him. I tell you the truth, I almost wept when I read your account of his encounter with Bill Alexander's dog. Not that I felt great apprehension for Rio's safety; but I feel an interest in that dog that I never did in the inferior animals, and never shall in any again, I am certain. And the reason of it is mainly on account of his attachment and fidelity to me. I dream of him frequently."[130]

In 1838 Stephens was able to make one of his boyhood dreams come true, as he describes in the following letter, dated June 3, 1856:
☞ "I assure you that that part of my life which is by far the most interesting is that which was spent on the 'old homestead,' under the paternal roof, and in the family circle. That was the 'day-dawn' period with me. It was short, nor was it always happy,—far from it; but the remembrance of it has always been sweet though mournful. My strong attachment to the place, the hills, the springs, the brooks, the rocks, and even the gullies with which I was familiar from my earliest recollection, determined my whole course of life. By that alone my destiny has been controlled. It was this alone that caused me to settle in Crawfordville, close by, where I could visit them at pleasure. When I was admitted to the bar in 1834, the prospect of a young lawyer there without means was little short of starvation just ahead. The most liberal inducements were offered me to go to Columbus and become one of a firm, with a proffered guarantee of fifteen hundred dollars for the first year. This I declined for no

other reason but a fixed determination I had formed never to quit, if I could avoid it, those places nearest my heart, where I played as well as toiled in my youth, about which I had so often dreamed in my orphan wanderings, and which I was determined to own in my own name if I should ever be able to make the purchase. This is what kept me at Crawfordville. And often during the first year after my settlement there did I walk down (for horse I had none to ride) to see those old familiar scenes, and earnestly look forward to the day when by aid of propitious fortune I might call them my own, and feel that whatever else might betide me, I had the place which of all others I wished to live at, and to be buried at when I die. This local attachment, I tell you, warped, shaped, and controlled my destiny. . . . The great object of my youthful days, to buy it back again, I was unable to accomplish until 1838. The owner, wishing to remove to Alabama, came to terms upon which we agreed, and I own it still. I have added considerably to it since; but it is all esteemed by me as the 'old homestead,' about which cluster the brightest images in the memory of my whole existence."[131]

From a July 20, 1856, letter to his brother Linton:
☞ "This morning's mail brought me letters containing the sad intelligence that our only [living] brother [John Lindsay Stephens] was no more on earth. I am truly overwhelmed with grief, and hardly know what to say or how to write to you on the subject. The truth is I can hardly realize the fact. . . . This day week I wrote him a long letter. That letter I am informed he did not live to read; it reached his office the day after his eyes were sealed in death. And is it so that I shall never see his familiar face and form again? . . . It seems to me now that if I could recall any unkind word or look I may have given him, that it would afford me consolation. But this cannot be. I shall go home as soon as I can leave here. I did intend to go to New York next Saturday, but that is out of the question now. I was going there to make a speech; but I do not now feel as if I could make any speech this summer. I must see after the family of my poor brother, and must do what I can to keep those most dear to him from want."[132]

From an August 31, 1856, letter to his brother Linton:
☞ "I get great numbers of letters from Pennsylvania, Ohio, Indiana, Illinois, urging me to go to those States; but not a line from home. My intention is to go home as soon as I can get there. I do not like the tone of our Georgia papers. It makes me almost despair of the future of our section. I fear we are doomed to divisions and factions. I cannot believe, however, that the [Millard] Fillmore movement can result in anything more than in sowing seeds of mischievous divisions hereafter. . . . I understand that the Republicans [the Liberals of the

day] have spent five hundred thousand dollars on Pennsylvania. These merchants of the North, who have grown rich out of us, are shelling out their money like corn now to oppress us; and yet thousands, even of Georgians, would sing hosannahs at the triumph of our enemies!"[133]

From a December 30, 1856, letter to his brother Linton:
☛ "If you were to be called hence [that is, pass away], my existence would be

Zachary Taylor

miserable indeed. I do not know how I could bear it. But if I were to be called, your lot would not be so bad. You have other reliances for support and sustainment. The thought that by possibility I may be detained on the stage of action longer than you, fills me with the deepest gloom."[134]

From a January 15, 1857, letter to his brother Linton, whose wife Emmeline (Thomas) was deathly ill:
☛ "May He who rules over us and shapes our destinies guard and protect you, watch over and protect her who always puts trust in Him! I write this in the House [of Representatives] in the midst of confusion. I can only say, God be with you, and be merciful to you in sparing her who is so dear to you, and whose speedy recovery is my earnest desire and prayer."[135]

From a January 18, 1857, letter to his brother Linton. Emmeline has died:
☛ "I do wish I had been there; not only that I might have seen her once more in this life, but that I might have mingled my sorrow with yours, and thus have afforded you at least the small comfort of the sympathy of a heart not unused to the bitterest pangs that life can bear. Few mortals have suffered more than I have; and few that see me and associate with me daily, have a conception of what torture and misery I endure. But of all the sufferings I have ever yet been subjected to, the loss of dear ones is the worst. This is like cutting the very heart-strings of life. I felt it on the death of our dear father, whose dead form

now lies stretched before me in my mind's eye. Then my cup of grief was near running over. One more drop, and I should have sunk and died under it. I felt something of the same upon the death of my brother [Aaron] Grier [Stephens]. These were the most severe trials of my life. I have felt deep grief upon many other occasions; but on those, the very nerves of my life were touched. I have no doubt that you have felt, or do now feel, that deep agony of the soul that I then felt. Oh, how I sympathize with you, and how I wish I could be with you! I think of you day and night. If I were not afraid of being detained on the road in exposure that would jeopard my life, I would go immediately to see you. But such is the condition of the roads, I fear to start. The appearance this morning indicates another snow before tomorrow. I to-day raised blood upon coughing. . . . I want to see you and talk to you. But as this is impossible at present, let us commune as often on paper as we can. May Heaven watch over, guard, and protect you!"[136]

From a Spring 1857 letter to his brother Linton:
☛ "No mortal has ever had more reason to despair—to curse his fate and die—than I have had; and few men, I imagine, have ever suffered more deeply and intensely. I have sometimes been on the very brink of despair: but I have borne all, and believe that I am better in consequence. Out of the very bitterest weeds of life I draw sweetness and consolation; out of disappointments, crosses, and ills I extract comfort and hope. . . . The subject of the condition of the spirits of the dead [ghosts], whether they are in a conscious state or not, whether or not they are permitted to look on and see what we the survivors are doing, was once a matter of most perplexing thought to me. But these are matters not intended for mortals to know; and no good can come of thinking upon them. It is sufficient for me to be resolved that if the spirits of those most dear to me when living, who are now departed, do look on and see what I am doing, they will be gratified at what I do or try to do. In my severest grief for the death of friends, the best consolation I ever had was the reflection that those friends would be pained to know that I was suffering so much on their account. This thought has checked many a sigh and tear. . . . Father told me, two nights before he died, that he thought he should die. We were alone, and he talked a long time with me. He enjoined upon me how I should act in case he died. All my energy came from those dying injunctions. At least in my greatest grief, a resolve to perform them was the ruling passion that prevailed. And it is a ruling passion with me yet. His memory I can never forget. And it seems to me that I should never have been happy since his death had it not been for the reflection that he would take pleasure in seeing me happy. And now again good-by. May God, the God of our common father, protect and sustain you

and make you still useful and happy in your day and generation!"[137]

From a June 15, 1857, letter to his brother Linton:
☛ "I have no object on earth but you and your happiness to engross my mind. I am thinking of you nearly all the time. Business I have to attend to, but in business, at home or abroad, you are in my mind."[138]

From a December 25, 1857, letter to his brother Linton:
☛ "This morning I got your letter of the 20th, the one in which you spoke of Rio, and told me he had been howling, off and on, all the evening. Poor dog! How that news affected me! I wonder if he was howling for his master,—if he was grieving for my absence. The thought that he might be touched me deeply, and made me sad. I have been sad all day. . . . Mr. Toombs reached here this morning. He called up soon; but notwithstanding all his hilarity and flow of spirits, I could not drive off the melancholy which the thought of my poor dog's howling for me produced."[139]

From a January 20, 1858, letter to his brother Linton, from Washington, D.C.:
☛ "I never had so much work—hard work—to do before. I am at it night and day. I seldom get to bed before twelve and one o'clock, and am up at half-past seven. I am wearing out. I wish I had not consented to come here. I see but little good I can do. I am opposed to most of the policy, as far as I can perceive it, of the present [James Buchanan] Administration."[140]

From a February 5, 1858, letter to his brother Linton:
☛ "Last night we had a battle-royal in the House [of Representatives]. Thirty men at least were engaged in the fisticuff. Fortunately, no weapons were used. . . . Nobody was hurt or even scratched, I believe; but bad feeling was produced by it. It was the first sectional fight ever had on the floor, I think; and if any weapons had been on hand it would probably have been a bloody one. All things here are tending to bring my mind to the conclusion that the Union cannot or will not last long."[141]

From a February or March 1858 letter to his brother Linton:
☛ "I am wearing out my life for nothing. To mix daily with men who have no patriotism, and no object but their own little selfish ends, is disgusting to me. If the admission of Kansas is carried, I shall be done with politics. It is a business I take no pleasure in. . . . I have done my part. Some other must take my place. The rest of my life, whether long or short, I wish to spend in quiet retirement and uninterrupted solitude. Physical pains I am used to: mental pains as well.

No change can increase either. My fortitude, I trust, will never fail me in whatever may await me in the future. . . . If the South would but have the right sort of men here, there would not be the least difficulty. We should carry the Lecompton Constitution, and achieve the greatest triumph in our history. But patriotism is defunct, public virtue is gone, integrity is gone, or at least all these high qualities are fast dying out."[142]

From a March 11, 1858, letter to his brother Linton:
☛ ". . . in the call of the roll there were twenty-two Democrats [then the Conservatives]—Lecompton men—absent, and only five anti-Lecompton. Thirteen of the twenty-two were from the South. Had they been present we should have saved the question. How shamefully the South is represented! Some of the Southern men were too drunk to be got into the House. We got a postponement of the question until to-morrow. . . . I am very apprehensive that we shall be beaten, but it will be by the South. I am almost overwhelmed with mortification to think that the deed will be done by our own people. My heart is sad—sad—sad. . . . If we should separate [from the Union], what is to become of us in the hands of such representatives? Have we any future but miserable petty squabbles, parties, factions, and fragments of organizations, led on by contemptible drunken demagogues? My country—what is to become of it! It is the idol of my life. Her glory, her prosperity, her welfare, happiness and renown. Perhaps it is too much my idol; but it has been the absorbing object of my life's ambition; and yet all is, I fear, about to be blasted."[143]

From an April 17, 1858, letter to fellow Georgia politician Richard M. Johnston:
☛ "I have been overwhelmed with business. My time is taken up, day and night, with the absorbing question of the admission of Kansas. I am now on the Committee of Conference. I am sick, besides, and yet am compelled to be up to give audience to all sorts of views and suggestions. . . . If we can get a recognition of the principle we have been contending for, the right of the State to come in with slavery, or without objection on that score, it is all I can hope for."[144]

From a May 14, 1858, letter to his brother Linton:
☛ "When I received your letters I was thinking of this day thirty-two years ago. It was on that day your mother [Matilda Marbury Somerville Lindsay] followed our common father [Andrew Baskins Stephens] to the world of spirits, leaving you, as I was left before, an orphan in the complete sense of the word,—a helpless child, without father or mother. The day you have perhaps no recollection of; but well do I recollect it. It was the consummation of my woes

at that period of my life; that was the day on which the fate of our little family circle was sealed. Soon we were scattered; and never did the family hearth blaze in cheerfulness again. A few nights before my heart almost sank within me on hearing the screams of an ill-omened bird,——a raven it must have been,——which came near the house on the hill to the southwest, perched, I think, upon the mulberry that still stands there. Ben [a family servant] said, when he heard the croaking of the nightly messenger, that it was the sign of death. His remark sank deep into my soul. I have never heard such a bird before or since, and what kind of a bird it was I do not know. You may set this down to a sprinkling of superstition in my nature; I will plead guilty. . . ."[145]

From a June 11, 1858, letter to his brother Linton. A gloomy Stephens had just purchased a pair of eyeglasses:
☞ "Thus life passes away; time rolls on, years troop by, leaving their foot-prints in wrinkles in the face, gray hairs on the head, and dimmed vision in the eyes. In a few more years, loss of teeth, bending shoulders, and trembling limbs will close the scene."[146]

From a September 3, 1858, letter to Richard M. Johnston. Stephens had just returned home to Crawfordville, Georgia, from a trip to Chicago, Illinois:
☞ "We got home safely, and in time for our court. My health has been considerably benefited. I was a little annoyed when I returned and found that our newspapers had got into such a muss about the purpose of my visit to Illinois. I was really provoked at their ill-grounded surmises and unjust suspicions,——charging political motives and personal objects in forming political combinations,——but I don't care a button for it now. Politics had nothing in the world to do with my travels, and I had as little as possible to do with politics. I was, in reality, running away from the subject. I was in quest of rest

John Caldwell Calhoun

and relaxation, and, as far as possible, eschewed even the mention of the theme in conversation. When my opinion was asked I gave it; as I always have done and always shall. I did not hesitate to say in Ohio and Illinois and everywhere just what I said at home and in Athens before I left, that I should prefer to see [Stephen A.] Douglas elected to [Abraham] Lincoln, and I thought the war of the Washington *Union* on him ought to cease. I did not say that I considered it a 'wickedly foolish' war; but I did say that I thought it an unwise and impolitic war. This is my deliberate judgment; and it is perfectly immaterial with me who approves it and who disapproves it."[147]

In 1858 Stephens and Richard M. Johnston rode to the former's boyhood home, which Stephens referred to as "the homestead." While there Stephens made the following remarks to Johnston:

☛ [On finding the family graveyard, Stephens said:] "Here lie many who were dear to me in life, and here I wish to be buried when I die." [The pair sat on a hillside and Stephens, observing the family's creek below, said:] "How many, many events are associated in my heart with that spring! How many times I have been here when a child, often coming for no other purpose than to muse here undisturbed! Do you see my name carved upon that stone? That was done when I was a boy. Here I have often lain upon my back and looked up through the tops of the trees toward the sky and watched the flying clouds. My mother [who had died when he was child] I had only heard of from others, and when very young I used to come here and think where she then was, and fancied that she might be in one of those passing clouds, and might know how my heart longed for her. But no human being knew that I had such thoughts."[148]

From a January 28, 1859, letter to Richard M. Johnston, from Washington, D.C.:
☛ "I know you would pity me if you were to see my operations for one day. Now what do you think? I was just going to say, if you could see my work, interruptions, calls, and long sittings of visitors, etc.: but before I got the words penned here came a man who consumed a half-hour of my time; and so it is from morning until night, and from night till morning. I rise and breakfast at eight; then commence with my mail. Frequently I do not get half through that before I am bored almost to death with calls on business of all sorts; then to the Committee at ten: then to the House at twelve; then to dinner at four; then calls before I leave the table till twelve at night. Then I take up and get through my unfinished reading of letters and newspapers of the morning; and then at one o'clock get to bed. I now have about one hundred letters before me unanswered. Were you here, you would pity me. . . . But on one thing I am determined: when this session ends, with it will and shall end my connection

with politics forever. Then I can follow, and if life and strength allow, I can and will devote myself to pursuits more congenial to my tastes and nature."[149]

From a March 15, 1859, letter to Richard M. Johnston. Stephens is happy to be home in Georgia again, retired permanently, or so he believes, from politics:
☛ "I felt like a mariner after a long and perilous voyage, who, once more in safety, is permitted to tread the firm ground about his own mansion. God willing, he will remain there. This is my feeling. . . . I feel truly gratified myself that my public services have been closed as they have. Few men have passed more critical junctures with more uniform success, and none in my knowledge have ended their careers with more of the general good will and esteem of men of all parties than I have. This is no small compensation, for the cares, anxieties, and perplexities attending the labors I have performed, in all which I can assure you I have looked to nothing so much as the public good. In all my public acts that has been the leading object and controlling motive. The remainder of my days, whether few or many, I wish to devote to objects more congenial to my nature than looking after and watching the interest and welfare of a restless, captious, and fault-finding people. It is true, I have less to complain of on that score than any one who ever occupied the position I have so long. Indeed, I do not complain at all. Still, it is more agreeable to me to look after my own affairs than other people's. In this course I shall at least be free from that intense sense of responsibility which ever pressed so heavily upon me while occupying a post of public trust and confidence."[150]

From a March 16, 1859, letter to his brother Linton, from home in Crawfordville:
☛ "A part of my daily duties is to doctor poor Rio. Poor fellow, he is blind. When I got home, driving into the yard, just before dark, and saw him at a distance, and called to him, and saw from the motion of his head and body that he could not see me, I almost wept. He knew my voice and came as fast as he could in a devious way, turning right as I spoke to him, until he scented me out, and then put up the most piteous rejoicing bark in evident tones of lamentation. My heart was overcome, but I could do and say nothing but, 'Poor dog! you know your master, do you?' whereupon he seemed to utter something like a cry himself. He now follows me about wherever I go. He barks incessantly if I leave him. He keeps close after me, and follows the sound of my feet. I usually carry a cane, and let that drag along behind for him to hear it more distinctly than he can my tread. He goes thus with me to town; knows when he gets to the court-house steps, knows when he gets to the platform of the depot, knows when he is on the hill-side of the Spring-branch. For two days I have been washing his eyes with sugar of lead: I think it helps them. To-day in walking out

Stephens' dog Rio

in the old fields, I fancied he could see a little. I thought he shunned a bush. Usually he will butt against anything in the way. When I noticed him going round the bush as I thought, I called him to me and said, 'Why, Rio, can master's dog see again?' He opened his inflamed eyes wide, and looked me in the face. Whether he could see or not, I do not know, but he barked joyously and frisked off as he used to do in play. I said, 'Do you want to catch a rabbit?' whereupon he barked as before and seemed to have life enough if he had had his sight. I am going to do my best to cure him."[151]

From a March 18, 1859, letter to his brother Linton:
☛ "My daily recreation and amusement, apart from books and writing, is the melancholy pastime of strolling about the lot and grounds, lending, or rather guiding, a blind dog. Who knows what he will come to? But I tell you it is a great thing for a man to take pleasure in whatever lot he finds himself cast in. This is the secret of life; and I assure you I find more pleasure in thus exercising Rio, and witnessing the pleasure it affords him, than I ever did in the enjoyment of all the honors this world has ever seen fit to bestow upon me, though some of the papers say that no man ever retired from public life with more general good will and favor than I have. So be it: I am content; and whether it be so or

not, I am content."[152]

From a letter to his brother Linton at the close of 1859:
☞ "I like law better than politics, but like being at home better than either; and am now inclined to the opinion that very soon I shall quit the courts, and devote all my time to myself, or with myself. Not this year; but very soon,—if I live."[153]

From a January 29, 1860, letter to his brother Linton:
☞ "I have been down to the old homestead place, over the play-grounds and work-grounds of my youth. These but brought in review their many soul-touching memories. You cannot conceive how deeply I am touched by your tone of depression. But what can I say for your relief? Nothing—absolutely nothing. That must come from yourself, and from Him in whose hands we all are held. Sometimes I am totally bewildered, as if stunned by the incomprehensibilities around me. However, I recover with the confidence that all will be right in the end, if I do my duty. This is the only light by which my faith is guided. This is my only stay, my only staff. The calls of duty, activity, and exertion keep me up, and they are all that do. But for a will which I believe few possess, and for which I am truly thankful, I should long since have sunk into hopeless despair. But that will seems sometimes weak and faltering, as it does this day. Shall it fail me? I trust not. But who can tell? . . . Shall I be able to hold on to the end? That is the question. For twenty-odd years you have been the polar [North] star of my existence. In you all my hopes have been centred. Should you by any means be removed from me, I fear my stay, my staff, would break. You may know, therefore, how keenly I feel anything that concerns you."[154]

From a May 6, 1860, letter to Richard M. Johnston. The Democratic (Conservative) candidates for the upcoming presidential election had just been selected. Unfortunately, with four sets of candidates, the entire Democratic field was weakened, opening up the door for a probable Republican (Liberal) win in November. Stephens was not happy:
☞ "As to the blow-up at Charleston, all I can say is that I deeply regret it, though I was not much disappointed with it. The country is in a bad state, much worse than the people are aware of. This may be the beginning of the end. . . . I am sorry things are as they are; sorry as I should be to see the paroxysms of a dear friend in a fit of delirium tremens. On such occasions it is useless to indulge in complaints or upbraidings; the only question is, can any relief be afforded? But enough. I am taken up with plantation business and with law business, and have but little time to devote to public affairs. I can get along

with any sort of government as well as anybody else."[155]

When asked in May 1860 if he thought "it was entirely right to forbid your name from going before the Charleston Convention as a Democratic (Conservative) candidate for U.S. president?" he replied:
☛ "Yes: I think so, decidedly. The Democratic [Conservative] party had quite enough men from whom to choose. I did not wish the office. In perfect sincerity with you, I should exceedingly dislike to be President. I do not wish that office nor any other. What amazes me in [Stephen A.] Douglas is his desire to be President. I have sometimes asked him what he desired the office for. It has never yet added to the fame of a single man. You may look over the list of the Presidents: which of them made any reputation after he became President? Four years, or even eight, are too short a time to enable a man to pursue a policy which will be permanent enough to give him reputation. Louis Napoleon, as President of France under the Constitution, could have made no reputation. He is beginning now to make it. When he shall have been where he is as long again as he has been already, he may then, if his abilities are really great, become illustrious. I could never see why so many men in this country should be anxious to be President. People don't generally believe me in what I say about myself in this respect; but that is all very indifferent to me. Some of your people in Athens [Georgia] will insist on believing that I opposed the nomination of Governor [Howell] Cobb by the State Convention at Milledgeville. I had nothing upon earth to do with that, neither for nor against him. No, sir; I far prefer living here—right here—to being President of the United States. If I had loved office I should have continued in the House of Representatives. That office to me is preferable to the Presidency. If I were ambitious to make a reputation, I should be able to make it faster in that place than in the other."[156]

From a June 19, 1860, letter to his brother Linton. Stephens expresses his disdain for the Southern secession movement. Though he supports secession as a constitutional right, he denounces it as a solution to the growing conflict between the South and the North:
☛ "The post-office is beginning to be a nuisance. It is now the field for almost as much espionage and villainy, from the prying into a private note to the stealing of a package of bank-bills, as ever the same institution was in Spain, or is now in Cuba. . . . I have no idea what will be done in Baltimore; my conjecture is that they will blow up in a row. The seceders intended from the beginning to rule or ruin; and when they find that they cannot rule, they will then ruin. They have about enough power for this purpose; not much more; and I doubt not but they will use it. Envy, hate, jealousy, spite,—these made

the war in heaven, which made devils of angels, and the same passions will make devils of men. The secession movement was instigated by nothing but bad passions. Patriotism, in my opinion, had no more to do with it than love of God had with the other revolt. . . . I am always more or less an invalid in summer. Last year was the exception with me. I enjoyed better health that summer than I ever did in my life, taking the whole summer together. I have no hope of doing so well this summer, if ever again."[157]

From a July 12, 1860, letter to his brother Linton:
☛ "I am surprised that anybody could have supposed it possible for me to support the seceders' nomination. I should have to blot out my own record for several years past to do this. Others may eat their words, but I do not feed on such diet. It is to me the worst sign of the times to see so many of our public men doing this thing. The surest sign that a dog is going mad is to see him eat his own ordure; and this eating of words and old party principles is, in my judgment, a like sign of approaching rabies among the people. But good-by. I am out of politics, and mean to stay out."[158]

From a November 21, 1860, letter to his brother Linton. Big government Illinois Liberal Abraham Lincoln was elected a few weeks earlier:
☛ "I see by the [Georgia] *Constitutionalist* [the leading conservative Democratic paper of the State] of last night that my plan [to be patient and try to avoid secession at all costs] is not to be backed by that paper. It is going, I suppose, for immediate secession. What else to make of it I do not know. This disheartened me a good deal. I shall patiently wait for further developments, and shall, in the mean time, hold on to my line of policy without wavering or faltering. I think it is right. If that paper is now following the lead of Mr. Toombs, as I apprehend, I do not know what he meant by saying that he did not want the issue in our election to be made on union or disunion per se. Why did he say that he did not want any disunion man elected to the Convention? Secession or separation and disunion mean the same thing. I do not see how, under the idea of the *Constitutionalist*, the Convention can be chosen but upon the issue of union or disunion without further effort. We have indeed fallen upon sad times; and I doubt if there is enough patriotism in this country to save us from anarchy, either in the Union or out of it."[159]

Pro-Union Stephens, who, as mentioned, was against secession as a remedy to the South-North struggle, wrote the following to his brother Linton on November 30, 1860:
☛ "I am daily becoming more confirmed that all efforts to save the Union will be unavailing. The truth is, our leaders and public men who have taken hold of

this question do not desire to continue it on any terms. They do not wish any redress of wrongs; they are disunionists per se, and avail themselves of present circumstances to press their objects; and my present conviction is that they will carry the State by a large majority."[160]

From a December 3, 1860, letter to his brother Linton:
☛ "Letters from all parts of the country continue to pour in on me. I find it impossible to answer them all. Last night I got one from Richard Brodhead, of Pennsylvania, former Senator. He was greatly pleased with my speech, and gave it as his opinion that the present Republican [Liberal] Legislature of Pennsylvania would immediately, in January, repeal their Personal Liberty Laws. He thinks that if we would be moderate as well as firm, all will be right. Other letters, of the most fulsome character, I have received, from Memphis, Detroit, New York. But I will say no more. I fear it will all come to nought; that it is too late to do anything; that the people are run mad. They are wild with passion and frenzy, doing they know not what.

"This is a beautiful, clear, cool day, a big frost in the morning with a considerable freeze, but now pleasant and charming. The air is still, and all things look pleasant in the calm, placid sunshine. If I were well enough to be out in it, it seems that I should rejoice to walk abroad in such an elastic atmosphere. But I can only indulge in fancy as I peep through my windows, sitting as I am by a comfortable fire with Rio, poor fellow, sleeping at my feet. He has been looking for me to go out with him for some time, until he got wearied at that, and then, child-like, fell asleep."[161]

What follow is Stephens' December 30, 1860, letter to President-Elect Lincoln. South Carolina had seceded a few days earlier on December 20. In a December 22 letter to Stephens, Lincoln had said: "Do the people of the South really entertain fears that a Republican Administration would, directly or indirectly, interfere with the slaves, or with them about the slaves? If they do, I wish to assure you, as once a friend, and still, I hope, not an enemy, that there is no cause for such fears. The South would be in no more danger in this respect than it was in the days of [George] Washington. I suppose, however, that does not meet the case. You think slavery is right, and ought to be extended; while we think it is wrong, and ought to be abolished. That, I suppose, is the rub. It certainly is the only substantial difference between us." Here is Stephens' reply:
☛ "Dear Sir—Yours of the 22nd instant was received two days ago. I hold it and appreciate it as you intended. Personally I am not your enemy—far from it—and however widely we may differ politically, yet *I trust we both have an earnest desire to preserve and maintain the Union of the States, if it can be done upon the principles and in furtherance of the objects for which it was formed.* It was with such

feelings on my part, that I suggested to you in my former note the heavy responsibility now resting on you, and with the same feelings I will now take the liberty of saying in all frankness and earnestness, that *this great object can never be attained by force.* This is my settled conviction. Consider the opinion, weigh it, and pass upon it for yourself. An error on this point may lead to the most disastrous consequences. I will also add, that in my judgment the people of the South do not entertain any fears that a Republican Administration [the Liberal Party of the day], or at least the one about to be inaugurated [in March 1861], would attempt to interfere directly and immediately with Slavery in the States. Their apprehension and disquietude do not spring from that source. They do not arise from the fact of the known Anti-Slavery opinions of the President elect. [George] Washington, [Thomas] Jefferson, and other presidents are generally admitted to have been Anti-Slavery in sentiment. But in those days Anti-Slavery did not enter as an element into Party organizations. [Emphasis added, L.S.]

"Questions of other kinds, relating to the foreign and domestic policy—commerce, finance, and other legitimate objects of the General Government—were the basis of such associations in their day. The private opinions of individuals upon the subject of African Slavery, or the state of the Negro with us, were not looked to in the choice of Federal officers, any more than their views upon matters of religion, or any other subject over which the Government under the Constitution had no control. But now this subject, which is confessedly on all sides outside of the Constitutional action of the Government so far as the States are concerned, is made the 'central idea' in the Platform of principles announced by the triumphant Party. The leading object seems to be simply, and wantonly, if you please, to put the Institutions of nearly half the States under the ban of public opinion and national condemnation. This, upon general principles, is quite enough of itself to arouse a spirit not only of general indignation, but of revolt on the part of the proscribed. Let me illustrate. It is generally conceded, by the Republicans [Liberals] even, that Congress cannot interfere with Slavery in the States. It is equally conceded that Congress cannot establish any form of religious worship. Now, suppose that any one of the present Christian Churches or Sects prevailed in all the Southern States, but had no existence in any one of the Northern States—under such circumstances suppose the people of the Northern States should organize a political Party—not upon a foreign or domestic policy, but with one leading idea of condemnation of the doctrines and tenets of that particular Church, and with the avowed object of preventing its extension into the common Territories, even after the highest judicial tribunal of the land had decided they had no such Constitutional power! And suppose that a Party so organized should carry a Presidential election! Is it not apparent that a general feeling of resistance to the success, aims, and objects of such a Party would necessarily and rightfully ensue? Would it not be the inevitable consequence? And the more so, if possible, from the admitted fact that it was a matter beyond their control, and one that they ought not in the spirit of comity between co-States to attempt to meddle with. I submit these thoughts to you for your calm reflection. We at the South do think African Slavery, as it exists with us, both morally and politically right. This opinion is founded upon the [cultural] inferiority of the Black race. You, however, and perhaps a majority of the North, think it wrong. Admit the difference of opinion. The same difference of opinion existed to a more general extent amongst those who formed the Constitution, when it was made and adopted. The changes have been mainly to our side. As Parties were not formed on this difference of opinion then, why should they be now? The same difference would of course exist in the supposed case of religion. When Parties or combinations of men, therefore, so form themselves, must it not be assumed to arise not from reason or any sense of justice, but from *Fanaticism?* The motive can spring from no other source, and when men come under the influence of fanaticism, there is no telling where their impulses or passions may drive them. *This is what creates our discontent and apprehension.* You will also allow me to say, that it is neither unnatural nor unreasonable, especially when we see the extent to which this reckless spirit has already gone. Such, for instance, as the avowed disregard and breach of the Constitution, in the passage of the statutes in a number of the Northern States against the rendition of fugitives from service, and such exhibitions of madness as the John Brown raid into Virginia, which has received so much sympathy from many, and no open condemnation from any of the leading men of the present dominant Party. For a very clear statement of the prevailing sentiment of the most moderate men of the South upon them, I refer you to the speech of Senator [A. O. P.] Nicholson, of Tennessee, which I inclose to you. Upon a review of the whole, who can say that the general discontent and apprehension prevailing is not well founded? [Emphasis added, L.S.]

"In addressing you thus, I would have you understand me as being not a personal enemy, but as one who would have you to do what you can to save our common country. A word 'fitly spoken' by you now, would indeed be 'like apples of gold, in pictures of silver.' I entreat you be not deceived as to the nature and extent of the danger, or as to the remedy. *Conciliation and harmony, in my judgment, can never be established by force. Nor can the Union, under the Constitution, be maintained by force. The Union was formed by the consent of Independent Sovereign States. Ultimate Sovereignty still resides with them separately, which can be resumed, and will be, if their safety, tranquillity and security in their*

"Liberty Hall," Stephens' home outside Crawfordville, Georgia

judgment require it. Under our system, as I view it, there is no rightful power in the *General Government to coerce a State, in case any one of them should throw herself upon* *her reserved rights, and resume the full exercise of her Sovereign Powers. Force may* *perpetuate a Union. That depends upon the contingencies of war. But such a Union* *would not be the Union of the Constitution. It would be nothing short of a Consolidated* *Despotism.* Excuse me for giving you these views. Excuse the strong language used. Nothing but the deep interest I feel in prospect of the most alarming dangers now threatening our common country, could induce me to do it. Consider well what I write, and let it have such weight with you, as in your judgment, under all the responsibility resting upon you, it merits. Yours respectfully, Alexander H. Stephens."[162] [Emphasis added, L.S.]

From a long January 1, 1861, letter to his brother Linton. It was statements like those *in this letter that would soon earn Stephens a reputation for being a "traitor" to the* *South. In his defense however, later he would be the first to admit that prior to the War* *he had assumed far too much on the part of Lincoln and his Yankee constituents:*

☛ "It is night. I have just received your letter. I think the views you give as to the outline of what you intend to say to-morrow, so far as relates to the course our own State ought to take, and the policy she ought to pursue towards South Carolina, are entirely correct. This letter, of course, you will not get until after your speech and until the election is over. But I assure you I feel the deepest concern in the progress of events on the other side of the Savannah River. By force of circumstances they will necessarily involve the interests and fate of

Georgia.

"I have read the [secession] address put forth by the Convention at Charleston to the Southern States. It has not impressed me favorably. In it South Carolina clearly shows that it is not her intention to be satisfied with any redress of grievances. Indeed, she hardly deigns to specify any. The Slavery question is almost entirely ignored. Her greatest complaint seems to be the Tariff, though there is but little intelligent or intelligible thought on that subject. Perhaps the less she said about it the better. For the present tariff from which she secedes is just what her own Senators and members in Congress made it. There are general and vague charges about consolidation, despotism, etc., and the South having, under the operation of the General Government, been reduced to a minority incapable of protecting itself, etc. This complaint I do not think well founded. It arises more from a spirit of peevishness or restless fretfulness than from calm and deliberate judgment. The truth is, the South, almost in mass, has voted, I think, for every measure of general legislation that has passed both Houses and become law for the last ten years. Indeed, with but few exceptions, the South has controlled the Government in its every important action from the beginning. The protective policy was once, for a time, carried against the South; but that was subsequently completely changed. Our policy ultimately prevailed. The South put in power—or joined a united country in putting in power and sustaining the Administration of [George] Washington for eight years. She put in and sustained [Thomas] Jefferson eight years, [James] Madison eight years, [Andrew] Jackson eight years, [Martin] Van Buren four years, [John] Tyler four years, [James K.] Polk four years, [Franklin] Pierce four years, and [James] Buchanan four years. That is, they have aided in making and sustaining the Administration for sixty years out of the seventy-two of the Government's existence. Does this look like we were or are in an abject minority at the mercy of a despotic Northern majority, rapacious to rob and plunder us? It is true we are in a minority, and have been a long time. It is true also that a party at the North advocate principles which would lend to a despotism, and they would rob us if they had the power,—I have no doubt of that. But by the prudent and wise counsels of Southern statesmen this party has been kept in the minority in the past, and by the same prudent and wise statesmanship on our part I can but hope and think it can be so for many long years to come. Sound Constitutional men enough at the North have been found to unite with the South to keep that dangerous and mischievous faction in a minority. And though Lincoln has been elected, it ought to be recollected that he has succeeded by a minority vote, and even this was the result of a dissension in the ranks of the Conservatives [Democrats] or Constitutional men North and South; a most unfortunate and lamentable event, and the more so from the fact that it was designedly effected by men who wished to use it for ulterior ends and objects."[163]

Stephens' January 1, 1861, letter to his brother Linton continues:
☛ "Now we have real causes of complaint against the North,—or at least against certain States of the North,—causes which, if not redressed, would justify the extreme course, the *ultima ratio* [that is, secession], on the part of the South. These, however, are barely glanced at in the South Carolina address. These causes are the 'Personal Liberty Acts,' as they are called, in several of the Northern States. Other acts of their Legislatures which openly and avowedly refuse obedience to, or compliance with, their constitutional obligation to return fugitive slaves. These acts are in flagrant violation of constitutional obligations; and they constitute the only cause, in my opinion, which can justify secession. All other complaints are founded on threatened dangers which may never come, and which I feel very sure could be averted if the South would pursue a judicious and wise course. Whether we ought to secede in consequence of the faithlessness of those Northern States alluded to is simply a question of policy. It is one on which able men and true may differ. One thing is certain: the South would be justified in doing it. For nothing is better settled by all law, recognized by savage as well as by civilized people, than that a compact broken by one party to it is not binding on the other. But if we [Georgia] secede, I should like to see it put on the right ground; and while I think the ground would fully justify the act, yet I do not think it would at present be wise to resort to that remedy. For I feel confident that, if we should adopt the right course, those States would recede and repeal their obnoxious statutes. Hence I am mortified and grieved when I read such papers as the South Carolina manifesto. It is not on the right line."[164]

Stephens' January 1, 1861, letter to his brother Linton continues:
☛ "But I am grieved at almost everything I see and hear every day. The times are fearfully distempered. I am fully persuaded of one thing, and that is, there is no power on earth that can bring any good out of the present state of things. The progress of events cannot be arrested. I tell you now, as you cannot get this until after your election, and it cannot, therefore, influence your action in the matter. If you were not a candidate I should not allow my name to be used to-morrow for the Convention. I have no desire to be in that body. I have a repugnance to the idea. I believe the State [of Georgia] will go for secession,—have believed it ever since I left Milledgeville. I have no wish to be in a body of men that will give that vote. My judgment does not approve it. But when the State acts I shall abide by her decision, with the fidelity of one

who imagines he feels the dictates of patriotism as sensibly and as strongly as any one who ever breathed the breath of life."[165]

Stephens' January 1, 1861, letter to his brother Linton continues:
☞ "I must confess in the darkness and gloom that hang upon the future I see no prospect and but little hope for good government ever again in this country, North or South. The mischievous faction at the North will bear sway there. Constitutional liberty they never understood, or did not like, if they did. How it will be with us at the South time must disclose; but when our public men act so unwisely under present circumstances, I cannot hope for much under their rule in the days of real peril. We are on the high road to ruin I verily believe. How far a man can, consistently with a proper sense of duty to his country, abandon it to its fate when he sees its fate inevitable, I will not undertake to say. But this country, as it was and has been, is entirely demoralized if not ruined. It is beyond the power of salvation. If I am elected, and you are, I shall go to the Convention simply to share your fate, and to link my destiny with yours and that of our State, just as I would, if I could, in the blow-up of a steamer at sea, get on the same fragment of the wreck with you and other dear ones, that we might in the last hour have the consolation of going down together."[166]

Stephens' January 1, 1861, letter to his brother Linton continues:
☞ "I am communing with you now as I do with no one else; and I would not have you mention my feeling to any one. I would give no one unnecessary pain in the anticipation of impending evils. Let all enjoy themselves who can; all indulge better hopes who can. Despair is a terrible feeling for one who has but the nerve to bear it. I feel as if I can bear anything. After all, perhaps what I apprehend will not take place. Don't, therefore, let what I write affect your cheerfulness. It may be a misfortune to have our lives cast upon such evil times. But still we have duties to perform, and these should be performed, to the best of our abilities, with fidelity under all circumstances, whether of good or evil. All that a man can do is to discharge his own duty, whatever that may be. This I shall do, to the best of my understanding of it, in whatever fortunes betide me or the country. I have ceased to put much confidence in our public men. Most of them are destitute of principle. I will not particularize. It is painful to me to think of it."[167]

Stephens' January 1, 1861, letter to his brother Linton continues:
☞ "To-day, after reading Judge Ezzard's late letter, coming out for immediate secession, on the back of Judge Nisbet's speech in Macon, to drown my thoughts on these disagreeable subjects, I took a long walk. The evening was

Stephen Arnold Douglas

cloudy, cold, and bleak. But I felt as if I wanted to get away from all company,—human company and human society at least. I took my poor old blind dog, string in hand, and sought solitude. I went through the old fields over on the Berry Little place, through the pines, sighing in the chill wind. I went until I came to the Bristow place,—the place your grandmother settled. Old memories were here awakened. I approached the old houses. What a wreck was before me! The inclosures and fences were all down. I went up to the spot where I first met you on my first visit to your grandmother after you went there to live. You were then a very little boy. You had run out at the gate to meet me. Do you remember the time and the spot? There this evening I stood and gazed on all around me. Emotions, deep and strong, swelled my breast, and for a time public affairs were all lost in contemplations of another sort.

"Rio, though sightless and almost deaf, seemed to be impressed, through some strange instinct, with the agitations of my mind. He whined in sympathy, and raised a mournful howl. I was looking at the old house, in all its present dilapidation and ruin,—the doors all broken down, and rooms now become a shelter for stray goats and sheep in foul weather. A few old peach-trees stood, the survivors of the orchard. A lonely cedar, on the edge where the yard used to be, remains to the memory of some kind hand that planted it. These scenes I had in full view when Rio gave utterance to his sympathetic melancholy howl. Aroused by this, I went on to the spring, leading him by the string down the rough hill-side path. That bold and pure fountain of cool waters in other days I found all covered with mud and sand. What a change in all things about this once human habitation from what I saw on my first visit to it! How changed those who imparted so much life and cheerfulness to this now dreary and desolate place! Many of them gone to the grave,—all of them, I believe, but yourself,—all gone from the land of the living. . . .

"With these reflections I wended my way back through the woods, the pines, and old fields, with a heart as bare, as desolate, and as shattered as the waste places I had been gazing and meditating upon. But enough of these gloomy midnight thoughts. Good-by. My best wishes attend you now and forever. It may be that I am too desponding as to the fate of our country. I hope and trust I am; but I give you my feelings as they are and have been for some time."[168]

From a January 3, 1861, letter to his brother Linton:
☛ "Yesterday was an awful day. The elements of nature seemed to be in accordance with the distemper of the times. I suffered severely with a headache, and should not have gone out, but was sent for to go to the

court-house to make a speech. I went up,—found about one hundred persons standing about, some by the stove, some on the stair-steps, some in the jury-boxes, all dripping with wet, and exhibiting as hopeless a spectacle of men in dark and doubt, oppressed with some appalling calamity about to come upon them, as I ever beheld.

"I gave them a talk of about an hour and a half. The speech was well received by a large majority, though I gave them but little encouragement. I gave them many illustrations, but above all guarded them against panic. There was nothing to cause real alarm. If the worst came, we were abundantly able to defend and protect ourselves. The greatest danger was from fear or panic. I felt none of it. The sensation telegraphs from Washington had no effect on me. As to what our [Georgia Secession] Convention would do or ought to do I could not tell them,—that depended upon circumstances to be disclosed. All that I could say as to myself was that I should keep two things constantly in view. The first was the right, honor, safety, and security of Georgia,—that I should maintain at all hazards and to the last extremity. The second was the maintenance of the Union, if it could be done consistently with the other object. If I became satisfied that this could not be done, then I was for taking such measures as would by co-operation with other States lead to another Union on the basis of the present Federal Constitution, taking within it all who would comply with its existing obligations. I thought the Constitution as it is good enough. I saw no necessity for any new guaranty. South Carolina seems to think so too. She wants the Southern States to unite with her upon that; and if that be the basis, we have the admission of the present States,—Congress could not ask any but the adoption of the fundamental law of union, etc.

"When I got through, J_____ H_____ cried out ' Three cheers for South Carolina!' This he repeated three or four times, but got no response. . . .

"Yesterday was the worst day for an election I ever saw in Georgia. It has told greatly against the Conservative [then the Democrats] cause, I have no doubt. It really appears as if Providence was on the other side [that is, the Republicans, the Liberals of the day]. From the beginning of this movement last spring every incident of what is termed luck seems to be against the Conservatives. I call it Providence. My reading of it is that a severe chastisement for sins of ingratitude and other crimes is about to be inflicted upon us,—'when the wicked rule the nation mourns.'[(169)] We are about to suffer as we have never suffered before. This is my apprehension."[170]

From a February 2, 1861, letter to Richard M. Johnston. A reluctant Stephens had been asked to attend the Montgomery Convention in Alabama, to help in establishing the Southern Confederacy's new government:

☛ ". . . this country is in a great deal worse condition than the people are at all aware of. What is to become of us I do not know. I shall go to Montgomery,—do all I can to prevent mischief, if possible.—and if the new Government shall be successfully launched, as I sincerely hope it may be, then I shall again go into that retirement so congenial to my feelings. If my efforts in this last movement shall fail,—if I see no prospect of doing good at Montgomery, I shall retire and give up all as lost. Don't think me desponding,—I write to you exactly as I feel: and what I write is for yourself alone. Whatever feelings of despondency I have in looking to the future come from my knowledge of the men in whose hands we are likely to fall. They are selfish, ambitious, and unscrupulous. Republics cannot be built up or successfully administered without the strictest and sternest virtue and purest patriotism on the part of those at the head of affairs."[171]

From a February 5, 1861, letter to his brother Linton. Stephens is at Montgomery, participating in the convention:
☛ "Nothing was done after organization except the appointment of a Committee to prepare and report rules. This was on my motion, and of course I was put on the Committee, though I requested [Howell] Cobb [President of the Provisional Government] not to do it. I did not wish to be on it. I made the motion merely because the crowd generally seemed green and not to know how to proceed. South Carolina and Mississippi had instructed their delegations to vote by States; and Louisiana members said the same of their State. I saw, therefore, that there was no doing anything until some rules of proceeding were adopted. The Committee appointed was Stephens, Keitt, Curry, Harrison, of Mississippi, and Perkins, of Louisiana. All were in my parlor last night except Curry, who sent word that he was sick. Before they came I had drawn up a set of rules which I submitted to them, and, with one or two exceptions, they were adopted by the Committee. I culled them partly from the rules of the United States Senate and House of Representatives, and there were some entirely new ones that I introduced. After the report was agreed upon, I went to the printing-office, after ten o'clock at night, and got them to promise to strike off fifty copies by twelve o'clock to-day for me, at my expense."[172]

From a February 9, 1861, letter to his brother Linton:
☛ "We agreed last night at about midnight to a Constitution for a Provisional Government for the Confederate States. That is the name. It is the Constitution of the United States, with such changes as are necessary to meet the exigencies of the times. Two new features have been introduced by me: one, leaving out the clause that excluded Cabinet Ministers from being

members of Congress; the other, that Congress should not have power to appropriate any money unless it be asked for by the Executive or some one of the heads of Departments. Wright and myself were on the Committee from Georgia to report the Constitution. Each State had two members on it. [Christopher G.] Memminger, of South Carolina, who moved the raising of the Committee, was Chairman.

"We have just elected the President and Vice-President of the Confederacy. Mr. [Jefferson] Davis, of Mississippi, was unanimously chosen President, and I was unanimously chosen Vice-President. I knew that such was the understanding as to what would be the result, and did not go to the hall when the election took place. The vote was cast by States. I have a good deal to say about this and other matters transacted here when I see you."[173]

From a February 10, 1861, letter to his brother Linton:
☛ "To-morrow I am to be inaugurated, or signify my acceptance and take the oath of office publicly in the Congress hall at twelve o'clock. . . . I almost shrink from the responsibilities I shall assume. To making any speech on the occasion I have a strong aversion; but such is the request in the letter asking my acceptance."[174]

From a February 11, 1861, letter to his brother Linton:
☛ "This, as you know, is my birthday; and this day at the hour of one I was inaugurated (if such be the proper term for the proceeding) Vice-President of the Confederate States of America. The coincidence, altogether accidental, made a marked impression upon my mind. The remarks I made you will of course see. They were delivered as if extemporaneous, though they had been written and committed to memory. As you will see, they were very short. I wrote them down this morning before going to the Capitol. There was, I suspect, great disappointment at their brevity. I had been urged to make a speech, and a very large crowd was assembled to hear it. I was satisfied that such a course would be injudicious, indelicate, and improper. Since it is all over, a great many have told me that I did exactly right. I was governed entirely by my own judgment and sense of propriety in the matter."[175]

From a February 21, 1861, letter to his brother Linton, from Montgomery, Alabama:
☛ "I am bored to death with company and calls. . . . Sometimes it does seem to me that it will kill me. I cannot get ten minutes of solitude during the twenty-four hours. As one leaves another calls."[176]

From a February 21, 1861, letter to Richard M. Johnston:

George Washington

☛ "I am occupied day and night; never did I have such a heavy load of work on my hands. Sometimes I think I shall sink under it. If it was not for calls and visitors I could get along; but almost every moment of the day, when I am out of Congress, until twelve at night, I have to receive and talk to people calling to see me on business. As to public affairs here, I am gratified in feeling able to say that they promise better for the future than I expected. I am, however, still filled with, solicitude and anxiety. My every effort is devoted to the public weal, and my earnest hopes are that all will yet end well. Greater difficulties surround us than I fully realize: perhaps I am more apprehensive in relation to their extent and magnitude than I ought to be. I know I am much more so than the majority of those with whom I come in contact. Still, I cannot divest myself of deep anxiety, and a consideration that we have more troubles ahead than many of our more sanguine friends see or realize. There is more conservatism, as it is called, in Congress than I expected to see, and this increases my hopes.

"I was induced to accept the place under the Provisional [Confederate] Government assigned to me from no motive in the world but a desire to promote the public weal. I thought it would have that effect, and therefore could not decline. As far as my individual wishes are concerned, I assure you I would not exchange the pleasures of one day at my quiet home for all the honors or emoluments of all the offices and powers this world could bestow.

"It will require a great deal of patience, forbearance, and patriotism on the part of the people to bear us successfully through the dangers that surround us. All must be content with knowing that we will do the best we can under the circumstances: this, I think, is the desire of [the Confederate] Congress, and to this end their labors will be devoted. And what they do will be sustained by a generous patriotism on the part of the people. Many inconveniences incident to a change of government will be looked for and borne with fortitude by the people. War I look for as almost certain. Every effort should be made to avoid it, if possible, consistent with honor and right. But we are told by high authority that 'offences must needs come'; and I think this is one of the occasions on which we may expect such a result."[177]

From a February 26, 1861, letter to his brother Linton:
☛ "I am now in hopes we shall get through with the permanent [Confederate] Constitution by an early day in next week. I intend to go home then. . . . I am getting home-sick. I fear that the appointing power will not act with sufficient discretion and wisdom."[178]

From a February 27, 1861, letter to his brother Linton:
☛ "The debates in this body are becoming a great bore to me. Only occasionally a member speaks whom I have any patience with. I fear we shall not get through with the permanent Constitution in time for the Georgia Convention next week."[179]

From a February 28, 1861, letter to his brother Linton:
☛ "In public business we are getting on slowly but harmoniously. I may be mistaken, but I think we have great troubles ahead,—not with this body but

with the [Southern] people. I have a great deal to say to you when I see you, but I cannot write. I am anxious to see you. I want to get home badly."[180]

From a March 1, 1861, letter to his brother Linton:
☞ "The reason I have said so little on public affairs is twofold: first, the great uncertainty of anything I might say getting safely to you; and, secondly, the great uncertainty of my mind upon the course of events. All I can say would be speculative. I have thought, and still think, we shall have war. Still we may not, and I earnestly hope not. In all my letters to friends who have written to me for my views on particular questions I have concluded with these general ideas, that great forbearance and patience must be exercised by the people in sustaining those necessary inconveniences and burdens incident to a change of government,—the derangements of the mails, the derangements of commerce, the increase of taxes, these and a thousand other things not thought of must be borne with nerve and patriotism. If the public or body politic cannot stand this shock, I don't know what will become of us. We are getting along harmoniously here, but still I see great troubles ahead that nobody I meet with seems to be in the least aware of. This annoys me. We lack statesmanship of what I consider the highest order. We have but little, if any, of real forecast. This renders me uneasy."[181]

From a March 3, 1861, letter to his brother Linton:
☞ "Upon the whole, this [Confederate] Congress, taken all in all, is the ablest, soberest, most intelligent, and conservative body I was ever in. . . . Nobody looking on would ever take this Congress for a set of revolutionists."[182]

From a March 5, 1861, letter to his brother Linton:
☞ "We have run against a snag, that is, a disturbing question in the formation of the fundamental law, not yet decided,—cannot say how it will be decided. Some feeling has been thrown into the debate, and some temper exhibited. . . . The general opinion here is that war is almost certain. This has been my opinion all the time. I see great troubles ahead."[183]

From a March 8, 1861, letter to his brother Linton:
☞ "The most exciting of all the questions we have had was decided to-day. If we have no motion to-morrow to reconsider, I shall be glad. This was the clause relating to the admission of other States."[184]

From a March 10, 1861, letter to his brother Linton:
☞ "This is Sunday night. We got through the permanent Constitution last

night. I do not like all its provisions. . . . The only hard contests were in keeping it from being greatly worse than it is. I was in an agony all day yesterday for fear that some serious mischief might be done. A divided State only saved us several times upon points almost vital. I even still dread to-morrow, for fear that some new motion may be brought forward, though we have ordered it to be engrossed. There are some very bad passions and purposes beginning to develop themselves here. I am constantly suspended between hope and fear for the future. I have not yet any settled conviction or confidence on which I can rely. I am anxious to see you, when I can confer freely with you upon all these questions."[185]

From a March 13, 1861, letter to Richard M. Johnston:
☛ "As to public affairs, I can only say that in my judgment our destiny, under Providence, is in our own hands. What our course shall be will depend upon our people. We are in the position of a young man of talent and ability setting out in life. As such a one, we shall be the architects of our own fortunes. With truth, fidelity, integrity, and industry a young man of parts in this world, under the smiles of Heaven, will seldom fail to succeed; and with virtue, patience, and patriotism on the part of our people, I doubt not the success, the complete success, of this our new enterprise. But should dissensions, strifes, and factions spring up among us, all will go to ruin. This is the riddle of our present position. We have all the elements of a great empire. All that is necessary for us to become so is the intelligence, virtue, and patriotism to wield them to that high end. I am not without hope that our people will prove themselves equal to the demand of the times."[186]

From an April 17, 1861, letter to his brother Linton. The Battle of Fort Sumter, in which Lincoln had wickedly tricked the South into firing the first shot, had been waged on April 12, and on April 15 Lincoln had illegally called for 75,000 Northern troops to invade the South:
☛ "There is no truth whatever in the telegraphic despatches that the [Confederate] President [Jefferson Davis] intends to head an expedition to Washington, and to leave me at the head of the Government here. He has no idea at present to take command of the army. The matters he wished to consult me about were the subjects of receiving volunteers from the Border States, the issuing of letters of marque, and other matters relating to the state of the country. A proclamation will be forthcoming to-morrow, I expect, inviting privateering. The proposals will be received and held ready for the action of Congress when that body meets. The proclamation will be put forth to let the Northern merchants know what they may expect, and to have privateers ready.

"It is expected here that Virginia will secede, and all the Border States will follow her; and then, I think, the whole North will consolidate. This will keep the Republicans [Liberals] in power. This is perhaps what they are mainly aiming at. But events happen so rapidly now that it is useless to speculate two days ahead."[187]

From an April 18, 1861, letter to his brother Linton
☛ "The news came that Virginia was out [seceded]. Great rejoicing—firing cannon, etc. The day is brilliant. The news this morning is that General [Winfield] Scott has resigned [his position as Commander-in-Chief of the U.S. Army]. This is important, if true."[188]

From an April 19, 1861, letter to his brother Linton
☛ "In a few hours I am to start for Richmond. I shall, if nothing Providential prevents, pass by home to-morrow evening, and shall mail this on the road. I go to Virginia as a representative of this Government in forming a treaty of alliance offensive and defensive between this Government and that State. She, of course, will soon be a member of this Confederacy. But Governor [John] Letcher has telegraphed for a Commission to be sent on forthwith, that the two Governments may act in concert in the impending dangers. They want help, expecting a hard fight soon. They are about, I take it, to seize Harper's Ferry and the Navy Yard at Portsmouth. Perhaps they are looking for an attack from Washington.

"I was strongly inclined not to accept the position, owing to my health and the apprehension that night travel might make me sick; but upon the urgent request of the President [Davis] and all his Cabinet I have consented to go. The subject admits of no delay: Letcher telegraphed for immediate action."[189]

From an April 19, 1861, letter to Richard M. Johnston:
☛ "Events of the greatest magnitude are now almost hourly developing. When the war that has now commenced will end no human power can divine. The issues are with Him who rules the universe, in whose hands are the destinies of nations. . . ."[190]

From an April 22, 1861, letter to his brother Linton. On April 19 Lincoln had illegally issued a naval blockade on the then seven secedes states:
☛ "I arrived this morning at six o'clock; came through without stopping or any detention. All is excitement here. Warlike preparations are seen at every corner and along every street. . . . The Governor of Maryland [Thomas H. Hicks] is with us. They are making strong resistance to the march of Federal

troops through that State. Ten or fifteen thousand troops are detained on the other side of Baltimore. They are for Washington. A desperate and sanguinary conflict is at hand there. Maryland will be the battle-ground at first,—this I think probable. General [Winfield] Scott has not resigned and will not, from best advices. We are on the eve of a tremendous conflict between the sections. Sentiment is rapidly consolidating on both sides of the line. North Carolina is in a blaze from one extremity to the other. Yesterday, Sunday as it was, large crowds were assembled at all the stations along the railroad,—at Wilmington five thousand at least, the Confederate flag flying all over the city. I had to make them a speech at all the places,—only a few words at some, and longer

Alexander Hamilton Stephens

at others; at Wilmington nearly half an hour. I alluded to the Sabbath, and made the remarks as appropriate as possible. They were more like a sermon than a political speech.

"To-morrow, at one o'clock, I am to meet the State Convention here in closed-doors session. The mails north are all stopped, and there is no travelling even to Alexandria without special passport. Our people in Georgia have no idea of the feelings entertained here of the dangers of impending war hanging on their immediate borders. All the cities and towns of Virginia are under guard day and night; and all persons not able to give an account of themselves taken up. There is a strong inclination on the part of some here to make an attack upon Washington [D.C.]. What course and policy will be adopted is not yet determined upon. . . .

"The people are in apprehension this city will be attacked by the [U.S.] forces now in the Chesapeake and Potomac below. There are no forts on the James River to prevent armed ships from coming up. The Pawnee, Cumberland, and others, with a large force of soldiers at Old Point, are below. I must now close for the mail. May God bless you and save our land from bloodshed!"[191]

From an April 25, 1861, letter to his brother Linton, from Richmond:
☛ "The work of my mission is in suspense before the Convention,—been so hung up since yesterday. I am anxious as to its fate. The Virginians will debate and speak, though war be at the gates of their city. I shall be highly gratified if the convention I have entered into with the Committee of the Convention shall be ratified by that body. If it be rejected, I hardly know what course to pursue.

"This city is all excitement. Fifteen thousand troops are now here. All Virginia is in arms. Unless things have greatly changed in Georgia since I left, you can have no idea of the state of things here. Yet the Convention acts slowly: they are greatly behind the times. The first night I got here I made a speech in response to a serenade. The next day I addressed the Convention in secret session. All that I have said here, I am told, has been well received by all parties.

"My health holds up tolerably well; though I was very much relaxed and rather feeble the first two days. I am now stronger and better. Though I cannot be with you in person, my thoughts are with you."[192]

From an April 29, 1861, letter to his brother Linton. On April 27 Lincoln had illegally suspended the writ of habeas corpus near military lines:
☛ "What is to be the end of this impending conflict, or when the end will be, is beyond my conjecture. Never was the country so thoroughly roused, from

the Rio Grande to the Canada line. The feeling at the North is just as intense, from all I can learn, as it is at the South. If one general battle ensue, it will take many men to end the strife. All things are in the hands of an overruling Providence, and He will shape events according to the counsels of His own will. The race is not to the strong nor the swift. Let us trust in Him, and that in His mercy the country may be saved from the terrible curse of a general fratricidal war. . . . I feel anxious to see the message of President Davis delivered to-day. I trust he will recommend defensive measures only, not aggressive or offensive. If we act on the defensive strictly, we may yet avoid a general war. This should be done, if it can be, honorably."[193]

From a May 4, 1861, letter to his brother Linton:
☞ "I think we shall move the Government in summer, perhaps to Richmond. That will be nearer the theatre of war. I am prepared for, and expect, a prolonged and bloody conflict. It may not be so. I hope it may not. But I have never believed that a separation of the States of the old Confederation would take place without a severe conflict of arms. How long it will last none can tell. Our Congress will have recognized the existing war, and made all arrangements and preparations possible to meet it by the time this reaches you, I expect. It will require great sacrifice on the part of the people to secure the success of our cause; but I feel entirely assured their patriotism is fully equal to the crisis."[194]

From a May 5, 1861, letter to his brother Linton:
☞ "We have no news here; all in Congress goes on smoothly. But very little is doing except preparing for war on an extensive scale. It will take not less than forty millions per annum, I think, to maintain our cause while the conflict lasts. This, of course, to some extent, is conjecture. May God be with you and bless you! Don't fail to rely on Him and put your trust in Him."[195]

From a May 13, 1861, letter to his brother Linton:
☞ "We shall adjourn on the 18th, or perhaps on the 23rd at farthest, to meet in Richmond in July. This has not been made public, and you will therefore keep it secret. I am glad you have determined to go into the volunteer service for the war. That bill for the war is a good one: we shall get a large force under it, but will not get all we shall need to meet the requirements, and have passed another bill to authorize the President to receive for any time he may think proper. Both bills will accommodate all and bring a very effective force into the field. Do not let the military ardor of our people be lessened. . . . I am very unwell to-day."[196]

From a May 14, 1861, letter to his brother Linton:

☛ "Another memorable anniversary of an epoch of great grief and affliction to me. This day of May, 1826, your mother [Matilda Lindsay] died, and with her death the fate of our little family was sealed. [Our] Father [Andrew B. Stephens] died on the 7th and she died on the 14th. . . . . My grief was great on the death of my father,—almost greater than I could bear; but the cup of affliction did not run over until 'ma' [Margaret Grier, Stephens' mother], as we called her, was also taken from us. Then I felt that we should have to be dispersed; and we were dispersed. Who can tell what I suffered at that period of my life! The anniversary always fills me with sadness."[197]

From a May 14, 1861, letter to Richard M. Johnston:

☛ "I have been, and am still, overwhelmed with public affairs. We are in the midst of a war of the hugest magnitude.—in every issue and consequence nothing short of political, and, it may be, of physical existence. What is to be the end is beyond the reach of human speculation. . . . The destiny of nations is in the hands of Him who directs all things according to the counsels of His own will. When I say that no one can tell what is to be the end of the conflict, I do not intend to be understood as expressing any apprehensions as to the success of our arms,—far from that. We cannot, I think, be conquered or subjugated under proper counsels. But when is the conflict to end, and what is to come after it? These are to me perplexing questions. I have but little doubt that the North will go into anarchy. What is to become of us? That depends upon the virtue, intelligence, and patriotism of our people. These noblest of all public traits (if I may so express myself in designating the character of bodies political) will, with us, soon be put to the severest test. I will not permit myself to doubt that the people of the South will prove equal to the crisis. I do not concur with those who think we shall have a short war. I wish I could. . . . I do not see any prospect of immediate peace, nor can I see how it will ever be attained.—I mean fixed and permanent peace between the sections. We may have suspension of hostilities,—truces,—temporary stipulations, etc. But how or on what principles a treaty of permanent peace is ever to be effected, I cannot now see. For instance, will the Confederate States ever make a treaty that will not provide for and secure the rendition of fugitive slaves? Certainly not. Will any Administration of the United States ever agree to such a treaty? or if it should, will the people of those States ever sustain such an Administration, unless utterly exhausted by war?

"[The Confederate] Congress will probably adjourn in a few days. The next session will most probably meet in Richmond, Virginia. The President [Davis], it is expected, will take command in person of our forces now in the field on the border. He will doubtless convene Congress at some place convenient for him to communicate with at his headquarters.

"One of the great pressures now upon us is the want of money. We have plenty just now; but our expenditures are upon a basis of not less, I suppose, than forty millions per annum. How are we to get the money? Loans, treasury-notes, and direct taxes are our only expedients. Taxes to meet interest on bonds and treasury-notes must be raised. It is thought that one-quarter of one per cent, on the property of the Confederate States will be sufficient. This will make the Confederate tax in Georgia about four times what our State tax has been for several years. Independence and liberty will require money as well as blood. The people must meet both with promptness and firmness.

"But I can indulge in this scribbling no further. My attention has been frequently called off since I commenced. To this fact ascribe any incoherency in the line of thought in it you may perceive. It is written for yourself only, not for the public in any sense of the term. We are all here harmonious and perfectly united. Every one feels the dangers that surround us, and every one seems determined to do his whole duty. Private considerations have all merged in the public safety.

"With best wishes for you individually, your family, and for our common cause and common country, I will say no more except that I am not well."[198]

From notes made by Richard M. Johnston concerning a May 30, 1861, meeting he attended at Stephens' Georgia home. Judge Thomas M. Thomas accompanied Johnston:
☛ Mr. Stephens: "All Lincoln's Cabinet, except [Francis P.] Blair [Sr.], were opposed to the war at first,—honestly, as I think. They were driven into it by such men as Cassius M. Clay, Jim Lane, and the Republican Governors.

"The North, I believe, will go into anarchy. They have lost all appreciation of constitutional liberty. They may hold up for some time, and they may break down in six months. The ruin is certain to come. They never before had any just idea of the value of the South to them. Four hundred millions would not cover the losses they have already suffered by our breaking from them. They are now like leeches that have been shaken from a horse's legs, and are beginning to find out what it was that fattened them. We are the horse; and what they are determined to do is to get the horse back again."

Judge Thomas: "Governor [Howell] Cobb thinks that when [the U.S.] Congress meet, the showing which [Salmon P.] Chase will make, of money, will drive them to a cessation of hostilities."

☛ Mr. Stephens: "I wish from my heart it might be so. But I tell you that there is not the slightest chance for such a thing. You might as well expect

Benjamin Harvey Hill

two men, after they have stripped and exchanged blows, to pause and put their hands in their pockets in order to see if they have money or not. When that Congress meets, it will become an assembly of Jacobins, and will raise money if they have to lay assignats upon [Yankee slave trade businessmen John] Astor and the other rich ones there. The [U.S.] Administration cannot stop the war. They are pushed on by the people, and those in the lead who hesitate will be hung or banished. The mild must give way to the violent, as the Girondists gave way to the Mountain. [William H.] Seward may be clever enough to become another [Maximilien de] Robespierre."

Judge Thomas: "What do you think of the South having a dictator?"

☛ Mr. Stephens: "That would never do. That would be the very worst thing we could do. We are the only people on this continent who have constitutional liberty. We must hold on to that and not part from it for a day.

"The [C.S.] War Department is managed badly. The Secretary [LeRoy P. Walker] is very inefficient. He'll 'do and do and do,' and at last do nothing. He is like a man who in playing chess thinks and thinks and thinks before moving, and at last makes a foolish move. He is very rash in counsel, and lamentably irresolute and inefficient in action. There were twenty thousand stand of arms offered us for sale. He postponed it until after the fall of Sumter; then tried to get them, but it was too late. Toombs ought to have been there. He is the brains of the whole concern.

"If the [Confederate] Government would now buy one million of bales, for which they might afford to give ten cents a pound, which is two cents more than the market price, with these they could raise a navy that could compete successfully with the North. It is vain to expect relief from the blockade from foreign powers. We alone could relieve ourselves of that; and our cotton, unless it was put to the use suggested, would be of little importance to us."[199]

From a June 7, 1861, letter to his brother Linton, concerning the death (on June 3) of Yankee conservative and friend of the South and the Constitution, Stephen A. Douglas:
☛ "Douglas, we have seen, is dead. I almost wish he had either lived longer or died sooner. It is, however, best as it is, since it is as it is. Had he lived he might have had great power in staying the North from aggressive war. I can but think this would have been his position. He would have been against attempted subjugation. He would have been for a treaty, for recognition, and for peace. This is my opinion. But it may be he could have done nothing; it may be he would have been overwhelmed; it may be [that] it is better for him, and with an end [?] for the country that he is removed. I have but little doubt that the state of the country had a great deal to do with his death. A diseased body has but little recuperative or reactive energy when the spirits are low. The vital powers depend greatly upon mental stimulus. I can but mourn his loss, though he was nominally an alien enemy. He was a man of great ability and many virtues. Few public men had more nerve than he had to oppose what he thought wrong, and to advocate what he thought right, against the prevailing popular sentiment. He had his faults; but who has not? He was

ambitious,——too aspiring, perhaps, for his own true fame. Had he died just twelve months earlier, what a difference, perhaps, would our country present in its political aspect! But for him there would have been no [Democratic party] split at Charleston, and but for that split there would have been no disunion as yet. Whether that would have been better for us is known only to Him who shapes the fortunes of men and guides the destinies of nations. From present indications it would seem that we did not cut loose from the North too soon. They will go into anarchy or despotism. The only hope of constitutional liberty on this continent is now with us; and whether we shall successfully pass the ordeal in store for us time alone can determine."[200]

From a July 29, 1861, letter to Richard M. Johnston. On July 21, according to at least one 19th-Century report, some 20,000 Confederates defeated around 60,000 Yankees at the Battle of First Manassas[201]:
☛ "We shall probably have before long several such fights as took place at Manassas on the 21st. I have no idea that the North will give it up. Their defeat will increase their energy. This is what I expect, and we should be prepared to meet this result. The [Confederate] victory at Manassas was great and complete. May all our conflicts to come be as triumphant!"[202]

From a September 3, 1861, letter to Richard M. Johnston:
☛ "I see no end to the war,——not the slightest prospect of peace. So far from it, all the signs of a protracted conflict are more portentous to me than they have ever been. *The war on the part of the North is founded upon no rational principle. It is against principles, against interest, and against reason*; and with nations it is as with individuals when they act against reason, there is no accounting for their conduct or calculating upon it on any rational principles. . . . [Emphasis added, L.S.]
    "This is but the beginning. The guillotine, or its substitute, will soon follow. The reign of terror there has not yet fully commenced. The mob, or 'wide-awake' spirit, has not the control there yet, but it will have before the end. All the present leaders will be swept from the board. They will be deposed or hung to make way for worse men who are yet to figure in this great American drama. . . . We have a great conflict before us, and it will require all our energy, our resources, and patriotism, under a favoring Providence, to bear us safely through it."[203]

From a January 12, 1862, letter to Richard M. Johnston. When he felt well enough, Stephens made it a habit to visit Confederate military hospitals and help in caring for the wounded and the dying:

☛ "I am now up and out, though suffering to-day with neuralgia in the jaw and face. But I went to the hospitals,—the first time I have visited them in five weeks. By 'the hospitals,' I mean the three Georgia hospitals. There are a great many hospitals in the city. I went to the Georgia buildings and to two others. I was looking up some Alabama men I had been telegraphed about.

"I saw but few of those whose faces had become so familiar to me before. There was another generation of sufferers from those who were in the same places six or eight weeks ago. I was gratified to see that the number of faces was a great deal smaller than it was in September and November. There were to-day many empty beds in all three of our buildings. Several bad cases, however, met my eye: several in the agonies of death,—none that I knew. The scenes I witnessed were exceedingly painful. I thought of the homes of the dying men, and the dear ones there who, if where I was, could have administered consolation and comfort that neither I nor any of those around could administer. It is a sad thing to sicken, languish, and die, with no kind friend near.

". . . As to the war, I have nothing of interest to write. I see no prospect of peace; and yet the indications of a break-down at the North are more favorable than they have been. My greatest apprehensions now are that there will be a corresponding break-down of the war spirit on our part. The conduct of our military operations and the discipline of our army are well calculated to produce this result. . . . We have a fiery ordeal to go through yet.

"Liberty Hall," with Stephens' grave site and monument on the right

It is that patience under wrong and suffering to which our people are so little accustomed,—this test we have yet to be submitted to, and it is the severest to which our human nature can be subjected. It is that to which the army under [George] Washington was submitted when they were about to mutiny, and he made them a speech (at Newburg) which, all things considered, I look upon as the greatest speech ever made by man. In its conclusion he called upon the neglected and ill-provided-for soldiers who had suffered so much wrongfully from their Government 'still to bear—to be patient—to suffer on,—and to show the world by their conduct that but for that day's trial mankind would have lacked the highest example of virtue that human nature is capable of exhibiting.' I do not give the words, but something of the idea. And yet Washington is not usually counted among our orators."[204]

From a February 26, 1862, letter to his brother Linton. Near the start of Lincoln's War Linton had been made Confederate lieutenant colonel of the Fifteenth Regiment Georgia Infantry. Within a few months, however, he was taken ill (probably with dyspepsia) and forced to resign:

☛ "I urge you not to return to the army. If, in the spring, you are well enough, go and present yourself to General Toombs as a volunteer aide. He will accept you. You can then control your time; leave when no danger is at hand, and be present when danger is threatened. You will in this way be more useful, I think, than in having a regiment; for your greatest usefulness, in my judgment, will be in your advice. As an aide you will be on intimate terms with the general.

"General [Robert E.] Lee, I think, will be made Secretary of War. I think well of him as a prudent, safe, and able general, but do not think he will make a good War Minister. Toombs, I think, would make the best in the Confederacy. . . . The message of the President [Davis], sent into [the Confederate] Congress yesterday, surprised me. It is not such a paper as I or the country expected. But we have to bear what we cannot mend. The country must work out its own deliverance. The present Congress [now part of the new permanent C.S. government] is not what I could wish to see it, either in the Senate or House. Our new Government is now in its crisis: if it can stand, and will stand, the blow that will be dealt in the next eighty or ninety days, it may ride the storm in safety. . . .

"P.S.—Hereafter my letters to you will be without address or signature, for fear the enemy may get them at Weldon or Wilmington."[205]

From an April 8, 1862, letter to his brother Linton, concerning the death of Confederate General Albert Sidney Johnston at the Battle of Shiloh, April 6:

☛ "I am truly sorry to hear of the fall of General Albert Sidney Johnston. I fear he was reckless in the fight. I don't regard the action as a decisive one, as far as heard from. The enemy will make another, and perhaps several other desperate stands at other places before they are driven out of West Tennessee. But we have abundant reason to rejoice over our success, as far as it has gone. I do not, however, permit myself to be much elated by successes, just as I do not permit myself to be much depressed by reverses. We shall have many bloody battles yet before our independence is achieved. This will ultimately be done, however, if our people will but have the patience, fortitude, and patriotism to stand the ordeal before them. These, I trust, will not fail them."[206]

By the Spring of 1862, Stephens was becoming disillusioned with some of President Davis' military and economic policies, including the Confederate draft, the suspension of habeas corpus, and what he considered the mishandling of "King Cotton." During this period Richard M. Johnston took notes from several meetings he had with Stephens on these topics, some excerpts which follow:

☛ "This is a very poor [C.S.] Congress. There are few men of ability in the House. In the Senate not more than two or three. Tom [Thomas J.] Semmes is the ablest. The next are [Robert W.] Barnwell, [Robert M. T.] Hunter, and [Clement C.] Clay [Jr.].

". . . If the West Point policy [that is, fighting strictly by the book] should prevail fully we shall be beaten. If the Southern volunteer should ever come to forget that he is a gentleman (and that is what the West Point men say he must do), then it will be merely a struggle between matter and matter, and the biggest and heaviest body will break the other. We have less matter, and to have equal momentum we must have greater velocity than our enemies,—so to call our spirit and the consciousness of being gentlemen.

". . . The energy [of the Confederate government] I discover now seems to me like that of a turtle after fire has been put upon his back.

". . . [I do not expect to return to the Confederate White House at Richmond very soon.] I can do no good there. The policy of the [C.S.] Government is far against my judgment, and I am frequently embarrassed on account of this difference. I am frequently called upon to give my opinions, and I do so always with frankness, but without asperity. I do all I can to avoid even the appearance of that.

". . . The Conscription Act was very bad policy. Heavy fighting maybe expected within the next few months. We should have called for volunteers for the war, and no doubt they would come. It would have been better to rely upon soldiers thus recruited. Conscripts will go into battle as a horse goes from home; volunteers, as a horse goes towards home: you may drive the latter hard and it does not hurt him. . . . But the day for a vigorous policy is past. It is too late to do anything. I fear we are ruined irretrievably. . . .

    ". . . What stupendous ignorance we have shown of the value of cotton! The Government and those who favored its policy did not undervalue cotton, but misunderstood the character of its value. In their opinion, cotton was a political power. There was the mistake. It is only a commercial power. If it had been understood and employed in that way, it would have been easy to manage the Government by getting enough ironclad ships in Europe to keep several ports open. It is now too late for that. Our portal system is closed effectually, and we cannot stand that any more than a man can stand it in his own case. He dies of strangury and such evils. Nationally, we must do the same thing."[207]

From an August 17, 1862, letter to his brother Linton. Stephens had just returned to the Confederate capitol at Richmond to attend the reassembling of the C.S. Congress:
☛ "I have heard nothing officially since I have been here. I called to see the President yesterday evening, but he was in Cabinet meeting,—had been for two days. I could see none of the Secretaries. . . . I am now looking for an early recognition abroad,—say by the 1ˢᵗ of October. Still, I may mistake. The North seems in a great ferment. Something will come of this: either the mellow wine of reaction and peace, or the gall of a more determined and bitter hostility."[208]

From an August 27, 1862, letter to his brother Linton:
☛ "I was much struck by your views on the tendency of things toward the merging of all power and authority in the hands of the [Confederate] military. I have been deeply impressed with these convictions for several weeks past. [C.S. General Hugh W.] Mercer's impressment orders without the shadow of authority, either military or civil; [C.S. General Earl] Van Dorn's orders establishing martial law in parts of Mississippi, with stringent rules abridging the freedom of speech and the liberty of the press; and, last of all, [C.S. General Braxton] Bragg's order establishing martial law in Atlanta and appointing a civil (?) governor for that city, with numerous subordinates, etc.,—these things aroused my indignation, and I have not been idle in attempting to arouse our members of Congress, both in the Senate and House, to the importance of arresting these proceedings. . . . At this time, I am glad to say, a reaction is in active progress here. I think I have done some good. I first called on the [C.S.] Secretary of War [George W. Randolph] about Mercer's orders, and upon a review of the matter he telegraphed Mercer that he must not resort to force. . . . I got Mr. [Thomas J.] Semmes, the most sensible man in the Senate, to

Jefferson Davis

introduce a resolution there requiring the Judiciary Committee to report upon these questions. That Committee is now at work, and matters are progressing favorably. I have got Semmes to agree with me that no power in this country can establish martial law; neither the President, nor Congress, much less a general in the field. Congress may suspend the writ of *habeas corpus*; but that is the utmost extent to which they can go. And then some nice questions arise as to the effect of the suspension of the *habeas corpus*. It does not interfere, in my opinion, with the regular and speedy trial to which the party is entitled, nor with his full redress in action at law for an illegal arrest, against the party making it, be he general or what not. All arrests are at the peril of the party making them. They must be upon oath and upon probable cause. I have pointed out six plain and palpable violations of the Constitution in these military orders. I am unremitting in my efforts, in a calm and dispassionate manner, to get Congress to awaken to the heavy responsibility resting upon them at this crisis to save our constitutional liberties; and I am glad to say that my efforts thus far have met with more success than I anticipated when I saw the general apathy prevailing at first. The truth is, I believe the fault of our people to which you allude, and which I saw and felt, arose from an excess of patriotism. They wanted to do all that was proper and right for the advancement of our cause, and were not, and are not, sufficiently watchful of great vital principles. I hope we shall come out right. The President [Davis], I am informed, has written to all the generals revoking these orders of martial law, and telling them they have no power to assume such authority."[209]

From an August 31, 1862, letter to his brother Linton:
☛ "Nothing has yet been done in [the C.S.] Congress on the Martial Law, Provost-Marshal, and Passport systems, or the usurpations of generals in passing their unlawful orders in violation of the Rules and Articles of War, wherein is established the military law of the country, by which officers as well as men are governed. But the reaction is going on. We are beginning to look to and understand it, and I think as well as hope that proper action will be taken before long. It is strange what ignorance prevailed on this subject, and how little the representatives of the people know of the nature of the Government under which they live. This generation of men, from the highest to the lowest classes, seems to have lost all sight of principles. Born and reared under free institutions, they seem never to have understood or cared to understand anything about them any more than the constituent elements of the air they breathe. They seem to have looked upon constitutional government as a matter of course, without knowing anything of its original cost, its constant hazards, and the only securities for its perpetuation. I hope they will be brought to think

and to act before it is too late. What we most need now is wise, well-informed, bold, firm, and patriotic legislation, as well in the States as in Congress."[210]

From a September 1, 1862, letter to Richard M. Johnston:

☛ "In regard to our prospects in general, I can only say that I can see no approach to the end. I did think some days ago that foreign powers would offer their mediation,—England and France especially. I have changed that opinion. I had not seen the Queen's [Victoria] speech to which you allude. That and [Lord] Palmerston's since the adjournment of Parliament put an end to such ideas. England and France do not intend ever to recognize us, I think, so long as we show ability to weaken, cripple, and injure the Northern Government. I am somewhat in doubt whether even this is the turning-point with them, or whether they are looking for the extinction of slavery first. They want the final separation to take place, and they want slavery abolished also [Stephens was completely wrong in this view].[211] They may think that the North can uproot the institution among us without being able to subjugate us to their rule. To this extent they may weaken and cripple us, while we, in the mean time, greatly weaken and cripple them by the wasting of their resources and the accumulation of the enormous debt attending the continuation of the struggle.

"Were I the [Confederate] President I should forthwith recall all my Ministers or Commissioners abroad. European powers look upon this war with a complication of views, if I may so express myself. They have no real sympathy with either side. Their interests prompt them to side with us, but the feelings prompted by these interests are about equally balanced by their aversion to slavery [again, Stephens is incorrect]. They had become very jealous of the United States Government as a great and growing power. Its example as a republican government was becoming dangerous to them. They therefore rejoice to see that strife now racing here which, if left alone, will, in their judgment, end in the destruction of republicanism on both sides of the line. It requires no statesmanship to see that the North is already a despotism, complete and fearful. The powers of it are daily becoming more widely displayed and more intensely felt. Its march is onward. Blood will soon flow there as it did in France under the Directory. There will never, I apprehend, be anything like constitutional liberty in that country again. European powers, looking to the history of the world, doubtless think the same fate is in store for us. And I must confess the tendency of things with us for the last few months is well adapted to stimulate and strengthen such speculations. The readiness with which our people surrender most important and essential constitutional rights to what for the moment they consider the necessity of the case, is an indication of their character. Such, for instance, is the submission, without a murmur, to the

Abraham Lincoln

usurpations of commanding generals in their orders of impressment, establishing martial law, appointing provost-marshals and governors in certain localities, etc. All such orders are palpable and dangerous usurpations, and if permitted to continue will end in military despotism. Of this I feel as certain as I do that the sun will go down to-day and rise to-morrow. There is nothing that has given me half so much concern lately as these same military orders and usurpations. Not the fall of New Orleans, or the loss of the Virginia. Better, in my judgment, that Richmond should fall, and that the enemy's armies should sweep our whole country from the Potomac to the Gulf, than that our people should submissively yield obedience to one of these edicts of our own generals. I do not mean to question the patriotism with which they were issued, the object supposed to be attainable by them, nor the patriotism of the people thus far in yielding to them. But, my dear sir, it is the principle involved. We live under a constitutional government, with clearly-defined powers. By our constitution, the law-making power, as well for the army as for the citizens not in military service, is vested in Congress. This power is limited even in their hands. Martial law sets at defiance the Constitution itself. It is over and above it. It is directly against its most important prohibitions, put there for the protection of the rights of the people. Congress cannot establish martial law. No power under this Government can do it. Congress may suspend the writ of *habeas corpus*, but that is not martial law by any means. It does not interfere with the redress that one injured by an illegal arrest may have against the party making the arrest. It does not authorize anybody to arrest another, except upon probable cause, supported by oath. It does not dispense with the right to a speedy and public trial by a jury under an indictment found by a grand jury. It does not authorize any infringement of the liberty of the press or the freedom of speech. These great bulwarks of liberty and barriers against the encroachments of power remain untouched. My apprehensions on this point have been more thoroughly aroused from the fact that the people seem willingly and even patriotically to be yielding to usurpations. They do not consider what they are doing. They do not recollect that the price of liberty is eternal vigilance. They forget that the first encroachments of power are often under the most specious guises. But you may be assured that, in the forcible language of [Jean-Louis de] Delolme, 'our acts, so laudable when we only consider the motive of them, will make a breach at which tyranny will one day enter.' The North to-day presents the spectacle of a free people having gone to war to make freemen of slaves, while all they have as yet attained is to make slaves of themselves. We should take care and be ever watchful lest we present to the world the spectacle of a like free people having set out with the object of asserting by arms the correctness of an abstract constitutional principle, and losing in the end every principle of constitutional liberty, and every practical security of personal rights.

"I have not time, however, to continue this subject. I must go to the Senate. But my whole soul is in it, and I am laboring day and night, in season and out, to awaken attention to the dangers that threaten us."[212]

Around this time, the Fall of 1862, Stephens wrote a letter to Richard M. Johnston concerning his practice of paying for the education of indigent children:

☛ "I have assisted upwards of thirty young men in getting an education. About a third of these I have taken from the stump and put through college. The other two-thirds I assisted to graduation, but most of them at a medical college. Out of the whole number only three who have lived have failed to refund the money. The three I have alluded to are, I think, scamps, except perhaps one. One who refunded I think is a scamp also, though he is a preacher. Nine of the number I assisted are dead; five of these died before refunding: two died while at school. Only four of the number studied law. Six are preachers: four Baptists, one Presbyterian, and one Methodist. One of them is (or was when last heard from) a man of distinction in Tennessee, a professor and author. Another is at the head of a high school in Mississippi, and another at the head of a high school in Georgia. Mr. _____, the preacher, is, I think, a shabby fellow. He showed some ingratitude. The other three I spoke of I think shabby, but I never heard of any ingratitude. Take the whole lot, all in all, I think very well of them. The per centum of black sheep in the flock is small: not more than one in twelve or thereabouts. Of the number I assisted in getting medical diplomas, there are now living in the State six, all clever physicians of good standing. Two of the physicians died some years ago."[213]

A week later Stephens again wrote to Richard M. Johnston on this topic:

☛ "In my letter a few days ago about those whom I had assisted in getting an education, I omitted one fact which ought perhaps to have been stated. Fourteen of the number, at one time, or some time after quitting school, became teachers. Several of them are still teaching. It is proper also to state that none of them, that I am aware of, was ever addicted to intemperance except one. He sometimes drank too much; but he abandoned liquor entirely before he died. I ought to say also that the four I spoke of as shabby fellows all maintain what is considered respectable positions in society. . . . A great majority of those I have aided have done good in their day and generation in their quiet spheres of life. This is a source of great gratification to me."[214]

During the Winter of 1862 Stephens was asked about his relationship with President Jefferson Davis. Were they on good terms?:

☛ "Very good. Whenever we meet he is quite cordial and agreeable. We meet but seldom, however, lately. He used to send for me often to consult with me; but since the Government has been removed to Richmond he has done so but once. What caused a change in him I do not know. He has never shown any change in his bearing when I called to see him."[215]

When asked about Confederate General Robert E. Lee, Stephens said:

☛ "I have always regarded him as the ablest man in our army; indeed, the first military man on the continent. I have always placed a very high estimate upon him; not only as a general, but as a man, from my first acquaintance with him. . . . It requires a rare combination of qualities to make a great leader of armies.

"The last time the President consulted with me on any question, it was about who should be sent to command at Charleston. I urged him to send Lee.

Alexander Hamilton Stephens

Lee was sent. This was in November, 1861. The President thinks very highly of his abilities. Yet I think Lee was surprised at Sharpsburg. I do not think that he knew the enemy were pressing so close on his rear after he went over into Maryland. Still he gained the fight, and I think him vastly superior to [U.S. General George B.] McClellan, or any other one on the board at present, except [Confederate General] J. E. Johnston, who perhaps is a better tactician than even Lee."[216]

When it was suggested to Stephens that the Southern people seemed to regard the "great experiment of self-government" as a failure, and that the South then might as well accept the strong centralized "big government" of the North, he replied:

☛ "By no means. I shall never be willing to give up constitutional liberty, or the doctrine that the people can easily and safely govern themselves upon the principles upon which our institutions rest. In our system these principles rest upon the rights and sovereignty of the States. For their support are requisite virtue, intelligence, patriotism, and constancy on the part of the great body of the people. When I see the apparent indifference of so many among us on the questions involving these essential principles of our liberties, and the success of our system, I must confess I have fears for the future. Still, I am far from giving it up. I think the system at the North is a failure. But our people are different. We have more virtue, and by far more political intelligence in the masses of our people than they have. The great body of our people are honest, industrious, frugal, pure, and not disposed to look to Government for anything but wise and equal laws. In other words, they look to Government for nothing but justice. At the North the great mass look to Government as a means for living by their wits in some way. Government with them is a license to rob and plunder in some way or other; and to get control of Government for these purposes is the highest object of their ambition. The people there, as well as their rulers, have been corrupted for years,—at least a large portion of them, if not the majority. The same thing is true of a portion of our people, and we have some corrupt leaders. But the great majority are not so. They understand their rights, and all they want of rulers is to give them good government. So long as this shall predominate I shall never despair of the principles of self-government with our people."[217]

When asked about the secession of the Southern states, Stephens answered:

☛ "If the South had not seceded, Lincoln's Administration would have broken down in sixty days. He was utterly powerless to do harm."[218]

From a January 18, 1863, letter to his brother Linton:

☛ ". . . I now think that the war will break down in a twelvemonth somewhere. We may not have peace, but we shall have a smash-up. The present armies cannot be sustained. Gold is going up rapidly at the North. If we can stand before the enemy and hold our own until May, a large part of the Federal army will go out of service,—three hundred thousand of those called for in August last were for nine months. Meantime, it will be no easy matter for us to hold on. Our expenditures are enormous,—to meet them we have nothing as yet but the new issue of treasury-notes. These swell the currency until prices are frightful,—expenditures increasing in the same ratio. Taxation cannot itself reduce it. Four hundred millions are now required, I see by the Treasury Report. We cannot stand a tax for more than a hundred and twenty millions,—that would be very heavy. I think it would be better to tax in kind,—take produce and army supplies, and quit issuing treasury-notes."[219]

From a January 22, 1863, letter to his brother Linton. Lincoln's second illegal Emancipation Proclamation had been issued on January 1, 1863:
☛ ". . . What [President Jefferson] Davis means by Lincoln's [Emancipation] proclamation being irrevocable, or its admitting 'of no retraction,' I suppose is this: it is not in its nature executory, as his first one was [that is, the Preliminary Emancipation Proclamation, issued September 22, 1862, and which called for the deportation of all African-Americans]; it is not menacing, but absolute and final action. It is a declaration of emancipation absolutely within the extent of its limits. The power that issued it is forever estopped by the act in opposing or changing it. It is like a pardon,—final, absolute, and beyond retraction. It would, I think, be impossible upon any public principles, or those recognized among nations, for Lincoln to agree to any terms of peace which would change that fact; or I do not mean exactly that, but I mean it would be impossible for the States to go back into the Union with their slaves. He, as President, could not hereafter ignore his act, and put back into slavery those now declared free. The proclamation utterly destroys all prospect of a restored Union with slavery as it was. But I am not in condition to express myself clearly, and I will quit. My pen, too, is abominable, and I never could write or think either when I am trying to write with a mean pen."[220]

From a January 25, 1863, letter to his brother Linton, who has recently given Stephens a new dog (a bull-terrier pup), which the latter named "Sir Bingo Binks":
☛ "When I got home the other morning, I found that Sir Bingo Binks had created quite a stir on my lot. He bad greatly rumpled Rio's feelings by his rude familiarity, he had provoked sundry snaps from Troup for biting and catching at his legs, which had greatly alarmed Ellen [the chambermaid] for the

puppy's safety, the more so as she laid claim to him as hers. When I arrived, I found Binks after the chickens, which had brought old Mat [a female servant] out, greatly disturbed at this new pest in her poultry-yard. She was driving him from one brood, where he had produced considerable confusion, but the mischievous rascal immediately put out after another, when an old hen, nothing daunted by his appearance, flew upon him with impetuous fury, which turned the tide of war, or fun, as the case happened to be viewed by different sides. Binks gave a squall, tucked his tail and fled, much to old Mat's gratification. Now whether the dog perceived this, and determined upon his own revenge in his own way, or not, I cannot undertake to say; but a change came over the spirit of his humors. He broke out in a new direction. This time he took after old Mat herself, caught the skirts of her dress, running round first on one aide and then the other, and almost tripping her up. She looked to me very strongly tempted to kick or stamp the insolent whelp, and perhaps would have done it if Binks's good fortune had not come to his timely relief by bringing my presence on the ground. I was surprised to see him so well grown and sprightly. By supper-time every room, corner, and nook of the house into which he could find entrance was explored, and all the grounds and houses round about; even under the kitchen he had found his way in pursuit of a chicken, and there he found a place which it seems suited him better for lodgings than any he elsewhere discovered. To this place soon after supper he betook himself for the night, and no calling or coaxing was effectual in getting him out. It was amusing to hear the different names that were given him. Frank Bristow calls him 'Binger'; the parson calls him 'Mingo'; I call him sometimes 'Sir Bingo Binks,' but usually 'Binks'; while Anthony gives the Dutch sound of the B, and calls him 'Pinks.' Old Mat, whether from spite or not, calls him 'Minks'; while Ellen, Tim, and the younger fry, seeing such confusion among the elders, content themselves with simply styling him the 'puppy.' So he is likely to have names enough. And if you think there is really anything in a dog's name, I should like to have your prognostications in this case."[221]

From a January 29, 1863, letter to Richard M. Johnston:
☛ "I do not think much of the demonstration spoken of by the Democrats [Conservatives] in the Northwestern States. I have no idea of anything like armed resistance to the Lincoln Administration there; and indeed I don't put much faith in what is said of the extent of the disaffection or the degree to which it has gone in that section. It is very much like accounts heralded in Northern papers of the disaffection among us. What do you suppose a Yankee paper would say over [Georgia] Governor [Joseph E.] Brown's proclamation about bands of traitors or tories in our State that require the military to put them

The inauguration of Confederate President Jefferson Davis, February 18, 1861, Montgomery, Alabama. He is being introduced by Howell Cobb, from the viewer's perspective, standing to Davis' right. Stephens is just visible, seated to the left of Davis.

down? Nothing of that sort has occurred in any part of the North yet; and we know, or ought to know, how little confidence is to be attached to it from what we see among ourselves. The great majority of the masses, both North and South, are true to the cause of their side, no doubt about that. A large majority on both sides are tired of the war; want peace. I have no doubt about that. But as we do not want peace without independence, so they do not want peace without union. There is the difficulty. I think the war will break down in less than a twelvemonth: but I really do not see in that any prospect for peace, permanent peace. Peace founded upon a treaty recognizing our separate independence is not yet in sight of me."[222]

From a February 7, 1863, letter to Richard M. Johnston:
☛ "I have from the beginning looked upon [Robert E.] Lee as our ablest general. Before the Government was removed to Richmond, and before any reputation was won by any man in either army, except by [Confederate General Pierre G. T.] Beauregard at Charleston, I gave it frequently as my opinion that Lee was our best officer and McClellan the best the Yankees had. I have never changed that opinion in the slightest degree from that day to this. The President [Davis] always thought that General Albert Sydney Johnston was the ablest general on the continent. This I have heard him say, or its equivalent. I did not know General Johnston, but thought highly of him on account of the President's opinion, until he had been at the head of the army awhile in Kentucky. I then came to the conclusion that the President was mistaken in his estimate of him, and that conclusion of my mind has not been shaken since, not even by the battle of Shiloh. General Joseph E. Johnston is, I think, General Sydney Johnston's superior. In some things I think he is Lee's superior, or has some qualities essential for a general in a superior degree; but he lacks others which Lee possesses. So, taken on the whole, he is, in my judgment, Lee's inferior. I regard Lee as one of the first men I ever met. I was wonderfully taken with him in our first interview. I saw him put to the test which tries the metal of character.—the stuff that a man is made of. He came out of the crucible pure and refined gold, so far as integrity and patriotism are concerned."[223]

From a February 8, 1863, letter to Richard M. Johnston, concerning what Stephens considered violations of the C.S. Constitution by the Davis administration:
☛ "In my opinion the power to raise armies delegated to Congress is precisely the power given by the Secretary of War to any person he may select 'to raise a regiment.' Nothing more and nothing less. Suppose such authority given, as it has often been done, 'with full power to raise a regiment;' would anybody in this day, in this country, ever dream that such an agent had power to impress freemen into his corps? An attempt to do so would excite wonder as well as indignation; but not a whit more, in my opinion, than would have been excited in the Convention that formed the Constitution in 1787, if it had been told them that their agent, Congress, under this clause would attempt that thing.

". . . There are two ways of levying troops: one by enlistment, the other by compulsion. Congress has power to raise a levy in both ways,—no doubt about that,—with a qualification, however, in the latter mode. The power in the first clause to raise extends only to the former mode. The following clause relates only to the subject how troops are to he ordered into service when necessary. For the power to provide for culling out the militia means nothing more than the power to order out or compel those to go into service who are able to go and who will not go without the call, the order, or the compulsion. All those who stand in this class are militia, whether organized or not, *ex vi termini* ["from the force of the term"] though they are to be organized before they are called out. This is what Congress has power to provide for by law: to have that class of people put into companies, regiments, etc., and trained ready to be 'called out,' 'ordered out,' or 'compelled' to go out when required."[224]

From a March 8, 1863, letter to Richard M. Johnston:
☛ "If our [the Confederate] Congress will not do something, and that speedily, to sustain our finances, the break-down will be on our own side. Our credit is suffering greatly. Nothing will save it but immediate taxation, and high taxation at that. Lincoln is no more a dictator now than he has been all the time; and as for the *Herald*, I am not surprised at anything in it. It is a mercenary sheet, and utterly destitute of any principle whatever, either moral, social, or political. The Yankee Conscript Law was what I was apprehensive they would adopt. Its main object is to retain in the service those whose terms were about to expire. I don't think Lincoln will call out a great many more troops. He will keep his army at about a million strong. [Editor's note: by War's end Lincoln would eventually enlist nearly 3 million soldiers.] I have been expecting our recognition by [French Emperor] Napoleon [III] early in the spring. One or two items of news from Northern papers within the last ten days tend to check this expectation. These are the correspondence which has come to light between [U.S.] Secretary [William H.] Seward and the Mexican Minister at Washington. From this it is clearly seen that Seward is currying favor with Napoleon by affording indirect aid in his Mexican War. That war he must feel a deep interest in, and such favor as the Washington [Yankee] Government may show him will go a long way in keeping him from making it his enemy. Again, I see it stated that Lincoln has been closeted with [French minister to the U.S., Edouard-Henri] Mercier [de Lostende] at Washington. There is no foundation for the assertion in our papers that Seward had given the lie direct to Mercier's statement touching his visit last year to Richmond. I have read Mercier's letter and Seward's; there is no contradiction in them."[225]

From a March 19, 1863, letter to his brother Linton:

☛ "It is all over with poor old Rio! He died soon after I left the house for the [railroad] cars on Monday. I left him in the passage between the library and the main building. He was very quiet and seemed to be in a sleep. I took a last look at him, for I never expected to see him again. After I got out of the gate near the academy, I heard him bark loud and repeatedly, just as he used to bark when I left home. It seemed to me that he knew I had gone. I verily believe he did.—by what strange instinct I cannot say. I told Anthony [a servant], who was with me, to go back and be with him, and keep him from falling out at the door, and to take care of him. Before the cars left the depot, Harry [a servant] sent word to me that he was dead.

"Anthony says that after he stopped barking he got up and staggered into the library and went towards my room. His strength failed just at my room door: then he fell and died without any struggle or evidence of suffering. I had given orders about his burial before I left.—these were followed. He lay in the library all night, in the position in which he usually slept, with his face on his fore-feet. Next day he was put into a box or coffin made by George [a servant], and buried in the garden, between the rock-pile and the palings. He was placed in the coffin as he lay.

"It is just two weeks this evening since he and I took our last evening walk. That night he had a cough and seemed unwell: next day he was worse. The last two days he did not seem to suffer so much as he did two or three days before, but slept quietly most of the time.

"He was a remarkable dog,—most devoted in his attachment to me: and I do heartily sorrow and grieve for him. After his afflictions, when he was deaf and blind, it was a source of melancholy pleasure to me to lead and direct him about, and think of his acts in his better days; and now the remembrance of these walks with him in his infirmities awakens associations of as much interest as any connected with his whole life. . . .

"The world will never see another Rio. And few dogs ever had, or ever will have, such a master. Over his grave I shed a tear, as I did over him frequently as I saw nature failing."[226]

From a March 20, 1863, letter to Richard M. Johnston, concerning the death of Rio:

☛ "I shed tears at his grave yesterday, and feel as if I shall shed many more for him before he passes from my memory. The infirmities of his old age rather increased than lessened my attachment to him. His devotion to me was, I believe, stronger than life. For nearly thirteen years he has been my constant companion, day and night, when I have been at home, and until he became blind a few years ago, he always attended me wherever I went, except to

Washington City. You may well imagine then how I miss him! Miss him in the yard, in the house, in my walks: for, though blind, he used to follow me about the lot wherever I went. When I was reading or writing he was always at my feet. At night, too, his bed was the foot of my own. His beautiful white thick coat of wool was soft as silk. But you know him and need no description. He is gone. You, nor I, nor any one will ever see his like again. Who that knew him as I did could refrain from shedding a tear for Rio?"[227]

From a March 29, 1863, letter to his brother Linton:
☛ "This is a dull and gloomy day,—well adapted in my loneliness to increase that sadness which your last two letters produced; but I have long since learned not to indulge such feelings. They always increase as they are nurtured. . . . I have much to make me melancholy: indeed, I should have been a victim of melancholy long ago if I had not resisted it with all my might. I now feel as if I had conquered in the conflict. It was not, however, without great danger from another source which I perceived and had to guard and strive against with equal vigilance and energy,—that was misanthropy. These have been the Scylla and Charybdis in my life. Melancholy and misanthropy,—the rocks and the whirlpool. I have, I think, escaped both. This I do not think I have accomplished by myself: I feel within that I have been sustained by an unseen power on whom I have relied and to whom I have locked in my worst trials, even in the darkest hours, with hope and assurance that all would be well under His guidance and protection. I do not feel justified before Him; but I do feel that with his long-suffering and loving-kindness my frailties will be graciously pardoned, my weakness strengthened, and patience and fortitude imparted sufficient to enable me to bear all the ills of this life, and that by discharging my duties fully and to the best of my ability during this probationary existence, I shall be fitted for that higher sphere hereafter, where there will be no more pain and no more suffering, no more trouble and no more sin. These are the principles and convictions on which I act. I have for years made it my business to devote a portion of each day to prayer—in communing with this unseen, all-pervading Power—with God. I was in early life deeply impressed with what is called religious feeling; but after I grew up and entered the world these feelings greatly subsided. I at one time became skeptical, callous. The world was a mystery: I could see nothing good in it. I was miserable, and that continually. But coming to the conclusion, after a close self-examination, that the error might be in myself, I determined to adopt a new line of policy for my conduct. The first resolution was to cease finding fault with, or thinking about, what I could not understand. The second was to nurture and cultivate assiduously the kindlier affections of the heart, and with this every day, at some

hour, to put myself in communion with God to the best of my ability, asking Him to aid, assist, direct, and protect me in doing right.

"The effect of this upon my mind and feelings, and general views of things, was soon felt by me. The exercise which at first seemed meaningless and senseless, soon appeared to bring a certain inexplicable satisfaction to the spirit. The earlier impressions of life soon revived. I felt a better—a much more contented and happier man. The feeling grew with its culture,—it softened the temper, awakened deeper emotions of reverence, gratitude, and love. It gave consolation in grief, strength in resisting temptation. It impressed the mind with man's weakness and frailties, and his dependence on God. It seemed to elevate the soul and put it in unison with its Maker. This is what sustains me.

"Such is the character of my religion. I make no boast of it; and perhaps very few people who know me have any idea of its existence, even to this extent. For I heard last year that _____ had expressed the opinion that I was an unbeliever; and some years ago Toombs told me that a gentleman whom I will not name—now dead—said in speaking of me that I was an infidel—or atheist, I forget which. These opinions produced but one effect on me, and that was the rather painful reflection that I had perhaps not set the world such an example of the real faith that was in me, as I ought to have done. But I have always had such an aversion to what I consider the cant of religion, that I have been rather inclined to suppress than to exhibit to others what I really think and feel in such matters. So far as it concerns the world's judgment in my case, it must look to my acts and conduct.

"I must ask pardon from even you for what I have said in this digression on the subject. I only meant briefly to say a few things about that inward, and I believe spiritual, Power that sustains me in hours of doubt and darkness, as well as in periods of sunshine and good fortune, and to assure you that my life, upon the whole, for many years, has not been an unhappy one. . . . I can say no more now. Indeed, I have said a great deal more than I intended. I have never before said, even to you, so much about some of my heart's secrets. May God be with you, sustain you, guide you, and protect you!"[228]

From a March 29, 1863, letter to Richard M. Johnston:

☛ "So soon as the spring opens, I expect to go on to Richmond. I am in lower spirits than usual. The signs of the times are dark and gloomy to me: darker and gloomier than they ever have been here, except during the summer and fall of 1860, when I saw portended so clearly all the troubles we now have upon us, and those still worse which I fear are ahead of us. . . .

"Our country is in a sad condition: worse than the people are at all

Anti-South Yankee propaganda sketch linking the Confederacy (left) with the Devil and his minions (right). Vice President Stephens is to the right of President Davis (near the left center).

aware of. It is painful to me to look towards the future. I shrink from it as from a frightful gulf towards which we are rapidly tending. This is a general fast-day, dedicated to humiliation and prayer,—most appropriate duties. . . .

"My motto is patience, fortitude, and duty, at all times and under all circumstances. The world and its events are beyond my control: all I can do is to perform my part faithfully to the best of my ability, with the firm conviction that all in the end will be right, whether it is as I wish it or not."[229]

From an April 2, 1863, letter to his brother Linton:
☛ "I spent three pleasant days and nights down at my homestead place. Did a great deal of work, and have had a great deal done which I think will be useful, mostly in hill-side ditching to save the old hills over which I wandered and worked when a boy. My mind all the time was filled with recollections of my earliest youth."[230]

From an April 3, 1863, letter to his brother Linton:
☛ "I do hope our State will not endorse the Confederate bonds; but I see A. [?] expresses the opinion that the bill for this purpose will pass by a large majority. It will be a great error and blunder if it is done; and those who vote for it will rue it if they live. The whole scheme is radically wrong in purpose. The

responsibility of creating debt, and paying it, or providing for its payment, ought to rest on the same shoulders. No possible good can result from the measure. For the power to tax is plenary in the Confederate Government,—State endorsement cannot add a particle to the credit of the bonds in case of success in establishing independence. No good then can possibly come of it; but much mischief may. For if Congress has let its credit run by appropriating without the nerve to tax, what will they not do when they are relieved from that responsibility, or imagine themselves relieved, and turned loose to spend without limit? Many do not understand this matter: they do not consider that if Congress does not pay the interest on these bonds, say next year, that the State will have to tax the citizens to meet this payment. The debt now is not much short of one thousand millions. Georgia's part of this would be, in round numbers, about one hundred millions. The annual interest on this will be, in round numbers, about eight millions. Are these people who will vote for this bill of endorsement ready to vote this annual tax on their constituents? The truth is, they are not, and will not do it. Why, then, should they say they will? Why give the pledge? They unwisely think they nor their successors will never be called on to redeem it. In this they are sadly mistaken. I feel deeply upon the subject. It is utterly wrong, and the worst consequences will follow the policy, if adopted."[231]

From a June 26, 1863, letter to his brother Linton:
☛ "I learned an important fact in North Carolina, which I suppose is the cause of the President's [Davis] call for militia for State defence. Correspondence intercepted between [Yankee General John G.] Foster, of North Carolina, and Montgomery, on the Georgia coast, shows that a plan was concocting to have a general insurrection among the slaves on the 1st day of August. Indeed, the plan is concocted and perfected on a limited scale. They are to make it as extensive as possible by the time. From prudential reasons the correspondence has not yet been made public."[232]

From a June 27, 1863, letter to his brother Linton:
☛ "To-day I had an interview with the President [Davis]. I may go further before my return. There is great excitement in the city: no doubt a formidable force is advancing on it from below, far superior in numbers to any that can be brought against it. It may be a feint, but is believed to be real. We have now five steamers running from a Southern port to a neutral one. These are not armed vessels. The *Alabama*, *Florida*, *Virginia*, *Georgia*, and *Clarence* are armed ships afloat. We have got by our commercial steamers about eighty thousand stand of arms lately, powder, etc., and eight hundred cases of bacon and other

army supplies. Vicksburg has been replenished with provisions from the other side. No news from Lee. Nobody here knows where he is. I am still very anxious to hear from home, but would advise you to trust nothing of importance to the mails."[233]

From a June 28, 1863, letter to his brother Linton:
☛ "The state of the controversy on the condition of affairs between the two Governments in regard to the exchange of prisoners is in a very unsatisfactory condition. We are upon the eve of the bloodiest and most barbarous system of retaliation. The enemy refuses to exchange any prisoner: they hold all our prisoners to retaliate upon if we execute such officers as may be captured loading negro troops. Whether anything can be done to avert this result I do not know. I am willing to do all I can to avert it, but am not hopeful."[234]

From a June 30, 1863, letter to his brother Linton, from Richmond, Virginia:
☛ "It is desired, I believe, by the Government that I should go farther, or at least attempt to go farther, and see if any agreement can be made on the disputed points. It is not certain that I would be received. . . . From what I can see of the state of the questions, I have but little hope of being able to effect anything, even if negotiations should be entertained. . . . It is thought important to have the effort made and the overture rejected before resort to retaliation, which is now apparently the next step before us. . . . No news from Lee. None from Vicksburg. The enemy at [the] White House [in Washington, D.C.] are increasing their forces, it is said. The citizens are all out under arms this evening."[235]

From a July 1, 1863, morning letter to his brother Linton:
☛ "I believe it is pretty well settled that I shall go farther. . . . I saw the President [Davis] again this morning. He is quite sick with dysentery, and was suffering greatly. He has conversed with me very freely, unreservedly, and most confidingly on all matters pertaining to the present position of our affairs. So have all his Cabinet. Would that my powers, under the guidance and aid of the Ruler of the universe, were equal to what they desire me to accomplish! But I assure you that I have but little hope of succeeding in the least one of these objects. They urged me to go, though I told them candidly that in the present condition of things I could effect nothing. I yielded my judgment to theirs."[236]

From a July 1, 1863, evening letter to his brother Linton:
☛ "[Confederate Secretary of War James A.] . . . Seddon has just left me. It is determined that I go. Expect to start the day after to-morrow. . . . I have

to-day read the 'Montgomery correspondence,' as it is called. Montgomery is the Kansas 'Jay-hawker.' The correspondence is nothing but a letter from him to Foster, dated Washington, D.C., May 12th. It is in the nature of a circular to the commanders of Federal forces in the several Southern districts, stating in substance that a plan was arranged to sever the communications throughout the Southern States. The plan was for the negroes, as far as possible, and as far as information could be got to them by agents,—slaves from their lines, seeming to be escaped, while really sent on this business.—to be induced to rise in mass on the night of the 1st of August, and tear down all bridges, railroad bridges, telegraphic wires, etc., using any and all weapons they could find, and then to make for the swamps or mountains until they could get communication with the enemy. They were not to use arms except in self-defence. They were to live on roasting-ears, etc. As the letter has not been made public, I do not wish you to make any allusion to it; but there is no doubt of its genuineness. We have no further information from the enemy on the Peninsula. . . . A party crossed the Pamunkey [River] day before yesterday,—cavalry,—it was thought with the intention of making a raid on Gordonsville. The militia up there were called out. The citizens of that place drill every day: the number is said to be two thousand four hundred, all armed."[237]

From a July 9, 1863, letter to his brother Linton:
☞ "The news from Lee's army is bad. What will befall Virginia in case he has met, or should meet, with a great disaster no one can tell. . . . I was very sorry that he crossed the Potomac [River]. If I had known he was going to do it, I should not have written the President [Davis] the first letter I did. My policy and the policy of invasion were directly opposite."[238]

From a July 10, 3, 1863, letter to his brother Linton:
☞ "I am about to leave this place for home again. I am through with the business that brought me here, or at least have done all that I can in it. The object was to hold a conference with the enemy upon several points of disagreement on the existing cartel for the exchange of prisoners. These points of disagreement present questions of the gravest character. Both sides are about to begin retaliation. I was exceedingly anxious to avoid such revolting scenes, and undertook a mission for this purpose. The proposition was rejected by the enemy [Lincoln and his cabinet], after deliberating on it for two days. I went as far as Newport News. There my arrival and object were telegraphed to Washington City by [U.S.] Admiral Stephen P. Lee, of the North Atlantic squadron. I deeply regret the result. The final determination not to receive the mission may have been induced by news received of the fall of Vicksburg, and

Horace Greeley

a turn in the tide of war at Gettysburg. How this was I do not know. My object was made known on the 4th, and the rejection of the mission, or refusal to receive it, was notified to me in the afternoon of the 6th. We have no news—none reliable at least—from General [Robert E.] Lee. The greatest anxiety is felt for the fate of his army. Misfortunes seldom come singly. The prospect before us presents nothing cheering to me. But my rule is neither to be elated by good news nor depressed by bad."[239]

Remarks recorded from the Summer of 1863:
☛ "The hardships growing out of our military arrangements are not the fault of the President [Davis]. I once thought they were. But they are due to his subordinates, the [dogmatic] devotees of West Point. Cases arise, and are brought to the attention of the President, who must decide upon them almost at once. He is often sick, and having abundant confidence in [Confederate Inspector] General [Samuel] Cooper, gives his consent to whatever he proposes."[240]

From a September 21, 1863, letter to Richard M. Johnston:
☛ "As to what I was saying in the conversation to which you allude, about the future relations of the Confederate and Western States, it was in substance this: We must govern the Northwest by ideas, or they will govern us by force. There is no reason in the world why we should not be upon the most intimate and friendly terms with them, so far as trade and commerce are concerned. It is to the interest of both parties that such should be the case. Whether both sections shall ever again be under a common government is beyond all satisfactory conjecture or speculation at this time. But this is not necessary for the purposes I indicate. Their policy could be controlled by ideas emanating from us without the exercise by us of any governmental authority over them, or by them over us, when the war is over, and it must end at some time in some way; we must, if we succeed, have some treaty or compact with these people, regulating our trade and intercourse with them. What will be the nature of such treaty or compact we now cannot say. But in my opinion now is a fitting time,—indeed, from the beginning the time has been fitting to throw out such ideas as may be the nucleus on which the future compact may be formed. These ideas should be well considered and matured, looking to their interests as well as ours."[241]

From an October 28, 1863, letter to Richard M. Johnston, who asked Stephens if he had thought about how he would handle the War should Jefferson Davis die and Stephens be made president:

☛ "I should regard the death of the President as the greatest possible public calamity. What I should do I know not. I have never permitted my mind to contemplate the future so far. Should the contingency happen while I hold my present position, I should be governed in my action by circumstances: I should look to such men as I might find agreeing with me in the line of policy I might think it best to pursue. Who they might be I do not know. I have many strong personal friends; but such would not do to rely on in matters of state. Men of the greatest ability, united with me in opinions, whose services I could command on such a line of policy as I might adopt, would be those I would seek after. My first and great object would be to secure the confidence of the people; to make the Administration acceptable to all classes; to make every man who fights or suffers by privation or sacrifice in any way, feel that it is all for his rights and liberties, and not for a mere dynasty. Good government and constitutional liberty, the birthright of our people, should be the governing principle. This I state to you, not as the result of any reflection on the subject, but as the instincts of my nature. Hence I think it not improbable that among the first acts I should perform would be the clearing of the hospitals of thousands of sick and invalid soldiers, who are doing nothing but wasting what of life is left them where they can do the public no good, but are exhausting supplies which will soon be very much needed. Every provost-marshal should soon be dismissed, and the whole passport system abolished. Fifty thousand men now engaged all over the country in this sort of annoying business should either be sent to the army where they belong, or sent home to some profitable occupation. All impressments, except in case of actual necessity for the army, should be instantly discontinued. Supplies should be bought at market value. Virtue, honesty, justice, and patriotism, that lofty sentiment which looks to good government as something worth living for and dying for, should be inculcated in every possible way."[242]

From a November 3, 1863, letter to Richard M. Johnston:
☛ "In my letter of last week, written just before starting for Atlanta, I did not say as much as I intended on one point alluded to. That was, my reason for looking upon the death of the President, should such an event happen, as one of the greatest public calamities that could befall us. This is an unpleasant subject to me; but as your letter brought it to my mind, and I gave you the opinion I did, it is but proper to state the reasons upon which it was founded. The general and profound shock such an event would produce throughout the country in its present restless and dissatisfied condition, would of itself tend to gender and increase a spirit of dissension and faction. Such a spirit at all times exists in a country situated as ours is; and with us it would almost certainly

manifest itself in a formidable way, from the fact that a large party in the country, or at least a large number of prominent and active men in the country, who would, in all probability, soon form a party for concert of action, really and honestly would distrust my ability to conduct affairs successfully. They have now, and would have, no confidence in my judgment or capacity for the position that such an untimely misfortune would cast upon me. They believe, I am confident, that under my administration all would go to ruin. To what extent these demonstrations might go I cannot conjecture; but quite far enough greatly to weaken and cripple my efforts on any line of policy I might adopt, even assuming that it might be the best. The unhinging and upturning and unsettling things so little settled at present; the greater confounding of things even now confused: the uncertainties, the disquietudes, the breakings-up of hopes and expectations that such an event would occasion, would render it unquestionably one of the greatest calamities that could befall us, to say nothing of the correctness of the views of those who entertain such serious doubts of my ability to direct affairs. On that point I assure you I have the strongest distrust of myself. I know that affairs in many particulars would not be managed as they are; but would they be managed for the better or the worse? I know not; and it would be with trembling and fear I should take the helm if the necessity should ever arise. I wish never to advert to this subject again."[243]

From a November 4, 1863, letter Stephens expounds on his wretched experience teaching school for four months at Madison, Georgia, in 1832:

☛ "I left Madison with a good impression of the people toward me, who knew not how miserable I was while I was there. My health was not good; before I left college I had become dyspeptic, and was subject to severe nervous headaches, which increased greatly in severity while I was at Madison. My long walks, I am now convinced, were injurious to me. Before the expiration of the term I had, through my old classmate and room-mate, William Le Conte, made arrangements to teach a private school for his father the next year. The trustees at Madison wished to retain me, but I told them of my engagement, and we parted in friendship and with good feelings on both sides. I shall never forget the day I left the town,—that house, that office. . . . Nor shall I forget the night after this parting. My brother, Aaron Grier [Stephens], came for me in a buggy, and we drove all the way to Crawfordville. I had a terrible headache,—a most horrible headache!"[244]

On November 17, 1863, Stephens wrote out the following detailed description of his father, Andrew Baskins Stephens, who died May 7, 1826, in Taliaferro County, Georgia:

☛ [Walking with a friend in the field where his father used to work, Stephens said:] "My father was a wise man. The more I think of him the more deeply I am impressed with the fact, not only in reference to his knowledge of the world and of men, but in all the relations and business of life. And this brings the whole subject we were talking of the other day back to my mind. One of his traits . . . was rarely to lose his temper. He very seldom suffered himself to get angry, and when he did, he suppressed all outward show of it. He never quarrelled with his neighbors, nor scolded his servants, children, or scholars [students]. He took great care to give no cause of offence to others.

"A common remark of his own was, 'Haste makes waste.' His rule was to keep constantly going, moderately but regularly, and never to lose any time. He never allowed his oxen or horses to be pushed; rarely himself rode faster than a walk, and he would have punished a child or servant for trotting a horse from the plough, or galloping to or from the mill, even without a load. His rules were rigid, and his discipline strict. Punishment invariably followed their infraction, through negligence or inattention,—punishment sure, but never severe.

"There was nothing about the farm that more provoked him than bad ploughing, whether in breaking up the land or in the cultivation of the crop. He took great pains with his ploughs, seeing that they were properly proportioned, and that the share and coulter were rightly pitched to run easily, both for horse and man. He made his plough-stocks himself, and saw that every part was rightly adjusted. He allowed no loitering or stopping after a start was made for the field. Two hours were allowed for rest and feeding at noon in the summer, less in the other seasons.

"My duty, from childhood, was to attend to the sheep. I had to see that they were up every night, summer and winter. I shall never forget a punishment that I got about the sheep soon after the duty was assigned me. One evening, after a snowy day, I went to call them up, fold them and feed them as usual. I found them all but one. It was almost dark, and the snow was several inches deep on the ground. I called for some time, but the sheep did not come, and I returned, and did not report that one was missing. The next evening the sheep was still missing, and still I made no report. The following morning my father went with me himself to look at the sheep, as was his custom from time to time to go around and see how every one was attending to his duty. He missed the sheep, which was a ewe, and immediately asked how long she had been missing. I told him. 'Why had I said nothing of it before?' he sternly asked. I could say nothing, for the true reason of my silence was the fear that I should be sent out to look for the lost ewe in the dark and snow; and as I did not tell of it the first night, I held my peace the next day. I had no idea that anything serious had happened to the ewe, but supposed she would come up in a day or two, and that no one but myself would know that she had ever been missing.

"The affair, however, turned out very differently from my expectations. I got a sound chastisement for my carelessness and disobedience; but the evident anger of my father at my misconduct caused me much severer pain than did the stripes he inflicted. He and I set out to search for the ewe: and at last we found her dead, with a lamb she had borne lying dead beside her. The whole affair made a deep and lasting impression on my mind, and I do not think I was ever again guilty of a similar piece of negligence. It was not from the fear of the punishment: indeed, looking back, I do not remember that I ever had a whipping in my life that did me any good; and I certainly was never deterred from doing anything by the fear of one. Perhaps I never deserved one more than I did this; and I did not feel that I had been wronged by it, which is more than I can say of many that I did get. But such was my reverence and love for my father, and such my trust in his justice and goodness, that I did not think he would act in any matter of this sort from any motive but the sense of duty. But I thought then, and still think, that if he had not whipped me, but had explained the reason of his injunction to me to report any missing sheep at the time, and had gone with me as he did, and we had found the sheep dead in consequence of my neglect, this would have had all the effect upon me that the punishment was intended to produce. For it was a matter of deep and painful thought to me for a long time afterwards, that old 'Mottle-face,' as we used to call the ewe, had suffered and died through my neglect. No darkness, cold, or snow could have kept me from hunting her up if I had thought of her being in such a condition.

"My father's habits as a teacher, and his manner of teaching, I well recollect. He never scolded; never reprimanded a scholar in a loud voice; never thumped the head, pulled the ears, or used a ferula [a thick-stemmed plant], as I have often seen other teachers do. He took great pleasure in the act of teaching, and was unwearied in explaining everything to his scholars, the youngest as well as the oldest. He had no classes, except in spelling and reading, in which exercises he insisted on a clear, full enunciation. He was himself one of the best readers I have ever heard, and he was very particular in making his scholars attend to the pauses, and deliver the passages with the proper emphasis and intonation; and to instruct them in this he would take the book and show the school how it ought to be read. In this way even the dullest scholar understood what was required of him, and what good reading was. His 'cipherers,' as those used to be called who studied arithmetic, and such as were in higher branches, such as surveying, etc., were allowed to study outside the school-house.

"His scholars generally were much attached to him. He was on easy and familiar terms with them without losing their respect; and the smallest boys would approach him with confidence, but never with familiarity. He had one custom I never saw or heard of in any other school. About once a month, on a Friday evening, after the spelling classes had got through their tasks, he had an

Judah Philip Benjamin

exercise on ceremony, which the scholars called 'learning manners,' though what he called it—if I ever heard him call it anything—I cannot remember. The exercise consisted in going through the usual form of salutation on meeting an acquaintance, and introducing persons to each other, with other variations occasionally introduced. These forms were taught during the week, and the pupils' proficiency was tested on the occasions I am speaking of. At the appointed hour on the Friday evening, at a given signal, books were laid aside and a recess of a few minutes given. Then all would reassemble and take seats in rows on opposite benches, the boys on one side and the girls—for he taught both sexes—on the other. The boy at the head of the row would rise and walk toward the centre of the room, and the girl at the head of her row would rise and proceed toward the same spot. As they approached, the boy would bow and the girl drop a curtsey,—the established female salutation of those days,—and they would then pass on. At other times they were taught to stop and exchange verbal salutations, and the usual formulas of polite inquiry, after which they retired, and were followed by the next pair. His leading object was to teach ease and becoming confidence of manner, and gracefulness of movement and gesture. He was very particular about a bow; and when a boy was awkward in it, he would go through the motion himself, and show how it ought to be done. These exercises were varied by meetings in an imaginary parlor,—the entrance, introduction, and reception of visitors, with practice in 'commonplace chat,' to use his own phrase, suited to the supposed occasion. Then came the ceremony of introductions. The parties in this case would walk from opposite sides of the room in pairs, and upon meeting, after the salutations of the two agreed upon, would commence making known to each other the friends accompanying them: the boy saying, 'Allow me, Miss Mary, to present to you my friend Mr. Smith. Mr. Smith, Miss Jones.' Whereupon, after Miss Mary had spoken to Mr. Smith, she would in turn introduce her friends.

"These exercises, trivial as the description may seem, were of great use to raw country boys and girls, removing their awkwardness and consequent shyness, and the painful sense of being at a disadvantage, or the dread of appearing ridiculous; and I have no doubt many or all of them, in after-life, had frequent occasion to be grateful for my father's lessons in 'manners.' They were delighted in by the scholars, especially the large boys and girls, and in the old-field schools some of these were nearly or quite grown. Frequently, when the weather was fine, parents and neighbors would come to the school-house on these Friday evenings to witness the ceremonies. When such visits were expected, the girls would dress a little smarter than usual, and the boys would fix themselves up at the spring, washing, combing, and giving an ornamental adjustment, popularly called a 'roach,' to their hair; and the conversation, of surpassing politeness and elegance, was extremely amusing.

"My father was very fond of dramatic exercises in school, and while, as I said before, he was never much given to mirth, meaning by that excessive laughter or joke-telling, yet he was very fond of the humorous in dramatic form. He seldom had public examinations, but almost always had what he called an 'exhibition' some time during the year. At these exhibitions speeches were delivered by the boys, pieces of poetry or prose recited, and dialogues or dramatic scenes acted. The speeches of the small boys he wrote himself. They were short, and usually took a humorous turn. The larger boys recited pieces of his selection, among which there was sure to be [Alexander] Pope's 'Universal Prayer,' which was a great favorite with him. My brother Aaron had this assigned to him on one occasion, when a short piece of poetry called 'The Cuckoo'—I forget the author—fell to my lot. I also recited a piece on Charity, by Blair, and took parts in several plays.

"These exhibitions were numerously attended,—surprisingly so, under the circumstances. At one I think there were at least three thousand persons, and the crowd was like that of a camp-meeting, the spectators having assembled from a circuit of many miles: indeed, the exhibition was a great gala-day, not only for the school, but for all the surrounding country. A stage was constructed at the end of the school-house, and dressing-rooms, as I may call them, partitioned off by curtains. The green-room was in the school-room, and was entered through a window behind the curtain. The scenes for action were selected with a good deal of taste. None were chosen from tragedy proper, or from farce, but chosen with an eye to improve manners and morals. Some of the dialogues of this kind he wrote himself. He devoted great care to the rehearsals, showing each performer how his part should be recited and acted. His versatility of talent in this line was surprising, and the scholars used to enjoy the rehearsals quite as heartily as the spectators did the performance. In this, as in everything else, he carried out his principle that whatever was to be done ought to be well done. Half-way modes of doing things, make-shifts and failures, were an abomination in his sight.

"His scholars had a strong attachment for him, and those who had once been his pupils seemed to feel as deep regard and respect for him as for their own parents. This feeling, I have found, adhered to them through life. Whenever in my travels I have fallen in with any of my father's old scholars, their hearts seemed to warm into a glow towards me. He talked to them, counselled them, instilled into them principles of sobriety, morality, industry, energy, and honor. Cheating, lying, and everything mean or dishonest he held up to scorn and abhorrence. He was, so far as I know, the only old-field teacher of those days on whom the boys never played the prank of 'turning out.' They had probably too much respect and regard for him.

"In early life he was very healthy and robust, and unusually strong for one of his size, as I have often heard him say. He never met one of his own weight whom he could not out-jump. Wrestling had been a favorite amusement with him in his youth; but in after-life he never allowed his children, scholars, or servants to engage in it. His reason for this prohibition grew out of an incident of his life which he sometimes related with much feeling. When he first grew up, Sherod Young, a friend of his of about the same age, and his equal in strength, to whom he was much attached, and with whom he had had many a wrestling-bout without any very decided advantage on either side, proposed to him that they should go out alone, and by one final trial determine which was the better of the two. For a long time neither had much the advantage, until at last Young by some movement lost his footing, and my father threw him a heavy fall, and fell himself upon him. For some time he lay insensible, and apparently dead. No one was present to help. My father used every effort to revive him, but in vain, until finally he gave up in despair, believing him dead. Life, however, at last returned; but it was long before he entirely recovered from the effects of the fall. From that day my father never again wrestled with any one, nor would he allow it to take place wherever he could prevent it.

"But in later years, and as far back as my earliest recollection of him, he suffered from some affection of the spine, and could not lift anything of much weight, nor stoop without pain. He suffered also much from ear-ache, of a rheumatic or neuralgic character, and I have known him tormented for many sleepless nights in succession with this painful malady. He often expressed the opinion that he would not live to old age. In speaking of death he used to express a strong desire to retain his consciousness to the last. 'I should like to meet him' [Death], he would say, 'in my right mind.' This, however, was not the case with him. He died of pneumonia, or, as it was then called, influenza. He was confined to his bed nine or ten days, but was not thought to be dangerously ill until the day before he died. About twenty-four hours before he died he became delirious, then fell into a stupor, after which he recognized nothing. The evening on which he was first taken, he told all the family that he thought he should die, though he was not suffering much pain. He had all the children and servants called into his bedroom, where my step-mother was lying ill herself, and told them what he thought would be the issue of the disease. Several days passed, and no bad symptom had made its appearance. The Thursday before he died—which happened on Sunday—he sent for my first teacher, Nathaniel Day, to draw up his will. This was done, and he seemed cheerful enough. On that night, or the next, I now forget which, I was in the room alone with him for a while, and he told me he was going to die, and gave me a long talk and much advice, speaking with a great deal of feeling. I then had no idea that he was really going to die. I was deeply impressed by what he said, but the fact or even the probability of his dying I could not realize. When I saw him breathe his last it came near killing me. It seemed as if I could not live. Never was human anguish greater than that which I felt upon the death of my father. He was the object of my love, my admiration, my reverence. It seemed to me impossible that I could live without him; and the whole world for me was filled with the blackness of despair. His whole life, from the time of my earliest recollection, was engraven upon my memory; his actions, his conversations, his admonitions, his counsels, were before me by day and by night for many a month afterwards. Whenever I was about to do something that I had never done before, the first thought that occurred to me was, What would my father think of this? Sometimes I indulged the fancy that perhaps his spirit was watching over me, and that he saw what I was doing and even knew my thoughts; and this fancy was soothing and pleasing to me. I sometimes dreamed of him, and always awoke from such dreams weeping, for in them I could never have such intercourse with him as I longed for. There was nothing in them life-like, nothing real; all was shadowy, and he was dead! The *inanis imago* ['empty image'] was all that I could see.

"But the principles and precepts he taught me have been my guiding-star through life. Nothing could have induced me to do anything which I thought he would have disapproved if he had been alive. My strongest desire was to do in all things what I thought would have pleased him. Even now the thought often occurs to me: I wonder what my father thinks of this? But the thought brings sad memories to life and awakens anew the old sorrow!"[245]

From Stephens' diary concerning his father's death:
☛ "I was young, without experience, knew nothing of men or their dealings, and when I stood by his bedside and saw him breathe his last, and with that last breath my last hope expired, such a flood of grief rushed into my heart as almost burst it. No language can tell the deep anguish that filled a heart so young; the earth, grass, trees, sky, everything looked dreary; life seemed not worth living, and I longed to take my peaceful sleep by my father's side."[246]

From a November 25, 1863, letter to his brother Linton. Stephens has traveled to Linton's house, but finding him away, left these words for him:
☛ "I did great injustice to a member of your household in my letter of Monday. I fully intended to make the *amende honorable* yesterday, but forgot it. In my letter I said that when I got here I found nobody at home, when the truth was,

Edwin McMasters Stanton

Pompey [Linton's dog] was on the steps and gave me a most cordial welcome. He said nothing, but conducted me into the library with a great deal of canine gallantry. He has ever since kept close to me. Last night he slept in my room (your room, I should say), but did not make any attempt on the bed. This showed better breeding, I think, than his grandson Binks [Stephens' dog] would have shown under the circumstances. Sir Bingo always looks out for soft places and warm ones in cold weather.

"Dr. Berckmans came over yesterday evening to play piquet [a card game] with me. We had several games. After supper he and Cosby [a family friend] played: I sat in the corner and smoked my pipe. They played on until I got sleepy: the game between them about equal from what I could gather. . . . In this way it went on until I got up and went to bed."[247]

From a December 9, 1863, letter to his brother Linton, from Crawfordville:
☛ "I see it stated that [Confederate General Joseph E.] Johnston is to take command of the Army of Tennessee. I am glad of this. . . . One thing about Johnston I like,—or at least I have the opinion of him that he will not fight unless he feels assured of victory. Our ultimate success now depends as much upon not fighting as fighting."[248]

From a December 31, 1863, letter to his brother Linton:
☛ "Your last letter has awakened my deepest sympathy. Could I say or do anything to afford relief or even consolation, most cheerfully would I do it. But I can do no more than give you my own experience. I can but hope that you may perhaps profit by it. I have in my life been one of the most miserable beings, it seemed to me, that walked the earth,—subject to occasional fits of depression that seemed well-nigh bordering on despair. Without enjoyment, without pleasure, without hope, and without sympathy with the world. Everything seemed to render me more and more miserable. The first lesson I learned in this condition that did me any good was this great truth: that man's happiness or misery depends more upon himself than everything else combined. Every one carries with him passions and emotions with which, according to their cultivation, he may make a heaven or a hell. The first rule of conduct deduced from this lesson was the strict and absolute avoidance of everything that annoyed, or tended to excite those passions that rendered me unhappy, and the assiduous cultivation of those feelings that were attended with the opposite effect. Great and heroic effort was necessary at first and for a long time. . . . Never let the mind dwell upon anything disagreeable,—turn it to something else. Even in the worst state of things that befall us there are some prospects more agreeable than others: let the mind be directed to them. With a proper discipline of one's self in this way, ever keeping the passions in perfect subjection, contentment and happiness are attainable by all, with a constant culture of the moral faculties, and a firm reliance on the great Father of the universe."[249]

3

Personal Letters & Observations

Part Three

From a January 1, 1864, letter to Richard M. Johnston:

☛ "Our affairs [that is, of the Confederate states], in my judgment, have been growing worse and worse for the last four years, and will be greatly worse yet, I fear, unless there be a radical change in our military policy,—if indeed we have any, which I very much question. It seems to me that those at the head of our affairs on this subject have had no policy, no definite line of action with a view to fixed objects. They have all along been like the Tennessee lawyer, 'trusting to the sublimity of luck, and floating upon the surface of the occasion.' . . . But I will not croak or grumble. I am a patient looker-on,—that is all."[250]

From a January 21, 1864, letter to Richard M. Johnston:

☛ "If the pending proposition before [the Confederate] Congress passes, to put the whole country under martial law, with the suspension of the writ of *habeas corpus*, and the President [Davis] signs and enforces it, and the people submit to it, constitutional liberty will go down, never to rise again on this continent, I fear. This is the worst that can befall us. Far better that our country should be overrun by the enemy, our cities sacked and burned, and our land laid desolate, than that the people should thus suffer the citadel of their liberties to be entered and taken by professed friends."[251]

From a February 1864 letter:
☛ "Just as I was concluding that letter, Dr. _____ and his family came in,—wife, children, and servants,—'frustrating' me a little, as it was dinnertime, and I knew that only three names beside my own had been put into the pot, and as I was unwell, and besides it was Eliza's [Stephens' cook and laundress] wash-day, I thought of but little during the winding-up of my letter but the scanty showing for dinner we should have for so many more than were expected, unless new arrangements were immediately put in motion. For, besides the doctor and his family, I soon saw two others coming.

"And now if you have any curiosity to know how the little affair of dinner at short notice on a wash-day was managed, I will state for your satisfaction that Eliza very soon had us an excellent meal of fried ham and eggs, quite enough for all, which all seemed to relish very well, too. The bread was hasty corn-cake, good enough for hungry people. This, with butter and buttermilk, constituted our dessert. The children pitched into sorghum syrup with as keen a relish as if it had been apple-pie. Upon the whole I do not know if it did not all pass off as well as if I had delayed dinner an hour or two and had tried to do better. My rule in such cases is, never to fix up anything for persons dropping in at mealtime. If I have not enough cooked, as in this case, I set them to cooking that which can be got ready in the quickest time."[252]

From a February 20, 1864, letter to his brother Linton:
☛ "I see by the telegrams yesterday that the *habeas corpus* suspension is not general; but the limitations are not, as to totality, as I expected. They are as to causes of arrest. The efforts to suspend the act were once defeated, I think. The matter then, as the bill shows, was brought forward at the instance of the President [Davis]. [The C.S.] Congress, I suspect, granted only part of the request,—not, probably, what was wanted. So the courts are still left open for the protection of ordinary legal rights. But I trust the new Congress will repeal the present act. Power should not be allowed to make any encroachment."[253]

From an April 17, 1864, letter to his brother Linton:
☛ "I see the Mississippi Legislature has unanimously passed the Resolutions against *habeas corpus* suspension. Have you seen their Resolutions? They are jam

up on our line. What will Mrs. Grundy now say? Is Mr. Davis's own State in unanimous opposition to his Administration in this particular? Are they all factionists and malcontents?"[254]

From an April 18, 1864, letter to his brother Linton:
☞ "This is certainly a very late and extraordinary spring. I have seen crops as late as they are now; but never did I see the 16th of April come with so little start in vegetation generally. For instance, on this day of this month, in 1849, I saw a frost that killed everything,—wheat in the head, corn half-leg-high (some of it ploughed over once), young peaches as large as the end of your thumb. Not only the fruit, but the leaves of the trees were killed, and the whole forest was rendered almost black. The leaves on all trees were full-grown when the frost came. . . . One of the singular things or facts to be noticed in this spring is that peach-trees on high land bloomed about as early as they usually do, while those in the low land held back like the apple-trees. The red oaks, post oaks, hickories, and black locusts in my yard still present a wintry appearance; the buds have hardly commenced to swell. The Spanish oak has made more advance; the buds show plainly on it, and some tasselled blooms are to be seen. But the forest still looks wintry. Such a state of things on the 16th day of April I never saw before, and I have a distinct recollection for the last forty-five years. The latest spring I

LeRoy Pope Walker

ever saw before this, in respect to planting, was in 1843. All March was cold that year,—big snows on the 19th and 29th, succeeded by hard frosts. But when that spell broke up, as it did on the night of the 31st of March, it was in one of the most wonderful thunder-storms ever witnessed in this country, and the more noted at the time by the superstitious from the fact that that was the day the world was to come to an end, according to the Millerites [a Yankee apocalyptic group], who had been cutting some figure for a few years."[255]

From a May 12, 1864, letter to his brother Linton. Stephens was on a train bound for Richmond, Virginia:

☞ "About dark it began to rain. I had before discovered that there was another train following in our rear, about five minutes behind us. I inquired of the conductor about the danger of being run into in the dark, and learned that the only precaution was a lamp in the rear of our car. On we went, making slow speed up the grades, and dashing at a furious rate down them. All fell asleep. I was stretched out on two benches, dozing. The cars were halting,—jerking up a high grade. Presently I felt a big jerk, and soon heard a soldier say, 'The cars have broken loose, and we are running back down the grade.' I jumped up, looked out, and saw it was so. Our speed was increasing rapidly; the rain was pouring, and all outside was dark,—black as pitch. I went to the rear end of the car to look out for the train behind us, and there I found the conductor standing with the signal-lamp. No sign of the other cars. The rain pouring, all black with darkness, the cars gaining in speed every moment, I woke up Hidell and Myers; this woke all in the car. On we went to the foot of the grade, about two miles, and then we began to ascend. Our speed now began to slacken,—this brought hope and relief to all. In about half a mile farther we stopped. I asked the conductor if he knew where we were, or the nature of the road immediately in our rear? Were we on a curve, or was there a straight stretch on the line the rear cars would come? He said it was a straight stretch for a mile and a half to the Catawba River. This put me at ease, and I took my bed again. Soon Hidell, who remained at the end door, came and reported to me that the conductor was mistaken,—we were on a curve. He saw by the lightning. I went and looked, and when it lightened saw that the road could not be seen more than fifty yards. I looked for the conductor; he was gone and could not be found: the signal-lamp was held by one of the train-hands. Upon a survey of the premises I discovered that the step of the car was exactly opposite a bridge across the side ditch. A fence was near the road, inclosing woods and a pair of bars right opposite the little bridgeway across the ditch. So I concluded it safest to get out. All followed except two or three, who remained watching for the approaching cars. We who got out passed over the bridge, got into the woods, and just at this time the other train came dashing down the grade. On it came until it turned the curve,—the lantern man gave a whoop, left his lantern standing where it could be seen, and followed us. The whistle instantly sounded, all brakes were put down, and the engine reversed. The train halted within the distance, and no harm was done. Our engine came back for us after awhile. We all got off in the course of an hour, and reached here at the time stated."[256]

Stephens' a May 12, 1864, to his brother Linton continues:

☛ "No definite news from Richmond this morning, and no news at all from Dalton. No news I am always inclined to look upon as bad news. I am uneasy about the state of affairs at both points, Dalton and Richmond. I am fearful that our authorities have under-estimated [U.S. General Ulysses S.] Grant's force. If he has two hundred thousand, as I think he must have, it seems to me that if he has disposed of them as he might have done, we must be in great peril there. Suppose, for instance, he brought against Lee eighty thousand,—about Lee's number, perhaps,—and suppose he landed twenty thousand on the Rappahannock [River] below Fredericksburg [Virginia], and fifty thousand at the head of navigation on the Pamunkey [River], and fifty thousand near City Point. Suppose his object in attacking Lee was to detain him, skirmish with him for four or five days as he was making his way down on the south side of the Rappahannock to Fredericksburg, while the twenty thousand were moving up to reinforce him if he should be hard pressed, and while the fifty thousand landed at West Point or higher up were moving up on the south side of the South Anna towards Beaver Dam and the Central Railroad, thus putting fifty thousand men between Lee and Richmond, and cutting off Lee's supplies by railroad, on which he is solely dependent,—then his army, or what remains of it, say at least fifty thousand, reinforced by the twenty thousand coming up the river, could easily join the other fifty thousand between Lee and Richmond, making in all one hundred and twenty thousand, most of them fresh troops, to face Lee's reduced and fatigued forces. In the mean time, the fifty thousand at or about City Point would hold Beauregard, with not over fifty thousand, in complete check. If Grant has adopted any such programme as this, it seems to me that we are in great peril; and if he has not, he is not the military chieftain he is asserted to be. I am anxious. I hope all will end well. Lee is a man of great ability; but Bragg is controlling everything at Richmond now."[257]

From a May 23, 1864, letter to his brother Linton. Stephens is traveling across the South via railroad:

☛ "As notified by the conductor of the trains on the Piedmont Road, I appeared at the depot to start for Greensboro, North Carolina, a little before one o'clock P.M. . . . The day was hot and sultry,—no sign of any train in readiness, or any conductor. Remained for two hours,—no sign of making ready to start. Another hour passes. A train is brought out, and seven hundred and fifty Yankee prisoners marched out to be put on it. All the cars filled with prisoners,—the tops of the cars filled. Another train brought out, and two hundred and fifty more Yankee prisoners marched out and put in. At the end of this train a passenger-car is attached, all the others and all the cars of the first train being boxcars. My conductor appears; apologizes for his delay,—had not control of the trains,—under Government officers; but we would get off in this last train in half an hour. Takes me to the car and gives me a good seat. Baggage put on. I walk out on the platform before the car leaves. A great number of wounded soldiers standing about trying to get passage home: some with bandages on the head, some with arms in slings, and some on crutches. In reply to their questions the conductor says they cannot go,—they must wait until to-morrow. Great murmuring in the crowd: 'They had been there two days waiting and without money.'—'No more care or thought is given to a wounded soldier than if he were a dog,'—such exclamations were common. I stepped up to one poor fellow who had his arm in a sling: 'Are you from the army?' 'Yes, sir.' 'What regiment?' 'Twenty-fifth Georgia.' 'What is your name?' 'Roberts.' 'At what place were you wounded?' 'I was wounded in the Wilderness, the first day's fight.' 'Can you tell me anything about the other wounded or killed in the regiment?' 'No, sir; I was wounded about the first of the action, and sent back to Orange Court-House.'

"I take my seat in the car,—the man with a gun at the door lets me in. On this quite a number of the wounded soldiers get in at the windows. Conductor comes and makes them get out,—they complain bitterly. Some one tells them, I suppose, that I was the Vice-President, for I hear some vociferous fellow say aloud, in a passion, 'I'll be d——d if I don't go; I am as good as the Vice-President!' Time rolls on,—the Yankee train rolls off. Half-past five comes,—the conductor tells the wounded about the car that as many as can fill the car may go,—that the worst cases should have preference. The car is soon full. Those outside look sad,—the conductor tells them that a train will leave at eight o'clock and take them all. This pacifies them. By the by, when I had seen the state of things, I had gone to see Major Morphet, who had come down in charge of the prisoners, whom I knew, and who had charge of the trains, and urged upon him to send the wounded soldiers forward as soon as possible. Among the loudest complaints they were making was one that the Yankees should be sent on before them. Some of them swore in their wrath that the Yankees ought to be killed; but instead of that they were cared more for than the men who had been wounded in defending their country. I was truly sorry for them. . . . Our train rolled off at last. We had forty-eight miles to go, and the conductor told me we should get there, or were due, at nine o'clock. But it was three when we got to Greensboro. The water on the road had given out, and the hands had to haul it up with buckets at the creeks and branches. . . . Soon after starting, a soldier looking very weak and sick, and much emaciated, passed by me, looking for a seat. The conductor had given me a seat to myself, so I touched the soldier and told him to take a seat by me. He did so with a

James Alexander Seddon

good deal of modesty as well as thankfulness. He evidently, from his manner, knew who I was. He seemed to be sick and not wounded. 'Do you belong to the army?' said I. 'Yes, sir,' he replied, looking steadily but timidly in my face, when for the first time I saw he was a mere boy. 'What regiment?' 'The Fifteenth Georgia.' 'What's your name?' 'Noel Monroe Humphrey. I live in Hancock County, but joined the Taliaferro company last winter. Don't you recollect the night that Ed. Johnson and all of us took supper at your house?—that's the time I joined. I was going on then. I got to the company and was taken sick,—was sent back to the hospital at Liberty, Virginia, where I have been ever since, until last week they furloughed me. I have been here three days trying to get on, but couldn't.' . . . The poor fellow looked very badly. I recollected all about his stopping at my house and taking supper. On my asking him if he had any money, he said he had not a cent. I asked him how he got along for something to eat. The only chance, he said, was at the wayside houses. I asked him if he had had anything that day. Nothing since breakfast, as he had been waiting ever since twelve for the train to start. I asked him if he was not hungry; he said he was. I hauled out my basket and gave him as much as he wanted. Seeing others about looking anxiously on, I passed the basket round,—about half a dozen ate up what was laid in for our travelling lunch for some days. I was sorry I did not have enough for all. Among those who did get some, I noticed a sprightly-looking fourteen-year old boy, who said he was from Marion County. . . .

    "At Winsboro three ladies and a young gentleman got in,—the young gentleman of a pale, rather sallow, complexion. I was half asleep, but heard the young gentleman whisper, 'The Vice-President is aboard.' 'Which is he?' asks one of the ladies in a whisper;—'that man there? that little man?' 'No, that one on the seat right behind you.' 'This little man?' says she, in a very low voice. I heard no reply, but heard her utter a guttural sound that you are well acquainted with, but I know not how to write or spell. It was all guttural, and may be imagined from my expressing it as well as I can with the letters '*eh en*'—with the French sound of the *en*. I opened my eyes and thought she was laughing. I felt badly; not at my own bad looks, but at the great disappointment I had caused one of my constituents."[258]

From a June 23, 1864, letter to Richard M. Johnston:
☞ ". . . I feel intense interest and anxiety about the condition of things in Virginia and Upper Georgia. If we can but hold our own for six months longer, I shall then indulge stronger hopes than I can possibly feel now. I think [Confederate General Joseph E.] Johnston acts wisely in not hazarding his army in a fight, if this be his reason for falling back as he has done. Unless he has the prospect of doing the enemy a great injury by crippling and routing them, he should avoid an encounter of arms as long as possible. Temporary invasion is not conquest. The loss of property may be great, the devastation appalling; still, so long as our army is preserved the work of the enemy is unaccomplished. We may all be subjected to privations and sacrifices; these can be borne, not only for six months, but for years, if the right spirit is kept alive with our people. This depends as much upon the policy of the Administration as anything else; indeed, I believe more."[259]

From a June 28, 1864, letter to Richard M. Johnston:
☞ "Without fail come by to see me. I have some old papers that I wish to hand you. Whether you or I live longer in the contingencies of war, they may be safer in your hands, or where you may put them, than they would be here. Should the enemy make incursions into the interior of our State (which I do not think improbable, whatever may be my hopes that they may not), this place would probably be in their line of march, towards Augusta. In that case, of course, my house would be rifled. . . . I am still feeble, but better than when I wrote you last. I am confined pretty much to the house. It is too hot for me to go out: I cannot even drive to the plantation."[260]

From a September 4, 1864, letter to Richard M. Johnston:
☞ "The Chicago Convention [to nominate a U.S. presidential candidate for the upcoming November 1864 election] did not do as well as I hoped they would, and as I think they would have done if our authorities had backed the leading peace men there from the beginning, as they should have done. Still, I am not without hope that good will result from their action. The prospect for the early

dawn of the day of peace is not so good as it would have been if an out-and-out peace man had been nominated on an out-and-out peace platform. Still, under the circumstances, it may be that many of the real advocates of peace on the basis of a separation of the States thought it best to pursue the course they have, which, in their judgment, will ultimately lead to the same result. I think they made a mistake. Still, they may be better informed as to the state of the popular mind at the North than I am. They may have thought it was hazarding too much to submit the naked question of separation to the people there now, and, moreover, it may be that while a large majority of that body would to-day be for separation rather than a continuation of the war, yet the same majority would greatly prefer a restoration of the Union with every fair and just guaranty to the South if such restoration can be effected. And it may be that they felt it a patriotic duty with these views to make the effort; while at the same time they are prepared, if the effort fails, to have peace even upon the basis of ultimate separation. This is my reading and understanding of their action, knowing as I do the sentiments of several men who would give that action their sanction. This idea, I think, is about this [from the North's perspective]: we will first elect [Yankee General George B.] McClellan if possible, and in order to do this we will put ourselves upon the most plausible platform entirely consistent with the dictates of the highest patriotism working to a restoration of the Government in its pristine purity. If we elect McClellan on this platform, we will then do everything that can be done by the most patriotic efforts to effect such a restoration by negotiation, not by arms. If that fail, then we will take peace as the last alternative on the basis of separation. This is my rendering of their action [at the North]. For their [McClellan's] platform is out and out for a suspension of hostilities,—for opening negotiations,—and if they fail of restoring the Union, their platform stops them from a return to a coercive policy. So, upon the whole, if our authorities commit no blunders, all may yet be well. But who can count upon anything that depends upon the contingency that our authorities will commit no blunders?"[261]

From a September 14, 1864, letter in which Stephens replied to a gentleman from Georgia who had written him, asking about the possibility of co-founding a peace movement with Northern conservatives to help bring an end to Liberal Lincoln's War:
☛ "The Resolutions of the Georgia Legislature, at its last session, upon the subject of peace, in my judgment, embodied and set forth very clearly those principles upon which alone there can be permanent peace between the different sections of this extensive, once happy and prosperous, but now distracted country. The easy and perfect solution to all our present troubles, and those for more grievous ones which loom up in prospect and portentously

threaten in the coming future, is nothing more than the simple recognition of the fundamental principle and truth upon which all American constitutional liberty is founded, and upon the maintenance of which alone it can be preserved; that is, the sovereignty—the ultimate, absolute sovereignty—of the States. This doctrine our [Confederate] Legislature announced to the people of the North and to the world. It is the only keynote to peace—permanent, lasting peace—consistent with the security of public liberty. The old [U.S.] Confederation was formed upon this principle. The old Union was afterwards formed upon this principle; and no union or league can ever be formed or maintained between any States, North or South, securing public liberty upon any other principle. The whole framework of American institutions, which in so short a time had won the admiration of the world, and to which we were indebted for such an unparalleled career of prosperity and happiness, was formed upon this principle. All our present troubles spring from a departure from this principle; from a violation of this essential, vital law of our political organism. In 1776 our ancestors and the ancestors of those who are waging this unholy crusade against us proclaimed the great and eternal truth, for the maintenance of which they jointly pledged their lives, their fortunes, and their sacred honor, that 'governments are instituted amongst men, deriving their just powers from the consent of the governed;' and that whenever any form of government becomes destructive of those ends [for which it was formed], it is the right of the people to alter or abolish it, and to institute a new government, laying its foundations on such principles, and organizing its powers in such form, *as to them* shall seem most likely to effect their safety and happiness.

"It is needless here to state that by 'people' and 'governed' in this annunciation is meant communities and bodies of men capable of organizing and maintaining government, not individual members of society. 'The consent of the governed' refers to the will of the mass of the community or State in its organized form, and expressed through its legitimate and properly-constituted organs. It was upon this principle the colonies stood justified before the world in effecting a separation from the mother-country. It was upon this principle that the original thirteen co-equal and co-sovereign States formed the Federal compact of the old Union in 1787. It is upon the same principle that the present co-equal and co-sovereign States of our Confederacy formed their new compact of union. The idea that the old Union, or any union between any of the sovereign States, consistently with this fundamental truth, can be maintained by force, is preposterous. This war springs from an attempt to do this preposterous thing. *Superior power may compel a union of some sort; but it would not be the Union of the old Constitution nor of our new; it would be that sort of union that results from despotism. The subjugation of the people of the South by the people of the North would necessarily involve the destruction of the Constitution and the overthrow of their liberties as well as ours. The men or party at the North, to whom you refer, who favor peace, must be brought to a full realization of this truth in all its bearings before their efforts will result in much practical good; for any peace growing out of a union of the States established by force will be as ruinous to them as to us."*[262] [Emphasis added, L.S.]

In one of the more remarkable incidents of Lincoln's War, on September 2, 1864, Yankee war criminal General William T. Sherman requested an interview with Stephens, with the "truly noble and humane desire to devise some plan for terminating the war without further bloodshed." Stephens replied from Crawfordville on October 1, 1864, directly to Sherman's intermediary:

☛ "William King, Esquire: Sir,——I have considered the message you delivered me yesterday from General Sherman with all the seriousness and gravity due the importance of the subject. That message was a verbal invitation by him through you to me to visit him at Atlanta, to see if we could agree upon some plan of terminating this fratricidal war without the further effusion of blood. The object is one which addresses itself with peculiar interest and great force to every well-wisher of his country,——to every friend of humanity,——to every patriot,——to every one attached to the principles of self-government, established by our common- ancestors. I need not assure you, therefore, that it is an object very dear to me,——there is no sacrifice I would not make, short of principle and honor, to obtain it, and no effort would I spare, under the same limitations, with reasonable or probable prospect of success.

"But, in the present instance, the entire absence of any power on my part to enter into such negotiations, and the like absence of any such power on his part, so far as appears from his message, necessarily precludes my acceptance of the invitation thus tendered. In communicating this to General Sherman, you may also say to him that if he is of opinion that there is any prospect of our agreeing upon terms of adjustment to be submitted to the action of our respective Governments, even though he has no power to act in advance in the premises, and will make this known to me in some formal and authoritative manner (being so desirous for peace himself, as you represent him to have expressed himself), I would most cheerfully and willingly, with the consent of our authorities, accede to his request thus manifested, and enter with all the earnestness of my nature upon the responsible and arduous task of restoring peace and harmony to the country, upon principles of honor, right, and justice to all parties. This does not seem to me to be at all impossible, if truth and reason should be permitted to have their full sway. Yours most respectfully, Alexander H. Stephens."[263]

From an October 2, 1864, letter to Richard M. Johnston:

☛ "I was very much pleased with [Georgia] Governor [Joseph E.] Brown's reply to the message of Sherman. As to the prospects of peace, they do not appear so hopeful to me as when I wrote to you last on the subject, soon after the Chicago nomination, and before McClellan's letter of acceptance. That letter, I think, will greatly lessen his chances of election, and it also weakens any hopes of peace at an early day, even in case he should be elected. Still, I should prefer his [McClellan's] election to that of Lincoln. He will, or would, of course, suspend hostilities and try negotiation. Efforts failing in that line, he would renew the war for the restoration of the Union and the old Constitution with all its guaranties. These include the perpetuation of slavery. Whenever the war assumes this attitude on the part of the North, England will no longer be silent. She will recognize us. France and other powers will join. With our recognition abroad, the moral power of the war at the North will be greatly crippled. Peace after awhile will follow. The position of England and France for the last two years is owing to their strong desire to have slavery exterminated. I believe Lincoln's emancipation policy was dictated by England. He was told if the war had no great object in view in aid of the progress of civilization and Christianity, such, for instance,

Christopher Gustavus Memminger

as the abolition of slavery, as they viewed it, recognition would take place. Lincoln was compelled to issue his emancipation proclamation, or witness immediate foreign recognition after the battles of Richmond in 1862; and whenever the war is renewed, if that should be the case, with a view to continue the old Union, Constitution, and slavery, England will no longer regard it as a war for any high and noble purpose, but as a war for subjugation and havoc, and she will say it must be stopped."[264]

From an October 9, 1864, letter to his brother Linton. Stephens is commenting on a "published letter in which the writer expressed his views that the people of the Confederacy were living 'under a complete despotism, worse than Lincoln's,' but one that was a necessary result of their position":

☛ "This is the great mistake which has deluded thousands. Despotism is not necessary to put into active operation the maximum of military power of any nation or people. What nation in modern times has put forth greater military energy than Great Britain? My opinion is that our institutions, even freer in their organic law, are capable of calling forth and putting into exercise quite as great a maximum of military power as England, and without the sacrifice of a single constitutional right. All that is wanting are brains and integrity in properly administering and working the machinery of Government.

"This idea that any amendment to the Constitution is necessary before there can be called a convention of the States, is all wrong. The two Governments could give their assent to this form of adjustment, or initiation of adjustment, as well as any other. . . . My opinion is, that if such a convention should be called by the consent of both Governments, and it should be agreed in that body that the Sovereignty of each State separately should be recognized with all its legitimate and rightful consequences as a basis of peace, there would, or ought to be, no difficulty on the part of either Government in ratifying these terms. The whole scheme would work easily and conformably to the Constitutions of both Governments. Each State at the ballot-box would decide—as she ought to be permitted to do—her own destiny."[265]

From an October 5, 1864, letter to his brother Linton:

☛ "I concur entirely with you in your views upon the subject of good or bad faith on the part of the several States in relation to their action in severing or not their connection with others, either during war or peace. The war makes no difference. The right ground on which to meet any proposition for a severance at this time is, not that it would be an act of bad faith, but an act highly injurious to the interest of any such State. The [Southern] Confederation was formed for the mutual advantage and interest of all. Should any State at any time become satisfied that the war is not waged for purposes securing her best interests, future safety, and protection, she has a perfect right to withdraw, and would commit no breach of faith, either expressed or implied, in doing so.

"What I meant by both Governments [C.S. and U.S.] giving their consent to a convention of the States, was, that such consent could be given without any violation of the Constitution. In this way the meeting of the States in convention could be regularly, rather than constitutionally, assembled. As under our [Confederate] Constitution the initiation of peace properly belongs to the Executive, it seems to me that to have all things done regularly and properly, should a Convention of the States be resorted to, the proposition should be made by one, and acceded to by the other Government. Each State in our Confederacy, and each in the old Union, has delegated the treaty-making power, and all powers relating to foreign intercourse, to the Federal Head; and if any State should be disposed to take control of the present issues of peace and war without the consent of the Federal Head, I am inclined to think that she would first have to resume her sovereign powers,—in other words, she would first have to secede. But with the consent of the Federal Head this would not be necessary,—the delegates to such convention would be but commissioners on the part of each Confederation, who might be appointed in this way as well as any other. At least they could be appointed in this way without any violation of the Constitution. Mr. Davis, in his speech at Columbia, says such a convention would be against the Constitution! I do not see how this is. Should McClellan be elected [in the upcoming November election], this may, and perhaps will, become a great question; but if not, it will pass away, most probably, as a thousand other shadows of the day, without leaving any impression, and without indicating anything even to the most observing minds, except the real substance to which they owe their origin. Hence I said so little on the subject in my letter: that little was said barely for the purpose of making a favorable response to the Chicago movement, that it might have all the influence that anything coming from me could have. That, I know, would not be much. But I did think, and do think, if President Davis had said even as little as I did on that general line, or favoring the idea to the extent I did, it would have had a telling effect at the North. He, however, has chosen to repel the offer at the threshold."[266]

In response to growing criticism that he was working at cross purposes with President Davis and the Southern Cause, Stephens addressed this public letter to his constituents on November 10, 1864:
☛ "To The Public: The following old address [which was given by Stephens at Crawfordville, Georgia, on July 4, 1834] is now reprinted in this form, not with any special view to its own merits, but for the purpose of self vindication. Insinuations and flings, if not direct charges, have repeatedly been made of late against me as a new light on States' Rights, in my advocacy of the doctrine of 'the ultimate absolute sovereignty of the several States' as the only sure basis of a permanent peace between the States of the old Union.

"This address was the first written political speech ever made by me. It was made while I was a student of law, and notwithstanding its many very apparent defects (of which however as a first production I am not ashamed), it clearly shows that States' Rights and State Sovereignty are no new or latter day ideas with me. For this purpose only I ask its perusal at this time by all who may be disposed to do me justice in this particular.

174   THE QUOTABLE ALEXANDER H. STEPHENS

"It is true I was not a Nullifier. Nullification as I understood its exposition at that day claimed the right of any State, in effect, to render null and void, or inoperative within her limits, any law of Congress, and still remain within the Union. Without any desire to revive any of the questions that then divided State Rights men, I may simply add that in my judgment then and now, the reserved Sovereign Powers of the States could be properly resorted to for ultimate protection only by a full resumption of all powers delegated; in other words by secession. In this way only could the sovereign veto of a State against actual or threatened aggression be effectually and properly interposed. When thus interposed there was no constitutional power in the Central Government to command obedience by coercion.

"It is also true that I opposed secession in 1850 and 1860, as a question of policy, but not as a matter of right. The charge that I ever at any time or on any occasion uttered the sentiment that secession would be 'a crime' is entirely without the shadow of a foundation. The clear right of a State under the compact of 1787 to resume the full exercise of all her delegated powers by a withdrawal from the Union whenever her people in their deliberate and solemnly expressed judgment should determine to do so, was never questioned by me. This was the doctrine of the States' Rights party of Georgia under the lead of the illustrious and renowned Troup—the correct teachings of the Kentucky and Virginia Resolutions of 1798 and 1799. In these principles I was reared, by them I have ever been governed in my political acts, and by them I expect to live and die. Hence when Georgia seceded in 1861, even against my own judgment, I stood by her act. To her alone I owed ultimate allegiance. Her cause became my cause. Her destiny became my destiny. From that day to this that cause has engaged every energy of my heart, head and soul, and in it they will continue to be enlisted to the bitter end. Should that end be the establishment of this principle of 'the ultimate absolute sovereignty of the several States,' it will in my judgment more than compensate for the loss of blood and treasure of this war so unjustly waged against her and her confederates, great as it has been or may be. This doctrine once firmly established will, I doubt not, prove to be the self-adjusting principle—the Continental Regulator—in our present or any future systems of associations or confederations of States that may arise. I make no boast of consistency so far as party relations are concerned—these I have often changed, but principles never."[267]

Speaking of the depreciation of Confederate currency, Stephens wrote the following from Richmond, Virginia, December 5, 1864:

☛ "I pay thirty dollars [$500 in today's currency] a day for meals and a room.

Robert Edward Lee

Fuel, lights, and extras generally will be about thirty dollars per day more; so it will not take long to consume my salary."[268]

From a December 23, 1864, letter to his brother Linton. Stephens was at Richmond to attend the Confederate Congress. Disillusioned and despondent over events within the C.S. government, he considers resigning the vice presidency:

☞ "I am satisfied that I can do no good here. Yesterday I got hold of Judge [Roger B.] Taney's decision on the *Habeas Corpus* question in the case of John Merryman, in Baltimore, May, 1861. It is a great paper. I will try to have it republished in Georgia. It sets at nought the prevailing opinions here on the power of Congress over this great writ of right.

"I have strong inclinations to resign my position as Vice-President. I shall do nothing hastily or rashly, but I can never approve doctrines and principles which are likely to become fixed in this country. Judge Taney uses this language,—speaking of the President of the United States: 'He is not empowered to arrest any one charged with an offence against the United States, and whom he may from the evidence before him believe to be guilty; nor can he authorize any officer, civil or military, to exercise this power, for the Fifth Article of the Amendments to the Constitution expressly provides that no person shall be deprived of life, liberty, or property without due process of law,—that is, judicial process.' This is very high authority for the position that warrants for arrest under the Constitution must be judicial warrants,—emanating from the Judicial Department of the Government and not the Executive. In another part of the decision he quotes another of the Amendments to the Constitution, and then says: 'And these great and fundamental laws which Congress itself could not suspend have been disregarded.' . . . The decision is 'jam up' to [in accord with] your resolutions; and if you had had it before you, and had been drawing resolutions founded upon its principles, you could not have done it more exactly than you did in the Georgia Resolutions of last March."[269]

From a December 24, 1864, letter to his brother Linton:

☞ "You will see by a vote of the House taken in open session to-day, that the indications are strong that it is the intention of that body again to suspend the privilege of the writ of *habeas corpus*. . . . I went to the Whig office this morning and offered them two hundred and twenty dollars to republish Judge Taney's decision. I could not get a positive answer whether they will do it or not. I offered their price. . . .

"If this bill passes in such form as it is most likely to pass, I do trust [Georgia] Governor [Joseph E.] Brown will issue his proclamation advising the justices of the inferior courts in the State to disregard it until the matter may be adjudicated by our own [Confederate] Supreme Court. If that court shall decide the act to be constitutional, I shall feel very little further interest in the result of the conflict. It will simply be a contest between dynasties,—a struggle between two powers,—not for rights or constitutional liberty, but for despotism."[270]

Regarding the suspension of habeas corpus *by the Confederate government, some Southerners promoted the idea that "the loss of liberty should be, for a time, endured, for the sake of securing independence, and that Davis would be a better master than Lincoln." To this Stephens replied:*
☛ "I will never choose between masters. Death, rather than any master whatever."[271]

From a January 5, 1865, letter to his brother Linton. Attorney Stephens had just visited a Richmond prison to confer with a murder suspect he was representing:
☛ "I was glad that I went to see the prisoner. Liberty,—the bare right of locomotion,—to walk out in the open air and enjoy the light of day,— what an inestimable blessing it is! How many millions enjoy [it] and never think of its value! How many thousands daily walk the streets of Richmond by the numerous prisons in it, and never think of the unfortunate beings who repine and often die in the cold dusky walls on which they direct not a glance nor bestow a thought! Whenever I see a head at an iron grate, my heart is interested in behalf of the sufferer; and I often speculate on the history, or tragedy it may be, of that life. Good-night. I dreamed of you last night. May I dream of you again to-night."[272]

From a January 6, 1865, letter to his brother Linton:
☛ "The feeling here is better than it was. The present indications are that the *habeas corpus* suspension will be abandoned, and several other follies as well as mischievous measures. I sent you a copy the other day of a rehash of your Resolutions [the 'Georgia Resolutions' of March 1864] which I did up for Atkins of the House to be offered by him to the Committee of Foreign Affairs, hoping to get their endorsement of them in a report to the House recommending their adoption. The Committee consisted of nine members: the vote stood four to four. The Chairman, [William C.] Rives, cast the vote against them; but it is thought he will reconsider, and that they will pass the House.

"The Senate to-day held a meeting after adjournment,—[Robert M. T.] Hunter in the chair,—and passed a resolution unanimously requesting me

George Brinton McClellan and his wife Ellen

to address them on the present condition of the country. It was with closed doors. The whole took me by surprise; but I complied with the request and spoke to them two hours. I gave them my views very freely."[273]

Of this speech (January 6, 1865) Stephens later wrote:
☞ "I urged the importance of offering to the North negotiations on the basis of the Resolutions alluded to. I told them that we had ten friends at the North to one in any other part of the world. Our external policy should look to co-operation with these. By 'friends at the North,' I did not mean men who were in favor of disunion, or those who would even avow a willingness for our separation, but men who really had the same interests at stake in the contest that we have,—the preservation of State Rights and Constitutional liberty. This made them our natural allies; and we should pursue such a course of policy towards them as to bring their efforts in maintaining their own liberties to co-operate with us to maintain ours. We should let them know that, after the contest was over, we would then consider with them all questions looking to new union, and settle them upon rational considerations in view of reciprocal advantages and mutual convenience.

"The speech was delivered off-hand, without a moment's reflection, but it made, I think, a very decided impression. . . . Whether anything can be made of the concern, I do not know. I shall labor to the last and do all I can. I am not sanguine, but am not by any means depressed. I am prepared for anything, and have a spirit that I trust will prove equal to any crisis. With duty discharged with fidelity, I shall have a clear conscience, and feel content, let events take what direction, under Providence, they may."[274]

On February 3, 1865, Stephens, along with Confederate commissioners Robert M. T. Hunter and John A. Campbell, met with Lincoln and William H. Seward at Hampton Roads, Virginia, to discuss the possibility of ending the War "honorably." Here, Lincoln made the statement that if the Southern states agreed to come back into the Union, they could continue to practice slavery as long as they wanted for all he cared.[275] Seward also made a remarkable statement, suggesting that Louisiana should secede from the Union permanently! In the end, as neither side would budge on their principles, the meeting was a failure. On February 20, 1865, Stephens wrote to Richard M. Johnston about the four-hour long meeting, now known as the "Hampton Roads Conference":
☞ "The objects of the mission to Fortress Monroe have not been understood by the people generally. It was to endeavor if possible to obtain an armistice. [Yankee Francis P.] Blair [Sr.] had stated in Richmond that President Lincoln was very much pressed by the Radical party [that is, Northern abolitionists] at home to employ the most extreme measures with what he termed 'the rebels':

and that now, as the relations with France were becoming embarrassing, it would be a good time to make overtures to the United States Government on the basis of the 'Monroe doctrine.' I believed that, if Blair was sincere, much could be done by the exercise of prudence. When the President [Davis] made known the matter to me, I urged him to keep it a profound secret, and to go himself to meet Lincoln. He expressed himself as decidedly opposed to that. I then advised him to send some one whose absence would not be especially noticed, and suggested Judge [John A.] Campbell. The President maintained that the Commission must consist of more than one; so I suggested in addition Thomas S. Flournoy, who was then in Richmond, and [C.S.] General [Henry L.] Benning, in which suggestion I thought he acquiesced. But the next day the President sent for me, and said that the Cabinet had agreed upon Campbell, [Robert M. T.] Hunter, and myself. I found that the appointment was already generally known in Richmond. I was very reluctant to go, because I felt that the President did not fully sympathize with the real objects of that mission; but I concluded to go because of even a slight hope of doing some good.

"Lincoln and Seward, of course, would not agree to consider any terms of truce which did not recognize a return of the Southern States to the Union. I urged an armistice, allowing the States to adjust themselves as suited their interests. If it would be to their interests to reunite, they would do so; but that according to the principle of State rights and State sovereignty, they could not be compelled. Seward made the supposition that Louisiana, bordering as she does for a great distance on both sides of the Mississippi, the great outlet of the West, should secede. I answered that he took indeed an extreme case; but that if France would treat her better than the Union of which she was a member, she ought to secede."[276]

From a March 17, 1865, letter to Richard M. Johnston, in which Stephens elaborates on the Hampton Roads Conference:
☞ "I have, from the first, not been without some suspicion that the whole arrangement with Blair was planned with a view to stop and forestall, just as it did, the action of [the Confederate] Congress on the line (indicated by my resolutions) they were about to adopt. This would have been done in ten days, or perhaps sooner, but for the denouement of the Blair affair. What Congress most probably would have done is this: they would have passed the resolutions submitted, and would have appointed Commissioners to seek an informal conference with the [Yankee] authorities at Washington, to ascertain upon what terms peace could be obtained; and would have been instructed to propose a convention of all the States as a mode of initiating negotiations. This would not have been done under any expectation that Lincoln would agree to it; but to

Howell Cobb

show to the people of the North and the world the fairness of our course, and to make allies at the North of all friends of constitutional liberty there. It was to be the first step in the change of our foreign policy in the conduct of the war. It was to unite our people and divide the North; and was to be followed up by a like change of policy in this. Hereafter the question of the future relations of the States toward each other was to be left for adjustment among themselves, when the great principle of the sovereignty—ultimate, absolute sovereignty—of each was first acknowledged. If it should be first settled by the friends of constitutional liberty, North and South, that there is no rightful power in the central Government to coerce a State; with this principle once acknowledged and settled as the basis of American institutions, then all other questions as to the relations of the States among themselves were to be left for time and reason to adjust upon the principle of 'reciprocal advantages and mutual convenience.' This was my programme for continuing the war on this line. On no other did I see much chance of success; and on no other did I see much good to be obtained even by success. For independence without liberty had no attractions for me; and I see no prospect of liberty except upon the acknowledged principle of the rights and sovereignty of the separate States, North or South."[277]

Though on April 9, 1865, Lee surrendered his army to Grant at Appomattox, many Confederate troops continued to fight, either not having heard the news yet, or having heard it, suspected it to be a Yankee inspired rumor. Some Rebel soldiers, like Edmund Ruffin, committed suicide rather than become veritable slaves under Yankee imperialism. Other Southerners moved to Europe or Mexico. And though Lincoln was by now gone (assassinated by disgruntled Copperhead John Wilkes Booth on April 14), still other Rebels promised to keep Lincoln's War going by hiding in the mountains and engaging in guerilla attacks on Union troops. In the midst of all this Stephens wrote the following to his brother Linton on April 20, 1865:

☞ ". . . I hear the enemy have possession of Macon and are moving on Augusta. These reports will keep me from going over to Sparta this week. While I do not know that I shall attempt to get out of their way if they do pass through here, I do not feel disposed to get voluntarily in their way. I wish you would come over here and let us stand or fall together. I have positive information that General Lee's army surrendered on the 10th inst. Johnston must soon do the same. Organized war is, or soon will be, over with us. If I knew when a letter from me to Governor Brown would reach him, I would write him advising him to convene the Legislature and recommend the call of another State convention to consider our present condition and provide for the future. Almost anything is better than guerilla warfare."[278]

On May 11, 1865, Stephens was illegally arrested at his home on charge of "treason" and taken to Fort Warren in Boston Harbor, Massachusetts, where he was placed in a cold damp cell under armed guard. During the middle of his sentence, on July 21, 1865, he penned the following letter to his good friend James A. Stewart, who had written to the current U.S. President Andrew Johnson on Stephens' behalf. Stephens asks for a fair trial before a jury, something no liberal Northerner wanted—or ever allowed. Why? Because it would have exposed the unconstitutionality of Lincoln's War and his many crimes. Thus Stephens was freed from prison without explanation after five months:

☛ "21st July, 1865. Mr. J. A. Stewart, Louisville, Ky.: My Dear Sir:—Yours of the 10th inst. was received to-day. Language would fail to express to you the thanks I feel for it. I cannot write to you as fully as I wish. I am suffering from rheumatism in the hand, and cannot use the pen without pain. You will please take the will for the deed.

"You understand me thoroughly, I think. I went with the State [of Georgia] on secession from a sense of duty only. No more ardent or devoted friend to the Constitution of the United States, and the principles of civil and religious liberty therein embodied and guaranteed, than I was and am, ever breathed the vital air of heaven; and no one can rejoice more than I at the prospect of seeing peace and prosperity restored to our once happy land. This appears from the indications of the President's policy. No one would take more pleasure in using his powers to the utmost extent in that direction, if permitted, than I should, if my counsels should be sought. I have no desire, on my own account, however, ever to have anything to do with public affairs again. But if I were at liberty, and the people should desire to know my sentiments, I should take great pleasure in giving them. Perhaps in Georgia they are in better condition to listen to me than they ever were before. I know this was the case when I was taken away; and I know my counsel was peace and the full and perfect acceptation of the new order of things. I mean the abolition of slavery.

"I am sincerely thankful to you for your letter to the President. Why I am confined here, and that too under such rigorous orders, is a mystery to me. . . . I do not understand why I, who exerted my every effort to prevent the strife, and then my every effort to end it in the speediest manner, reasonably, by peaceful adjustment of some sort, should be the victim of such sufferings as I am. This is what is strange, mysterious, and unaccountable to me. I therefore thank you for your letter to the President. You have known my course throughout. I feel assured, if I could but confer with him face to face, that I could satisfy him that I am, upon all principles of justice, entitled to parole. If, from the office I held under the Confederate organization, and which was accepted with the sole view of doing all in my power to maintain the principles of the government under the circumstances, it should be thought proper to make an example of me by trial for treason—that, it seems to me, is no reason why I should be punished as I am, in advance of the punishment first to be found to be right, by judgment of the law. My parole would be most sacredly adhered to.

"But I can say no more, except again to thank you for your letters—the one to me just received, and the one you wrote to the President. I should be

The Confederate Founding Fathers: President Davis and his cabinet in 1861. From left to right: Stephen Russell Mallory (secretary of the Navy), Judah Philip Benjamin (attorney general), LeRoy Pope Walker (secretary of war, standing), Jefferson Davis (president), Robert Edward Lee (general-in-chief of Confederate forces), John Henninger Reagan (postmaster general), Christopher Gustavus Memminger (secretary of the Treasury), Alexander Hamilton Stephens (vice president, sitting), Robert Augustus Toombs (secretary of state).

glad to hear from you often.

"This I shall send to Louisville, with directions to be forwarded to Rome, Ga., in case you shall have left the former place before it reaches there. Yours truly, Alexander H. Stephens."[279]

Still in prison at Fort Warren, Stephens wrote the following letter to "Miss Van Lew" in the fall of 1865:

☛ "My dear Miss Van Lew: I am truly obliged to you for your message through my brother. You will please accept my sincere thanks for your kind remembrance, and especially for the interest you manifest in having me released from this place. I was elated some weeks ago with the hopes of an 'early' release, but I say to you frankly that I am now free from such illusory anticipations. I have settled down into a quiet state of mental composure, prepared patiently to wait the course of events. Whether the objection to my release, which you mention as having heard, has anything to do with my prolonged imprisonment, or has effected a change of purpose once formed in my favour on the part of authorities at Washington, I do not know. My continued imprisonment has, at times, seemed to me so unaccountable that I have been forced to attribute it to some malign influence, springing from motives of vindictiveness to me personally for some cause or other to me entirely unknown. [Editor's note: Stephens was right. It was Yankee vindictiveness, pure and simple.]

"There is not the slightest foundation in fact for the 'objection' which you have heard mentioned, to wit, that my 'Union speech at Milledgeville, in 1860, was a prearranged thing for Secession service, to win influence, and that at the time it was made, the other speech, so contrary and opposite, was already written,' etc.

"My speech for the Union, in November, 1860, was an earnest and honest outpouring if ever such emanated from human heart and head. And never before or since have I uttered a sentiment inconsistent with it. Since I have been here, I have been taunted by anonymous communications calling my attention to certain extracts from speeches made by me, which were published at the North in pamphlet form under the heading of 'Campaign Tract for 1864.' These are forgeries outright. None such, either in words or sentiments, were ever made by me. One other remark on the statement of facts on which this objection rests. I never wrote a speech to be delivered in my life, except college essays or addresses. The Union speech was extemporaneous. The only report ever made was that by Mr. Marshall. Upon that speech and its sentiments, even down to abiding by and sharing the fortunes and fate of my State if she should go against my counsels, I now stand. This much I feel it is my duty to you and myself to state.

"My course, whether right or wrong, has been at least uniform, conscientious, and consistent with my principles. I opposed the movement that led to the war with my utmost power in the most perfect good faith. I opposed it on grounds of policy alone, not on grounds of abstract right. I am in no way responsible before God or man for the origin of the war (at least intentionally), nor for its continuance, much less its atrocities. I did all I could to avert the monster evil in the beginning, and after it was upon us, I did all I could to mitigate its horrors and to end them as speedily as possible. After the war was commenced, all my energies were directed to getting the questions involved taken from the arena of arms and submitted to the forum of reason and justice for peaceful solution and adjustment, not upon a sectional but upon a broad and continental basis. My offending has this extent. No more.

"Please excuse so much about myself. Your message seemed to make it not only proper but almost necessary for your own correct understanding of my true position in these matters. With sentiments of the highest esteem toward you and kindest regards toward your mother, I remain, Yours Truly, Alexander H. Stephens."[280]

Much to Stephens' amazement, he was released from prison early, as he recorded in his journal that day, October 12, 1865:

☛ "This never-to-be-forgotten day of the week is again upon me. It is a blustering morning. Linton went up by the boat.

"Soon, Dr. Seaverns appeared and stated that orders had come for my release. Major Livermore soon followed with the telegram. It embraced Judge Reagan and myself. So, I am again free as far as personal locomotion is concerned. It is just twenty-two weeks to the day since the first keys were turned upon me as a prisoner. What events come to me on Thursday! Major Livermore said he would give me a copy of the order. Meantime I see in the Boston *Post* the General Order embracing Judge Campbell, General Clark, Judge Reagan, myself, and Trenholm. I wish Linton were here. Wrote letters to John A. Stephens, C. T. Bruen, S. J. Anderson, Lieut. W. H. Woodman.

"Linton returned by the evening boat. He, Reagan, and I took a last evening walk on the rampart [of Fort Warren]. Dr. Seaverns called after supper and sat some time.

"Oct. 13.—I rose early and now make this last entry. I expect to start by this evening's boat for my dear home. It is a long and hazardous trip for me, beset with many dangers, and I am beset in the outset with many anxieties concerning many things. But, O God, in whom I put my trust, deliver me from all evil!

"Crawfordville, Ga., Oct. 27, 1865—Thanks be to the Giver of all good, the Father of all mercies, and the Bestower of all blessings, I am once more at home! I am sitting in the same room and at the same table from which I arose to suffer arrest on the 11th of May."[281]

Safely back at his Georgia estate, "Liberty Hall," Stephens resumed his life as an attorney. During his absence, Stephens' loyal "slaves" had kept his plantation in order, and upon his return he divided up the land and rented out small farms to them. Almost immediately Stephens was invited back into politics, and was pushed forward as a candidate for the U.S. Senate. He was also invited to speak before the Legislature on "the state of the country." On January 22, 1866, he wrote this reply to "Messrs. J. F. Johnson, Charles H. Smith, and others":

☛ "Gentlemen,—Your note of invitation to me to address the General Assembly on the state of the country, and assuring me that it is the almost universal desire of the members that I should do so, if consistent with my feelings, etc., was received two days ago. I have considered it maturely; and be assured, if I saw any good that could be accomplished by my complying with your request, I would cheerfully yield any personal reluctance to so general a wish of the members of the General Assembly thus manifested. But as it is, seeing no prospect of effecting any good by such an address, you and your associates will, I trust, excuse me in declining. My reasons need not be stated; they will readily suggest themselves to your own minds upon reflection.

"In reference to the subject of the election of United States Senators, which is now before you, allow me to avail myself of this occasion to say to you, and through you to all the members of the General Assembly, that I cannot give

my consent to the use of my name in that connection. This inhibition of such use of it is explicit and emphatic. I wish it so understood by all. As willingly as I would yield my own contrary inclinations to what I am assured is the general and unanimous wish of the Legislature in this respect, if I saw any prospect of my being able, by thus yielding, to render any essential service to the people of Georgia; and as earnestly desirous as I am for a speedy restoration of civil law, perfect pence, harmony, and prosperity throughout the whole country, yet, under existing circumstances, I do not see any prospect of the availability of my services to these ends in any public position. Moreover, so far as I am

John Letcher

personally concerned, I do not think it proper or politic that the election should be postponed with any view to a probable change of present circumstances or a probable change of my position on the subject; and I do trust that no member will give even a complimentary vote to me in the election. Yours truly, Alexander H. Stephens."[282]

After some coaxing from friends and political colleagues, Stephens relented, writing the following to "Messrs. H. R. Casey, William Gibson, and others" on January 29, 1866:
☛ "The right claimed by you in your note to me, of this date, I do not wish to be understood as at all calling in question.

"In reply to your interrogatory. I can only say that I cannot imagine any probable case in which I would refuse to serve, to the best of my ability, the people of Georgia in any position which might be assigned to me by them or their representatives, whether assigned with or without my consent. Yours truly, Alexander H. Stephens."[283]

Subsequently Stephens was elected, but was prohibited from taking his seat by certain vengeful Yankees. A few of Stephens' comments from this period (1866) are of interest:

☛ "My convictions on the original abstract question [as to the reserved rights of the States] have undergone no change; but I accept the issues of the war and the result as a practical settlement of the question."[284]

☛ "The cause which was lost by the surrender of the Confederates was only the maintenance of this principle [that of a Federation of Sovereign States] by arms. It was not the principle itself that they abandoned. They only abandoned their attempt to maintain it by physical force."[285]

☛ "Nobody is more misunderstood than [U.S. statesman William H.] Seward. He is frequently spoken of as a leader of public opinion; but it is a great mistake,——it leads him. He is always quick to see its drift, and when he does, he instantly follows, and seems to lead, like boys at a military procession, who seem to lead the march by following in front of the music."[286]

☛ ". . . [U.S. President Andrew] Johnson prefers to do things indirectly. He looks one way and rows another. It is difficult to understand him fully; but I think he really desires to see the South restored to all its rights. As for [U.S. politician Edwin M.] Stanton, he is a monster of evil. It is strange the influence he has to keep himself in the Cabinet. In the case of Mrs. [Mary E. J.] Surratt [who was wrongly hanged for allegedly participating in the murder of Lincoln] his conduct was sickening to humanity."[287]

☛ "[I still have a high opinion of U.S. General Grant.] He is an unsophisticated, honest, and, I think, as yet unambitious man. There is a great deal of development for Grant yet. He is young, and will yet have a more important destiny than he has had thus far. I do not doubt that he is a patriot. The Radicals [liberal Northern abolitionists] pretend to claim him; but they know that he is not with them. He says little about politics, but what he does say is to the point. For instance, one day when I called to see him, he was speaking about the Radical policy, and said, 'The true policy should be to make friends of enemies. The policy of the present majority is to make enemies of friends.' One of the party asked him if it was true that he had been fined for fast driving on the street. He answered, 'Yes, I was. I expect the next thing will be that they will take me before the Freedmen's Bureau' [a so-called 'pro-black' Yankee governmental department]."[288]

Nathan Bedford Forrest

From a June 6, 1866, letter to J. Barrett Cohen:

☞ "My Dear Sir: Allow me to return you many thanks for your very able and interesting argument on the *Habeas Corpus* case in your court. The pamphlet came to the office here during my absence from home, or it would have been acknowledged sooner. Be assured I was very much pleased indeed with the views you presented. I need hardly add that I consider the argument conclusive upon the points raised.

"I have thought of you often since the collapse of the Confederate [government] and was exceedingly glad to know from this pamphlet that you are still in the land of the living, once more in the old city of Charleston and in the full vigor of your manly intellect. Please remember me kindly to your father. I hope he is with you and well. I should be highly gratified to hear from you by letter and to know what your prospects are—what hopes if any you have for the future of our country."[289]

From a July 15, 1867, letter to J. Barnett Cohen:

☞ "My Dear Sir: Your welcome letter of the 10th inst. was received some days ago. I have not been able to reply sooner. I am quite out of health. . . . [It] is . . . my opinion that the action of the majority of Congress is governed by no fixed principles or settled policy. They themselves do not know what they may do. The ruling principle with them is power, and they will do anything to secure that. I think they will secure their object without resorting to [the] confiscation [policy of Liberal Pennsylvania politician Thaddeus Stevens, in which the slaves of Southern slave owners would be seized if their owners were found to have aided the Confederacy]. As I wrote to you before, I think constitutional liberty on the continent is in its last death struggles. Did you get that letter?"[290]

In late 1867 Stephens made the following remarks concerning the North's "organized outrage" known as "Reconstruction":

☛ "We are now just entering that dark region in our future, that impenetrable cloud in our destiny, embracing what I have so often spoken of to you as the 'pessimus' point in our affairs, to which we have been tending for many years. From the hideous outlines of the portentous prospect the soul instinctively recoils as from the visage of death. Our political doom is sealed: the great and dreaded night has come upon us. My soul is in anguish at the death of American constitutional liberty!"[291]

In 1867 Stephens began work on his monumental two-volume tome A Constitutional View of the Late War Between the States. *Volume One was published in 1868, Volume Two in 1870. On June 3, 1868, he wrote the following letter to his friend James A. Stewart of Rome, Georgia, who had sent the vice president a sharp letter criticizing several points in the first volume:*

☛ "Liberty Hall, Crawfordville, Ga., 3ʳᵈ June, 1868. My Dear Sir:—Yours of the 1ˢᵗ instant, was received yesterday. I have read it with that interest, which I have told you before, I read all you write upon public matters. There is, in what you say on such questions, a tone of candor, frankness and patriotism which always commend your views and opinions to my most careful and serious consideration.

"To the sentimental portions of the communication now before me—to the deep devotion and love of country, and ardent attachment to the principles of good government and constitutional liberty manifested in them throughout, you have the warmest response from my heart. Yea, more; I will go farther and say, no more earnest devotee of our glorious Union under the Constitution of the United States, than I am, ever breathed the breath of life.

"It is indeed in my opinion, as it was in Mr. [Thomas] Jefferson's, 'the world's last hope.' But what is that Union? Is it a Union or a consolidation of the whole American people in one body politic, or is it a Union of separate and distinct Bodies politic? Is it not in truth and in fact, a Federal Union of States? This is the great question discussed in the first Volume of the *Constitutional View of the late War.* It is the object of history to give a truthful narrative of facts. Just or proper conclusions are but logical sequences of undisputed and indisputable facts, with the legitimate logical and philosophical conclusions which necessarily follow from them upon the same unerring principles of reason which lead to the establishment of all truth.

"If the facts of our history be as they are set forth in the work referred to, (and you will pardon me for saying that I think it would be as difficult to disprove any single one of them as it would be to disprove the fact that America was discovered by Columbus,)[292] then the only remaining question is whether the conclusions drawn from them be logical and philosophical, and not whether they be in accordance with either our previous theories or present wishes.

"Is it true as a matter of historical fact that the people occupying the geographical Territories known as the United States of America, were never at any period, either before, during or since the war of the Revolution of 1776, 'one people,' in a strict national sense? This, I think, is clearly and fully demonstrated in the work referred to. Before their separation from the British Crown, the people of the Colonies, now known as States, were as distinct from each other in their political organizations as the people of Jamaica and Australia, or Canada now are; and they were no more 'one people,' in any political sense, than the people of these last mentioned portions of the present British dominions now are: they were territorially nearer together, but just as separate and distinct in all their national governmental polity.

"Moreover, it was the leading object with them in resorting to independence not to become 'one people,' but to maintain the right of each Colony or State for itself, to govern itself absolutely as it pleased; the Sovereign right of each to thus govern itself as it pleased, was the common bond that united them all in joint action for their Separate Independence. Singly, they were not able to cope successfully with England in the assertion and maintenance of this right. But by Confederation, as the small Grecian Republics did against the Medes and Persians, they were and did. The Declaration of Independence was not by representatives of the people of the Colonies in mass as 'one people.' But it was by States in Congress assembled. It was voted upon by States as separate and distinct bodies politic, and proclaimed as the unanimous declaration of Thirteen States, which, by articles of confederation then before them, assumed the name and style of the United States of America. This was the state of things, and such were the political relations existing between the people of the different Colonies or States of this country on the 4th day of July, 1776. They were certainly not one body politic then. Each Colony or State had its own internal government to itself, clothed with absolute sovereignty over the life and property of every person within its jurisdiction. Did they by the Declaration of Independence become 'one people,' or nation? Most assuredly not, as the Articles of the first confederation fully demonstrated and the treaty of peace firmly establishes. Did they then afterwards become 'one people'—one body politic by the adoption of the new Federal Constitution in 1787? The bare statement of the Act refutes such an idea. A Federal Constitution means an organic law for distinct and separate peoples or

States, just as the preamble of this Constitution declares it to be ordained and established for States—'for the United States of America.'

"Now these great leading and controlling facts of our history are as indisputable as that [George] Washington commanded our armies. The legitimate inference and logical conclusions from these and other great facts of

John Henninger Reagan

our history as to where, under our system, so emanating, and so constituted that ultimate, absolute sovereignty which can rightfully make and unmake Constitutions still resides, are matters which properly fall within the domain of reason—the facts can never be upset. They are as firm as the everlasting hills and mountains which mark our geographical conformation.

"The conclusion I draw from them is set forth in the colloquies [contained in *A Constitutional View*]. To me it seemed and seems irresistible, as much so as any truth in mathematics. It was on this point, the logical sequence from the facts, I expressed a wish to hear from you. The object, of course, was not controversy—far from it; but only in a private way to interchange views with one toward whom I have ever entertained so much esteem and respect, however widely we differed sometimes as to policy. As to our earnest desire for good government, I believe there is not and never has been any difference between us. It is only as to the surest means of attaining it we have differed. And, though this letter is longer than I intended it to be, you must bear with me in saying, further, that in my judgment good government never could be attained by the consolidation of the people of the United States in one grand Republic, as you seem to think they now are. No surer or speedier road to despotism could be taken than such a concentration of sovereignty.

"The only hope of Constitutional liberty over so large a country as ours is not in one Republic, but in a Union of Several Republics. In other words, in just such a Federal or Confederate Republic as our fathers, in their profound wisdom, devised at Philadelphia, in 1787. I did and do think it the best system of government, or rather of governments that the world ever saw. It is, however, be it ever remembered, founded upon the separate sovereignty of the several States. This, my dear sir, is no delusion. It is an irrefutable truth. It is, moreover, an essential element and power in the harmonious working of the system. It is a power that may be misused or abused, or unwisely exercised, as it was, in my judgment, in the case of secession. Yet the great mischief and ruinous results of that unwise and impolitic act are not to be attributed so much to the act itself as to the denial of the right to perform the act.

"Madness seems to have ruled the hour on both sides. While I did not think the bare election of Mr. Lincoln justified secession, yet I did believe and do believe that the breach of faith on the part of several of the Northern States, in the matter of the rendition of fugitives from service, did. But an act that is perfectly right in morals and law is not therefore either wise, politic or expedient. This was my view of secession in 1860. But if, at the time, this great fundamental principle of our system had not been denied, we should have had no war, and the Union would have been restored upon its original principles, sooner or later—most probably before this time—and we should have escaped the rule of that fanatical spirit [of the Northern Liberals] which, under the pretext of saving the Union, aims at nothing but the overthrow of the Constitution.

"That, indeed, was their object at the beginning; for the Constitution they ever held to be nothing better than a 'covenant with hell and an agreement with death.' As much as I disagreed with those who advocated secession as a policy, yet I doubted not that many of them, even a majority of them, really and earnestly believed it was the only hopeful way of escaping the terrible evils now upon us.

"But enough. Excuse this long scrawl. I had no idea of writing at any length when I

George Wythe Randolph

commenced. I only intended to say I had read what you had written, with that interest I always feel in what you say on public questions; but if the great facts of our history be as I have set them forth, (and about which I think there can be no doubt), then the people of the United States do not constitute one people or nation, in the usual sense of that word; but through the State organizations, as States, they are united in one great Federal [that is, Confederate] Republic. Hence, while I cordially respond to the truly patriotic tone of your sentiments, yet I find very little in what you said which has any bearing upon the deductions of my argument, based upon the premises on which it rests. Yours truly, Alexander H. Stephens."[293]

On June 10, 1868, Stephens responded to another letter from James A. Stewart concerning his book A Constitutional View:

☛ "Liberty Hall, Crawfordville, Ga., 10th June, 1868. My Dear Sir:—Yours of the 6th instant has just reached me. I am very much pleased with its tone and temper. You will excuse me in saying a few words in the same spirit in reply.

"Are you correct in your position that demonstrable truth never gives rise to controversy? Is any thing more clearly demonstrable than that the earth turns on its axis? Was there not great controversy about this truth? Was not Galileo threatened with torture for maintaining it? Truths are logical deductions from facts. Between intelligent, rational minds there can be no controversy or disagreement as to the '*quod erat demonstrandum*,' etc., (the matter to be demonstrated), where the facts are agreed upon. All the controversy or disagreement that has arisen or existed between men of undoubted ability and patriotism in our country, upon the questions discussed in the work alluded to, has its origin in a disagreement between them as to matters of fact. If the facts of our history be as I have set them forth, then the conclusions, or truths which they establish, are demonstrable. They are as demonstrable as any truth in mathematics. All depends upon the correctness of facts. I agree with you entirely, when you say that 'it is only points not susceptible of positive proof that engage the controversial powers of intellect;' or, rather, I would say that it is only such points as are not susceptible of positive proof that ought to engage controversial powers of intellect long. For all such as are susceptible of proof ought, in the forum of reason, to be settled by the proof. Some controversy, in such cases, may arise as to the character of the proof; but if this is undisputed, or indisputable, then the truth—the legitimate logical deduction from the facts—becomes the demonstration. Hence it is hardly correct to say, as you do, that 'the very fact of a matter being in controversy is evidence of a want of power to demonstrate;' for very often, in settling premises—or arriving at facts capable of proof, on which facts, when established, the argument is to be erected, in demonstration of the great proposed truth—controversy, or discussion pro and con, may arise. Assumed premises are often not granted. These are frequently disputed; but, when established by evidence or proofs that can not be controverted in the forum of reason, they then become facts—incontrovertible facts—upon which the argument may proceed, to the complete demonstration of the ulterior truth.

"This ulterior truth, which I think is completely demonstrated in the 'Constitutional View,' is that the Constitution of the United States was formed, agreed to, assented to, and ratified by States, as separate, distinct political sovereign powers—that it was made by States and for States; that is, it was made by States, and for the government of States, in all their foreign and inter-State affairs, and not for the government of any people whatever, apart from the several States' authority, in any sense whatever. In other words, that it is a purely Federal [Confederate] Government, founded upon compact between independent sovereign States. This, I repeat, is the ulterior truth, which I think is demonstrated in the book. Whether the demonstration be conclusive or not, depends upon the proofs on which rest the preliminary facts. If it be established as an incontrovertible fact, as a matter of history, that the

Declaration of Independence was but the joint act of several distinct colonies, for the independence of each colony by itself, and not for the independence of all the American colonies, as one people or nation; if, further, it be a fact that these colonies did afterwards become separate and independent sovereign States, and did so acknowledge themselves to be in their first Articles of Confederation; and if, in a word, all the facts connected with the formation of the present Constitution be as set forth in the book—then the conclusion is nothing short of a demonstration that the Constitution itself is a compact between sovereign States, with all the incidents and consequences resulting therefrom.

"You suggest to me to change the word 'Constitutional,' in the title of the book, to the word 'Compact,' etc.

"This would be improper, because it would not give the specific as well as the generic character of the work. Every Constitution of government, formed by the consent of a free people—either in mass (as those of one society or body politic, like our State Constitutions were formed), or by the assent of organized political bodies (as the Constitution of the United States was)—is a compact, but every compact is not a constitution. Two or more nations may make a treaty simply: this would be a compact, but not a constitution. Constitution, when used in reference to bodies of men, implies or means the organic law which establishes the channels through which political powers are to be exercised, as well as the nature and extent of the powers to be exercised by the agents it provides for the execution of them. It is, therefore, properly applied to such organic law, when made for a single society or State, or for an aggregation of distinct societies or States, as integral members of a government. When so made by the people of a single society or State, it is a social compact. When so made by an aggregation of societies or States (each society or State acting as a separate body politic), it is a Federal [Confederate] compact. Our State Constitutions are all social compacts. The Constitution of the United States is a Federal [Confederate] compact: it is a compact between States.

"It is a compact, however, by which each State, as a State, agrees that a certain portion of her sovereign powers (but only those which relate to foreign and inter-State matters) may be exercised by a designated class of agents, who are the common agents of all the States. This makes it a government, and gives it a specific character, distinguishing it from other kinds of compacts. It is, moreover, a government proper, too; but no more a government proper, however, than the Articles of Confederation were. It has more powers conferred, and more agents, and different machinery for its operations; but its nature is the same. The Articles of Confederation were the first Constitution for the United States. That was a compact—'a league,' said Judge [John]

Marshall; but it was, nevertheless, a Constitution for the States, conferring the exercise of important, though not absolute, but delegated, governmental powers. The present Constitution is also a compact between the same sovereign powers, though it confers, by like delegation, several additional governmental powers. Therefore, as it is a compact, conferring governmental powers of some sort, it is a Constitution. It is properly styled a Constitutional compact; and it is also, as its preamble asserts, a Constitution for States, and not for any people whatever in a municipal or social point of view, in any sense of the word whatever. Hence 'Constitutional View' is right and most appropriate.

Joseph Emerson Brown

"Now all these things, I insist, are demonstrated by me, if the facts upon which the argument is built are true. All depends upon the truth of these great leading facts of our history. If the proofs upon which they rest cannot be successfully assailed, then, for the future, all controversy on these questions heretofore at issue may cease; all bare theories or opinions must be abandoned. The world—the intellectual world—must acknowledge the truth, that the Constitution of the United States is a compact between sovereign States, and that powers delegated by the sovereign States may be resumed by them; or, at least such was the condition and the rights of the parties under their organic law, at the beginning of the late unfortunate and ever to be lamented war between the States. And hence, I repeat that 'a Constitutional View (one that looks into this organic law) of the late War between the States,' is, I think, an exceedingly appropriate title.

"One word in reference to Mr.[Daniel] Webster's speech in reply to Mr. [Robert Y.] Hayne. His whole argument was based upon the assumption that the Constitution was made by the whole people of the United States as one body politic; he assumed it to be a social compact and not a Federal

[Confederate] compact. The overwhelming proofs establishing the great facts of our history, which I have brought to light, show that this assumption was groundless—utterly untenable—and that his reasoning from erroneous premises, however logical and grand these premises, led him to erroneous conclusions. The same applies to his reply to Mr. [John C.] Calhoun; but later in life, as I show, he himself admitted that the Union was one—not of the whole people as 'one people' or nation—but that it was a 'Union of States.'

"Do pardon this long letter. My whole soul is in the theme, and when I begin to write I hardly know when to quit.

"With sentiments of the highest esteem and kindest regards, I remain as ever, Yours truly, Alexander H. Stephens."[294]

The publication of the first volume of Stephens' A Constitutional View in 1868 caused a sensation, in particular in the North, where the author was attacked with illogical ferocity from all sides. Stephens was also criticized by some in the South, who believed that his vote against secession in 1860 meant that he was pro-North. In response to the many viciously critical articles being printed, Stephens wrote the following to Richard M. Johnston on August 3, 1868:

☛ "The truth is, there seems to be a great covert spite against me by a certain class of our politicians. This is shown in a striking manner by several of their papers throughout the South in starting and propagating slanders against me. . . . They were all equally groundless and false; or at least they had this ground and this only to rest upon: I had expressed the opinion in Atlanta that it would be best for the State [of Georgia] and for the whole country that the Radicals [Liberal Northern abolitionists and anti-South partisans] in the Legislature should adopt the Constitutional Amendment. I advised no Democrat [Conservative] to vote for it. On the contrary, I urged all I saw and talked with—and they were few—to vote against it. I said that if I were in the place of any one of them, I would not vote for it. That would be endorsing what I thought utterly unconstitutional. But if my not voting against it would permit the Radicals to pass it, I would not vote on the question. To defeat it at this step of the question could do us no possible good that I could see, but might do us harm. It would continue us under military rule, and would put it out of our power to aid in electing Seymour, which we might do if the election was left to the people and our counsels prevailed in the canvass.

"Enough States had already adopted it to make it part of the Constitution in case it should be held to be valid. Georgia's action therefore would not affect that question. The great and vital question now was to elect the Democratic [Conservative] nominees. If they carried the country, this Constitutional Amendment would be held to be a nullity. Its passage, therefore, by the Radicals in our State could not possibly do us any practical harm, and its adoption by them would not only remove us from under military government, but enable us, if we were wise, materially to aid, by nine electoral votes, to bring those into power who would hold it, as we did, null and void from the beginning.

"Divers other reasons I gave why statesmanship should be directed to the policy of letting the Radicals pass it. One was that if the Radical nominees were elected to the offices of President and Vice-President, we could not expect to get a better State Constitution than that which we now have. Under it all whites, as well as blacks, are entitled to vote. If this Constitution should be rejected, another, disfranchising a large class of whites, as in Tennessee and Alabama, might be put upon us. While this would be no reason for me to vote for what I believed to be unconstitutional, yet it would be a reason why I should not vote at all."[295]

In October 1868 the editor of the Southern Review, *Dr. A. T. Bledsoe, published a scathing critique of Stephens'* A Constitutional View. *On October 11, 1868, Stephens wrote to Richard M. Johnston on the matter:*
☞ "It is my intention to reply, under my own name, to Dr. Bledsoe's tirade against the *Constitutional View*; or rather his attack on me under guise of reviewing the book. While the occasion and provocation might justify considerable passion, yet he shall see that I can and will show up his outrages on me with as much cold-bloodedness as that with which I have exhibited the enormous and infamous wrongs of those who wielded the Federal authority in the subjugation of the Southern States. As my object in the former case was not to disgust the world with my own passions, however deep and intense, but to present truth in such a light as to arouse the just indignation of all candid and unprejudiced minds by such a wanton violation of justice and right as the war was, so will it be in the other. My vindication against Dr. Bledsoe's assertions and misrepresentations shall be as full and complete as the vindication of our cause in the *Constitutional View* is against all the malign assaults of our enemies; and it shall be equally temperate in manner and expression."[296]

In the Winter of 1868 Stephens was elected Professor of Political Science and History by the University of Georgia, which had bestowed upon him a degree of "Doctor of Laws." On December 28, 1868, Stephens penned the following to Richard M. Johnston:
☞ "I expect to go to Athens to-morrow to look into matters touching the Professorship before deciding on my acceptance of it. . . . I don't intend to notice Dr. Bledsoe's 'Rejoinder,' so called. I laid it aside on first perusal to take it up afterwards in order to see if there was really anything in it that would

justify a notice from me. On a careful examination I can see nothing of the kind. His position in asserting that there is an inconsistency between the speech and the book, on the question of secession, is astonishing to me."[297]

From a January 5, 1869, letter to Richard M. Johnston. Stephens has been forced to decline the professorship due to a "severe attack" of rheumatism and insufficient salary:
☛ "I have been very badly off lately, and am now hardly able to sit up. . . . I shall not accept the Professorship. I am not now able to walk, except to hobble about the house. Pain in the knee. I cannot assume the duties of the chair in the University. Moreover, I could not live upon the salary."[298]

Around this time, at Johnston's request, Stephens collected together his letter correspondence with his brother Linton and sent the package off to Johnston—who was soon to become one of the vice president's most enthusiastic biographers. Along with the collection of letters, Stephens sent the following note:
☛ "I glanced over the last cursorily, and I came to the conclusion that my character was more completely embodied in them than any personal likeness was ever set forth by daguerreotype or photograph. They expressed the most secret thoughts of my heart without reserve upon many questions, public and private. . . . I was almost amazed at finding that I had said so little that I would now wish unsaid, or would even wish to see modified in any way. What I said of Judge [Joseph] Story I would not modify in the slightest degree; and yet when I wrote these letters I had never read that portion of his Commentaries upon the Constitution of the United States which treats of our early history, and which I so thoroughly review in my work. At that time, too, I did not think very well of Mr. [Thomas] Jefferson. I never understood his character until I read his life by [Henry Stephens] Randall many years afterwards. It was not published, I think, until 1858 or 1859. . . . This is all the explanation I have to make about anything you may see in these letters.
        ". . . I have formally declined the Professorship, at least for the present. I had a very severe attack of my old disease two days ago, and am now barely able to be up."[299]

In early 1869 a heavy gate fell on Stephens, injuring his sciatic nerve and aggravating his rheumatism. The effects of the accident and illness were so severe that he was confined to his home for the next four years. It was from this time forward that he walked on crutches and was pushed about in a wheel chair. On March 12, 1869, he wrote the following in a personal letter:
☛ "I am still almost helpless. I cannot move the body without assistance. This I write propped up with pillows. I fear it will be a long time before I get on

"The Confederate Capitol." Stephens is at the top center right.

foot again, if I ever do. I am weak, and grow weaker, it seems, every day, and have no lessening of the pain. You ask if I feel lonely. No, I do not. I read a little every day, and scribble a little too. . . . The delay of my [literary] work worries me a great deal. But I have made up my mind not to be worried with it. I have directed all the MS. [the manuscript of the second volume of *A Constitutional View*, which he was then working on] to be burned, except a small part, in case I should not be able to finish it. The part excepted is the chapter on the Hampton Roads Conference."[300]

From a March 16, 1869, letter:
". . . As for myself, I am so-so; and every day increases my apprehension that I am to be an invalid the rest of my life. I mean that I am to be a cripple, and never to be on foot as of yore. An invalid I have been all my days. With assistance, I can get out of bed and sit up in a chair supported by pillows, and can move from chair to chair in the room. But I see no prospect of being able to walk again soon. I can do nothing on the *History* [the second volume of *A Constitutional View*] in this condition."[301]

From a June 22, 1869, letter:
☛ "I am barely able to be up: cannot walk or stand without assistance of some sort. I am at work [on my books], however, part of most of the days. Some days I can do nothing."[302]

From a January 23, 1870, letter to Richard M. Johnston:
☛ "I have been very much annoyed by company. Two or three strangers have been here all the time visiting: I should say, however, that only one of them was an absolute stranger."[303]

From a February 26, 1870, letter. As usual, Stephens' house was full of guests, some of them unwanted, such as a correspondent from the New York Herald*:*
☛ "I feel exceedingly annoyed by this visit. I told him I did not wish him to make me an object of his correspondence, and how much I was annoyed by such things. I was almost rude to him in the positiveness with which I expressed myself on that subject. What he will do I cannot say, for there is no telling what this class of men will do. . . . P.S.—I forgot to tell you my old dog Troup is dead. He died the night before my [rheumatism] attack, worn out with old age."[304]

From an April 11, 1870, letter. Stephens has just completed the second volume of A Constitutional View*:*
☛ "I have just time enough to say before the mail closes, and just strength enough also to say, that the book is done. The last sheets went off by express this morning. . . . I have been in a bad way lately, and could do nothing: hence the delay. What the papers said about my health was all utterly false. When they said I was better I was greatly worse."[305]

From a September 1870 letter. Stephens has decided to write a history book for school children:

☛ "You ask me what I expect to do when I get through with the *School History*. Well, I do not exactly know. If in life, I shall do what my hands may find to do at that time. I cannot be idle. I am compelled to do something in some department of labor for a support while I remain here; and I prefer that sort of work which, in my opinion, will be most useful to mankind, while it yields a comfortable living."[306]

From an October 10, 1870, letter:

☛ "I have another little matter on hand,—a little matter of recreation. I have five

Frederick Douglass

law-students in my office, to whom I devote about one hour every evening when I am able. . . . I make no charge against them for instruction or use of books. I do what I can for them by way of recreation from my own labors, and they agree to reimburse me hereafter for their board. . . . The order of the day is close application to books and work during the morning, recitation and conversation during the afternoon, and whist [a card game] at night. I cannot use my eyes in reading or writing by candle- or gas-light, so we have a whist-party every night."[307]

From a March 2, 1871, letter to Richard M. Johnston:

☛ "You ask what I now think of [Liberal U.S. President Ulysses S.] Grant. I think of him just as I did on first acquaintance. My opinion of the man has not changed, either as to his ability or future career since our interview at City Point, in 1865. I am now inclined to think, from his surroundings, that his policy is tending to empire, and whether he will succeed or not will depend upon whether there are brains and patriotism enough combined in the land to defeat his purpose. I have not yet reached a satisfactory solution of this question. I am upon it as I was upon the question of our success during the war. The difficulty was not with the people, but with their leaders. An overwhelming majority of the people of the United States are devoted to the institutions of their ancestors, and are utterly opposed to anything like monarchy or imperialism. All they want to drive usurpers from power is the lead of bold, wise, sagacious, discreet, patriotic standard-bearers, through constitutional channels and instrumentalities."[308]

From a February 27, 1872, letter to Richard M. Johnston. Stephens has just finished his School History:

☛ "I am still absorbed,—not on the same subjects, but in the fifty other matters that are on my table to be attended to. It is impossible under such circumstances to write an old-fashioned letter, springing from a full heart in its spontaneous pourings-forth to a bosom-crony."[309]

From a July 5, 1872, letter to Richard M. Johnston:

☛ "I have had another attack since you were here, from which I am still suffering, but am able to sit up. I am a little more depressed and low-spirited than I have been for some time. This springs from the clear indications of the times, that the Southern people will most likely, in the coming Presidential canvass, cast their lot with [Yankee Liberal] Mr. [Horace] Greeley. This greatly increases the apprehension that I have felt for the last twelve years, that our people are really incapable of self-government; that they do not possess the essential requisites, the necessary intelligence, virtue, and patriotism. No people can be free long, no self-governing people, I mean, who do not study and understand the principles of the Government, and who do not have the virtue and patriotism to maintain these principles.

"The reflection that our people—the Southern people—are getting ready and ripe for a master, is a sad, sad one to me. But it presses heavily upon me just now, and renders me not only depressed but gloomy in spirits sometimes."[310]

On July 14, 1872, Stephens' brother Linton died after a short illness, leaving behind two wives (one an ex) and three small children. Stephens was then the last surviving member of his father's family. Heartbroken and melancholy, he wrote the following to Richard M. Johnston on July 16, 1872:

☛ "I am now passing through one of the bitterest agonies of my life. Before this reaches you, you will have heard of the death of my dearest of brothers. He died at his home on the evening of Sunday last.

". . . Oh that I had you to comfort me!—some one to whom I could talk, and in this way find relief from an overpressed heart, which converse with friends alone can afford. The light of my life is extinguished. How long I can survive it, God in His infinite mercy alone knows. The bitterest pang I have is that all the world to me is now desolate. I have no one to whom I can talk and unbosom my woes. Heretofore, when heavy afflictions of any sort came upon me, for thirty years or more, he was my prop and stay. Towards him my thoughts constantly turned for relief and comfort. Now that prop and stay is gone. I am indeed most miserable. All around me is dark, gloomy, cheerless, hopeless. I am not able even to go and take a last look at that noble form who has so long been my life's support. Oh, how little did I think, when he bade me adieu with you two weeks ago, last Saturday, that it would be the last time I should see him! But so it was. To the decrees of the Most High we must all submit with whatever resignation He shall afford us grace through faith in His mercy to command.

"In this most afflictive bereavement I am not without some consolation—some comfort. This springs from reflecting upon his well-rounded life. He was in the full prime of manhood, and in the zenith of a well-earned and enduring fame, with a character for honor and integrity unsullied, with deeds that will live after him, leaving a deep impress upon the times, not only at the bar and in the forum of popular discussion, but in the halls of legislation and in the records of our judiciary. What more could I desire? All must die. He has but paid the debt of nature,—has passed from the stage of earthly existence where he had acted an honorable, a useful, and a noble part. He did not remain to be subject to the infirmities, either of body or mind, which seem to be the inevitable attendants of old age. What he has done is a rich inheritance for his posterity. Why, then, should I weep? Why should my heart be torn with such anguish?

"These are the consoling thoughts which come to my relief and comfort.

"But, oh! the bitter consciousness that I shall never see him more; that I now have no one to whom I can look for support in distresses of body and mind,—this overwhelms me. May you, my dear friend, while you live, be spared the deep agony I now feel! . . .

"My brother was perfectly in his senses to the last, and was entirely conscious of his condition and rapidly-approaching end. He expressed a willingness to die, and showed no fear at the approach of dissolution. Did not suffer any very severe pain, and had no struggle. He was calm and resigned, and spoke to within a few moments of his last breath. Thus passed away my dearest brother."[311]

From a July 19, 1872, letter to Richard M. Johnston:

☞ "Your consoling letter was received this morning. . . . The accidents of every

Napoleon III

day seem only to add deeper pangs to my grief. The more I realize my situation, the deeper I am impressed with the sense of my utter isolation from anything that can bind me to this world. I can write nothing—I can do nothing. My thoughts are upon him [Linton] all the time. . . ."[312]

From a September 9, 1872, letter to Richard M. Johnston:

☛ "I have been overwhelmed with work. Have had no time to do anything but work on business connected with the [Atlanta] *Sun.* . . . Politics in Georgia are now greatly mixed and confused. What turn events will take depends upon what is done in Louisville next week. If a sound Democratic [Conservative] platform is adopted, and a ticket of sound men put upon it who will accept, we shall have a lively time of it."[313]

From a November 20, 1872, letter to Richard M. Johnston. After being house-bound for four years due to various illnesses, Stephens was about to leave for Atlanta:

☛ "How shall I stand this trip? Oh, if I had my dear brother to go with me! My poor dog [Rio], what will become of him? How he will grieve and lament for me! For nearly four years he has seldom, and for a few moments only at a time, been out of my sight. Day and night he has been with me and depended on me, blind and unable to take care of himself.

"I go to Atlanta on business, and hope to be able to return on Saturday, but no one can imagine what it costs me in feeling to make this adventure, to leave my home once more. . . .

"You seem to be despondent at Grant's election. In my opinion the country is better off with Grant than with Greeley. I opposed Grant for the principles of his party, not for any principles of his own. Grant seems to have no principles but to execute the mandates of Congress; Greeley has principles, and the worst now avowed by any public man in this country."[314]

From a December 14, 1872, letter to Richard M. Johnston:

☛ "Just at this time there is evidently, both North and South, a strong disposition to crush my character and suppress all I write. Did you see in the *Herald* the other day in which Judge [John A.] Campbell is represented to have expressed most ungenerous and unjust things against me? This article is now being republished at the South. All this causes me much pain,—pain to think that I should be so unjustly treated by those who are really so much indebted to me for the vindication of their characters with the cause and character of the Southern people.—P.S.: It is a wonder to me, or at least a matter of serious thought, why I am permitted to live. Why do I linger on the stage? What is it for? Why am I here hobbling about and Linton gone? I constantly feel as if I had nothing to live for, nothing that I can do. I do not court death, yet it seems to me that I would not shun it."[315]

From an April 7, 1873, letter to Richard M. Johnston:

☛ "You ask me what I am so busy about. Why, my dear sir, I am busy with company; busy with answering letters,—fifteen or twenty sometimes a day:—busy with giving legal advice—gratuitously in most cases—to neighbors, widows, and the poor: even the blacks come to me constantly for advice; busy with my law-class. I have another class of five law students now who make a constant draft on my attention. They are not in a class, but all in separate books. Then I write a great deal more for the [Atlanta] *Sun* than you seem to be aware of,—two or three and sometimes four articles in the week. This is not all. Every once in a while comes a long manuscript for me to read over and advise about, and tell how it is to be published."[316]

From an 1877 note to Richard M. Johnston, written by Stephens' secretary (as the vice president was by now too feeble to hold a pen):

☛ "I was full to overflowing when you left me last night. Had you lingered another moment, or said another word, I should have gushed into tears. Your reading the letters about Linton had stirred my grief afresh, and brought vividly to my mind the remembrance of the day you and he last spent together at my house. Oh, the memories of that day!"[317]

From a Winter 1879 letter to Richard M. Johnston:

☛ "I have peculiar feelings. It seems that my days are drawing near their end, and yet I am as well as usual. I am impressed with a recollection of the feelings

William Cabell Rives

expressed by Linton the last night he spent with me. He said he felt as if his days were approaching their end. It does not fill me with sadness, and yet it makes me anxious to be as much with devoted, life-long friends as possible."[318]

From a March 10, 1879, letter to Richard M. Johnston, from Washington, D.C.:

☛ "The contest for the Speakership is waxing fierce. Democrats

[Conservatives] are fighting Democrats as angrily as they ever fought Radicals [Liberals]. I am somewhat removed from the seat of war, but the din of the battle is heard all over the city. The contest is not for the Speakership only, but for the clerkship and office of doorkeeper, while the strife and struggle for the good positions in the Senate under the new organization of that body is quite characteristic of the times."[319]

From a March 12, 1879, letter to Richard M. Johnston:
☞ "Such is the intense feeling on the subject of the organization of the House on Tuesday that I am almost afraid to leave the city lest some accident should happen that would prevent my presence when required."[320]

In 1879 former Confederate General Richard Taylor (son of U.S. President Zachary Taylor, and brother of C.S. President Jefferson Davis' first wife, Sarah K. Taylor), wrote a surprising article attacking Stephens. According to Taylor, Stephens had "received with coldness an application made by him to aid in obtaining the release of President Davis" from imprisonment at Fort Warren, Boston, Massachusetts. Though this was impossible, as Stephens himself was a prisoner at Fort Warren at the time, Taylor stuck to his story. In an April 28, 1879, letter to Richard M. Johnston, Stephens made the following comments on this topic:
☞ "As for Dick Taylor's attack on me, I care very little about it. The statement in his note that the interview referred to was in the latter part of October instead of July is as utterly unfounded as his first assertion. I was at home the latter part of October. I did pass through Washington on my return home after my parole from Fort Warren. I left that fort on the 13th of October, and spent one day in Washington in going to Georgia. I stopped at Willard's Hotel, but saw no man connected with the Government here during the day I remained over except President [Andrew] Johnson. I called and paid my respects to him. I was a paroled prisoner, and the statement that I was in favor with the Government officials at that time is utterly untrue. I do know that General Taylor did not call upon me at that time upon the subject he states. The idea is utterly preposterous. Indeed, I have no remembrance of ever seeing General Taylor to speak to him in my life; but the idea that he should have called upon me for the purpose he states at that time, even if he had called and I had not known him, is, as I have said, utterly preposterous."[321]

From a January 10, 1880, letter to Richard M. Johnston, from Washington, D.C.:
☞ "I think it probable that Congress will adjourn early next week. We are getting all things in right shape. The limitations on appropriations to the army at the polls as deputy marshals are just where I wanted them at the

beginning."[322]

From a January 26, 1880, letter to Richard M. Johnston. It concerns an article by Howard Carroll in the New York Times, in which Carroll had fabricated various aspects of Stephens' life in order to flesh out the piece:

☞ "I considered Howard Carroll's article a sort of romance. I never had twenty minutes' talk with him in my life. He called to see me at Long Branch for an interview for a general sketch, and especially my views upon the General Government. As to the latter, he took down in shorthand what he has very well produced in the last chapter. As to the former, I handed him a copy of your and Dr. [William H.] Browne's biography, and told him that in that he would find all the material facts of my life accurately set forth. The greatest fault, I thought, in his article was the absence of any allusion whatever to that book. All the facts he got from me was my statement to him that the book was substantially correct on all matters relating to my life, quite as much so as if I were to go over the whole of it with him. In using several

Thomas Holliday Hicks

ideas gathered from the book, and re-vamping the matter in his own words, he made several mistakes."[323]

In 1880 Stephens held one of his usual dinners at his home. He called his guests' attention to one of the main courses, cooked opossum, saying:
☛ "Let no Georgian go back on his raising to-day."[324]

From a September 11, 1880, letter to Richard M. Johnston:
☛ "The weather is still very dry and hot. I think the thermometer will nearly reach 100° to-day. I sent off about half my MS. [*History of the United States*] last week, and hope to get it all off by the first of November, if my health does not fail. The book is a big one, and I am engaged at it ten hours a day, sometimes more."[325]

In the Spring of 1882 Stephens was at Washington, D.C., where his friends put him up as a candidate for governor of Georgia. As the campaign progressed, Richard M. Johnston asked Stephens if he thought he would ever serve as a senator again, to which the venerable old Rebel replied:
☛ "Never, never. My days are nearly over. This may be, and probably is, the last time that we shall ever see each other; and I tell you solemnly that if I were to consult my own feelings, I should prefer to be beaten in this race. I have consented to be a candidate only because of the hope of healing the wounds in the Democratic [Conservative] party of Georgia."[326]

From an October 12, 1882, letter to Richard M. Johnston. Stephens had just won the Georgia governorship by over 60,000 votes:
☛ "My majority turns out to be something over sixty thousand. [Lucius J.] Gartrell carries only six counties. This is certainly a triumph signal enough for any one to be gratified at, if not proud of. I assure you, however, that I have none of the feeling of pride about it, and quite as little disposition to exult over it. The sense of responsibility resting upon me greatly oppresses me with its weight. I have about ten offices to fill, and already have at least one thousand applications for them. Think of that, my dear friend!"[327]

From a January 3, 1883, letter to Richard M. Johnston:
☛ "My health is just about as it has been. I usually write from seven o'clock in the morning to eight o'clock at night, pretty constantly engaged every hour in the day. The letters I have to answer number usually daily from twenty to forty. The number to-day is about forty. But when Mr. [John] Slidell is with me I endeavor to clear the table every night.

"... We are getting along very well at the executive mansion. We gave a reception on New Year's day. It was the first time that the Governor [that is, Stephens himself] ever gave a New Year's reception in the day, or, I believe, at any hour. The custom in Atlanta is for ladies to give receptions at night on New Year. The example set at the mansion was said to be a rather unexpected success."[328]

Lucius Jeremiah Gartrell

4

Government

☛ "No system of Representative Government can be long maintained by any People who have not the Intelligence to understand it, the Patriotism to approve it, and the Virtue to maintain inviolate both its form and principles as established."[329]

☛ "Power is corrupting. It fascinates, intoxicates, turns the brain, and changes the nature of man; it transforms those who touch and handle it. Such is its unvarying tendency. This is an eternal truth, and no wise man or people will ever disregard it. People are never in so much danger as they are when unlimited power is in the hands of those in whom they perfectly confide."[330]

☛ "Governments, philosophically considered, are but the outward coverings, the skins or shells of society, or political organisms thrown out or developed by a natural process for the protection of the inner life, according to the laws of its being. Hence the constitutions of States must grow—they can never be made—they must spring from natural development. What is to be the future of this country [the Southern Confederacy] time must disclose upon this principle. For dead governments or defunct empires there is no resurrection. After dissolution their elements may come up in some other living form; not upon the principle, however, of reconstruction, but upon that of new assimilation."[331]

☛ "[Concerning political] . . . parties and party organizations. They are the curse and bane of republics. They can exist nowhere else. They are generally considered, to some extent, the life of free institutions; at least they seem to be so to the casual observer; and yet they have never failed to be the cause of their ultimate overthrow. This is somewhat paradoxical. Perhaps they are not what they even seem to some extent to be—the life of free institutions. This, I think, is the truth; and a little analysis will show it. Free thought, free speech, and free discussion, are the life as well as soul of free institutions. Parties generally spring from these, and necessarily, under our present modes of deciding questions. They never arise, however, except when questions are to be decided by a count of votes. The freest and most enlightened discussion may exist, and progress without any party organization, until arrangements are made for marshalling the forces for a decision of the question. How then can the bad effects of this marshalling of the forces (which soon becomes so corrupt) be best guarded against, or prevented consistently with the progress of thought, interests, and welfare of society. I have thought of it a good deal recently. To my mind the remedy is now clear. It lies in a modification of the bare plurality principle, in the decision of all questions affecting the general interest of society. A larger portion than a bare half of these, who are to decide all such questions, should be required to be consentient to any decision before it is binding upon the whole. The jury trial, which has worked so well for centuries in England, and with us, requires unanimity to give validity to the verdict. This principle might, with great profit, be carried also to the halls of legislation and the forums of election. I will not undertake to say to what extent, above plurality, and short of unanimity, it could be properly carried in either. But in a resort to this principle, lies the surest guarantees against corrupt party organizations in a republic. One of the most erroneous ideas generally entertained is, that a majority barely should govern, and that any measure is right which secures the greatest good to the greatest number. This dogma, or these dogmas, are both fundamentally wrong. That society, or the body politic, should govern itself, is true. This, however, does not imply that a bare plurality should govern all the rest. If this were so, no constitutional barriers or checks would ever be proper. The objects to be aimed at in providing a proper system for society to govern itself justly, so as that the rights of each shall be secured and the common interests of all promoted, should be to require, as far as practicable, the consentient will of the whole, expressed through its proper channels, to give validity and sanction to any measure affecting the general interests or welfare of all."[332]

☛ "No doctrine or principle is more unjust or pernicious than that 'of the greatest good to the greatest number.' The true rule is the greatest good to all,

Wood engraving of Davis and the Confederate cabinet. From left to right: Attorney General Judah P. Benjamin, Secretary of the Navy Stephen R. Mallory, Secretary of the Treasury Christopher G. Memminger, Vice President Alexander H. Stephens, Secretary of War Leroy Pope Walker, President Jefferson Davis, Postmaster John H. Reagan, and Secretary of State Robert A. Toombs.

to each and every one, without injury to any. No one hundred men on earth have the moral right to govern any other ninety-nine men or, less number, and to make the interests of the ninety-nine, or less number, subservient to the interests of the hundred, because thereby the greatest good to the greatest number will be promoted."[333]

☞ "Society in its government should look not to the greatest good to the greatest number, but to the greatest attainable good to all without injury or detriment to any. This should be the universal rule. The best way to secure its practical application in republics or popular governments, in my opinion, is to make approaches toward the unanimity principle, at least in legislation. How nearly perfect unanimity should be required, or what proportion of the votes in legislative bodies should be required to pass any law, I am not prepared to say. While great mischiefs grow out of the bare majority principle as our own, as well as the history of many other countries shows, very little danger need be apprehended from such modification of it as I speak of—not even if it should be extended to a requisition of perfect unanimity. All proper laws are steps in progress by society. Society can much more safely stand still awhile as a general rule, than to venture a step without a full and clear conviction that it is in the right direction. No truth is better established than that 'the world is governed too much.' No new law ought ever to be passed until the wants and needs of society as a whole in its progress requires it. All checks upon legislation looking to this end are not only proper, but eminently wise. With free speech, free discussion, and a free press, the power of truth, amongst an enlightened people, would not be long in bringing the general opinion of the whole body of legislators to a proper and just appreciation of any new measure or proposed advanced step in progress—quite soon enough for that prudent, safe, and stately step, that all governments should be careful to make. Many, I am fully aware, would be disposed to consider these views utterly impracticable, if not chimerical; such persons are but superficial observers. They do not understand the true philosophy of government. It is a lamentable fact, that there has been less improvement in the progress of civilization from the lights of experience in the science of government, than in any other branch of human knowledge."[334]

Stephens, who uttered these words in 1846 before the U.S. Senate, was speaking of the Mexican-American War. However, he would maintain these same sentiments fifteen years later when Abraham Lincoln began threatening war on the South:
☞ "I hold all wars to be great national calamities. I do not maintain that war can or should always be avoided. I do not belong to the peace party, so called; I am no non-resistance man [pacifist]; I am far from holding that all wars are wrong. But I do hold that they ought never to be rushed into blindly or rashly. This *ultima ratio*—this last resort of nations to settle matters of dispute or disagreement between them, should always be avoided, when it can be done without a sacrifice of national rights or honor. And the greatest responsibility rests upon those at the head of affairs, to whom are confided the interests and destinies of a country, that they do not disregard the heavy obligations of this most important trust."[335]

Stephens did not believe that socialistic Europeans, steeped in centuries of monarchical rule, understood the principles of true liberty:
☞ "Brutus and a few associates found no difficulty in removing Caesar from an imperial throne. But they did not thereby restore lost freedom to Rome. France found but little difficulty in bringing Louis the XVI to the block; but France did not thereby establish a republic. She found even less difficulty in driving Charles the X from the kingdom he had so badly governed; but she did not thereby succeed in establishing a good government for the people. Louis Philippe had in like manner in a short time to be carried to her Tarpeian Rock. It is now just four years since she made her last effort at republicanism. And what do we now behold? Louis Napoleon [III]—a President King!

"And so it will be, I fear, with all the nations of Europe, until there be a change in the minds, habits, education, and modes of thinking on the part of their people. Liberty, in their estimation, is licentiousness, lawlessness. They do not understand or appreciate its first principles. Men, to be capable of maintaining law and order in a free government, must be schooled in the elementary principles."[336]

5

Constitutional

Principles

On January 25, 1845, Stephens spoke before the U.S. Congress concerning the admission of Texas to the Union. A debate arose over whether or not slavery should be extended to the Lone Star State:

☛ "My objection is, that the General Government has no power to legislate for any such purpose. If I understand the nature of this Government, and the ground always heretofore occupied by the South upon this subject, it is that slavery is peculiarly a domestic institution. It is a matter that concerns the States in which it exists, severally, separately, and exclusively; and with which *this Government has no right to interfere or to legislate, further than to secure the enforcement of rights under existing guaranties of the Constitution, and to suppress insubordinations and insurrections if they arise.* Beyond this there is no power in the General Government to act upon the subject, with a view either to strengthen or to weaken the institution. For, if the power to do one be conceded, how can that to do the other be denied? I do not profess to belong to that school of politicians who claim one construction of the Constitution one day, when it favors my interests, and oppose the same, or a similar one, the next day, when it happens to be against me. Truth is fixed, inflexible, immutable, and eternal;

unbending to time, circumstances, and interests; and so should be the rules and principles by which the Constitution is construed and interpreted. And what has been the position of the South for years upon this subject? What has been the course of her members upon this floor in relation to the reception of abolition petitions? Has it not been that slavery is a question upon which Congress cannot act, except in the cases I have stated, where it is expressly provided by the Constitution: that Congress has no jurisdiction, if you please, over the subject, and that, therefore, it is improper and useless, if not unconstitutional, to receive petitions asking what Congress cannot constitutionally grant? This has been the ground assumed by the South, and upon which these petitions have been rejected for years by this House, until the rule was rescinded at the beginning of this session. And however much gentlemen from different parts of the Union have differed in opinion upon the extent of the abstract right of petition, and the propriety and expediency of receiving all kinds of petitions, whether for constitutional objects or not, yet I believe they have always been nearly all agreed in this, that Congress has no right or power to interfere with the institutions of the States. This, sir, is our safeguard, and in it is our only security; it is the outpost and bulwark of our defence. Yield this and you yield everything. Grant the power to act or move upon the subject, yield the jurisdiction, call upon Congress to legislate with the view presented in that correspondence, and instead of strengthening they might deem it proper to weaken those institutions; and where, then, is your remedy? I ask Southern gentlemen where, then, is their remedy? We were reminded the other day by a gentleman from South Carolina [Mr. Holmes] that we were in a minority on this floor. It is true we are in a minority; and is it wise in a minority to yield their strong position, their sure and safe fortress, to the majority, for them to seize and occupy to their destruction? No, sir; never. Upon this subject I tell gentlemen from the South, and the people of the South, to stand upon the Constitution as it is, and that construction which has been uniformly given to it upon this point, from the beginning of the Government. This is our shield, wrought in the furnace of the Revolution. It is broad, ample, firm, and strong; and we want no further protection or security than it provides."[337] [Emphasis added, L.S.]

From Stephens' January 25, 1845, speech before Congress, in which he addressed a New York Congressman who declared that the measure to allow Texas (considered by Stephens to be an "independent sovereign power") to decide the slavery question for herself is a "fraud upon the Constitution":

☞ ". . . When I cast my eyes, Mr. Chairman, over the surface of the world, and survey the nations of the earth, and see that the people of the United States alone, of all the millions of the human family who live upon the habitable globe, are really free and fully enjoy the natural rights of man; that all other parts are dreary, wild, and waste; and that this is the only green spot, the only oasis in the universal desert, and then consider that all this difference is owing to our Constitution; that all our rights, privileges, and interests are secured by it, I am disposed to regard it with no trifling feelings of unconcern and indifference. It is, indeed, the richest inheritance ever bequeathed by patriot sires to ungrateful sons. I confess I view it with reverence; and, if idolatry could ever be excused, it seems to me it would be in allowing an American citizen a holy devotion to the Constitution of his country. Such are my feelings; and far be it from me to entertain sentiments in any way kindred to a disregard for its principles, much less in contempt for its almost sacred provisions."[338]

From the same January 25, 1845, speech before Congress. Here Stephens addresses the objection that the U.S. government has no right to "acquire territory":

☛ "Suppose I grant his position and his premises entirely, does his conclusion, in reference to the proposition I advocate, necessarily follow? Do the resolutions of the gentleman from Tennessee propose to acquire territory? We are often misled by the use of words. . . . We have had 'annexation' and 'reannexation,' and 'acquisition of territory,' until there is a confusion of ideas between the object desired and the manner of obtaining it. To acquire conveys the idea of property, possession, and the right of disposition. And to acquire territory conveys the idea of getting the rightful possession of vacant and unoccupied lands. If this be the sense in which the gentleman uses it, I ask, does the plan of the gentleman from Tennessee propose to do any such thing? It is true it proposes to enlarge and extend the limits and boundaries of our Republic. But how? By permitting another State to come into the Union with all her lands and her territory belonging to herself. The Government will acquire nothing thereby, except the advantages to be derived from the union. And if I understand the original substantial design of the Constitution, the main object of its creation, it was not to acquire territory, it is true, but to form a union of States, a species of confederacy; conferring upon the joint government of the confederation, or union, the exercise of such sovereign powers as were necessary for all foreign national purposes, and retaining all others in the States, or the people of the States, respectively. This was the design, this was the object of the Constitution itself, which is but the enumeration of the terms upon which the people of the several States agreed to join in the union for the purposes therein specified; and in this way all the States came into it, Georgia among the rest, with her rich western domain extending to the Mississippi, out of which two States have since grown up, and have been likewise admitted.

When the Government was first formed, North Carolina and Rhode Island refused to come in for some time. It was not until after it was organized and commenced operations, by eleven of the States, that these two consented to become members of the Union. Could the United States, those eleven which first started this General Government, be said to have acquired territory when North Carolina was admitted? or the twelve which composed the United States when Rhode Island came in? There was in each of those cases an addition of a State and enlargement of the confederated Republic, just as there will be if Texas be admitted, as proposed by the gentleman from Tennessee; but no acquisition of territory in the common acceptation of that term."[339]

Continuing his January 25, 1845, speech before Congress, Stephens argued in defense of Texas and the Constitution:

☛ "The authority on which I rely is no forced construction, but the plain, simple language of the Constitution, which declares that—

> 'New States may be admitted by Congress into this Union: but no new State shall be formed or erected within the jurisdiction of any other State; nor any State be formed by the junction of two or more States, or parts of States, without the consent of the Legislatures of the States concerned as well as of Congress.'

"The terms here used are broad, unqualified, and unrestricted. 'New States may be admitted by Congress into this Union.' But it is said that it was only meant by those words to give the power to admit States formed out of the territory of the United States, and within their jurisdiction, and not to include a foreign State. To this I might reply that it is a *petitio principii*,—a begging of the question. Whether that was the meaning and intention is the main inquiry; and from the words used no such inference can be drawn. But the gentleman from New York says he believes that was the meaning and intention; and further, that he believes if any other opinion had been entertained the Constitution would never have been ratified. Well, sir, his belief is not argument. . . . We are taught that we should not only believe, but be able to give a 'reason for the faith that is in us.' And here again I listened for the reasons of the gentleman's faith, but heard nothing better than a repetition of his belief.

"Let us, then, examine the matter. If there is any difficulty, we must look to the words, the objects, and contemporaneous history. As to the words, they are quite unambiguous. The term State is a technical word, well understood at that time. It means a body politic,—a community clothed with all the powers and attributes of government. And any State, even one of those growing up in the bosom of our own territory, upon admission, may be considered to some extent foreign. For if it be a State, it must have a government separate from, and to some degree independent of, the Union. For if it be in the Union, then it could not be admitted; that cannot be admitted in which is already in. And if it is a State, and out of the Union, seeking admission, it must be considered *quoad hoc* ["to this extent"] to be foreign. Now, as to contemporaneous and subsequent history. What relation did North Carolina hold to the Union under the new organization of 1787? She refused to ratify the Constitution, and was most clearly out of it. The last article of the Constitution declared,—

> 'The ratification of the conventions of nine States shall be sufficient for the establishment of this Constitution between the States so ratifying.'

"But more than nine ratified: eleven did; leaving North Carolina and Rhode Island out, as before stated. The Union was formed, and the Constitution established for those that had ratified, and the Government proceeded to organization. North Carolina was then certainly out of the Union. She had the right and power to remain out. If she had, would she not have been foreign to it? And, consequently, was she not foreign whenever the

"Liberty Hall"

Government went into operation under the new Constitution without her ratification? The case of Vermont is more in point. She was a separate and independent community, with a government of her own. She was not even one of the original revolting thirteen colonies. She had never been united in the old Confederation, and did not recognize the jurisdiction of the United States."[340]

Stephens concluded his January 25, 1845, address with these words:
☛ "With this question is also to be decided another and a graver one; which is, whether the limits of the Republic are ever to be enlarged? This is an important step in settling the principle of our future extension. Nor do I concur with gentlemen who seem to apprehend so much danger from that quarter. We were the other day reminded by the gentleman from Vermont of the growth of the Roman Empire, which went on increasing and enlarging until it became unwieldy and fell of its own weight; and of the present extent of England, stretching to all sections of the world, governing one-sixth of the human family, and which is now hardly able to keep together its extensive parts. But there is a wide difference between these cases. Rome extended her dominions by conquests. She made the rude inhabitants of her provinces subjects and slaves. She compelled them to bear the yoke: *jugum subire* ["shake off the yoke"] was the requisition of her chieftains. England extends her dominion and power upon a different principle. Hers is the principle of colonization. Her distant provinces and dependencies are subject to her laws, but are deprived of the rights of representation. But with us a new system has commenced, suited to and characteristic of the age. It is, if you please, the system of a Confederation of States, or a republic formed by the union of the people of separate independent States or communities, yielding so much of the national character or sovereign powers as are necessary for national and foreign purposes, and retaining all others for local and domestic objects to themselves separately and severally. And who shall undertake to say to what extent this system may not go? . . .

"We live, sir, not only in a new hemisphere, but, indeed, in a new age; and we have started a new system of government, as new and as different from those of the old world as the Baconian system of philosophy was novel and different from the Aristotelian, and destined, perhaps, to produce quite as great a revolution in the moral and political world as his did in the scientific. Ours is the true American system; and though it is still regarded by some as an experiment, yet, so far, it has succeeded beyond the expectations of many of its best friends. And who is prepared now to rise up and say, 'Thus far it shall go, and no farther'?

"But I am in favor of this measure for another reason. It is, as the honorable chairman of the Committee on Foreign Affairs said in his opening speech, in one sense and in one view, a sectional question,—a Southern question. It will not promote our pecuniary interests, but it will give us political weight and importance; and to this view I am not insensible. And though I have a patriotism that embraces, I trust, all parts of the Union, which causes me to rejoice to see all prosperous and happy; and though I believe I am free from the influence of unjust prejudices and jealousies toward any part or section, yet I must confess that my feelings of attachment are most ardent towards that with which all my interests and association are identified. And is it not natural and excusable that they should be? The South is my home—my fatherland. There sleep the ashes of my sires; there are my hopes and prospects; with her my fortunes are cast; her fate is my fate, and her destiny my destiny. Nor do I wish to 'hoax' gentlemen from other sections upon this point, as some have intimated. I am candid and frank in my acknowledgment. This acquisition [of Texas] will give additional power to the southwestern section in the national councils; and for this purpose I want it,—not that I am desirous to see an extension of the 'area of slavery,' as some gentlemen have said its effects would be. I am no defender of slavery in the abstract. Liberty always had charms for me, and I would rejoice to see all the sons of Adam's family, in every land and clime, in the enjoyment of those rights which are set forth in our Declaration of Independence as 'natural and inalienable,' if a stern necessity, bearing the marks and impress of the hand of the Creator himself, did not, in some cases, interpose and prevent. Such is the case with the States where slavery now exists. But I have no wish to see it extended to other countries; and if the annexation of Texas were for the sole purpose of extending slavery where it does not now and would not otherwise exist, I should oppose it. This is not its object, nor will it be its effect. Slavery already exists in Texas, and will continue to exist there. The same necessity that prevails in the Southern States prevails there, and will prevail wherever the Anglo-Saxon and African races are blended in the same proportions. It matters not, so far as this institution is concerned, in the abstract, whether Texas be in the Union or out of it. That, therefore, is not my object: but it is the political advantages it will secure, with the questions settled as proposed,—leaving no door open for future agitation,—and thus preserving a proper balance between the different sections of the country. This is my object; and is it not proper and right?

"If we look around, we see the East [portion of the U.S.], by her economy, her industry, and enterprise, by her commerce, navigation, and mechanic arts, growing opulent, strong, and powerful. The West, which a few years ago was nothing but an unbroken wilderness, embracing the broad and fertile valley of the Mississippi, where the voice of civilization was never heard, is now teeming with its millions of population. The tide of emigration, still rolling in that direction, has already reached the base of the Rocky Mountains, and will soon break over those lofty barriers, and be diffused in the extensive plains of Oregon. Already the West vies for the ascendancy on this floor, and why should not the South also be advancing? Are her limits never to be enlarged, and her influence and power never to be increased? Is she to be left behind in this race for distinction and aggrandizement, if you please? As one of her sons, I say, no. Let her, too, enter the glorious rivalry; not with feelings of strife, jealousy, or envy,——such sentiments are not characteristic of her people,——but with aspirations prompted by the spirit of a laudable emulation and an honorable ambition."[341]

Northern Liberals in Stephens' day were determined to dominate the South politically, economically, and socially, an attitude just alive today as it was in the 1800s. In 1848 a bill regarding slavery was presented to Congress by Yankee progressives that would have limited the spread of slavery while taking away many of the South's constitutional rights. In an August 7 speech that year, conservative Southerner Stephens voiced his opinion on the matter:

☛ ". . . [W]hat are we of the South to gain by this Compromise? Nothing but what we would have, even with the Wilmot Proviso,——the poor privilege of carrying our slaves into a country where the first thing to be encountered is the certain prospect of an expensive lawsuit which may cost more than any slave is worth; and, in my opinion, with the absolute certainty of ultimate defeat in the end, and with no law in the mean time to protect our rights and property in any way whatever! This, sir, is the substance of the Compromise, even in the most favorable view in which it can be presented. And this is the security for the South which I had the temerity to reject! Would that the people of that section may ever have men upon this floor of such temerity! I did reject it, and I shall continue to reject all such favors. If I can get no better compromise, I shall certainly never take any at all. As long as I have a seat here, I shall maintain the just and equal rights of my section upon this as well as upon all other questions. I ask nothing more, and I shall take nothing less. All I demand is common right and common justice; these I will have in clear and express terms, or I will have nothing. I speak to the North, irrespective of parties. I recognize no party association in affiliation upon this subject. If the two parties at the North combine and make a sectional issue, and by their numerical strength vote down the South, and deny us those equal rights to which I think we are in justice entitled, it will be for the people of the South then to adopt such a course as they may deem proper. I do not stand here to make any threats in their name, nor have I authority to commit even my own constituents to any course of policy. They must do that for themselves. My commission here extends only to the maintenance of their rights upon all questions and measures that may come before me in this House. And this I shall do at all hazards.

". . . The late treaty is not the supreme law of the land yet, and will not be till the laws necessary to give it effect are passed. Mr. [U.S. President James K.] Polk has not yet asked us to appropriate the money, and when he does, it will be our constitutional right and duty to deliberate on the expediency of making the appropriation. And I now state that, if I am here when that appropriation is made, I shall exercise this constitutional right, and I shall never vote one dollar from the common treasure of this Union to pay for these Territories, if the institutions of my section are to be wholly excluded from them. Nor will I vote one dollar to carry this treaty into effect until I have this matter settled, and what I consider the great rights of the South secured. And I believe this is the great lever of the South upon this question. Let the bill organizing Territorial governments be linked with the appropriation of the money, and let the South present an unbroken front against paying a dollar, if their institutions are to be excluded, and I shall have some hopes yet of obtaining justice.

"Now, sir, you know something of the only plans upon which I intend to compromise this business. But, as I said before, if in all this I should be defeated,—if the South will not stand with me upon this point,—if the combined vote of the North carry the Wilmot Proviso,—then, sir, it will be for the people of the South to take their own course, such as they may deem their interest and honor demand. It is not for me to indicate that course. But one thing I will say, that I shall be with them in whatever course they may take. Their interests are my interests; their fortunes are my fortunes , their hopes are my hopes; and whatever destiny awaits them awaits me also."[342]

Around 1850 or 1851, Stephens made this remark in regards to the South-North agitation over the Missouri Compromise:
☛ "The South has no compromise to offer but the Constitution."[343]

Stephens to Judge Thomas W. Thomas, May 5, 1855:
☛ "True Americanism, as I have learned it, is like true Christianity—disciples in neither are confined to any nation, clime, or soil whatsoever. Americanism is not the product of the soil; it springs not from the land or the ground; it is not of the earth, or earthy; it emanates from the head and the heart; it looks upward, and onward and outward; its life and soul are those grand ideas of government which characterize our institutions, and distinguish us from all other people; and there are no two features in our system which so signally

James Buchanan

distinguish us from all other nations as free toleration of religion and the doctrine of expatriation—the right of a man to throw off his allegiance to any and every other State, prince or potentate whatsoever, and by naturalization to be incorporated as a citizen into our body politic. Both these principles are specially provided for and firmly established in our constitution."[344]

Stephens to Atlanta, Georgia, Mayor James M. Calhoun (a cousin of John C. Calhoun), September 8, 1862:

228 C/C THE QUOTABLE ALEXANDER H. STEPHENS

☛ "[Confederate] Soldiers in the service, as well as the officers, are subject to the Rules and Articles of War, and if they commit any offence known to the Military Code therein prescribed, they are liable to be tried and punished according to the law made for their government. If these Rules and Articles of War, or in other words, if the Military Code for the government of the army is defective in any respect, it ought to be amended by [the Confederate] Congress. There alone the power is vested. Neither Generals nor the Provost-Marshals have any power to make, alter or modify laws, either military or civil; nor can they declare what shall be crimes, either military or civil, or establish any tribunal to punish what they may so declare. All these matters belong to Congress; and I assure you, in my opinion, nothing is more essential to the maintenance and preservation of Constitutional Liberty than that the Military be ever kept subordinate to the Civil Authorities."[345]

Stephens to the Honorable Herschel V. Johnson at Sandy Grove, Georgia, June 22, 1864:
☛ ". . . while I live and breathe I shall do, and continue to do, what I can to preserve the liberties of the people from overthrow and ruin."[346]

Stephens to the Honorable Alexander J. Marshall, at Richmond, Virginia, November 4, 1864:
☛ "Without busying ourselves much about the future, or making efforts to shape its destinies, the great object at present of every well-wisher to his country should be to direct all energies, moral, intellectual, and physical, to the vindication and establishment of the principle for which the war now upon us is waged on our part—that is the ultimate absolute sovereignty of the several States. This principle once recognized, permanently fixed and adhered to, affords the surest grounds for the hope of a lasting peace. This, and this only, so far as I can see, will prove the self-adjusting principle, the perfect regulator in the working of our present or any new system of association of States that may arise. With this principle settled the future may well be left to take care of itself. Mutual safety, security, protection, and interest are the natural affinities that draw people or States into alliances and confederations. When these natural laws are left perfectly free in their operation, they never fail to produce their legitimate results—the peace, prosperity, and happiness of the people in whatever associations or alliances they may arrange themselves. After the long struggle of the first war of independence [i.e., the American Revolutionary War], both parties came to the conclusion that 'reciprocal advantages and mutual convenience are found by experience to be the only permanent foundation for peace and friendship between States.'"[347]

Stephens' November 4, 1864, letter to the Honorable Alexander J. Marshall continues:
☛ "This great truth [state sovereignty], found after the most painful analysis of years in the crucible of blood, was set forth in the preamble of the provisional treaty of peace. It is for the statesman a far more useful truth than was ever the fancied philosopher's stone for the alchemist. Had it been recognized and acted upon this war with its horrors, its cruelties, sufferings, and desolation never would have occurred. To illustrate:—If, after the secession of the southern States, clearly justified by the breach of faith on the part of their northern confederates, the latter States had discovered, as they seem to have done, that the Union was of so much benefit to them, they would have looked to its restoration not by force but by a correction of their own error—by renewed assurance of good faith in the future. If, after that, the seceded States had found it to their benefit and advantage, all things duly considered, to be in union on the original terms, with good faith maintained by all, they would, as naturally as every thing in the material world obeys the law of affinity, have adjusted themselves accordingly. If they had not so found it to be their interest to renew that confederation, they would have remained separate and independent, as they ought to have done. For safety, security, and self-preservation is the first law of nature with States as well as with individuals. In the latter event, whatever treaties or leagues the reciprocal advantages and mutual convenience of both or each and all required, would have been entered into and nothing more. There would have been no war—no force—but each and all would have moved on peacefully and prosperously in their own rightful spheres. The surest way to preserve the health and vigor of the physical body, is strictly to conform to the laws of its existence. The same is true of States or governments. A fundamental principle in the old Union and constitution, one of the laws of its existence, was the reserved sovereignty of the several States."[348]

From a June 16, 1846, speech in the U.S. House of Representatives:
☛ "The limits or boundaries of a country can be fixed in two ways only: one is by negotiation, and the other is by the sword. The President by himself can do neither. He may make the initiative in the former case; but Congress can alone constitutionally draw the sword for any purpose."[349]

From an 1846 speech:
☛ "I am no enemy to the extension of our [U.S.] domain, or the enlargement of the boundaries of the republic. Far from it. I trust the day is coming, and not far distant, when the whole continent will be ours; when our institutions shall be diffused and cherished, and republican government felt and enjoyed throughout the length and breadth and width of this land—from the far south

to the extreme north, and from ocean to ocean. That this is our ultimate destiny, if wise councils prevail, I confidently believe. But it is not to be accomplished by the sword. Mr. Chairman, republics never spread by arms. We can only properly enlarge by voluntary accessions, and should only attempt to act upon our neighbors by setting them a good example. In this way only is the spirit of our institutions to be diffused as the 'leaven,' until 'the whole lump is leavened.' This has been the history of our silent but rapid progress, thus far. In this way Louisiana, with its immense domain, was acquired. In this way the Floridas were obtained. In this way we got Oregon, connecting us with the Pacific. In this way Texas, up to the Rio Grande, might have been added; and in this way the Californias, and Mexico herself in due time may be merged in one great republic. There is much said in this country of the party of progress. I profess to belong to that party; but am far from advocating that kind of progress which many of those who seem anxious to appropriate the term exclusively to themselves are using their utmost exertions to push forward. Theirs, in my opinion, is a downward progress. It is a progress of party—of excitement—of lust of power—a spirit of war—aggression—violence and licentiousness. It is a progress which, if indulged in, would soon sweep over all law—all order—and the constitution itself."[350]

From an 1852 speech at Baltimore, Maryland:
☞ "I wish that all nations had as good a government as we have. But we should not peril our own life in hopeless efforts to rescue that of others. Let us not, in a fit of misguided zeal for the liberties of mankind, lose our own. All men are not suited for constitutional free government. One of the most common of the popular errors of the day is that any people having the wish to be free also have the ability to be free. This is a great mistake. Constitutional liberty, or liberty regulated by law—the only liberty that is worth the name—is not so easily acquired. If it were, we would not to-day be the only people on earth in its enjoyment. It is true, the people of almost any nation, with a firm resolution, can overthrow the strongest of despotisms, but they can not build up a republic in its stead. This requires more than physical force. It requires virtue, intelligence, morality, patriotism, and statesmanship."[351]

Prior to Lincoln's War, Stephens defended slavery using both the Bible (which sanctions and in some cases even requires it) and the Constitution (under which it was legal up until December 6, 1865). In the following excerpt from a September 1860 speech at City Hall Park, Atlanta, Georgia, he discussed the latter defense in relation to the great European-American expansion into the Western Territories:
☞ "I am perfectly willing for the pioneers of civilization who quit the old States

for new homes in the west, to form and regulate their own domestic Institutions in their own way, and make all other laws according to their liking. It was in this way our fathers settled this goodly land, and made the wilderness to blossom as the rose. They were all 'squatters,' in the popular slang of the day. When they wanted slaves of the African race, they had them, and I am perfectly willing that their descendants, with emigrants from all the other States who colonize and settle our broad Territories, shall exercise the same rights of Self-government that they did. If these opinions make a man a 'squatter sovereign,' then I am one. Nicknames will never drive me from the maintenance of sound principles."[352]

In 1868 Stephens wrote:
☛ "The Southern States were ever loyal and true to the Constitution. This I maintain as a great truth for history. The only true loyalty in this country is fidelity to the principles of the Constitution! The openly 'disloyal,' or those avowedly untrue to the Constitution, were those [Liberals in the North] who instigated, inaugurated, and waged this most unrighteous war against their Confederate neighbors!"[353]

After Lincoln's War, in 1870, Stephens took aim at the rank hypocrisy of the Northern states:
☛ "The proverb, about casting stones, is a very good one, when properly applied. In this instance, however, the whole force of its logic, as well as its rhetoric, recoils with damaging effect upon him who uses it. These Northern States . . . were the dwellers in glass houses, who charged the Southern States with violating the Constitution when they were the only violators of it themselves."[354]

In 1870 Stephens made special mention of the North's and the South's divergent views of the U.S. Constitution, and how this led to Lincoln's War:
☛ "What I have said clearly shows the political position of both Parties to the war, at the time of its inauguration and the fall of Fort Sumter, so far as concerns the principles on which they acted. The principles actuating the Washington authorities were those aiming at Consolidated Power; while the principles controlling the action of the Montgomery authorities were those which enlisted devotion and attachment to the Federative [Confederate] system as established by the [Founding] Fathers in 1778 and in 1787. The [Liberals'] object on the one side—the aggressive side—the Federal side, so miscalled—was to overthrow the very principles upon which every Federal [Confederate] system is based; while, on the other, it was to defend and

maintain those principles. In short, the cause of the Confederates was State Sovereignty, or the Sovereign Right of local Self-Government on the part of the States severally. It was the same cause, to maintain which all the Colonies at first, and all the States afterwards, united, in the ever memorable conflict with the Mother Country [Great Britain], in 1776; and on the success of which, in that contest, depended the whole fabric of American Free Institutions. The cause of their assailants [i.e., the Yankees] involved the overthrow of this entire fabric, and the erection of a Centralized Empire in its stead! This is the issue, in a Constitutional point of view, fairly presented."[355]

With the hindsight of Lincoln's War behind him, Stephens made this comment in 1870:
☛ "The only way in which wars are to be avoided in this country, is for Rulers to abstain from usurpations of power."[356]

6

The United States
& Her Government

From an 1846 speech before the U.S. Senate:

☛ "I wish to remind gentlemen of what they appear sometimes to forget, that the executive and his cabinet are not the country, and that it is quite possible for him and them to be wrong without putting the country in the same condition. There is a wide difference between the ministers and the sovereign. In this country sovereignty resides, not in the throne or the executive, but in the people. The administration is but the ministry; they are but public servants, and should be held to strict accountability. I hope never to see the day when the executive of this country shall be considered identical with the country itself in its foreign relations, or when any man, for scanning his acts, however severely when justly, shall on that account be charged with opposition to his country. Such is the case only where allegiance is due to a crown, where the people's rulers are their masters; but, thank God, in this country we can yet hold our rulers to an account. How long we shall be permitted or be disposed to do so I know not; but whenever we cease to do it we shall become unfit to be free."[357]

Stephens, who was thoroughly against the Mexican-American War (1846-1848), uttered these words on June 16, 1846, before the U.S. House of Representatives:

☛ "[Is this a war of conquest?] If so, I protest against that part of it. I would shed no unnecessary blood; commit no unnecessary violence; allow no outrage upon the religion of Mexico; have no desecration of temples, or 'revelling in the halls of the Montezumas;' but be ready to meet the first offers of peace. I regret that General Taylor did not have the authority to accept the proffered armistice when it was tendered. In a word, I am for a restoration of peace as soon—yes, at the earliest day it can be honorably effected. I am no enemy to the extension of our domain, or the enlargement of the boundaries of the republic. Far from it. I trust the day is coming, and not far distant, when the whole continent will be ours; when our institutions shall be diffused and cherished, and republican government felt and enjoyed throughout the length and breadth and width of this land—from the far south to the extreme north, and from ocean to ocean. That this is our ultimate destiny, if wise councils prevail, I confidently believe. But it is not to be accomplished by the sword. Mr. Chairman, republics never spread by arms. We can only properly enlarge by voluntary accessions, and should only attempt to act upon our neighbors by setting them a good example."[358]

From an 1847 speech on the Mexican-American War:

☛ "[I greatly question the current policy of the Mexican-American War, and ask whether] . . . a line of military posts should now be established and defended, until our enemy shall get in a humor to treat; or whether the most desolating invasion should be pushed forward. . . .

"[I personally oppose all wars that are waged for conquest!] . . . [For, as we all well know,] free institutions never did and never will enlarge the circuit of their extent by force of arms. The history of the world abounds with many melancholy examples in illustration of the truth of this position. No principle is more dangerous to us, than that of compelling other nations to adopt our form of government. It is not only wrong in itself, but it is contrary to the whole spirit and genius of the liberty we enjoy; and, if persisted in, must inevitably result in our downfall and ruin. No instance is to be found upon record of any republic having ever entered upon such a hazardous crusade which did not end in the subversion of its own liberties, and the ultimate enslavement of its own people. And before embarking upon so dangerous an enterprise, I trust we shall have some security and guarantee that we shall at least escape the fate of those whose example we follow."[359]

From a February 12, 1847, speech concerning the North's Wilmot Proviso—which sought to prohibit slavery from being permitted in the newly developing Western

Territories. Stephens uncannily predicts the coming "Civil War":

☞ "Who can sit here and listen to the debates daily on this question and look unmoved upon the prospect before us? . . . This Wilmot Proviso and the resolutions from the legislatures of the States of New York and Pennsylvania and Ohio, all of the same character and import, speak a language that cannot be mistaken—a language of warning upon this subject, and which the country would do well to heed in time. They show a fixed determination on the part of the North, which is now in a majority in this House and ever will be hereafter, that, if territory is acquired, the institutions of the South shall be forever excluded from its limits. What is to be the result of this matter? Will the South submit to this restriction? Will the North ultimately yield? When the elements of discord are aroused, who will direct the storm? Who does not know how this country has been shaken to its very centre by the Missouri agitation!

James Knox Polk

". . . As a political institution I shall never argue the question of slavery here. I plead to the jurisdiction. The subject belongs exclusively to the States. There the Constitution wisely left it; and there Congress, if it acts wisely, will let it remain. Whether the South will submit to the threatened proscription, it is not my province to say. The language of defiance should always be the last alternative. But as I value this Union, and all the blessings which its security and permanency promise, not only to the present but coming generations, I invoke gentlemen not to put this principle to the test. I have great confidence in the strength of the Union, so long as sectional feelings and prejudices are kept quiet and undisturbed—so long as harmony is preserved amongst the States. But I have no disposition to test its strength by running against that rock upon which Mr. [Thomas] Jefferson predicted we should be finally wrecked. And the signs of the times, unless I greatly mistake them, are not of a character to be left unheeded. With virtue, intelligence and patriotism on the part of the people; and integrity, prudence, wisdom, and a due regard to all the great interests of the country on the part of our rulers, a bright and glorious destiny awaits us. But if bad counsels prevail; if all the solemn admonitions of the present and the past are disregarded; if the policy of the administration is to be carried out; if Mexico, the 'forbidden fruit,' is to be seized at every hazard, I very much fear that those who control public affairs, in their eager pursuit of the unenviable distinction of despoiling a neighboring republic, will have the still less enviable glory of looking back upon the shattered and broken fragments of their own confederacy [i.e., the U.S.A.]. And instead of gloating over the ruins of the ancient cities of the Aztecs, they may be compelled to turn and behold in their rear another and a wider prospect of desolation, carnage and blood."[360]

On January 21, 1850, writing from Washington, D.C., Stephens brings up the topic of Southern secession:
☛ "When I look at the causes of the present discontent I am persuaded there will never again be harmony between the two great sections of the Union. When California and New Mexico and Oregon and Nebraska are admitted as States, then the majority in the Senate will be against us. The power will be with them to harass, annoy and oppress. . . . It is a great mistake to suppose that the South can stave off this question. We have ultimately to submit or fight. . . . Could the South maintain a separate political organization? The result of my reflection is that she could, if her people be united."[361]

In a February 10, 1850, letter to his brother Linton, Stephens speaks of the "Second Hartford Convention," the upcoming Nashville Convention, and the secession of the Southern states, of which the following is an excerpt:
☛ "I would not for the world court the good will of either a knave or a fool by the sacrifice of principle; but I would not quarrel with them, nor change my conduct towards them because of their not appreciating my motives or conduct. I look upon _____ _____ as a most consummate knave, and yet I suppose he will be sent to the N[ashville] C[onvention] and there take a high stand on Southern Rights! . . . What is to become of us I cannot tell. But everything I see around me augurs the approach of anarchy. The opinion I gave you some time ago is strengthened by time. I see no prospect of a continuance of this Union long. The Nashville Convention will be held. It will be the nucleus of another sectional assemblage. A fixed alienation of feeling will be the result. The antislavery feeling and feeling of dismemberment may be abated, but it will return with increased force. It is the idea of the age, the monomania of the century in which we live. Its march is onward, steady and stealthy, like the approach of some mysterious epidemic. When, where, or how it is to end,

God only knows. If we had virtue and patriotism among our people and not demagogism, I should hope much from a Southern Confederacy. But I fear such men as _____ and _____, and all of that class, cannot safely control the destinies of any people. They may create a revolution, but they cannot build up a good government. Other heads, other hands, and other hearts will be necessary for such a work. We have the ability, the natural position, and the resources for a great and prosperous people. All the elements of power and progress are still within reach. All we want is the good sense, the forecast, the sound judgment, and the proper principles to exert them rightly, in order to give us all that a nation ought to have for its elevation and renown. But I fear we should soon degenerate into factions headed by bad leaders who would look only to their own distinction. We must, however, make the most and the best [of events?] as they pass. Great ones are ahead of us, of this I feel certain. The next quarter of a century will be an important epoch in the history of the Western Continent. Those who are now entering into life will necessarily be conspicuous actors in it."[362]

From an 1852 speech at Baltimore, Maryland:
☛ "It was and is the policy of attending to our own business, and letting other nations alone. It was and is the policy, the time-honored policy, of non-intervention. It may not be a foreign policy, but it is a [George] Washington policy; by an observance of which we have come to be what we are—one of the first nations of the earth."[363]

From the same 1852 speech:
☛ "Intervention to prevent intervention is very much like getting into a fight to prevent a fight. Intermeddlers with other people's business generally come off worsted."[364]

During a speech in January 1856 Stephens commented on the topic of "popular sovereignty," which held that sovereign power is invested in the people, not the government (as many Liberals then believed—and still do):
☛ "I am for maintaining the steadfastness of the territorial bills of 1850—the principle of leaving the people of the territories, without Congressional restriction, to settle this question for themselves, and to come into the Union, when admitted as States, either with or without slavery as they may determine. This principle was recognized and established after the severest sectional struggle this country has ever witnessed, and after the old idea, whether right or wrong in itself, whether just or unjust, whether constitutional or unconstitutional, of dividing the territories between the sections (by the 36° 30'

Richard Henry Lee

line) was entirely abandoned and repudiated by the party that at first forced it as an alternative upon the other."[365]

From an 1857 speech before the U.S. House of Representatives:
☛ "This, sir, is a government of limited powers. All the powers it can rightfully exercise or confer, are such as are expressly delegated in the constitution, and such as may be necessary to carry out those which are expressly named. . . . But I am asked: 'Is not the government of the United States sovereign?' and 'whether it is not the representative of the sovereignty of the people of the United States over the territories?' In reply, I state, that the government of the United States, in my judgment, is clothed with certain sovereign powers; but these powers are limited to specified objects. In the legitimate and proper exercise of these powers, to the extent of their grant, it may be considered as sovereign or supreme as any other government, just as sovereign as the Autocrat of Russia, in whom is concentrated all power; but these powers with which it is clothed, extend only to such subjects as are covered by the grant delegating them. Over all others, it has no power or authority to act at all. So far from being sovereign as to these, it is perfectly impotent. It cannot rightfully exercise any authority whatever upon any matter not committed to its charge by grant from the people of the States respectively; and it can wield the sovereign powers of the people thus delegated to it only over such subjects, and to accomplish such objects, as the people have authorized it to exercise authority upon. To this extent it is the representative, or rather the active and living embodiment of the sovereignty of the people. It is, in other words, the organ, or constitutes the channels through which their sovereignty acts on the subjects specified in the grant of its powers. But the appropriation of the public domain to one class of citizens, to the exclusion of another, is not to be found in the scope of these powers, or the objects for which they were conferred."[366]

Stephens wrote the following to a friend on January 22, 1860:

☛ "When the passions of men are once let loose, without control legal or moral, there is no telling to what extent of fury they may lead their victims. Republicks can only be maintained by virtue, intelligence and patriotism. We have but little public virtue, heroic virtue or patriotism now amongst our public men. They are generally selfish, looking not to country but to individual aggrandisement. There are but few now in Congress who consider anything so much as how their own votes affect them at home. This is a lamentable truth. And if we should break up, all these fellows would be striving to get the inner track of each other, each to take the lead of all the rest. It would be a race between demagogues to see who could pander most to the passions, prejudices and ignorance of the people, that they might profit thereby . . ."[367]

From a November 14, 1860, speech before the Georgia legislature:
☛ ". . . this Government of our Fathers, with all its defects, comes nearer the objects of all good Governments than any other on the face of the earth . . ."[368]

From the same November 14, 1860, speech:
☛ "I look upon this country with our Institutions as the Eden of the world, the Paradise of the Universe."[369]

Did the Declaration of Independence make the entire population of the United States one people, one political society, bound together under one National Government, one nation, as Liberals have long maintained? This is an important question, because if it is true, the idea of the constitutional legality of secession is thrown into question. In 1868 Stephens responded to it this way:
☛ "The Declaration [of Independence] . . . was made by the people of each Colony, for each Colony, through representatives acting by the Paramount authority of each Colony, separately and respectively. The Declaration of Independence was, in this way, a joint act of all the Colonies, for the benefit of each severally, as well as for the whole. The Congress that made it was a Congress of States. The deputies or delegates from no State assumed to vote for it until specially instructed and empowered so to do. Massachusetts had instructed and empowered her delegation so to act as early as January before; South Carolina in March; Georgia in April; North Carolina in April; Rhode Island in May; Virginia in May; New Hampshire in June; Connecticut in June; New Jersey in June; Maryland in June; Pennsylvania and New York were the last. The powers and instructions from these States did not arrive until after the 1st day of July, which caused a postponement of final action of the Congress on the Declaration until the 4th day of that month, when, full powers being received from all the States, it was then, after being voted upon by States and

carried by States, unanimously proclaimed by all the States, so in Congress assembled. The Declaration of Independence was, be it remembered, voted upon and carried by States, and proclaimed by and in the name of States."[370]

Stephens' line of thought continues:

☛ "This is the true history of the matter. . . . That these men did look forward hopefully for a continued Union of the States, under a Compact to be formed securing the Independence and Sovereignty of each, I do not doubt; but that they did not then consider each as an Independent Sovereign power, is wholly at variance with all the attending facts. The very Declaration itself shows this conclusively without going farther into a detail of these facts. The very title shows how it was made. Here it is: 'In Congress, July 4th, 1776, the unanimous Declaration of the thirteen United States of America.' It was the Declaration of States in Congress assembled, by their deputies, empowered by the Paramount authority of each, to make it. The Declaration was not that they were to be one State, as New Hampshire had instructed her representatives to make it, but, in their own language, 'thirteen free, Sovereign and Independent States.' This was in strict accordance with the instructions of their constituents. The people of the several Colonies would not consent for a Declaration to be made in any other way. This appears from the instructions of all the Colonies or States except New Hampshire. In their several instructions and powers for the Declaration of Independence, were instructions and powers for forming a Confederation of Independent States. So universal was this sentiment, that Richard Henry Lee's [the first cousin of Confederate General Robert E. Lee] first motion for the Declaration of Independence, early in June, was not only for Independence, but farther—for 'a plan of Confederation, to be prepared and transmitted to the respective Colonies for their consideration and approbation.'"[371]

From 1868:

☛ "Our history at this period rests not upon legends or fables. That Congress itself did not . . . consider the Declaration of Independence as a National act, or put any such construction upon it, as [Liberals have so often] . . . done, appears clearly from what they were then doing. At the very time the Declaration of Independence was made, a Committee, consisting of one delegate from each State, was organized to prepare articles of Confederation between the States, as separate, distinct Sovereign political Communities."[372]

From 1868:

☛ "So far from the Federal Government assuming a national character at that

A sheet from *Frank Leslie's Illustrated Newspaper*, concerning the secession of South Carolina. Stephens is pictured in the bottom right corner.

time, it would not presume to bind the States or enter into an obligation upon matters that related to their own separate Sovereign Jurisdiction. That Government only engaged to use its influence in recommending to the Sovereign States respectively certain stipulations. This statement of [my Liberal friends, that the Founding Fathers did not consider the original thirteen colonies to be separate and independent states] . . . is the more remarkable, because it is in direct conflict with numerous decisions of the Supreme Court of the United States."[373]

From 1868:
☛ "[In 1824 Chief Justice John] . . . Marshall . . . distinctly [affirmed], judicially [affirmed], from the Bench of the Supreme Court of the United States, that the States were separate and distinct Sovereignties when the Articles of Confederation were entered into, and that these articles were but a league between Sovereign Powers."[374]

From 1868:
☛ ". . . the Government of the United States is not, by virtue of it, supreme or Sovereign in the sense in which . . . [Liberals] use that term; and so far from being entitled thereby to claim the ultimate or any sort of allegiance of the citizens of the several States, it is not entitled even to claim their obedience to its laws except within the strict limit of its specifically-delegated powers."[375]

Stephens was well versed on the background of the U.S. Constitution's clause concerning the limited powers of the U.S. government (Article 1, Section 8), as he showed in 1868:
☛ "The history of this clause of the Constitution is this. It is well known, or, at least, it may be here stated, as it will be established without question, that, in the Convention that formed the Constitution, there was a party who were strongly in favor of doing away with the Federal [Confederate] system that existed before that time, and substituting, in its stead, a General National ['big'] Government over the whole people of all the States, as one body politic. This [Liberal] party wished to do away entirely with the Sovereignty of the several States. Their object was to give the Central National Government Paramount authority over the Sovereignty of the States. With this view, a proposition was brought forward, to give the National Government power 'to negative all laws, passed by the several States, contravening, in the opinion of the National Legislature, the articles of Union, or any treaties subsisting under the authority of the Union.' This proposition, if it had been adopted, would have greatly favored the object of the Nationals [i.e., the big government Liberals], but it was rejected by a decided vote."[376]

From 1868:
☛ ". . . the acts of the General Government, under the present Constitution, are no more binding on the States, or the citizens of the States, by virtue of it, than they were under the [U.S.] Confederation [1781-1789]."[377]

Stephens wrote the following to a friend in 1868:
☛ "I did consider the Constitution, as made by the Fathers, as embodying the best system of Government ever devised by man. While the breaches of faith on the part of some of our Northern Confederated States, were sufficient to justify a withdrawal from the Union, on the part of the Southern States, yet I did not think a withdrawal the wisest or best, or even surest policy, to obtain a redress of the grievances of which they so justly complained. The state of things then existing, sprung from no defect in the Constitution; it was the work of demagogues, both South and North; chiefly, however, at the North. I, moreover, greatly doubted if we had statesmanship enough at the South to guide our fortunes safely and successfully, in case this course should be adopted. I had the liveliest apprehensions that the end would be just what it is. These views, however, did not weaken in the least, my devotion to the great principles—the eternal truths—upon which our Government was established, and upon which, alone, you will allow me to say, in my judgment, Constitutional Liberty, on this continent, can be maintained and perpetuated. Had these principles been adhered to—if no war had been waged against the seceding States, I feel quite sure we should, sooner or later—perhaps before this time—as I have said before, have had a restoration of the whole Union, upon the same principles of voluntary agreement, that it was at first formed upon."[378]

In 1868 Stephens clarified some of the confusion over the party designations "Federalist" and "Anti-Federalist":
☛ "The administration of John Adams, who succeeded Washington in the Presidency, in 1797, bearing the popular name of Federal [an abbreviation of the word Confederal; thus identical to the word Confederacy], had endeavored, as was believed and charged, by construction and implication, to give that effect to the Constitution which Patrick Henry thought would be done in its practical workings. The party still bearing this name, during Mr. Adams's term of office, claimed virtually, it was said, for the Federal [Confederate] Government, general, absolute power, and maintained that the Supreme Court was the only arbiter between the General Government and State Governments, or the people, on all questions arising from the action of the General Government. They passed the Alien and Sedition laws, and acted generally upon the principle

"Liberty Hall," rear view

that the Federal Government was a consolidated Union of the people of all the States in one single, great Republic. They still kept the Party name of Federal [Confederate], because it was popular. This Party name, however, with their avowed principles, was nothing but a mask. It was but 'the livery of Heaven,' stolen 'to serve the Devil in.' [In other words, the Federalists of this period were actually anti-Confederalists, big government Liberals who wanted to consolidate all power in Washington and nationalize the central government. Adding to the confusion, after this, conservatives—originally called "Federalists"—became known as "Anti-Federalists." L.S.][379]

From 1868:
☛ "That the Government of the United States is a Confederated Republic, or Confederacy, of some sort, and not a Consolidated Government, is now no longer a matter of investigation or question. Whatever other characteristics, peculiar or anomalous, it possesses, it is beyond doubt, cavil, or dispute, Federal [Confederate] in its nature and character.

"That it presents, in its structure, several new features, wholly unknown in all former Confederacies of which the world's history furnishes examples, all admit. This was well understood at the time of its formation, as well as ever since. No exactly similar model is to be found amongst all the nations of the earth, or in the annals of mankind, in the past or present. But we have seen the model which was in the minds of its authors at the time it was framed, and which formed the basis of their conceptions and designs. That was the model of a Confederated Republic given by [Baron de] Montesquieu. This model was not only in the minds of the Convention which framed the Constitution, but in the minds of all the Conventions of the States which adopted it. This has been shown from the proceedings of those bodies. That model exhibited several small Republics so united into a larger one, for foreign and inter State purposes, as to present themselves in joint Combination to the world, as one Nation, while as between themselves each one retained unimpaired its own inherent, innate Sovereignty and Nationality. This was the ideal before all the States of this Union, at the time of the formation of the Constitution. According to this model, which was as far as the wisdom of men then had gone in forming Governments for the preservation of free institutions, and to prevent the principle of universal Monarchical Rule, the action of the larger and conventional State or Nation so, formed for external or foreign purposes, was confined in its internal operations exclusively to the integral members of the Union or Confederation. No power was conferred upon this joint agent of all to interfere, in any way or under any circumstances, with the individual citizens of the separate Republics.

"But a new idea had for sometime been in embryo. It was then struggling into birth. [Thomas] Jefferson's brain had first felt the impulse of its quickening life. The framers of the Constitution saw its star, as the wise men of the East saw the star of Bethlehem. They did homage to it, even in the manger, where it then lay in its swaddlings, as the political Messiah just born for the regeneration of the down trodden Peoples of the Earth. That idea was to apply a new principle to the model before them, to improve upon it by a division of its Powers, and by extending its operations, without changing the basis upon which it was formed. It was simply for these separate Republics to empower their joint agent, the artificial or conventional Nation of their own creation, to act, in the discharge of its limited functions, directly upon their citizens respectively, and to organize these functions into separate departments, Executive, Judicial and Legislative, as their own separate systems were organized. This, it is true, was a new and a grand development in the progress of the science of Government, which, of all sciences, unfortunately for mankind, is the slowest in progress."[380]

From 1868. Stephens explains the mystery of the true nature of the U.S. government:
☞ "A little analysis and generalization may enable us to bring order out of this confusion. In one sense it is a National Government. In this, however, there is nothing new or peculiar in the Government established by the New Constitution. In the same sense in which it is National, and none other, was the old Confederation National. The United States, under that, we have seen was called and properly called a Nation, for certain purposes. For the same purposes, and in the same sense, and none other, may they now properly be called a Nation. Their present Government is National in the same sense in which the Governments of all Confederated Republics are National, and none other. The very object in forming all Confederated Republics is to create a new and an entirely artificial or conventional State or Nation, which springs from their joint Sovereignties, and which has no existence apart from them, and which is but the Corporate Agent of all those Sovereignties creating it, and through which alone they are to be known to Foreign Powers, during the continuance of the Confederation. This Conventional Nation is but a Political Corporation. It has no original or inherent powers whatever. All its powers are derived—all are specific—all are limited—all are delegated—all may be resumed—all may be forfeited by misuser, as well as non-user. It is created by the separate Republics forming it. They are the Creators. It is but their Creature—subject to their will and control. They barely delegate the exercise of certain Sovereign powers to their common agent, retaining to themselves, separately, all that absolute, ultimate Sovereignty, by which this common agent,

with all its delegated powers, is created. This is the basis, and these are the principles, upon which all Confederated Republics are constructed. The new Conventional State or Nation thus formed is brought into being by the will of the several States or Nations forming it, and by the same will it may cease to exist, as to any or all of them, while the separate Sovereignties of its Creators may survive, and live on forever."[381]

From 1868:

☛ "A Government so constructed, being itself founded on Compact between distinct Sovereign States, is necessarily Federal [Confederate] in its nature, while it at the same time gives one national character and position amongst the other Powers of the world, to all the Parties constituting it! In this sense, all Confederated Governments are both Federal and National. The Government of the United States is no exception to the rule. In this sense, Washington, Jefferson, and Jackson, spoke of the United States under the Constitution as a Nation, as well as a Confederated Republic. In this sense, it is properly styled by all a Nation. This was the idea symbolized in the motto, '*E pluribus unum.*' One from many. That is, one State or Nation—one Federal [Confederate] Republic—from many Republics, States, or Nations. This is what is meant by the Nation when properly applied to the United States. It is not the whole people, in the aggregate constituting one body united on the principles of a social Compact, but that conventional State which

Mary Elizabeth Jenkins Surratt

springs from and is dependent upon the several State Sovereignties creating it, as in all other cases of Confederated Republics. The bare fact that it operates on the individual citizens of the several States, in specified cases, and has in its organization the requisite functions for this purpose, does not change, in the least, the nature of the Government, if this arrangement is agreed upon in the Compact between the Sovereign Parties to it. That depends entirely upon the great fact which we were so long in establishing, that the Government itself, with all its powers as well as machinery, was founded upon Compact between separate and distinct Sovereign States. If this be so, as has been conclusively established, then the Government, so constructed, must of necessity be Federal [Confederate], and purely Federal [Confederate], in its character."[382]

From 1868:

☞ "The great question, therefore, in this investigation was, is the Constitution a Compact between Sovereignties? If so, the Government established by it is purely, entirely, and thoroughly Federal in its nature, and no more National in any sense than all former Federal Republics. All those features in its operations directly upon individuals, instead of upon States, which give rise to ideas of Nationality, or of its being of a mixed nature, spring themselves from the Federal Compact. Ours, therefore, is a pure Confederated Republic, upon the model of Montesquieu, with the new principle referred to incorporated into the system, without changing, in the least, the basis of its organization—at least, so thought the Fathers by whom it was established. It is true we have as yet no apt distinctive word in political nomenclature, by which to characterize this specific distinctive improvement in the purely Federal system. This only shows the barrenness of language. Actualities often precede nomenclature. And, hence, De Tocqueville, perceiving this in our system, said of it, that 'the new word, which ought to express this novel thing, does not yet exist.' 'The human understanding,' says he, 'more easily invents new things than new words, and we are hence constrained to employ many improper and inadequate expressions.' No truer remark was ever made about the Government of the United States. All the difficulty or confusion on the subject, however, relates only to the name. It is one of nomenclature, and not substance. That stands out perfectly distinct in all its features, however unlanguaged it, with these features, may yet be. This want of a suitable name applies, also, only to its specific character, that name which will perfectly characterize its specific difference from other Confederacies, ancient or modern. There is no difficulty as to the proper generic term applicable to it. That is unquestionably Federal [Confederate]. Its genus, with all the incidents of the class, is a Federal or Confederated Republic. That is fixed by the fact that it is founded upon Compact—Confederation between distinct Sovereign Powers."[383]

From 1868:

☞ "The Government of the United States, however new some of its features are in the machinery of its operation, is no exception to the general rule, applicable to all Federal [Confederate] Republics, as to where the ultimate absolute Sovereign or Paramount authority resides. According to that rule, in all of them, it is retained by the Parties to the Compact. Such was the case in the model of [Baron de] Montesquieu. Such is the case in all Confederacies of this character, according to [Emerich de] Vattel, as we have seen. Such is, necessarily, the case in our system, built upon these models. All unions of separate States, under Compacts of this sort, are founded upon the same essential basis. Sovereignty, with us, therefore, upon these fixed and indisputable principles, now resides, as I said before, just where it did in 1776—just where it did in 1778—and just where it did in 1787: that is, with

the people of the several States of the Federal Union. This Sovereignty, so residing with them, is the Paramount authority to which allegiance is due. Allegiance, a word brought from the Old World, of Latin origin, from *ligo*, to bind, means the obligation which every one owes to that Power in the State, to which he is indebted for the protection of his rights of person and property. Allegiance and Sovereignty, as we have seen, are reciprocal. 'To whatever Power a citizen owes allegiance, that Power is his Sovereign.' To what Power are the citizens of the several States indebted for protection of person and

Robert Young Hayne

property, in all the relations of life, for the regulation of which Governments are instituted? Certainly not to the Federal Government. That Government, in its operations, has no right to interfere, in any way whatever, with the citizens of the several States, but in a few exceptional cases; and then, not for protection, but in the enforcement of laws, which the State would have been bound, by her plighted faith, to execute herself, had not this new feature been introduced into the Federal system. The Government of the United States, in its internal polity, is known to the citizens of the several States only by its requisitions upon individuals, instead of States, except in a very few specified cases. In its National character, it gives ample protection abroad. This was one of its main objects. In its postal arrangements, it furnishes many conveniences, for which it is duly paid. In these particulars, there is no difference between the Constitution and the first Articles of Confederation. But it was no part of the objects of either to afford protection to the citizens of the States, respectively, in all those relations of life which mark the internal polity of different States and Nations. These, now, as before, all depend upon the Sovereign will of the States. This Sovereign will fixes the status of the various elements of Society, as well as their rights. In the States, severally, remains the great right of Eminent Domain, which reserves to them complete jurisdiction and control over the rights of person and property of their entire population. With them remains, untrammelled, the power to establish codes of laws—civil, military, and criminal. They may punish for what crimes they please, and as they please, and the Government of the United States cannot interfere. To their own Legislatures, their own Judiciaries, their own Executives, their own laws, established by their own Paramount authority, do all the citizens of all the States look for whatever protection and security they receive, possess, or enjoy, in all the civil relations of life. In all such matters as require that protection to which allegiance is due, the Government of the United States is unknown to them."[384]

In 1868, during so-called "Reconstruction," Stephens was asked by a Liberal if it was not true that that Federal (Central) government had unlimited powers:
☛ " . . . our fathers made no such government. Further, I will add that any government in this country, administered on these principles, as ours has been for the last eight years, will and must end, in a short time, in Empire and Despotism."[385]

What is the correct way to define the U.S. government? Stephens gave this reply in 1870:
☛ "It is not a Nation of individuals, blended in a common mass, with a consolidated Sovereignty over the whole; but a Nation the constituent elements, or members of which, are separate and distinct political organizations, States, or Sovereignties. It is a 'Confederated Republic,' as Washington styled our present Union. This is the same as if he had styled it a Confederated Nation. It is, in truth, a Confederated Nation [i.e., a Confederacy]. That is, it is a Nation of States, or in other words, a Nation of Nations. In this sense, these States, thus united, do constitute a Nation, and a Nation of the highest and grandest type the world ever saw!"[386]

When asked about the Missouri Compromise of 1820, a bill that sought to regulate slavery in the Western Territories, Stephens made this response in 1870:

☛ ". . . the conflict in this Missouri Controversy, was not one between the advocates and opponents of Slavery [as Northern Liberals pretend], but between the advocates and opponents of our true Federal [Confederate] system under the Constitution.

". . . This was the Missouri Compromise, so-called. It did not come from the South. It was not moved by any member, or Senator from the South. Even Mr. [Henry] Clay [of Kentucky], whose name has been so erroneously connected with it, had nothing to do with its origination. It was proposed . . . by Mr. [Jesse B.] Thomas, a Senator from Illinois, as an additional section to the bill providing for the admission of Maine and Missouri, without any restriction on either, as all the other new States had been admitted. It related to matter entirely extraneous to the bill, and passed the Senate the 17th day of February, by a vote of thirty-four to ten. Of the ten noes, every one was from the South, except two. [James] Noble and [Waller] Taylor, Senators from Indiana, voted against it."[387]

From 1872:
☛ "Ours, therefore, being a Federal Government, is and must be, as all other Federal Governments are, 'a Government of States, and for States,' with limited powers directed to specific objects; and not a Government in any sense or view for the masses of the people of the respective States in their internal and municipal affairs. This great Sovereign Power of Local Self-Government, for which Independence was declared and achieved, resides with the people of the respective States."[388]

7

The Union

In September 1860 Stephens uttered the following words during a speech at Atlanta, Georgia:

☞ ". . . there is no cause in which I would more willingly die than in the cause of my country; and I would just as soon fall here, at this time, in the advocacy of those principles upon which its past glory has been achieved, its present prosperity, and its future hopes depend, as anywhere else, or on any other occasion. I told you, at the outset, that the signs of the times portend evil. I gave you this as my deliberate judgment; the future must make its own disclosures. But you need not be surprised to see these States, now so peaceful, contented, prosperous, and happy, embroiled in war in less than twelve months. There are occasions too grave for excitement, or any appeal to the passions. Believe me, I mean all I say; the most terrific tornadoes, those which demolish cities, destroy whole fleets, and sweep everything before them, come most unexpectedly. So do the most violent revolutions amongst men. The human passions are the same everywhere. They are dangerous elements for public men, politicians, and Party leaders to deal with.

"The condition of the country threatens the most violent conflict of sectional feeling, antipathy, and animosity, at no distant day. Should an outbreak occur, where is the power that can control it? A ball may be put in motion by one who cannot stop it; a fire may be kindled by hands that cannot quench it. Those who begin revolutions seldom end them. I do not mean to say that the secession movement at Charleston and Baltimore was a Disunionist movement, or intended as such by all those who joined in it. I do not mean to say that Messrs. [John C.] Breckinridge and [Joseph] Lane, who gave that movement their countenance, by accepting nominations under it, are Disunionists. I know both these gentlemen well, and doubt not their patriotism. Had either of them, or both, received the nominations from the regular Democratic Convention, I should have given them as warm a support as I do Messrs. [Stephen A.] Douglas and [Herschel V.] Johnson. Neither do I mean to say that the great mass of those who support the Seceders' ticket are Disunionists—no, far from it. But I do mean to say that the movement, whatever may have been the motive

Jesse Burgess Thomas

in which it originated, and by which it is countenanced and supported, whether by good men or bad, tends to disunion—to civil strife—may lead to it—and most probably will, unless arrested by the virtue, intelligence, and patriotism of the people. Is the cause assigned sufficient to put in hazard such even probable results? If it is, let the hazard be made; but if not, let us pause and consider. Much as I am attached to the Union, and as clearly convinced as I am that it is best for the interests and welfare of all sections, that it shall be preserved and maintained, if it can be, consistently with the rights, honor and security of all parts, yet I hold it subordinate to these great objects of its formation: life itself, dear as it must be held by all subordinate to essential rights and honor. This is true of individuals, and it is true of States and Nations. It was with these views and feelings, the ultimatum of our State was set forth in what is known as the Georgia Platform, in 1850. As I did then, so do I now, hold the Union subordinate to the objects therein set forth. On that Platform Georgia planted herself then, and on it I trust she will continue to stand. On the principles of that Platform I believe the Union ought to be maintained, and can be, if our Southern people are but true to themselves."[389]

Stephens speaking before the Virginia Secession Convention on April 23, 1861:
☛ "I was attached to the Union, however, not on account of the Union per se, but I was attached to it for what was its soul, its vitality and spirit; these were

the living embodiments of the great principles of self-government, springing from the great truth, that the just powers of all governments are derived from the consent of the governed, as it was transmitted to us by our fathers. This is the foundation on which alone all constitutional liberty is and must be based—and to these principles I am to-day attached just as ardently as I ever was before, and I now announce to you my solemn conviction that the only hope you have for the preservation of these principles, is by your alliance with those who have rescued, restored, and re-established them in the constitution of the Confederate States—there is no hope in the States north."[390]

☞ "[It is clear] . . . that the Union existing between these States, anterior to the formation of the new Constitution, was a Compact, or as Judge [John] Marshall expressed it, nothing but 'a league' between Sovereign States . . . [and that] in remodelling the Articles of the old Confederation, it was not the object, or design of any of the parties, to change the nature or character of that Union; but only to make it more perfect, by an enlargement of the delegation of powers conferred upon the Government thereby established with such changes in its organic structure, touching the mode and manner of exercising them, as might be thought best to attain the object of their delegation."[391]

Concerning dictator Lincoln and his numerous unconstitutional acts and war crimes against the Union, all which he perpetuated under the alleged "plea of necessity," Stephens wrote:
☞ "The maxims [my Liberal friends] . . . quote, I admit, are older than the Constitution. So is Tyranny! The latter sprung from the former. The object of written Constitutions is to put an end to both. No Statesman should ever be trusted in this country in the exercise of any power under the 'plea of necessity' or who 'consults' the 'safety of the people,' or attempts 'to preserve the life of the Nation' upon any maxims outside of the Constitution. The life of the Nation is the Constitution! From this springs all the life our wonderful Nation, constituted as it is, ever had. In it alone this Conventional Nation, as we have seen it is, lives, and moves, and has its being! It is this alone which gave it existence, and it is this alone which can give it immortality! Of all the absurdities, (you will please excuse the expression,) I ever heard uttered, the strangest to me is that set forth in the proposition, that the preservation of the life of anything can be effected by its destruction or extinguishment! I know nothing approximating it, unless it be that other most preposterous notion from which all these proceedings sprung, that a voluntary Union of separate Independent States could be preserved and maintained by coercion! The life of the Nation can only be preserved, as the life of anything else, by maintaining the

principles of its organic law!"[392]

To this day the uninformed continue to believe that the South fought the North in attempt to crush the Union. According to Stephens, nothing could have been further from the truth:

☛ ". . . we were not fighting against the Union, but for the [constitutional] Principles upon which the Union was based."[393]

☛ ". . . the Union, in my judgment, can be maintained and perpetuated—not by physical power, but by the much stronger attractive principle of 'mutual convenience and reciprocal advantage' . . ."[394]

Stephens to the Honorable Alexander J. Marshall, at Richmond, Virginia, November 4, 1864:

☛ "The old [U.S.] Union was founded upon a compact between sovereign and independent States. This compact was based upon the idea or assumption that it was for the best interests of all to be united upon its terms, each performing and discharging faithfully to all the rest the obligations imposed by it. That assumption, in my judgment, was sound and correct."[395]

8

Causes of the War

In May 1860, Georgia politician Richard M. Johnston recorded the following brief interview with Stephens. Lincoln's election, the secession of South Carolina, and Lincoln's War on the South and the Constitution were only months away:

Mr. J.—"Well, the Charleston Convention has adjourned without a nomination. What do you think of matters now?"

Mr. S.—"Think of them? Why, that men will be cutting one another's throats in a little while. In less than twelve months we shall be in a war, and that the bloodiest in history. Men seem to be utterly blinded to the future. You remember my reading to you a letter which I wrote to a gentleman in Texas, asking the use of my name in his State as a candidate for the Presidency?"

Mr. J.—"The one in which you said that we should make the Charleston Convention a Marathon or a Waterloo?"

Mr. S.—"Yes. Well, we have made it a Waterloo."

Mr. J.—"Do you not think that matters may yet be adjusted at Baltimore?"

Mr. S.—"Not the slightest chance for it. The [Democratic, that is, Conservative] party is split forever. [Stephen A.] Douglas will not retire from the stand he has taken, and the party will nominate somebody else. The only hope was at Charleston. If the party could have agreed there we might carry the election. As it is, the cause is hopelessly lost. The election cannot be carried without the support of Douglas."

Mr. J.—"I hope he will give his support yet."

Mr. S.—"Never."

Alexis de Tocqueville

Mr. J.—"What a misfortune it was that he did not support the Lecompton Constitution."

Mr. S.—"Yes. But he knew, as all men knew, that it was procured by stratagem. I supported it, not in consideration of any matters connected with its formation, except that it was framed in strict and technical conformity with the enabling act. I thought it ought to be adopted, and think so yet, because it gave us only what we were entitled to under the Kansas Act."

Mr. J.—"You think Douglas entitled to the nomination?"

Mr. S.—"I won't say that he is entitled to it; but I will say that he is one of the foremost defenders of constitutional rights in the country. And then his name has been the strongest in two Conventions. He voluntarily withdrew it in 1852; the same in 1856. I suppose he has made up his mind not to withdraw it a third time. The greatest alleged objections to Douglas are his ambition and the hordes of office-seekers that are in his suite. If the party would be satisfied with the Cincinnati platform, and would cordially nominate Douglas, we should carry the election; but I repeat to you that is impossible."

Mr. J.—"But why must we have civil war, even if the Republican [Liberal] candidate should be elected?"

Mr. S.—"Because there are not virtue and patriotism and sense enough left in the country to avoid it. Mark me, when I repeat that in less than twelve months we shall be in the midst of a bloody war. What is to become of us then God only knows. The Union will certainly be disrupted; and what will make it so disastrous is the way in which it will be done. The Southern people are not unanimous now, and will not be, on the question of secession. The Republican [Liberal] nominee will be elected. Then South Carolina will secede. For me, I should be content to let her have her own way, and go out alone. But the Gulf States will follow her example. The people are by no means unanimous; but the majorities will follow her. They are what we will start off with in our new nation—the Gulf States following South Carolina. After that the Border States will hesitate, and their hesitation will encourage the North to make war upon us. If the South would unanimously and simultaneously go out of the Union we could make a very strong government. But even then, if there were only Slave States in the new confederacy, we should be known as the Black Republic, and be without the sympathy of the world. Still, if we had wise and patriotic men, and men that were statesmen, we could make a great country of the South."[396]

During Lincoln's War Stephens was asked about his criticisms of the U.S. Constitution, about its alleged "defects," and how these caused "the present alienation and disruption of the States." He replied:

☞ "My opinion, as to the origin and cause of these troubles, is that it existed more with the people than with the government; or rather it may more properly be assigned to the prejudices and passions of the people, excited, aroused, and inflamed by unprincipled, ambitious, and selfish demagogues, North and South, than to any radical defect in the constitution. The ship was strong enough, large enough, safe enough; the real difficulty was with the crew, or those of the crew who strove amongst themselves for some share in the guidance and control of the noble, stately old craft. Of course she was not perfect in all her parts, as nothing from human hands ever was or ever will be; still, in my judgment, there was in the old constitution no inherent radical defect. As expounded by [Thomas] Jefferson and the States rights men in the Kentucky and Virginia resolutions of 1798 and 1799, it was intended to, and did, in deed and in truth, establish the 'best government on earth.' This is my deliberate judgment. So far as our troubles in their origin can be traced to the constitution, I think, without doubt, they are attributed to the consolidating tendency with which it was administered. It was the centralizing idea that carried protection into the halls of Congress; then internal improvements [known today as 'corporate welfare']; and lastly, satan-like, the slavery question."[397]

Stephens continues on the same topic:
☛ "This, after being agitated there until the popular mind was greatly excited, was carried back to the northern States by their demagogues, and made the test of party organizations. In this way those States at the North, before alluded to, were brought to their open breach of faith under the constitution, and to their virtual disruption of the Union under the compact. But for the centralizing, consolidating ideas under which the constitution was administered, (not as it was made and intended to operate by the States which formed it,) these disturbing questions would never have been entertained by Congress. But for getting seats in Congress on this hobby, there would have been no such parties formed at the North; and no such breach of faith would ever have been committed, nor would any of the other evils and excitements growing out of the slavery question, which so agitated the public mind North and South, and which did so much in the hands of demagogues in both sections, in producing the actual and final rupture, ever have occurred. In this view our present troubles may be mainly attributed to this tendency in the administration of the government to centralism and consolidation. That clause in the constitution, to which you refer, did work injuriously to the South: but that (I speak of the whole clause) was one of the compromises of the constitution. The southern States yielded that to the North in consideration of some concession, (which one I forget now,) made by them upon the subject of slavery. That whole clause, giving Congress power to regulate commerce, was the source of more injury to southern interests than every thing else together. This clause authorized the navigation acts under the operation of which southern importations, and their direct trade from abroad, were crippled, and soon amounted to little or nothing. The financial system adopted, centralizing the capital of the funded

Salmon Portland Chase

public debt at the North, in combination with the navigation laws, completely revolutionized commerce, or at least changed its channels and marts in the States. Charleston, before the constitution was formed, was not much, if in any degree, inferior in trade and commerce to Boston or New York. I do not recollect the statistics exactly, but all southern ports lost largely in their trade by the operation of these navigation acts. This principle was not well understood by our people; much that was attributed to the tariff, and other imaginary causes, was due to this. The monied capital was at the North; the shipping was owned at the North. The whole coast trade was secured to American bottoms. No foreign vessel was allowed to break, bulk, or unload parts of her cargo in different ports. Hence nearly all importations in foreign bottoms were thrown into New York, Boston, or Philadelphia. These became the great marts. A ship from Liverpool coming for cotton, rice, or tobacco, would first leave her cargo of imports at New York, thence sail in ballast to Savannah, Charleston, or Norfolk for her return cargo. Northern shipping, then, under the monopoly secured by the navigation laws, distributed the assorted cargoes accumulated in the great marts as the demands in other ports required. Southern cities thus became nothing but tributaries and dependencies upon those of the North. The latter grew and prospered, while the former remained stationary or declined. This is but a glance at the system. All growing out of that clause of the constitution agreed to on compromise as stated."[398]

Stephens continues:
☞ "But these navigation laws might have been revised and amended, so as to break down this monopoly of New England shipping, if the southern members of Congress had united with those of the west upon the question, and exerted half the efforts they wasted upon many very trifling subjects. I am not prepared to say what would be the practical workings of the system, with the omission in this clause of the words 'between the States.' I should have to think about it and study it more than I now have time to do, before arriving at any opinion satisfactory even to myself upon it. I am so much of a States rights man, however, by nature; my first impulse is strongly in favor of the opinion that it would have been better to leave that matter to the States. Had the States retained that power under the old system, we might perhaps under it have been enabled to bring the covenant breakers to a reconsideration of their acts of bad faith, in the matter before alluded to, without resorting to secession. This power, retained by States thus confederated, might be an important and useful check in bringing delinquent members up to the full discharge of their duties and obligations under the compact. Still I could not venture a positive opinion one way or the other, without more reflection. I should, however, never favor

its exercise, simply with a view to the protection of any of the mechanic arts or industrial pursuits. That whole theory, in my judgment, is radically wrong."[399]

Stephens, like all Southerners at the time, understood the true cause of Lincoln's War—and it was not slavery, as the former Confederate vice president discusses in these brilliant excerpts from his two-volume work A Constitutional View of the Late War Between the States *(published in 1868 and 1870):*

☛ "It is a postulate, with many writers of this day, that the late War was the result of two opposing ideas, or principles, upon the subject of African Slavery. Between these, according to their theory, sprung the 'irrepressible conflict,' in principle, which ended in the terrible conflict of arms. Those who assume this postulate, and so theorize upon it, are but superficial observers.

"That the War had its origin in opposing principles, which, in their action upon the conduct of men, produced the ultimate collision of arms, may be assumed as an unquestionable fact. But the opposing principles which produced these results in physical action were of a very different character from those assumed in the postulate. They lay in the organic Structure of the Government of the States. The conflict in principle arose from different and opposing ideas as to the nature of what is known as the General [Central] Government. The contest was between those who held it to be strictly Federal [Confederate] in its character, and those who maintained that it was thoroughly National [Monarchical]. It was a strife between the principles of Federation [Confederation], on the one side, and Centralism, or Consolidation [Nationalism], on the other.

"Slavery, so called, was but the question on which these antagonistic principles, which had been in conflict, from the beginning, on divers other questions, were finally brought into actual and active collision with each other on the field of battle."[400]

Stephens' continues his line of thought from A Constitution View:

☛ "Some of the strongest Anti-slavery men who ever lived were on the side of those who opposed the Centralizing principles which led to the War. Mr. [Thomas] Jefferson [of Virginia] was a striking illustration of this, and a prominent example of a very large class of both sections of the country [South and North], who were, most unfortunately, brought into hostile array against each other. No more earnest or ardent devotee to the emancipation of the Black race, upon humane, rational and Constitutional principles, ever lived than he was. Not even [William] Wilberforce [leading British abolitionist] himself was more devoted to that cause than Mr. Jefferson was. And yet Mr. Jefferson, though in private life at the time, is well known to have been utterly opposed

James M. Calhoun

to the Centralizing principle, when first presented, on this question, in the attempt to impose conditions and restrictions on the State of Missouri, when she applied for admission into the Union, under the Constitution. He looked upon the movement as a political manœuvre to bring this delicate subject (and one that lay so near his heart) into the Federal Councils, with a view, by its agitation in a forum where it did not properly belong, to strengthen the Centralists [Liberals] in their efforts to revive their doctrines, which had been so signally defeated on so many other questions. The first sound of their movements on this question fell upon his ear as a "fire bell at night." The same is true of many others. Several of the ablest opponents of that State Restriction, in Congress, were equally well known to be as decidedly in favor of emancipation as Mr. Jefferson was. Amongst these, may be named Mr. [William] Pinkney and Mr. [Henry] Clay, from the South, to say nothing of those men from the North, who opposed that measure with equal firmness and integrity.

"It is the fashion of many writers of the day to class all who opposed the Consolidationists [Liberals] in this, their first step, as well as all who opposed them in all their subsequent steps, on this question, with what they style the Pro-Slavery Party. No greater injustice could be done any public men, and no greater violence be done to the truth of History, than such a classification. Their opposition to that measure, or kindred subsequent ones, sprung from no attachment to Slavery; but, as Jefferson's, Pinkney's and Clay's, from their strong convictions that the Federal Government had no rightful or Constitutional control or jurisdiction over such questions; and that no such action, as that proposed upon them, could be taken by Congress without destroying the elementary and vital principles upon which the Government was founded.

"By their acts, they did not identify themselves with the Pro-Slavery Party (for, in truth, no such Party had, at that time, or at any time in the History of the Country, any organized existence). They only identified themselves, or took position, with those who maintained the Federative [Confederate or Conservative] character of the General Government."[401]

Stephens' explanation of the true cause of Lincoln's War continues:

☛ ". . . out of the million and a half, and more, of the votes cast, in the Northern States, in 1860, against Mr. [Abraham] Lincoln how many, could it, with truth, be said, were in favor of Slavery, or even that legal subordination of the Black race to the White, which existed in the Southern [and in the Northern] States?

"Perhaps, not one in ten thousand! It was a subject, with which, they were thoroughly convinced, they had nothing to do, and could have nothing to do, under the terms of the Union, by which the States were Confederated, except to carry out, and faithfully perform, all the obligations of the Constitutional Compact, in regard to it.

"They simply arrayed themselves against that Party which had virtually hoisted the [liberal/socialistic] banner of Consolidation. The contest, so commenced, which ended in the War, was, indeed, a contest between opposing principles; but not such as bore upon the policy or impolicy of African Subordination. They were principles deeply underlying all considerations of that sort. They involved the very nature and organic Structure of the Government itself. The conflict, on this question of Slavery, in the Federal Councils, from the beginning, was not a contest between the advocates or opponents of that peculiar Institution, but a contest, as stated before, between the supporters of a strictly Federative [Conservative] Government, on the one side, and a thoroughly National [Liberal] one, on the other."[402]

From 1868:

☛ "[. . . most of my Northern friends completely misunderstand the true cause of Mr. Lincoln's War, wrongly attributing the main problem to slavery. Yankee abolitionist] Mr. [Horace] Greeley [for example], one of the ablest and fairest writers of the class I have alluded to, in his 'American Conflict,' treats the whole war as the culmination of a strife, for more than half a century, about 'Negro Slavery,' without scarcely giving a passing word upon the subject of the nature of the Government of the United States, or attempting to show that it had any rightful authority whatever over the subject matter of this strife. He writes as if it were conceded that the United States is one great Nation, one people, divided in sentiment upon the subject of African Slavery, or the legal status of the African race in some of the States. He traces and treats the discussion of this question just as a British historian might treat the discussions on the Corn Laws, or the extension of the franchise in his country. All this manner of treatment of the subject is radically defective. It utterly ignores the true causes of the war, on which alone its Rightfulness depends. Slavery, so called, or that legal subordination of the black race to the white, which existed in all but one of the States, when the Union was formed, and in fifteen of them when the war began, was unquestionably the occasion of the war, the main exciting proximate cause on both sides, on the one as well as the other, but it was not the real cause, the '*Causa causans*' of it. That was the assumption on the part of the Federal authorities, that the people of the several States were, as [Liberals] . . . say, citizens of the United States, and owed allegiance to the Federal Government, as the absolute Sovereign power over the whole country, consolidated into one Nation. The war sprung from the very idea [Liberals] .

Amos Tappan Akerman

. . have expressed, and from the doctrine embraced in the question propounded to me. It grew out of different and directly opposite views as to the nature of the Government of the United States, and where, under our system, ultimate Sovereign power or Paramount authority properly resides."[403]

From 1868:

☛ "[Let us discuss the authentic reason the Southern states departed from the Union.] Considerations connected with the legal status of the Black race in the Southern States, and the position of several of the Northern States toward it, together with the known sentiments and principles of those just elected to the two highest offices of the Federal Government (Messrs. Lincoln and [Hannibal] Hamlin), as to the powers of that Government over this subject, and others which threatened, as was supposed, all their vital interests, prompted the Southern States to withdraw from the Union, for the very reason that had induced them at first to enter into it: that is, for their own better protection and security. Those [i.e., Northern Liberals] who had the control of the Administration of the Federal Government, denied this right to withdraw or secede. The war was inaugurated and waged by those at the head of the Federal Government, against these States, or the people of these States, to prevent their withdrawal from the Union. On the part of these States, which had allied themselves in a common cause, it was maintained and carried on purely in defence of this great Right, claimed by them, of State Sovereignty and Self-government, which they with their associates had achieved in their common struggle with Great Britain, under the Declaration of 1776, and which, in their judgment, lay at the foundation of the whole structure of American free Institutions.

"This is a succinct statement of the issue, and when the calm and enlightened judgment of mankind, after the passions of the day shall have passed off, and shall be buried with the many gallant and noble-spirited men, who fell on both sides in the gigantic struggle which ensued, shall be pronounced, as it will be, upon the right or wrong of the mighty contest, it must be rendered in favor of the one side or the other, not according to results, but according to the right in the issue thus presented.

". . . if the History of this most lamentable and disastrous conflict, disastrous I fear to all the great principles of Self-government, established or attempted to be secured by the Constitution of the United States, shall ever be written, the Right and Justice of the cause will be found to be on the side [the South's] of those with whom my fortunes were cast, and with whom, in all their heroic struggles and unparalleled sacrifices, my feelings and sympathies were ever thoroughly enlisted, and my utmost exertions put forth for their success.

Whatever errors in policy they may have committed, either in the inception of the difficulties or in their subsequent management, the real object of those who resorted to Secession, as well as those who sustained it, was not to overthrow the Government of the United States; but to perpetuate the principles upon which it was founded. The object in quitting the Union was not to destroy, but to save the principles of the Constitution. The form of Government therein embodied, I did think, and do still think, the best the world ever saw, and I fear the world will never see its like again."⁴⁰⁴

☛ ". . . I do stand upon facts, and these are the incontestable facts of this case, which will forever perpetuate the truth of my assertion, that upon the head of the Federal Government will forever rest the inauguration of this most terrible war which did ensue.

"No part of its responsibility rests upon the Southern States. They were the aggressors in no instance. They were ever true to their plighted faith under the Constitution. No instance of a breach of its mutual covenants can be ever laid to their charge. The open and palpable breach was committed by a number of their Northern Confederates [i.e., Yankee comrades]. No one can deny this. Those States at the North, which were untrue to their Constitutional engagements, claimed powers not delegated, and elected a Chief Magistrate pledged to carry out principles openly in defiance of the decision of the highest Judicial Tribunal known to the Constitution. "Their policy tended inevitably to a Centralized Despotism. It was under these circumstances that Secession was resorted to, as before stated; and, then, the war was begun and waged by the North to prevent the exercise of this Right. All that the Southern States did, was in defence, even in their firing the first gun."⁴⁰⁵

What transpired just prior to Lincoln's War that helped bring the two sections to blows?
☛ ". . . all the dangers which then threatened [the Union's] . . . continuance arose from the Centralizing tendency of the Government [at the North]. This had, by its Tariffs, and by several other measures . . . , given a preponderance to the population of the non-slaveholding [Northern] States, and the tendency was towards Consolidation."⁴⁰⁶

Following Lincoln's War Stephens was repeatedly asked his opinion on the true cause of the conflict, and each time he gave the same answer:
☛ "[The cause of the War Between the States can be traced to] . . . the open, palpable, and avowed violation of the Constitution by the Centralists [Liberals] and [Northern] Restrictionists in the matter of the rendition of fugitives from service. [It is conclusive] . . . that in that matter the wrong, the aggression, the

acknowledged 'breach of faith,' was on the side of the non-slaveholding [i.e., Northern] States . . . , and that in no instance pointed out by [my Liberal friends,] . . . as an excuse or palliation, was there any aggression or breach of faith by the Southern States. They were ever true to their Constitutional obligations, and resorted to a withdrawal from the Union only when it became the thorough conviction of their leading men, that it was the object of the Centralists [i.e., the Northern Liberals], by using this question, to accomplish their purpose of effecting a Consolidated Empire instead of continuing the Federal [Confederate] Republic. [It is clear to anyone with even a trace of knowledge of the U.S. Constitution and American history] . . . that by public law they had a perfect right to withdraw. In denial of this right to withdraw, the war was inaugurated . . . . The cry, on the part of those [i.e., the Republicans, the Liberal party of the day] controlling the Federal Government at the time, of saving the Union, was but a pretext to cover their design of overthrowing the Principles of the Constitution."[407]

☛ ". . . the origin of all these late troubles as well as present ills, and the still greater ones now threatening, have been traced to their proper source—to their primal cause. That, we have seen, was a violation of one of the essential principles of the organic structure of our new and wonderful system of a Federative [Confederate] Union of Sovereign States [i.e., the right of secession]. From this violation of principle, all these direful consequences have come, as effects follow causes."[408]

9

Secession, Home Rule, & State Sovereignty

From Stephens' speech on the joint resolution for the annexation of Texas, delivered January 25, 1845, before the U.S. House of Representatives:

☛ "[Vermont] . . . was a separate and independent community with a government of her own. She was not even one of the original revolting thirteen colonies. She had never been united in the old [U.S.] Confederation. . . . She was a distinct, independent government within herself. She had her own constitution, her own legislature, her own executive, judiciary and military establishment, and exercised all the faculties of a sovereign and independent state. She had her own post-office department and revenue laws and regulations of trade. The United States did not attempt to exercise any jurisdiction over her. . . . The gentleman from Vermont says New York claimed jurisdiction over her and finally gave consent for the admission of Vermont as a State. This is true. But Vermont did not recognize the jurisdiction of New York; she bade defiance to it. And after years had rolled on in this situation, she treated with New York, as one sovereign treats with another, and paid thirty thousand dollars for a relinquishment of that jurisdiction which she would not allow to be exercised, and was then admitted into the Union as one of the

States."[409]

From May 9, 1860:

☛ "I assume as an unquestioned and unquestionable fact that non-intervention has for many years been received, recognized and acted upon as the settled doctrine of the South. By non-intervention, I mean the principle that Congress shall pass no law upon the subject of slavery in the Territories, either for or against it in any way—that they shall not interfere or act upon it at all,—or in the express words of Mr. [John C.] Calhoun, the great Southern leader, that Congress shall 'leave the whole subject where the Constitution and the great principles of self-government placed it.' This has been eminently a Southern doctrine. It was announced by Mr. Calhoun in his speech in the Senate on the 27th of June, 1848, and after two years of discussion was adopted as the basis of the adjustment made in 1850. It was the demand of the South, put forth by the South, and since its establishment finally has been again and again affirmed and reaffirmed as the settled policy of the South by party conventions and State legislatures. . . . It was not a new question and, whether rightly or wrongly, it has been decided—decided and settled just as the South asked that it should be,—not, however, without great effort and a prolonged struggle. The question now is, shall the South abandon her own position in that decision and settlement? This is the question virtually presented by the action of the seceders from the Charleston convention; or, stated in other words, it amounts to this: whether the Southern States, after all that has taken place, should now reverse their previous course, and demand Congressional intervention for the protection of slavery in the Territories as a condition of their remaining longer in the Union? Shall the South make this demand of Congress, and when made, in case of failure to obtain it, shall she secede from the Union, as a portion of her delegates (some under instructions and some of their own free will) seceded from the Charleston convention on their failure to get it granted there? . . . My judgment is against the demand."[410]

On November 14, 1860, shortly after Lincoln's election on the 6th, Stephens was asked to speak before the Georgia legislature, where he used the podium to discuss his anti-secessionist views:

☛ "My countrymen, if we shall in an evil hour rashly pull down and destroy those institutions which the patriotic hand of our fathers labored so long and so hard to build up, and which have done so much for us and for the world, who can venture the prediction that similar results will not ensue? There were many amongst us in 1850 zealous to go at once out of the Union, to disrupt every tie that binds us together. Now do you believe, had that policy been carried out at that time, we should have been the same great people we are to-day?

". . . Our position on this point is, and ought to be, at all hazards, for perfect equality between all the States and the citizens of all the States in the Territories, under the Constitution of the United States. If Congress should exercise its power against this, then I am for standing where Georgia planted herself in 1850. These were plain propositions which were then laid down in her celebrated platform, as sufficient for the disruption of the Union if the occasion should ever come; on these Georgia has declared that she will go out of the Union; and for these she would be justified by the nations of the earth in so doing. I say the same . . . if Mr. Lincoln's policy should be carried out. I have told you that I do not think his bare election sufficient cause; but if his policy should be carried out, in the violation of any of the principles set forth in the Georgia platform, that would be such an act of aggression, which ought to be met as therein provided for. If his policy should be carried out in repealing or modifying the Fugitive Slave Law so as to weaken its efficacy, Georgia has declared that she will, in the last resort, disrupt the ties of the Union—and I say so, too. I stand upon the Georgia platform and upon every plank of it; and if these aggressions therein provided for take place, I say to you and to the people of Georgia, be ready for the assault when it comes; keep your powder dry and let your assailants then have lead if need be. I would wait for an act of aggression. This is my position."[411]

From the same November 14, 1860, speech:
☞ "Northern States on entering the Federal compact pledged themselves to surrender such [slave] fugitives. . . . They have violated their plighted faith. What ought we to do in view of this? By the law of nations you would have the right to demand the carrying out of this article of agreement, and I do not see that it should be otherwise with respect to the States of this Union; and in case it be not done, we would by these principles, have the right to commit acts of reprisal on those faithless governments, and seize upon their property, or that of their citizens wherever found. The States of this Union stand upon the same footing as foreign nations in this respect. But by the law of nations we are equally bound, before proceeding to violent measures, to set forth our grievances before the offending governments, to give them an opportunity to redress the wrong. . . . Let us, therefore, not act hastily. Let your committee on the state of the republic make out a bill of grievances; let it be sent to the governors of those faithless States; and if reason and argument shall be tried in vain—if all shall fail to induce them to return to their Constitutional obligations, I would be for retaliatory measures, such as the Governor [Joseph E. Brown] has suggested to you. This mode of resistance in the Union is in our

power. It might be effectual, and if not, in the last resort, we would be justified in the eyes of nations, not only in separating from them but in using force. . . . My own opinion is that if this course be pursued, and they are informed of the consequences of refusal, these States will recede, will repeal their nullifying acts; but if they should not, then let the consequences be with them, and the responsibility of the consequences rest upon them."[412]

Stephens' November 14, 1860, speech continues:
☞ "Should Georgia determine to go out of the Union, I speak for one, though my views might not agree with them, whatever the result may be, I shall bow to the will of her people. Their cause is my cause, and their destiny is my destiny; and I trust this will be the ultimate course of all. The greatest curse that can befall a free people, is civil war."[413]

Stephens' November 14, 1860, speech continues:
☞ "I am for exhausting all that patriotism demands before taking the last step. I would therefore invite South Carolina to a conference. I would ask the same of all the other Southern States, so that if the evil has got beyond our control, which God in His mercy grant may not be the case, we may not be divided among ourselves, but if possible secure the united cooperation of all the Southern States; and then, in the face of the civilized world, we may justify our action, and, with the wrong all on the other side, we can appeal to the God of battles to aid us in our cause. But do nothing in which any portion of our people may charge you with rash and hasty action. It is certainly a matter of great importance to tear this government asunder. You were not sent here for that purpose. I would wish the whole South to be united if that is to be done. . . . In this way our sister Southern States may be induced to act with us; and I have but little doubt that the States of New York, Pennsylvania, and Ohio and the other Western States, will compel their legislatures to recede from their hostile attitude, if the others do not. Then with these we would go on without New England, if she chose to stay out."[414]

Stephens' November 14, 1860, speech continues:
☞ "My position, then, in conclusion, is for the maintenance of the honor, the rights, the equality, the security, and the glory of my native State in the Union, if possible; but if these cannot be maintained in the Union, then I am for their maintenance, at all hazards, out of it."[415]

On January 16, 1861, Stephens attended Georgia's Secession Convention at Milledgeville, where he pled for calm, reason, and patience in the face of the ever growing secessionist movement across the South. While he accurately predicted the horrors of the coming war with the North, the pro-Union sentiments he expressed only added to his already undeserved reputation (among Southerners) as being a "Southern Yankee."[416] *His passionate address did little good. Three days later, on January 19, Georgia left the Union, and a dismayed Stephens went with it:*

☞ "This step [of seceding from the Union] once taken, can never be recalled; and all the baleful and withering consequences that must follow will rest on the

Thomas Jonathan "Stonewall" Jackson

convention for all coming time. When we and our posterity shall see our lovely South desolated by the demon of war, which this act of yours will inevitably invite and call forth; when our green fields of waving harvests shall be trodden down by the murderous soldiery and fiery car of war sweeping over our land; our temples of justice laid in ashes; all the horrors and desolation of war upon us; who but this convention will be held responsible for it? and who but him who shall have given his vote for this unwise and ill-timed measure, as I honestly think and believe, shall be held to strict account for this suicidal act by the present generation, and probably cursed and execrated by posterity for all coming time, for the wide and desolating ruin that will inevitably follow this act you now propose to perpetrate?

"Pause, I entreat you, and consider for a moment what reasons you can give that will even satisfy yourselves in calmer moments—what reasons you can give to your fellow-sufferers in the calamity that it will bring upon us. What reasons can you give to the nations of the earth to justify it? They will be the calm and deliberate judges in the case; and what cause or one overt act can you name or point on which to rest the plea of justification?"[417]

From Stephens' January 1861 speech:

☛ "What right has the North assailed? What interest of the South has been invaded? What justice has been denied? and what claim founded in justice and right has been withheld? Can either of you to-day name one governmental act of wrong, deliberately and purposely done by the Government of Washington, of which the South has a right to complain? I challenge the answer.

"While, on the other hand, let me show the facts (and believe me, gentlemen, I am not here the advocate of the North; but I am here the friend, the firm friend and lover of the South and her institutions, and for this reason I speak thus plainly and faithfully, for yours, mine, and every other man's interest, the words of truth and soberness), of which I wish you to judge, and I will only state facts which are clear and undeniable, and which now stand as records authentic in the history of our country. When we of the South demanded the slave-trade, or the importation of Africans for the cultivation of our lands, did they not yield the right for twenty years? When we asked a three-fifths representation in Congress for our slaves was it not granted? When we asked and demanded the return of any fugitive from justice, or the recovery of those persons owing labor or allegiance, was it not incorporated in the Constitution, and again ratified and strengthened in the Fugitive Slave Law of 1850?

"But do you reply that in many instances they have violated this compact and have not been faithful to their engagements? As individual and local communities they may have done so; but not by the sanction of Government; for that has always been true to Southern interests. Again, gentlemen, look at another fact, when we have asked that more territory should be added, that we might spread the institution of slavery, have they not yielded to our demands in giving us Louisiana, Florida, and Texas, out of which four States have been carved, and ample territory for four more may be added in due time if you by this unwise and impolitic act, do not destroy this hope, and perhaps by it lose all, and have your last slave wrenched from you by stern military rule, as South America and Mexico were, or by the vindictive decree of a universal emancipation, which may reasonably be expected to follow."[418]

From Stephens' January 1861 speech:

☛ "But, again, gentlemen, what have we to gain by this proposed change of our relation to the general Government? We have always had the control of it, and can yet, if we remain in it and are as united as we have been. We have had a majority of the Presidents chosen from the South; as well as the control and management of most of those chosen from the North. We have had sixty years of Southern Presidents to their twenty-four, thus controlling the executive department. So of the judges of the Supreme Court, we have had eighteen from the South, and but eleven from the North; although nearly four-fifths of the judicial business has arisen in the Free States, yet a majority of the court has always been from the South. This we have required so as to guard against any interpretation of the Constitution unfavorable to us.

"In like manner we have been equally watchful to guard our interest in the legislative branch of Government. In choosing the presiding Presidents (*pro tem.*) of the Senate, we have had twenty-tour to their eleven. Speakers of the House we have had twenty-three, and they twelve. While the majority of the representatives, from their greater population, have always been from the North, yet we have so generally secured the Speaker, because he, to a greater extent, shapes and controls the legislation of the country. Nor have we had less control in every other department of the general Government. Attorney-Generals we have had fourteen, while the North have had but five. Foreign ministers we have had eighty-six and they but fifty-four. While three-fourths of the business which demands diplomatic agents abroad is clearly from the Free States, from their greater commercial interests, yet we have had the principal embassies, so as to secure the world's markets for our cotton, tobacco, and sugar on the best possible terms. We have had a vast majority of the higher offices of both army and navy, while a larger proportion of the soldiers and sailors were drawn from the North. Equally so of clerks, auditors, and comptrollers filling the executive department, the records show for the last fifty years that of the three thousand thus employed, we have had more than two-thirds of the same, while we have but one-third of the white population of the Republic."[419]

From Stephens' January 1861 speech:
☛ "Again, look at another item, and one, be assured, in which we have a great and vital interest; it is that of revenue, or means of supporting Government. From official documents we learn that a fraction over three-fourths of the revenue collected for the support of the Government has uniformly been raised from the North.

"Pause now, while you can, gentlemen, and contemplate carefully and candidly these important items. Leaving out of view, for the present, the countless millions of dollars you must expend in a war with the North; with tens of thousands of your sons and brothers slain in battle, and offered up as sacrifices upon the altar of your ambition—and for what? we ask again. Is it for the overthrow of the American Government, established by our common ancestry, cemented and built up by their sweat and blood, and founded on the broad principles of right, justice, and humanity? And, as such, I must declare here, as I have often done before, and which has been repeated by the greatest and wisest of statesmen and patriots in this and other lands, that it is the best and freest Government—the most equal in its rights, the most just in its decisions, the most lenient in its measures, and the most inspiring in its principles to elevate the race of men, that the sun of heaven ever shone upon.

"Now, for you to attempt to overthrow such a Government as this, under which we have lived for more than three-quarters of a century—in which we have gained our wealth, our standing as a nation, our domestic safety while the elements of peril are around us; with peace and tranquillity accompanied with unbounded prosperity and rights unassailed—is the height of madness, folly, and wickedness, to which I can neither lend my sanction nor my vote."[420]

Prior to Lincoln's War Stephens had voted against the secession of his home state of Georgia. After she decided to leave the Union, however, he made the following comment on April 23, 1861, before the Virginia Secession Convention:
☞ ". . . when the State in her sovereign capacity determined otherwise, my judgment was yielded to hers. My allegiance was due to her. My fortunes were linked with hers; her cause was my cause; and her destiny was my destiny."[421]

Stephens' April 23, 1861, speech before the Virginia Secession Convention continues:
☞ "The cause of Georgia was the cause of us all; and so I trust it will be in Virginia. Let all past differences be forgotten. Whether, if some other course had been adopted, our rights could have ultimately been secured in the old Union, is a problem now that can never be solved. I am free to confess, as I frankly do, that the late indications afford strong evidence that the majority at the North were bent upon our destruction at every cost and every hazard. At all events, we know that our only hope now is in our own strong arms and stout hearts, with unity among ourselves. Our course is adopted. We can take no steps backward. The time for compromise, if it ever existed, is past. Many entertained hopes from the 'Peace Congress'—that failed. Even an extension of the Missouri line, which was offered by prominent southern men, was sullenly rejected. Every indication of northern sentiment on the part of the dominant party there, since the election last fall, shows that they were and are bent upon carrying out their aggressive and destructive policy against us. This they insidiously expected to succeed in, by relying upon the known strong Union sentiment in the border States. They evidently relied strongly on this in Virginia. Their policy being to divide and conquer. In this, I think, however, they counted without their host.

"The people of Virginia may have been attached to the Union; but they are much more attached to their homes, their firesides and all that is dear to freemen—constitutional liberty.

"All hopes of preserving this in the old Union are gone forever. We must for the future look to ourselves. It is cheering to feel conscious that we are not without hope in that quarter. At first, I must confess, that I was not without serious apprehensions on that point. These apprehensions were allayed at Montgomery.

"The men who were sent there were not such materials as revolutions usually throw up. They seemed to understand thoroughly the position of affairs—the past, the present, and the future. They duly appreciated the magnitude of the responsibilities resting upon them, and proved themselves, I trust, not only determined to overthrow one government, but capable of building up another. Their work . . . is before you. One leading idea runs through the whole—the preservation of that time-honored constitutional liberty which they inherited from their fathers."[422]

From a November 4, 1864, letter to Alexander J. Marshall:
☛ "Secession, with us [in the South], I regarded as one of those moral or political epidemics to which States and communities are often subject—like other epidemics of a physical character to which humanity in general is subject. It was both infectious and contagious, baffling all skill and defying all treatment. Logically speaking, there was but one real and substantial cause for it. That was the open, palpable, and avowed breach of the compact of 1787, by a number of the States at the North in the matter of rendition of fugitives from service. A compact broken by one party to it is broken as to all. This is a universal rule of law amongst all people, civilized or savage. The old Union was, therefore, virtually broken by those faithless States at the North. Other irritating causes and apprehended dangers contributed to the consummation of the result at the South. But for this cause by itself, the seceding States will ever be justified in what they did by an impartial and enlightened world. The wisdom or policy of their course looking to their own interest is not now the question. That was a matter for them to determine for themselves in view of all the consequences attending it. What they [the Southern states] did they had a perfect right, moral as well as civil, to do."[423]

From November 4, 1864:
☛ "The right to resume the exercise of all powers delegated when safety required it, was declared by Virginia in her act of ratification. The Union was one eminently of consent. An attempt to continue it by force, violates the law

"Liberty Hall," servants' quarters and outbuildings

of its existence. As paradox[ic]al as it appears to many, yet it is nevertheless true, that the doctrine of the reserved sovereignty of the State, under the old constitution, carrying with it the perfect right on the part of any State to secede at pleasure, subject to no control but moral obligation, was the strongest Union doctrine consistent with the preservation of liberty ever proclaimed. . . . Governments to be strong must indeed be held together in its parts by force. The universe is held together by force, by the strongest of all forces, by Omnipotence itself; yet the power that controls its every part, preserving forever one indissoluble whole, is nothing but the simple law of attraction. This is the force that should be looked to in binding States indissolubly. This is the force that gives governments irresistible strength in the union of all their parts. . . ."[424]

From 1868:

☛ "Sovereignty is the highest and greatest of all political powers. It is itself the source as well as embodiment of all political powers, both great and small. All proceed and emanate from it. All the great powers specifically and expressly delegated in the Constitution, such as the power to declare war and make peace; to raise and support armies, to tax and lay excise duties, etc., are themselves but the incidents of Sovereignty."[425]

In an August 1868 letter to a Georgia scallywag, Stephens touched on the topic of Southern secession and Lincoln's War. Amidst the debate, Stephens asked his friend to reread his book A Constitutional View of the Late War Between the States:

☛ "[Let us focus on] . . . the great questions of the right, or wrong of secession; the right and the wrong of the war; which are so fully discussed in the book. It has nothing to do with the question of State Sovereignty, on which depends the right of secession; and with it the solution of the question, on which side, in the war that followed, is to be placed the right of the contest; and also, on which side the present evils, so seriously felt by all of us, are chargeable—on the side of secession, or on the side of those who made war to prevent it.

"Let me again ask you to re-read the book. Study it closely. Examine its array of facts—not my statement of them, but the records therein produced themselves—these enduring monuments of history. When you have done so, put to yourself these questions. Is it true that the Colonies, before their Declaration of Independence, were separate and distinct political organizations?

"Is it true, that in making the Declaration of their Independence, they voted by Colonies, and thus unanimously declared themselves to be Free and Independent (not nation) but States?

"Is it true that before this Declaration was made, a committee was raised by the Congress that made it to prepare Articles of Confederation between them as separate, distinct, sovereign States, to go into effect after the Declaration should be made?

"Is it true that these Articles of Confederation were afterwards reported and entered into, and in them it was declared:

'Each State retains its Sovereignty, Freedom and Independence, and every Power, Jurisdiction and Right which is not by this Confederation expressly delegated to the United States in Congress assembled'?

"Is it true that this Congress expressly declared that the allegiance of the citizens of the several States was due to the State?

"Is it true that in the Treaty of Peace, in 1783, Great Britain acknowledged the Independence and Sovereignty of each of the States separately, and by name?

"Is it true that the Supreme Court of the United States, in 1805, decided that 'on the 4th of October, 1776, (after the general Declaration of Independence on the 4th of July before,) the State of New Jersey was completely a Sovereign and Independent State, and had a right to compel the inhabitants of the State to become citizens thereof'?

"Is it true that Judge [Samuel] Chase, from the same bench, in 1796, gave forth these utterances:

> 'In June, 1776, the Convention of Virginia was a Free, Sovereign,
> and Independent State, and on the fourth of July, 1776, following,
> the United States, in Congress assembled, declared the thirteen
> United Colonies Free and Independent States; and that as such they
> had full power to levy war, conclude peace, &c. I consider this as
> a declaration, not that the United Colonies jointly, in a collective
> capacity, were Independent States, &c, but that each of them had
> a right to govern itself by its own authority, and its own laws
> without any control from any other power on earth'?

"Is it true that Chief Justice [John] Marshall, from the same bench, as late as 1824, declared that under the Confederation the States were completely Sovereign and Independent?

"If, after a thorough examination, the answer is Yes, as it must be, to each of these questions—for the proofs of the facts embraced in them, adduced in the volume referred to, are incontestable—then allow me, without submitting any more of a like character, now to ask you—barely for your reflection, and with a view to elicit an answer—if these be really the facts of history, does it avail anything against them, for you to inform me, however honestly and sincerely, that you do not believe that absolute paramount State Sovereignty ever did exist in this country, either before or after the adoption of the present Constitution? This is about the substance of what you say upon that subject."[426]

Stephens' August 1868 letter to the Georgia scallywag continues:
☛ "It is not my purpose to argue the case at this time. I simply ask if the facts be as set forth, were not your previous opinions, which are now repeated, founded in error? You say, for instance, 'the Government of the United States, as I understand it, is of the nature of an indissoluble partnership.'

"But is this a correct understanding of it, if the facts of its history be as set forth in the *Constitutional View*? Must not these facts be assailed and demolished, or must not this understanding be abandoned? Is not one or the other of these alternatives a logical necessity? Can opinions, theories, assumptions, or understandings of any sort be maintained against unquestionable and indisputable facts, when intellect, guided by reason is the arbiter?

"This is the view I have endeavored, and still endeavor to impress upon you. The real undeniable facts of history, and not our crude understanding of them, must prevail in this matter. Moreover, allow me to say that I do not

A note from Lincoln to Stephens, dated November 30, 1860. U.S. President-elect Lincoln is asking the soon-to-be C.S. vice president for a copy of one of his speeches. The two were on friendly terms in Washington, D.C. before the start of Lincoln's War.

know that I exactly comprehend what you mean by an indissoluble partnership. There is, and can be no such thing in law, as an indissoluble partnership between persons in any of the business transactions of life, much less can there be any such thing between Sovereign States or Nations.

"Again, what avail is it for you to tell me that the question of difference between the advocates of a strong Government [i.e., Liberals] and the advocates of a Government of delegated and limited powers [i.e., Conservatives] in the Convention that formed the present Constitution, was settled by that body 'ordaining a National Congress, a National Judiciary, and a National Executive,' &c, if the records taken from the Journal show directly the reverse of this to be the fact of the case, as those adduced in the volume referred to do most explicitly show? Is it or not true that the word *National* was stricken out of the draft of the proposed plan of Government, then before them, wherever it occurred, and the words 'United States,' or 'Congress' substituted in its place?

"Was not *National Legislature* stricken out and *Congress* put in its stead? Was not the meaning of the word *Congress* well understood? Did it not then and now mean an assemblage of States?

"*Congress*, under the first Articles of Confederation, was the meeting in council of the several separate sovereign States, through their duly appointed and accredited representatives. This well-known word, with its proper and legitimate meaning, was retained in the present Constitution. There was no change in this particular in the present Articles of Union from those of the first Confederation. *Congress* means the same now that it did before the Convention of 1787 met. It means the assemblage of sovereign States in grand council. It was known not as the National Legislature, as by some it is called, but as 'the Congress of the United States.'"[427]

Stephens' August 1868 letter continues:

☞ "Then again, what avail is it for you to tell me that 'the power to each State at its own will and pleasure to withdraw from the Union and resume the delegated powers, was not reserved' under the Constitution, if it be true, as matter of fact, that the sovereignty of the States was not surrendered by the adoption of the Constitution? That they were sovereign before must be received as an unquestionable fact. And the bare fact that all the powers possessed by the Federal Government are by universal accord admitted to be delegated only, ought to be of itself sufficient to satisfy any one that the Paramount Authority delegating must of necessity have continued to exist. So general was this opinion in the minds of those who framed the Constitution, that nothing was said on that subject in the instrument, as it first came from their hands. But, to quiet the apprehensions of many upon that point, it was soon after expressly stated in an amendment unanimously adopted by the States, that 'the powers not delegated to the United States by the Constitution, nor prohibited by it to the States, are reserved to the States respectively, or to the people.' This settled the question that sovereignty, the source of all political power, was reserved or retained by the States severally, under the second Articles of Union, as it had been under the first. So stated Samuel Adams when this amendment was before the Massachusetts Convention. No one in the Convention that framed the Constitution questioned the sovereign right of the States severally to secede from the first Articles of Union, though upon their face they were declared to be perpetual. Eleven States did thus, of their own will and pleasure, withdraw from the first Union, by virtue of this power or right, which was incident to their sovereignty, and entered into the new articles. The two other States left by them soon followed. The same power or right to withdraw in like manner from the second Articles of Union necessarily remained as an incident of the same sovereignty. Hence, if the facts of our history be as set forth in the book referred to, it must be admitted that the power to withdraw at pleasure was reserved to the States. Judge [Joseph] Story and Mr. [Daniel] Webster fully admitted this. All rational minds must admit it. The whole question therefore turns upon the truth of the facts of our history set forth in the book. These I cannot repeat here, but re-invite your attention to them.

"What you say about the power to disturb the domestic tranquillity, or injure the general welfare, not being reserved, I fully admit. The power wrongfully to disturb the domestic tranquillity of neighboring States, is not a natural right of Sovereignty. The powers reserved to the States were all the natural rights of nations, as established by the laws of nations; except such as were delegated to their co-States, and such as were covenanted not to be exercised by them separately, while the bond of their associated union should continue. In this respect there is not the slightest difference between the provisions of the present Constitution and the first Articles of Confederation. It was because the right to disturb the domestic tranquillity of their neighbors was not reserved to the States, and did not by nature belong to their Sovereignty, that the Southern States so justly complained of the settled policy of many of their Northern Confederates to disturb their domestic tranquillity, and even to stir up insurrections in them."[428]

To those, mainly uneducated Yankees, who frequently attacked Stephens (as they did all Southerners) for being a secessionist and allegedly "anti-Union," he gave this 1868 reply in his book A Constitutional View:

☞ "No stronger or more ardent Union man ever lived than I was. Not a man in the Convention which framed the Constitution of the United States, which sets forth the terms of "the Union," was or could have been more devoted to it than I was. But what Union? or the Union of what? Of course, the Union of the States under the Constitution. That was what I was so ardently devoted to. The Union is a phrase often used, I apprehend, without considering its correct import or meaning. By many it is used to signify the integrity of the country as it is called, or the unity of the whole people of the United States, in a geographical view, as one Nation.

"[My liberal colleagues maintain that the original Union created by the Founding Fathers was national in character. To them] allow me . . . to say that there never was in this country any such union as [they] . . . speak of; there never was any political union between the people of the several States of the United States, except such as resulted indirectly from the terms of agreement or Compact entered into by separate and distinct political bodies. The first

Union so formed, from which the present Union arose, was that of the [American] Colonies in 1774. They were thirteen in number. These were distinct and separate political organizations or bodies. After that the Union of States was formed under the Articles of Confederation, in 1777; and then, the modifications of the terms of this Union by the new Compact of 1787, known as the present Constitution [of the United States]. To this last Union, at first, only eleven of the original thirteen States became parties.

William Wilberforce

Afterwards the other two (North Carolina and Rhode Island) also acceded and became members. The last of these (Rhode Island) rejoined her former associates in 1790. Subsequently, twenty new members were admitted into the association, on an equal footing with those first forming it. Whatever intimate relationships, therefore, existed between the citizens of the respective thirty-three States constituting the Union in 1860, they) were created by, or sprung from, the terms of the Compact of 1787, by which the original States as States were united. These terms were properly called the Constitution of the United States; not the Constitution of one people as one society or one nation, but the Constitution of a number of separate and distinct peoples, or political bodies, known as States. The absolute Sovereignty of these original States, respectively, was never parted with by them in that or any other Compact of Union ever entered into by them."[429]

From 1868:

☛ "However strongly opposed I was to the policy of Secession, or whatever views I gave against it as a policy, or wise measure . . . I declared my convictions to be, that if the people of Georgia, in their majesty, and in the exercise of their resumed full Sovereignty, should, in a regularly constituted Convention called for that purpose, withdraw from the Compact of Union, by which she was confederated, or united, with the other States under the

Constitution, that it would be my duty to obey her high behest. [My pro-Union Speech of 1860] . . . was made mainly, it is true, against the policy of Secession for then existing grievances complained of, but also against the unconstitutionality of measures proposed to be passed by the State Legislature, with a view of dissolving the Union. The Sovereign power of the people of the State, which alone could regulate its relations with the other States, was not vested in the Legislature. That resided with the people of the State. It had never been delegated either to the State authorities, or the authorities created by the Articles of Union. It could be exercised only by the people of the State in a regularly-constituted Convention, embodying the real Sovereignty of the State—just such Convention as had agreed to and adopted the Constitution of the United States. It required the same power to unmake as it had to make it. Hence, I said—'Let the sovereignty of the people of Georgia be first heard on this question of severing the bonds that united them with the other States;' and that, whatever decision the State might thus and then make, 'my fortunes would be cast with hers and her people.'"[430]

From 1868:

☛ "In this country it is equally admitted on all hands that Sovereignty, which is the Paramount authority, resides with the People. All government, according to our axioms and maxims, is but the exercise in trust of delegated powers. The exercise of supreme or Sovereign powers may be by delegation. In this country it is entirely by delegation; but whatever is delegated may be resumed by the authority delegating. No postulate in mathematics can be assumed less subject to question than this. The exercise of supreme law-making power, even over the authority delegating it, may be legitimate so long as the delegated power is unresumed. Obedience to laws passed under such delegation of power, is, as I have said, a very different thing from allegiance which is due to the authority delegating the exercise of the supreme law-making power. Whenever the delegated powers are resumed, allegiance must be due to the resuming Sovereign power; to that which can rightfully make and unmake Constitutions.

"The Government of the United States was created by the States. All its powers are held in trust by delegation from the States. These powers are specific and limited. They are supreme within the sphere of their limitations—supreme so long as the authorities delegating them continue the trust even over the authorities delegating them; but being held entirely by delegation, they exist no longer than the party or parties delegating see fit to continue the trust. In this sense alone is the authority of the General Government supreme, even over the subjects which lie within the sphere of the

For your own eye only
Springfield, Ills. Dec. 22. 1860
Hon. A. H. Stephens—
My dear Sir

Your obliging ans-
wer to my short note is just received,
and for which please accept my
thanks— I fully appreciate the
present peril the county is in, and
the weight of responsibility on me.
Do the people of the South really
entertain fears that a Republican
administration would, directly, or
indirectly, interfere with the slaves,
or with them, about their slaves?
If they do I wish to assure you, as
once a friend, and still, I hope,
not an enemy, that there
is no cause for such fears—
The South would be in no more
danger in this respect, than it
was in the days, of Washington

Page one of another letter from Lincoln to Stephens, this one dated December 22, 1860.
Lincoln promises Stephens that he will not interfere with slavery.

I suppose, however, this does not mean this case — You think slavery is right and ought to be extended; while we think it is wrong and ought to be restricted — That I suppose is the sub— It certainly is the only substantial difference between us —

Yours very truly
A. Lincoln

Page two of the foregoing letter. Lincoln states that the only difference between them is that Stephens wants to extend slavery while he wants to restrict it (to the South).

powers with which it was intrusted by delegation. The Paramount authority in this country, Sovereignty, that to which allegiance is due, is with the People somewhere. There is no Sovereignty either in the General Government or the State Governments. These are permitted to exercise certain Sovereign powers so long only as it shall suit the Sovereign will that they shall so do, and no longer. Sovereignty itself, from which emanates all political power, I repeat, remains and ever resides with the People somewhere. And with what People? Why, of necessity, it appears to me, with the same People who delegated whatever powers the General Government has ever been intrusted with; that is, the People of the several States; not the whole People of the United States as one mass, as can be most conclusively demonstrated."[431]

From 1868:
☛ "Sovereignty cannot pass by implication. If the States were Sovereign when they entered into the Articles of Confederation, they must still remain so, unless they parted with that Sovereignty in those articles, or in the new articles—the new Constitution, as it was called—of 1787, which are the basis

of the present Union."[432]

From 1868:

☞ "Sovereign States cannot be deprived of any of their rights by implication; nor in any manner whatever but by their own voluntary consent or by submission to a conqueror."[433]

From 1868:

Stephens rightfully argued that the essential principles of our first constitution, known as "The Articles of Confederation," were not cast aside at the forming of our second one, called "The Constitution of the United States of America," asserting that:

☞ "Each State retained its Sovereignty, freedom and Independence, and every power and right which is not expressly delegated to the United States [while the] object of the Confederation was for their mutual defence, the security of their liberties and their mutual and general welfare, binding themselves to assist each other against all force offered to or attacks made upon them, or any of them, on account of religion, Sovereignty, trade, or any other pretence whatever."[434]

From 1868. The changeover from our first constitution to our second took place at the Philadelphia Convention of 1787. Of this important event in American history Stephens wrote:

☞ "No intimation was given, in any of the proceedings that led to the call of this Convention, of any wish, much less a desire, to change the character of the Federal system, or to transform it from a Confederate Republic, as it was then acknowledged to be, into a consolidated nation. It is important to pay strict attention to the proceedings at this time. The Convention was called, not to change the nature of the General Government, but to delegate to it some few additional powers, and to adjust its machinery, in accordance with these additional powers. It was with this view, and for this purpose, with this 'sole and express purpose,' that the States, in Congress, gave the movement their sanction. Now, then, how did this matter proceed? How did the States, in their Sovereign capacities, respond to this call for a Convention, to change the Articles of their Confederation, so as to remedy the evils complained of? Each of the States, be it remembered, at that time, was a perfect State, clothed with all the attributes of Sovereignty. . . . The responses of all the States show conclusively the great indisputable fact that they all, at that time, claimed to be Sovereign and Independent, and that their sole object in going into Convention at that time was barely to provide for such changes as could be made in their then Constitution, as experience had shown to be proper, and not to change its

Federal character."[435]

From 1868:
☛ "From all [the] . . . responses of the States, to the call for a Convention of the States, it clearly appears that the sole object of all was to change and modify the Articles of Confederation, so as better to provide for the wants and exigencies of 'the Union,' which must have meant the Union then existing, and which we have seen was a Union of Sovereign States. The object was not to change the Federative character of that Union. This is an important point to be kept constantly in view, and never lost sight of. The Convention was called with this sole view, and the call was responded to by every State with this sole view. . . . It was assembled as a Convention of the States. The Delegates represented distinct, separate, and acknowledged Sovereign powers."[436]

From 1868:
☛ ". . . the great controlling fact in the case, one that removes every particle of ground upon which [Liberals build their] . . . entire theory of the Government, is, that subsequently, on the 20th of June [1787], when the report of the Committee of the Whole was before the Convention, for consideration; after the whole plan, submitted by Governor [Edmund] Randolph, had been gone through with; after the ideas and objects of the members, generally, had been developed; and after the bearing of this word National, or the sense in which some used it, had been fully disclosed, and when eleven States were present, it was moved, by Mr. [Oliver] Ellsworth, of Connecticut, to strike out this resolution, that had been previously agreed to, as before stated, and to insert the following:—

> Resolved, That the Government of the United States ought to consist of a Supreme Legislative, Judiciary and Executive.

"This resolution was agreed to; and, after this action of the Convention upon this resolution, the word 'National,' wherever it occurred, throughout Governor Randolph's whole plan, was stricken out, and the 'Government of the United States,' or its equivalent, inserted. So, the 'fundamental proposition' upon which [Liberals build their] . . . whole superstructure, is completely knocked from under [them]. . . . The grounds, upon which it temporarily rested for the short space of twenty-one days, were completely removed by the Convention itself."[437]

From 1868:
☛ ". . . this is not a Government of the People of this Country as one Nation.

. . . It is still, under the Constitution, as it was under the Articles of Confederation, a Government of States, and for States. It was so agreed to in the [Philadelphia] Convention. It was so nominated in the bond. It was so submitted to the States for their approval and ratification, and not to the people of the whole country, in the aggregate, as . . . [Liberals] . . . maintain; but it was so submitted to the States, in their political organizations, and by them, as States, it was so agreed to and ratified. Each State retained the absolute power to govern its own people in its own way, in all their domestic relations, without any interference by the people of the other States, or the Federal Government, except in the specified cases set forth in the Constitution."[438]

In attacking the case for small government, states' rights, and secession, big government Liberals point to the Preamble to the Constitution, which says: "We, the people of the United States." Their claim is that this demonstrates that the Constitution "was submitted to the whole people, and by them [it was] acted upon, ratified and adopted, and not by the States, as States." Stephens' replied to this falsity in 1868:

☛ "[The Preamble] . . . shows no such thing; and it is a wonder to me how any one should ever have entertained such an idea. . . . what is the meaning of 'We, the people of the United States,' as they here stand? The meaning and sense of words must always be understood from the connection in which they are found. We have abundant and conclusive evidence that they could not have been intended to mean, in the connection where they here stand, what [Liberals] . . . would have them imply. Because, the very authority of the Delegates—their credentials—which, we have seen, stated that what they should do, should be referred back to the States, should be submitted to them, and should not be binding, unless approved by them, severally and respectively. And, besides, we know that this preamble, as it unanimously passed the Convention, on the 7th of August, 1787, was in these words:—

> We, the people of the States of New Hampshire, Massachusetts, Rhode Island and Providence Plantations, Connecticut, New York, New Jersey, Pennsylvania, Delaware, Maryland, Virginia, North Carolina, South Carolina, and Georgia, do ordain, declare, and establish the following Constitution . . .

"This shows what was the meaning of the Convention. It was we the people of each State. The change in the phraseology was made by a sub-committee on style, not by the Convention, except in their agreement to the Report of said committee. Why was it made? For a very obvious reason. It was not known which of the States would ratify it. Hence it was exceedingly inappropriate to set forth in advance the States by name. By the terms of the

Page one of Stephens' December 14, 1860, letter to Lincoln.

Page two of Stephens' December 14, 1860, letter to Lincoln.

Constitution, Article VII, it was to go into operation between such of the States as might ratify it, if as many as nine or more should do so. The committee on style readily perceived that it would be exceedingly out of place, to have, in the preamble to the organic law, terms embracing a people, or States, who might not put themselves under it. For instance, Rhode Island and North Carolina did not ratify the Constitution for some time. During this period they were entirely out of the Union. They might have remained out until now. Suppose they had. How oddly would this preamble to the Constitution have read: 'We the people of New Hampshire, Rhode Island, North Carolina, etc., in order to form a more perfect Union,' etc., when the people of Rhode Island and North Carolina had done no such thing. To preserve symmetry in their work, and retain the same idea was what the Committee did in their change of phraseology. As they put it, it would embrace the people of such States only as should adopt it. They would then be the people of the States, respectively, which would thereby be United. States United and United States mean the same thing. Upon a close scrutiny of the change of language in the Preamble, as it was at first adopted by the Convention, and as it was reported by the committee on style, some exceedingly interesting views are suggested, but these are far from favoring the inference usually drawn from it. Let me call your special attention to them, for they have a direct and important bearing upon the point. . . . The words, as agreed to at first, in Convention, as we have seen, were:

> We, the people of the States of New Hampshire, Massachusetts, Rhode Island and Providence Plantations, Connecticut, New York, New Jersey, Pennsylvania, Delaware, Maryland, Virginia, North Carolina, South Carolina, and Georgia, do ordain, declare, and establish the following Constitution for the government of ourselves and our posterity.

"Now look closely to the words substituted, and weigh nicely the import of the words left out, as well as those inserted. As the clause was changed by the committee on style, and afterwards unanimously adopted in the Convention, it reads as follows:

> We, the people of the United States, in order to form a more perfect Union, establish justice, insure domestic tranquillity, provide for the common defence, promote the general welfare, and secure the blessings of liberty to ourselves and our posterity, do ordain and establish this Constitution for the United States of America.

"The most striking difference in phraseology between the two, is that which sets forth the object in forming 'a more perfect Union,' etc., to be, to 'ordain and establish this Constitution,' not for the people in any sense, but for States as political societies. As the words originally stood, the inference might have been drawn from the bare words themselves, that the object was to form a government for the people in the aggregate. 'We, the people of the States of New Hampshire, Massachusetts, etc., do ordain and establish the following Constitution for the government of ourselves and our posterity.' From these words, I say, the inference might have been drawn that the object was to form a government for the people in the aggregate, but this inference is completely rebutted by the change of phraseology. As it stands, the instrument 'is ordained and established' as a Constitution for States—for the United States. The same as if it read 'for the States of this Union.'

"The change, in this particular, is very important, and the very Preamble, which is so often alluded to, for a directly opposite purpose, conclusively shows that the Government was intended to be, and is a Government States, and for States, as I said. In the change of phraseology the introduction of the word Union has a wonderful significance of itself. The new Constitution was proposed 'in order to form a more perfect Union,' that is, it was to make more perfect 'the Union' then existing. That, we have seen, was a Union of States under the Articles of Confederation. It was to revise these Articles, to enlarge the powers under them, or, in other words, to perfect that Union, that the Convention was called; and that was the object aimed at in all their labors to the conclusion of their work as set forth in this Preamble. So much for the evidence furnished by the Preamble."[439]

When asked what the purpose of the Philadelphia Convention of 1787 was, Stephens gave this response in 1868:
☛ "The object was to strengthen the Union of States. That was the only Union existing, and the only Union to which they could have referred. The object was to strengthen or consolidate the bonds of that Union, and not to weaken them, much less to sever and utterly destroy them, as would be the import of the word according to [the Nationalist's] . . . construction. The object was to render the Union of States more perfect or better calculated to accomplish the ends for which it was at first formed. Is not this perfectly clear and true beyond all question? Could any thing be more preposterous or absurd than to suppose that such a body of men, so called together, would, in giving an account of their labors to the body calling them, have stated that the great object with them had been to do the very reverse of what they had been called to do? . . . Do not the words of [the delegates] themselves, in their connection with their contemporaneous action, under all the circumstances and surroundings, most conclusively rebut the inference that you and others draw from them, and establish beyond the shadow of doubt that the object was not to merge the Sovereignty of all the States into one, and to abandon the Union of Sovereign States by the establishment of a great National Government? [It was, in essence, a] change of machinery in operating the system, and not a change of the basis of the system."[440]

From 1868:
☛ "[As further proof of the intention of the Founding Fathers, we have the letters of George Washington.] They show that [he] . . . clearly understood the new system to be a Federal system [i.e. a Confederacy], as the old one was

[under the Articles of Confederation]. That there was no change of the locus of ultimate absolute Sovereignty under it. That the Union, which was perfected and consolidated, was to be still a Union of States, each Sovereign as before, and not a Union of the entire people of the whole country, as [Liberals contend]. . . . Washington [in fact] emphatically styles it, 'the new Confederacy'—'the new Federal System.' [Liberals say] that the present Government is no Confederacy, that 'we had already enough of a Confederacy.' Here again, [they are] . . . directly at issue with Washington. Washington speaks of the new system, as of the old, and styles it 'the new Confederacy.'"[441]

William Pinkney

Nineteenth-Century Liberals, as they are today, were confused over the words "federal" and "confederate." As I discuss in my "Notes to the Reader," originally they both had the same meaning, as "federal" is merely an abbreviation of "confederal." In 1868, Stephens too found himself having to explain this to his progressive Northern colleagues:

☛ "Federal and Confederate mean substantially the same thing. When applied to States they both imply and import a Compact between States. Washington, in one of his letters . . . spoke of the new Government as 'a Confederacy.' In another, to Sir Edward Newenham, dated the 20th July, 1788, he speaks of the new Government then ratified by enough States to carry it into effect as a 'Confederated Government.' In his response to the reply of the Senate to his first speech to Congress after the new Government was organized, in 1789, he expressed his happiness in the conviction that 'the Senate would at all times co-operate in every measure which may tend to promote the welfare of this Confederated Republic.' These are the terms by which he characterized 'the Union,' after the present Constitution was formed and after it was in operation. There is no difference between the words Federal and Confederated as thus used and applied. We see that Washington used them both, at different times, to signify the same thing, that is, the Union of the American States under the Constitution."[442]

From 1868:

☛ "It being universally admitted, then, by the advocates of the Constitution at the time of its adoption, that it was Federal [Confederate] in its character, and that the Government under it would be a Confederated or Federal Republic, which means the same thing, [I would like to discuss] . . . what is the nature and very essence of all such Governments. Dropping Dictionaries, let us go to writers upon the Laws of Nations. Here is [Baron de] Montesquieu [the French philosopher]. In Book ix, chap. 1, he speaks first of Republics generally. These may exist either under Democratic or Aristocratic Constitutions.

> 'If a Republic is small, it is destroyed by a foreign force; if it be large, it is ruined by an internal imperfection.
>
> 'It is, therefore, very probable, that mankind would have been at length obliged to live constantly under the Government of a single person, had they not contrived a kind of Constitution that has all the internal advantages of a Republican, together with the external force of a Monarchical Government. I mean a Confederate Republic.
>
> 'This form of Government is a Convention, by which several small States agree to become members of a larger one which they intend to form. It is a kind of assemblage of societies, that constitute a new one, capable of increasing by means of new associations, till they arrive to such a degree of power, as to be able to provide for the security of the united body.
>
> 'The State (that is the State formed by the Confederation) may be destroyed on one side, and not on the other; the Confederacy may be dissolved, and the Confederates preserve their Sovereignty.
>
> 'As this Government is composed of petty Republics, it enjoys the internal happiness of each; and with respect to its external situation, it is possessed, by means of the association, of all the advantages of large monarchies.'

"This, by the highest authority, is the form and nature of all Federal or Confederated Republics. The Government of the United States, in the judgment of [President George] Washington, belongs to that class. All the States of the Union were small Republics [i.e., tiny nation-states] within themselves. By entering the Union for foreign and inter-State purposes, they did not, therefore, according to Montesquieu, forfeit or part with their separate sovereignty. On the same subject, [Emerich de] Vattel, another writer, universally admitted to be authority of high order, says:

'Several Sovereign and Independent States may unite themselves together by a perpetual Confederacy, without ceasing to be, each individually, a perfect State. They will together constitute a Federal Republic; their joint deliberations will not impair the Sovereignty of each member, though they may, in certain respects, put some restraint on the exercise of it in virtue of voluntary engagements.'

"That, I maintain, was exactly what the States of our Union did, by the adoption of the Constitution. . . . This, I think, is quite enough to satisfy [the Liberals] . . . that whatever apprehensions were indulged in by many as to results from abuse of powers, yet it was universally admitted by the advocates of the Constitution that a Federal Republic [i.e., a Confederacy] was to be established by it, and not a National Consolidation."[443]

In 1868, concerning the U.S. Constitution and state sovereignty, Stephens said:
☞ ". . . after scanning the whole, taken together, what section, clause, phrase or word, on the face of the Constitution itself, shows any intention, on the part of the framers, to merge the separate Sovereignty of all the States into one, under it; and, by its adoption, to establish a National Government, instead of perfecting and continuing, under a new organization, with enlarged powers, the Federal Union, then existing between the States, and for the remedying of which, the Convention was called? It was made, we see, by States. It was to be established, we see, not over, but between, the States ratifying it.

"[For those familiar with the U.S. Constitution, is] . . . not the leading idea, throughout the whole instrument, that the new Government was to be a Compact between States, as the old one was? States pervade the whole instrument. The Senators are to be elected by the Legislatures of the several States. The House of Representatives is to be composed of members, chosen by the people of the several States; and to be chosen by electors, possessing such qualifications as each State, for itself, may prescribe for the electors of the most numerous branch of its own State Legislature."[444]

From 1868:
☞ "Every law that has been passed, from the beginning, under this Constitution, as under the Articles of Confederation, derives its sole authority, as its face shows, from States in Congress assembled!

"The whole operation of the Government, from its first starting, depended upon the action of the States. The election of President and Vice President, from the first to the last, depended entirely upon the States, as States, and, also, the election of Senators. Nor can there be a House of

Representatives in the Congress without the co-operation of the States! The General Government, created by the instrument, has no authority, as appears from its face, to enter any State, or take jurisdiction over a foot of her soil, even for the erection of forts and arsenals, etc., except by her consent, first had and obtained by contract or purchase. This shows that the Right of Eminent Domain, the indisputable attribute and accompaniment of Sovereignty, remained with the States, severally, even over such places as might thus pass, in fee, from them, or their citizens, to the United States, as in like purchases, in all cases whatsoever.

"What is there, then, in this whole instrument, that looks towards such a consolidation of the whole people of this country into one community or Nation, as [Liberals and Nationalists contend]?"[445]

From 1868:

☛ "[Under the U.S. Constitution it] . . . is especially stipulated, that no amendment shall ever be made, which shall deprive the States of their equal suffrage in the Senate! Does not this clearly show where ultimate Sovereign power rests under this system? That is, that it remains with the States severally, now, just as it did under the Confederation."[446]

From 1868:

☛ "Were States ever more Providentially, yea, Divinely, established, than [ours in the U.S. have] . . . these had been? Under their whole superstructure, in their Declaration of Independence, lie the great truths, announced by political bodies for the first time in the history of the world, of the capacity and right of man to self-government. That all Governments 'derive their just powers from the consent of the governed,' and that, 'whenever any Government becomes destructive of the ends' for which it is

David Wilmot

established, 'it is the right of the people to alter or abolish it, and to institute a new Government, laying its foundation on such principles, and organizing its powers in such forms, as to them may seem most likely to effect their safety and happiness.' This is asserted to be the inalienable right of all Peoples and all States! On these immutable principles, the Governments of these States had been established, separately, and severally. Were States ever established that so well deserved to live forever?"[447]

On February 6, 1788, Massachusetts ratified the U.S. Constitution. Stephens often referred to this particular document in order to prove that the U.S. was based on and around the right of state sovereignty, as he did in the following excerpt from 1868:
☛ "Here we see potent words! The instrument is recognized as a new Constitution! New in contradistinction to the old one! That was the Articles of Confederation. It is distinctly declared to be a Compact to form a more perfect Union—a more perfect Union, of course, between the same parties. Those parties were the several States, or the people of the several States, in their Sovereign character. We see it was adopted as 'a Constitution for the United States of America'—not, as I have often said, for the whole American people, but for the American States united by the Compact. The Government, we see, was to be Federal [Confederate]. The Supreme Court of the United States is styled 'the Supreme Judicial Federal [Confederate] Court.' The whole proceedings, from beginning to end, show upon their face Federal [Confederate] action and Federal [Confederate] engagements. The instrument, ratified, was directed to be sent 'to the United States in Congress assembled.'"[448]

From 1868:
☛ "[In Virginia's June 25, 1788, ratification of the U.S. Constitution] . . . is to be noted that . . . they expressly declare and make known that the powers granted under it may be resumed by them whensoever they may be perverted to their injury."[449]

From 1868. After reviewing all of the state's ratification assemblies and documents concerning the U.S. Constitution, Stephens noted:
☛ "The leading idea in all the Conventions was that a Confederate Republic was to be established by it upon the model set forth in Montesquieu. According to that model an artificial State is created for Foreign or National, as well as inter State purposes, and these only, by several small Republics, thus Confederating, for their common defence and happiness; each retaining its separate Sovereignty, and the artificial State so created by them being, at all

times, subject to their will and power. That this artificial State so created may be dissolved, and yet the separate Republic survive, retaining, at all times, their State organization and Sovereignty. This model of a Confederate Republic, by Montesquieu, was the leading idea with the advocates of the system, as appears from their debates, in every State where we have access to them.

"Now, then, after this review, is it not clear that the United States are, or constitute, a Confederated Republic (as Washington styled it), bound together by the solemn Compact of Union, entered into by the several members thereof, under the Constitution? . . . Is not the Constitution, as appears not only from the history of its formation thus given, but from its face, a Compact between Sovereign States?"[450]

From 1868. On January 3, 1838, the U.S. Senate passed a resolution in which:
☛ "More than two to one of the Senate of the United States affirmed most positively and solemnly that the Union of the States was Federal [Confederate], and that in entering into it under the Constitution, the States did so severally as free, independent, Sovereign Powers. That the Union was one of States, formed by States, and not by the people in the aggregate as one nation."[451]

In his book A Constitutional View, *after reviewing numerous documents and letters from the period of the Founding Fathers, Stephens made this statement in 1868:*
☛ "[It is obvious then] . . . that the Constitution of the United States was formed by separate, distinct, and Sovereign States. This is the conclusion to which we are all, however willingly or reluctantly, compelled to come at last, not only by the testimony of witnesses of the highest order, and by the decisions of the judicial tribunal of the highest authority, the Supreme Court of the United States, Chief Justice [John] Marshall at its head, but by the everlasting records themselves, by all the great facts of our history, which can never be obliterated or effaced."[452]

From 1868:
☛ "Now as to the rightfulness of the State's thus resuming her Sovereign powers! In doing it she *seceded* from that Union, to which, in the language of Mr. [Thomas] Jefferson, as well as General Washington, she had *acceded* as a Sovereign State. She repealed her ordinance by which she ratified and agreed to the Constitution and became a party to the Compact under it. She declared herself no longer bound by that Compact, and dissolved her alliance with the other parties to it. The Constitution of the United States, and the laws passed in pursuance of it, were no longer the supreme law of the people of Georgia, any more than the treaty with France was the supreme law of both countries,

after its abrogation, in 1798, by the same rightful authority which had made it in the beginning. [Emphasis added, L.S.]

"In answer to [the Liberals'] . . . question, whether she could do this without a breach of her solemn obligations, under the Compact, I give this full and direct answer: she had a perfect right so to do, subject to no authority, but the great moral law which governs the intercourse between Independent Sovereign Powers, Peoples, or Nations. Her action was subject to the authority of that law and none other. It is the inherent right of Nations, subject to this law alone, to disregard the obligations of Compacts of all sorts, by declaring themselves no longer bound in any way by them. This, by universal consent, may be rightfully done, when there has been a breach of the Compact by the other party or parties. It was on this principle, that the United States abrogated their treaty with France, in 1798. The justifiableness of the act depends, in every instance, upon the circumstances of the case. The general rule is, if all the other States—the Parties to the Confederation—faithfully comply with their obligations, under the Compact of Union, no State would be morally justified in withdrawing from a Union so formed, unless it were necessary for her own preservation. Self-preservation is the first law of nature, with States or Nations, as it is with individuals.

"But in this case the breach of plighted faith was not on the part of Georgia, or those States which withdrew or attempted to withdraw from the Union. Thirteen of their Confederates had openly and avowedly disregarded their obligations under that clause of the Constitution which covenanted for the rendition of fugitives from service, to say nothing of the acts of several of them, in a like open and palpable breach of faith, in the matter of the rendition of fugitives from justice. These are facts about which there can be no dispute. Then, by universal law, as recognized by all Nations, savage as well as civilized, the Compact, thus broken by some of the Parties, was no longer binding upon the others. The breach was not made by the seceding States. Under the circumstances, and the facts of this case, therefore, the legal as well as moral right, on the part of Georgia, according to the laws of Nations and nature, to declare herself no longer bound by the Compact, and to withdraw from the Union under it, was perfect and complete. These principles are too incontestably established to be questioned, much less denied, in the forum of reason and justice."[453]

From 1868:

☛ "This right of a State to consider herself no longer bound by a Compact which, in her judgment, has been broken by her Confederates, and to secede from a Union, formed as ours was, has nothing about it, either new or novel.

It is incident to all Federal Republics. It is not derived from the Compact itself. It does not spring from it at all. It is derived from the same source that the right is derived to abrogate a treaty by either or any of the parties to it. That is seldom set forth in the treaty itself, and yet it exists, whether it be set forth or not. So, in any Federal Compact whatever, the parties may or may not expressly provide for breaches of it. But where no such provision is made, the right exists by the same laws of Nations which govern in all matters of treaties or conventions between Sovereigns. The admission of the right of Secession, under this law, on the part of the several States of our Union, by Mr. [Daniel] Webster and Judge [Joseph] Story, if it be true that the Constitution is a Compact between the States, might be considered ample authority, in answer to [the Liberals'] . . . question on that point; since the conclusion, to which we arrived, that it is such a Compact."[454]

Contrary to Northern mythology, the Southern states were not the first to consider secession from the Union. The movement actually got its start, like both the American slave trade and American slavery, in the North—with New England, specifically. In December 1814 and January 1815, several of the New England states gathered at the Hartford Convention in Connecticut to consider seceding from the Union to form what was to be called the 'New England Confederacy." Stephens referred to this event in his book A Constitutional View, *in 1868:*

☞ ". . . the right of a State to withdraw from the Union was never denied or questioned, that I am aware of, by any jurist, publicist, or statesman of character and standing, until Kent's Commentaries appeared, in 1826, nearly forty years after the Government had gone into operation! From the weight of evidence, therefore, the conclusion follows, that in the opinion of the [Founding] fathers generally, as well as of the great mass of the people throughout the country, the right existed. It has been stated by high authority [U.S. President James Buchanan], that 'the right of Secession is not a plant of Southern origin—it first sprung up in the North.' A more accurate statement would be that it was not sectional but continental in its origin. It was generally recognized in all parts of the Union during the earlier days of the Republic."[455]

From 1868:
☞ "In what [Liberals] . . . consider . . . the weakness of our Government [i.e., state sovereignty], according to my idea of its nature, I repeat, its chief strength, its great beauty, its complete symmetry, its ultimate harmony, and, indeed, its very perfection, mainly consist; certainly, so long as the objects aimed at in its formation are the objects aimed at in its administration. And, on this principle, on the full recognition of the absolute ultimate Sovereignty of the several States,

Stephens' residence at Richmond, Virginia

I did consider it the best, and the strongest, and the grandest Government on earth! My whole heart and soul were devoted to the Constitution, and the Union under it, with this understanding of its nature, character, objects, and functions!

"When, therefore, the State of Georgia seceded, against my judgment, viewing the measure in the light of policy, only, and not of right (for the causes, as we have seen, and shall see more fully, hereafter, were more than ample to justify the act, as a matter of right), I felt it to be my duty to go with her, not only from a sense of the obligations of allegiance, but from other high considerations of patriotism of not much less weight and influence. These considerations pressed upon the mind the importance of maintaining this principle [the right of secession], which lies at the foundation of all Federal systems; and to which we were mainly indebted, in ours, for all the great achievements of the past. It was under this construction of the nature of our system, that all these achievements had been attained. This was the essential and vital principle of the system, to which I was so thoroughly devoted. It was that which secured all the advantages of Confederation, without the risk of Centralism and Absolutism; and on its preservation depended, not only the safety and welfare, and even existence, of my own State, but the safety, welfare, and ultimate existence of all the other States of the Union! The States were older than the Union! They made it! It was but their own creation! Their preservation was of infinitely more importance than its continuance! The Union might cease to exist, and yet the States continue to exist, as before! Not so with the Union, in case of the destruction or annihilation of the States! With their extinction, the Union necessarily becomes extinct also! They may survive it, and form another, more perfect, if the lapse of time and changes of events show it to be necessary, for the same objects had in view when it was formed; but it can never survive them! What may be called a Union may spring from the common ruins, but it would not be the Union of the Constitution!—the Union of States! By whatever name it might be called, whether Union, Nation, Kingdom, or any thing else, according to the taste of its dupes or its devotees, it would, in reality, be nothing but that deformed and hideous Monster which rises from the decomposing elements of dead States, the world over, and which is well known by the friends of Constitutional Liberty, everywhere, as the Demon of Centralism, Absolutism, Despotism! This is the necessary reality of that result, whether the Imperial Powers be seized and wielded by the hands of many, of few, or of one!"[456]

From 1868:
☞ "Had this foundation principle of the system [state sovereignty] then been generally acknowledged [by Abraham Lincoln in 1861]—had no military force been called out to prevent the exercise of this right of withdrawal on the part of the seceding States—had no war been waged against Georgia and the other States, for their assertion and maintenance of this right, had not this primary law of our entire system of Government been violated in the war so waged, I cannot permit myself to entertain the shadow of a doubt, that the whole controversy, between the States and Sections, would, at no distant day, have been satisfactorily and harmoniously adjusted, under the peaceful and beneficent operation of this very law itself. Just as all perturbations and irregularities are adjusted in the solar system, by the simple law of gravitation, from which alone it sprung in the beginning, and on which alone its continuance, with its wonderfully harmonious workings, depends!"[457]

From 1868:
☞ ". . . if . . . the whole assumption on which the Union was formed was wrong,—if it were not for the true and best interests of all the States, constituted as they were, to be so united,—if it were true, as asserted by the controlling [Liberal] spirits of the derelict [Northern] States, that the

Constitution itself as to them, was but a 'covenant with death and an agreement with Hell,'—then, of course, the re-adjustment would not have taken place, and ought not to have taken place. But I did not believe that the masses of the people in these States entertained any such sentiments towards the work of their Fathers!

"My opinion was, that it only required those masses to see, feel, and appreciate the great advantages of that Union to them; and to realize the fact that a Compact, broken by them, could not longer be binding upon others, as Mr. [Daniel] Webster had said, to cause them to compel their officials to comply with the terms of an engagement, which, upon the whole, was of so great importance to their best interests. My convictions were equally strong that, when this was done, the masses of the people at the South, influenced by like considerations, would have controlled all opposition to their cheerful and cordial return to their proper places.

"There would have been no war, no bloodshed, no sacking of towns and cities, no desolation, no billions of treasure expended, on either side, and no million of lives sacrificed in the unnatural and fratricidal strife; there would have been none of the present troubles about restoration, or reconstruction; but, instead of these lamentable scenes, a new spectacle of wonder would have been presented for the guide and instruction of the astonished Nations of the earth, greater than that exhibited after the Nullification pacification, of the matchless workings of our American Institutions of Self-Government by the people!"[458]

Stephens made this reply in 1869 to a critique of him by Northern abolitionist Horace Greeley:

☛ "What he says about Secession having been carried in the Southern States by 'a violent, subversive, bullying, terrorizing, minority, overawing and stifling' a majority of the people of these States, is nothing but bald and naked assertion, which cannot be maintained against the facts of history. The question was as thoroughly discussed as any ever was before the people. Conventions were regularly called by the duly constituted authorities of the States, and members duly elected thereto, according to law in all the States, which seceded before Mr. Lincoln's Proclamation of War. These elections were as orderly as elections usually are in any of the States on great occasions. In these Conventions, Ordinances of Secession were passed by decided majorities! It is true that a large minority in all these Conventions, save one, and in all these States, were opposed to Secession as a question of policy; very few in any of them questioned the Right, or doubted their Duty to go with the majority. But after Mr. Lincoln's Proclamation of War—after his illegal and unconstitutional

Alexander Hamilton Stephens

call for troops—after his suspension of the Writ of *Habeas Corpus*, no people on earth were ever more unanimous in any cause than were the people of the Southern States, in defence of what they deemed the great essential principles of American Free Institutions! There was not one in ten thousand of the people, in at least ten of the Southern States, whose heart and soul were not thoroughly enlisted in the cause! Nor did any people on earth ever make greater or more heroic sacrifices for its success, during four long years of devastation, blood, and carnage!

"A majority of the people overawed and terrorized by a minority! Indeed!"

"If so, what became of this majority when the Confederate Armies, which stood between them and their deliverers, were overpowered? Where is this majority now, even with the sweeping disfranchisement which silences so many of the overawing tyrants? Why has it not been permitted to exercise the inalienable Right of Self-Government, even with the reinforcement of the enfranchised blacks? Why are so many of these States, till this day, held under military rule, with their whole populations 'pinned' to very bad Government by Federal [U.S.] bayonets, under the pretext of their continued 'disloyalty?' This assertion, as to the state of things in the beginning, is as utterly groundless in fact, as it is utterly inconsistent with the gratuitous assumptions on which the present pretext is based!

"Is it not amazing . . . that Mr. Greeley in the face of the facts for the last four years, to say nothing of those of the war, when, according to his own showing, the Administration at Washington in rushing into it, were in 'the wrong'—I say, to omit all mention of the wrongs of the war, its immense sacrifices of blood and treasure, is it not amazing in the highest degree, that Mr. Greeley, in the face of the facts of the last four years only, should now repeat to us the Principles of American Independence as his creed? Have not the Constitutions of ten States, as made and adopted by the people thereof, 'founded on such principles and organized in such form as seemed to them most likely to effect their safety and happiness,' been swept from existence by military edict? Have not the people in these ten States, including the arbitrarily enfranchised blacks, been denied the right to form new Constitutions, laying their foundations on such principles and organizing its powers in such form as to them shall seem most likely to effect their safety and happiness? Have they not been required, and literally compelled, to form such Constitutions as seemed most likely to effect the safety and security of the dominant faction at Washington?"[459]

On September 21, 1870, Stephens replied publicly to U.S. Attorney General Amos T. Akerman, who had savaged the vice president's book A Constitutional View of the Later War Between the States. *Stephens does an excellent job of popping the inflated ego of the meddling, self-righteous, uninformed, anti-South Yankee—who evinced an attitude that is, sadly, still prevalent among many Northerners to this very day. The essay later appeared in Stephens' 1872 book* The Reviewers Reviewed:

☞ "Liberty Hall, Crawfordville, Ga., September 21, 1870. To the Editor of the *Constitutionalist*, Augusta, Georgia: Dear Sir:—You will, I trust, allow me the use of your columns to take such notice of two speeches recently made by Hon. Amos T. Akerman, Attorney-General of the United States, as I think due to myself, due to him, and due to some, at least, of the very grave matters referred to by him in both.

"In the first of these speeches, made at Washington City, I am directly charged and accused by him with having promulgated doctrines which he characterizes as '*pernicious*,' and which he says '*must be suppressed*.'

"In the other of these speeches, delivered at Atlanta, Georgia, while my name is omitted; yet his official denunciations, in like spirit, are chiefly directed against the same political heresies, according to his standard.

"These dangerous and 'pernicious doctrines' he is pleased to say, are to be found in the two volumes published by me upon the 'Late War between the States.'

"This quasi public arraignment by the Attorney-General of the United States, and would-be, perhaps, 'Crown Officer' of a firmly established Empire, I am by no means disposed to evade; and, therefore, ask the favor, through the medium of the *Constitutionalist*, to enter a traverse, and to make known to him and to the world, that I hold myself in readiness to meet him, or any body else, upon the merits of his 'Bill of Information,' thus filed; and without any technical exceptions on my part, as to the informality in which it has been brought forward.

"The only tribunal I desire is the bar of an enlightened public opinion. The only arena I wish, for the settlement of all the questions involved, is the forum of reason; where no weapons or force are to be used, but the power of truth and logic. So armed on such a field, I do not shrink from the fullest investigation of all matters discussed in the work, to which he alludes, nor from the judgment which may be rendered upon them, after such a hearing, by the intelligent and unbiased of the present or future generations.

"What, then, are the errors in fact or argument in either of the volumes referred to, which, in the opinion of this high officer, are so dangerous and '*pernicious*'—so *poisonous and death-producing*—as that they ought not to be thus inquired into, or even tolerated by discussion, but ought to be summarily and arbitrarily '*suppressed?*'

"1st. Is it an erroneous, and 'pernicious doctrine' to maintain, as the book does, that the United States constitute, not a single Republic, but a Federal Republic; and that the Union, about which Mr. Attorney-General says so much, is a Federal Union—a Union of separate, distinct States, each State of the Union being a perfect State, as known in Public Law?

"2nd. Is it an error in fact or doctrine to maintain, as the book does, that these States, upon entering into this Union, were recognized by themselves, as well as other powers, as separate, independent, Sovereign States?

"3rd. Is it an error in fact or doctrine to maintain, as the book does, that the Constitution of 1787 is the basis of the present Union; and that it was formed by the States in their sovereign character, and for them in their sovereign character: or, in other words, that it is a Constitution 'made by States and for States;' and that the Sovereignty of the States was not parted with by them in its ratification?

Stephen Russell Mallory

"4th. Is it an error in fact or doctrine to maintain, as the book does, that the Federal Government is entirely Conventional in its character— that it was created by the States solely with a view to the better regulation of their inter-State and foreign affairs, and the greater security of their perpetual existence as Sovereign States, by their mutual pledge and guaranty to this end—and that the Federal Government, so created, possesses no inherent powers whatever—that all the powers it rightfully holds, or can rightfully exercise, are held from the States, and from them by delegation only?

"5th. Is it an error in fact or doctrine to maintain, as the book does, that all the powers, so held by this Federal or Conventional Government, are particularly enumerated and limited in the Constitution; and that the exercise of any power outside of these limitations is nothing but a usurpation, and should be set aside by the courts as a nullity?

"6th. Is it an error in fact or doctrine to maintain, as the book does, that the Constitution of the United States, so made, was a Compact between the States ratifying it—the States being the parties to it; and that it is binding between them, as all other like Compacts by the laws of nations?

"7th. Is it an error in fact or doctrine to maintain, as the book does, that all delegated powers by Sovereign States can, by the laws of nations, be rightfully resumed by the party delegating them, when the purposes for which they were delegated are not attained?

"8th. Is it an error in fact to assert, as the book does, that quite a number of the Northern States of the Union, before the Secession of any of its Southern members, (under the influence of that faithless [Northern Liberal] faction which now rules this country by fraud and usurpation,) did openly and confessedly refuse to perform their covenanted obligations under a clause of the Constitution, without which that Compact never would have been agreed to, or the Union, under it, entered into by the Southern States?

"9th. Is it an error in fact to state, as the book does, that the present Chief-Justice [Salmon P.] Chase fully admitted this breach of faith on the part of these Northern States; and openly declared in the Peace Congress in February, 1861, that they never would perform these admitted obligations on their part?

"10th. Is it an error in fact to maintain, as the book does, that no one of the Southern States which seceded or attempted to secede from the Union, because of this breach of faith, on the part of their Confederates, was ever untrue to her covenants in the Compact of Union?

"11th. Is it an error in fact or doctrine to maintain, as the book does, that this open and confessed breach of faith on the part of their Northern Confederates, according to the laws of all nations, whether savage or civilized, completely absolved the Southern States from their obligations under the Compact, and fully justified their withdrawal?

"12th. Is it an error in fact to maintain, as the book does, that the Covenant-Constitution-breaking [Northern] States did afterwards hold, that the Seceding States were still bound to perform their part of the Compact, notwithstanding their own acknowledged breach of faith, and that they went to war against them to compel them to remain in the Union, and discharge their obligations under the Constitution?

"13th. Is it an error in fact or doctrine, to maintain, as the book does, that the war, thus inaugurated, was a 'War between States,' and in no proper or just sense a Rebellion or Civil War?

"14th. Is it an error in fact to maintain, as the book does, that the only pretext on the part of the Northern States, for waging this war, thus inaugurated between the States, was 'the preservation of the Union of the States, with all the dignity, equality, and rights of the several States unimpaired?'

"15th. Is it an error in fact to maintain, as the book does, that when the Seceding States abandoned their struggle for a separation, and agreed to the terms of capitulation, which was substantially an acquiescence, so far as armed resistance was concerned, in the declaration upon which the war was waged against them; the other States, the Covenant-breakers themselves—under the rule of the same revolutionary faction—after the sacrifice of hundred of thousands of lives and thousands of millions of dollars, changed their position in Congress, and said that they could not safely permit that to be done for which they had waged the war—that they could not safely allow a restoration of the Union of the States under the Constitution for which they had shed so much blood and expended so much treasure! But that these acquiescing States should be shorn of their 'dignity, equality and rights' by a process of 'Reconstruction' according to their liking, though outside of the Constitution, before being allowed representation in the Congress of the States?

"16th. Is it an error in fact or doctrine, on the review of this conduct, to ask, as the book does, 'Is there to be found in the annals of mankind a parallel of such unblushing, double-faced, insolent, and infamous iniquity?'

"These, Mr. Editor, are a few of the positions and doctrines maintained in the two volumes referred to by Mr. Attorney-General; and if they, founded, as they are, upon indisputable facts, set forth irrefutable truths, to what or whom, let me ask him and the world, is their promulgation either dangerous or 'pernicious?' Is it to the cause of public liberty, or to the true friends of the institutions of our ancestors, or only to the policy and secret designs of those who are aiming at their overthrow and subversion?

"Mr. Attorney-General in his Bill of Information makes very few distinct specifications touching the 'pernicious' doctrines of the two volumes which, he says, 'must be suppressed.' Two only of these are deemed worthy of notice at this time.

"The first is, that I have asserted that 'the Reconstruction measures were monstrous, and pronounced that all the Government had done for four years was monstrous, and threatened the liberties of the people.'

"In answer to this I have simply to say, that if the foregoing positions maintained in the book are unassailable, is it not undeniably true that the whole of 'these Reconstruction measures,' with all their concomitants, are not only monstrous outrages, but most deadly blows directed at the very vitals of the Constitution, as well as the liberties of the people?

"The other of these specifications is, that I have attempted to show that '[John] Marshall,' and others named by him, 'were wrong, and that Calhoun was right' in his views of the Constitution.

St. George Tucker

"In answer to this charge it is only necessary to refer to the book itself, which Mr. Attorney-General may very well wish to have suppressed, if for no other object than to shield himself from the exposure of having made a very unfair statement, not to say palpable misrepresentation. In the book no opinion of Marshall is assailed; but, on the contrary, some of the most important positions in it—those doubtless deemed by the would-be 'Crown Officer,' most 'pernicious' to his own views, aims, and objects—are not only fortified but in contestably established by the authority of this eminent Chief-Justice of the Supreme Court of the United States.

"It was he who announced from the Bench of that Court the most 'pernicious doctrine,' that the States composing this Union at the time, formed their present Constitution as Sovereign States.

"It was he who held and proclaimed from the same Bench, that all the

Legislative powers of the Congress of States, under the Constitution, depended upon the will of a majority of the States.

"It was he who held in the Convention of Virginia that ratified the Constitution, that the powers conferred by that instrument could be rightly resumed by those who conferred them.

"This, perhaps, is the most 'pernicious' of all the doctrines set forth in the book, which Mr. Attorney-General is so anxious to have 'suppressed.' And perhaps, moreover, the true solution of his unqualified denunciation of the whole work is, that the array of facts presented in the two volumes, and the irresistible conclusions established by them, are so 'pernicious' to the schemes of the would-be 'Crown Officer' and his co-workers in the erection of a Centralized Empire over the ruins of the principles of that wonderful Federal Union, established by the 'Fathers,' that they cannot be tolerated by them; and hence the official mandate, that the doctrines therein set forth 'must be suppressed!' Potent words these, and of most ominous significance, coming from the quarter they do! They express the unmistakable language of tyrannical men in power in all ages and countries, when they feel the force of truths which are indeed dangerous and most 'pernicious' to their own guilty acts of usurpation upon the rights of States, as well as the liberties of outraged peoples! This language from the present Attorney-General smacks strongly of like Cabinet anathemas of the Nationalists, Centralists, and Consolidationists of this country in 1798-99 which ended in the ever-memorable Alien and Sedition 'laws, so called' of that period.

"The doctrine of the advocates of Constitutional Liberty under our Federative System at that day, as promulgated, not by Mr. [John C.] Calhoun, as Mr. Attorney-General most adroitly attempts to make the people believe, but by Mr. [Thomas] Jefferson and his associates, was, that these acts of usurpation were not laws but nullities.

"The doctrines inculated in the two volumes referred to, Mr. Attorney-General well knows, are the doctrines of Mr. Jefferson—the great apostle of the American Federative system, for the maintenance and preservation of free institutions by neighboring States. They are the doctrines which in 1798-1799 were, as now, considered exceedingly 'pernicious' to their schemes by all the enemies of these institutions. By the earnest promulgation of these doctrines, and a firm maintenance of them, at the polls, by the peoples of the several States of this Union, the rights of the States, as well as their own, were rescued from the hands of usurpers at that time; and on a like promulgation and maintenance of the same doctrines at this time, rests the only sure hope of the future rescue and preservation of the same rights and liberties from the hands of the usurpers who now bear sway. One of the most important as well as saving of the principles of these doctrines is that no danger need ever be feared in a free country from any error of opinion or doctrine however great, 'where reason is left free to combat it.'

"This Cabinet ukase [imperial decree] of Mr. Attorney-General shows nothing more clearly than the power of the truths promulgated in the two volumes thus denounced. He and his associates know and feel, that, by nothing short of a suppression of these truths directly or indirectly, and the obliteration, if possible, of all the great facts of our history, can-they bring the public mind to receive the doctrine attempted to be instilled by him in his Atlanta speech; which amounts to this: that the States of this Union have no higher position in the scale of existence than mere legal, corporations.

"Shades of Ames, Samuel Adams, Parsons, Ellsworth, Hancock, Madison, Hamilton, Marshall, Jackson, Jefferson, and Washington!

"I will not say that such a doctrine ought to be suppressed; but with all the respect for high official position which I can command, I will say, that the Attorney-General of the United States, in putting forth such sentiments ought to have blushed; if not for his own reputation, at least, from a proper sense of reverence for the memories of the illustrious dead!

"The Union of these States, nothing but a Union of a sort of corporations to be fashioned, moulded, controlled, and shorn of their rights by and at the will of the Central Government!

"This 'Confederacy' of States, as [John] Marshall styled it on the Bench of the Supreme Court—this 'Confederated Republic,' as [George] Washington styled it in his message to the Senate—this 'Union of Sovereign Members,' as [Andrew] Jackson spoke of it in his Inaugural Address, according to the teachings of the present Attorney-General, is nothing but an aggregation of corporations! Bare creatures of municipal law! This, in substance, is my understanding of his most insidiously-inculcated imperializing doctrine.

"If by the suppression of truth, this doctrine can be established, then, indeed, will be consummated that most lamentable result which [Alexander] Hamilton thought need never be feared, even by the most vigilant and zealous guardians of popular rights, when he declared in the Convention of New York, which ratified the Constitution, that 'The States can never lose their Powers till the whole people of America are robbed of their Liberties.' Yours, most respectfully, Alexander H. Stephens."[460]

From 1870:

☛ "Politically, this failure to perform their obligations under the existing Compact [i.e., to obey the Fugitive Slave Law as found in the U.S. Constitution], as it was, on the part of the Northern States, according to the

"Liberty Hall"

universal principles of public law, totally absolved their Southern Confederates from any further obligations under it. This principle of public law cannot be denied. If that [Liberal] Party, then controlling these derelict [Northern] States, from an enlightenment of their consciences, had been brought to see that this Compact of their Fathers was founded in sin, or, in other words, if they had come to see that the Constitution, as it was made, and as it then stood, was but '*a Covenant with Death and an Agreement with Hell*,' as many of the leading [Liberal Yankee] men of this party declared, and as nearly all really believed, not excepting even the Judge himself, (as we may legitimately infer from his remarks,) what, then, was their proper course as a truly moral and upright people? Was it not peacefully to withdraw from an alliance founded upon such '*a summation of all iniquity*,' or at least to permit those peacefully to withdraw with whom they were bound in stipulations, which they confessed they could not in conscience perform? Ought they not to have agreed to separate in peace? If the Compact was in truth so founded in sin, in violation of the laws of God, it was utterly void from the beginning. No rights or obligations could arise under it on either side. The parties were remitted to their original positions. They stood towards each other just as they did before it was made. I fully agree to the doctrine of a higher law—that Supreme law of right, ordained by the Most High, which governs the moral universe, and to which all human laws, as well as Compacts, must conform."[461]

From 1870:

☛ "Sovereignty is not in the Legislature. We, the People, are Sovereign! I am one of them, and have a right to be heard; and so has every other citizen of the State. You Legislators—I speak it respectfully—are but our servants. You are the servants of the people, and not their masters. Power resides with the people in this country. The great difference between our country and most others, is, that here there is popular Sovereignty, while there Sovereignty is exercised by kings or favored classes. This principle of popular Sovereignty, however much derided lately, is the foundation of our Institutions. Constitutions are but the channels through which the popular will may be expressed. Our Constitutions, State and Federal, came from the people. They made both, and they alone can rightfully unmake either."[462]

From 1870:

☛ "The only true equilibrium, or balance of power, in my opinion, under our system, which it was essential to maintain, was the recognized Sovereignty of the several States. This was the all powerful check against aggression upon the rights of any State. This was the complete Regulator of the entire system."[463]

From 1870:

☛ ". . . the Sovereign Right of each State, within the limitations mentioned, to withdraw from a Union formed as ours is admitted to have been, was perfect, considered either morally or politically. On the same principles, too, the Sovereign Right of all the States so withdrawing, to enter into a new Confederation, as they had done, was equally perfect. Where any party has a perfect right to perform an act, no other party can have a right, either legal or moral, to prevent the doing of it. This seems to me to be a perfectly rational conclusion. In the domain of reason, moreover, the conclusions of logic are inexorable!"[464]

Stephens explains why the Founding Fathers did not think to put the words "sovereignty" and "states' rights" in the U.S. Constitution:

☛ "It is true, the word Sovereignty is not in the 'national [U.S.] Constitution,' nor had it any business there. But the words 'State' and 'States' abound in it. From its Preamble to its close it shows that it was made 'by States' and 'for States,' and to be binding 'between States' only; and binding between them only as all Compacts are between States! The word State of itself imports Sovereignty as fully as the word Nation, Kingdom, or Empire. When the Constitution upon its face showed that it was made 'by States' and 'for States,' it was needless to speak of them as Sovereign States; for there cannot be any such thing as a State, known and recognized by public law, without Sovereignty."[465]

When asked how the Southern states could justify secession in 1860 and 1861, Stephens gave this answer in 1870:

☛ "If eleven States, in 1788, rightfully seceded or withdrew from the Confederation of 1778, which was so declared, 'to be perpetual,' and entered into the new Union, under the present Constitution, leaving North Carolina and Rhode Island out, as they did, why could not the same eleven, or any other eleven, in 1861, just as rightfully withdraw from the Union of 1788, which was not declared to be perpetual? If there was no treason or rebellion in the first 'Secession movement,' it seems to me, that he ought to have seen there could not be in the second, which was based on the same identical principle.

"Nor is this principle of a Union of States, formed and held together by a voluntary assent, one of 'disintegration upon which no Government can endure.' Upon it many Governments, as we have seen, have been formed, which did endure, and continued to grow and prosper until this principle was departed from by them. It is the principle of real strength as well as aggregation upon which our Government endured and increased in the number of States, from eleven to thirty-three, and prospered as no other Government ever did, for sixty years, under the teachings of Mr. [Thomas] Jefferson! All such Governments will endure and increase by aggregation and accession, and not go to pieces by disintegration or Secession, so long as the cohesive principle of mutual interests and reciprocal advantages binds the States together. No Federal Government ought to endure or last any longer than this principle is recognized. Mutual interests and reciprocal advantages are the main objects aimed at in the formation of all such Governments. These are the ends for which they are created. It was for these reasons, and to secure these objects, that the original joint Declaration of Independence was made by the several States of our Union. It is true, their joint Declaration was not made with a view of the States being severally independent of each other, but with the view that, by joint and Federal action, all would be better enabled to achieve, establish, and secure, permanently, the Sovereignty of each severally. Continued union on the same principles was doubtlessly expected and desired. But the right of each to its own Sovereignty and Independence was what was achieved."[466]

In 1870, Stephens once again explains why he left the Union with his home state of Georgia:

☛ "When the higher and grander objects to which I looked, and which I also thought not only attainable but also the surest means of preventing ultimate

subjugation—the most disastrous result according to my opinion that could
befall us as well as the people of all the States—became, therefore, altogether
impracticable, the whole of my energies, heart and soul, were then directed to
the next best alternative which was practisable, and that was the establishment
of the separate Independence of the Confederacy. This I considered as not only
essential to the maintenance of our own liberties; but the surest means of
preserving Constitutional Liberty on the Continent. All this, in my judgment,
was involved in the issue. The whole depended upon the successful
maintenance of the Principle of the Sovereignty of the States."[467]

From 1870:

☛ "One of the greatest errors in the policy of Secession, as I viewed it, was the
separation which it necessarily produced between the real friends of the
principles of the Constitution, North and South, in a common contest between
them and the Centralists. It was in truth a great battle—the Political
Armageddon of America—in which there should have been a concentration of
forces instead of that dispersion which of necessity resulted from Secession.
But, still, true friends of Constitutional Liberty, as true Christians, are animated
by the same essential principles everywhere. They can but be allies in the great
cause in whatever different organizations they may be placed. It was our true
policy, therefore, as it seemed to me, while struggling for our own
Independence, to use every possible means of impressing upon the minds of the
real friends of liberty at the North, the truth that if we should be overpowered
and put under the heel of Centralism, that the same fate would await them
sooner or later. That it would be better for them to permit us to enjoy our
separate Independence, and for them to do the same, than for both to be
subjected to a Consolidated Despotism."[468]

From 1870:

☛ "Depend upon it, there is no difference between Consolidation and Empire;
no difference between Centralism and Imperialism. The consummation of
either must necessarily end in the overthrow of Liberty and the establishment
of Despotism. To speak of any Rights as belonging to the States, without the
innate and inalienable Sovereign power to maintain them, is but to deal in the
shadow of language without the substance. Nominal Rights without Securities
are but Mockeries!

"Nothing can be truer than that the States under our system possess no
Rights but Sovereign Rights. All their reserved Rights are necessarily Sovereign
Rights. They hold nothing by grant or favor from the Federal Government. On
the contrary, the Federal Government itself possesses no Right, and is intrusted

with the exercise of no Power, except by delegation from the Sovereignty of the several States. Sovereignty itself, as [I have shown], . . . is, from its very nature, indivisible! There never was a greater truth, more pointedly uttered than that by Mr. [Thomas] Jefferson, that the States of this Union 'are not united upon the principle of unlimited submission to their General Government.' The Administration of our Government, therefore, must be brought back and made to conform in its action, to these principles thus announced by the Great Author of the System [i.e., God], and under which all the great achievements of the past were made. If this is not done, it is utterly vain to look for, or expect anything, but ultimate Centralism and Despotism!"[469]

10

Anti-South Propaganda

In his book A Constitutional View of the Late War Between the States, *Stephens offered a number of speeches by John C. Calhoun and Robert A. Toombs, commenting:*

☛ "In sampling these debates with the view to present the tone and temper of the times, I purposely select the speeches made by Mr. Calhoun and Mr. Toombs, because they have been generally regarded as the extremest of the Ultras on that side, and have both been very greatly misrepresented on this subject. No man was ever more so than Mr. Toombs. It has been the object of many to hold him up as the embodiment of Slavery Propagandism. Even histories have been written in which the statement is made that he had declared that he would yet call the roll of his slaves on Bunker Hill. This has been done, too, without a particle of proof, and after the most positive denial by him of his ever having made such a declaration."[470]

Liberals have long painted the South as "aggressively" and "wrongfully" pushing through the Kansas-Nebraska Act of 1854, which overturned the Missouri Compromise of 1850 and opened up the territories of Kansas and Nebraska to slave owning settlers. In reply to this particular piece of anti-South propaganda Stephens wrote:

☞ ". . . the legislation of 1854 did nothing but carry out, in good faith, the Territorial principle established in 1850. There was no aggression in it on the part of the South. There was no 'perfidy,' or 'breach of Compact,' or 'wrong,' perpetrated by anybody in securing its accomplishment. Apart from its being the fulfilment of a pledge to maintain the principle of 1850, was it not perfectly just and right in itself? What wrong did the Act contain? Wrong to whom? Was it wrong to the people of the South, one large section of the Union, to permit them to enjoy an equal and fair participation of the public domain, purchased by the common blood and common treasure of all? Was it wrong to the people of the North to permit those of them who might emigrate to these Territories, to be as free there, as they were in their native homes? Was it wrong and unjust to allow all, from all the States, who might be disposed to quit their father-land and to seek to better their fortunes in these rich and fertile plains, to enjoy the same rights which their fathers did in the early formation of their State Constitutions and Governments? Whom did the bill wrong? To whom did it deal any injustice? Was it the slave—the African—whom a Southern master might take there? How could it be unjust, even to him? Was not his condition as much bettered by new lands and virgin soils, as that of his master? Was not expansion of that portion of Southern population quite as necessary for their comfort and well-being, as it was for the whites? Was it either just, right, or humane to keep them hemmed in within their then limits, until by failure of subsistence they should be reduced to starvation, even in the Slavery view of the subject?"[471]

Another popular piece of Northern fiction concerns the Kansas Border War (1854-1861), or "Bleeding Kansas," as it is more popularly known. Pro-North writers have long blamed Southern slave owners for the entire affair. However, Southerners like Stephens knew the Truth:

☞ "[The election of James Buchanan to U.S. president in 1856] . . . was another most signal condemnation of the principles as well as policy of the Restrictionists by the people and States of the Union. It was the more so from the fact that after their utter defeat in the Halls of Congress, on the principles of the legislation of 1854, they had openly resorted to the policy of stirring up bloody strife in the Territories. Large amounts of money were raised for what were called 'Emigrant Aid Societies.' The object of these was to send to these Territories as many as possible of the most daring characters to drive Southern settlers from the Territories by force. Arms were bought and put in the hands of these desperadoes, thus sent out as warriors and not as peaceful colonists. This was done, too, by many who styled themselves Ministers of the Gospel! The result, for a time, was what during this Presidential campaign, was called

Philip Henry Sheridan

the 'Civil War in Kansas,' which was charged by them and their allies upon the Legislation of 1854 [the Kansas-Nebraska Act], while in truth the whole strife was instigated and gotten up by the avowed enemies of that legislation, enraged by their defeat, and with the view to kindle a general war in the States, for the total abolition of Slavery. It was in these Kansas scenes of blood in 1856, that the noted John Brown first figured, who afterwards closed his career by his most infatuated 'raid' on the United States Armory at Harper's Ferry, in 1859. All these wild, reckless and revolutionary measures, so instigated and controlled by these mischievous malcontents, did not prevent the general condemnation stated, in 1856. There can be no question that there was then a very large majority of the people of the United States, South as well as North, devotedly attached to the Union under the Constitution and who were resolved to maintain, if possible, the Federal [Confederate] system against all [the Liberals'] attempts, whether covert or open, at Centralism or Consolidation.

"Allow me to say, further, that my opinion then was, and now is, if Mr. Buchanan had adhered to the principles on which he was so triumphantly elected, in 1856, he, or whoever else might have been nominated on the same platform at Charleston, on which he had been nominated at Cincinnati, would have been even more triumphantly elected in 1860. For, by the Kansas policy of the Restrictionists, and from their avowed sympathy for John Brown in his desperate undertaking in getting up civil war in Virginia, the supporters of the Constitution and Union, everywhere, saw that revolution was their real object, and were ready to give them a sterner rebuke than ever before. But Mr. Buchanan did not adhere to the principles on which he had been elected. He insisted upon another plank being introduced into the Party Platform, which, however right it might have been on principle, as an original question, was, nevertheless, a distinct departure from the doctrine of strict Non-intervention on the part of Congress, with Slavery in the Territories in any way, either for or against, which had been agreed upon as the basis of the final settlement in

1850. This we shall have occasion, perhaps, to look into hereafter. The result of his policy, which may be here stated, was the rupture of the Party by which he had been elected, and the success of Mr. [Abraham] Lincoln, the [Liberal] candidate of the Restrictionists, by a popular vote of only 1,857,610, against the combined vote of 2,787,780, cast for the other three candidates voted for, even with the distractions and bitter feelings growing out of the rupture."[472]

Just as in Stephens' time, today pro-North advocates and scallywags continue to promote the myth of the so-called "Irrepressible Conflict," maintaining that it was the South's stubborn adherence to the Constitution and states' rights that inevitably pushed the South and the North into war. Stephens, like all Southerners, knew that this was nothing but another Yankee myth, fabricated to cast further blame for the conflict on the Southern people:

☛ "The doctrine of the 'Irrepressible Conflict' between the Institutions of the several States, was, in my view, itself the embodiment of Centralism [Northern Liberalism]. The Federal Government, in my judgment, so far from being weakened, was strengthened by the heterogeneous interests of the several States [i.e., states' rights]. Nothing tends more to Centralization of power, even in a separate State or Nation, than homogeneousness of interests on the part of its constituent elements. All progress in Governments, as well as progressive developments in everything else, is marked by successive steps from the 'simplex to the complex,' from the homogeneous to the heterogeneous. This is the true law of progress in all things. In nature, in art, and in science in all their departments. The chief safe-guards of liberty, in every political organization, owe their origin to a diversity of pursuits and a conflict of interests between its various members."[473]

One of the most pernicious Northern fictions was "the charge of cruelty and inhumanity towards prisoners, which has been so extensively made at the North, against Mr. Jefferson Davis and the Confederate authorities . . ." There was also the Yankees' outrageous claim that President Davis had been part of a "plot" to murder Lincoln. To these preposterous accusations Stephens responded this way:

☛ "[It] . . . is utterly without foundation in fact. From the commencement and throughout the war, the whole course of Mr. Davis towards prisoners shows conclusively the perfect recklessness of the charge. His position on this subject, in the beginning, clearly appears from what we have seen, and that fully sustains this statement. The efforts which have been so industriously made to fix the odium of cruelty and barbarity upon him, and other high officials under the Confederate Government, in the matter of prisoners, in the face of all the facts, constitute one of the boldest and baldest attempted outrages upon the truth of history, which has ever been essayed: not less so than the infamous attempt to fix upon him and other high officials on the Confederate side, the guilt of Mr. Lincoln's assassination! Whatever unnecessary privations and sufferings prisoners on both sides were subjected to, the responsibility of the whole rested not upon Mr. Davis or the Confederate authorities.

"... [I can say with complete certainty that the] horrors of Libby and Belle Island [prisons], as well as of Salisbury and Andersonville [prisons], so pathetically set forth by many, and great as they really were, were not his fault, or in any way justly chargeable upon him. . . . It was the fault of the Federal [U.S.] authorities in not agreeing to, and carrying out an immediate exchange, which Mr. Davis was, at all times, anxious to do. The [Liberal] men at the head of affairs at Washington were solely responsible for all these sufferings. Upon these officials, and upon them only, can these sufferings be justly charged! Neither Libby, nor Belle Island, nor Salisbury, nor Andersonville would have had a groaning prisoner of war, but for the refusal of the Federal authorities to comply with the earnest desire of the Richmond [C.S.] Government, for an immediate exchange, upon the most liberal and humane principles. Had Mr. Davis's repeated offers been accepted, no prisoner on either side would have been retained in confinement a day. This all the facts clearly show. All the sufferings and loss of life, therefore, during the entire war, growing out of these imprisonments on both sides, and they were great on both sides, (it is not my wish to understate or underrate them on either,) are justly chargeable to but one side, and that is the Federal side."[474]

Another great lie put forth by the anti-South propaganda machine in the North is that, because of the Confederacy's alleged "deplorable treatment" of Yankee soldiers, more Union soldiers died in Southern prisons than Rebel soldiers in Northern ones. Stephens was quick to dismantle this fabrication:

☛ "It now appears that a larger number of Confederates died in Northern, than of Federals in Southern prisons, or stockade. The Report of Mr. [Edwin M.] Stanton, as [U.S.] Secretary of War, on the 19th of July, 1866, exhibits the fact that, of the Federal prisoners in Confederate hands during the war, only 22,576 died; while of the Confederate prisoners in Federal hands 26,436 died. This Report does not set forth the exact number of prisoners held by each side respectively. These facts were given more in detail in a subsequent Report by Surgeon-General [Joseph K.] Barnes, of the United States Army. His Report I have not seen, but according to a statement, editorially, in the 'National Intelligencer'—very high authority—it appears from the Surgeon-General's Report, that the whole number of Federal prisoners captured by the Confederates and held in Southern prisons, from first to last during the war,

The Stephens family's "Old Homestead" burial ground

was, in round numbers, 270,000; while the whole number of Confederates captured and held in prisons by the Federals was, in like round numbers, only 220,000. From these two Reports it appears that, with 50,000 more prisoners in Southern stockades, or other modes of confinement, the deaths were nearly 4,000 less! According to these figures, the per centum of Federal deaths in Southern prisons was under nine! while the per centum of Confederate deaths in Northern prisons was over twelve! These Mortality statistics are of no small weight in determining on which side there was the most neglect, cruelty, and inhumanity!"[475]

One of the North's most deeply cherished myths is that Stephens was "at war" with Confederate President Jefferson Davis. This fairy tale is frequently used, in fact, to explain why Stephens was seldom at his office in the Confederate capitol at Richmond, Virginia. Stephens explains, for example, his absence during the Summer of 1864:
☛ "[It is not that] . . . I had withdrawn from the Seat of Government with any intention of heading an opposition to the Administration, with the object of abandoning the war. Far, indeed, was I from being actuated during that absence by any such motives as these. I was confined at home the greater part of that summer by a protracted attack of severe disease.[476] . . . [Actually, there] was . . . at no time . . . a personal breach, or anything like a feud between us."[477]

Even Stephens' last exit from Richmond on February 9, 1865, premature as it was (the War would not end until two months later on April 9), was devoid of any and all acrimony, as he himself stated in 1870:

☞ "I left Richmond in no ill-humor with Mr. Davis, or with any purpose of opposing or obstructing the execution of the designs of the Administration, in any way; but because I could not sanction a Policy which I thought would certainly end in disaster, and I did not wish to be where my opinions might, by possibility, be the cause of divisions and dissensions, which would just as certainly lead to the same result. General confidence in the Administration was essential to success on any line, and this I did not wish to weaken or impair in others at this most critical juncture, though I could not, myself, approve the course which had been taken."[478]

11

The Confederacy

On February 9, 1861, following the formation of the Confederate Constitution and his election to the position of Confederate vice president, Stephens made the following speech:
☛ "Gentlemen And Fellow-citizens, for though we met as strangers from different and independent States, we are once more citizens of a common country. [Applause.] Allow me briefly and sincerely to return you my unfeigned thanks for this compliment. The state of my health, my voice and the night air, apart from all other considerations, will prevent me from doing more. This is not the time or the place to discuss those great questions which are now pressing upon our public counsels. We are in a transition condition—in the process of a new formation.

"Sufficient to say, that this day a new republic has been born—the Confederate States of America has been ushered into existence, to take its place amongst the nations of the earth—[cheers]—under a temporary or provisional government, it is true; but soon to be followed by one of a permanent character, which, while it surrenders none of our ancient rights and liberties, will secure more perfectly, we trust, the peace, security, and domestic tranquillity that should be the objects of all governments. [Applause.]

"What is to be the future of this new government—the fate of this new republic—will depend upon ourselves. Six States only, at present, constitute it—but six stars, as yet, appear in our constellation—more, we trust, will soon be added. By the time of the adoption of the constitution of the permanent government, we may have a number greater than the original thirteen—of the original Union, and with more than three times their population, wealth, and power. [Applause.] With such a beginning, the prospect of the future presents strong hopes to the patriot's heart, for a bright and prosperous career. But what that future shall be, depends, I say, upon ourselves and those who shall come after us. Ours is a republic. And all republics, to be permanent and prosperous, must be supported by the virtue, intelligence, integrity, and patriotism of the people. These are the corner-stones upon which the temple of popular liberty must be constructed, to stand securely and permanently. Resting ours upon these, we need fear nothing from without or from within. With a climate unsurpassed by any on earth; with staples and productions which control the commerce of the world; with institutions, so far as regards our organic and social policy, in strict conformity to nature and the laws of the Creator, whether read in the Book of Inspiration or in the great book of manifestations around us, we have all the natural elements essential to the attainment of the highest degree of honor, glory, and renown. [Applause.]

"These institutions have been much assailed. It is our mission to vindicate the great truths on which they rest—and with them to exhibit the highest type of civilization which it is possible for human society to reach. In doing this, our policy should be marked by a desire to preserve and maintain peace with all other States and peoples. If this cannot be done, let not the fault lie at our door. While we should make aggressions on none, we should be prepared to repel them if made by others; let it come from whatever quarter it may. [Applause.] We ask of all others simply to be let alone, and to be permitted to work after our own safety, security, and happiness, in our own way, without molesting or giving offence to any other people.

"Let then peace, fraternity, and liberal commercial relations with all the world, be our motto. [Cheers.] With these principles, without any envy toward other States in the line of policy they may mark out for themselves, we will rather invite them to a generous rivalship in all that develops the highest qualities of our nature. [Applause.]

"With best wishes for you, gentlemen, and the success of our common government, this day announced, I bid you goodnight."[479]

The following excerpts are from Stephens' famous, or rather, infamous "Cornerstone Speech" delivered at the Athenæum in Savannah, Georgia, on March 21, 1861. Seven Southern states had already seceded. The beginning of the "Civil War" was only three weeks away. We will note here that this speech has been repeatedly and "grossly misrepresented" by the pro-North and New South movements. In fact, it was widely known at the time that Stephens delivered it "impromptu" and that the transcriptions later made of it were "imperfectly" reported. Despite these facts, as well as the ignorant and vengeful manner in which anti-South proponents have tried to twist the import of this address, as Richard M. Johnston says, its entire content can be summed up in this manner: "On the subject of slavery there was no essential change in the new [U.S.] Constitution from the old [that is, the Articles of Confederation]. As Judge [Henry] Baldwin [1780- 1844], of the Supreme Court of the United States, had announced from the Bench several years before, that slavery was the corner-stone of the old Constitution, so it is of the new"[480]:

☛ ". . . we are passing through one of the greatest revolutions in the annals of the world. Seven States have within the last three months thrown off an old government and formed a new [the C.S.A.]. This revolution has been signally marked, up to this time, by the fact of its having been accomplished without the loss of a single drop of blood. [Applause.] This new constitution [the C.S. Constitution], or form of government, constitutes the subject to which your attention will be partly invited. In reference to it, I make this first general remark. It amply secures all our ancient rights, franchises, and liberties. All the great principles of Magna Charta are retained in it. No citizen is deprived of life, liberty, or property, but by the judgment of his peers under the laws of the land. The great principle of religious liberty, which was the honor and pride of the old [U.S.] constitution, is still maintained and secured. All the essentials of the old constitution, which have endeared it to the hearts of the American people, have been preserved and perpetuated. [Applause.] Some changes have been made. Of these I shall speak presently. Some of these I should have preferred not to have seen made; but these, perhaps, meet the cordial approbation of a majority of this audience, if not an overwhelming majority of the people of the Confederacy. Of them, therefore, I will not speak. But other important changes do meet my cordial approbation. They form great improvements upon the old constitution. So, taking the whole new constitution, I have no hesitancy in giving it as my judgment that it is decidedly better than the old."[481]

Stephens' "Cornerstone Speech" continues:

☛ "Allow me briefly to allude to some of these improvements. The question of building up class interests, or fostering one branch of industry to the prejudice of another under the exercise of the revenue power, which gave us so much trouble under the old constitution, is put at rest forever under the new. We allow the imposition of no duty with a view of giving advantage to one class of persons, in any trade or business, over those of another. All, under our system, stand upon the same broad principles of perfect equality. Honest labor and enterprise are left free and unrestricted in whatever pursuit they may be engaged. This subject came well nigh causing a rupture of the old Union, under the lead of the gallant Palmetto State, which lies on our border, in 1833. This

Ulysses S. Grant

old thorn of the tariff, which was the cause of so much irritation in the old body politic, is removed forever from the new. [Applause.]

"Again, the subject of internal improvements [known today as 'corporate welfare'], under the power of Congress to regulate commerce, is put at rest under our system. The power claimed by construction under the old constitution, was at least a doubtful one—it rested solely upon construction. We of the South, generally apart from considerations of constitutional principles, opposed its exercise upon grounds of its inexpediency and injustice. Notwithstanding this opposition, millions of money, from the common treasury had been drawn for such purposes. Our opposition sprang from no hostility to commerce, or all necessary aids for facilitating it. With us it was simply a question, upon whom the burden should fall. In Georgia, for instance, we have done as much for the cause of internal improvements as any other portion of the country according to population and means. We have stretched out lines of railroads from the seaboard to the mountains; dug down the hills, and filled up the valleys at a cost of not less than twenty-five millions of dollars. All this was done to open an outlet for our products of the interior, and those to the west of us, to reach the marts of the world. No State was in greater need of such facilities than Georgia, but we did not ask that these works should be made by appropriations out of the common treasury. The cost of the grading, the superstructure, and equipments of our roads, was borne by those who entered on the enterprise. Nay, more—not only the cost of the iron, no small item in the aggregate cost, was borne in the same way—but we were compelled to pay into the common treasury several millions of dollars for the privilege of importing the iron, after the price was paid for it abroad. What justice was there in taking this money, which our people paid into the common treasury on the importation of our iron, and applying it to the improvement of rivers and harbors elsewhere?

"The true principle is to subject the commerce of every locality, to whatever burdens may be necessary to facilitate it. If Charleston harbor needs improvement, let the commerce of Charleston bear the burden. If the mouth of the Savannah river has to be cleared out, let the sea-going navigation which is benefitted by it, bear the burden. So with the mouths of the Alabama and Mississippi river. Just as the products of the interior, our cotton, wheat, corn, and other articles, have to bear the necessary rates of freight over our railroads to reach the seas. This is again the broad principle of perfect equality and justice. [Applause.] And it is especially set forth and established in our new [Confederate] constitution."[482]

Stephens' "Cornerstone Speech" continues:

☛ "Another change in the constitution relates to the length of the tenure of the presidential office. In the new constitution it is six years instead of four, and the President rendered ineligible for a re-election. This is certainly a decidedly conservative change. It will remove from the incumbent all temptation to use his office or exert the powers confided to him for any objects of personal ambition. The only incentive to that higher ambition which should move and actuate one holding such high trusts in his hands, will be the good of the people, the advancement, prosperity, happiness, safety, honor, and true glory of the confederacy."[483]

What follows is the portion of Stephens' "Cornerstone Speech" that has been long and widely hailed by the anti-South movement as "proof" that the Old South was "inherently racist," that "slavery was the cause of the American Civil War," that Dixie's economic system was based "solely on slavery," and that the South's participation in that conflict was only to "preserve slavery." We in the South, of course, heartily disagree with this biased and uninformed assessment of Stephens' words.

It is true, at the time, that he believed blacks were ordained by God to be subordinate to whites (an idea he later rejected), and it is equally true that he here declares that slavery was the "cornerstone" of the South's economy. Yet, since less than 5 percent of the South owned slaves, it is obvious that the latter statement is impossibly incorrect. Why then did he make it?

With only a tiny minority of the South being interested in slavery, Stephens needed to say something that would get both his constituents' attention and their support in the terrible partisan political battles with the North. The most efficient way to accomplish this was to use the tried and true tactics of exaggeration, fear-mongering, and hyperbole, the same ones routinely used by politicians to this day.

We must also consider the bold fact that if slavery had been the "cause of the War," as pro-North advocates continue to maintain, then why did the conflict not end with Lincoln's Emancipation Proclamation on January 1, 1863? Instead, the War dragged on for another two years, proving once and for all that the North was only fighting to install an empire, and the South was only fighting to prevent it:[484]

☛ "The new constitution has put at rest, forever, all the agitating questions relating to our peculiar institution—African slavery as it exists amongst us—the proper status of the negro in our form of civilization. This was the immediate cause of the late rupture and present revolution. [Thomas] Jefferson in his forecast, had anticipated this, as the 'rock upon which the old Union would split.' He was right. What was conjecture with him, is now a realized fact. But whether he fully comprehended the great truth upon which that rock stood and stands, may be doubted. The prevailing ideas entertained by him and most of the leading statesmen at the time of the formation of the old constitution, were that the enslavement of the African was in violation of the laws of nature; that it was wrong in principle, socially, morally, and politically. It was an evil they knew not well how to deal with, but the general opinion of the men of that day was that, somehow or other in the order of Providence, the institution would be evanescent and pass away. This idea, though not incorporated in the constitution, was the prevailing idea at that time. The constitution, it is true, secured every essential guarantee to the institution while it should last, and hence no argument can be justly urged against the constitutional guarantees thus secured, because of the common sentiment of the day. Those ideas, however, were fundamentally wrong. They rested upon the assumption of the equality of races. This was an error. It was a sandy foundation, and the government built upon it fell when the 'storm came and the wind blew.' [Emphasis added, L.S.]

"Our new government is founded upon exactly the opposite idea; its foundations are laid, its corner-stone rests upon the great truth, that the negro is not equal to the white man; that slavery—subordination to the superior race—is his natural and normal condition. [Applause.]

"This, our new government, is the first, in the history of the world, based upon this great physical, philosophical, and moral truth. This truth has been slow in the process of its development, like all other truths in the various departments of science. It has been so even amongst us. Many who hear me, perhaps, can recollect well, that this truth was not generally admitted, even within their day. The errors of the past generation still clung to many as late as twenty years ago. Those at the North, who still cling to these errors, with a zeal above knowledge, we justly denominate fanatics. All fanaticism springs from an aberration of the mind—from a defect in reasoning. It is a species of insanity. One of the most striking characteristics of insanity, in many instances, is forming correct conclusions from fancied or erroneous premises; so with the anti-slavery fanatics; their conclusions are right if their premises were. They assume that the negro is equal, and hence conclude that he is entitled to equal privileges and rights with the white man. If their premises were correct, their conclusions would be logical and just—but their premise being wrong, their whole argument fails. I recollect once of having heard a gentleman from one of the northern States, of great power and ability, announce in the House of Representatives, with imposing effect, that we of the South would be compelled, ultimately, to yield upon this subject of slavery, that it was as impossible to war successfully against a principle in politics, as it was in physics or mechanics. That the principle would ultimately prevail. That we, in maintaining slavery as it exists with us, were warring against a principle, a principle founded in nature, the principle of the equality of men. The reply I made to him was, that upon his own grounds, we should, ultimately, succeed, and that he and his associates, in this crusade against our institutions, would ultimately fail. The truth announced, that it was as impossible to war successfully against a principle in politics as it was in physics and mechanics, I admitted; but told him that it was he, and those acting with him, who were warring against a principle. They were attempting to make things equal which the Creator [as is clearly evident in the Bible, according to Stephens] had made unequal."[485]

The controversial portion of Stephens' "Cornerstone Speech" continues:
☛ "In the conflict thus far, success has been on our side, complete throughout

the length and breadth of the Confederate States. It is upon this, as I have stated, our social fabric is firmly planted; and I cannot permit myself to doubt the ultimate success of a full recognition of this principle throughout the civilized and enlightened world.

"As I have stated, the truth of this principle may be slow in development, as all truths are and ever have been, in the various branches of science. It was so with the principles announced by Galileo—it was so with Adam Smith and his principles of political economy. It was so with [English physician William] Harvey, and his theory of the circulation of the blood. It is stated that not a single one of the medical profession, living at the time of the

William Henry Seward

announcement of the truths made by him, admitted them. Now, they are universally acknowledged. May we not, therefore, look with confidence to the ultimate universal acknowledgment of the truths upon which our system rests? It is the first government ever instituted upon the principles in strict conformity to nature, and the ordination of Providence, in furnishing the materials of human society. Many governments have been founded upon the principle of the subordination and serfdom of certain classes of the same race; such were and are in violation of the laws of nature. Our system commits no such violation of nature's laws. With us, all of the white race, however high or low, rich or poor, are equal in the eye of the law. Not so with the negro. Subordination is his place. He, by nature, or by the curse against Canaan [modern Mormons continue to embrace and teach this concept], is fitted for that condition which he occupies in our system. The architect, in the construction of buildings, lays the foundation with the proper material—the granite; then comes the brick or the marble. The substratum of our society is made of the material fitted by nature for it, and by experience we know that it is best, not only for the superior, but for the inferior race, that it should be so. It is, indeed, in conformity with the ordinance of the Creator. It is not for us to inquire into the wisdom of his ordinances, or to question them. For his own purposes, he has made one race to differ from another, as he has made 'one star to differ from another star in glory.'

"The great objects of humanity are best attained when there is conformity to his laws and decrees, in the formation of governments as well as in all things else. Our confederacy is founded upon principles in strict conformity with these laws. This stone which was rejected by the first builders 'is become the chief of the corner'—the real 'corner-stone'—in our new edifice."[486]

During his March 21, 1861, "Cornerstone Speech" Stephens reassured the Southern people that they had all they needed to launch and maintain a successful Confederate Republic, despite the naysayers in the North:
☛ "We have all the essential elements of a high national career. The idea has been given out at the North, and even in the border States, that we are too small and too weak to maintain a separate nationality. This is a great mistake. In extent of territory we embrace five hundred and sixty-four thousand square miles and upward. This is upward of two hundred thousand square miles more than was included within the limits of the original thirteen States. It is an area of country more than double the territory of France or the Austrian empire. France, in round numbers, has but two hundred and twelve thousand square miles. Austria, in round numbers, has two hundred and forty-eight thousand

square miles. Ours is greater than both combined. It is greater than all France, Spain, Portugal, and Great Britain, including England, Ireland, and Scotland, together. In population we have upward of five millions, according to the census of 1860; this includes white and black. The entire population, including white and black, of the original thirteen States, was less than four millions in 1790, and still less in 1776, when the independence of our fathers was achieved. If they, with a less population, dared maintain their independence against the greatest power on earth, shall we have any apprehension of maintaining ours now?

"In point of material wealth and resources, we are greatly in advance of them. The taxable property of the Confederate States cannot be less than twenty-two hundred millions of dollars! This, I think I venture but little in saying, may be considered as five times more than the colonies possessed at the time they achieved their independence. Georgia, alone, possessed last year, according to the report of our comptroller-general, six hundred and seventy-two millions of taxable property. The debts of the seven confederate States sum up in the aggregate less than eighteen millions, while the existing debts of the other of the late United States sum up in the aggregate the enormous amount of one hundred and seventy-four millions of dollars. This is without taking into the account the heavy city debts, corporation debts, and railroad debts, which press, and will continue to press, as a heavy incubus upon the resources of those States. These debts, added to others, make a sum total not much under five hundred millions of dollars. With such an area of territory as we have—with such an amount of population—with a climate and soil unsurpassed by any on the face of the earth—with such resources already at our command—with productions which control the commerce of the world—who can entertain any apprehensions as to our ability to succeed, whether others join us or not?"[487]

Stephen's "Cornerstone Speech" continues:
☛ "What is to be the result of this revolution? Will everything, commenced so well, continue as it has begun? In reply to this anxious inquiry, I can only say it all depends upon ourselves. A young man starting out in life on his majority, with health, talent, and ability, under a favoring Providence, may be said to be the architect of his own fortunes. His destinies are in his own hands. He may make for himself a name, of honor or dishonor, according to his own acts. If he plants himself upon truth, integrity, honor and uprightness, with industry, patience and energy, he cannot fail of success. So it is with us. We are a young republic, just entering upon the arena of nations; we will be the architects of our own fortunes. Our destiny, under Providence, is in our own hands. With

wisdom, prudence, and statesmanship on the part of our public men, and intelligence, virtue and patriotism on the part of the people, success, to the full measures of our most sanguine hopes, may be looked for. But if unwise counsels prevail—if we become divided—if schisms arise—if dissensions spring up—if factions are engendered—if party spirit, nourished by unholy personal ambition shall rear its hydra head, I have no good to prophesy for you. Without intelligence, virtue, integrity, and patriotism on the part of the people, no republic or representative government can be durable or stable.

"We have intelligence, and virtue, and patriotism. All that is required is to cultivate and perpetuate these. Intelligence will not do without virtue. France was a nation of philosophers. These philosophers become Jacobins. They lacked that virtue, that devotion to moral principle, and that patriotism which is essential to good government. Organized upon principles of perfect justice and right—seeking amity and friendship with all other powers—I see no obstacle in the way of our upward and onward progress. Our growth, by accessions from other States, will depend greatly upon whether we present to the world, as I trust we shall, a better government than that to which neighboring States belong. If we do this, North Carolina, Tennessee, and Arkansas cannot hesitate long; neither can Virginia, Kentucky, and Missouri. They will necessarily gravitate to us by an imperious law. We made ample provision in our constitution for the admission of other States; it is more guarded, and wisely so, I think, than the old constitution on the same subject, but not too guarded to receive them as fast as it may be proper. Looking to the distant future, and, perhaps, not very far distant either, it is not beyond the range of possibility, and even probability, that all the great States of the north-west will gravitate this way, as well as Tennessee, Kentucky, Missouri, Arkansas, etc. Should they do so, our doors are wide enough to receive them, but not until they are ready to assimilate with us in principle."[488]

Stephen's "Cornerstone Speech" continues:
☞ "The process of disintegration in the old Union may be expected to go on with almost absolute certainty if we pursue the right course. We are now the nucleus of a growing power which, if we are true to ourselves, our destiny, and high mission, will become the controlling power on this continent. To what extent accessions will go on in the process of time, or where it will end, the future will determine. So far as it concerns States of the old Union, this process will be upon no such principles of reconstruction as now spoken of, but upon reorganization and new assimilation. [Loud applause.] Such are some of the glimpses of the future as I catch them.

"But at first we must necessarily meet with the inconveniences and difficulties and embarrassments incident to all changes of government. These will be felt in our postal affairs and changes in the channel of trade. These inconveniences, it is to be hoped, will be but temporary, and must be borne with patience and forbearance.

"As to whether we shall have war with our late confederates, or whether all matters of differences between us shall be amicably settled, I can only say that the prospect for a peaceful adjustment is better, so far as I am informed, than it has been."[489]

Stephen's "Cornerstone Speech" continues:

☛ "Our object is peace, not only with the North, but with the world. All matters relating to the public property, public liabilities of the Union when we were members of it, we are ready and willing to adjust and settle upon the principles of right, equity, and good faith. War can be of no more benefit to the North than to us. Whether the intention of evacuating Fort Sumter is to be received as an evidence of a desire for a peaceful solution of our difficulties with the United States, or the result of necessity, I will not undertake to say. I would fain hope the former. Rumors are afloat, however, that it is the result of necessity. All I can say to you, therefore, on that point is, keep your armor bright and your powder dry. [Enthusiastic cheering.]

"The surest way to secure peace, is to show your ability to maintain your rights. The principles and position of the present administration of the United States—the republican [Liberal] party—present some puzzling questions. While it is a fixed principle with them never to allow the increase of a foot of slave territory, they seem to be equally determined not to part with an inch 'of the accursed soil.' Notwithstanding their clamor against the institution, they seemed to be equally opposed to getting more, or letting go what they have got. They were ready to fight on the accession of Texas, and are equally ready to fight now on her secession. Why is this? How can this strange paradox be accounted for? There seems to be but one rational solution—and that is, notwithstanding their professions of humanity, they are disinclined to give up the benefits they derive from slave labor. Their philanthropy yields to their interest. The idea of enforcing the laws, has but one object, and that is a collection of the taxes, raised by slave labor to swell the fund, necessary to meet their heavy appropriations. The spoils is what they are after—though they come from the labor of the slave."[490]

☛ "Here [in the American South] . . . all the landmarks of English liberty have been preserved and maintained, while at the North scarcely a vestige of them is left. There [in the North], instead of courts of justice with open doors, the

William Tecumseh Sherman

country is dotted all over with prisons and bastiles. No better argument in behalf of a people struggling for constitutional liberty could have been presented to arouse sympathy in our favor. It showed that we were passing through a fiery furnace for a great cause, and passing through unscathed. It showed that whatever may be the state of things at the North, that at the South at least the great light of the principles of self-government, civil and religious liberty, established on this continent by our ancestors, which was looked to with encouragement and hope by the down-trodden of all nations, was not yet extinguished, but was still burning brightly in the hands of their southern sons, even burning the more brightly from the intensity of the heat of the conflict in which we are engaged. To us, in deed and in truth, is committed the hopes of the world as to the capacity and ability of man for self-government. Let us see to it that these hopes and expectations do not fail. Let us prove ourselves equal to the high mission before us."[491]

Here, from his book A Constitutional View, *Stephens describes the ancient and noble roots of the Southern Confederacy:*

☛ "Now all these Governments, the Grecian, the Germanic, as well as our own first Confederation, were founded . . . upon just such a principle. . . . The principle of voluntary consent. This is the principle upon which are founded all Confederations. Just such Governments are all Confederated Republics. And these are the only kinds of Governments, as Montesquieu informs us, which have saved the human race from universal monarchical rule. Low as [the Liberal's] . . . estimate of them may be, they are the only escape yet discovered by man for free institutions, among bordering States or Nations. Governments which have done so much for mankind certainly do not deserve, nor have they received from them, such sentiments as you imagine.

"But [it is obvious] . . . that our present system is a great improvement upon all former models of this kind of Confederation. While it is founded upon the same basis of consent and voluntary agreement, as I hope I have clearly shown, yet it has several new and important features in its organization, unknown before, and to which we are mainly indebted for its unparalleled success in the past. It is because of these new features, all resting upon the same basis as all other Confederations, placing it far above all other systems, that I considered it the best Government the world ever saw.

"The same view was entertained by John Hancock, when, in his message to the Legislature of Massachusetts, as we have seen, he said, that if the proposed amendments, which he had himself offered in the State Convention, should be adopted, the chief one of which was the expressly declared reservation of the Sovereignty of the States, he should 'consider it the most perfect system of Government as to the objects it embraces that has been known amongst mankind.'"[492]

12

The Confederate
Constitution

These excerpts are from Stephens' April 23, 1861, speech before the Virginia Secession Convention:

☞ "The first thing [on the new Confederacy's agenda] was to organize a provisional government. This was done by the adoption of the provisional constitution. It is to last but one year, and conforms to our ancient usages as nearly as practicable. No changes in essential or fundamental principles. We have but one legislative body. This possesses the powers of the old Senate and House combined; but the rights of the States and the sovereign equality of each is fully recognized—more fully than under the old constitution, which was the basis of the action of the convention; for, during the provisional government, on all questions in Congress, each State has an equal vote. This provisional government was only a temporary arrangement to meet the exigencies until a permanent constitution could be formed and put into operation. This was really the great work before them.

"In this, as in the provisional government, the old constitution of our fathers—the constitution of Madison and Washington, was their model. I said I might say something touching its provisions. Time will not allow me to go

342 cɟ THE QUOTABLE ALEXANDER H. STEPHENS

much into details. You will please read and examine it minutely for yourselves. While the old constitution was the basis and model of its construction, you will find in it several changes and modifications. Some of them important. But of them all I make in passing this general remark—they are all of a *conservative* character. This is the most striking characteristic of our revolution or change of government thus far, that none of the changes introduced are of a radical or downward tendency.

"But all the changes—every one of them—are upon what is called the *conservative* side. Now, this I ask your special attention to. It is an important fact. I wish you specially to mark it, for I know that efforts has been made to create prejudice against our movement by telling the conservative men of the country that it sprung from some of the hot heads down South, and should not be relied on or trusted. But take the [Confederate] constitution and read it, and you will find that every change in it from the old constitution is conservative. In many respects it is an improvement upon the constitution of our fathers. It has such improvements as the experience of seventy years showed were required. In this particular our revolution thus far is distinguished from popular revolutions in the history of the world. In it are settled many of the vexed questions which disturbed us in the old confederacy. A few of these may be mentioned—such as that no money shall be appropriated from the common treasury for internal improvements [corporate welfare]; leaving all such matters for the local and State authorities. The tariff question is also settled. The presidential term is extended [to six years], and no re-election allowed. This will relieve the country of those periodical agitations from which sprang so much mischief in the old government. If history shall record the truth in reference to our past system of government, it will be written of us that one of the greatest evils in the old government was the scramble for public offices—connected with the Presidential election. This evil is entirely obviated under the constitution which we have adopted.

"Many other improvements, as I think, could be mentioned, but it is unnecessary. I have barely alluded to the subject to show you that we do not invite you to any wild scheme of revolution. We invite Virginia to join us in perpetuating the principles upon which she has ever stood—the only hope of constitutional liberty in the world, as I now seriously apprehend. If it fails with us, where else can we see hope? But for the South, what would have become of the principles of Jefferson, Madison, and Washington, as embodied in the old constitution long ago? Whatever the United States government has done in advancement of civilization, by solving the great principles of self-government by the people, through representatives clothed with delegated powers, is due mainly to the South. The achievement has been by southern statesmen."[493]

In 1870 Stephens made these comments about the Constitution of the Confederate States of America:

☛ "The whole document utterly negatives the idea which so many have been active in endeavoring to put in the enduring form of history, that the Convention at Montgomery was nothing but a set of 'Conspirators,' whose object was the overthrow of the principles of the Constitution of the United States, and the erection of a great 'Slavery Oligarchy,' instead of the free Institutions thereby secured and guaranteed. This work of the Montgomery Convention, with that of the Constitution for a Provisional Government, will ever remain not only as a monument of the wisdom, forecast and statesmanship of the men who constituted it, but an everlasting refutation of the charges which have been brought against them. These works together show clearly that their only leading object was to sustain, uphold, and perpetuate the fundamental principles of the Constitution of the United States."[494]

13

The Confederate Government

Concerning the Confederacy's unconstitutional suspension of habeas corpus:
☛ "Power is ever insidious in its encroachments, or at least is usually so. Give it an inch and an ell [a right-angled bend] is soon taken. Various attempts had been made to get some such policy fixed upon the country; all had failed of perfect success. This was started and had been adopted under far more favorable auspices than any of its predecessors. It was, therefore, by far the more dangerous. When error once gets foothold, it seldom ever voluntarily abandons its advantage. Power, however insidious in its approaches, is ever insolent in a position once gained. The only sure way to meet it successfully, is with a bold, unyielding defiance at the beginning. Whoever trifles with it or dallies with it at first, is certain to become its victim in the end. This was my view of this matter when I first heard of the passage of this most monstrous act. The only sure hope of preventing its principles from becoming fixed upon the country, was such an immediate, prompt, bold, and harsh, if you please, expression of popular indignation and reprobation of it as to cause, if possible, its immediate abandonment. It was no time for soft words or temporizing. Usurpation never did and never will yield to gentle suasion. Power never let[s]

go its grasp, and never will upon mild entreaty. I speak to you eternal truths in all soberness."[495]

Speaking of the Confederate politicians who voted to suspend habeas corpus:

☞ "I have nothing to do with the motives of men; I wish this distinctly understood, not only for once, but always. I arraign no one, and pronounce judgment upon no one. I speak of things, acts, and measures, and their inevitable tendency. My deliberate opinion is, that very few men understand, know, or appreciate the nature of their acts, the character or tendency of them. Men, at best, are but grown up children. In legislatures, or other deliberate bodies, they generally act in masses; the individual is merged in the multitude; he exercises very little of his own private judgment. This is the general rule with a large majority according to my experience and observation. To assign bad motives to such, would be as cruel, as unjust. I have no disposition to do it. As well might one poor wretch be held responsible for the sins of society. But this cannot prevent or modify my judgment of the acts of the aggregate mass, the great sins of the whole, or the ruinous tendency of them. My experience has also taught me that men hardly ever understand themselves. The wisest uninspired maxim that ever was uttered, I think is this: 'Know thyself.' Millions have repeated it, and other millions still repeat it, without the slightest comprehension of its import; hence it not unfrequently happens, when the nature or tendency of one's acts are stated to him, he flares up in a passion and in a rage, because he thinks his motives have been impugned."[496]

On November 1, 1862, Stephens gave a speech in his hometown of Crawfordville, Georgia. Of this address Johnston and Browne write: "He made a strong appeal to the patriotism and sympathy of his audience, dwelt upon the rightfulness and justice of the cause of the South, which he pronounced a war 'for home, for firesides, for our altars, for our birthrights, for property, for honor, for life,—in a word, for everything for which freemen should live, and for which all deserving to be freemen should be willing, if need be, to die.' He explained the plan, which he had urged upon the Government, of making the cotton the basis of a system of finance." It is unfortunate that President Davis did not implement Stephens' idea, for it might have changed the course of Lincoln's War, allowing a Confederate victory:

☞ "I was in favor of the [Confederate] Government taking all the cotton that would be subscribed for eight per cent, bonds at a rate as high as ten cents a pound. Two millions of bales of the last year's crop might have been counted upon as certain on this plan. This at ten cents, with bales of the average commercial weight, would have cost the Government one hundred millions of bonds. With this amount of cotton in hand and pledged, any number, short of fifty, of the best iron-clad steamers could have been contracted for and built in Europe,—steamers at the cost of two millions each could be procured. Thirty millions would have got fifteen of these, which might have been enough for our purpose. Five might have been ready by the 1ˢᵗ of January last [1862] to open some one of the ports blockaded on our coast. Three of these could have been left to keep the port open, and two could have convoyed the cotton across the water, if necessary. Thus the debt could have been promptly paid with cotton at a much higher price than it cost, and a channel of trade kept open till others, and as many more as necessary, might have been built and paid for in the same way. At a cost of less than one month's present expenditure of our army, our coast might have been cleared. Besides this, at least two more millions of bales of the old crop on hand might have been counted on: this, with the other, making a debt in round numbers to the planters of two hundred million dollars. But this cotton, held in Europe until its price shall be fifty cents a pound, would constitute a fund of at least one billion dollars, which would not only have kept our finances in sound condition, but the clear profit of eight hundred million dollars would have met the entire expenses of the war for years to come."⁴⁹⁷

Though Stephens was never "at war" with his boss Confederate President Jefferson Davis, as the Northern newspapers of the day claimed, he did disagree with Davis on several key issues: taxation, the military draft, and the Confederacy's suspension of habeas corpus. The following comments were made by Stephens on March 16, 1864, before the Georgia legislature at Milledgeville, Georgia. First he touches on the topic of the Confederacy's "currency":

☛ "It is the beauty of our system of government, that all in authority are responsible to the people. It is, too, always more agreeable to approve than to disapprove what our agents have done. But in grave and important matters, however disagreeable or even painful it may be to express disapproval, yet sometimes the highest duty requires it. No exceptions should be taken to this when it is done in a proper spirit, and with a view solely for the public welfare. In free governments men will differ as to the best means of promoting the public good. Honest differences of opinion should never beget ill feelings, or personal alienations. The expressions of differences of opinion do no harm when truth alone is the object on both sides. Our opinions in all such discussions of public affairs, should be given as from friends to friends, as from brothers to brothers, in a common cause. We are all launched upon the same boat, and must ride the storm or go down together. Disagreements should never arise, except from one cause—a difference in judgment, as to the best means to be adopted, or course to be pursued, for the common safety. This is the spirit by which I am actuated in the comments I shall make upon these acts of [the Confederate] Congress.

"As to the first two of these measures, the Tax Act and Funding Act, known together as the financial and currency measures, I simply say, in my judgment, they are neither proper, wise or just. Whether in the midst of conflicting views, in such diversity of opinion and interests, any thing better could not be obtained, I know not—perhaps not. With that view we may be reconciled to what we do not approve. It is useless now to go into discussions of how better measures might have been obtained, or how bad ones might have been avoided—the whole is a striking illustration of the evils attending first departures from principle—the *'facilis descensus Averno'* [Latin: 'the decent to Hell is easy']. Error is ever the prolific source of error. Our present financial embarrassments had their origin in a blunder at the beginning, but we must deal with the present, not the past. These two acts make it necessary for you to change your legislation to save the State from loss. As to the course you should adopt to do this, I know of none better than that recommended by the governor [Joseph E. Brown]. His views and suggestions on this point seem to be proper and judicious."[498]

Jefferson Davis

As Stephens' speech before the Georgia legislature continues, he turns to the issue of the military draft:

☛ "The military act by which conscription is extended so as to embrace all between the ages of seventeen and fifty, and by which the State is to be deprived of so much of its labor, and stripped of the most efficient portion of her enrolled militia, presents a much graver question. This whole system of conscription I have looked upon from the beginning as wrong, radically wrong in principle and in policy. Contrary opinions, however, prevailed. But whatever differences of opinion may have been entertained as to the constitutionality of the previous conscript acts, it seems clear to my mind that but little difference can exist as to the unconstitutionality of this late act. The act provides for the organizing of troops of an anomalous character—partly as militia and partly as a portion of the regular armies. But, in fact, they are to be organized neither as militia or part of the regular army. We have but two kinds of forces, the regular army and the militia—this is neither. The men are to be raised as conscripts for the regular forces, while their officers are to be appointed as if they were militia. If they were intended as militia, they should have been called out, through the governor, in their present organizations—if as regular forces, they cannot be officered as the act provides. It is most clearly unconstitutional. Who is to commission these officers? The governor [Brown] cannot, for they are taken from under his control; the President cannot constitutionally do it, for he can commission none except by and with the advice and consent of the Senate. It is for you to say whether you will turn over these forces, and allow them to be conscripted, as is provided, leaving the question of constitutionality for the courts, or whether you will hold them in view of agricultural and other interest, or for the execution of your laws, and to be called out for the public defence in case of emergency by the governor when he sees the necessity, or when they are called for as militia by the President. The act upon its face, in its provisions for details, seems to indicate that its object is not to put the whole of them in the field. Nothing could be more ruinous to our cause if such were the object and intention, and should it ever be carried into effect. For if all the white labor of the country, from seventeen to fifty—except the few exemptions stated—be called out and kept constantly in the field, we must fail, sooner or later, for want of subsistence and other essential supplies. To wage war successfully, men at home are as necessary as men in the field. Those in the field must be provided for, and their families at home must be provided for. In my judgment, no people can successfully carry on a long war, with more than a third of its arms-bearing population kept constantly in the field, especially if, cut off by blockade, they are thrown upon their own internal resources for all necessary supplies, subsistence and munitions of war. This is a question of arithmetic on well settled problems of political economy. But can we succeed against the hosts of the enemy unless all able to bear arms up to fifty years of age are called to and kept in the field? Yes, a thousand times yes, I answer, with proper and skilful management. If we cannot without such a call, we cannot with it, if the war last long. The success of Greece against the invasion by Persia—the success of the Netherlands against Philip [II of Spain]—the success of Frederick against the allied powers of Europe—the success of the colonies against Great Britain, all show that it can be done. If our only hope was in matching the enemy with equal numbers, then our cause would be desperate indeed. Superior numbers is one of the chief advantages of the enemy. We must avail ourselves of our advantages. We should not rely for success by playing into his hand. An invaded people have many advantages that may be resorted to, to counterbalance superiority of numbers. These should be studied, sought, and brought into active co-operation. To secure success, brains must do something as well as muskets.

"Of all the dangers that threaten our ultimate success, I consider none more imminent than the policy embodied in this act, if the object really be, as its broad terms declare, to put and keep in active service all between the ages of seventeen and fifty, except the exempts named. On that line we will most assuredly, sooner or later, do what the enemy never could do, conquer ourselves. And if such be not the object of the act—if it is only intended to conscript men not intended for service, not with a view to fill the army, but for the officials, to take charge of the general labor of the country and the various necessary vocations and pursuits of life, then the act is not only wrong in principle but exceedingly dangerous in its tendency."[499]

Stephens' speech before the Georgia legislature continues, with the focus shifting to the issue of the suspension of habeas corpus:

☞ "I come, now, to the last of these acts of [the Confederate] Congress. The suspension of the writ of *habeas corpus* in certain cases. This is the most exciting as it is by far the most important question before you. Upon this depends the question, whether the courts shall be permitted to decide upon the constitutionality of the late conscript act, should you submit that question to their decision, and upon it also depend other great essential rights enjoyed by us as freemen. This act upon its face, confers upon the President, secretary of war, and the general commanding in the trans-Mississippi department, (the two latter acting under the control and authority of the President,) the power to arrest and imprison any person who may be simply charged with certain acts, not all of them even crimes under any law; and this is to be done without any oath or affirmation alledging probable cause as to the guilt of the party. This is attempted to be done under that clause of the constitution, which authorizes Congress to suspend the privilege of the writ of *habeas corpus*, in certain cases.

"In my judgment this act is not only unwise, impolitic and unconstitutional, but exceedingly dangerous to public liberty. Its unconstitutionality does not rest upon the idea that Congress has not got the power to suspend the privilege of this writ, nor upon the idea that the power to suspend it is an implied one, or that clearly implied powers are weaker as a class and subordinate to others, positively and directly delegated.

"I do not understand the executive of this State to put his argument against this act upon any such grounds. He simply states a fact, as it most clearly is, that the power to suspend at all is an implied power. There is no positive, direct power delegated to do it. The power, however, is clear, and clear only by implication. The language of the constitution, that 'the privilege of the writ of *habeas corpus* shall not be suspended unless, when in cases of rebellion or invasion, the public safety may require it,' clearly expresses the intention that

the power may be exercised in the cases stated; but it does so by implication only, just as if a mother should say to her daughter, you shall not go unless you ride. Here the permission and authority to go is clearly given, though by inference and implication only. It is not positively and directly given. This, and this only, I understand the governor [Brown] to mean when he speaks of the power being an implied one. He raises no question as to the existence of the power, or its validity when rightfully exercised, but he maintains, as I do, that its exercise must be controlled by all other restrictions in the constitution bearing upon its exercise. Two of these are to be found in the words

Alexander Hamilton

accompanying the delegation. It can never be exercised except in rebellion or invasion. Other restrictions are to be found in other parts of the constitution—in the amendments to the constitution adopted after the ratification of the words as above quoted. These amendments were made, as is expressly declared in the preamble to them, to add 'further declaratory and restrictive clauses,' to prevent 'misconstruction or abuse of the powers' previously delegated. To understand all the restrictions, therefore, thrown around the exercise of this power in the constitution, these additional 'restrictive clauses' must be read in conjunction with the original grant, whether that was made positively and directly, or by implication only. These restrictions, among other things, declare, that 'no person shall be deprived of life, liberty, or property, without due process of law,' and that the right of the people to be secure in their persons, houses, papers and effects, against *unreasonable* searches and seizures, shall not be violated, and no warrants shall issue but upon probable cause, supported by oath or affirmation, and particularly describing the place to be searched, and the person or thing to be seized.

"All admit that under the clause as it stands in the original grant, with the restrictions there set forth, the power can be rightfully exercised only in cases of rebellion or invasion. With these additional clauses, put in as further restrictions to prevent the abuse of powers previously delegated, how is this clause conferring the power to suspend the privilege of the writ of *habeas corpus*, now to be read? In this way, and in this way only:

> The privilege of the writ of *habeas corpus* shall not be suspended, unless when in cases of rebellion or invasion the public safety may require it. [And no person] shall be deprived of life, liberty, or property, without due process of law. [And further.] The right of the people to be secure in their persons, houses, papers and effects against unreasonable searches and seizures, shall not be violated, and no warrants shall issue but upon probable cause, supported by oath or affirmation, and particularly describing the place to be searched, and the persons or things to be seized.

"The attempted exercise of the power to suspend the privilege of the writ of *habeas corpus* in this act, is in utter disregard in the very face and teeth of these restrictions, as much so, as a like attempt in time of profound peace would be in disregard of the restrictions to cases of rebellion and invasion, as the constitution was originally adopted. It attempts to provide for depriving persons 'of liberty, without due process of law.' It attempts to annul and set at naught the great constitutional 'right' of the people, to be secure in their persons against 'unreasonable seizures.' It attempts to destroy and annihilate the bulwark of personal liberty, secured in our great chart to the humblest as well as the highest, that 'no warrants shall issue but upon probable cause, supported by oath or affirmation,' and 'particularly describing the person to be seized.' Nay, more, it attempts to change and transform the distribution of powers in our system of government. It attempts to deprive the judiciary department of its appropriate and legitimate functions, and to confer them upon the President, the secretary of war, and the general officer commanding the trans-Mississippi department, or rather to confer them entirely upon the

Ambrose Everett Burnside

President, for those subordinates named in the act hold their places at his will, and in arrests under this act are to be governed by his orders. This, by the constitution, never can be done. Ours is not only a government of limited powers, but each department, the legislative, executive and judicial, are separate and distinct. The issuing of warrants, which are nothing but orders for arrests, against civilians or persons in civil life, is a judicial function. The President, under the constitution, has not the power to issue any such. As commander-in-chief of the land and naval forces, and the militia when in actual service, he may order arrests for trials before courts-martial, according to the rules and articles of war. But he is clothed with no such power over those not in the military service and not subject to the rules and articles of war. This act attempts to clothe him with judicial functions, and in a judicial character to do what no judge, under the constitution, can do: issue orders or warrants for arrest, by which persons are to be deprived of their liberty, imprisoned, immured in dungeons, it may be without any oath or affirmation, even as to the probable guilt of the party accused or charged with any of the offences or acts stated. This, under the constitution, in my judgment, cannot be done. Congress can confer no such power upon our chief magistrate. There is no such thing known in this country as political warrants, or 'lettres de cachet' [an arbitrary order issued by a king]. This act attempts to institute this new order of things so odious to our ancestors, and so inconsistent with constitutional liberty.

"This act, therefore, is unconstitutional, not because Congress has not power to suspend the privilege of the writ of *habeas corpus*, but because they have no power to do the thing aimed at in this attempted exercise of it. Congress can suspend the privilege of the writ—the power is clear and unquestioned—neither is the power, as it stands, objectionable. Georgia, in the convention, voted against the clause conferring it in the constitution as originally adopted—that, perhaps, was a wise and prudent vote. But, with the restrictions subsequently adopted there can be no well grounded objection to it. It is, under existing restrictions, a wise power. In time of war, in cases of rebellion or invasion, it may often be necessary to exercise it—the public safety may require it. I am not prepared to say that the public safety may not require it now. I am not informed of the reasons which induced the President [Jefferson Davis] to ask the suspension of the privilege of the writ at this time, or Congress to undertake its suspension as provided in this act. I, however, know of no reasons that require it and have heard of none. But in the exercise of an undisputed power, they have attempted to do just what cannot be done—to authorize illegal and unconstitutional arrests. There can be no suspension of the writ, under our system of government, against unconstitutional arrests—there can be no suspension allowing, or with a view to permit and authorize, the seizure of persons without warrant issued by a judicial officer upon probable cause, supported by oath or affirmation—the whole constitution must be read together, and so read and construed as that every part and clause shall stand and have its proper effect under the restrictions of other clauses."[500]

Stephens' speech before the Georgia legislature continues:
☛ "Some seem to be of the opinion, that those who oppose [these acts] . . . are for a counter-revolution. No such thing; I am for no counter-revolution. The object is to keep the present one, great in its aims and grand in its purposes, upon the right track—the one on which it was started, and that on which alone it can attain noble objects and majestic achievements. The surest way to prevent a counter-revolution, is for the State to speak out and declare her opinions upon this subject. For as certain as day succeeds night, the people of this confederacy will never live long in peace and quiet under any government with the principles of this act settled as its established policy, and held to be in conformity with the provisions of its fundamental law. The action of the Virginia legislature in 1799, saved the old government, beyond question, from a counter and a bloody revolution; kept it on the right track for sixty years afterward, in its unparelleled career of growth, prosperity, development, progress, happiness, and renown. All our present troubles, North and South, sprang from violations of those great constitutional principles therein set forth."[501]

Stephens' speech before the Georgia legislature continues:
☛ "Let no one, therefore, be deterred from performing his duty on this occasion by the cry of counter-revolution, nor by the cry that it is the duty of

all, in this hour of peril, to support the government. Our government is composed of executive, legislative and judicial departments, under the constitution. He most truly and faithfully supports the government who supports and defends the constitution. Be not misled by this cry, or that you must not say any thing against the administration, or you will injure the cause. This is the argument of the preacher, who insisted that his derelictions should not be exposed, because if they were, it would injure his usefulness as a minister. Derelict ministers are not the cause. Listen to no such cry. And let no one be influenced by that other cry, of the had effect such discussions and such action will have upon our gallant citizen soldiers in the field. I know something of the feeling of these men. I have witnessed their hardships, their privations, and their discomforts in camp. I have witnessed and ministered to their wants and sufferings from disease and wounds, in hospitals. I know something of the sentiments that actuated the great majority of them, when they quit home, with all its endearments, and went out to this war—not as mercenaries or human machines, but as intelligent, high-minded, noble-spirited gentlemen, who were proud of their birthright as freemen, and 'who knowing their rights,' dared maintain them, at any and every cost and sacrifice. The old Barons who extorted Magna Charta from their oppressor and wrongdoer by a resort to arms, did not present a grander spectacle for the admiration of the world when they went forth to their work, thoroughly imbued with a sense of the right for the right's sake, than this gallant band of patriots did when they went forth to this war [against Lincoln], inspired with no motive but a thorough devotion to and ardent attachment for constitutional liberty. To defend this and maintain it inviolate for themselves and those who should come after them, was their sole object. Their ancient rights, usages, institutions, and liberties were threatened by an insolent foe [liberal Yankees], who had trampled the constitution of our common [Southern] ancestors under foot. They and we all had quit the Union, when the rights of all of us were no longer respected under it, but we had rescued the constitution—the ark of the covenant—and this is what they went forth to defend. These were the sentiments with which your armies were raised, as if by magic. These are the sentiments with which re-enlistments for the war have been made. These are the sentiments with which your ranks would have been filled to the last man whose services can be relied upon in action if conscription had never been resorted to. You cannot, therefore, send these gallant defenders of constitutional liberty, a more cheering message than that, while they are battling for their rights and the common rights of all in the field, you are keeping sacred watch, and guard over the same in the public councils. They will enter the fight with renewed vigor, from the assurance that their toil, and sacrifice and blood will not be in vain, but that when the strife is over and independence is acknowledged, it will not be a bare name, a shadow and a mockery, but that with it they and their children after them shall enjoy that liberty for which they now peril all. Next to this, the most encouraging message you could send them is, that while all feel that the brunt of the fight must be borne by them, and the only sure hope of success is in the prowess of their arms, yet every possible and honorable effort will be made by the civil departments of the government to terminate the struggle by negotiation and adjustment upon the principles for which they entered the contest."[502]

Stephens finished his speech before the Georgia legislature with these words:
☛ "What fate or fortune awaits you or me, in the contingencies of the times, is unknown to us all. We may meet again, or we may not. But as a parting remembrance, a lasting memento, to be engraven on your memories and your

Baron de Montesquieu

hearts, I warn you against that most insidious enemy which approaches with her siren song, 'Independence first and liberty afterward.' It is a fatal delusion. Liberty is the animating spirit, the soul of our system of government, and like the soul of man, when once lost it is lost forever. There is for it, at least, no redemption, except through blood. Never for a moment permit yourselves to look upon liberty, that constitutional liberty which you inherited as a birthright, as subordinate to independence. The one was resorted to to secure the other. Let them ever be held and cherished as objects co-ordinate, co-existent, co-equal, co-eval, and forever inseparable. Let them stand together 'through weal and through woe,' and if such be our fate, let them and us all go down together in a common ruin.

Without liberty, I would not turn upon my heel for independence. I scorn all independence which does not secure liberty. I warn you also against another fatal delusion, commonly dressed up in the fascinating language of, 'If we are to have a master, who would not prefer to have a southern one to a northern one?' Use no such language. Countenance none such. Evil communications are as corrupting in politics as in morals.

". . . I would not turn upon my heel to choose between masters. I was not born to acknowledge a master from either the North or South. I shall never choose between candidates for that office. Shall never degrade the right of suffrage in such an election. I have no wish or desire to live after the degradation of my country, and have no intention to survive its liberties, if life be the necessary sacrifice of their maintenance to the utmost of my ability, to the bitter end. As for myself, give me liberty as secured in the constitution with all its guaranties, amongst which is the sovereignty of Georgia, or give me death. This is my motto while living, and I want no better epitaph when I am dead.

"Senators and representatives! the honor, the rights, the dignity, the glory of Georgia, are in your hands! See to it as faithful sentinels upon the watchtower, that no harm or detriment come to any of those high and sacred trusts, while committed to your charge."[503]

From Stephens to Confederate Secretary of War James A. Seddon, April 29, 1864:
☞ "[No one] . . . cannot possibly regret more sincerely or profoundly my disagreement with members of the administration upon some of the late measures of legislation than I do myself. And nothing could have induced me to take public position against them, but a sense of public duty arising from a strong conviction of the mischievous and dangerous tendency of those measures—founded as they were, in my judgment, upon great and radical errors. But in this, as in all differences amongst common friends in a great common cause, I assure you I was influenced by nothing except what I regarded as the public good. I was not influenced in the slightest degree by feelings of hostility or bitterness, to say nothing of malignancy, toward a single mortal who disagreed with me."[504]

In response to growing criticism that he was working at cross purposes with President Davis and the Southern Cause, Stephens addressed this letter to "the Public" on November 10, 1864:
☞ "Insinuations and flings, if not direct charges, have repeatedly been made of late against me as a new light on States' Rights, in my advocacy of the doctrine of 'the ultimate absolute sovereignty of the several States' as the only sure basis of a permanent peace between the States of the old Union. . . . States' Rights and State Sovereignty are no new or latter day ideas with me. . . .

"It is true I was not a Nullifier. Nullification as I understood its exposition at that day claimed the right of any State, in effect, to render null and

Henry Wager Halleck

void, or inoperative within her limits, any law of Congress, and still remain within the Union. Without any desire to revive any of the questions that then divided State Rights men, I may simply add that in my judgment then and now, the reserved Sovereign Powers of the States could be properly resorted to for ultimate protection only by a full resumption of all powers delegated; in other words by secession. In this way only could the sovereign veto of a State against actual or threatened aggression be effectually and properly interposed. When thus interposed there was no constitutional power in the Central Government to command obedience by coercion.

"It is also true that I opposed secession in 1850 and 1860, as a question of policy, but not as a matter of right. The charge that I ever at any time or on any occasion uttered the sentiment that secession would be 'a crime' is entirely without the shadow of a foundation. The clear right of a State under the compact of 1787 to resume the full exercise of all her delegated powers by a withdrawal from the Union whenever her people in their deliberate and solemnly expressed judgment should determine to do so, was never questioned by me. This was the doctrine of the States' Rights party of Georgia under the lead of the illustrious and renowned Troup—the correct teachings of the Kentucky and Virginia Resolutions of 1798 and 1799. In these principles I was reared, by them I have ever been governed in my political acts, and by them I expect to live and die. Hence when Georgia seceded in 1861, even against my own judgment, I stood by her act. To her alone I owed ultimate allegiance. Her cause became my cause. Her destiny became my destiny. From that day to this that cause has engaged every energy of my heart, head and soul, and in it they will continue to be enlisted to the bitter end. Should that end be the establishment of this principle of 'the ultimate absolute sovereignty of the several States,' it will in my judgment more than compensate for the loss of blood and treasure of this war so unjustly waged against her and her confederates, great as it has been or may be. This doctrine once firmly established will, I doubt not, prove to be the self-adjusting principle—the Continental Regulator—in our present or any future systems of associations or confederations of States that may arise. I make no boast of consistency so far as party relations are concerned—these I have often changed, but principles never."[505]

Despite his few differences with Davis, Stephens and his superior at the Confederate White House agreed on nearly every other issue, as the following excerpt from 1870 reveals. Stephens is referring to President Davis' Inaugural Address given on February 18, 1861:
☛ "This address affords additional evidence, if any were wanting, to show the objects aimed at by the Confederate States in their separation from their former associates. It clearly shows, as the Acts of the Convention show, that these States had quit the Union only to preserve for themselves, at least, the principles of the Constitution. It shows, also, that there was no purpose, wish, design, or intention, on the part of Mr. Davis, to make war, commit aggression, or do any wrong to those States, or the people of those States which remained in the old Union, or to interfere improperly in any way, with the Government of their choice."[506]

Before and throughout the entire duration of Lincoln's War, the Confederate government sent one peace commission after another to Washington, D.C., to meet with the U.S. president or any of his cabinet members, in an attempt to end hostilities. Here Stephens remarks on their reception by the Yankees:
☛ "The whole conduct of the [Confederate Peace] Commissioners was marked with perfect frankness and integrity of purpose, while they were met with an equivocation, a duplicity, a craft, and deceit, which, taken altogether, is without a parallel in modern times!"[507]

Stephens went on to note "the duplicity of the Washington authorities," who continually lied to the Confederate commissioners just prior to the Battle of Fort Sumter. It was at this time that Lincoln, who by now desperately wanted to invade and crush the Confederacy, nefariously tricked the South into firing the first shot. Of this period Stephens writes:
☛ "[Important changes in plans and policy were] . . . not communicated to the [Confederate] Commissioners. They were . . . kept uninformed and left to rest

upon the assurances given, while the most energetic measures and active preparations for war and subjugation were being concocted and executed."[508]

It is a little known fact that Stephens wanted not only the Border states to join the Southern Confederacy, but eventually both the Northwestern and the Northern states as well. Here is how he phrased it:

☛ ". . . the leading object with me was not only to secure the accession of the Border States, so-called, but the accession, at no distant day, of all the great Northwestern States so intimately connected with us geographically and politically; and moreover, if possible, by inducing our late derelict Confederates [i.e., the Northern states] to reconsider their course, also, in the end, to secure the accession of all these States of the old Union into our new Confederacy! To use a common phrase for illustrating the idea, my object was to Nationalize our new Articles of Union, and to cause them to become the common Bond of a new and still more perfect Union of the whole, by bringing all the States to their voluntary adoption through a process not exactly of a Reconstruction of the old Union, but of a Reorganization of its constituent elements, and a new Assimilation upon the basis of our new Constitution, just as the original thirteen States had passed from the first Articles of Confederation of seventeen hundred and seventy-eight to the second of seventeen hundred and eighty-seven!

"[In a word, I was quite willing to] make Peace on the basis of a 'Reorganization of the Union,' as [the Liberals] . . . call it, under . . . the Montgomery Constitution, . . . or upon renewed and reliable guarantees on the part of the derelict Northern States to return to the discharge of their obligations, and to maintain the Federal system according to the true spirit and intent of the Constitution of 1787; or I would have been willing to make Peace simply upon the recognition of the principle that lies at the foundation of that System—the absolute Sovereignty of the several States—leaving any Re-union or Unions in the future to their own voluntary choice, according to their own views of their own interests, safety, security, and happiness, as time with the lights of experience, patriotism, and wisdom might determine.

"[I was never in favor of erecting a permanent separate Slave States' Confederacy.] . . . I did not consider such a Confederacy as either desirable in itself, or permanently practicable under the circumstances. The heterogeneousness of the interests of the different States under the Federal [Confederate] system, when administered according to its true principles, in my opinion, gave it real stability. This was the tightening principle which when left to its own free action gave steadiness to all its parts, and that beauty and grandeur exhibited in all its complicated motions."[509]

Stephens continues on with this line of thought:

☞ "Concerning the idea that the Northern States would ever be induced to adopt the Confederate States Constitution] . . . I entertained scarcely a doubt upon the subject, with prudent and wise statesmanship on the part of our Rulers, looking to that end; indeed, but for the war, this result, with a proper policy for its attainment, would have been almost inevitable. An overwhelming majority of the people of the Northern States was thoroughly opposed to the principles of the Centralists [Liberals]. The repeated popular condemnations of their principles referred to show this conclusively. But for the war the Centralists, then controlling the Federal Government by accident and not popular confidence, would, as a Party, have gone to pieces in ninety days. They would hardly have been sustained in New England at the next elections; the re-action there was already ominously felt by them. The war was a necessity for their continued hold of Power, even in those States. Hence, the conspiracy of the 'seven Governors' who demanded of Mr. Lincoln a change of his policy, as to the withdrawal of the Federal forces from the Southern Forts. War, with bold usurpations which it was to cover and excuse, was their only hope.

"But even after the war was thus begun, if the Confederate Authorities had desired it, and had directed their energies to the attainment of that object, it could, in my opinion, have still been accomplished—not so speedily or easily, but almost as surely in the end. The real war-spirit at the North, at first, was confined exclusively to the Abolitionists proper, and other Centralists [Liberals], who, from political affinity, cordially co-operated with them. But these two elements combined did not constitute, in the aggregate, much, if any, over one-third of the people of, the Northern States. The great majority of the people of these States, however strongly they were opposed to Slavery, were nevertheless more strongly attached to the Federal [Confederate] System, and utterly opposed to the consolidating principles of the [Liberal] Party then in power. Thousands, and

Benjamin Franklin

hundreds of thousands of those who rushed to the rescue of the Capital in the manner we have seen, no more approved the usurpations of Power on the part of the Washington Authorities, nor the policy which inaugurated the war, than did the people of the Confederate States. They, it is true, were all opposed to Secession. They belonged to the mercantile and shipping classes, who were opposed to interrupting the old-established channels of trade, and to that very large class throughout the North, of all interests and occupations, who were thoroughly devoted to what they called 'the Union,' without any very well defined ideas of its nature or character. These different elements, actuated by such sentiments, constituted the masses on whom the 'old flag' produced such magical effect in those eventful days; and these were the masses on whom the Party now in power so adroitly used this 'old flag' for their ulterior purposes, though for it they themselves had neither reverence nor respect. It was now held up by them [Northern Liberals] as a sacred emblem of patriotic devotion, though by many of their leaders it had been for years before denounced as 'a flaunting lie' and 'hate's polluted rag.' It now, however, served their purpose, and they understood well how to use it, in misguiding the patriotic impulses of a confiding people. A very large majority, not only of the entire people of the North, but even of those who voluntarily entered the war, were thoroughly wedded to the Institutions of the Country, as established by the [Founding] Fathers. The main object with them was to maintain what they called 'the integrity of the Country.' 'The Union' under the Montgomery Constitution of 1861, would have been just as acceptable to them, as the 'Union' under the Philadelphia Constitution of 1787. Arch-Bishop [John] Hughes was an eminent representative man of this large portion of the Northern population. In this condition of things it seemed to me that the prospect of effecting an adjustment of the differences between the States upon the basis of the Montgomery Constitution was by no means hopeless, notwithstanding the formidable obstacles produced by the war, if the Confederate Authorities could but be induced to approve it, and direct all their civil and military operations with a view to its accomplishment. If our policy and course had been to make common cause with all true friends of the Federal [Confederate] System throughout the United States, upon this basis, against the usurpations and Centralizing principles of the Washington Government, the war, in my opinion, then and now, would have been a short one."[510]

14

Slavery & Blacks

From an 1847 speech before the U.S. House of Representatives:
☛ "Upon the subject of slavery, about which so much has been said in this debate, I shall say but little. I do not think it necessary to enter into a defence of the character of the people of my section of the Union, against the arguments of those who have been pleased to denounce that institution as wicked and sinful. It is sufficient for me and for them, that the morality of that institution stands upon a basis as firm as the Bible; and by that code of morals we are content to abide until a better be furnished. Until Christianity be overthrown, and some other system of ethics be substituted, the relation of master and slave can never be regarded as an offence against the Divine laws. The character of our people speaks for itself. And a more generous, more liberal, more charitable, more benevolent, more philanthropic, and a more magnanimous people, I venture to say, are not to be found in any part of this or any other country. As to their piety, it is true they have 'none to boast of.' But they are free from that pharisaical sin of self-righteousness, which is so often displayed elsewhere [i.e., in the North], of forever thanking the Lord that they are not as other men are."[511]

The following excerpt is from Stephens' letter to his brother Linton Stephens, dated March 14, 1850. This missive not only shows Stephens' great humanity toward blacks, but it also destroys one of the most common Northern myths, that "Southern slaves were prohibited from marrying." This particular letter concerns the marriage of one of

Stephens' house servants, Eliza, to Harry, a servant belonging to another family, the Googers. Subsequently, Stephens purchased Harry so he and Eliza could be together. Over time Harry became Stephens' favorite and most valuable "slave." That the affectionate feelings were mutual is clear from the fact that Harry voluntarily took his master's surname as his own. Harry Stephens served under the great Georgia statesman from before Lincoln's War to his death in 1880, three years before Stephens' own passing. Sometime after their marriage, Stephens gave the couple the "gift" of a beautiful two-story house he owned. Eliza was still living in the home as late as 1904. Eliza and Harry had saved so much money over the years that Eliza was wealthier than the always generous Stephens at the time of his death in 1883. In fact, when Stephens was arrested in May 1865, Harry offered to lend his master money:

Beriah Magoffin

☛ "In my letter written at the House to-day I forgot to reply to the request of Googer's Harry to take Eliza for his wife. Say to him that I have no objection. And tell Eliza to go to Solomon & Henry's [store] and get her a wedding dress, including a pair of fine shoes, etc., and to have a decent wedding of it. Let them cook a supper and have such of their friends as they wish. Tell them to get some 'parson man' and be married like 'Christian folks.' Let the wedding come off some time when you are at home, so that you may keep order amongst them. Buy a pig and let them have a good supper. Let Eliza bake some pound cake and set a good wedding supper."[512]

From a December 28, 1853, letter to his brother Linton, regarding Bob, one of Stephens' servants. Contrary to Yankee myth, which likes to portray Stephens as a racist and cruel slave owner, this letter reveals the warm, personal, and respectful relationships he had with the blacks who served under him:

☞ "And poor Bob! he went over in the sleet and snow with his wife and little ones. I fear the exposure will make some of them sick. By the way, Bob was not obnoxious to your apprehension that he had made too free with the mules and buggy. He had my permission to make you the visit, before I left. It was a darling visit to Bob. It had been near his heart all summer. I suspect he enjoyed it right well, if the simple-hearted, good-natured fellow did not get drunk!

"Bob, with all his faults, has many excellent traits of character, and some substantial virtues. He is honest, faithful, and truthful. Just before I left home, he came up to town on Sunday, and stayed with me all day. I was sitting in the front parlor alone, reading, when he came and sat on the steps. He began to talk in a very serious mood about my leaving home. I turned the subject to a religious talk. I asked him if he ever thought what would become of him if he should die. He said yes: that subject occupied more of his mind every day than all other things put together. I asked him if he ever prayed. He said he tried to pray. . . . Towards sundown I walked down to the back lot to take some exercise, and Bob went with me. He, Rio, and I were the trio. We looked at some young pigs, then walked through the apple-orchard, peach-orchard, and potato-patch, back to the house, Bob still talking and forgetting to go home. But about sundown he rose with, 'Well, this won't do for me; I must be gwine [going]. Good-by, Mass' Ellick.' This ended the last evening I ever had the pleasure of spending with Bob."[513]

From an October 27, 1854, letter to his brother Linton. It concerns a Southern tradition called "corn shucking," in which the normal restraints between master and "slave" are loosened. Again we see Stephens' true nature in regard to African-Americans:

☞ ". . . Last night I had a corn-shucking. About thirty or forty negroes assembled, shucked out all the pile, and after that, according to custom, claimed the right of carrying me, the boss, about over the yard and through the house, singing and cutting all sorts of capers. I thought discretion was the better part of valor, and did not resist the 'toting' custom. The sport seemed to amuse the negroes very much, and when they had got their hands in with me, they took brother John and John Tilly and carried them both through the rocking and tossing process. This sport, as you may know, is like that which Sancho Pansa fell in with once. They put their victim in a chair, and then swing him to and fro in the air as high as their long arms will permit."[514]

From a January 24, 1854, letter to his brother Linton, regarding "Uncle Ben," an old family servant who was visiting Stephens:

☞ "I saw Ben at the plantation to-day. He looked sad. He had been all over the old stamping- and hunting-grounds. In vain had he looked for the old persimmon-tree. Perkins (the former owner) had cut it down. Ben cried when he talked about the grave-yard to-day. He said, 'When Missis planted that cedar-tree at the children's graves, she told me if I should live the longest to take care of it; but many has been the year since I saw it. When I went to Upson County it was a little bit of a bush; now it looks like an old tree. Mass' Grier planted the poplar. He just cut a twig and stuck it in the ground, and it grew. Now the tree has grown up, lived out its life, and is dead.' I almost cried to hear Ben talk."[515]

From a January 26, 1854, letter to his brother Linton, again regarding a visit with "Uncle Ben":
☞ ". . . When I got to the grave-yard I found Ben, as Old Mortality, gazing on brother's tombstone trying to read the inscription. We remained about the sacred spot for some time. When we were about starting he said with tears in his eyes and faltering voice that he wanted me to get Mass' John [John Lindsay Stephens, Alexander's half-brother] to let him come back and stay on the old place. He wanted to live there the rest of his life, and when he died to be buried with the rest. I answered that I would see about it."[516] [Upon Uncle Ben's death, Stephens granted his wish.]

From a December 14, 1854, speech before the U.S. House of Representatives. Despite Stephens' firsthand knowledge of blacks and his friendly relations with them, at this early date he is still possessed with a desire to keep them in bondage. Why? As we will see in the following pages, he was a devout Christian with a profound belief in the Bible—a book that not only sanctions slavery, but in some passages actually requires it. In defending slavery then, Stephens felt that he was merely following biblical principles. Other aspects of this speech reveal Stephens' strong adherence to the Constitution and states' rights:
☞ "Why is it that gentlemen object so much to the introduction of slavery into Kansas, if the people of that Territory desire it to go there? When I made a speech at the last session upon this subject, I stated that I would vote for the principle of allowing the people of any section of the country to come into the Union and form institutions as they please. This I said when I knew there might be twice as many people there from the North as from the South, and the chances of emigration I knew would greatly preponderate in favor of the North. I am willing, now, to abide by that principle. I have no desire to deprive the people of any State or Territory, in our common country, of the right of adopting such institutions for their government, when they become States, as

they please. It is anti-American, and entirely at war with the spirit of the age, about which we hear so much. I ask why the people of any section of the country should be prevented from adopting the institutions of the South, if they wish them? Socially, morally, or politically, or in any respect of the question, is there any reason for depriving them of that right? Is it for the sake of humanity that gentlemen are not willing for the people of Kansas to assign the African the same condition there that he occupies in the South, if they think it best to do so? Are gentlemen willing to degrade their own race by not permitting them to vote upon matters relating to their own Government, while they are endeavoring to elevate the negro to the standard of the white man?

You may degrade the white man, but you cannot raise the negro to the level you purpose. It is impossible. You have to reverse a law of nature first. Men may indulge in philanthropic speculations as much as they please, but here is the great immutable law of nature, and they cannot avoid it. I am not here to argue whether decrees of the Most High are right, wise, and just. There is a difference, a vast difference, established by the Creator between the different races of men. For myself, I believe that He who made all is just, and that He made the white man as He made him, and that He made the negro as He made him—for wise and just purposes.

Braxton Bragg

Some vessels are made for honor, and some for dishonor; one star differeth from another star in magnitude as well as brilliancy.[517]

". . . I believe . . . that the system of government, as adopted by the South, defining the status or relation of [the white and black] . . . races, is the best for both of them; and I am prepared to argue that question with the gentleman, here or anywhere. Take the negroes in Indiana, take them in the North generally, and compare their condition with those of the South. Take them in Africa; take them anywhere on the face of the habitable globe; and then take them in the southern States, and the negro population of the South are better off, better fed, better clothed, better provided for, enjoy more happiness, and a higher civilization, than the same race has ever enjoyed anywhere else on the face of the world. Could [John] Howard the [British] philanthropist [and social reformer], who has left an undying fame for his deeds of humanity, have taken the same number of Africans from their native country and raised them from their barbarous condition to that of the slaves of the South, he would have added much to that stature of immortality which, in his day, he erected to himself. It would have greatly added to that reputation, which now sanctifies his memory in the hearts and affections of mankind.

"Look at the three millions of Africans as you find them in the South; and where is the man so cold-hearted, and cold-blooded, as would wish to put them in the condition that their forefathers were, or their kindred now are in Africa? What has done so much for these people but that which is so much denounced by inconsiderate fanatics; men and women, too, who find fault with what they know nothing about?"[518]

From the same December 14, 1854, speech:

☛ ". . . take our negroes, and compare their condition with that of the free negroes of the North. I have the result of the census returns before me, and from that it appears that the increase of the free people of color in the United States, from 1840 to 1850, was only ten and ninety-five hundredths *per centum*. This shows that their condition cannot be very good, or desirable; and to this increase is to be added, too, the fugitive slaves, and those who have been emancipated. With all these sources of increase, that increase has only been ten and ninety-five hundredths *per centum*.

"Now, how is it with the [Southern] slaves—the [so-called] down-trodden, the abused, the half-starved slaves? Their increase, during the same period, was twenty-eight and fifty-eight hundredths. Is there any such result to be presented at the North, where they are free and left to themselves? How can your missionaries in philanthropy and crusaders in benevolence account for this?

"But some people say that slavery is a curse to the white man. They abandon the idea that it is a curse to the negro. They say it weakens, impoverishes, and demoralizes a State. Let us see. They say there can be no high social, moral, or material development under the institution of slavery. I have before me some statistics on this point—statistics relating to material development. But, before alluding to them, I will say upon the subject of morals, that I saw a table of crimes made out in the census office for 1850. From those statistics it appeared—I speak from memory; I have not the paper before me—that the number of convictions for crimes of every grade, in

Charles Sumner

Massachusetts, the land of 'steady habits,' and where we hear so much of the immoral effects of slavery, with a population under one million, was several thousand; while in the State of Georgia, with a population not so great, the similar convictions are less than one hundred. I say, then, upon the score of crime, upon the score of morals, I am ready to compare my State with that of Massachusetts, or any one of the free States. Where, then, is the moral curse which arises from slavery?"[519]

From the same December 14, 1854, speech. Note that contrary to Northern myth, Stephens is not defending slavery so much as he is the right of the American people (whites, blacks, browns, yellows, and reds) to decide if they wanted to practice slavery or not, as guaranteed in the U.S. Constitution. Here he is speaking of the debate over whether or not to allow slavery into the new Western Territories (the as of yet unformed and unnamed Western states):

☛ "Now, then, if the people of Kansas, the people of Nebraska, or the people of any other portion of our territory, going from old Massachusetts, going from New York, or from Indiana, or from the South, learning and consulting wisdom from the past, and profiting by experience from all parts of the Union, should think it practically best for the happiness of themselves and for their posterity in the far distant future, to adopt the social institutions of Georgia in preference to those of Indiana, if they prefer the institutions of the South to those of the North, I say they should not be deprived of their right to do it, and the gentleman from Indiana, and those who act with him, should not set themselves up as judges and 'masters' to control the matter."[520]

The following excerpt is from Stephens' June 28, 1856, speech before the U.S. House of Representatives. During his discussion on the bill to admit Kansas as a state under the Topeka Constitution, he paused to give his opinion on "slavery at large," using both the U.S. Constitution and the Bible as a defense. We will note here that—from God himself to the Old Testament prophets, from Jesus to Paul—the Bible not only allows and encourages slavery, it literally demands it in several sections. Thus in defending slavery using the Bible, Stephens was only following the Christian interpretation of the Good Book as it was then understood by most Americans South and North. While modern America has condemned slavery, to this day the most learned Bible scholars and theologians are still unable to explain why, far from prohibiting or even disapproving of slavery, the Bible clearly and repeatedly condones, approves, and even requires it:

☛ ". . . Even, however, if slavery be sinful, as they [abolitionists] affirm, or their language implies, permit me here to ask, is not the sin the same whether the slave be held in Georgia, Carolina, or in Kansas? Is it any more sinful in one place than another? But are these gentlemen correct? Is African slavery, as it exists in the South, either a violation of the laws of nature, the laws of nations, or the laws of God? I maintain that it is not. It has been recognized by the laws of nations from time immemorial. [In our Constitution, the] . . . highest court in this country, the Supreme Court of the United States, has so decided the laws of nations to be. . . .

"Then as to the law of God—that law we read not only in his works about us, around us, and over us, but in that inspired Book wherein he has revealed his will to man. When we differ as to the voice of nature, or the language of God, as spoken in nature's works, we go to that great Book, the Book of books, which is the fountain of all truth. To that Book I now appeal. God, in the days of old, made a covenant with the human family—for the redemption of fallen man: that covenant is the corner-stone of the whole Christian system. Abram, afterwards called Abraham, was the man with whom that covenant was made. He was the great first head of an organized visible church here below. He believed God, and it was accounted to him for righteousness. He was indeed and in truth the father of the faithful. Abraham, sir, was a slaveholder. Nay, more, he was required to have the sign of that covenant administered to the slaves of his household.

". . . Here is the passage, Genesis 17:13. God said to Abraham:

> 13. He that is born in thy house and he that is bought with thy money must needs be circumcised; and my covenant shall be in your flesh for an everlasting covenant.

"Yes, sir, Abraham was not only a slaveholder, but a slave dealer it seems, for he bought men with his money, and yet it was with him the covenant was made by which the world was to be redeemed from the dominion of sin. And it was into his bosom in heaven that the poor man who died at the rich man's gate was borne by angels, according to the parable of the Saviour. In the 20th chapter of Exodus, the great moral law is found—that law that defines sin—the ten commandments, written by the finger of God himself upon tables of stone. In two of these commandments, the 4th and 10th, verses 10th and 17th, slavery is expressly recognized, and in none of them is there any thing against it—this is the moral law. In Leviticus we have the civil law on this subject, as given by God to Moses for the government of his chosen people in their municipal affairs. In . . . 25:44-46, I read as follows:

> 44. Both thy bondmen and thy bondmaids which thou shalt have, shall be of the heathen that are round about you; of them ye shall buy bondmen and bondmaids.
>
> 45. Moreover, of the children of the strangers that do sojourn among you, of them ye shall buy, and of their families that are with you which they begat in your land: and they shall be your possession.
>
> 46. And ye shall take them as an inheritance for your children after you, to inherit them for a possession; they shall be your bondmen forever; but over your brethren, the children of Israel, ye shall not rule one over another, with rigor.

"This was the law given to the Jews soon after they left Egypt, for their government when they should reach the land of promise. They could have had no slaves then. It authorized the introduction of slavery amongst them when they should become established in Canaan. And it is to be noted that their bondmen and bondmaids to be bought, and held for a possession and an inheritance for their children after them, were to be of the heathen round about them. Over their brethren they were not to rule with rigor. Our southern system is in strict conformity with this injunction. Men of our own blood and our own race, wherever born, or from whatever clime they come, are free and equal. We have no castes or classes amongst white men—no 'upper tendom' or 'lower tendom.' All are equals. Our slaves were taken from the heathen tribes—the barbarians of Africa. In our households they are brought within the pale of the covenant, under Christian teaching and influence; and more of them are partakers of the benefits of the gospel than

Clement Laird Vallandigham

ever were rendered so by missionary enterprise. The wisdom of man is foolishness—the ways of Providence are mysterious. Nor does the negro feel any sense of degradation in his condition—he is not degraded. He occupies and fills the same grade or rank in society and the State that he does in the scale of being; it is his natural place; and all things fit when nature's great first law of order is conformed to."[521]

From the same 1856 speech:

☞ ". . . Job was certainly one of the best men of whom we read in the Bible. He was a large slaveholder. So, too, were Isaac and Jacob, and all the patriarchs. But, it is said, this was under the Jewish dispensation. Granted. Has any change been made since? Is any thing to be found in the New Testament against it? Nothing—not a word. Slavery existed when the gospel was preached by Christ and his Apostles, and where they preached: it was all around them. And though the Scribes and Pharisees were denounced by our Saviour for their hypocrisy and robbing 'widows' houses,' yet not a word did He utter against slaveholding. On one occasion He was sought for by a centurion, who asked him to heal his slave, who was sick. Jesus said he would go; but the centurion objected, saying: 'Lord, I am not worthy that thou shouldst come under my roof; but speak the word only, and my servant shall be healed. For I am a man under authority, having soldiers under me; and I say to this man, go, and he goeth; and to another come, and he cometh; and to my slave, do this, and he doeth it.' Matthew 8:9. The word rendered here 'servant,' in our translation, means slave. It means just such a servant as all our slaves at the South are. I have the original Greek.

"The word in the original is *doulos*, and the meaning of this word, as given in [Edward] Robinson's Greek and English Lexicon, is this—I read from the book: 'In the family the *doulos* was one bound to serve, a slave, and was the property of his master—"a living possession," as Aristotle calls him.' And again: 'The *doulos*, therefore, was never a hired servant, the latter being called *misthios*,' etc. This is the meaning of the word, as given by Robinson, a learned doctor of divinity, as well as of laws. The centurion [a non-Christian Pagan] on that occasion said to Christ himself, 'I say to my slave do this, and he doeth it, and do Thou but speak the word, and he shall be healed.' What was the Saviour's reply? Did he tell him to go loose the bonds that fettered his fellow man? Did he tell him he was sinning against God for holding a slave? No such thing. But we are told by the inspired penman, that:

> When Jesus heard it he marvelled, and said to them that followed: Verily I say unto you, I have not found so great faith, no, not in Israel. And I say unto you that many shall come from the east and west and shall sit down with Abraham, and Isaac, and Jacob, in the kingdom of heaven. But the children of the kingdom shall be cast out into utter darkness; there shall be weeping and gnashing of teeth. And Jesus said unto the centurion, Go thy way, and as thou hast believed so be it done unto thee. And his servant [or slave] was healed in the selfsame hour.

"Was Christ a 'doughface' [i.e., a Yankee who sanctioned slavery in the South; who sympathized with the South]? Did He quail before the slave power? And if he did not rebuke the lordly centurion for speaking as he did of his authority over his slave, but healed the sick man, and said that he had not found so great faith in all Israel as he had in his master, who shall now presume, in His name, to rebuke others for exercising similar authority, or say that their faith may not be as strong as that of the centurion."[522]

From the same 1856 speech:

☛ "In no place in the New Testament, sir, is slavery held up as sinful. Several of the Apostles alluded to it, but none of them——not one of them, mentions or condemns it as a relation sinful in itself, or violative of the laws of God, or even Christian duty. They enjoin the relative duties of both master and slave. Paul sent a runaway slave, Onesimus, back to Philemon, his master. He frequently alludes to slavery in his letters to the churches, but in no case speaks of it as sinful. To what he says in one of these epistles I ask special attention. It is 1st Timothy, chapter 6th, and beginning with the 1st verse:

> 1. Let as many servants (*douloi*, slaves in the original, which I have before me) as are under the yoke (that is, those who are the most abject of slaves) count their own masters worthy of all honor, that the name of God and his doctrine be not blasphemed.
>
> 2. And they that have believing masters, (according to modern doctrine, there can be no such thing as a slaveholding believer; so did not think Paul,) let them not despise (or neglect and not care for) them, because they are brethren; but rather do them service, because they are faithful and beloved, partakers of the benefit. These things teach and exhort.
>
> 3. If any man teach otherwise and consent not to wholesome words, even the words of our Lord Jesus Christ, and to the doctrine which is according to godliness:
>
> 4. He is proud, (or self-conceited,) knowing nothing but doting about questions and strifes of words, whereof cometh envy, strife, railings, evil surmisings.
>
> 5. Perverse disputings of men of corrupt minds, and destitute of the truth, supposing that gain is godliness: from such withdraw thyself.

"This language of St. Paul, the great Apostle of the Gentiles, is just as appropriate this day, in this House, as it was when he penned it eighteen hundred years ago. No man could frame a more direct reply to the doctrines of the gentleman from Ohio, [Joshua R. Giddings,] and the gentleman from Indiana, [Mr. Dunn,] than is here contained in the sacred book. What does all this strife, and envy, and railings, and 'civil war' in Kansas come from, but the Teachings of those in our day who teach otherwise than Paul taught, and 'do not consent to wholesome words, even the words of our Lord Jesus Christ?'

"Let no man, then, say that African slavery as it exists in the South, incorporated in, and sanctioned by the constitution of the United States, is in violation of either the laws of nations, the laws of nature, or the laws of God!

"And if it 'must needs be' that such an offence shall come from this source, as shall sever the ties that now unite these States together in fraternal bonds, and involve the land in civil war, then 'woe be unto them from whom the offence cometh!'"[523]

In an 1857 speech before the U.S. House of Representatives, Stephens contradicts Northern mythology by stating the true reason why he and much of the rest of the South voted to allow the Western states to come into the Union as slave states if they wished: the Constitution:

☞ "Those from the South who supported the New Mexico and Utah bills, did so because this principle of Congressional restriction was abandoned in them. It was not from any confidence, in a practical point of view, that these territories ever would be slave States. The great constitutional and essential right to be so if they chose was secured to

Edmund Jennings Randolph

them. That was the main point. This, at least, was the case with myself; for, when I looked out upon our vast territories of the west and northwest, I did not then, nor do I now, consider that there was or is much prospect of many of them, particularly the latter, becoming slave States. Besides the laws of climate, soil, and productions, there is another law not unobserved by me, which seemed to be quite as efficient in its prospective operations in giving a different character to their institutions, and that is the law of population. There were, at the last census, nearly twenty millions of whites in the United States, and only a fraction over three millions of blacks, or slaves. The stock from which the population of the latter class must spring, is too small to keep pace in diffusion, expansion, and settlement, with the former. The ratio is not much greater than one to seven, to say nothing of foreign immigration, and the known facts in relation to the tardiness with which slave population is pushed into new countries and frontier settlements. Hence the greater importance to the South of a rigid adherence to principles on this subject vital to them. If the slightest encroachments of power are permitted or submitted to in the territories, they may reach the States ultimately. And although I looked, and still look, upon the probabilities of Kansas being a slave State, as greater than I did New Mexico and Utah, yet I voted for the bill of 1854, with the view of maintaining the principle much more than I did to such practical results. As a southern man, considering the relation which the African bears to the white race in the southern States, as the very best condition for the greatest good of both; and as a national man, looking to the best interests of the country, the peace and harmony of the whole by a preservation of the balance of power, as far as can be, (for after all, the surest check to encroachments is the inability to make them,) I should prefer to see Kansas come into the Union as a slave State; but it was not with the view or purpose of effecting that result that I voted for the Kansas bill, any more than it was with the view or purpose of accomplishing similar results as to New Mexico and Utah that I supported the measures of 1850. It was to secure the right to come in as a slave State, if the people there so wished, and to maintain a principle, which I then thought, and still think, essential to the peace of the country and the ultimate security of the rights of the South."[524]

Stephens uttered the following words during a speech before the U.S. House of Representatives on February 12, 1859. It concerned the admission of the state of Oregon. Here Stephens took the opportunity to expose the hypocrisy of those Northerners, like Abraham Lincoln and his fellow members of the American Colonization Society, who only wanted to free black slaves in order to ship them, as "Honest Abe" put it, "back to their native land":

☛ ". . . those [Northerners and Westerners] who profess to be the exclusive friends of negroes, as they now do, so far as that constitution was concerned, voted to banish them forever from the State, just as Oregon has done. Whether this banishment be right or wrong, it is no worse in Oregon than it was in Kansas. But, on the score of humanity, we of the South do not believe that those who, in Kansas or Oregon, banish this race from their limits, are better friends of the negro than we are, who assign them that place among us to which by nature they are fitted, and in which they add so much more to their own happiness and comfort, besides to the common well-being of all. We give them a reception. We give them shelter. We clothe them. We feed them. We provide for their every want, in health and in sickness, in infancy and old age. We teach them to work. We educate them in the arts of civilization and the virtues of Christianity, much more effectually and successfully than you can ever do on the coasts of Africa. And, without any cost to the public, we render them useful to themselves and to the world. The first lesson in civilization and Christianity to be taught to the barbarous tribes, wherever to be found, is the first great curse against the human family—that in the sweat of their face they shall eat their bread. Under our system, our tuition, our guardianship and fostering care, these people, exciting so much misplaced philanthropy, have attained a higher degree of civilization than their race has attained anywhere else upon the face of the earth. The Topeka [Kansas] people excluded them; they, the like neighbors we read of, went round them; we, the like good Samaritans, shun not their destitution or degradation—we alleviate both."[525]

Stephens did not believe that slavery was a moral issue, but rather a sociopolitical one, one founded on the Constitution and the tacit guarantee of states' rights (as noted in the Tenth Amendment):
☛ "[The slave's] . . . status in society is a question, not of moral right, but one of political and social economy; and . . . every State and organized Community have the right to fix and settle this status for themselves."[526]

Despite Stephens' support of slavery, he felt that it should be abolished if it did not "stand upon the immutable principles of nature":
☛ "We live in an age of discussion—all questions of science and arts, morals and governments, must pass this ordeal. The Institution of African slavery amongst us cannot escape it. If it does not stand upon the immutable principles of nature, as I believe it does, it must go down, and ought to go down."[527]

The following remarks, delivered by Stephens before the Virginia Secession Convention on April 23, 1861, are based on his literal interpretation of the Bible, which, as we have seen, clearly makes no prohibition against slavery, but instead both authorizes and demands it:
☛ "The condition of the negro race amongst us presents a peculiar phase of republican civilization and constitutional liberty. To some, the problem seems hard to understand. The difficulty is in theory, not in practical demonstration; that works well enough—theories in government, as in all things else, must yield to facts. No truth is clearer than that the best form or system of government for any people or society is that which secures the greatest amount of happiness, not to the greatest number, but to all the constituent elements of that society, community or State. If our system does not accomplish this; if it is not the best for the negro as well as for the white man; for the inferior as well as the superior race, it is wrong in principle. But if it does, or is capable of doing this, then it is right, and can never be successfully assailed by reason or logic. That the negroes with us, under masters who care for, provide for and protect them, are better off, and enjoy more of the blessings of good government than their race does in any other part of the world, statistics abundantly prove. As a race, the African is inferior to the white man. Subordination to the white man is his normal condition. He is not his equal by nature, and cannot be made so by human laws or human institutions. Our system, therefore, so far as regards this inferior race, rests upon this great immutable law of nature. It is founded not upon wrong or injustice, but upon

the eternal fitness of things. Hence, its harmonious working for the benefit and advantage of both. Why one race was made inferior to another, is not for us to inquire. The statesman and the Christian, as well as the philosopher, must take things as they find them, and do the best he can with them as he finds them.

"The great truth, I repeat, upon which our system rests, is the inferiority of the African. The enemies of our institutions ignore this truth.

Edward Everett

They set out with the assumption that the races are equal; that the negro is equal to the white man. If their premises were correct, their conclusions would be legitimate. But their premises being false, their conclusions are false also. Most of that fanatical spirit at the North on this subject, which in its zeal without knowledge, would upturn our society and lay waste our fair country, springs from this false reasoning. Hence so much misapplied sympathy for fancied wrongs and sufferings. These wrongs and sufferings exist only in their heated imaginations. There can be no wrong where there is no violation of nature's laws. We have heard much of the higher law. I believe myself in the higher law. We stand upon that higher law. I would defend and support no constitution that is against the higher law. I mean by that the law of nature and of God. Human constitutions and human laws that are made against the law of nature or of God, ought to be overturned; and if [Yankee William H.] Seward was right the constitution which he was sworn to support, and is now requiring others to swear to support, ought to have been overthrown long ago. It ought never to have been made. But in point of fact it is he and his [Northern] associates in this crusade against us, who are warring against the higher law—we stand upon the laws of the Creator, upon the highest of all laws. It is the fanatics of the North, who are warring against the decrees of God Almighty, in their attempts to make things equal which he made unequal. My assurance of ultimate success in this controversy is strong from the conviction, that we stand upon the right. Some years ago in the Hall of the House of Representatives, a very prominent gentleman from Ohio, announced with a great deal of effect, that we at the South would be obliged to yield upon this question of slavery, because we warred against a principle; and that it was as impossible to war successfully against principle in politics as it was in mechanics. The principle, said he, would ultimately prevail. He announced this with imposing effect, and endeavored to maintain that we were contending against the great principle of equality in holding our fellow men in the unnatural condition of bondage. In reply, I stated to him, that I admitted his proposition as he announced it, that it was impossible to war successfully against a principle in mechanics and the same was true in politics—the principle would certainly prevail—and from that stand point I had come to the conclusion that we of the South would ultimately succeed, and the North would be compelled to yield their ideas upon this subject. For it was they who were contending against a principle and not we. It was they who were trying to make the black man a white man, or his equal, which was nearly the same thing. The controlling laws of nature regulate the difference between them as absolutely as the laws of gravitation control whatever comes within their action—and until he could change the laws of gravitation, or any other law of nature, he could never make the negro a white man or his equal. No human efforts or human laws can change the leopard's spots or the Ethiopian's skin. These are the works of Providence—in whose hands are the fortunes of men as well as the destiny of nations and the distinctions of races."[528]

After Lincoln's War Stephens did as he promised: now convinced that he was wrong about the "natural inferiority" of blacks and the "rightness" of slavery, he completely altered his views on African-Americans and the North's "peculiar institution" and began championing black civil rights. The following excerpts are from a speech he gave before the Georgia General Assembly on February 22, 1866:

☛ "One of the results of the war is a total change in our whole internal polity. Our former social fabric has been entirely subverted. Like those convulsions in nature which break up old incrustations, the war has wrought a new epoch in our political existence. Old things have passed away, and all things among us in this respect are new. The relation heretofore, under our old system, existing between the African and European races, no longer exists. Slavery, as it was called, or the status of the black race, their subordination to the white, upon which all our institutions rested, is abolished forever, not only in Georgia, but throughout the limits of the United States. This change should be received and accepted as an irrevocable fact. It is a bootless question now to discuss, whether the new system is better for both races than the old one was or not. That may be proper matter for the philosophic and philanthropic historian, at some future time to inquire into, after the new system shall have been fully and fairly tried.

"All changes of systems or proposed reforms are but experiments and problems to be solved. Our system of self-government was an experiment at first. Perhaps as a problem it is not yet solved. Our present duty on this subject is not with the past or the future; it is with the present. The wisest and the best often err, in their judgments as to the probable workings of any new system. Let us therefore give this one a fair and just trial, without prejudice, and with that earnestness of purpose which always looks hopefully to success. It is an ethnological problem, on the solution of which depends, not only the best interests of both races, but it may be the existence of one or the other, if not both.

"This duty of giving this new system a fair and just trial will require of you, as legislators of the land, great changes in our former laws in regard to this large class of population. Wise and humane provisions should be made for them. It is not for me to go into detail. Suffice it to say on this occasion, that ample and full protection should be secured to them [blacks], so that they may stand equal before the law, in the possession and enjoyment of all rights of person, liberty and property. Many considerations claim this at your hands. Among these may be stated their fidelity in times past. They cultivated your fields, ministered to your personal wants and comforts, nursed and reared your children; and even in the hour of danger and peril they were, in the main, true to you and yours. To them we owe a debt of gratitude, as well as acts of kindness. This should also be done because they are poor, untutored, uninformed; many of them helpless, liable to be imposed upon, and need it. Legislation should ever look to the protection of the weak against the strong. Whatever may be said of the equality of races, or their natural capacity to become equal, no one can doubt that at this time this race among us is not [culturally] equal to the Caucasian. This inequality does not lessen the moral obligations on the part of the superior to the inferior, it rather increases them. From him who has much, more is required than from him who has little. The present generation of them, it is true, is far above their savage progenitors, who were at first introduced into this country, in general intelligence, virtue, and moral culture. This shows capacity for improvement. But in all the higher characteristics of mental development, they are still very far below the European type. What further advancement they may make, or to what standard they may attain, under a different system of laws every way suitable and wisely applicable to their changed condition, time alone can disclose. I speak of them as we now know them to be; having no longer the protection of a master, or legal guardian, they now need all the protection which the shield of the law can give."[529]

Stephens' February 22, 1866, speech continues:
☛ "But, above all, this protection [of Southern blacks] should be secured, because it is right and just that it should be, upon general principles. All governments in their organic structure, as well as in their administration, should have this leading object in view; the good of the governed. Protection and security to all under its jurisdiction, should be the chief end of every government. It is a melancholy truth that while this should be the chief end of all governments, most of them are used only as instruments of power, for the aggrandizement of the few, at the expense of, and by the oppression of, the many. Such are not our ideas of government, never have been and never should be. Governments, according to our ideas, should look to the good of the whole, and not a part only. 'The greatest good to the greatest number,' is a favorite dogma with some. Some so defended our old system. But you know this was never my doctrine. The greatest good to all, without detriment or injury to any, is the true rule. Those governments only are founded upon correct principles, of reason and justice, which look to the greatest attainable advancement, improvement and progress, physically, intellectually and morally, of all classes and conditions within their rightful jurisdiction. If our old system was not the best, or could not have been made the best, for both races, in this respect and

Elbridge Thomas Gerry

upon this basis, it ought to have been abolished. This was my view of that system while it lasted, and I repeat it now that it is no more. In legislation, therefore, under the new system, you should look to the best interest of all classes; their protection, security, advancement and improvement, physically, intellectually, and morally. All obstacles, if there be any, should be removed, which can possibly hinder or retard, the improvement of the blacks to the extent of their capacity. All proper aid should be given to their own efforts. Channels of education should be opened up to them. Schools, and the usual means of moral and intellectual training, should be encouraged amongst them. This is the dictate, not only of what is right and proper, and just in itself, but it is also the promptings of the highest considerations of interest. It is difficult to conceive a greater evil or curse, that could befall our country, stricken and distressed as it now is, than for so large a portion of its population, as this class will quite probably constitute amongst us, hereafter, to be reared in ignorance, depravity and vice. In view of such a state of things well might the prudent even now look to its abandonment. Let us not however indulge in such thoughts of the future, nor let us, without an effort, say the system cannot be worked. Let us not, standing still, hesitatingly ask, 'Can there any good thing come out of Nazareth?' but let us rather say as Gamaliel did, 'If this counsel or this work be of men, it will come to naught, but if it be of God ye cannot overthrow it, lest haply ye be found even to fight against God.' The most vexed questions of the age are social problems. These we have heretofore had but little to do with; we were relieved from them by our peculiar institution. Emancipation of the blacks, with its consequences, was ever considered by me with much more interest as a social question, one relating to the proper status of the different elements of society, and their relations toward each other, looking to the best interest of all, than in any other light. The pecuniary aspect of it, the considerations of labor and capital, in a politico-economic view, sunk into insignificance, in comparison with this. This problem, as one of the results of the war, is now upon us, presenting one of the most perplexing questions of the sort that any people ever had to deal with. Let us resolve to do the best we can with it, from all the lights we have, or can get from any quarter. With this view, and in this connection, I take the liberty of quoting for your consideration, some remarks even from the [Yankee abolitionist] Rev. Henry Ward Beecher. I met with them [i.e., Beecher's remarks] some months ago while pondering on this subject, and was as much struck as surprised, with the drift of their philosophy, coming from the source they did. I give them as I find them in the *New York Times* where they were reported. You may be as much surprised at hearing such ideas from Mr. Beecher, as I was. But however much we may differ from him on many questions, and on many questions connected with this subject, yet all must admit him to rank amongst the master spirits of the age. And no one perhaps has contributed more by the power of his pen and voice in bringing about the present state of things, than he has. Yet, nevertheless, I commend to your serious consideration, as pertinent to my present object, what he was reported to have said, as follows:

> 'In our land and time facts and questions are pressed upon us which demand Christian settlement—settlement on this ground and doctrine. We cannot escape the responsibility. Being strong and powerful, we must nurse, and help, and educate, and foster the weak, and poor, and ignorant. For my own part I cannot see how we shall escape the most terrible conflict of classes, by and by, unless we are educated into this doctrine of duty, on the part of the *superior to the inferior*. We are told by zealous and fanatical individuals, that all men are equal. We know better. *They are not equal. A common brotherhood teaches no such absurdity.* A theory of universal, physical likeness, is no more absurd than this. *Now, as in all times, the strong go to the top, the weak go to the bottom. Its natural, right and can't be helped.* All branches are not at the top of the tree, but the top does not despise the lower; nor do they all despise the limb or the parent trunk; and so with the body politic, there must be classes. *Some must be at the top and some must be at the bottom.* It is difficult to foresee, and estimate the development of the power of classes in America. They are simply inevitable. They are here now, and will be more. If they are friendly, living at peace, loving and respecting and helping one another, all will be well. But if they are selfish, unchristian; if the old heathen feeling is to reign, each extracting all he can from his neighbor, and caring nothing for him; society will be lined by classes as by seams—like batteries, each firing broadside after broadside, the one upon the other. If, on the other hand, the law of love prevails, there will be no ill-will, no envy, no disturbance. Does a child hate his father because he is chief, because he is strong and wise? On the contrary, he grows with his father's growth, and strengthens with his strength. And if in society there should be fifty grades or classes, all helping each other, there will be no trouble, but perfect satisfaction and content. This Christian doctrine carried into practice, will easily settle the most troublesome of all home present questions.' [Emphasis added, L.S.]

"What [Beecher] . . . here said of the state of things where he spoke in the State of New York, and the fearful antagonism of classes there, is much more applicable to us. Here, it is true, only two great classes exist, or are likely

Francis Wilkinson Pickens

to exist, but these are deeply marked by distinctions bearing the impress of nature. The one is now beyond all question greatly superior to the other. These classes are as distinct as races of men can be. The one is of the highest type of humanity, the other of the lowest. All that he says of the duty of the superior, to protect, to aid, to encourage, and to help the inferior, I fully and cordially indorse and commend to you as quite as applicable to us and our situation, as it was to his auditors. Whether the doctrine, if carried out and practiced, will settle all these most troublesome home questions with us as easily as he seemed to think it would like home questions with those whom he was addressing, I will not undertake to say. I have no hesitancy, however, in saying that the general principles announced by him are good. Let them be adopted by us as far as practicable. No harm can come from it, much good may. Whether the great barrier of races which the Creator has placed between this, our inferior class and ourselves, shall prevent a success of the experiment now on trial, of a peaceful, happy, and prosperous community, composed of such elements and sustaining present relations toward each other, or even a further elevation on the part of the inferior, if they prove themselves fit for it, let the future, under the dispensations of Providence, decide. We have to deal with the present."[530]

☛ "[From even a casual perusal of my thoughts and words the reader will] . . . readily perceive . . . how thoroughly, looking to the grand results, my entire feelings, heart, and soul, with every energy of mind and body, became enlisted in the success of this cause [the Southern one: Constitutional liberty], when force was invoked [by Lincoln], when war was waged to put it down. It was the cause, not only of the Seceding States, but the cause of all the States, and in this view it became, to a great extent, the cause of Constitutional Liberty everywhere. It was the cause of the Federative [Confederative] principle of Government, against the principle of Empire! The cause of the Grecian type of Civilization against the Asiatic! So, at least, I viewed it, with all the earnestness of the profoundest convictions. The matter of Slavery, so-called, which was the proximate cause of these irregular movements on both sides, and which ended in the general collision of war, as we have seen, was of infinitely less importance to the Seceding States, than the recognition of this great principle. I say Slavery, so-called, because there was with us no such thing as Slavery in the full and proper sense of that word. No people ever lived more devoted to the principles of liberty, secured by free democratic institutions, than were the people of the South. None had ever given stronger proofs of this than they had done, from the day that Virginia moved in behalf of the assailed rights of Massachusetts, in 1774, to the firing of the first gun in Charleston Harbor, in 1861. What was called Slavery amongst us, was but a legal subordination of the African to the Caucasian race. This relation was so regulated by law as to promote, according to the intent and design of the system, the best interests of both races, the Black as well as the White, the Inferior, as well as the Superior. Both had rights secured, and both had duties imposed. It was a system of reciprocal service, and mutual bonds. But even the two thousand million dollars invested in the relation thus established, between private capital and the labor of this class of population, under the system, was but as the dust in the balance, compared with the vital attributes of the rights of Independence and Sovereignty on the part of the several States. For with these whatever changes and modifications, or improvements in this domestic institution, founded itself upon laws of nature, time, and experience, might have shown to be proper in the advancing progress of civilization, for the promotion of the great ends of society in all good Governments—that is the best interest of all classes, without wrong or injury to any—could, and would have been made by the superior race in these States, under the guidance of that reason, justice, philanthropy, and statesmanship, which had ever marked their course, without the violent disruption of the entire social fabric, with all its attendant ills, and inconceivable wrongs, mischiefs, and sufferings; and especially without those terrible evils and consequences which must almost necessarily result from such disruptions and reorganizations as make a sudden and complete transfer of political power from the hands of the superior to the inferior race, in their present condition, intellectually and morally, in at least six States of the Union!

"The [Southern] system [of servitude], as it existed, it is true, was not perfect. All admit this. No human systems are perfect. But great changes had been made in it, as this class of persons [African-Americans] were gradually rising from their original barbarism, in their subordinate sphere, under the operation of the system, and from their contact, in this way, with the civilization of the superior race. Other changes would certainly have been made, even to the extinction of the system, if time, with its changes, and the progress of attainments on the part of these people had shown it to be proper—that is, best for both races. For if the system, as designed, was not really the best, or could not have been made the best for both races, or whenever it should have ceased to be so, it could and would have been thoroughly and radically changed, in due time, by the only proper and competent authority to act in the premises."[531]

☛ "The erroneous dogma of the greatest good to the greatest number, was not the basis on which this Institution [i.e., slavery] rested. Much less was it founded upon the dogma of principle of the sole interest or benefit of the white race to the exclusion of considerations embracing the interests and welfare of the other. It was erected upon no such idea as that might, barely, gives right, but it was organized and defended upon the immutable principles of justice to all, which is the foundation of all good Governments. This requires that society be so organized as to secure the greatest good possible, morally, intellectually, and politically, to all classes of persons within their jurisdictional control, without necessary wrong or detriment to any. This was the foundation principle on which this institution in these States was established and defended.

"These questions are not now, however, before us. We are at present considering the workings of the Federal [Confederate] system, and not the wisdom or policy of the social systems of the several States, or the propriety of the status of their constituent elements respectively.

"This whole question of Slavery, so-called, was but one relating to the proper status of the African as an element of a society composed of the Caucasian and African races, and the status which was best, not for the one race or the other, but best, upon the whole, for both.

"Over these questions, the Federal Government had no rightful control whatever. They were expressly excluded, in the Compact of Union, from its jurisdiction or authority. Any such assumed control was a palpable violation of the Compact, which released all the parties to the Compact, affected by such action, from their obligations under the Compact. On this point there can be no shadow of doubt.

"Waiving these questions, therefore, for the present, I repeat that this whole subject of Slavery, so-called, in any and every view of it, was, to the Seceding States, but a drop in the ocean compared with those other considerations involved in the issue. Hence, during the whole war, being thoroughly enlisted in it from these other and higher considerations, but being, at the same time, ever an earnest advocate for its speediest termination by an appeal from the arena of arms to the forum of reason, justice, and right, I was wedded to no idea as a basis of peace, but that of the recognition of the ultimate absolute Sovereignty of all the States as the essential basis of any permanent union between them, or any of them, consistent with the preservation of their ultimate existence and liberties. And I wanted, at no time, any recognition of Independence on the part of the Confederate States, but that of George III, of England. That is, the recognition of the Sovereignty and Independence of each, by name.

"The Confederate States [of 1860-1861] had made common cause for this great principle [state sovereignty], as the original thirteen States had done in 1776. The recognition of this I regarded as essential to the future well-being,

George Mortimer Bibb

happiness, and prosperity of all the States, in existence and to be formed, as well as the countless millions of people who are hereafter to inhabit this half of the Western Hemisphere."[532]

Stephens was always keen to discuss the facts surrounding the South's institution of black "slavery" (as distinct from white, red, yellow, and brown slavery—which have also been widespread and endemic throughout world history)[533] and the War for Southern Independence:

☞ "[Regarding] the immediate and exciting question, which brought the organic principles of the Government into such terrible physical conflict in the inauguration of the war. This was, as stated in the outset, the question of negro Slavery, or more properly speaking that political and legal subordination of the black race to the white race, which existed in the Seceding States.

"I thus speak of Slavery as it existed with us, purposely. For, it is to be remembered in all our discussions on this subject, that what was called Slavery with us, was not Slavery in the usual sense of that word, as generally used and understood by the ancients, and as generally used and understood in many countries in the present age. It was with us a political Institution. It was, indeed, nothing but that legal subordination of an Inferior race to a Superior one [Note: Stephens is referring here to what he believed was the cultural, social, moral, and religious superiority of Anglo-Saxon society, just as the African has long considered his society culturally, socially, morally, and religiously superior to that of the European; L.S.] which was thought to be the best in the organization of society for the welfare politically, socially, morally and intellectually of both races. The slave, so-called, was not in law regarded entirely as a chattel, as has been erroneously represented. He was by no means subject to the absolute dominion of his master. He had important personal rights, secured by law. His service due according to law, it is true, was considered property, and so in all countries is considered the service of all persons, who according to law are bound to another or others for a term, however long or short. So is the legal right of parents to the service of their minor children in all the States now considered as property. A right or property that may be assigned, transferred or sold. [Alexander] Hamilton expressed the idea of this peculiar Institution, as it existed with us, clearly, when he said:

> 'The Federal Constitution, therefore, decides with great propriety on the case of our slaves, when it views them in the mixed character of persons and of property. This is in fact their true character. It is the character bestowed on them by the laws under which they live.'

"They [Southern black 'slaves'] were so viewed and regarded by the Constitutions and laws of all the States. The relation of master and slave under the Institution, as before said, was but one of 'reciprocal service and mutual bonds.' The view of them as property related to their services due according to law."[534]

☞ "This matter of negro subordination, I repeat, was the exciting question in 1860. There were, it is true, many other questions involving the same principles of the Government, which had agitated the public mind almost from the time it went into operation, still exciting the public mind to a greater or less degree: but this question of the status of the Black race in the Southern States, was by far the most exciting and all-absorbing one, at that time, on both sides, and was the main proximate cause which brought those principles of the

Government into active play, resulting in the conflict of arms. This relation of political and legal subordination of the Inferior to the Superior race, as it existed in 1860, in all the Seceding States, had at one time, be it constantly kept in mind, existed in all the States of the Union, and did so exist in all, save one, in 1787, when the present Articles of Union were entered into.

"By these Articles this relation was fully recognized, as appears from the solemn covenant therein made, that fugitives from service, under this system, as it then thus existed, escaping from one State into another, should, upon claim, be delivered up to the party to whom the service was due. This was one of the stipulations of the Compact upon which the Union was formed, as we have seen, and of which Judge [Joseph] Story said, on an important occasion, in delivering an opinion from the Bench of the Supreme Court of the United States, 'it cannot be doubted that it constituted a fundamental article, without the adoption of which the Union could not have been formed.'

"These are all great facts never to be lost sight of in this investigation of the rightfulness of this most terrible war, and in determining correctly and justly upon which side the huge responsibility of its inauguration, and of the enormous wrongs, and most disastrous consequences attending its subsequent conduct, must, in the judgment of mankind, forever rest."[535]

☛ "It is not at all germane to [my] . . . purpose in this investigation, at this time, to inquire into the Right, or Wrong of the Institution of Slavery itself, as it thus existed in what were then [incorrectly and unfairly] known as the Slave

Gouverneur Morris

States. Neither is it in the line of my argument now, to treat of the defects, or abuses of the system. Nor is it at all necessary, or pertinent to my present object, to trace from its inception to its culmination, the history or progress of that movement against it, which was organized for the purpose of bringing the questions it involved into the arena of Federal Councils, and within the range of Federal action. Suffice it here barely to say, and assume as a fact what is known to us all so well, that, in 1860, a majority of the Northern States, having long previously of their own accord abolished this Institution, within their own limits respectively, had, also, by the action of their Legislatures, openly and avowedly violated that clause in the Constitution of the United States [i.e., the Fugitive Slave Clause], which provided for the rendition of fugitives of this class from service.

"To give a history of that movement to which I allude, to trace its progress from its origin, would require a volume of itself. A volume both interesting and instructive, might be devoted to it. This is what is known as the Abolition movement in this country, and this is what Mr. [Horace] Greeley is pleased to style the 'American Conflict.' But from entering into an investigation of that sort, I now forbear. It is in no way pertinent or essential to my purpose. Whoever feels an interest in the subject, will see it treated fully, truthfully, and ably by the master hand of Mr. George Lunt, of Boston, in his history of the 'Origin of the War.'"[536]

Stephens next lays out the Truth about so-called Southern "slavery" and the real cause of the War for Southern Independence:
☞ "Suffice it, therefore, for me, at present, on this subject, only to say, generally, that such a movement was started, such a conflict was begun at an early day after our present system of Government went into operation. As early as the 12th day of February, 1790, within twelve months after [George] Washington was inaugurated as President, a petition invoking the Federal authorities to take jurisdiction of this subject, with a view to the ultimate abolition of this Institution in the States respectively, was sent to Congress, headed by Dr. [Benjamin] Franklin. This movement, in its first step thus taken so early, was partially checked by the Resolution to which the house of Representatives came, after the most mature consideration of the petition and its objects. That Resolution declared:

> That Congress have no authority to interfere in the emancipation of slaves, or in the treatment of them within any of the States; it remaining with the several States alone to provide any regulations therein, which humanity and true policy may require.

"This clear exposition of the nature of the Federal Government, and its utter want of power to take any action upon the subject, as sought for by the petitioners, checked, I say, for a time, this movement, or conflict so started and commenced. The conflict, however, was only partially checked; it went on until in 1860, when those who so entered into this movement standing forth as the Abolition or Anti-Slavery Party under the [erroneous] name of Republican, but which in truth was the [Liberal] party of Centralism and Consolidation, organized upon the principle of bringing the Federal Powers to bear upon this

Hannibal Hamlin

Institution in a way to secure its ultimate Abolition in all the States, succeeded in the election of the two highest officers of the Government [Liberal President Abraham Lincoln and Liberal Vice President Hannibal Hamlin], pledged to carry out their principles, and to carry them out in open disregard of the decision of the Supreme Court, which highest Judicial Tribunal under the Constitution, had by solemn adjudication denied the power of the Federal Government to take such action as this Party and its two highest officers stood pledged to carry out. With all these questions, I repeat, I have nothing now to do, except to say that the conflict from its rise to its culmination, was not a conflict between the advocates and opponents of the Institution itself. It seems to have been Mr. [Horace] Greeley's leading object, throughout his work, to give this idea of the nature of the conflict, as I stated in the beginning. This, however, was in no sense the fact of the case. The [slavery] conflict, fierce and bitter as it was for seventy years, was a conflict between those who were for maintaining the Federal [Confederate] character of the Government, and those who were for centralizing all power in the Federal Head [in Washington, D.C.]. This was the conflict. It was a conflict between the true [Conservative] supporters of the Federal [Confederate] Union of States established by the Constitution, and those [Liberals] whose object was to overthrow this Union of States, and by usurpations to erect a National Consolidation in its stead."[537]

☛ "The same conflict arose upon divers other questions, also, at an early day. It exhibited itself in the discussions of the first Judiciary Act. In the financial measures submitted by Mr. [Alexander] Hamilton, the then Secretary of the Treasury. In the assumption of the State debts. In the first Apportionment Bill, which was vetoed on these grounds by [George] Washington, in 1792, and much more formidably it exhibited itself in the passage of the Alien and Sedition Acts, in 1798, under the elder [John] Adams. This [big government Liberal] Party, as we have seen, then [wrongly] assumed the popular name of Federal, as it [wrongly] assumed the popular name of Republican in 1800. These latter measures of 1798 came near stirring up civil war, and would most probably have resulted in such a catastrophe, if the Party, so organized with such principles and objects, had not been utterly overthrown, and driven from power by the advocates of our true Federal [Confederate] system of Government, under the lead of [the Confederacy advocate] Mr. [Thomas] Jefferson, in 1800. It was after this complete defeat on these other questions, that the Centralists rallied upon this question of the Status of the Black race in the States, where it continued to exist, as the most promising one for them to agitate and unite the people of the Northern States upon, for the accomplishment of their sinister objects of National Centralization or Consolidation."[538]

In the following excerpts Stephens comments on the underhanded ploys instigated by big government Northern liberals, who used slavery as a false issue to try and push through their anti-South agenda:
☛ "On this question, Mr. Greeley and other writers speak of only two Parties during the entire conflict. The Pro-Slavery party, and the Anti-Slavery or Liberty party. *The truth is there never was in the United States, or in any one of them, an organized Pro-Slavery party. No such antagonism, as he represents, ever existed in the Federal Councils. The antagonism on this question, which was clearly exhibited in the*

beginning, as appears from the Resolution of the House of Representatives referred to, was an antagonism growing out of Constitutional principles, and not any sort of antagonism growing out of the principles involved in the right or wrong of negro Slavery, as it then existed in the several States of the Union. It was an antagonism growing out of principles lying at the foundation of the common Government of the States. Of those men, for instance, who voted for the Resolution referred to, in 1790 [which proposed that the central government be prohibited from interfering with the institution of slavery in the individual states], how many can be supposed to have been Pro-Slavery in their sentiments, or in favor of the Institution? Let us look into it. Here is the record of the vote. Amongst the prominent supporters of the Resolution, and on the list of those who voted for it, is the name of Roger Sherman, of Connecticut. Here is Benjamin Huntington, also of the same State. From Massachusetts, we see the names of Theodore Sedgwick, Elbridge Gerry, and Benjamin Goodhue. From New Hampshire, we see the name of Nicholas Oilman. From New Jersey, Elias Boudinot and Lambert Cadwallader. From Pennsylvania, Frederick A. Muhlenberg, Thomas Hartley, and Daniel Heister. These were all prominent men in the formation of the Constitution. All from the Northern States. The vote shows, that not only a majority of the members from the Northern States voted for the Resolution, but that a majority of those who did vote for it, were from the Northern States. Those from the South who voted against it, the debate shows so voted, because they did not think the petition should be considered, or acted upon at all, as it related to subjects not within their Constitutional jurisdiction. But how many of this majority of the Northern members who voted for it, can be reasonably supposed to have been Pro-Slavery in sentiment? In their action in entertaining the petition, they intended only to show what they considered a due regard to the right of petition, and at the same time prove themselves true to the Constitution of their country. This the debate conclusively shows. So in all after times up to the election in 1860. Those who resisted the action of the Abolitionists did so, because it was based upon revolutionary principles—principles utterly at war with those upon which the Union was established. As a striking illustration of this, Mr. [Thomas] Jefferson himself is well-known to have been as much opposed to the Institution of Slavery, as it then existed in the United States, as any man in either of them; and yet he headed the great party in opposition to this mode of effecting the object of those who desired its Abolition, as he had led the same party to success over the Centralists on other questions, in 1800. He utterly denied that the Federal Government could rightfully exercise any power with the view to the change of any of the Institutions of the States respectively. [Emphasis added, L.S.]

"The same is true of all the prominent leaders of this party, as well as the great mass of the people composing it, from the days of Jefferson to those of General [Lewis] Cass and Mr. [Stephen A.] Douglas. Mr. [William] Pinkney and Mr. [Henry] Clay, though Southern men as Mr. Jefferson was, were decidedly Anti-Slavery in their sentiments, and yet they ever acted with the party of Mr. Jefferson upon this question. General Cass and Mr. Douglas were Northern men with sentiments equally averse to Slavery, and for the same reasons opposed the Abolition movement in the Federal Councils. Even Chief Justice [Roger B.] Taney, who delivered the opinion of the Supreme Court in the case referred to, was by no means individually Pro-Slavery in his sentiments. His views upon the Institution are understood to have been very similar to those of Mr. Pinkney and Mr. Clay. Out of the million and half, and more, of men in the Northern States who voted against Mr. [Abraham] Lincoln, in 1860, perhaps not ten thousand could be said, with truth, to be in favor of the Institution, or would have lived in a State where it existed. It was a subject with which they were thoroughly convinced they had nothing to do, and could

Henry Stuart Foote

have nothing to do under the terms of the Union by which the States were confederated, except to carry out and faithfully perform all the obligations of the Constitutional Compact in regard to it. *In opposing the 'Liberty Party,' so-called, they enlisted under no banner of Slavery of any sort, but only arrayed themselves against that [Liberal] organization, which had virtually hoisted the banner of Consolidation. The struggle or conflict, therefore, from its rise to its culmination, was between those who in whatever State they lived, were for maintaining our Federal [Confederate] system as it was established, and those who were for a consolidation of power in the Central Head.*"[539] [Emphasis added, L.S.]

Stephens explains the actual origins of the "Civil War":

☛ ". . . the great fact now to be considered in this investigation, is, that this Anti-Constitutional Party [i.e., the Republicans, the Liberals of the day], in 1860, came into power upon this question in the Executive branch of the Federal Government.

"*This is the state of things which produced so much excitement and apprehension in the popular mind of the Southern States at that time. This Anti-Slavery Party had not only succeeded in getting a majority of the Northern States to openly violate their Constitutional faith in the avowed breach of the Compact, as stated; but had succeeded in electing a President and Vice President pledged to principles which were not only at war with the domestic Institutions of the States of the South, but which must inevitably, if carried out, ultimately lead to the absorption of all power in the Central Government, and end sooner or later in Absolutism or Despotism. These were the principles then brought into conflict, which, as stated, resulted in the conflict of arms.* [Emphasis added, L.S.]

"The Seceding States feeling no longer bound by a Compact which had been so openly violated, and a majority of their people being deeply impressed with the conviction that the whole frame-work of the Constitution would be overthrown by this Party which would soon have control of the Executive Department of the Government, determined to withdraw from the Union, for the very reasons which had induced them to enter it in the beginning. Seven of these States, South Carolina, Georgia, Florida, Alabama, Mississippi, Louisiana, and Texas, did withdraw. Conventions of their people, regularly called by the proper authorities in each of these States respectively—Conventions representing the Sovereignty of the States similar in all respects to those which by Ordinances had ratified the Constitution of the United States—passed Ordinances resuming the Sovereign Powers therein delegated. These were the Secession Ordinances. . . . These Conventions also appointed Delegates, to meet in Montgomery, Alabama, on the 4th of February, 1861, with a view to form a new Confederation among themselves, upon the same essential basis of the Constitution of the United States.

"It was not in opposition to the principles of that Government that they withdrew from it. They quit the Union to save the principles of the Constitution, and to perpetuate, on this Continent, the liberties which it was intended to secure and establish. Mr. [James] Buchanan was then President of the United States. He held that the Federal Government had no power to coerce a Seceding State to remain in the Union, but, strangely enough, at the same time held, that no State could rightfully withdraw from the Union. Mr. Lincoln came into power on the 4th of March, 1861. He held that the Federal Government did possess the Constitutional Power to maintain the Union of

States by force, and it was in the maintenance of these views, the war was inaugurated by him."[540]

Stephens was often called upon, by the uninformed, to defend and explain so-called "slavery" as it existed in the Old South:

☞ "One digression I am here compelled to make here [concerns various anti-South remarks made by my Liberal friends regarding Slavery]. . . . [They speak] . . . of Slavery as it existed with us, as a 'sin in the sight of men and in the sight of God'—as the 'summation of all iniquity!' I stated in the outset that the right or wrong of this Institution did not legitimately come within the purview of our present discussion. That related exclusively to the rightful powers of the Federal Government over it, to interfere with it in any way, except as is expressly provided in the Compact. But these remarks of [the Liberals] . . . demand notice. They require a reply. In replying briefly as possible, but pointedly, [concerning Slavery] I have to say I know of but one sure standard in determining what is, and what is not sin or sinful. That standard is the written law of God as prescribed in the Old and the New Testament. By that standard the relation of master and slave, even in a much more abject condition than existed with us, is not founded in sin. Abram, afterwards called Abraham, the father of the faithful, with whom the Divine Covenant was made for man's salvation and the redemption of the world from the dominion of sin, was a slave-holder. He was enjoined to impart the seal of this everlasting covenant not only to those who were born in his house; but to those who were 'bought with his money.' It was into his bosom, in Heaven, that the poor man, who died at the rich man's gate, was borne by angels, according to the Parable of the Saviour. Job certainly was one of the best men we read of in the Bible. He was a large slave-holder. So, too, were Isaac and Jacob and all the Patriarchs. The great moral law which defines sin, the Ten Commandments given to Moses on Mount Sinai, written on stone by the finger of God himself, expressly recognizes Slavery, and enjoins certain duties of masters towards their slaves. The chosen people of God, by the Levitical Law, proclaimed under divine sanction, were authorized to hold slaves—not of their own race—(of these they were to hold bondmen for a term of years)—but of the Heathen around them—of these they were authorized to buy slaves 'bondmen and bondwomen,' for life, who were to be to them 'an inheritance' and 'possession forever.'

"Slavery existed when the gospel was preached by Christ and his Apostles, and where they preached it was all around them. And though the Scribes and Pharisees were denounced by Christ for their hypocrisy and robbing widows' houses and divers other sins, yet not a word did he utter, as far as we

Herschel Vespasian Johnson

are informed, against slaveholding. On the contrary, he said he had not found so great faith in all Israel, as in the slave-holding Centurion! Was he truckling to [i.e., flattering] a Slavery Oligarchy when he made this declaration? In no place in the New Testament is the relation of master and slave spoken of as sinful. Several of the Apostles alluded to it; but none of them, not one of them, condemned it as sinful in itself, or as violative of the laws of God, or even of Christian duty. They enjoin the relative duties of both masters and slaves. Paul sent a fugitive slave, Onesimus, back to Philemon his master. He did not consider it any violence to his conscience to do this, even when he was under no stipulated obligation to do it.

"He frequently alludes to Slavery in his letters to the Churches, but in no case speaks of it as sinful. What he says in one of these epistles, I must read to you. It is the first five verses of chapter vi. of the First Epistle to Timothy:

1. 'Let as many servants [slaves] as are under the yoke count their own masters worthy of all honor, that the name of God and his doctrine be not blasphemed.

2. 'And they that have believing masters,' (according to the [Liberal's] . . . idea, there could be no such thing as a Slave-holding believer, but so did not think Paul,) 'let them not despise them, because they are brethren; but rather do them service, because they are faithful and beloved, partakers of the benefit. These things teach and exhort.

3. 'If any man teach otherwise, and consent not to wholesome words, even the words of our Lord Jesus Christ, and to the doctrine which is according to godliness;

4. 'He is proud, knowing nothing, but doting about questions and strifes of words, whereof cometh envy, strife, railings, evil surmisings,

5. 'Perverse disputings of men of corrupt minds, and destitute of the truth, supposing that gain is godliness: from such withdraw thyself.'

"Can we suppose that Paul would have so written, if he had considered that there was anything morally wrong in the relation of master and slave, much less if he had looked upon it as the 'summation of all iniquity;' and if our Ministers of the Gospel did continue to teach the same doctrine, to enjoin the same duties upon master and slave, can it be justly said that they thereby 'desecrated the Temples of the Living God?' If they withdrew themselves from those who taught otherwise, and whose doctrines brought 'envy, strife, railings,' and finally war, did they not follow the advice of the great Apostle of the Gentiles, and likewise the words, as he affirms, of our Lord Jesus Christ, 'that the name of God and his doctrine be not blasphemed?'

"It is not, as I have said, within the purview of this discussion, to speak of the right or wrong of Slavery morally, or the evils of the Institution politically, arising from an abuse of power under it, any more than it is to speak of the institution of marriage, or the relation of parent and child, as it is regulated in any State.   These are matters which under the Federal [Confederate] system belong exclusively to the several States. What I have here said in reply to [the accusations of the Liberals] . . . is therefore a digression. From this I will now return, with but one single additional remark upon what [the Liberals have] . . . said on this point; and that is this: To maintain that Slavery is in itself sinful, in the face of all that is said and written in the Bible upon the subject, with so many sanctions of the relation by the Deity himself, does seem to me to be little short of blasphemous! It is a direct imputation upon the wisdom and justice, as well as the declared ordinances of God, as they are written in the inspired oracles, to say nothing of their manifestation in the universe around us."[541]

☛ "James H. Hammond, of South Carolina, one of the most intellectual men this country ever produced, when Governor of his State, in 1844, in reply to a communication he received from the Free Church of Glasgow, Scotland, upon the subject of Slavery, amongst other things, said:

> 'Your memorial, like all that have been sent to me, denounces Slavery in the severest terms; as 'traversing every law of nature, and violating the most sacred domestic relations, and the primary rights of man.' You and your Presbytery are Christians. You profess to believe, and no doubt do believe, that the laws laid down in the Old and New Testaments for the government of man, in his moral, social and political relations, were all the direct revelation of God himself. Does it never occur to you, that in anathematizing Slavery, you deny this divine sanction of those laws, and repudiate both Christ and Moses; or charge God with downright crime, in

regulating and perpetuating Slavery in the Old Testament, and the most criminal neglect, in not only not abolishing, but not even reprehending it, in the New? If these Testaments came from God, it is impossible that Slavery can 'traverse the laws of nature, or violate the primary rights of man.' What those laws and rights really are, mankind have not agreed. But they are clear to God; and it is blasphemous for any of His creatures to set up their notions of them in opposition to His immediate and acknowledged Revelation. Nor does our system of Slavery outrage the most sacred domestic relations. Husbands and wives, parents and children, among our Slaves, are seldom separated, except from necessity or crime. The same reasons induce much more frequent separations among the white population in this, and, I imagine, in almost every other country.'[542]

Stephens continues with his discussion on black servitude in the American South, including an explanation of his infamous "Cornerstone Speech." He begins by demolishing the long held Northern myth that the South possessed a great "Slavery Dynasty":

☞ "In [only] one thing [have the Liberals] . . . done me full justice, and that was in [their] . . . assumption, that I had no sympathy with any conspirators or conspiracy aiming at the overthrow of the Constitution of the United States, with the view of establishing a '*Slavery Dynasty*' in its stead. If any such body of men existed in the country, they certainly had no sympathy from me. Nay, more, if any such body was organized in Washington or elsewhere, or had any existence anywhere, it was wholly unknown to me. *I think it had existence, if [my Liberal friends] . . . will allow me respectfully to say so, only in [their] . . . imagination[s], and that of others who have written fictions called histories. The only real conspiracy against the Constitution organized in Washington, as I understand it, was that of the seven Governors, from seven Northern States, who assembled there, and by their mischievous machinations caused Mr. [Abraham] Lincoln to change his purpose as to the evacuation of Fort Sumter. Caused him to fail to 'keep faith as to Fort Sumter.' This was the conspiracy which inaugurated the war. It was a conspiracy well typified by the Seven Headed monster Beast in the Apocalypse!* The analogy I will not stop to trace, striking as it is, but will follow the [Liberals]. . . . [Emphasis added, L.S.]

"[They quote] . . . from my speech on the annexation of Texas. [They] . . . did not, however, quote fully. In that speech I said, and said truly, that I was 'no defender of Slavery in the abstract.' I was speaking of it politically and not morally, and of Slavery in the general sense of that term applied to men of the same race, and not as it existed in the States of this Union. This was true then, and now, and always with me. I said also on that occasion, in the next sentence, and now repeat, that

'Liberty always had charms for me, and I would rejoice to see all
the sons of Adam's family, in every land and clime, in the
enjoyment of those rights which are set forth in our Declaration of
Independence as 'natural and inalienable,' if a stern necessity,
bearing the marks and impress of the hand of the Creator himself,
did not, in some cases, interpose and prevent. Such is the case with
the States where Slavery now exists.'

"Here is that speech. [The Liberals were] . . . as much at fault in [their]
. . . memory in regard to it, as [they were] . . . in regard to the Union speech
of 1860.

"There is, moreover, nothing in the 'Corner-Stone' speech, as [they
call it] . . . , inconsistent with the sentiments delivered in the Texas speech.
Here is the 'Corner-Stone' speech, also. In it I said:

'Many Governments have been founded upon the principle of the
subordination and serfdom of certain classes of the same race; such
were, and are in violation of the laws of nature. Our system
commits no such violation of nature's laws. With us, all of the
white race, however high or low, rich or poor, are equal in the eye
of the law. Not so with the negro. Subordination is his place. He,
by nature, or *by the curse against Canaan*, is fitted for that condition
which he occupies in our system. The architect, in the construction
of buildings, lays the foundation with the proper material—the
granite; then comes the brick or the marble. The substratum of
our society is made of the material fitted by nature for it, and by
experience we know that it is lest, not only for the Superior, but
for the Inferior race, that it should be so. *It is, indeed, in conformity
with the ordinance of the Creator. It is not for us to inquire into the
wisdom of his ordinances, or to question them. For his own purposes, he has
made one race to differ from another, as he has made "one star to differ
from another star in glory."* [Emphasis added, L.S.]
'The great objects of humanity are best attained when
there is conformity to his laws and decrees, in the formation of
Governments as well as in all things else. Our Confederacy is
founded upon principles in strict conformity with these laws. This
stone which was rejected by the first builders "is become the chief
of the corner"—the real "corner-stone"—in our new edifice.'

"In the corner-stone metaphor, I did but repeat what Judge [Henry]
Baldwin of the Supreme Court of the United States, had said of the Federal
Government itself, in the case of *Johnson* vs. *Tompkins*. In that case he declared
that 'the foundations of this Government are laid, and rest on the rights of

property in slaves, and the whole fabric must fall by disturbing the corner-stone.'

"It was disturbed, as we have seen, and the only intended difference between the old 'edifice' and the 'new,' in this respect, was to fix this corner-stone more firmly in its proper place in the latter, than it had been in the former. This is the substance of that speech; and there is no conflict between the sentiments expressed in both upon the same subject matter.

James Madison

"So much for all these points, irrelevant as all of them, and *ad hominem* as some of them are, which have been presented by the [Liberals]. . . . I assure [them], . . . none of them announced any truth which hurts in the least. . . . But what bearing have they upon the matter under immediate consideration?

"How stands the issue between us as to the character of the conflict about Slavery? My position was that in the Federal Councils and before Federal Authorities it was not a conflict between the advocates of the system of Slavery, as it existed, and its opponents, as Mr. [Horace] Greeley has treated it throughout; but that it was in all its stages and phases so far as Federal Politics were concerned, a conflict between those who claimed, and those who denied, that the Federal Authorities had any rightful power, under the Constitution, to take any action whatever upon it, with a view to its immediate or ultimate extinction, or its regulation in any way in contravention of the Rights of the States."[543]

☛ "Why was the Declaration [of Independence] finally made without any allusion to the subject [of slavery]? Was it not because it was a matter over which each Sovereign State was to exercise its own discretion as it ought to? Was not Mr. [Thomas] Jefferson, the draftsman of that instrument, as much opposed to Slavery as Mr. [John] Adams, or Dr. [Benjamin] Franklin, or Roger Sherman, or Robert R. Livingston, his colleagues on the committee, and all of whom, except himself, were Northern men?

"... In a word, ... [have my Liberal friends] ... ventured to deny a single fact, stated by me ... in relation to the nature of this conflict, and the position of the great names mentioned upon it, from the time of its first introduction in Congress down to the election of Mr. Lincoln? [They have] . . . not, and I am sure [they] ... will not. We are bound, therefore, to take it as a fact, admitted by silence, at least, that *the conflict on this subject in the Federal Councils and before Federal Authorities, was not one between the 'principles of human rights and human bondage' at all; but that it was a conflict between the [Conservative] advocates and supporters of a Federal [Confederate] Government, with limited and specific powers, on the one side, and those [Liberals] who favored Centralism and Consolidation on the other.* [Emphasis added, L.S.]

"The States South were all on the side of the Constitution. They never invoked any stretch of Federal power to aid or protect that peculiar Institution, either in the States or Territories. Their position from the beginning to the end, upon the Territorial question, was 'non-intervention,' by Congress, either for or against the Institution. All they asked of Congress, in this particular, was simply not to be denied equal rights in settling and colonizing the common public domain, and that the people in these inchoate States [mainly the Western Territories] might be permitted to act as they pleased upon the subject of the status of the Negro race amongst them, as upon all other subjects of internal policy, when they came to form their Constitutions for admission into the Union, as perfect States upon an equal footing with the original Parties, without dictation or control from the Federal Authorities, one way or the other. They claimed the same Sovereign Right of local Self-government on the part of these new States which was the moving cause of the Declaration of Independence, and was the basis upon which our whole system of Government rested. This was their position on the admission of Missouri, and their position throughout. They never asked the Federal Government to extend, or strengthen their particular interest in any such way, as stated. No case of the kind can be named."[544]

Another point on which the North has long berated the South is the "Three-Fifths Clause" in the Constitution (Article 1, Section 2, Clause 3), which allowed slave owners to count each servant as three-fifths of a person so that those states with heavy slave populations would be more fairly represented in Congress (as the number of representatives allowed from each state is based on the state's population). Stephens dissembles this particular fiction piece by piece, beginning with the fact that the idea was proposed by a

Martin Van Buren

Northerner, *James Wilson:*

☛ "On this point of the 'three-fifths' representation clause of the Constitution, I should have been amazed at what [my Liberal friends say] . . . if I had not so often heard the same thing stated by others of equally high position and equally distinguished for general intelligence: but [they] . . . will allow me to say, most respectfully, that it is utterly without foundation, in fact. There is no clause [i.e., the Three-Fifths Clause] in the Constitution, the history or effects of which seem to be so little understood by men of note and high standing, both at the North and South, as this. It is not among the compromises, so-called, of the Constitution at all. It was not carried by any bluster, insolence, or dictation, or even demand of Southern members in the Convention. It did not emanate in that body from the Slavery interest, so-called, or any one connected with it, and its effects whether so designed or not, have been greatly to weaken and lessen the just powers in the Federal Government of these States, in which Slavery existed, instead of strengthening and enlarging them."[545]

Stephens continues his remarks on the Three-Fifths Clause:

☛ "The debates on it, when and where it originated, and when it was agreed to by the States, show that there was nothing sectional in it. When agreed to it had no reference whatever to representation, nor any rule or ratio of representation in Congress, of either persons or property. The States all, then, had an equal vote in the Congress, without regard to the number or character of their respective populations. But this counting of five negro slaves as equal to three white persons, was agreed upon after mature consideration, and a thorough investigation of the subject for years, as a proper basis of direct taxation, when population was resorted to as the proper standard of fixing the quotas of the States respectively.

"It was offered by Mr. [James] Wilson [of Pennsylvania] in the Convention that framed the Constitution, and was adopted by that body . . . unquestionably upon the then universally admitted doctrine, that representation in Legislative Bodies and direct taxation should go together. It was with this view, and upon this principle solely, and with no view to a property representation at all, that it was incorporated, as it is, in the Constitution."⁵⁴⁶

Stephens continues his remarks on the Three-Fifths Clause:

☛ ". . . whatever may have been the design when it was offered, the effect of this 'three-fifths' clause was greatly to weaken instead of strengthening the political power of the States in which Slavery existed. For very soon, the number of slaves in the Southern States was considerably increased by accessions from the Northern States. The acts of these Northern States, to which the [Liberals have] . . . referred, abolishing the Institution within their limits, were generally prospective in their character. Under the operation of these acts, humane as they were, in his estimation, the slaves in these [Northern] States, were to some extent, to what is not and never will be exactly known, brought South, and sold before the period fixed for their final emancipation. Less than half, it is believed by some, in point of fact, ever became free under these acts, however philanthropic, and however inspired by the 'Christian principles of the age,' they may be considered by him to have been. This is the way in which many of them [slaves], at least, found a resting-place in the more Southern States.

"But besides this, and mainly, it must be borne in mind, that the system of direct taxation, which was looked to at the time, as the chief mode of raising the ordinary revenues of the Federal Government, was soon virtually abandoned; and the Southern States, in which the slaves had almost entirely 'found a resting-place,' under the Northern system of Abolition, lost their full and just popular representation under it, without the compensating advantages contemplated at the time of its adoption, in the matter of the assessment of the taxes. The taxes were raised in another way, and by this clause these States were deprived of their equal and just voice in their imposition, though they had to pay their full part of them."⁵⁴⁷

☛ "This legal right, on the part of the owner [to employ the services of his servants for life], was truly called 'property,' but it in no respect differed in kind or species of property from the legal right of every employer, to the service of those who, by contract or law, are bound to service for any time shorter than that of life. This legal right to services so due for a term ever so short, is as much 'property' in the one case as the other. It is a 'property' that is maintained in all Courts, without reference to the length of the term for which it is due. On this view, therefore, which is just and correct, there is no reason why all those persons in the Southern States, who were bound to service for life, 'should not have been counted in a census for a basis of popular representation, as well as all minors, apprentices, or others,' bound to service for a shorter term in all the States. The owner of five slaves at the South, therefore, was not endowed, under this clause of the Constitution, with as much political power as three white men at the North. The owner of five, or a hundred, or a thousand, was endowed with no political power under it. No more than the employer of five, or a hundred, or a thousand of operatives at the North."[548]

When Stephens was asked to elaborate on the difference in the relation of a free laborer of the North towards his employer, and that of a slave at the South towards his owner, he replied:

☞ "I did not say that there was no difference, whatever, between these relations. What I maintained is, that there was no difference in the 'property' view of them so far as relates to this clause of the Constitution. The right to the service, or labor of the one, under contract, whether, for a short or long term, was as much 'property' as the right to the service of the other, under law, though it was for life. The only difference, in this respect, (and that is what we are considering,) is that the labor of the one, was for a term only, and that of the other, was for life [though Southern "slaves" could purchase their freedom at any time]. The laborers in each case were equally recognized by the laws, North and South, as persons; and they were so equally recognized in the Constitution. In this respect there was no difference; and in this respect there is no reason why there should have been any difference in the count for arriving at an equal basis of popular representation.

"The slave-owner was endowed with no political power by this clause, no more than the employer of other kinds of labor at the North. This was, and is, my position; and from all this it clearly appears, I think, that this 'three-fifths' clause of the Constitution, was no 'Slavery Oligarchical,' or 'aristocratic provision' of the Constitution, carried at the dictation of the Southern States, and for their especial benefit. On the contrary, it was a curtailment of their just powers, as the Government has been administered. But for it, the Southern States would have had six more members than they had under the first census. But for it, and the consequent want of her full and just power in Congress, at the time, the Alien and Sedition laws, might not, and, most probably, would not have been passed; and the other centralizing acts of the Government, passed during that decade, which have since been claimed as

Roger Brooke Taney

precedents might, and, most probably, never would have had existence. But for it, in 1820, the Southern States would have had twelve more members in the House of Representatives, than they then had, and the Missouri Restriction of that year, which [Liberals] . . . call a Solemn Compact, would not have been carried as it was. Here I might properly reply to the points made on that subject, and show that the conflict on that measure, however portentous, was not a conflict, as I have before said, between the advocates and opponents of the Institution of Slavery, as it existed in the States, but a conflict, as all others of a like character, between those who defended the Federal [Confederate] principles of the Government, and those who were endeavoring to centralize its powers. It can be easily shown that, for these political ends, this subject of Slavery was then seized upon, by leaders defeated on other questions, as one which would be most likely to enlist the general sympathy of the people, and one on which, from conscientious scruples, they might more easily be led to disregard the obligations of Compacts."[549]

From a July 19, 1872, letter to Richard M. Johnston. Stephens' brother Linton had passed away only days earlier on July 14. Still, the vice president takes time to write about the health of one of his black servants, Uncle Ben:

☛ ". . . To-day my sorrows were increased by a message from old Uncle Ben, the old family servant down at the homestead, now in his seventy-second year, who has been an invalid nearly all his life, that he is in low condition. I fear from what George said that he too may soon pass away. Linton's death greatly affected all down there, and old Uncle Ben in particular, who was his nurse in childhood, as his rheumatism kept Ben about the house for several years. When Linton went to his Uncle Lindsay's, in Upson County, in 1828 or 1829, Ben went with him, and was with him until I became his guardian, in 1837. He was much attached to him, and the old man was greatly afflicted by his death. I sent him a doctor, and will go to see him just as soon as I can. I feel as if it would be a relief to me to visit the old man on his sick-bed, and mingle my tears with his for one whom he loved so much as well as I. I am grieved that he is suffering so much. May God have mercy on us all!"[550]

15

Abraham Lincoln

Shortly after Lincoln's election to U.S. president, he began making veiled threats toward the South, which became bolder with each passing week. It was at this time that Stephens began a written correspondence with his old friend (Lincoln and he had been members of the Whig Party together in the 1840s) in an attempt to calm nerves and stave off potential bloodshed. The following excerpt is from Stephens' letter to Lincoln dated December 30, 1860. Dishonest Abe, of course, ignored his Southern counterpart's sage advice:

☛ "In addressing you thus, I would have you understand me as being not a personal enemy, but as one who would have you to do what you can to save our common country. A word 'fitly spoken' by you now, would indeed be 'like apples of gold, in pictures of silver.' I entreat you be not deceived as to the nature and extent of the danger, or as to the remedy. Conciliation and harmony, in my judgment, can never be established by force. Nor can the Union, under the Constitution, be maintained by force. The Union was formed by the consent of Independent Sovereign States. Ultimate Sovereignty still resides with them separately, which can be resumed, and will be, if their safety, tranquillity and security in their judgment require it. Under our system, as I view it, there is no rightful power in the General Government to coerce a State, in case any one of them should throw herself upon her reserved rights, and resume the full exercise of her Sovereign Powers. Force may perpetuate a Union. That depends upon the contingencies of war. But such a Union would not be the Union of the Constitution. It would be nothing short of a Consolidated Despotism. Excuse me for giving you these views. Excuse the strong language used. Nothing but the deep interest I feel in prospect of the most alarming dangers now threatening our common country, could induce me to do it."[551]

From a speech by Stephens given November 14, 1860, before the Georgia legislature—one week after Lincoln's election:

☛ "We are now, indeed, surrounded by evils. Never since I entered upon the public stage, has the country been so environed with difficulties and dangers that threatened the public peace and the very existence of our

Jean-Jacques Burlamaqui

Institutions as now. . . . The consternation that has come upon the people is the result of a sectional election of a President [Lincoln] of the United States, one whose opinions and avowed principles are in antagonism to our interests and rights, and we believe, if carried out, would subvert the Constitution under which we now live."[552]

Stephens' November 14, 1860, speech continues:

☛ "Whatever fate is to befall this country, let it never be laid to the charge of the people of the South, and especially to the people of Georgia, that we were untrue to our national engagements. Let the fault and the wrong rest upon others. If all our hopes are to be blasted, if the Republic is to go down, let us be found to the last moment standing on the deck with the Constitution of the United States waving over our heads. [Applause.] Let the fanatics of the North break the Constitution, if such is their fell purpose. Let the responsibility be upon them. . . . but let not the South, let us not be the ones to commit the aggression."[553]

Stephens' November 14, 1860, speech continues. Here, after beseeching his fellow Georgians to resist the temptation to secede from the Union, he accurately predicts the eternal condemnation of the South that would surely follow:

☛ "We went into the election with this people [the Yankees]. The result was different from what we wished; but the election has been constitutionally held.

Were we to make a point of resistance to the Government and go out of the Union merely on that account, the record would be made up hereafter against us."⁵⁵⁴

Stephens, a devout Christian, always tried to think the best of people. Unfortunately, in the case of Abraham Lincoln, he could not have been a worse judge of character, as is plain from the following excerpt from Stephens' November 14, 1860, speech. In fact, the future Confederate vice president vastly underestimated Lincoln's ego, greed, and ignorance, as well as his innate criminalistic talents for subterfuge, chicanery, and double-dealing:

☞ "But it is said Mr. Lincoln's policy and principles are against the Constitution, and that, if he carries them out, it will be destructive of our rights. Let us not anticipate a threatened evil. If he violates the Constitution, then will come our time to act. Do not let us break it because, forsooth, he may. If he does, that is the time for us to act. [Applause.] I think it would be injudicious and unwise to do this sooner. I do not anticipate that Mr. Lincoln will do anything, to jeopard our safety or security, whatever maybe his spirit to do it; for he is bound by the Constitutional checks which are thrown around him, which at this time render him powerless to do any great mischief. This shows the wisdom of our system. The President of the United States is no Emperor, no Dictator—he is clothed with no absolute power. He can do nothing, unless he is backed by power in Congress."⁵⁵⁵

From an April 19, 1861, letter to Richard M. Johnston:
☞ ". . . The idea of Mr. Lincoln to urge a general war of subjugation against us seems to me to be too preposterous for a sensible man to entertain. But what his real designs are I suppose it would be difficult to imagine. The worst feature about it in prospect is the possibility that he has no real design on the subject, that he has no settled policy, that he is, like the fool, scattering fire without any definite purpose."⁵⁵⁶

From a March 8, 1863, letter to Richard M. Johnston:
☞ ". . . Lincoln is no more a dictator now than he has been all the time . . ."⁵⁵⁷

Stephens' Liberal opponents maintained that they could "see nothing in either of Lincoln's Proclamations [that is, declaring war on the South and instituting a naval blockade] which was not required of him in the faithful discharge of his duties, under his oath of office." In 1870 the former Confederate vice president responded to this statement:
☞ "There again is where we shall, perhaps, have to agree to disagree, I suppose; for this not being a matter involving a question of fact, so much as the proper

conclusion which should be drawn from admitted facts, will, as other like points, have to be left to the judgment of mankind. For myself, I can only say that, so far from his oath of office requiring him to do anything of the sort, its requirements were just the other way. [Abraham Lincoln] . . . was sworn to 'preserve, protect and defend the Constitution,' and 'faithfully to execute the office of President of the United States.' This oath imposed a solemn obligation on him not to violate the Constitution, or to exercise, under color of his office, any power not conferred upon him by that instrument. He was required to see to the faithful execution of the laws of the United States, us passed by the Congress of States, and as construed by Judiciary. He said in the first of these Proclamations be made the call for the militia 'in virtue of the vested in him by the Constitution and the laws.' But no such power was vested in him by the Constitution, nor was there any law of the United States authorizing to call out the militia for any such purposes as those for which he made this call, nor was there any law authorizing him 'to set on foot' the Blockade he did in Second of these Proclamations. It is true, he said he did it in pursuance of law, but there was no such law. As these two papers did produce such an effect, they deserve special notice. We will, therefore, take them up in order. In reference to the first, I have this to say, that Congress alone has power, under the Constitution, to declare war and to raise armies. Congress alone has power to provide by law for calling out the militia of the several States. This Congress had done, but had not provided for calling them out under any such state of things as existed when this Proclamation was issued by Mr. Lincoln."[558]

From 1870:

☛ "Mr. Lincoln's election was not, in any proper sense, an endorsement of the principles of his [Republican] Party [the Liberals of the day] by a majority of the people of the non-slaveholding States. I did not think it was to be considered as anything like a fair exponent of the fixed sentiments of a majority of even all those States which had cast their Electoral votes, as they had, for Mr. Lincoln. I considered it as nothing but the result of the unfortunate rupture of the Democratic Party, at Charleston, in 1860 [in which the Southern conservatives unwisely split up their votes, allowing Lincoln to win]. This rupture I also attributed directly to the very injudicious and unwise policy of Mr. [James] Buchanan . . . in insisting upon a new article in the creed of the Democratic [Conservative] Party, or a new plank in the Platform, as it was called."[559]

From 1870:

☛ "When the candidates entered the field in June [of 1860], not a man of this class [i.e., Northern Liberals], perhaps, thought it to be within the range of

Simon Cameron

probability even, that Mr. Lincoln and [his vice president] Mr. [Hannibal] Hamlin would receive a majority of the Electoral votes, as they did."[560]

From 1870:

☛ "I regarded the success of the Centralists and Restrictionists [Northern Liberals] in the [1860] election of Mr. Lincoln, as a great public calamity . . ."[561]

Because it has been carefully suppressed by enemies of the South, most Americans are not aware of the fact that Lincoln did not just wage war on the Southern people. He also committed hundreds of unconstitutional acts against his own constituents in the North. One example is Maryland, where Lincoln shut down the state's government and arrested its entire legislature, as well as ordinary citizens. For what? For merely discussing secession and supporting the Southern Confederacy! In 1870 here is how Stephens described what he referred to as Lincoln's "reign of terror":

☛ "Under [Lincoln's many] . . . acts, suspending the privilege of the writ of *Habeas Corpus*, Northern prisons were soon filled with hundreds, if not thousands, of the best and truest citizens of the country, for no reason except that of raising their voice against these utterly indefensible assumptions of Executive power which Mr. [Stephen A.] Douglas, and even Mr. [Daniel] Webster, had clearly stated would be crimes for which an impeachment should be made. Fort McHenry, Fort La Fayette, and Fort Warren were turned into Bastiles! Strange means these to preserve the liberties of the people, except upon the maxim, that the best way to preserve Liberty, as well as life, is to destroy it!

"The Members of the Legislature of Maryland were prevented from assembling for the performance of their public duties by arrests and imprisonments under military orders issued in pursuance of these Executive edicts. The Mayor and Marshal, and most, if not all the civil officers of Baltimore, besides many other of the most respectable and worthy citizens of that State and other States, were seized and immured in prison without any charge of crime or violation of law against them. Not only was the freedom of speech denied, but the liberty of the press was openly assailed and effectually suspended throughout all the Northern States. Here is a list of a hundred and seventy-five of some of the best citizens in this country, who were thus seized and imprisoned in Fort La Fayette alone, in less than one hundred days, without any charge of crime against them, and in open violation of an express clause of the Constitution! Maryland, of all the States, however, suffered most from these arbitrary and tyrannical proceedings."[562]

After the War, knowing that he disagreed with nearly everything Lincoln did during his

War on the South and the Constitution, Stephens' Liberal friends asked him what he thought Lincoln should have done. The former Confederate vice president replied:

☛ "I have a two-fold answer. I will, in the first place, state what, in my opinion, he ought not to have done; and in the second place, what he ought to have done. He ought not, then, to have ordered the forcible supply of the troops at Fort Sumter. He ought to have withdrawn those troops, as advised by Mr. Douglas, General [Winfield] Scott, and all the leading real friends of the Union, under the Constitution, in all parts of the country. In other words, he ought not to have inaugurated the war as he did. If he really believed that the Union of the States under the Constitution was such as could and ought to be maintained by force, then he ought to have convened the Congress of the Non-Seceding States, and asked that body by law to put at his command the military force necessary to meet the exigencies of the crisis. He ought not to have assumed the exercise of this power himself, for it is clear the Constitution vested no such power in him. This is what he ought not to have done, as well as what he ought to have done, in that view of the powers of the Federal Government.

". . . I will now go further, and tell you what I think the Congress of States ought to have done under the circumstances, if they had been so convened by him. They should have called a Convention of all the States, with a view to a readjustment of their relations. If the Seceded States had responded to that call, well and good. In that event, I have but little doubt that the result would have been a peaceful adjustment of all matters in controversy, by the derelict States heretofore referred to—those which had openly and avowedly refused to perform their obligations under the Constitution—receding from their position . . . , and that upon this redress of grievances and righting of the wrong complained of, the Seceded States would have returned to their positions; and the whole Federal machinery, at no distant day, would have been restored to its normal and harmonious action in all its parts, as peacefully and joyously as when it first went into operation.

". . . [In short, there] would have been no war, nor any of those outrages upon public liberty to which I have alluded, and which have brought so much reproach upon our Institutions of Self-government throughout the world, and which have but one inevitable end, if not abandoned, and that is absolute Despotism!

"My own opinion, as I have said, is, that if Mr. Lincoln had pursued the course which I think he ought to have done, there would have been a speedy restoration of the Union, by all the States returning to their duties and obligations under the Constitution, and the Federal Government would have entered upon a new and a grander career of greatness."[563]

Nineteenth-Century Liberals adored Lincoln, just as they do today. Unable to understand Stephens' animosity toward America's sixteenth chief executive, they asked him: "Was President Lincoln not eminently distinguished for his frankness, good nature and general kindness of heart"? Stephens answered this question in 1870:

☛ "So were many men who have figured in history, and who have brought the greatest sufferings and miseries upon mankind. [French Revolutionary leaders Georges J.] Danton and [Maximilien de] Robespierre, the bloodiest monsters in the form of men we read of in history, were distinguished for the same qualities. They both had the personal esteem as well as the strong attachment of some of the best men in France, who were utterly opposed to their public acts and policy.

Henry Ward Beecher

". . . A man may possess many amiable qualities in private life—many estimable virtues and excellencies of character, and yet in official position commit errors involving not only most unjustifiable usurpations of power, but such as rise to high crimes against society and against humanity. This, too, may be done most conscientiously and with the best intentions. This, at least, is my opinion on that subject. The history of the world abounds with apt instances for illustration. Mr. Lincoln, you say, was kind-hearted. In this, I fully agree. No man I ever knew was more so, but the same was true of Julius Caesar. All you have said of Mr. Lincoln's good qualities, and a great deal more on the same line, may be truly said of Caesar. He was certainly esteemed by many of the best men of his day for some of the highest qualities which dignify and ennoble human nature. He was a thorough scholar, a profound philosopher, an accomplished orator, and one of the most gifted, as well as polished writers of the age, in which he lived. No man ever had more devoted personal friends, and justly so, too, than he had. And yet, notwithstanding all these distinguishing, amiable and high qualities of his private character, he is by the general consent of mankind looked upon as the destroyer of the liberties of Rome!"[564]

Victorian Lincolnites, who worshipped at the "Church of Father Abraham," believed their president could do no wrong, that everyone of his wartime acts, even the heinous and unnecessary deaths of some 3 million Americans South and North, was for the benefit of the people and the Union. In 1870 Stephens responded to this notion:

☛ "I ask, what is there about the maintenance of Government, of any sort, which justifies such conduct? Are not Governments made for the security and peace of the people, and not the people for the maintenance of Governments which gives them neither? What other end or object has any just Government, or one that deserves to be maintained, but to afford protection and security to all those for whom it is instituted? The resistance [the Liberals] . . . speak of, was to his acts, and the measures adopted to maintain Government. But for his acts, and these measures thus to maintain Government, this resistance, and the consequences, would not have taken place. These occurrences, therefore, are not to be attributed to the resistance, but to his acts. The resistance itself was but a consequence of his acts. Had he not acted as he did, there would have been no resistance, and none of these scenes and consequences would have followed. This [my Liberal friends] . . . must admit."[565]

☛ "It must be borne in mind . . . that [even midway into his War] there had been no 'step backward' in Mr. Lincoln's usurpations of power. The only change in this view was bolder and more glaring forward strides in the same direction. Proclamations of even more extraordinary character than these heretofore noticed, had been issued by him during the second year of the war. Two of these deserve special notice in this connection. The first was his celebrated [Preliminary] Emancipation Proclamation, so-called [which contained Lincoln's racist clause asking the U.S. Congress for money to deport all African-Americans out of the country]. It was issued on the 22nd of September, 1862, to take effect on the 1st of January, 1863 [known as the Final Emancipation Proclamation]. In this he avowedly assumed to do what he had repeatedly declared in the most public and solemn manner he had no rightful power to do. No usurpation could be more palpable or flagrant than this. By the other of these edicts, issued two days afterwards, Martial Law throughout the United States was virtually declared, and a new class of officers under military commission for the execution of this high-handed measure, unknown to the laws and Constitution, was created by Imperial orders through the [U.S.] War Department.

"These measures, to say nothing of others, had awakened a most serious alarm throughout the entire North, for the stability and security of their own liberties, even amongst those who favored the prosecution of the war for the preservation of 'the Union.'"[566]

The following excerpts from Stephens' A Constitutional View *concern the infamous four-hour long Hampton Roads Conference held on February 3, 1865, and which was attended by Stephens, Robert M. T. Hunter, and John A. Campbell on the Southern side, and Lincoln and William H. Seward on the Northern side. How did this celebrated meeting originate? Whose idea was it, and why did it fail? What actually occurred at the interview between the Confederate Commissioners and Lincoln and Seward?*

John Cabell Breckinridge

Many lies about this conference have been fabricated by enemies of the South. However, Stephens, a stalwart Christian whose word was impeccable, was in attendance. And it is from him that we learn the Truth of what went on behind closed doors that chilly Virginia day—the only known time that President Lincoln deigned to meet with what he considered to be lowly Southern "Rebels" and "treasonous anarchists."

Though, because of Lincoln's inflexible Hitler-like approach to his War, the meeting was unsuccessful in yielding any results toward ending it with full Southern rights intact (the Confederates' main objective), several remarkable facts emerged; facts that fly in the face of pro-North propaganda:

• Lincoln and Seward admitted that only 200,000 (a mere 5 percent) of the South's 4 million slaves were affected by the Emancipation Proclamation.

• Lincoln admitted that "the people of the North were as responsible for slavery as the people of the South." [Note: Since both the American slave trade and American slavery got their start in the North (Massachusetts, to be precise), and the American abolition movement began in the South,[567] Lincoln is only half correct.]

• *Lincoln admitted that the Emancipation Proclamation was nothing more than a military measure (indeed, he openly referred to it as a "military emancipation"[568] and a "military necessity"),[569] and as such, would end with the termination of the War. After that, for all he cared, the Southern states could vote against the upcoming Thirteenth Amendment and continue to practice slavery. His main interest was, and always had been, the reunion of the Southern states—and nothing more. The only stipulation was that slaves who had been freed could not be re-enslaved.*

Though Lincoln does not say here why he did not want emancipated servants put back in bondage, we know the two main reasons from his earlier speeches and letters, and Stephens, Hunter, and Campbell, were no doubt well aware of them as well. The reasons:

A) As the Emancipation Proclamation itself intimates, Lincoln desperately needed blacks to fill the vacancies left by the thousands of his white U.S. soldiers who had died, deserted, defected to the South, or were wounded and could no longer fight.

B) As a white racist, white separatist, and black colonizationist (that is, one who wanted America to be a white-only nation), Lincoln had to free the slaves so that he could legally deport them out of the country (preferably, as he put it, "back to their native land") after the War.[570] The mass deportation of African-Americans was impossible as long as they were considered "private property." Lincoln had made his feelings on this topic perfectly clear during a public speech at Springfield, Illinois, on July 17, 1858, when he said: "What I would most desire would be the separation of the white and black races."[571] Here is a selection from Stephens' 1870 report on the Hampton Roads meeting:

☛ "I asked Mr. Lincoln what would be the status of that portion of the Slave population in the Confederate States, which had not then become free under his Proclamation; or in other words, what effect that Proclamation would have upon the entire Black population? Would it be held to emancipate the whole, or only those who had, at the time the war ended, become actually free under it?

"Mr. Lincoln said, that was a judicial question. How the Courts would decide it, he did not know, and could give no answer. His own opinion was, that as the Proclamation was a war measure, and would have effect only from its being an exercise of the war power, as soon as the war ceased, it would be inoperative for the future. It would be held to apply only to such slaves as had come under its operation while it was in active exercise. This was his individual opinion, but the Courts might decide the other way, and hold that it effectually emancipated all the slaves in the States to which it applied at the time. So far as he was concerned, he should leave it to the Courts to decide. He never would change or modify the terms of the Proclamation in the slightest particular. Mr. Seward said there were only about two hundred thousand slaves, who, up to that time, had come under the actual operation of the Proclamation, and who were then in the enjoyment of their freedom under it; so, if the war should then cease, the status of much the larger portion of the slaves would be subject to judicial construction. Mr. Lincoln sustained Mr. Seward as to the number of slaves who were then in the actual enjoyment of their freedom under the Proclamation. Mr. Seward also said, it might be proper to state to us, that [the U.S.] Congress, a day or two before, had proposed a Constitutional Amendment [what would become the Thirteenth Amendment] for the immediate abolition of slavery throughout the United States, which he produced and read to us from a newspaper. He said this was done as a war measure. If the war were then to cease, it would probably not be adopted by a number of States, sufficient to make it a part of the Constitution; but presented the case in such light as clearly showed his object to be, to impress upon the minds of the Commissioners that, if the war should not cease, this, as a war measure,

Harriet Beecher Stowe

would be adopted by a sufficient number of States to become a part of the Constitution, and without saying it in direct words, left the inference very clearly to be perceived by the Commissioners that his opinion was, if the Confederate States would then abandon the war, they could of themselves defeat this amendment, by voting it down as members of the Union. The whole number of States, it was said, being thirty-six, any ten of them could defeat this proposed amendment."[572]

Stephens' 1870 report on the Hampton Roads Conference continues:

☛ "I insisted that if he could, as a war measure, issue his Proclamation for Emancipation, which he did not venture to justify under the Constitution on any other grounds, he could certainly, as a like war measure, or as a measure for putting an end to the war rather, enter into some stipulation on this subject.

"He [Lincoln] then went into a prolonged course of remarks about the Proclamation. He said it was not his intention in the beginning to interfere with Slavery in the States; that he never would have done it, if he had not been compelled by necessity to do it, to maintain the Union; that the subject presented many difficult and perplexing questions to him; that he had hesitated for some time, and had resorted to this measure, only when driven to it by public necessity; that he had been in favor of the General Government prohibiting the extension of Slavery into the Territories, but did not think that that Government possessed power over the subject in the States, except as a war measure; and that he had always himself been in favor of emancipation, but not immediate emancipation, even by the States. Many evils attending this appeared to him.

"After pausing for some time, his head rather bent down, as if in deep reflection, while all were silent, he rose up and used these words, almost, if not, quite identical:

'Stephens, if I were in Georgia, and entertained the sentiments I do—though, I suppose, I should not be permitted to stay there long with them; but if I resided in Georgia, with my present sentiments, I'll tell you what I would do, if I were in your place: I would go home and get the Governor of the State to call the Legislature together, and get them to recall all the State troops from the war; elect Senators and Members to Congress, and ratify this Constitutional Amendment prospectively, so as to take effect—say in five years. Such a ratification would be valid in my opinion. I have looked into the subject, and think such a prospective ratification would be valid. Whatever may have been the views of your people before the war, they must be convinced now, that Slavery is doomed. It cannot last long in any event, and the best course, it seems to me, for your public men to pursue, would be to adopt such a policy as will avoid, as far as possible, *the evils of immediate emancipation*. This would be my course, if I were in your place.' [Emphasis added, L.S.]

"Mr. Seward also indulged in remarks at considerable length on the progress of the Anti-Slavery sentiment of the country, and stated that what he had thought would require forty or fifty years of agitation to accomplish, would certainly be attained in a much shorter time."[573]

Stephens' report on the Hampton Roads Conference continues:
☞ "Other matters were then talked over relating to the evils of immediate

emancipation, if that policy should be pressed, especially the sufferings which would necessarily attend the old and the infirm, as well as the women and children, who were unable to support themselves. These were fully admitted by Mr. Lincoln, but in reference to them, in that event, he illustrated all he could say by telling the anecdote, which has been published in the papers, about the Illinois farmer and his hogs.

"[Let me note here that] Mr. Lincoln had a wonderful talent for illustrations of this sort. His genius for Anecdotes was fully equal, if not superior, to that of Æsop for Apologues or Fables. They were his chief resort in conveying his ideas upon almost every question. His resources for producing them, seemed to be inexhaustible, and they were usually exceedingly pointed, apt, and telling in their application. The one on this occasion was far from being entitled to a place on a list of his best and most felicitous hits of this character. The substance of it was this:

"An Illinois farmer was congratulating himself with a neighbor upon a great discovery he had made, by which he would economize much

Chester Alan Arthur

time and labor in gathering and taking care of the food crop for his hogs, as well as trouble in looking after and feeding them during the winter.

'What is it?' said the neighbor.

'Why, it is,' said the farmer, 'to plant plenty of potatoes, and when they are mature, without either digging or housing them, turn the hogs in the field and let them get their own food as they want it.'

'But,' said the neighbor, 'how will they do when the winter comes and the ground is hard frozen?'

'Well,' said the farmer, 'let 'em root!'[574]

16

Lincoln's War

Concerning Lincoln's War, and all wars in general, Stephens said:

☛ "The result of wars generally depends quite as much upon diplomacy as upon arms—upon the proper use of the pen as of the sword. There is a time for each. It is a matter of the utmost importance to know when and how to use both."[575]

☛ "As to the future or any terms which our [Confederate] Government might grant or accept with a view to arrest further conflict, I can say nothing. I have no authority from the Confederate States government on the subject. But as a citizen desirous at all times to preserve peace, if it can be done on just and correct principles, I have no hesitancy in saying to you that the course of future events in these particulars will depend to a great extent, in my individual judgment, upon the course to be pursued by the government of the United States. From all evidences and manifestations of their design which have reached me, it seems to be their policy to wage a war for the recapture of former possessions, looking to the ultimate coercion and subjugation of the people of the Confed. States to their power and dominion. With such an object on their part persevered in, no power on earth can arrest or prevent a most bloody conflict."[576]

☛ "[Concerning] . . . the Proclamation of [Confederate] President [Jefferson] Davis inviting offers for commissions in Privateer service . . . it was intended as a justifiable and legitimate measure in defensive warfare against the war of

John Charles Frémont

aggression so clearly inaugurated by the Proclamation of President Lincoln."[577]

☛ "War, in one view, is eminently a business affair upon a large and magnificent scale; and it requires eminently business qualities to conduct it safely and successfully against such disadvantages as we labor under. But with the advantages we possess I have never doubted for a moment, but that we can wage it successfully in our defence, just as long as our enemies shall choose to prosecute it, if our resources of men and means are properly and efficiently wielded. From the beginning I believed it would very probably be ultimately a war for our subjugation or extermination."[578]

Anti-South proponents, pro-North writers, and Liberals in general have long put forth the notion that the South started the American "Civil War." "Did not Confederate General Pierre G. T. Beauregard in command of the Confederate forces, so-called, at Charleston, South Carolina, fire upon Fort Sumter in that Harbor?" they ask. "Did he not compel Union Major Robert Anderson, the United States officer in command of that Fort, to capitulate and surrender? Was it not this outrage upon the American flag that caused such deep and universal excitement and indignation throughout the entire North? Was it not this that caused the great meetings in New York, Boston and every Northern city? How can one maintain in the face of these notorious facts, that the war was begun by Mr. Lincoln, or the Federal authorities? Is it not as plain as day that the Insurgents, or Confederates launched this war?" Stephens knew the truth:

☞ "My whole argument is based upon facts, and upon facts that can never be erased or obliterated. It is a fact that the first gun was fired by the Confederates. It is a fact that General Beauregard did, on the 12th of April, 1861, bombard Fort Sumter, before any blow had actually been struck by the Federal authorities. That is not disputed at all. That is a fact which I have no disposition to erase or obliterate in any way. That is a great truth which will live forever. But did the firing of the first gun, or the reduction of Fort Sumter inaugurate or begin the war? That is a question to be first solved, before we can be agreed upon the fact as to who inaugurated the war; and in solving this question, you must allow me to say that in personal or national conflicts, it is not he who strikes the first blow, or fires the first gun that inaugurates or begins the conflict. [English historian Henry] Hallam has well said that 'the aggressor in a war (that is, he who begins it,) is not the first who uses force, but the first who renders force necessary.'

"Which side, according to this high authority, (that only announces the common sentiments of mankind,) was the aggressor in this instance? Which side was it that provoked and rendered the first blow necessary? The true answer to that question will settle the fact as to which side began the war.

"I maintain that it was inaugurated and begun, though no blow had been struck, when the hostile [U.S.] fleet, styled the 'Relief Squadron,' with eleven ships, carrying two hundred and eighty-five guns and two thousand four hundred men, was sent out from New York and Norfolk, with orders from the authorities at Washington, to reenforce Fort Sumter peaceably, if permitted—'but forcibly if they must.'

"The war was then and there inaugurated and begun by the [U.S.] authorities at Washington. General Beauregard did not open fire upon Fort

Yankee officers at John Bell Hood's headquarters, Atlanta, Georgia

Sumter until this fleet was, to his knowledge, very near the harbor of
Charleston, and until he had inquired of Major Anderson, in command of the
Fort, whether he would engage to take no part in the expected blow, then
coming down upon him from the approaching fleet. Francis W. Pickens,
Governor of South Carolina, and General Beauregard, had both been notified
that the fleet was coming, and of its objects, by a messenger from the authorities
at Washington. This notice, however, was not given until it was near its
destination. When Major Anderson, therefore, would make no such promise,

it became necessary for General Beauregard to strike the first blow, as he did; otherwise the forces under his command might have been exposed to two fires at the same time—one in front, and the other in the rear.

". . . It is true [then that] the first gun was fired on the Confederate side. That is fully admitted. But all the facts show that, if force was thus first used by them, it was so first used only, because it was rendered necessary in self-defence on the part of those thus using it, and so rendered necessary by the opposite side. This first use of force, therefore, under the circumstances, cannot, in fact, be properly and justly considered as the beginning of the war."[579]

Stephens' Northern Liberal friends held that Lincoln had every right to seize those forts in the Southern states that were claimed by the Confederacy. To this Stephens replied:
☛ "The Confederate States had offered to come to a fair and just settlement with the United States, as to the value of this property, as well as all other public property belonging to all the States in common, at the time of their separation. This Fort, as well as all else that belonged to the United States, belonged in part to these seven Seceded States. They constituted seven of the United States, to which all this joint property belonged. All the Forts which lay within the limits of the Seceded States, had been turned over by these States, respectively, to the Confederacy. . . . The Confederate States, therefore, through their authorities, had a right to demand, and take possession of all of these Forts, so lying within their limits, for their own public use, upon paying a just compensation for them to their former associates of the United States, who still adhered to that Union. These principles cannot be assailed. The offer so to pay whatever should be found to be due upon a general and just account, had been made. Mr. Lincoln, therefore, had no right under the circumstances, to hold any of these Forts by force, after the demand for the possession had been made; much less was it his duty either morally, or politically, when it was known that the attempt would inevitably lead to a war between the States. This is my answer to [the Liberals'] . . . property view."[580]

Stephens delivered the following before the Virginia Secession Convention on April 23, 1861. Though Lincoln had already illegally ordered troops to invade the South, the Old Dominion had not yet decided to secede from the Union:
☛ "A war is upon us—upon you and the Confederate States alike. The extent of this war no human ken at this moment can foresee. Whether it be short or prolonged; whether it will be bloody and waged on the part of our enemies, with a view to subjugation and extermination, are matters of uncertainty. In this free conference I may be permitted to give you my individual opinion on

these points, for what it is worth. We can lose nothing by looking dangers full in the face, however great; we may thereby be the better enabled to meet them. My own opinion, then, is, that it is to be a war for our subjugation and the extermination, if possible, of the whole fabric of our civil and social institutions. This is my view of its probable ultimate range; and that it will require all the resources of money and men of the southern people to maintain their cause successfully, unless, fortunately, by immediate and prompt action, such a decisive blow shall be given, on our part, as will turn the tide of victory in our favor at the outset, and show our full power to sustain independence. In this way it may be a war of short duration; but this is rather a hope than an expectation.

"As to the ultimate result—whether long or short, whether waged on a small or extensive scale—I do not permit myself to entertain a doubt. We have the means—the men, and those resources which will command the money. All will be put forth, if necessary. Still the issue of this war, as of all wars, as well as the destinies of the nation, we should not forget, are in the hands of the Great Sovereign of the universe. In Him and the justice of our cause, and our own exertions, our trust and confidence of success should be placed. Our enemies may rely upon their superiority of numbers, but the race is not always to the swift nor the battle to the strong; but it is with God who gives the victory to the right. The war has not been of our seeking. We have done all that we could to avoid it. We feel assured of the righteousness of our cause, and that 'thrice armed is he who hath his quarrel just.' We have committed no wrong on those who force the war on us; we have made no aggression on them or theirs; we have merely claimed and exercised the right of all free and independent States to govern ourselves as we please, and according to our own wishes, without interfering with or in any way molesting the other sovereign and independent States that formed the old Union. With those States we were united under a compact known as the constitution, that imposed obligations upon all the States. These obligations, on the part of the southern States, have been faithfully performed, while on the part of a large number of the northern States, they were openly and avowedly disregarded. The breach of faith was on their part. In the judgment of our people the only hope for safety was in a resumption of their delegated powers. Having resumed the powers delegated to the general government—a right which Virginia distinctly reserved to herself in the adoption of the Federal [U.S.] constitution—there is no power on earth that can rightfully call in question our acts as free, sovereign, and independent States, so far as the old Union is concerned."[581]

Stephens' speech before the Virginia Secession Convention continues:

☞ "The matter now before us is the formation of a new alliance that will better secure our rights and our safety—the first object of every State and community.

"The importance of a union or an alliance of some sort on the part of your commonwealth with the present Confederate States south, in this conflict for our common rights, I need not discuss before this intelligent body. Any one State, acting in its own capacity, without concert with other States, would be powerless, or at least could not exert its power efficiently. The cause of Virginia, and I will go further, the cause of Maryland, and even the cause of Delaware, and of all the States with institutions similar to ours, is the cause of the Confederate States—the cause of each, the interests of each, the safety of each is the same; and the destiny of each, if they could all but be brought to realize the dangers, would be the same. Therefore, where there is a common danger; where there is a common interest; where there is a common safety; where there is a common destiny, there ought to be a common and united effort."[582]

Rufus King

Stephens' speech before the Virginia Secession Convention continues:

☞ "Our people, from South Carolina to the Rio Grande, are in this movement heart and soul; and every dollar that can be raised will be used for the defence of the country in this emergency."[583]

Stephens' speech before the Virginia Secession Convention continues:

☞ "Because you stand on the border, it is not our desire that you should fight our battles. We don't wish you alone to fight these battles, or to bear yourself the expense of defending Virginia. I know that the intimation has been held out in other parts that we were not considering the peculiar circumstances of our brethren on the border States. I give you every assurance that our government feels thoroughly identified with you in interest, and we do not wish your great commonwealth to do more than bear her part in this contest. We know she is willing to do that. So far as the pecuniary matters are concerned then, I simply suggest whether it would not be wise and just and proper that all should share the burden equally—and whether we should not as our fathers did, in the first struggle for independence, look to each other, and bear equally the costs of a common cause? This I present, whether Virginia joins us ultimately or not. But to be entirely frank. I must say that we are looking to a speedy and early union of your State with our confederacy. Hence the greater importance for this immediate and temporary alliance. We want Virginia, the mother of States, as well as of statesmen, to be one of the States of our confederation. We want it because your people are our people—your interests are our interests; nay, more: because of the very prestige of the name of the old commonwealth. We want it, because of the memory of [Thomas] Jefferson, of [James] Madison, and [George] Washington, the father of his country—we want it for all the associations of the past—we want it because the principles in our constitution, both provisional and permanent, sprung from Virginia. They emanated from your statesmen—they are Virginian throughout—taught by your illustrious sages, and by their instrumentality mainly, were incorporated in the old constitution. That ancient and sacred instrument has no less of our regard and admiration now than it ever had. We quit the Union, but not the constitution—this we have preserved. Secession from the old Union on the part of the Confederate States was founded upon the conviction that the time-honored constitution of our fathers was about to be utterly undermined and destroyed, and that if the present administration at Washington had been permitted to rule over us, in less than four years, perhaps, this inestimable inheritance of liberty, regulated and protected by fundamental law, would have been forever lost. We believe that the movement with us has been the only course to save that great work of Virginia statesmen.

"On this point indulge me a moment. Under the latitudinarian construction of the constitution which prevails at the north, the general idea is maintained that the will of the majority is supreme; and as to constitutional checks or restraints, they have no just conception of them. The constitution was, at first, mainly the work of southern men, and Virginia men at that. The government under it lasted only so long as it was kept in its proper sphere with due regard to its limitations, checks, and balances. This, from the origin of the government, was effected mainly by southern statesmen. It was only when all further effort seemed to be hopeless to keep the federal government within its proper sphere of delegated powers, that the [original American] Confederate States [1781-1789], each for itself, resumed those powers and looked out for new safeguards for their rights and domestic tranquillity. These are found not in abandoning the constitution, but in adhering only to those who will faithfully sustain it.

"We have rescued the constitution from utter annihilation. This is our conviction, and we believe history will so record the fact. You have seen what we have done. Our [Confederate] constitution has been published. Perhaps most of you have read it. If not I have a copy here, which is at the service of any who may wish to examine it. It is the old constitution, with all its essentials and some changes . . ."[584]

The following is from Stephens' speech on March 16, 1864, before the Georgia legislature at Milledgeville, Georgia:

☞ "War is being waged against us by a strong, unscrupulous and vindictive foe; a war for our subjugation, degradation and extermination. From this quarter threaten the perils without. Those within arise from questions of policy as to the best means, the wisest and safest, to repel the enemy, achieve our independence, to maintain and keep secure our rights and liberties. Upon the decision of these questions, looking to the proper development of our limited resources, wisely and patriotically, so that their entire efficiency may be exerted in our deliverance, with at the same time a watchful vigilance to the safety of the citadel itself, as much depends as upon the skill of our commanders and the valor of our citizen soldiers in the field. Every thing dear to us as freemen is at stake. An error in judgment, though springing from the most patriotic motives, whether in councils of war or councils of state, may be fatal. He, therefore, who rises under such circumstances to offer words of advice, not only assumes a position of great responsibility, but stands on dangerous ground. Impressed profoundly with such feelings and convictions, I should shrink from the undertaking you have called me to, but for the strong consciousness that where duty leads no one should ever fear to tread. Great as are the dangers that threaten us, perilous as is our situation—and I do not intend to overstate or understate, neither to awaken undue apprehension, or to excite hopes and expectations never to be realized—perilous, therefore, as our situation is, it is far, far from being desperate or hopeless, and I feel no hesitation in saying to you, in all frankness and candor, that if we are true to ourselves, and true to our cause, all may yet be well.

"In the progress of the war thus far, it is true there is much to be seen of suffering, of sacrifice and of desolation; much to sicken the heart and cause a blush for civilization and Christianity. Cities have been taken, towns have been sacked, vast amounts of property have been burned, fields have been laid waste, records have been destroyed, churches have been desecrated, women and children have been driven from their homes, unarmed men have been put to death, States have been overrun and whole populations made to groan under the heel of despotism; all these things are seen and felt, but in them nothing is to be seen to cause dismay, much less despair; these deeds of ruin and savage barbarity have been perpetrated only on the outer borders, on the coast, and on the line of the rivers, where by the aid of their ships of war and gunboats the enemy has had the advantage; the great breadth of the interior—the heart of our country—has never yet been reached by them; they have as yet, after a struggle of nearly three years, with unlimited means, at a cost of not less than four thousand millions of dollars (how much more is unknown) and hundreds of thousands of lives, been able only to break the outter shell of the Confederacy. The only signal advantages they have as yet gained have been on the water, or where their land and naval forces were combined. That they should have gained advantages under such circumstances, is not a matter of much surprise. Nations in war, like individual men or animals, show their real power in combat when they stand upon the advantages that nature has given them, and fight on their own ground and in their own element. The lion, though king of the forest, cannot contend successfully with the shark in the water. In no conflict of arms away from gunboats, during the whole war, since the first battle of Manassas to that of Ocean Pond, have our gallant soldiers failed of victory when the numbers on each side were at all equal."[585]

Stephens' March 16, 1864, speech before the Georgia legislature continues:
☛ "Take courage from the example of your ancestors—disasters caused with them nothing like dismay or despair—they only aroused a spirit of renewed energy and fortitude. The principles they fought for, suffered and endured so much for, are the same for which we are now struggling—State rights, State sovereignty, the great principle set forth in the declaration of independence—the right of every State to govern itself as it pleases. With the same wisdom, prudence, forecast and patriotism; the same or equal statesmanship on the part of our rulers in directing and wielding our resources, our material of war, that controlled public affairs at that time, in the camp and in the cabinet, and with the same spirit animating the breast of the people, devotion to liberty and right, hatred of tyranny and oppression, affection for the cause for the cause's sake; with the same sentiments and feelings on the part of rulers and people in these days as were in those, we might and may be overrun as they were; our interior may be penetrated by superior hostile armies, and our country laid waste as theirs was, but we can never be conquered, as they never could be."[586]

In 1874 Stephens published his work, A Compendium of the History of the United

John Tyler

States: From the Earliest Settlements to 1872. *What follows is a brief excerpt from Stephens' chapters on "The Administration of Lincoln":*

☛ "The War Between the States: First Year.

"I. Abraham Lincoln, of Illinois, 16th President of the United States, was duly inaugurated at the usual place on the 4th of March, 1861, aged 52 years and 20 days. Borne in an open carriage, he was escorted and guarded from Willard's Hotel to the Capitol by an armed military force, under the direction of Gen. [Winfield] Scott, the General-in-chief of the Army of the United States. The oath of office was administered by Chief-Justice [Roger B.] Taney, in the presence of an audience estimated at 10,000. His Inaugural Address was read from a manuscript. It indicated no decisive policy, except the maintenance of the 'Union,' which he claimed to be 'older than the States,' and his purpose to collect the public revenues at the ports of the seceded States, as well as to 'hold, occupy, and possess' all the forts, arsenals, and other public property before held by the Federal authorities. . . .

"3. On the 12th of March the Confederate States Commissioners addressed a note to Mr. [William H.] Seward, Secretary of State, setting forth the character and object of their mission. In it they said:

> 'The undersigned are instructed to make to the Government of the United States overtures for the opening of negotiations, assuring the Government of the United States that the President, Congress, and people of the Confederate States earnestly desire a peaceful solution of these great questions; that it is neither their interest nor their wish to make any demand which is not founded in strictest justice, nor do any act to injure their late Confederates.'

". . . 4. From subsequent disclosures, it appears that it was the intention of Mr. Lincoln to withdraw the Federal forces from Fort Sumter at an early day, when the assurance to that effect was given; but when this intention became known in his party circles, the Governors of seven of the Northern

States, which were under the control of the Agitators, assembled in Washington, and prevailed on him to change his policy. It was after this that the war preparations mentioned were secretly commenced and carried on; and 'faith as to Sumter' was only so far 'kept' as to give notice, on the 8th of April, not to the Confederate Commissioners, but to Gov. [Francis W.] Pickens, of S.C., of a change of the policy of the Administration in regard to the assurance given, and that a fleet was then on its way to reinforce the fort, as stated.

". . . 6. This was the beginning of a war between the States of the Federal Union, which has been truly characterized as 'one of the most tremendous conflicts on record.' The din of its clangor reached the remotest parts of the earth, and the people of all nations looked on, for four years and upwards, in wonder and amazement, as its gigantic proportions loomed forth, and its hideous engines of destruction of human life and everything of human structure were terribly displayed in its sanguinary progress and grievous duration.

"About this war—its origin, causes, conduct, guilt, crimes, consequences, and results, as well as its sufferings, sacrifices, and heroic exploits—many volumes have already been published, and many more will doubtless be published; but in reference to the whole, it may with reverence be said, that if everything done in it, and 'every one' attending it deserving notice, should be duly recorded, 'even the world itself could not contain the books that should be written.'

". . . 7. The telegraphic announcement of the fall of Sumter enabled the Agitators to inflame the minds of the people of the Northern States under their influence to a higher pitch than ever, and to add to their ranks large accessions from the ranks of the Democratic [Conservative] and American parties. A cry was now raised by them for the maintenance of that Union which they had before denounced as 'a covenant with death, and an agreement with hell.' Upon the Confederates was charged the guilt of a desecration of the national flag, and with it the crime of treason. The beginning of the war with all its responsibilities was laid at their door. Mr. Lincoln, on the 15th of April, issued a Proclamation calling for 75,000 troops, and convening Congress to meet in Extra Session on the 4th of July. Thus stood the case on one side.

"On the other, the Confederates maintained that the silencing by them of the guns of Sumter was only an act of defence in anticipation of an approaching attack from a hostile fleet, as announced by the notification to Gov. Pickens of the intention of the Federal authorities to 'reinforce Fort Sumter, peaceably, if permitted; but forcibly, if necessary.' This they regarded as a declaration of war, already initiated by the Federals. They held that the war was in fact begun when this fleet put to sea for the purpose stated, and that it was formally declared by the notification given. They stood upon the well-established principle of public law, that 'the aggressor in a war' (that is, he who begins it) 'is not the first who uses force, but the first who renders force necessary.' They held, that under the Constitution of 1787, by which the previously existing Federal Union between the States had been strengthened and made 'more perfect,' the sovereignty of the several States was still reserved by the parties respectively, and with it the right of eminent domain was retained by each within its limits—that the Federal authorities had no rightful military jurisdiction over the soil upon which Fort Sumter was erected, except by the consent of the State of South Carolina. This was expressly stipulated in the Constitutional Compact, and when South Carolina had re-assumed her sovereign jurisdiction over her entire territory, the possession of this fort (erected by her consent, for the special protection of her own chief city, as well as the common defence of the other States) justly belonged to her. They maintained further that she and her new Confederates had the right legally and morally to claim and take possession of it; and that any attempt by force to resist the exercise of this right by any other Power, was an act of war upon her and them. Mr. Lincoln's call for troops, therefore, was met by the Government at Montgomery by a similar call for volunteers to repel aggressions. So matters stood on both sides."[587]

Having gone through the entire history of Lincoln's War, Stephens terminates this section of his 1874 Compendium *with these words:*
☛ "16. Thus ended the war between the States. It was waged by the Federals with the sole object, as they declared, of 'maintaining the Union under the Constitution;' while by the Confederates it was waged with the great object of maintaining the inestimable sovereign right of local self-government on the part of the Peoples of the several States. It was the most lamentable as well as the greatest of modern wars, if not the greatest in some respects 'known in the history of the human race.' It lasted four years and a little over, . . . with numerous sanguinary conflicts, and heroic exploits on both sides not chronicled in this Compendium; but many of which will live in memory, and be perpetuated as legends, and thus be treasured up as themes for story and song for ages to come.

"17. In conclusion, a few comments only will be added. One of the most striking features of the war was the great disparity between the numbers on the opposite sides. From its beginning to its end, near, if not quite, two millions more of Federals were brought into the field than the entire forces of the Confederates. The Federal records show that they had from first to last two million six hundred thousand men in the service; while the Confederates, all told, in like manner, had but little over six hundred thousand. The aggregate Federal population at its commencement was above twenty-two millions; that of the Confederates, was less than ten, near four millions of these being Negro slaves, and constituting no part of the arms-bearing portion of their population. [Note: Stephens is in error here. Modern research has determined that between 300,000 and 1 million armed Southern blacks fought both unofficially and officially for the Confederacy.] Of Federal prisoners during the war, the Confederates took in round numbers 270,000; while the whole number of Confederates captured and held in prisons by the Federals was in like round numbers 220,000. In reference to the treatment of prisoners on the respective sides, about which much was said at the time, two facts are worthy of note: one is, that the Confederates were ever anxious for a speedy exchange, which the Federals would not agree to; the other is, that of the 270,000 Federal prisoners taken, 22,576 died in Confederate hands; and of the 220,000 Confederates taken by the Federals, 26,436 died in their hands: the mortuary tables thus exhibiting a large per cent, in favor of Confederate humanity. The entire loss on both sides, including those who were permanently disabled, as well as those killed in battle, and

Roger Sherman

who died from wounds received and diseases contracted in the service, amounted upon a reasonable estimate 'to the stupendous aggregate of one million of men.' [When non-combatants of all races are added to these figures, modern Southern historians estimate that some 2 million Southerners died and 1 million Northerners died, making 3 million in total.] Both sides during the struggle relied for means to support it upon the issue of paper-money, and upon loans secured by bonds. An enormous public debt was thus created by each, and the aggregate of money thus expended on both sides, including the loss and sacrifice of property, could not have been less than eight thousand millions of dollars [or 110 billion dollars in today's currency]—a sum fully equal to three-fourths of the assessed value of the taxable property of all the States together when it commenced."[588]

When a Northern Liberal asked Stephens if he thought he could change his mind concerning Lincoln's War, Stephens replied:

☞ "There ought . . . to be no difference between intelligent minds as to Truth, which rests simply and entirely upon matters of fact; but, in practical life, there are great and wide differences, even on this, owing to a disagreement or a different understanding as to the facts merely. Justice and Right, depending on the Truth of the facts, must, of course, be the subjects of much wider differences in all cases where the facts are not first settled, or where the Truth is not admitted by both sides. Men's convictions as to Truth, or what they receive as the Truth, depend entirely upon their understanding of facts. Convictions are always sincere. There may be insincere professions of opinions, but there can be no insincere convictions, as to Truth, Justice, or Right, in any matter relating to human conduct. These depend upon laws of mind, over which volition has no control. . . . There is no such thing as convincing a man against his will. Galileo complied with the exactions of torture, by renouncing his belief in the rotatory motion of the earth; but his convictions of this great truth remained as firm as ever, notwithstanding. Belief and conviction are results with which the will has nothing to do, except in collecting and ascertaining the facts upon which depend the truth, or what is considered the truth, to which alone the mind yields its assent. Hence, the necessity of a very liberal charity in all discussions of this nature."[589]

Concerning the Battle of Fort Sumter, the opening conflict of Lincoln's War, Stephens had this to say:

☞ "I do maintain there was no rebellion, no resistance to lawful authority in the action of the Confederates in what occurred at Fort Sumter, but, on the contrary, I maintain that their resistance there was a resistance to open and palpable usurpations of power by the [Liberal Republican] authorities at Washington, and in the maintenance of that rightful authority to which both their obedience and allegiance were due."[590]

On April 15, 1861, Lincoln illegally issued his War Proclamation calling for 75,000 U.S. troops to invade the South. As part of his edict, Lincoln asked those Southern and Border States that had not yet seceded to raise specific quotas of soldiers for participation in the unconstitutional and immoral battle. Delaware was to furnish 780 men; Maryland, 3,123; Virginia, 2,340; North Carolina, 1,560; Kentucky, 3,123; Missouri, 3,123; and Arkansas, 780. There are only two logical reasons Lincoln would make such a request of the Southern and Border States that still belonged to the Union:

Joseph Lane

1) he was either so out of touch with reality that he did not realize what he was doing, or 2) more likely, he understood the situation perfectly well, knew that these particular states would refuse, and that posterity would later hold them accountable for contributing to the start of the War. Either way, the mad chief executive's ploy worked. Naturally, Stephens, along with nearly every other Southern leader and official, were horrified by Lincoln's proclamation. The Confederate vice president here lists some of the reactions by Southern governors:

☞ "In reply to the requisition for the quota of Delaware, Governor William Burton responded in substance, that he had no lawful authority for raising the troops.

"Governor [Thomas H.] Hicks, of Maryland, made no direct response for some days, but indirectly urged upon Mr. Lincoln not to have troops sent through the city of Baltimore, as the excitement there produced by the call was so great that violence would be almost inevitable. On the 18th of April, he issued a Proclamation to the people of Maryland, in which he said, he would not 'send any troops in obedience to the call, except to defend the National Capital.' On the fourth day after the Proclamation was issued, the 6th Massachusetts Regiment, in its passage through the city of Baltimore, was stopped by barricades in the streets, and was attacked with stones and other missiles by an infuriated mob. This gave rise to a great riot, in which several lives were lost on the part of the troops as well as the citizens. Every effort was made by George W. Brown, Mayor of the city, and George P. Kane, Marshal of Police, to prevent the outbreak, and to restore quiet to the excited multitude. After the Mayor had succeeded in suppressing actual violence, and had got the troops through the city, by going himself in front at the head of the column, he addressed the people publicly in Monument Square, where they had assembled. He there assured them, that he had conferred with Governor Hicks, who had united with him in telegraphing to Washington, that no more Northern troops should be sent through Maryland, and that Governor Hicks concurred with him in opinion against the policy of coercing the Seceded States. Governor Hicks was sent for, and made his appearance in this meeting, and is reported to have said:

> 'I coincide in the sentiment of your worthy Mayor. After three conferences we have agreed, and I bow in submission to the people. I am a Marylander; I love my State, and I love the Union; but I will suffer my right arm to be torn from my body, before I will raise it to strike a sister State.'

"This gave great satisfaction to the excited crowd, which thereupon dispersed. Mayor Brown also sent three persons of high character and the greatest respectability, to wit, H. L. Bond, J. C. Brune, and George W. Dobbin, as special messengers to Mr. Lincoln, with a dispatch in these words:

> 'The people are exasperated to the highest degree by the passage of troops, and the citizens are unusually decided in the opinion that no more troops should be ordered to come. The authorities of the city did their best to-day to protect both strangers and citizens, and to prevent a collision, but in vain; and but for their great efforts, a fearful slaughter would have occurred. Under these circumstances, it is my solemn duty to inform you, that it is not possible for more soldiers to pass through Baltimore, unless they fight their way at every step. I, therefore, hope and trust, and most earnestly request, that no more troops be permitted or ordered by the Government to pass through the city. If they should attempt it, the responsibility for the bloodshed will not rest upon me.'

"The very able and distinguished President of the Baltimore and Ohio Railroad, J. W. Garrett, fully concurred in this policy. He declined to transport any more troops over his road, in the then state of excitement.

"The Messengers of the Mayor sent to Washington, telegraphed back the next day that Mr. Lincoln had given them a letter to the Mayor of the city and the Governor of the State, that no more troops would be brought through Baltimore, if, in a military point of view, they could be marched around the city without opposition. So much for the effect of the proclamation upon Maryland.

"In reply to the call for the quota of Virginia, Governor [John] Letcher stated that it 'would not be furnished for any such purpose'—'an object' which, in his judgment, 'was not within the purview of the Constitution or the laws.' 'You have,' said he, 'chosen to inaugurate civil war.'

438 ᐸᏚᐳ THE QUOTABLE ALEXANDER H. STEPHENS

Governor [John W.] Ellis, of North Carolina, replied that he 'regarded the levy of troops made for the purpose of subjugating the States of the South, as in violation of the Constitution, and a usurpation of power; and that he could be no party to the wicked violation of the laws of the country, and to this war upon the liberties of a free people.'

"Governor [Beriah] Magoffin, of Kentucky, replied: 'Kentucky will furnish no troops for the wicked purpose of subduing her sister Southern States.'

"Governor [Isham G.] Harris, of Tennessee, replied: 'Tennessee will not furnish a man for purposes of coercion, but 50,000, if necessary, for the defence of our rights, and those of our Southern brothers.'

"Governor Henry M. Rector, of Arkansas, replied: 'No troops from Arkansas will be furnished to subjugate the Southern States. The demand is only adding insult to injury.'

"Governor Claiborne F. Jackson, the recently inaugurated Governor of Missouri, replied: 'The requisition is illegal, unconstitutional, revolutionary, inhuman, diabolical, and cannot be complied with.'

"I give but the substance of these replies. They clearly indicate the tone and temper of the times, and the impression the proclamation made upon the public mind in what were then styled the Border States."[591]

Concerning Lincoln's April 15, 1861, War Proclamation itself, Stephens had this to say:
☛ "There was not, at the time [he issued his edict], a civil officer of the [U.S.] Federal Government of any kind, in any of the Seceded States [C.S.]. There was no Federal Collector, or Federal Judge, or Federal Solicitor, or Federal Marshal throughout the limits of the Confederate States, to be resisted or interfered with in any way, by combinations of any sort, either 'powerful' or weak! Those in office had all resigned, and no new ones had been appointed. There was, of course, no judicial process to be resisted or obstructed in any way. There were no civil authorities to be aided in the execution of Federal laws. This call for troops, therefore, was neither in aid of the execution of any law, nor in pursuance of the provisions of any law. It was nothing short of a clear and palpable usurpation of power, under color of office!"[592]

On April 19, 1861, just days after publishing his War Proclamation, Lincoln illegally issued another proclamation, this one blockading the naval ports of the Confederate States. On this topic Stephens wrote:
☛ "This [act] is extraordinary, not only for its clear usurpations of power, but for the strange inconsistencies with itself, which so glaringly appear upon its very face.

"First. If the Ordinances of Secession were void, upon which assumption the Proclamation was based, then the Seceded States were still in the Union with all their Ports, and under the Constitution no discrimination could be made between them and other ports of the United States, either by Congress or the President, without a violation of this solemn Compact of Union. This provision of the Constitution, Mr. Lincoln's oath of office required him to 'preserve, protect, and defend;' and yet in this Proclamation, without any regard to the requirement of his oath in this particular, he openly, and avowedly, put under blockade the ports of seven States, which he claimed as still members of the Union! This too, he said he did in pursuance of law! What law? Did Congress ever pass any law for the blockading of our own Ports? Never!

"But, on the other hand, secondly: If the Secession Ordinances were valid, and the Confederate States were, as they claimed to be, a foreign power, so far as concerned their relations to the United States, then this Proclamation was equally a palpable violation of the Constitution, because it was an act of war, which the President had no right to resort to, unless first authorized and empowered by Congress.

"Viewed in either light, therefore, it was unquestionably a most flagrant usurpation of power! The Blockade was in no sense a measure to aid the civil authorities in the collection of revenues at Charleston, or elsewhere. It was in effect, as well as design, a war measure! Its purpose was to weaken an acknowledged Belligerent. If a blockade had been necessary or proper, either to suppress a rebellion or to weaken a neighboring foreign inimical Power, Congress alone had authority, under the Constitution, to 'set it on foot.'

"Then, again, the Proclamation was itself most strangely utterly inconsistent with the assumption on which it was based. The act of blockading the ports of the Confederate States, by the very laws of nations to which he refers, was an acknowledgment of Public War—not an Insurrection or Rebellion; which acknowledgment carried upon its very face a concession to the Confederate States of all the rights of Belligerents, in a Public War, under the laws of nations. This was the necessary effect and legitimate consequence of the measure itself. But this most extraordinary paper, after thus conceding, as it did, by its very terms, all the rights of Belligerents, under the laws of nations, went on to declare a purpose to consider and punish as pirates any persons who might engage, under 'letters of marque' on the high seas, on the opposite side, in this Public War, so recognized by him! By the laws of nations, Privateers are not pirates, as Mr. Lincoln himself afterwards admitted, at least by his acts."[593]

☛ "In the forum of reason, these Proclamations of Mr. Lincoln must be

Thomas Hart Benton

considered as gross violations of the Constitution, and most unscrupulous usurpations of power. The people of the Southern States were too well versed in Constitutional doctrines, and too thoroughly wedded to the principles of Liberty derived from their ancestors, not to be thoroughly aroused by the dangers thus portentously threatened against the very foundations of Free Institutions. They looked upon these Proclamations, and rightly too, as I think, as their English ancestors looked upon the royal edicts of Charles I, for ship money, and other equal outrages upon their well established Rights. Even the strongest Union men, as Mr. Zollicoffer, Neil S. Brown, and John Bell, of Tennessee, John Janney, Robert E. Scott, and William C. Rives, of Virginia, to say nothing of others of the same class in that State, and thousands of others of the same class in other States, who resisted Secession to the last, now saw that this claim of Executive power unless checked, sooner or later, would lead inevitably to a centralized Despotism. These are the considerations which produced the wonderful effect of these most extraordinary papers. [It is transparently obvious that] . . . the Administration at Washington was aiming at a complete overthrow of the Institutions of the country . . . ."[594]

☞ "[In a subsequent] . . . Proclamation, moreover, Mr. Lincoln actually increased the Army 64,748 men, and the Navy 18,000 men, by his own act, without the shadow of lawful or Constitutional authority. No ukase [czarist order] of the Autocrat of Russia was ever more imperial or absolute in its character!"[595]

☞ "Even before this, as early as the 27th of April, [Lincoln] . . . had, by an order to the Commanding General of the Army, authorized him to suspend the Privilege of the Writ of *Habeas Corpus* in certain localities, but it was not until the 10th of May that the initiative Proclamation for the general suspension of the privilege of this Writ made its appearance. This seems to have been a feeler to test public sentiment in the 'loyal States,' so-called. It was evidently experimental in its character; and as an experiment, it was tried first on the Islands, on the coast of Florida. Seeing by this experiment thus made, that he might, with impunity, proceed further in the same direction, this initiative step was not long afterwards followed by the bolder one of a virtual general suspension of the privilege of this Writ throughout the United States, by like orders to commanding [U.S.] Generals. By these acts successively, the most direct blows were struck at the very vitals of civil liberty as secured by England's Great Charter, and which was the priceless heritage of the people of all these States!

"It was in the full exercise of this despotic power that Mr. Seward boasted, in conversation with Lord Lyons, that he could do what her Majesty, Queen Victoria, could not do. In this conversation with the British Minister, Mr. Lincoln's Secretary of State [Seward] is reported to have said:

'I can touch a bell on my right hand and order the arrest of a citizen
of Ohio. I can touch the bell again and order the arrest of a citizen
of New York. Can Queen Victoria do as much?'

"He well knew that she could not, and that no Crowned Head in
Europe, not even the Czar of Russia, could do more!"[596]

*Stephens' friends on the Liberal side of the aisle believed Lincoln was fully justified in
issuing such edicts, despite their obvious unconstitutionality. In an attempt to buttress
their argument they declared: "If it was an extraordinary exercise of power, it was
completely justified by the necessity of the occasion. . . . 'Necessity has no law,' is an old
and time-honored maxim. . . . 'To consult the safety of the people, is the first great law,'
is also a maxim with all statesmen. It is much older than the Constitution. In all such
cases, the public safety is the supreme law, and all Constitutions, as well as all laws, must
yield to it. Upon these principles, it was necessary for Mr. Lincoln to exercise the powers
he did, to save the life of the Nation; and it was upon these principles, he was both
justified and sustained in what he did." To this Stephens replied:*

☛ "Necessity is always the usurper's, as well as the tyrant's plea. It is never
tolerated for an instant, by those who are jealous and watchful of their rights
and liberties. The '*solus populi*,' or 'safety of the people,' in all free
governments, is to be 'consulted' by those entrusted with delegated powers, by
a strict observance of those barriers and safeguards which the people have
themselves erected for their own protection and safety. The well-being of
every Body-Politic, like the well-being of every physical organism, is to be
consulted by a rigid conformity with the laws of its existence. These laws in the
Body-Politic are to be found in its Constitution. The object of all written
Constitutions established for the security of the ultimate safety of the people is,
as Mr. [Thomas] Jefferson says, 'to bind down their rulers' 'with the chains' of
the fundamental law, 'to prevent them from doing mischief' in the exercise of
their individual judgment, upon what concerns the safety of the people. Of
this, the people themselves are the only proper judges in the last resort."[597]

*What was the main object of the C.S.A. in taking up arms to fight the North? Stephens
replied:*

☛ "[Certainly] war, if it could possibly be avoided, was not the object, wish,
desire, or intention of the Confederate States—much less conquest. Peace was
their object. . . . It was, on their part, a war entirely in defence of what they
considered the inherent, sovereign, and inalienable Right of
Self-government."[598]

In describing Lincoln's War from the Southern perspective, Stephens had this to say in

1870:

☛ "The war . . . was no Insurrection or Rebellion, or even Civil War in any proper sense of these terms. A Rebellion or Insurrection is resistance to the Sovereign Power of any Society, Commonwealth, or State by those owing it allegiance, and may be justified or not, according to the facts of the case. A Civil War is but another name for the same sort of resistance, where it assumes so formidable a magnitude as to divide the members of the same Society or Commonwealth into two great Parties, between which ultimate supremacy becomes a matter of uncertainty and doubt. [Swiss legal authority Emerich de] Vattel has well and truly said, that 'custom appropriates the term of "civil war" to every war between the members of one and the same Political Society.' Further on he says, where such a

> 'war breaks the bands of society and Government, or, at least, suspends their force and effect, [it produces] two independent parties, who consider each other as enemies, and acknowledge no common judge. These two parties, therefore, must necessarily be considered as thenceforward constituting, at least for a time, two separate Bodies, two distinct Societies.'

"But this war [of Lincoln's], properly and truly considered, was not of this character at all. For, if the facts of our history be, as they appear incontestably to be from the review which we have made of them, the people of the United States never did form or constitute one Political Society, or Body-Politic. The Union of the States was a Union of distinct and separate Political Societies or Bodies-Politic. The States held no such relation to the Union as Departments or Provinces do to an Empire, or as Counties and Districts do to a State, as maintained by Mr. Lincoln. The citizens of each State owed allegiance, as we have seen, to their own separate States.

"The war, therefore, was a war between States regularly organized into two separate Federal Republics. Eleven States on the one side, under the name and style of 'The Confederate States of America' [or C.S.A.], and twenty-two States on the other side, under the like

John Marshall

name and style of 'The United States of America' [or U.S.A.]. In our further notice of the conduct of this war, we may properly enough, therefore, designate the Parties to it by the terms 'Confederates' and 'Federals,' though the latter term will by no means correctly represent the principles of those thus designated. In the beginning, and throughout the contest, the object of the 'Confederates' was to maintain the separate Sovereignty of each State, and the right of Self-government, which that necessarily carries with it. The object of the 'Federals,' on the contrary, was to maintain a Centralized Sovereignty over all the States, on both sides. This was the fundamental principle involved in the Conflict,' which must be kept constantly in mind."[599]

During the midst of Lincoln's War Stephens was asked, "What is it all for?" He replied this way:
☛ "The question, if replied to by the North, can have but one true answer. What is all this for on their part, but to overturn the principle upon which their own Government, as well as ours, is based—to reverse the doctrine that Governments derive "their just powers from the consent of the governed?" What is it for but to overturn the principles and practice of their own Government from the beginning? That Government was founded and based upon the political axiom that all States and Peoples have the inalienable right to change their forms of Government at will!

". . . If asked, on our side, what is all this for? the reply from every breast is, that it is for home, for firesides, for our altars, for our birthrights, for property, for honor, for life—in a word, for everything for which freemen should live, and for which all deserving to be freemen should be willing, if need be, to die!"[600]

Stephens gave frequent public speeches during Lincoln's War in order to maintain the support of the Southern people. Here is an excerpt from one of them:
☛ "We have our Independence to maintain, and Constitutional Liberty to preserve! With us now rest the hopes of the world! The North has already become a Despotism! The people, there, while nominally free, are in no better condition, practically, than serfs. The only plausibility they have for the war is to make freemen of slaves, and those of an Inferior race, while their efforts in this unnatural crusade thus far have resulted in nothing but making slaves of themselves. Presidential Proclamations supersede and set aside both laws and the Constitution. Liberty with them is but a name and a mockery. In separating from them, we quit the Union, but we rescued the Constitution. This was the Ark of the Covenant of our Fathers! It is our high duty to keep it, and hold it, and preserve it forever!"[601]

17

The

Southern People

On the corrosive effects of what Stephens called centralism and consolidationism, and what we now call liberalism, socialism, Marxism, and communism:
☛ "The people [of the United States] would have gone into anarchy long ago, if it had not been for the conservative influence of the more stable minded men of the South . . ."[602]

The following excerpts are from a December 14, 1854, speech Stephens gave before the House of Representatives. He is responding to an anti-South attack by Mr. Mace of Indiana, who charged the South with "claiming and extorting more than her just rights from the Federal government." In defending the South and her people, Stephens highlights some of the differences that existed between the two regions, and which still exist to this day:
☛ "But the gentleman says that when Southern men's measures are vetoed, they raise their voices in tones of thunder until they carry them. Sir, I do not believe there ever was a Southern measure vetoed. I do not recollect one. The South has never asked anything from your Government that called for a veto. There is the difference between us. The South asks but few favors from you.

Lewis Cass

It is a class of gentlemen from the North who ask aid from the Government. Why, we never come here in that attitude. Let me ask the gentleman when any measure from the South was ever vetoed? when the South ever asked anything that required the exercise of the veto power?

"But the gentleman said that he admired the South, because 'knowing their rights, they dared maintain them.' That I take as a compliment. And now, what is his position? Why the South, 'knowing their rights, and daring to maintain them,' he would have the North rise up and prevent her from getting her known and acknowledged rights! If we know our rights, and they are our rights, and we dare maintain them, why ought not the North,—why ought not the gentleman (I will not say the North) to grant us our rights? Have we ever asked anything but what was right? Now I say, with all due respect to the gentleman, that the true position of the South is this: we 'ask nothing but what is right, and we submit to nothing that is wrong.' That is the position that the South has always occupied, as I remember her history.

"Now, sir, upon the subject of internal improvements [today known as 'corporate welfare'] which the gentleman alluded to, has the South ever asked legislative aid in that particular? I do not speak now sectionally, or against the North; but look at the whole history of our Government. Who is it that is constantly appealing here for legislative aid and legislative patronage? Who ask for fishing bounties? Who ask for protection to navigation? Why, the people of the South, if they were permitted to use or employ foreign vessels in their coast trade, would be greatly benefited thereby. But American shipping must be protected; and who is it that asks that protection, not only upon shipping, but almost everything else? Who is it that wants a duty on coal? Who upon iron? Who upon woollen goods? Who upon shoes, leather, cotton fabrics,——everything? Why, the industrial interests of the North. We of the South, it is true, sometimes grumble and complain; but the great majority of the people of the South have yielded to what they consider in some instances very heavy exactions for the support of Government. But when did we ever come up and ask any aid from the Government of the United States? The constant prayer of the South to you has been to stay your hands. All that we ask of you is,——keep your hands out of our pockets. That is all that the South asks, and we do not get even that. If is true, sir, that in my own State we have asked some little favors, but very few. Some years ago we asked that you should take the obstructions out of the mouth of the Savannah River,——not obstructions that nature put there, but that were put there during the Revolutionary War, to keep out a foreign fleet,——put there not by the citizens of the State, but by public authority. It seems to us nothing but right and just that the General Government should remove those obstructions; but we have asked in vain for that. The gentleman says that the Representatives of the North come here and pass River and Harbor Bills, which are vetoed, and the wishes of their constituents are thereby defeated. Well, sir, we have some rivers in the South quite as navigable as those in Indiana; but when did Georgia, or South Carolina, or Virginia, or the South generally, come and ask Congress to clear out those rivers? . . .

"In the State of Georgia we have never asked for any harbor improvements except for the removal of those obstructions at the mouth of the Savannah River; and we never got that, as I have stated. We never asked the General Government to clear out our rivers. But we have a country of hill and valley, and we have to go to market with our products,——for we grow some things in Georgia, notwithstanding that, in the opinion of the gentleman from Indiana, we are a heaven-accursed, slavery-doomed land,——we grow some products in Georgia, I say, for market; and how do we get them to market? Do we come here and ask aid of the General Government? No, sir. Why, in my State, we have now upward of a thousand miles of railroad in full operation. How did we obtain it? We took our surplus capital, and with it we bought human labor, human energy, bone and sinew,——we bought the strong arms of our own citizens as well as of foreigners, to come and dig down the hills and fill up the valleys, and lay down the superstructure of our railroads,——we bought the iron, when we could get it, in this country, and we went abroad for it when we could not get it here; and notwithstanding all that, when we brought our iron into this country, we had to pay duty upon it to the General Government. Twenty millions of dollars have been spent in Georgia in constructing highways to our markets. That is the way we got our thousand miles of railroad. So far from coming here and receiving assistance from Government, we have actually had to pay a tax for the privilege of bringing our iron into the country. Georgia has paid not less than a million and a half of dollars as a duty on iron into the treasury for the privilege of building her own works of internal improvement. Now I would ask any candid man—I would ask the gentleman himself—if it is just, not only to tax Georgia for the privilege of constructing her highways, but then to take those very taxes that we have paid to open rivers in Indiana? It does not strike me that it is very just."[603]

After the War, in 1866, when asked by a member of the Reconstruction Committee why the Southern people seceded from the Union and fought the North, Stephens replied:
☛ "They [the Southern people] did what they did, believing it was best for the protection of constitutional liberty. Toward the constitution of the United States, as they construed it, the great mass of our people were as much devoted in their feelings as any people ever were toward any cause. This is my opinion. As I remarked before, they resorted to secession with a view of maintaining more securely these principles. And when they found they were not successful in their object, in perfect good faith, as far as I can judge from meeting with them and conversing with them, looking to the future developments of their country in its material resources, as well as its moral and intellectual progress, their earnest desire and expectation was to allow the past struggle, lamentable as it was in its results, to pass by, and to co-operate with the true friends of the constitution, with those of all sections who earnestly desire the preservation of constitutional liberty, and the perpetuation of the government in its purity. They have been a little disappointed in this, and are so now. They are patiently waiting, however, and believing that when the passions of the hour have passed away, this delay in restoration will cease. They think they have done every thing that was essential and proper, and my judgment is that they would not be willing to do any thing further as a condition precedent. They would simply remain quiet and passive."[604]

During this same interrogation by the Reconstruction Committee, Stephens was asked: "Suppose the States that are represented in Congress and Congress itself should be of the opinion that Georgia should not be permitted to take its place in the government of the country except upon its assent to one or the other of the two propositions suggested: is it then your opinion that under such circumstances Georgia ought to decline?" He responded:

☛ "Then I think she ought to decline under the circumstances, and for the reasons stated; and so ought the whole eleven [states of the former Confederacy]. Should such an offer be made and declined, and these States

Pierre Gustave Toutant Beauregard

should thus continue to be excluded and kept out, a singular spectacle would be presented. A complete reversal of positions would be presented. In 1861 these States thought they could not remain safely in the Union without new guaranties, and now, when they agree to resume their former practical relations in the Union under the constitution as it is, the other States turn upon them and say they cannot permit them to do so, safely to their interest, without new guaranties on their part. The Southern States would thus present themselves as willing for immediate Union under the constitution, while it would be the Northern States opposed to it. The former disunionists would thereby become unionists, and the former unionists the practical disunionists."[605]

When the Reconstruction Committee asked Stephens: "If the eleven States have at present an immediate constitutional right to be represented in Congress on a footing with the States at present represented, has that been a continuous right from the formation of the government, or from the time of the admission of the new States respectively, or has it been interrupted by war?," he replied:

☛ "I think, as the Congress of the United States did not consent to the withdrawal of the seceding States, it was a continuous right under the constitution of the United States, to be exercised so soon as the seceding States respectively made known their readiness to resume their former practical relations with the federal government, under the constitution of the United States. As the general government denied the right of secession, I do not think any of the States attempting to exercise it thereby lost any of their rights under the constitution, as States, when their people abandoned that attempt."[606]

When the Reconstruction Committee asked Stephens: "Will you state, if not indisposed to do so, the considerations or opinions which led you to identify yourself with the rebellion so far as to accept the office of Vice-President of the Confederate States of America, so called?," he replied:

☛ "I believed thoroughly in the reserved sovereignty of the several States of the Union under the compact of Union or constitution of 1787. I opposed secession, therefore, as a question of policy, and not one of right on the part of Georgia. When the State seceded against my judgment and vote, I thought my ultimate allegiance was due to her, and I preferred to cast my fortunes and destinies with hers and her people, rather than to take any other course, even though it might lead to my sacrifice and her ruin. In accepting position under the new order of things, my sole object was to do all the good I could in preserving and perpetuating the principles of liberty, as established under the constitution of the United States. If the Union was to be abandoned either with or without force—which I thought a very impolitic measure—I wished, if possible, to rescue, preserve, and perpetuate the principles of the constitution. This, I was not without hope, might be done in the new confederacy of States formed. When the conflict arose, my efforts were directed to as speedy and peaceful an adjustment of the questions as possible. This adjustment I always thought to be lasting, would have ultimately to be settled upon a continental basis, founded upon the principles of mutual convenience and reciprocal advantage on the part of the States, on which the constitution of the United States was originally formed. I was wedded to no particular plan of adjustment, except the recognition, as a basis, of the separate sovereignty of the several States. With this recognized as a principle, I thought all other questions of difference would soon adjust themselves, according to the best interests, peace, welfare, and prosperity of the whole country, as enlightened reason, calm judgment, and a sense of justice might direct. This doctrine of the sovereignty of the several States I regarded as a self-adjusting, self-regulating principle of our American system of State governments, extending, possibly, over the continent."[607]

Why did the Southern people take up arms against the North? Stephens, who frequently mentioned "the spirit and valor with which the Confederates battled on that sanguinary field for the inestimable right of Self-government," answered this way:
☛ "The struggle with them was not for power, dominion, or dynasty—nor for Fame; but to resist palpable and dangerous assumptions of power, and to repel wanton aggressions upon long established rights. They fought for those Principles and Institutions of Self-government which were the priceless heritage of their ancestors!"[608]

In 1870 Stephens made the following comments about the Southern people:
☛"However disastrous the results were to the Confederates; however extensive the misfortunes, losses, sufferings and sacrifices which attended and befell them in this second bloody conflict for the sovereign Right of local Self-government, on the part of the Peoples of the several States of this Federal Republic, whether composed of thirteen, thirty-three, or any other number; however utterly they failed to maintain this important principle, to which all that is truly great in the former history of the States is mainly attributable, and on which alone all sure hopes for general peace, prosperity and happiness, with good government for the whole in future, must be placed; however fruitless their efforts and blasted were their fondest anticipations in their highest objects of patriotic aim; however deplorable their present condition is, bereft of their estates and outlawed by the Government; and however worse the condition still to come may be for them; yet, notwithstanding all this, they have left to them

that which is inestimable in value, far above riches, wealth or power, and of which no oppression or tyranny can deprive them, and that is a Public Character, which after having passed the severest ordeal that can 'try men's souls,' stands forth with that moral grandeur which is ever imparted to the reputation of States as of individuals, by uprightness in conduct, integrity of purpose, truthfulness in words, and the 'crowning glory' of unsullied honor!

"Whatever other errors, faults, failings or shortcomings they may have

Oliver Ellsworth

had, no act of treachery, of perfidy, of hypocrisy or deceit, of breach of faith, or of turpitude—nothing of a low, mean, sordid or unmanly nature, can ever be justly laid to their charge in their State or Confederate organizations, either before or during the war; neither in the antecedents which led to it, nor in all the fury which marked its progress. Their whole public course shows them to have been a People as true, as brave, as generous, as frank, as refined, as magnanimous, as moral, as religious, and with all as honorable and patriotic, in the highest

and noblest sense of these words, as ever struggled against odds, and thus struggling, fell in battling for the Right. So the truth of history stands, and will continue to stand forever! These are facts which time will never obliterate or destroy. This record of their past is no small heritage, if they have nothing else left for them to transmit to their children, and to their children's children, for generations to come!"[609]

In 1870, five years after Lincoln's War ended, Stephens wrote:
☛ "No People on earth ever maintained the great Right of Self-government, so long as the Confederates did in this contest, with such sacrifices of blood and treasure, against such odds!"[610]

18

Yankees

Stephens to Judge Thomas W. Thomas, May 5, 1855:

☛ "I know of but one class of people in the United States at this time that I look upon as dangerous to the country. That class are neither foreigners or Catholics—they are those natives born at the North who are disloyal to the constitution of that country which gave them birth, and under whose beneficent institutions they have been reared and nurtured."[611]

From Stephens' April 23, 1861, speech before the Virginia Secession Convention:

☛ "The honor and glory of the western republic [i.e., the U.S.A.], to which the eyes of the world has been directed for years, was the work mainly of southern men, and my judgment is, if you will pardon its expression, that just so soon as the South is entirely separated from the North, and the government at Washington has no longer the advice and counsel of your statesmen and the men of the South, they will go into confusion and anarchy speedily. It gives me no pleasure to think so. It would be to our advantage, as well as theirs, for them, as we can no longer live in safety and peace under the same constitution, to go on and be prosperous, and leave us to do the same. But my conviction is that they will not. They do not understand constitutional liberty. It is an exotic in their clime. It is a plant of southern growth. I have, however, no war to make on their institutions. They seem to think them better than ours, and, not satisfied with this, they war upon ours. Now, the true policy of both sides, should be to let each other alone. Let both try their systems, not in war, but in friendly rivalship. Hence it is from no unkind feelings toward them or their

Winfield Scott

institutions, that I express the opinion I do. I believe that our institutions are by far the best. My judgment is that theirs will be a failure. I would give them every opportunity to try them thoroughly by themselves, and for themselves. I simply give my view of what I believe to be the prospect on both sides, as well as the true policy of both; but I seriously doubt whether the rivalry which I would fain indulge the hope of seeing carried out, will be engaged in. War is what they are bent on in the start. Where this will end, time alone can determine. What I have ventured to say of the probable future of the North, is founded upon the experience and associations of many years with their public men in Washington. They do not seem to understand the nature or workings of a federative [Confederate] system. They have but slender conceptions of limited powers. Their ideas run into consolidation.

"Whilst I was in [the U.S.] Congress I knew of but few men there from the North who ever made a constitutional argument on any question. They seemed to consider themselves as clothed with unlimited power. Mr. [Daniel] Webster was one of these distinguished few. Though he generally differed from southern men on points of constitutional power, yet he argued his side with great ability. Mr. [Stephen A.] Douglas is also another distinguished exception to the general remark. One or two others might be named as exceptions to the rule, but the great majority, the almost entire representation from the North in Congress, both in the House and Senate, seemed really to have no correct idea of the nature of the government they were engaged in carrying on. They looked upon it simply as a government of majorities.

"They did not seem to understand that it was a government that bound majorities by constitutional restraints. Now, nothing is more fixed or certain than that constitutional liberty can be maintained only by a rigid adherence to fundamental principles. Government is a science—the northern mind seems disinclined to that sort of study. Excuse this digression. It may not, however, be altogether inappropriate to the occasion—all things being duly considered. It springs from no disposition on my part wantonly to disparage northern character. It is intended rather to show where our future safety and security lies. We have our destiny under Providence in our own hands, and we must work it out the best we can. All we ask of our late confederates is to let us alone."[612]

Not all Yankees were enthusiastic about Lincoln and his War. In particular were those who originally enlisted in the U.S. army, supposedly, to defend Washington, D.C. against the "rebellious horde of Southern anarchists." As Stephens writes, this turned out to be just another one of "Dishonest Abe's" devilish tricks, for the South had no designs on the U.S. capitol or any other Northern region:

☛ "On the Federal side, thousands of those who were sent on this expedition, set out, not only with reluctance, but with a consciousness that the whole movement was wrong. They had volunteered for no such purpose. They had tendered their services with the sole view of defending the [U.S.] Capital [at Washington, D.C.]. It was under the impression and belief so extensively created at the North, that the Confederates intended to take Washington, that much the greater portion of this immense army had, with very patriotic motives, rushed to the rescue. Their object was to defend their own rights against an expected assault, and not to make aggression upon the rights of others. This entrapping them into this movement, when once mustered into service, and under military control, was but a part of the sinister purposes of the Federal authorities, which marked their policy throughout the war. The first false cry was to save the Capital, and after that came a second equally false one to save the Union; while their real object all the time was to use these popular catch words to mislead a confiding people, and under these specious pretexts to cover their ulterior designs of subverting and overturning the whole structure of the Government."[613]

Many of the Yankees Lincoln enlisted into his military were honest, law abiding, merciful, even gallant men. However, a sizeable percentage were of the very opposite type, as is evidenced by the enormous war crime statistics generated by the U.S. army between April 1861 and April 1865. The question was put to Stephens: "Upon whom rests the tremendous responsibility of all this sacrifice of human life, with all its indescribable miseries and sufferings?", to which he replied:

☛ "The facts, beyond question or doubt, show that it rests entirely upon the [Liberal] Authorities at Washington! It is now well understood to have been a part of their settled policy in conducting the war, not to exchange prisoners. The grounds upon which this extraordinary course was adopted were, that it was humanity to the men in the field, on their side, to let their captured comrades perish in prison, rather than to let an equal number of Confederate soldiers be released on exchange to meet them in battle! Upon the Federal [U.S.] Authorities, and upon them only, with this policy as their excuse, rests the whole of this responsibility. To avert the indignation which the open avowal of this policy by them, at the time, would have excited throughout the North, and throughout the civilized world, the false cry of cruelty towards prisoners was raised against the Confederates. This was but a pretext to cover their own violation of the usages of war in this respect among civilized nations.

"Other monstrous violations of like usages were not attempted to be palliated by them [the Yankees], or even covered by a pretext. These were, as you must admit, open, avowed and notorious! I refer not only to the general sacking of private houses—the pillaging of money, plate, jewels and other light articles of value, with the destruction of books, works of art, paintings, pictures, private manuscripts and family relics; but I allude, besides these things, especially to the hostile acts directly against property of all kinds, as well as outrages upon non-combatants—to the laying waste of whole sections of country; the attempted annihilation of all the necessaries of life; to the wanton killing, in many instances, of farm stock and domestic animals; the burning of mills, factories and barns, with their contents of grain and forage, not sparing orchards or growing crops, or the implements of husbandry; the mutilation of County and Municipal records of great value; the extraordinary efforts made to stir up servile insurrections, involving the wide-spread slaughter of women and children; the impious profanation of temples of worship, and even the brutish desecration of the sanctuaries of the dead!

"All these enormities of a savage character against the very existence of civilized society, and so revolting to the natural sentiments of mankind, when not thoroughly infuriated by the worst of passions, and in open violation of modern usages in war—were perpetrated by the Federal armies in many places throughout the conflict, as legitimate means in putting down the Rebellion so-called!

". . . All that I have stated, and much more, too, of a like character, were woefully realized by those who suffered from the deeds of [U.S. General Philip H.] Sheridan's men in the valley of Virginia, and by those who came

John Slidell

within the range of the atrocities attending [U.S. General William T.] Sherman's conflagrations and devastations in his 'grand march' through Georgia and the Carolinas, as well as by those who were subjected to the merciless ravages of [U.S. General James H.] Wilson's and [U.S. General John M.] Palmer's Marauders afterwards! Facts which have come to my own knowledge, established by indisputable proof, verify the statement in full, both to the letter and spirit. Private houses were sacked, pillaged, and then burnt; and after all family supplies were destroyed, or rendered unfit for use, helpless women and hungry children were left destitute alike of shelter and food. I know men—old men, non-combatants, men who had nothing to do with the war, further than to indulge in that sympathy which nature prompted—who were seized by a licensed soldiery and put to brutal torture, to compel them to disclose and to deliver up treasure that it was supposed they possessed. They were in many instances hung by the neck until life was nearly extinguished, and then cut down with the promise to desist if their demands were complied with, and threats of repeating the operation to death if they were not! . . . In some cases, where parties resisted, their lives, as well as their purses, watches and other articles of value, were taken!"[614]

19

After

Lincoln's War

In the Spring of 1865 Stephens was illegally arrested at his Georgia home, "Liberty Hall" in Crawfordville, and shipped to Boston, Massachusetts, where he was imprisoned for five months. The following excerpt is from his journal the day of his arrest:

☛ "Liberty Hall, Georgia, Thursday, May 11, 1865.—This was a most beautiful and charming morning. After refreshing sleep, I arose early. Robert Hull, a youth, son of Henry Hull, of Athens, Ga., had spent the night at my house. I wrote some letters for the mail, my custom being to attend to such business soon as breakfast was over; and Robert and I were amusing ourselves at casino, when Tim [a servant] came running into the parlour saying: 'Master! more Yankees have come! a whole heap are in town, galloping all about with guns.' Suspecting what it meant, I rose, told Robert I expected they had come for me, and entered my bedroom to make arrangements for leaving, should my apprehensions prove true. Soon, I saw an officer with soldiers under arms approaching the house. The doors were all open. I met him in the library. He asked if my name was Stephens. I replied that it was. 'Alexander H. Stephens?' said he. I told him that was my name. He said he had orders to arrest me. I

Millard Fillmore

asked his name and to see his orders. He said he was Captain Saint of the 4th Iowa Cavalry, or mounted infantry, attached to General Nelson's command; he was then under General Upton: he showed me the order by General Upton, at Atlanta, directing my arrest and that of Robert Toombs; no charge was specified; he was instructed to go to Crawfordville, arrest me, proceed to Washington and arrest Mr. Toombs, and then carry both to General Upton's headquarters.

"I told him I had been looking for something of this kind; at least, for some weeks had thought it not improbable; and hence had not left home; General Upton need not have sent any force for me; had he simply notified me that he wished me at his headquarters, I should have gone. I asked how I was to travel. He said: 'On the cars.' I then learned that his party had come down on the train arriving just before Tim's announcement. I asked if I would be permitted to carry any clothing.

"He said, 'Yes.' I asked how long I might have for packing. He said: 'A few minutes—as long as necessary.' I set to packing. Harry [a servant] came in, evincing great surprise and regret, to pack for me. The Captain then said: 'You may take a servant with you if you wish.' I asked if he knew my destination. He said: 'First, Atlanta; then, Washington City.' I called in Anthony, a black boy from Richmond who had been waiting on me several years, and inquired if he wished to go; I told him I would send him from Washington to his mother in Richmond. He was willing, so I bade him be ready soon as possible.

"In the meantime, Mr. [William H.] Hidell [Stephen's secretary] had come in; he was living with me and had gone out after breakfast. None of my [half] brother John's family residing at the old homestead happened to be with me; however, Clarence [Stephens, John's son], who was going to school at the Academy, hearing of what had occurred (I suppose), came over with some friends from town. It was about 10 A.M. when Captain Saint arrived. In about fifteen minutes—not much over—we started for the depot, Anthony and I with the Captain and squad; friends, servants, and Clarence following, most of them crying. My own heart was full—too full for tears."[615]

Stephens wrote the following in a letter while sitting in prison in Boston Harbor on July 1865. Lincoln's War had ended only four months earlier:
☞ "I went with the State [of Georgia] on secession from a sense of duty only. No more ardent or devoted friend to the Constitution of the United States, and the principles of civil and religious liberty therein embodied and guaranteed, than I was and am, ever breathed the vital air of heaven; and no one can rejoice more than I at the prospect of seeing peace and prosperity restored to our once happy land."[616]

Stephens' letter continues:
☞ "Why I am confined here, and that too under such rigorous orders, is a mystery to me. . . . I do not understand why I, who exerted my every effort to prevent the strife, and then my every effort to end it in the speediest manner, reasonably, by peaceful adjustment of some sort, should be the victim of such sufferings as I am. This is what is strange, mysterious, and unaccountable to me. I therefore thank you for your letter to the [U.S.] President [Andrew Johnson]. You have known my course throughout. I feel assured, if I could but confer with him face to face, that I could satisfy him that I am, upon all principles of justice, entitled to parole. If, from the office I held under the Confederate organization, and which was accepted with the sole view of doing all in my power to maintain the principles of the government under the circumstances, it should be thought proper to make an example of me by trial for treason—that, it seems to me, is no reason why I should be punished as I am, in advance of the punishment first to be found to be right, by judgment of the law. My parole would be most sacredly adhered to."[617]

Stephens gave the following speech before the General Assembly of the state of Georgia on February 22, 1866, George Washington's birthday. Against his own wishes he had been elected to the office of Georgia state senator by his friends and colleagues. Lincoln's War was now nearly a year in the past and the Yankees' vengeful, restrictive, punishing, and intentionally humiliating policy of "Reconstruction" was in full swing across the former Confederate states. Stephens used his address to console and encourage his fellow Southerners through an extremely trying time, one that would turn out to be a twelve year

period (1865-1877) in which the South was stripped of her rights and placed under harsh
military rule by the vindictive meddlesome North:

☛ "Gentlemen of the Senate and House of Representatives: I appear before you in answer to your call. This call, coming in the imposing form it does, and under the circumstances it does, requires a response from me. You have assigned to me a very high, a very honorable and responsible position. This position you know I did not seek. Most willingly would I have avoided it; and nothing but an extraordinary sense of duty could have induced me to yield my own disinclinations and aversions to your wishes and judgment in the matter. For this unusual manifestation of esteem and confidence, I return you my profoundest acknowledgments of gratitude. Of one thing only can I give you any assurance, and that is, if I shall be permitted to discharge the trusts thereby imposed, they will be discharged with a singleness of purpose to the public good.

"The great object with me now, is to see a restoration, if possible, of peace, prosperity, and constitutional liberty in this once happy, but now disturbed, agitated, and distracted country. To this end, all my energies and efforts, to the extent of their powers, will be devoted.

"You ask my views on the existing state of affairs; our duties at the present, and the prospects of the future? This is a task from which, under other circumstances, I might very well shrink. He who ventures to speak, and to give counsel and advice in times of peril, or disaster, assumes no enviable position. Far be that rashness from me which sometimes prompts the forward to rush in where angels might fear to tread. In responding, therefore, briefly to your inquiries, I feel, I trust, the full weight and magnitude of the subject. It involves the welfare of millions now living, and that of many more millions who are to come after us. I am also fully impressed with the consciousness of the inconceivably small effect of what I shall say upon the momentous results involved in the subject itself.

"It is with these feelings I offer my mite of counsel at your request. And in the outset of the undertaking, limited as it is intended to be to a few general ideas only, well may I imitate an illustrious example in invoking aid from on high; 'that I may say nothing on this occasion which may compromit the rights, the honor, the dignity, or best interests of my country.' I mean specially the rights, honor, dignity, and best interests of the people of Georgia. With their sufferings, their losses, their misfortunes, their bereavements, and their present utter prostration, my heart is in deepest sympathy.

"We have reached that point in our affairs at which the great question before us is—'To be or not to be?'—and if to be—How? Hope, ever springing in the human breast, prompts, even under the greatest calamities and adversities, never to despair. Adversity is a severe school, a terrible crucible; both for individuals and communities. We are now in this school, this crucible, and should bear in mind that it is never negative in its action. It is always positive. It is ever decided in its effects, one way or the other. It either makes better or worse. It either brings out unknown vices, or arouses dormant virtues. In morals, its tendency is to make saints or reprobates—in politics to make heroes or desperadoes. The first indication of its working for good, to which hope looks

John Jordan Crittenden

anxiously, is the manifestation of a full consciousness of its nature and extent; and the most promising grounds of hope for possible good from our present troubles, or of things with us getting better instead of worse, is the evident general realization, on the part of our people, of their present situation: of the evils now upon them, and of the greater ones [under so-called 'Reconstruction'] still impending. These it is not my purpose to exaggerate if I could; that would be useless; nor to lessen or extenuate; that would be worse than useless. All fully understand and realize them. They feel them. It is well they do."[618]

Stephens' February 22, 1866, speech continues:
☞ "Can these evils upon us—the absence of law; the want of protection and security of person and property, without which civilization cannot advance—be removed? or can those greater ones which threaten our very political existence, be averted? These are the questions.

". . . The first great duty, then, I would enjoin at this time, is the exercise of the simple, though difficult and trying, but nevertheless indispensable quality of patience. Patience requires of those afflicted to bear and to suffer with fortitude whatever ills may befall them. This is often, and especially is it the case with us now, essential for their ultimate removal by any instrumentalities whatever. We are in the condition of a man with a dislocated limb, or a broken leg, and a very bad compound fracture at that. How it became broken should not be with him a question of so much importance, as how it can be restored to health, vigor, and strength. This requires of him, as the highest duty to himself, to wait quietly and patiently in splints and bandages, until nature resumes her active powers—until the vital functions perform their office. The knitting of the bones and the granulation of the flesh require time; perfect quiet and repose, even under the severest pain, is necessary. It will not do to make too great haste to get well; an attempt to walk too soon will only make the matter worse. We must or ought now, therefore, in a similar manner to discipline ourselves to the same or like degree of patience. I know the anxiety and restlessness of the popular mind to be fully on our feet again—to walk abroad as we once did—to enjoy once more the free outdoor air of heaven, with the perfect use of all our limbs. I know how trying it is to be denied representation in Congress, while we are paying our proportion of the taxes—how annoying it is to be even partially under military rule—and how injurious it is to the general interest and business of the country to be without post-offices and mail communications; to say nothing of divers other matters on the long list of our present inconveniences and privations. All these, however, we must patiently bear and endure for a season. With quiet and repose we may get well—may get once more on our feet again. One thing is certain, that bad humor, ill-temper, exhibited either in restlessness or grumbling, will not hasten it."[619]

Stephens' February 22, 1866, speech continues:
☞ "Next to this, another great duty we owe to ourselves is the exercise of a liberal spirit of forbearance amongst ourselves."[620]

Stephens' February 22, 1866, speech continues:
☞ "The first step toward local or general harmony, is the banishment from our breasts of every feeling and sentiment calculated to stir the discords of the past. Nothing could be more injurious or mischievous to the future of this country, than the agitation, at present, of questions that divided the people anterior to, or during the existence of the late war. On no occasion, and especially in the bestowment of office, ought such differences of opinion in the past ever to be mentioned, either for or against any one, otherwise equally entitled to confidence. These ideas or sentiments of other times and circumstances are not the germs from which hopeful organizations can now arise. Let all differences of opinion, touching errors, or supposed errors, of the head or heart, on the part of any, in the past, growing out of these matters, be at once, in the deep ocean of oblivion forever buried.   Let there be no criminations or

Robert Mercer Taliaferro Hunter

recriminations on account of acts of other days. No canvassing of past conduct or motives. Great disasters are upon us and upon the whole country, and without inquiring how these originated, or at whose door the fault should be laid, let us now as common sharers of common misfortunes, on all occasions, consult only as to the best means, under the circumstances as we find them, to secure the best ends toward future amelioration. Good government is what we want. This should be the leading desire and the controlling object with all; and I need not assure you, if this can be obtained, that our desolated fields, our towns and villages, and cities now in ruins, will soon—like the Phoenix—rise again from their ashes; and all our waste places will again, at no distant day, blossom as the rose."[621]

Stephens' February 22, 1866, speech continues:
☞ "This view should also be borne in mind, that whatever differences of opinion existed before the late fury of the war, they sprung mainly from differences as to the best means to be used, and the best line of policy to be pursued, to secure the great controlling object of all—which was Good Government. Whatever may be said of the loyalty or disloyalty of any, in the late most lamentable conflict of arms, I think I may venture safely to say, that there was, on the part of the great mass of the people of Georgia, and of the entire South, no disloyalty to the principles of the constitution of the United States. To that system of representative government; of delegated and limited powers; that establishment in a new phase, on this continent, of all the essentials of England's Magna Charta, for the protection and security of life, liberty and

property; with the additional recognition of the principle as a fundamental truth, that all political power resides in the people. With us it was simply a question as to where our allegiance was due in the maintenance of these principles—which authority was paramount in the last resort—State or federal. As for myself, I can affirm that no sentiment of disloyalty to these great principles of self-government, recognized and embodied in the constitution of the United States, ever beat or throbbed in breast or heart of mine. To their maintenance my whole soul was ever enlisted, and to this end my whole life has heretofore been devoted, and will continue to be the rest of my days—God willing. In devotion to these principles, I yield to no man living. This much I can say for myself; may I not say the same for you and for the great mass of the people of Georgia, and for the great mass of the people of the entire South? Whatever differences existed amongst us, arose from differences as to the best and surest means of securing these great ends, which was the object of all. It was with this view and this purpose secession was tried. That has failed. Instead of bettering our condition, instead of establishing our liberties upon a surer foundation, we have, in the war that ensued, come well nigh losing the whole of the rich inheritance with which we set out.

"This is one of the sad realizations of the present. In this, too, we are but illustrating the teachings of history. Wars, and civil wars especially, always menace liberty; they seldom advance it; while they usually end in its entire overthrow and destruction. Ours stopped just short of such a catastrophe. Our only alternative now is, either to give up all hope of constitutional liberty, or to retrace our steps, and to look for its vindication and maintenance in the forums of reason and justice, instead of on the arena of arms—in the courts and halls of legislation, instead of on the fields of battle."[622]

Stephens' February 22, 1866, speech continues:
☛ "I have faith in the American people, in their virtue, intelligence and patriotism. But for this I should long since have despaired. Dark and gloomy as the present hour is, I do not yet despair of free institutions. Let but the virtue, intelligence, and patriotism of the people throughout the whole country be properly appealed to, aroused and brought into action, and all may yet be well. The masses, everywhere, are alike equally interested in the great object. Let old issues, old questions, old differences, and old feuds, be regarded as fossils of another epoch. They belong to what may hereafter be considered, the Silurian period of our history."[623]

Stephens' February 22, 1866, speech continues:
☛ "The old Union was based upon the assumption, that it was for the best

interest of the people of all the States to be united as they were, each State faithfully performing to the people of the other States all their obligations under the common compact. I always thought this assumption was founded upon broad, correct, and statesman-like principles. I think so yet. It was only [after Lincoln's election] when it seemed to be impossible further to maintain it, without hazarding greater evils than would perhaps attend a separation, that I yielded my assent in obedience to the voice of Georgia, to try the experiment which has just resulted so disastrously to us. Indeed, during the whole lamentable conflict, it was my opinion that however the pending strife might terminate, so far as the appeal to the sword was concerned, yet after a while, when the passions and excitements of the day should pass away, an adjustment or arrangement would be made upon continental principles, upon the general basis of 'reciprocal advantage and mutual convenience,' on which the Union was first established. My earnest desire, however, throughout, was whatever might be done, might be peaceably done; might be

John Wilkes Booth

the result of calm, dispassionate, and enlightened reason; looking to the permanent interests and welfare of all. And now, after the severe chastisement of war, if the general sense of the whole country shall come back to the acknowledgment of the original assumption, that it is for the best interests of all the States to be so united, as I trust it will; the States still being 'separate as the billows but one as the sea;' I can perceive no reason why, under such restoration, we as a whole, with 'peace, commerce, and honest friendship with all nations and entangling alliances with none,' may not enter upon a new career, exciting increased wonder in the old world, by grander achievements hereafter to be made, than any heretofore attained, by the peaceful and harmonious workings of our American institutions of self-government. All this is possible if the hearts of the people be right. It is my earnest wish to see it. Fondly would I indulge my fancy in gazing on such a picture of the future. With what rapture may we not suppose the spirits of our fathers would hail its opening scenes from their mansions above. Such are my hopes, resting on such contingencies."[624]

In August 1868 Stephens wrote the following to a fellow Georgian who had refused to secede from the Union at the start of Lincoln's War:
☛ "I believed . . . when it was resorted to (however strongly I was opposed to it as a politic or expedient remedy for then existing wrongs), that the only sure hope for the preservation of Constitutional liberty in this country, North as well South, was in the success of the measure; that is, in the successful maintenance and establishment of the principle of the sovereignty of the separate States. . . . it was a radical error to suppose that constitutional liberty with us could be maintained by attempting to perpetuate, by force, a Union of States voluntarily associated by compact!

". . . My object, as stated before, was not controversy. It was simply to impress upon your mind the great truths set forth in the work alluded to, establishing the sovereignty of the States; from a denial of which came the war with all its calamities—from which came all our present political ills—and from which, I fear, will come much greater and more disastrous ills of a like character hereafter."[625]

After Lincoln's War Stephens was asked why the South took up arms against the North:
☛ "[It is plain to see that our object] . . . was the perpetuation of that liberty and equality which was established by the Constitution of the United States. This [even my Liberal friends] . . . must admit. It was the same liberty and equality that the men of 1776 had perilled their lives, their honor, and all that they held sacred, to establish. [It is also obvious] . . . who were the real conspirators against our form of Government, as established by the Fathers. [For] . . . the 'naked question' presented by . . . the . . . leading men from the South at Washington [D.C.], at that time, was not, as [the Northern Liberals] . . . maintained, to overthrow that Government and to establish a 'Slavery Oligarchy' in its stead. On the contrary, it puts beyond all question the fact,

that the leading men of the South . . . aimed at nothing, and desired nothing, but the maintenance, in good faith, of the Constitution, with all its guarantees as they stood! They wanted and desired nothing but that Constitutional liberty and equality which the Fathers had established! They wanted no new Constitution, nor any new 'Slavery Dynasty!'"[626]

William Ballard Preston

☞ "The future destiny . . . of the Free Institutions of this Country, is now in the hands of the Peoples of the Northern States. We, at the South, are utterly powerless to do anything in shaping or controlling, at this time, the progress of coming political events. The only hope left to us is, that a reaction on all these questions, in the public mind, in the Northern States, will take place in time to save our Liberties as well as their own. This, [the reader] . . . may be assured, can be done only by driving the usurpers from their places, and bringing back the administration of the Federal Government to those principles on which it was so harmoniously and prosperously conducted for the first sixty years of its existence. This is to be done through the ballot-box alone. Should this take place, and the Judicial Department maintain its integrity, all may yet be well, even though this Fourteenth Amendment should go through the mockery of a ratification under the present programme; for, no Amendment of the Constitution proposed as this has been, and adopted as it must be, if at all, can ever be held to be valid by a firm and upright Judiciary."[627]

☞ "Immediately after the surrender . . . numerous arrests were made of high Confederate, as well as State Officials; but as yet not a single one of these has been put upon trial."[628] [Editor's note: None ever were.]

☞ "As to Mr. Davis, it is true, after the infamous charge upon which he was arrested—that is, of complicity in the assassination of Mr. Lincoln—was proven to have had no foundation whatever, except the perjury of suborned witnesses, a formal Bill of Indictment for Treason, in the matter of Secession and the War, was brought in against him. This has not yet been tried, though he has continuously demanded a trial, and urged it in the most earnest manner. His late enlargement on bail, without a trial, (through the unexampled generosity and magnanimity of Mr. Horace Greeley, Gerrit Smith, Augustus Schell, H. F. Clark, Aristides Welsch, of New York, David J. Jackman, of Pennsylvania, and others, in becoming sureties for his appearance to answer the charge when the Government shall be ready to proceed with it,) may be considered as settling the question, that the officials at Washington do not intend to allow that point on the principle involved in the issue, decided by the arbitrament of arms, to come before the Judicial Forum for decision and adjudication there. An arbitrament on the Arena of Reason, Logic, Truth, and Justice, they have, thus far, eschewed and avoided; so that the great fact is to be borne in mind, that up to this time, nothing really affecting this 'Corner-Stone' [states' rights] of our Federal Institutions, as Governor [Joseph E.] Brown styled the principle in his reply to General Sherman, has, as yet, been definitely settled, except the abandonment of an attempt to maintain it by a resort to arms."[629]

On February 12, 1878, Stephens was asked to give a speech before the U.S. House of Representatives for the unveiling of F. B. Carpenter's picture of Abraham Lincoln, entitled "The Signing of the Emancipation Proclamation." Stephens gave the speech "off-the-cuff," without notes or preparation, to the largest audience ever assembled in the House up to that time. His positive comments regarding the greatest enemy the South has ever had must be considered in context of the time, place, and situation. To his credit Stephens used the occasion to correct a number of Northern myths pertaining to not only Lincoln, but the Emancipation Proclamation, slavery, and the Old South. Emphasized text (that is, italics) are mine:

☞ "Mr. President [Rutherford B. Hayes] And Mr. Speaker: There is but little left to say in the performance of the part assigned me in the programme arranged for this August occasion. Upon the merits of the picture and the skill of the artist, my friend from Ohio [future U.S. president, James A. Garfield] has dwelt at large. I can but endorse all he has so well said on that subject. As to the munificent gift of the donor, he has also left me nothing to add. The present of a twenty-five thousand dollar painting to the Government well deserves commendation. Few instances of this sort have occurred in the history of our country; I know of none. The example of this generous lady in the encouragement of art may well be followed by others.

Joseph Eggleston Johnston

"Mr. President, with regard to the subject of the painting, I propose, if strength permits, to submit a few remarks; first, as to the central figure, the man; after that, as to the event commemorated. I knew Mr. Lincoln well. We met in the House in December, 1847. We were together during the Thirtieth Congress. I was as intimate with him as with any other man of that Congress, except perhaps one. That exception was my colleague, Mr. [Robert A.] Toombs. Of Mr. Lincoln's general character I need not speak. He was warm-hearted; he was generous; he was magnanimous; he was most truly, as he afterward said on a memorable occasion, 'with malice towards none, with charity for all.'

"In bodily form he was above the average; and so in intellect; the two were in symmetry. Not highly cultivated, he had a native genius far above the average of his fellows. Every fountain of his heart was ever overflowing with the 'milk of human kindness.' So much for him personally. From my attachment to him, so much the deeper was the pang in my own breast as well as of millions at the horrible manner of his 'taking off.' That was the climax of our troubles and the spring from which came afterward 'unnumbered woes.' But of those events no more now. Widely as we differed on public questions and policies, yet as a friend I may say:

'No farther seek his merits to disclose,
Or draw his frailties from their dread abode;
There they alike in trembling hope repose,
The bosom of his Father and his God.'

"So much I have felt it my duty on this occasion to say in behalf of one with whom I held relations so intimate, and one who personally stood so high in my estimation.

"Now as to the great historic event which this picture represents, and which it is designed to commemorate.

"This is perhaps a subject which, as my friend from Ohio has said, the people of this day and generation are not exactly in a condition to weigh rightfully and judge correctly. One thing was remarked by him which should be duly noted. That was this: *Emancipation was not the chief object of Mr. Lincoln in issuing the proclamation. His chief object, the ideal to which his whole soul was devoted, was the preservation of the Union. Let not history confuse events. That proclamation, pregnant as it was with coming events, initiative as it was of ultimate emancipation, still originated in point of fact more from what was deemed the necessities of war than from any pure humanitarian view of the matter. Life is all a mist, and in the dark our fortunes meet us.*

"This was evidently the case with Mr. Lincoln. He in my opinion was like all the rest of us, an instrument in the hands of that Providence above us, that 'Divinity which shapes our ends, rough-hew them how we will.' I doubt much, as was indicated by my friend from Ohio, whether Mr. Lincoln at the time realized the great result. *Mark you, the proclamation itself did not declare free all the colored people of the Southern States; it applied only to those parts of the country then in resistance to the Federal authorities. If the emancipation of the colored race, which is one of the greatest epochs in our day, and will be so marked in the future history of this country, be a boon or a curse to them (a question which, under Providence, is yet to be solved, and which depends much upon themselves),*

Rutherford Birchard Hayes

then, representing the Southern States here, I must claim in their behalf that the freedom of that race was never finally consummated, and could not be until the Southern States sanctioned the Thirteenth Amendment, which they did, every one of them, by their own former constituencies. Before the upturning of Southern society by the reconstruction acts[,] the white people there came to the conclusion that their domestic institution known as slavery had better be abolished. They accepted the proposition for emancipation by a voluntary, uncontrolled sanction of the proposed Thirteenth Amendment to the Constitution of the United States. This sanction was given by the original constituency of those States, the former governing white race, and without that sanction the Thirteenth Amendment never could have been incorporated in the fundamental law. That is the charter of the colored man's freedom. Mr. Lincoln's idea, as embodied in his first proclamation of September 22nd, 1862, as well as that of January 1st, 1863, was consummated by the adoption of the Thirteenth Amendment of the Constitution of the United States, and without that the proclamation had nothing but the continued existence of the war to sustain it. Had the States in resistance laid down their arms by the 1st of January, 1863, the Union would have been saved, but the condition of the slave so called would have been unchanged. Upon the subject of emancipation itself it may here be stated that the pecuniary view, the politico-economic question involved, the amount of property invested under the system, though that was vast, not less than two billion dollars, weighed, in my estimation, no more than a drop in the bucket compared with the great ethnological problem now in the process of solution.

"Mr. President [Hayes], *as to this institution called slavery in the Southern States many errors existed, and many exceedingly unjust prejudices.* Prejudice! What wrongs, what injuries, what mischiefs, what lamentable consequences have resulted at all times from this perversity of the intellect! Of all the obstacles to the advancement of truth and human progress in every department of knowledge, in science, in art, in government, and in religion, in all ages and climes, not one on the list is more formidable, more difficult to overcome and subdue than this horrible distortion of the moral as well as intellectual faculties.

"I could enjoin no greater duty upon my countrymen now, North and South, as I said upon a former occasion, than the exercise of that degree of forbearance which would enable them to conquer their prejudices. One of the highest exhibitions of the moral sublime the world ever witnessed was that of Daniel Webster, the greatest orator I ever heard, combining thought with elocution, when after Faneuil Hall was denied him, he in an open barouche in the streets of Boston proclaimed in substance to a vast assembly of his constituents—unwilling hearers—that they had conquered an uncongenial clime; they had conquered a sterile soil; they had conquered the winds and currents of the ocean; they had conquered most of the elements of nature, but they must yet learn to conquer their prejudices.

"I would say this to the people of the North as well as to the people of the South.

"Indulge me for a moment upon this subject of the institution of slavery, so called, in the Southern States. Well, Mr. President and Mr. Speaker, it was not an unmitigated evil. It was not, thus much I can say, without its compensations. It is my purpose now, however, to bury, not to praise, to laud, 'nor aught extenuate.'

"It had its faults, and most grievously has the country, North and South, for both were equally responsible for it, answered them. It also, let it be remembered, gave rise to some of the noblest virtues that adorn civilisation. But let its faults and virtues be buried alike forever.

"I will say this: If it were not the best relation for the happiness and welfare of both races or could not be made so, morally, physically, intellectually, and politically, it was wrong, and ought to have been abolished. This I said of it years before secession, and I repeat it still. But as I have said, this is no time now to discuss those questions.

"I have seen something of the world and travelled somewhat, and I have never yet found on earth a paradise. The Southern States are no exception. Wherever I have been I have been ready to exclaim with Burns.——

'But oh! what crowds in every land are wretched and forlorn!
Man's inhumanity to man makes countless thousands mourn.'

"It was so at the South. It was so at the North. It is so yet. It is so in every part of the world where I have been. The question of the proper relation of the races is one of the most difficult problems which statesmen or philanthropists, legislators or jurists, ever had to solve. The former policy of the Southern States upon this subject is ended, but I do not think it inappropriate on this occasion to indulge in some remarks upon the subject. Since the emancipation, since the former ruling race have been relieved of their direct heavy responsibility, for the protection and welfare of their dependents, it has been common to speak of the colored race as 'the wards of the nation.'

Andrew Johnson

"May I not say with appropriateness in this connection and due reverence, in the language of Georgia's greatest intellect (Toombs), 'They are rather the wards of the Almighty,' committed now under a new state of wings to the rulers, the law-makers, the law-expounders, and the law-executors throughout this broad land, within their respective constitutional spheres, to take care of and provide for, in that complicated system of government under which we live? I am inclined, sir, so to regard them and so to speak of them.——not as to exceptional cases, but as a mass. In the providence of God why their ancestors were permitted to be brought over here it is not for us to say, but they have a location and habitation here, especially in the South; and since the changed condition of their status, though it was the leading cause of the late terrible conflict of arms between the

States [editor's note: this is not true and Stephens knew it, making this comment all the more bizarre], yet I think I may venture to affirm there is not one within the circle of my acquaintance, or in the whole Southern country, who would wish to see the old relation restored.

"If there is one in all the South who would desire such a change back I am not aware of it. Well, then, this changed status creates new duties. The wardship has changed hands. Men of the North and of the South, of the East and of the West,—I care not of what party,—I would to-day, on this commemorative occasion, urge upon every one within the sphere of duty and humanity, whether in public or private life, to see to it that there be no violation of the divine trust.

"Mr. President and Mr. Speaker, one or two other reflections may not be out of place on this occasion. In submitting them I shall but repeat, in substance, what I said in my own State nearly twelve years ago. What is to be the future?

"During the conflict of arms I frequently almost despaired of the liberties of our country both South and North. War seldom advances, while it always menaces, the cause of liberty, and most frequently results in its destruction. The union of these States at first I always thought was founded upon the assumption that it was the best interest of all to remain united, faithfully performing each for itself its own constitutional obligations under the compact. When secession was resorted to as a remedy, it was only to avoid a greater evil that I went with my State, holding it to be my duty so to do, but believing all the time that, if successful (for which end I strove most earnestly), when the passions of the hour and of the day were over the great law which produced the Union at first, 'mutual interest and reciprocal advantage,' this grand truth which Great Britain learned after seven years of the Revolutionary War, and put in the preamble to the preliminary articles of peace in 1781, would reassert itself, and that at no distant day a new Union of some sort would again be formed.

"My earnest desire, however, throughout was that whatever might be done, might be peaceably done; might be the result of calm, dispassionate, and enlightened reason, looking to the permanent interests and welfare of all. And now, after the severe chastisement of war, if the general sense of the whole country shall come back to the acknowledgment of the original assumption, that it is for the best interests of all the States to be so united, as I trust it will,—the States still being 'separate as the billows but one as the sea,'—this thorn in the body politic being now removed, I can perceive no reason why under such restoration, the flag no longer waving over provinces but States, we as a whole, with 'peace, commerce, and honest friendship with all nations and entangling alliances with none,' may not enter upon a new career, exciting increased wonder in the Old World by grander achievements hereafter to be made, than any heretofore attained, by the peaceful and harmonious workings of our matchless system of American federal [confederate] institutions of self-government. All this is possible if the hearts of the people be right. It is my earnest wish to see it. Fondly would I indulge my fancy in gazing on such a picture of the future. With what rapture may we not suppose the spirits of our fathers would hail its opening

John Bell Hood

scenes from their mansions above. But if, instead of all this, sectional passions shall continue to bear sway; if prejudice shall rule the hour; if a conflict of classes, of labor and capital, or of the races shall arise; if the embers of the late war shall be kept a-glowing until with new fuel they shall flame up again, then our late great troubles and disasters were but the shadow, the penumbra of that deeper and darker eclipse which is to totally obscure this hemisphere and blight forever the anxious anticipations and expectations of mankind! Then, hereafter, by some bard it may be sung,—

> 'The Star of Hope shone brightest in the West,
> The hope of Liberty, the last, the best;
> It, too, has set upon her darkened shore,
> And Hope and Freedom light up earth no more.'[630]

20

Reconstruction

On April 16, 1866, Stephens was dragged before the U.S. kangaroo court known as the "Reconstruction Committee," where he was asked the usual insulting and absurd questions by meddling Yankees. Stephens did his best to represent the South against the dictatorial North. Of the inquisition the Richmond Dispatch wrote: "We publish this morning the evidence of Mr. Stephens given before the Committee on Reconstruction. Frankly, truthfully, and ably did Mr. Stephens reply to the Pharisees and Sadducees. Their artful and entrapping questions were turned against themselves. Mr. Stephens has more sense than all of them combined, and more patriotism to boot. Their whole study and vocation is to malign the South and excite against her the indignation of the northern people, that thus they and their party may control the officers, and the emoluments, and the fat shoddy contracts of the government. To this it is that the welfare and peace of a nation must be subordinate."[631] In answer to one particularly obnoxious question, Stephens had this say:

☛ ". . . my opinion is, that it would be best for the peace, harmony, and prosperity of the whole country that there should be an immediate restoration—an immediate bringing back of the States into their original practical relations—and let all these questions then be discussed in common council. Then the representatives from the South could be heard, and you and all could judge much better of the tone and temper of the people than you could from the opinions given by any individuals. You may take my opinion, or the opinion of any individual, but they will not enable you to judge of the condition of the State of Georgia so well as for her own representatives to be heard in your public councils in her own behalf. My judgment, therefore, is very decided that it would have been better, as soon as the lamentable conflict was over, when the people of the South abandoned their cause and agreed to accept the issue—desiring, as they do, to resume their places for the future in the Union, and to look to the halls of Congress and the courts for the protection of their rights in the Union—it would have been better to have allowed that result to follow, under the policy adopted by the administration, than to delay it or hinder it by propositions to amend the constitution in respect to suffrage or any other new matter. I think the people of all the southern States would, in the halls of Congress, discuss these

James Monroe

questions calmly and deliberately; and if they did not show that the views they entertained were just and proper, such as to control the judgment of the people of the other sections and States, they would quietly, patiently, and patriotically yield to whatever should be constitutionally determined in common council. But I think they feel very sensitively the offer to them of propositions to accept, while they are denied all voice in the common council of the Union under the constitution in the discussion of these propositions. I think they feel very sensitively that they are denied the right to be heard. And while, as I have said, they might differ among themselves in many points in regard to suffrage, they would not differ upon the question of doing any thing further as a condition precedent to restoration. And in respect to the alternate conditions to be so presented, I do not think they would accept the one or the other. My individual general views as to the proper course to be pursued in respect to the colored people are expressed in a speech made before the Georgia legislature, referred to in my letter to Senator Stewart, that was the proper forum, as I conceive, in which to discuss this subject. And I think a great deal depends in the advancement of civilization and progress, looking to the benefit of all classes, that these questions should be considered and kept before the proper forum."[632]

In July 1866 Stephens made the following remarks concerning so-called "Reconstruction." With former Confederate officials stripped of their powers and voting rights, and with the entire South under harsh military rule, Dixie and her people were searching for ways to resuscitate and reempower themselves:

☛ "Our only hope [now], the only hope for the country, is with the conservatives [then the Democrats] of the North. But outside the Democratic party at the North we have but few friends, and constitutional liberty has but few friends there outside of that organization. Hence a great deal will depend upon how they act towards the new movement."[633]

In the Spring of 1867 Stephens commented on the disastrous results stemming from the North's brutal and irrational Reconstruction policies:

☛ "I do not think that the [U.S.] Congress plan when carried out as it will be can be successfully worked—the two races can not coexist in their proportions in this country on this basis. What is to be the end I do not know. But reason and logic lead me to the conclusion that the system cannot be worked. The wish is not father to the thought with me in this instance. Far from it! Nothing could rejoice me more than the grand spectacle that the exhibition of the successful workings of our system of self govt. would thus present to an astonished world. But I do not think any such grand, moral and even sublime result is in store for us. I do not look to any such result. While I shall do nothing to hinder it or obstruct it yet I tell you candidly that I do not think humanity capable of such a demonstration. The system in my judgment will not work. It will break down and with its breaking down all semblance even of self govt. by both races will go with it. We are upon the verge of a consolidated centralized despotic empire. We are fast abandoning the Teutonic systems on which our institutions were based and are lapsing fast into the Asiatic system of empire."[634]

Stephens wrote the following in a July 1867 letter to a friend:

☛ "[It] is . . . my opinion that the action of the majority of [the U.S.] Congress is governed by no fixed principles or settled policy. They themselves do not know what they may do. The ruling principle with them is power, and they will do anything to secure that. . . . As I wrote to you before, I think constitutional liberty on the [American] continent is in its last death struggles."[635]

Stephens wrote the following to onetime Lincoln supporter Francis P. Blair, Sr., May 8, 1871:

☛ "I can well see how a man could have been most conscientiously and earnestly devoted to the emancipation of the negroes in this country. No man I think was more so or could have been more so than [Southerner] Mr. [Thomas] Jefferson was. However much therefore I may have differed with

Luther Martin

others upon that question while it was a living one, yet I can now not only cordially co-operate with all such men, since that question is forever out of the way, upon all the really practical and living questions of the present and future which involve the essentials and essence of liberty itself—and the more so when I meet with men of that class, who show by their acts that they were moved by earnest convictions and devotion to what they deemed the just rights of man on the question of emancipation. The only real difference, as I see it, between myself and [others on this point] . . . is the question of having an affirmance of the 14th and 15th amendments. . . . Now . . . the War was over, peace was declared, the 13th amendment was ratified. Slavery was forever abolished. All the states had returned to their obligations under the constitution. This was what the war had been waged for. At first it was waged solely with a view to compel the withdrawing states to return to their obligations under the constitution—when this was accomplished its end was attained—but under this negro slavery which was the prime exciting cause of it had been overthrown by it. It was abandoned in good faith by the returning states—these states were then certainly entitled to their seats in the Congress of States, for withdrawing from which the war had been waged against them, and which they [were assured during the while?—original editor's note] war was going on were vacant and awaiting their return. The denial of this return, and the Revolution forced by arms on their Govt. by which the 14th and 15th amendments were claimed to have been passed, was certainly a most glaring usurpation—after the war was over—after all its ends were attained and not as any thing growing out of the war. . . . The way is pointed out or clearly indicated in the Ky. Resolutions in the late Democratic Convention of that State, which have just reached me and with which as a whole I am greatly pleased. These Resolutions are brief but significant—they are potent not only in what they affirm but in what they do not affirm. . . . The great breaker ahead in the ranks of the Democracy is a positive affirmance of the validity of any usurpation caused by federal violence and perfidy."[636]

Stephens' letter to Blair continues:
". . . The ballot and the checks of the Constitution are the only sure safe guards of the people against the schemes of those who are now aiming at the overthrow of liberty and the establishment of a centralized Despotism in this country. On such a program, if power can be wrested from the hands of those who are now so outrageously abusing it for their ambitious and wicked purposes, all the questions growing out of the 14th and 15th amen[dmen]ts touching either their validity or effect can be practically easily settled through the instrumentality of the Constitution without wrong to any person or interest in the Country, by those who are really devoted to the great cause of maintaining and preserving free institutions on this continent—and that is now the only real living and absorbing question. . . ."[637]

Stephens wrote the following in 1870, in the midst of so-called "Reconstruction":
☞ "The Thirty-ninth [U.S.] Congress assembled in December, 1865. Soon after its assemblage, all the States embraced in these Proclamations, except Texas, were thoroughly reorganized under the Executive Policy, as just stated, with Senators and Members of Congress ready to take their seats, which Mr. [William H.] Seward, who was Mr. [Andrew] Johnson's as well as Mr. Lincoln's Secretary of State, had declared were still empty and ready for them in the National Councils. This [U.S.] Congress, both in the Senate and House of Representatives, it must be recollected, refused to admit the Senators and Members elected from the States thus reorganized under the Executive policy. They repudiated not only the Resolution of the 26th of July, 1861, referred to, as Mr. Johnson had done himself, but also repudiated the principles upon which he had acted; not upon the grounds, however,—which consistency required—that the Union was restored when the Insurrection, or Rebellion, so-called, had been put down; but upon the grounds, that Mr. Johnson had not gone far enough in his action towards the great object of Centralism aimed at from the beginning by the [Liberal] Party leaders of this Congress. They turned over the whole subject to a Joint Committee of the two Houses, known as the celebrated 'Reconstruction Committee.' To this grand Joint Committee, organized upon the model of a Jacobin Junto, was given the entire control of the whole subject. The Restoration of the Union as it was, (even with the abolition of Slavery, so-called,) was not what they wanted. They demanded a thorough Reconstruction, so far as the Confederate States were concerned. This [Liberal,

Northern, anti-South] Committee now openly proclaimed that the War had been waged, not for the preservation of the Union with the Rights, Dignity and Equality of all the several States unimpaired under the Constitution! The mask so long worn by the leading spirits of the War Party at the North, was now partly raised, and Mr. Johnson himself seems to have discovered for the first time, from the disclosures made, what were the real objects and purposes of the controlling leaders of his late associates and allies, from the beginning! The Monster Principle of ultimate complete Centralism, from clear indications, now stood before him in new lights, and as he had never viewed it before! This Committee assumed the position that not only the States reorganized under Mr. Johnson's policy, but even Tennessee, should never more take part in the Public Councils, without being first required not only to change their domestic Institutions so far as concerned the relations of the two races (constituting parts of their population), but without also being shorn of their Rights, Dignity, and Equality as members of the Union under the Constitution! They thus openly repudiated their many most solemn declarations during the war, and in so doing showed clearly that these declarations were nothing but specious pretexts resorted to at the time, by which thousands, and hundreds of thousands, and millions, perhaps, at the North, had been designedly misled and deceived!

"This position of the Reconstruction Committee upon these subjects is what led to the open rupture between Mr. Johnson and his late allies, and the mutual denunciations of treason and traitor, which are now [mid 1868] passing between them, and to which I referred some days ago. But, without commenting upon these, may it not most appropriately be here asked, if anything could more completely show the great

Jubal Anderson Early

wrong and injustice of the war on the part of the Federals throughout, than the position assumed by this Reconstruction Committee, and which was affirmed by Congress? During the whole period of four years' bloody strife, their avowed object was nothing more than to compel the Seceding States to return to a renewal of their obligations under the Constitution; and when this object was entirely effected, they stood before the country with the public declaration that they could not safely permit that to take place for which so much blood and treasure had been expended!

"What a spectacle they thus exhibited! To fully appreciate its monstrous character, it should be considered from two points of view: The war, remember, was waged by them for this avowed object of making other Parties perform their duties under a Compact, while they, themselves, were, at the very time and before, as we have seen, openly and confessedly faithless in the discharge of their own duties under the same Compact! Nay, more, this faithlessness on their part, remember also, was the cause of the Secession on the part of the others. Now, the spectacle would have been bad enough, if they had stopped with what they had, by superior power, been enabled thus to accomplish, and had been satisfied with results so most wrongfully attained! But how infinitely increased is the monstrousness of their conduct, when, not content with the result so wickedly and nefariously reached, they proceeded to make further exactions for their own special advantage and greater power! Is there to be found in the annals of mankind a parallel of such unblushing, double-faced, insolent and infamous iniquity?

"One thing which induced this extraordinary course, was doubtless the discovery of the fact that by the abolition of Slavery, so-called, the Confederate States would be entitled to thirteen more members in the House under the then Ratio of Representation, than they had theretofore been under the three-fifths count of their Black population, about which so much false clamor had been raised before the war! It now became clearly apparent, that the just and equal Rights of the South had been curtailed by that clause of the Constitution; and that her political power, in the Federal Government, would be considerably augmented by the change in this respect, which had been effected in the new order of things. The terms at first exacted of the Confederate States by this Reconstruction Committee, whose Report was agreed to in both Houses, were, that these States should agree to and ratify what they proposed to them as a further Amendment to the Constitution of the United States, known as the Fourteenth Amendment, as a condition precedent to their being allowed Representation in either branch of Congress. With these Congressional terms, Tennessee, on the 12th of July, 1866, complied. The other States all failed, or refused to do so."[638]

Of the unnecessarily harsh, cruel, ad revengeful Reconstruction Acts that the North continued to impose upon the South between 1865 and 1877, Stephens wrote:

☞ "The next great fact . . . to be here specially noticed, is the adoption by Congress of the 'Reconstruction Measures,' so-called, which are now pending before the people of those States which have been denied Representation in Congress. The first Act of this character passed Congress in February of this year. This Act more clearly shows the tendency of what may be looked to as the Ultimate Results of the War than any of the previous matters noted. The reasons assigned for this most extraordinary measure on the part of Congress, were no less extraordinary than the measure itself. It is amazing that men with intelligence and any regard for their character, could have had the audaciousness in the face of notorious truths to assign the reasons which they did for their action in this matter! These were given in the Preamble to the Act, and are as follows:

> Whereas, no legal State Governments, or adequate protection for life or property, now exists in the Rebel States of Virginia, North Carolina, South Carolina, Georgia, Mississippi, Alabama, Louisiana, Florida, Texas, and Arkansas; and, Whereas, it is necessary that Peace and Good Order should be enforced in said States, until loyal and Republican State Governments can be legally established! etc.

". . . how, with any regard for truth, could these States, in February, 1867, be said to be Rebel States? Was there a single man in arms against the General Government within their entire limits? Was not the whole mass of their entire people perfectly submissive, even to the unjust and unconstitutional demands of the [Liberal Lincolnian] Authorities at Washington? How, also, could they be said to be disloyal, in any sense? Had not every officer in them, from their Chief Executives to their lowest Magistrates, in the most bona fide manner, resumed their obligations to support and defend the Constitution of the United States? Is there any other test of loyalty but this known to the Constitution, either for State or Federal officers? This Preamble, thus fixed to this first Reconstruction Act, can be regarded in no other light, than as one of the most reckless perversions of truth ever put upon public record; while the Act itself must ever be regarded as one of the most palpable usurpations of Power to be found in the history of the world!"[639]

Stephens is speaking here of the passage of one of the North's numerous Reconstruction Acts:

☞ "To commend this monstrous outrage to the favor of their constituents, it was pretended to be justified by those who voted for it, as a proper measure of punishment for those who had engaged in the Rebellion, so-called, and as a necessary security in the future, for the Loyal States, so-called! But while this is the ostensible object, the real one was doubtless of a very different character. Viewed in its proper light—looking at its real design—it must be considered, with all its wrongs, as but another advanced step, stealthily taken, under false colors, towards that complete ultimate Consolidation of Power at which these leaders have been aiming all the time, but which they are not yet quite prepared openly to declare!"[640]

☞ ". . . in considering the Results of the War [we must bear this great fact in mind], . . . that the Centralists [Liberals] have not as yet openly proclaimed their ultimate object, much less have they acted in anything done by them up to this time, upon any claim of the actual consummation of that object, which we have seen, is Consolidation and Empire. They have not as yet openly denied the Federative [Confederate] character of the Government, however in direct war upon its Principles their acts have been covertly aimed. This is an exceedingly important fact to be specially noted and kept in mind. These monstrous Reconstruction Measures, with all their enormities and fatal tendencies towards ultimate complete Centralism and Empire, are still based upon the assumption that the States, as separate integral parts, constitute members of what is still, in words, at least, acknowledged to be a Federal Union! All these bold usurpations of power are, upon their face, nothing but resorts to induce, or to compel, under duress, the Peoples of the several Southern States to go through the forms of adopting the Fourteenth Amendment, as an additional Article to the Constitution. This policy is avowedly based upon the principle of voluntary consent on the part of these States. The programme of the Reconstructionists [anti-South Northern Liberals] thus far,

Patrick Henry

proceeds upon the assumption that the voluntary ratification of all Amendments to the Constitution by at least three-fourths of the integral members of the Union is essential to their validity. It is true, they did not pretend to have any Constitutional power to pass these measures. On the contrary, they openly and avowedly proclaim, that in adopting them they are acting 'outside of the Constitution!' This, too, they so proclaim to the world, immediately after taking solemn oaths to support that instrument!"[641]

☛ ". . . my opinion is, that the Cause which was lost at Appomattox Court House, was not the Federative [Confederate] Principle upon which American Free Institutions was based, as some have very erroneously supposed. This is far from being one of the Results of the War. The Cause which was lost by the surrender of the Confederates, was only the maintenance of this Principle by arms. It was not the Principle itself that they abandoned. They only abandoned their attempt to maintain it by physical force. This Principle on which rest the hopes of the world for spreading and perpetuating Free Institutions by neighboring States, in my judgment, like the principles of Christianity, ever advances more certainly and safely without resort to arms, than with it. Its teachings are Peace, Harmony and Good-will to all, and is much more sure of attaining its end, when the actions of its advocates are in conformity with its teachings. This Principle, therefore, though abandoned in its maintenance on battle-fields, still continues to live in all its vigor, in the Forums of Reason, Justice and Truth, and will. I trust, there continue to live forever!"[642]

☛ ". . . while the maintenance of the principle, or the maintenance of the Right of local Self-government was lost on the battle field; yet on other grounds, and in other Forums, it still lives in all its vigor. The issue decided by the sword, was the attempt on the part of the Confederates to maintain this principle and right, by physical force, in withdrawing from the Union. To this extent alone was the great cause affected by the arbitrament of arms; and to this extent alone was it then settled, by their abandonment of its further maintenance in that way; but the principle itself was not abandoned. It involves questions which cannot be settled by arms . . ."[643]

Stephens commented on the unconstitutional manner in which the North prosecuted its Reconstruction Acts upon the South:
☛ "Conquerors must govern their subjects according to the provisions of their own fundamental law. This is well established by the laws of Nations. The fundamental law of Congress, by which the Courts must be governed, is the Constitution of the United States. This gives Congress no power, in time of

John Brown

Peace, to suspend the Writ of *Habeas Corpus*, nor to declare Martial Law, to say nothing of the other enormities of these measures over any class of people, whether citizens, aliens, denizens or subjects."[644]

☛ "By our thus acting, perhaps after awhile, sooner or later, when the people of the Northern States become thoroughly impressed . . . with the dangerous tendencies of this whole Reconstructive policy to their own Institutions, a similar cry to that which went up from Virginia in Colonial days in regard to the Boston Port Bill, will again be raised and heard from one extent of the land to the other! The cry then was: 'The cause of Boston is the cause of us all!' These, we have seen, were the stirring notes which led to the establishment of our entire system of Constitutional Liberty. The only hope, in my view, now left for its preservation and maintenance on this Continent, is, that another like cry shall hereafter be raised, and go forth from hill-top to valley, from the Coast to the Lakes, from the Atlantic to the Pacific: 'The Cause of the South is the Cause of us all!'"[645]

Stephens ended his book, A Constitutional View, *with these words:*
☛ "If the worst is to befall us; if our most serious apprehensions and gloomiest forebodings as to the future, in this respect, are to be realized; if Centralism is ultimately to prevail; if our entire system of free Institutions as established by our common ancestors is to be subverted, and an Empire is to be established in their stead; if that is to be the last scene in the great tragic drama now being enacted: then, be assured, that we of the South will be acquitted, not only in our own consciences, but by the judgment of mankind, of all responsibility for so terrible a catastrophe, and from all the guilt of so great a crime against humanity! Amidst our own ruins, bereft of fortunes and estates, as well as Liberty, with nothing remaining to us but a good name, and a Public Character, unsullied and untarnished, we will, in the common misfortunes, still cling in our affections to 'the Land of Memories,' and find expression for our sentiments when surveying the past, as well as of our distant hopes when looking to the future . . ."[646]

At the end of Stephens' April 16, 1866, interrogation before the U.S. Reconstruction Committee of Congress, he was asked how he now felt about the "abstract right of secession and the reserved rights of the states," to which he answered:
☛ "My convictions on the original abstract question have undergone no change, but I accept the issues of the war and the result as a practical settlement of that question. The sword was appealed to decide the question, and by the decision of the sword I am willing to abide."[647]

On January 5, 1874, Stephens gave the following speech before the U.S. Congress concerning the North's outrageous Reconstruction policies, which it was then imperiously imposing on the Southern states. In particular he was incensed over the Liberals' so-called "Civil Rights Bill," which, based on the Fourteenth and Fifteenth Amendments, would coerce racial equality on the public. Stephens opposed the bill. Not because it granted civil rights to non-whites, but because it infringed on the Constitution:

☞ "The exercise of no new power was conferred by either of these new Amendments. The denial of the exercise of any number of powers by the United States, severally, does not, most certainly, confer its exercise upon the Congress of the States. Neither of these Amendments confers, bestows, or even declares any rights at all to citizens of the United States, or to any class whatever. Upon the colored race they neither confer, bestow, or declare civil rights of any character,—not even the right of franchise. They only forbid the States from discriminating in their laws against the colored race in the bestowment of such rights as they may severally deem best to bestow upon their own citizens. Whatever rights they grant to other citizens shall not be denied to the colored race as a class. This is the whole of the matter. The question then is, how can Congress enforce a prohibition of the exercise of these powers by a State? Most assuredly in the same way they enforced or provided for violations of like prohibitions anterior to these Amendments. The proper remedies before were and now are nothing but the judgments of courts, to be rendered in such way as Congress might provide, declaring any State act in violation of the prohibitions to be null and of no effect, because of their being in violation of this covenant between the States as set forth in the Constitution of the United States. No new power over this matter of a different nature or character from that previously delegated over like subjects was intended to be conferred by the concluding sections of either the Fourteenth or Fifteenth Article of Amendment. No such thing as the tremendous power of exercising general municipal, as well as criminal legislation over the people of the several States could have been dreamed of by the proposers of these Amendments. Such a construction would entirely upset the whole fabric of the Government, the maintenance of which in its integrity was the avowed object of the war.

"Interference by the [U.S.] Federal Government, even if the power were clear and indisputable, would be against the very genius and entire spirit of our whole system. *If there is one truth which stands out prominently above all others in the history of these States, it is that the germinal and seminal principle of American constitutional liberty is the absolute, unrestricted right of State self-government in all purely internal municipal affairs. The first Union of the colonies, from which sprung the Union of the States, was by joint action to secure this right of local self-government for each. It was when the chartered*

Joseph Story

rights of Massachusetts were violated by a British Parliament, the cry first went up from Virginia, 'The cause of Boston is the cause of us all!' This led to the declaration and establishment of the independence, not of the whole people of the united colonies as one mass, but of the independence of each of the original thirteen colonies, then declared by themselves to be, and afterwards acknowledged by all foreign powers to be, thirteen separate and distinct States. [Emphasis added, L.S.]

"It is not my purpose at this time even to touch upon any of the issues involved in the late war, or the chief proximate cause which led to it, or upon whom devolves the responsibility of its direful consequences. But, taking it for granted that the chief proximate cause was the status of the African race in the Southern States, as set forth in the decision of the Supreme Court to which I have first referred, suffice it to say on this occasion that that cause is now forever removed. This thorn in the flesh, so long the cause of irritation between the States, is now out for all time to come. And since the passions and prejudices which attended the conflict are fast subsiding and passing away, the period has now come for the descendants of a common ancestry, in all the States and sections of the country, to return to the original principles of their fathers, with the hopeful prospect of a higher and brighter career in the future than any heretofore achieved in the past. On such return depends, in my judgment, not only the liberties of the white and colored races of this continent, but the best hopes of mankind. And if any breach has been made in any of the walls of the Constitution, in the terrible shock it received in the late most lamentable conflict of arms, let it be repaired by appeals to the forums of reason and justice, wherein, after all, rest the surest hopes of all true progress in human civilization. If, 'in moments of error or alarm,' we have 'wandered' in any degree from the true principles on which all our institutions were founded, in the language of Mr. [Thomas] Jefferson, 'let us hasten to retrace our steps and to regain the road which alone leads to peace, liberty, and safety!'

"This I say in all earnestness to the members of this House from all sections of the Union,—South, East, West, and North; and especially to those who bear the party-name of Republican [the Liberals of the day]. If you, Mr. Speaker, and your political associates, be really and truly of the old Republican school [which originally was conservative], then be first and foremost to rally in the support of the principles of the great Chief who organized that party to rescue the Federal Government from centralisation in one of the most dangerous periods of its history; and under the auspices of whose doctrines, when the rescue was accomplished, the country was so happy, prosperous, and glorious for sixty years of its existence. If you do not, be assured your opponents will rally again under the banner of their ancient creed, and seize it from the hands of those who profess it by name, but reject it by their acts,—'keeping the word of promise to the ear while breaking it to the hope.'

"Excuse me, sir: please to pardon something to an ardent nature. The dawn of a new epoch in politics is upon us. There will soon be a breaking up of the elements of present party organizations. The great and vital issue between Constitutionalism and Centralism must soon be directly met by the people of the States. Seven-tenths of the people of the United States, in my judgment, are to-day as true to the principles of liberty, on which the Federal Constitution was founded, as were their ancestors who, in 1787, perfected its matchless and majestic structure. They are as much opposed to Centralisation and Empire, and the necessary consequence,—ultimate Absolutism and Despotism,—as the men of 1776 were. All that this immense majority now want for concert and co-operation are young and vigorous leaders, thoroughly in earnest, as well as thoroughly imbued with the importance and sacredness of the Cause. Nothing will hasten action in this direction more than the passage by Congress of this bill, or any like it, because its unnecessary and irritating effects will strike chords which will awaken opposition in every State of the Union, from the Atlantic to the Pacific, and from the Lakes to the Gulf.

William Lowndes Yancey

". . . In the workings of our complex system under our Federal Republic, each State is a distinct political Organism, retaining in itself all the vital powers of individual State government and development; while to all the States, in joint Congress assembled, are delegated the exercise of such powers, and such only, as relate to extra-State and Foreign affairs. The States are each perfect political Organisms, with all the functions of perfect government in themselves, respectively, on all matters over which they have not assigned jurisdiction to the Federal Head, or on which they have not restrained themselves by joint covenant in mutual prohibitions upon themselves. Under this system, adhered to, no danger need be apprehended from any extent to which the limits of our boundary may go, or to any extent to which the number of States may swell. For the maintenance of this model and most wonderful system of government, in its original purity and integrity, every well-wisher of his country should put forth his utmost effort. No better time for an effort on this line than now, right here in this House.

"Let us not do, by the passage of this bill, what our highest judicial tribunal has said we have no rightful power to do. If you who call yourselves Republicans shall, in obedience to what you consider a party behest, pass it in the vain expectation that the [conservative] Republican principles of the old and true Jeffersonian school are dead, be assured you are indulging a fatal delusion. The old Jeffersonian, Democratic, Republican principles are not dead, and will never die so long as a true devotee of liberty lives. They may be buried for a period, as Magna Charta was trodden under-foot in England for more than half a century; but these principles will come up with renewed energy, as did those of Magna Charta, and that, too, at no distant day. Old Jeffersonian, Democratic, Republican principles dead, indeed! When the tides of Ocean cease to ebb and flow, when the winds of Heaven are hushed into perpetual silence, when the clouds no longer thunder, when Earth's electric bolts are no longer felt or heard, when her internal fires go out, then, and not before, will these principles cease to live,—then, and not before, will these principles cease to animate and move the liberty-loving masses of this country. Dead, indeed! What mean these utterances just heard from the Chief Magistrate of the Old Dominion on his entering into office, to which he has recently been chosen by a majority of over twenty-seven thousand, in a State which General Grant carried last year by a majority I need not name? A notable point in these utterances is what he said in them of President Grant. Hear them, and judge whether they come from one dead or alive. Says [Virginia] Governor [James L.] Kemper in his first message:

'Adhering to those principles, Virginia seeks these ends: to secure and maintain her full constitutional rights and relations, and to perform all her constitutional duties, as one of the co-equal members of the Union; to exercise all rightful powers of self-government, and to determine, adjust, and regulate the internal, domestic, and municipal interests of her people, their relations and rights, including such as are known as civil rights, in strict conformity to the Federal Constitution and the late decision of the Supreme Court of the United States expounding recent amendments thereto, and the respective powers of the Federal and State Governments thereunder; to obtain an equitable settlement of her just claims against the common Government; to promote universal reconciliation upon the basis of equal justice to all the States and people; to cultivate harmonious relations with the common Government; and to yield a liberal support to every department thereof co-operating in the accomplishment of the ends thus sought. Virginia, recognizing no such obligations as bind her to any national party organization, maintaining her fidelity to all who are and who shall become allies in the defence of measures calculated to secure the ends named, is ready to co-operate cordially with men of whatever party in upholding those measures, by whomsoever proposed,—supporting those who support them, and opposing all opposition to them. One of the articles announcing the principles and purposes recently ratified by an overwhelming majority of our people declares that, disclaiming all purpose of captious hostility to the present Executive Head of the Federal Government, "we will judge him impartially by his official action, and will co-operate in every measure of his Administration which may be beneficent in design and calculated to promote the welfare of the people and cultivate sentiments of good will between the different sections of the Union." This article was no political expedient of the hour. It embodies the sentiments of honorable men, and binds by the obligations of good faith and justice. It pledges such liberal support as may be consistent with our principles and justified by the developments of the future.'

James Abram Garfield

"The principles here announced are in strict accordance with the old Jeffersonian, Democratic, Republican creed. As thus uttered they clearly indicate more than the dawn of that new epoch, and future new alignment of the elements of present party organizations in this country, to which I have referred. They are the key-note of that movement stirred by these old Jeffersonian principles, which, dead as some may suppose them to be, will, at no distant day, be the basis of as signal a triumph by that party which plants itself squarely upon them, whether styled Republican, Democratic, or by any other name, as was that achieved in 1800, under the guide of Jefferson himself. These are, indeed, the ever-living principles to which the country must return, and which alone lead 'to Peace, Liberty, and Safety!'"[648]

21

Quotes About

Alexander H. Stephens

Of Stephens' education as a boy Johnston and Browne write:
❦ "Mr. Stephens . . . did not acquire much learning in his youth from the schools of books, such as they were; but in the school of experience and practical knowledge, in the duties of the kitchen, the garden, and the field, in the heat and cold, on the bed of sickness, by the side of his mother's grave, at the pillow of his dying father, in his second orphanage, and in the breaking-up and scattering of the family,——in these, and things like these, he learned wisdom higher than any found in books, and by it he grew strong in endurance, strong in purpose, and strong in high resolves to do the right, resist the wrong, and help, wherever he might find them, the suffering and the weak."[649]

In 1907 Louis Pendleton wrote:
❦ "Alexander H. Stephens, stay of the weak and helpless and friend of all the world, was once asked, late in life, what he considered the highest compliment he had ever received, and gravely replied by telling how a white-haired old negro at Crawfordville, being asked by a visitor if he knew the master of 'Liberty Hall,' said: 'Tas suh, I knows Mars' Aleck——I knows him mighty well;

he's kinder to dawgs 'n other mens is to people.'"[650]

Stephens entered politics in the Fall of 1836, working in Georgia's state legislature. He began speaking in public for the first time, one of the earliest instances which was recorded by the Honorable Iverson L. Harris:

James Longstreet

❦ "The debate lingered for days, and when every one was worn down and tired of the name of 'Main Trunk,' from under the gallery a clear shrill voice, unlike that of any man of my acquaintance, was heard saying, 'Mr. Speaker!'

"Every eye was turned to the thin, attenuated form of a mere boy, with a black gleaming eye and cadaverous face. The attention became breathless, the House was enchained for half an hour by a new speaker, and one with new views of the question, such as had not been discussed or hinted at by others.

"When he sat down there was a burst of applause from a full gallery, and many of us on the floor joined in the chorus.

"That speech was electrical! It gave life to a dull debate, it aided immensely in the passage of the bill for the survey of the [rail]road, and the appropriation for it. It was the first and maiden speech in the Legislature of that gentleman.

"From that hour he has been a man of mark, and now he is recognized in the House of Representatives at Washington as its foremost man. Need I say that man was Alexander H. Stephens."[651]

The following review of public speech Stephens gave at Crawfordville, Taliaferro County, Georgia, on July 4, 1839, appeared shortly afterward in a Milledgeville newspaper. Stephens was announced to uproarious applause as "Taliaferro's native son":

❦ "After the cheering had subsided, Mr. Stephens arose in response. . . . He dwelt at length upon the history, character, position, principles, and objects of the Whig and the Administration parties, sparing neither, nothing extenuating, nor setting down aught in malice. While he held up the Whigs as embodying the reviving spirit of the old Nationals, he showed the leaders of the Administration party [that is, Democrats] to be the wolves in sheep's clothing who have crept into the ranks of the Republicans, by which that party is now literally scattered abroad, without any concert of action or any common head, as sheep indeed without a shepherd. That they were the Judas-like traitors by whom, for the spoils of office, the Republicans had been deceived and betrayed. They had been confided in by the people upon their professions of opposition to the Tariff, and when proved in person, were the first to attempt its enforcement at the point of the bayonet. They were among the loudest in their cry for retrenchment and reform, and promised the people, if entrusted with the power, to carry out these great measures, while they have increased the expenses of the Government from a little over eleven to nearly forty millions of dollars per annum! They were loud against a subsidized press and Executive interference with elections, while, since their promotion, they have taken the lead, far beyond all precedence, in those abuses, and openly defend and justify their course. They made common cause with the State banks in demolishing the United States Bank, and then turned against them with the cry of divorce ['of bank and state!'] when their whole object was to divorce the public money from the banks, it is true, but to their own pockets. [Stephens] . . . was in favor of divorces sometimes, but not from one to another adulterous bed. That these leaders profess to be the only true Republicans and standards of Democracy, while many of their members are known to have been ultra-Federalists, and even Hartford Conventionists [seceders]. They profess to be the only guardians of the people's rights, when they give the most important fiduciary trusts to notorious bankrupts in fame and in fortune, and for years ask not even a bond for the faithful discharge of their duty; thus permitting their sub-treasurers to pocket for themselves, or spend for the benefit of the party, hundreds of thousands of the public funds, and then, after taking a gentlemanly leave of the country, to spend the remainder of their days in splendor in foreign climes. They profess now to be the friends of the South, and only hope for the protection of our institutions, while many of them are the warm advocates of free negro suffrage, and their Magnus Apollo himself is a Missouri Restrictionist. That such a party, so marked with every badge of corruption, falsehood, and treachery, should be utterly spurned by a free people. [Stephens] . . . deprecated the day when we should be driven to the necessity—the forced choice—of appealing to such men for the protection and salvation of our liberties. . . . That two parties are now courting an alliance with

John Archibald Campbell

our State; and never was fair maiden more artfully allured by the wiles of seduction than was the integrity of the State now assailed by these political suitors. . . . The one is a known enemy, the other a traitor to our cause. It is no question upon which we should take sides or make any capitulations; nor should we suffer ourselves as Georgians to be forced into a choice as between such evils. Either is death to our principles; and we should uncompromisingly wage war against both. Though we be in the minority, let us be the Spartan band. Self-defence is the first law of our nature,—and the nearest enemy always first. [According to Mr. Stephens, after] . . . the extermination of the present occupant of the field, if another make his appearance, we can again rally to the onset. The price of liberty is not only 'eternal vigilance,' but continual warfare; and if we are to have an executioner, for our own and for our country's sake, let us at least leave it for others to provide him! The speaker concluded with this sentiment: 'Henry Clay and Martin Van Buren: candidates for the next Presidency. When the strife is between Caesar and Pompey, the patriot should rally to the standard of neither.' (Much cheering.)"[652]

In 1907 Lucian L. Knight wrote the following about Stephens:
❦ "To say that, in some respects at least, the most striking figure which the public life of this country has ever produced was Alexander H. Stephens, of Georgia, is to assert what is strictly within the bounds of sober judgment. The statement holds true not only of the latter years of the great statesman's career when, seated in his roller-chair [wheel chair], unable to stand upon his feet, he made the halls of Congress fairly ring with the echoes of his voice; but it also applies with equal force to the period of the great debates on slavery when national legislative scenes were by no means lacking in dramatic elements.

"The frailest human skeleton, Mr. Stephens rarely ever seemed to be assured at any one time of more than two weeks of earthly existence; but he possessed an intellect of gigantic proportions, well organized and far-sighted. It was in fact one of the psychological wonders of the age how a brain so massive could find enough to feed upon in a frame apparently so destitute of food supplies; but equally baffling was the marvelous power of compression by means of which he managed to condense such robust accents in lung spaces which were hardly large enough for sick-room whispers. He was frequently confined to his bed by violent attacks of ill-health from which it was thought he could never recover; but he managed to be on hand whenever important issues were pending and no man in American public life has stamped the impress of his mind more indelibly upon national legislation.

"Besides, he wrote books, had numerous personal mishaps and encounters, and issued several challenges [duels] which were not accepted. With the exception of four years spent in Richmond as Vice-President of the Confederate States, and some few years spent in retirement after the war, Mr. Stephens was in Congress almost continuously for nearly thirty years; and such was his feeble health, throughout all this long period, that he rarely ever spoke,

James Lawson Kemper

especially during the latter years of his congressional service, without recalling, in the dramatic spectacle which he presented, the famous death-bed scene of the Earl of Chatham in the House of Commons."653

In 1839, while visiting Charleston, South Carolina, the following incident occurred, highlighting one of Stephens' more common problems: being mistaken for a boy. This particular story is told by Henry Cleveland:

❧ "Being fatigued on his arrival at the hotel, Mr. Stephens availed himself of a comfortable sofa or lounge, and made the situation as easy as possible. His two travelling companions were Mr. Thomas Chafin and Dr. John M. Anthony, merchants, who had been frequent guests of the house. The good lady of the house came in just then, and found the two last-named gentlemen still standing, and what she took for some country boy occupying the easy lounge. Her manner was perfectly kind and somewhat patronising, as she said to him, 'My son, let the gentlemen have this seat.' The 'gentlemen' were amused, and the kind landlady much annoyed, when she afterward found that her 'son' was the [most] important personage of her house, and very soon the lion of the whole city."654

From Louis Pendleton:
❧ "By . . . [the 1840s] Stephens's [verbal] powers had been displayed in a wider field, and even those who had heard the greatest orators of the time, including [Henry] Clay, [John C.] Calhoun and [Daniel] Webster, rendered him their tribute. On February 2, 1848, when [Abraham] Lincoln and Stephens were in Congress together, both representing the Whig party, and were aged thirty-nine and thirty-six years respectively, the former wrote to his law partner in Springfield, Ill.: 'I take up my pen to tell you that Mr. Stephens, of Georgia,

a little, slim, pale-faced consumptive man, with a voice like Logan's has just concluded the very best speech of an hour's length I ever heard. My old, withered, dry eyes are full of tears yet.'"655

In 1851, while Stephens and his associate, fellow Georgia Robert A. Toombs, were trying to prevent disunion, Toombs said of his good friend:
❦ "Stephens carried more brains and more soul in the least flesh than any man God Almighty ever made."656

The public was fascinated by the frail Stephens, who it often compared to another eccentric, John Randolph of Roanoke, Virginia. It was not only his appearance that drew attention, but his intellectual prowess and brilliant oratory as well. A Virginia newspaper, The Compiler, *wrote the following of Stephens after a speech he gave in June 1844:*
❦ "[We regret] that Providence, which bestowed upon him such liberal intellectual powers, had not armed him with physical energies more in keeping with the energies of his mind. . . . His voice is very much of the same order as Randolph's, and he resembles him much in the disparity between the strength of his mental and physical constitution."657

Another Virginia paper, the Richmond Republican, *said of Stephens:*
❦ "In brilliant and cutting invective he has few equals among the public men of the day . . . and in this particular he frequently reminds his hearers of John Randolph."658

In September 1848 Stephens almost died in a physical altercation with a man named Judge Francis H. Cone. The violent episode, and its aftermath, was later described by Johnston and Browne in 1884:
❦ "Early in this [1848] campaign . . . an event occurred which disabled him for awhile for exertions, and indeed narrowly missed putting an end to his life. Mr. Stephens had heard that Judge Cone, a leading politician, had spoken in very acrimonious terms of his action, and had even gone so far, it was said, as to denounce him as a traitor to his country. This was reported to Mr. Stephens, who said that he did not believe that the judge had so spoken; but that as soon as he should meet him he would ask him about the matter, and if he avowed it, would 'slap his face.' Their first meeting occurred at a Whig gathering. After the speaking was over, the company sat down to a dinner in the grove, and during its progress Mr. Stephens took occasion to ask Judge Cone about the report, which the latter pronounced false. Mr. Stephens expressed his gratification, saying that he had never himself believed the report. He added,

'I do not mean to say anything offensive to you, Judge Cone; but I think it right to say, as it will certainly be repeated to you by others, that I said (after expressing my disbelief in the report) that if you avowed the expression attributed to you, I would slap your face.' The judge repeated his disavowal, and the matter seemed to have ended peaceably. But the affair was talked of all over the State, and the judge grew persuaded that it was the general opinion that he had shown cowardice. Heated by this, he wrote Mr. Stephens a letter, demanding a retraction of his threat, to which Mr. Stephens replied in the same way, saying that as the threat had been only contingent upon the avowal of the report, and as the judge had pronounced the report false, there was no occasion for any offence or angry feeling. Before the receipt of this reply of Mr. Stephens, Judge Cone and the latter accidentally met on the piazza of the Atlanta Hotel in that city. The judge, in an angry manner, again demanded a retraction. Mr. Stephens replied that the judge had made that demand of him in a letter, to which he had already replied in writing, and that he would give him no further answer. Upon this the judge called him a traitor, and Mr. Stephens instantly struck him across the face with a small cane in his hand. Livid with fury, the judge drew a dirk-knife, and attempted to stab him to the heart. In his left hand he had a closed umbrella, which Mr. Stephens caught, and interposed as a defence, the judge making furious thrusts with his knife,

John Randolph of Roanoke

and wounding Mr. Stephens eighteen times on the body and arms. At length the judge, who was a large, muscular man, rushed upon him violently, the umbrella broke, and Mr. Stephens fell upon his back, his adversary throwing himself upon him. Forcing Mr. Stephens's head back to the floor with his left hand, he held the knife above his exposed throat, crying, 'Retract, or I will cut your throat!' 'Never! Cut!' Mr. Stephens shouted. As the blade was descending Mr. Stephens caught it in his right hand, which was terribly mangled as his antagonist tried to wrench it away. Both men had risen to their feet again, still struggling, when friends rushed in and separated them, and Mr. Stephens was carried into the hotel, and his wounds immediately dressed. One of the stabs had penetrated to within less than a sixteenth of an inch from the heart; an intercostal artery had been cut, from which in a few minutes more he would have bled to death; and his right hand was cut almost to pieces. It was thought at first that he could not possibly survive.

"The news of this rencontre [meeting] quickly spread, and caused the greatest excitement throughout the State, but especially in Mr. Stephens's own county. Hundreds thronged into Crawfordville to meet the night-train from Atlanta and learn his condition, for the report had run that he could not survive his injuries. Mr. [Richard Malcolm] Johnston was present, and will never forget the intense anxiety and the deep and terrible feeling of resentment that filled all breasts. Men spoke to each other in low tones,—all were waiting to hear what the train would bring; they would control themselves, and do nothing until they knew the truth. When the train was heard approaching, their excitement was scarcely to be repressed. As it glided in, a passenger shouted that his life was in no danger, and such a shout arose from the multitude as was never heard in that village before.

"This painful affair was deeply regretted by all, but by none more than Judge Cone, who had always been an amiable man, and had never before been involved in any personal encounter. The taunts of his political opponents, and brooding over an imagined wrong, had for a time overthrown his judgment, and driven him to an act which he afterwards bitterly regretted. Mr. Stephens was very averse to the prosecution of Judge Cone for this assault, and refused to appear as prosecutor. The judge, however, was indicted, pleaded guilty to the lesser charge of stabbing, and was released on payment of a fine of one thousand dollars [about $120,000 in today's currency]. The amicable relations between the judge and Mr. Stephens were restored after some years, and were never again interrupted.

"As soon as Mr. Stephens had sufficiently recovered, he resumed his work in the canvass. His right hand had been so much disabled as to prevent his using it in writing . . . [and he was thus forced to begin writing with his left hand]."[659]

From the Macon Journal and Messenger, December 19, 1849:
❦ "Physically one of the most feeble, Alexander H. Stephens, of Georgia, is yet intellectually one of the ablest members of the House of Representatives. Short and slender in stature with the face and head of a young girl [he was then nearly thirty-eight years old], his appearance at once arrests attention, from its contrast with the more masculine figures around him. His voice, thin and sharp and shrill as the 'ear-piercing pipe,' cleaves the dense atmosphere of the sombre

Richard Taylor

chamber, startling the House and galleries by its clear, penetrating tones. Every eye is instantly turned upon the speaker, for he is one of the few members who always command attention. If he is introducing a bill, he presents a lucid and logically arranged statement of its character and object which reaches the dullest comprehension. Having thus laid it before the House, he calmly awaits the assaults of its adversaries. Should any misstatement of his remarks be made, he promptly corrects it on the spot. As the debate approaches to a close, he again takes the floor, and passing in review all the weightier arguments of his opponents, and mingling the most bitter sarcasm with the strongest invective that parliamentary decorum admits of, he tears asunder with the keen scimitar of his logic the finest webs of sophistry and the most ponderous mass of reasoning. Seeking exclusively the success of his measure, he avoids mere declamation, however tempting the occasion, and deals only with the facts that press most heavily against his case. When personally assailed, nothing can exceed the severity of his reply. When aroused, his tongue becomes a whip of scorpions. Of all the men in the House, he is the last for a new member to break a lance with. With a better arranged mind than John Randolph, he is probably more like him than any one who has been in Congress since his time."[660]

From the Georgia Telegraph, *March 6, 1849:*
❦ "[While we do not generally agree with his politics] . . . this ungainly-looking individual is considered by many the ablest member of the House, and of a House, too, that can boast some of the best minds of the country. . . . You look in vain for some outward manifestation of that towering, commanding intellect which has held the congregated talent of the whole country spellbound for hours. It is not in the eye, for it is dull and heavy. [Having just left a bed of severe illness, Stephens appeared at this time to be more emaciated than usual.] It is not in the face, for it is meaningless. It is not in the voice, for it is shrill and sharp; but still you feel convinced that the feeble, tottering being before you is all brain—brain in the head, brain in the arms, brain in the legs, brain in the body—that the whole man is charged and surcharged with electricity of intellect—that a touch would bring forth the divine spark!"[661]

Richard M. Johnston gives this interesting account connected with Stephens' retirement from Congress in the late Winter of 1859:
❦ "When leaving Washington, with a number of other Southern members, on the beautiful morning of the 5th of March, 1859, he stood at the stern of the boat for some minutes, gazing back at the Capitol, when some one jocularly said, 'I suppose you are thinking of coming back to those halls as a Senator.' (It was known that he had announced his intention not to return as a Representative.) Mr. Stephens replied, with some emotion, 'No; I never expect to see Washington again, unless I am brought here as a prisoner of war.' This was literally fulfilled in the latter part of October, 1865, when he passed through Washington on his way to his [Georgia] home as a paroled [Confederate] prisoner from Fort Warren."[662]

John Bell

In 1907 Lucian L. Knight wrote the following about the Hampton Roads Conference, held February 3, 1865. It was here that Stephens and Lincoln were to meet for the last time, and which was the occasion of a humorous comment uttered by the latter:

❦ "Controversy is still raging about the famous Hampton Roads conference which took place in the spring of 1865; and, without seeking to throw any new light upon this incident of the last bloody chapter of the war, it appears that the [Confederate] commissioners had no authority to act and little was accomplished beyond an exchange of diplomatic courtesies and personal felicitations. The kindly feelings existing between Mr. Stephens and Mr. Lincoln were attested by an interview in which Mr. Lincoln consented to use his friendly offices in having Lieutenant John A. Stephens, Mr. Stephens's nephew, then a prisoner on Johnson's Island, in Lake Erie, released or exchanged; and this promise he faithfully kept. An amusing incident of the conference was the joke which Mr. Lincoln perpetrated at the expense of Mr. Stephens. Amused at the spectacle of seeing the Confederate Vice-President peal off so many wraps on entering the room, he declared that Mr. Stephens was 'the smallest nubbin he had ever seen to have so many shucks.'"663

From a speech by Reverend W. H. Milburn, chaplain of the U.S. Congress:
❦ "[In spite of all the odds against him, Stephens was the] most powerful orator in Washington at that period [1840s-1850s]. How nearly disease and genius may be associated, is a question which I leave for psychologists to settle. But I feel sure that sleepless nights and days of pain have much to do with the brilliant intellect of this remarkable man. . . . [In comparing Stephens with John Randolph, both] have been the victims of disease whose origin dates far back in life, and each has consequently been the owner of a body, which, however

exquisitely it may have been strung, has been perilously sensitive. Both have exercised almost unequal sway on the floor of Congress; and both have been noted as masters in the art of offensive parliamentary warfare. Both have been admitted to be unimpeachably honest and fearless statesmen. But Mr. Randolph had scarcely a friend. Mr. Stephens has hardly an enemy. Bodily infirmity, if it did not master Mr. Randolph's will, soured his temper and gave to his perfect diction the poison of wormwood, and to his spirit the bitterness that verged upon misanthropy. Mr. Stephens has conquered suffering and made himself strong and noble by entering heartily into the sweet charities of life. . . . [While Randolph is] an intolerant aristocrat [Stephens is as] simple and genial in his manners as a child. . . . Whether Mr. Stephens continues in the House, which I presume he would prefer as the great popular body, or be removed to the Senate, I think that the country will one day adjudge him the finest orator and ablest statesman in either."[664]

In 1884 Richard M. Johnston and William H. Browne made the following observations about life at Stephens' home, "Liberty Hall," during Lincoln's War:
❦ "There was probably no home in Georgia where the old-fashioned virtue of hospitality was—and still is—practised on a more liberal scale than at Liberty Hall. . . . This name he gave his residence in 1845, when he first became its proprietor. The name was given because he expected all friendly visitors to act with as perfect liberty as if they were at home. The house was always open, whether Mr. Stephens was there or not. During the war many gave it the name of 'the Wayside Home,' where sick and crippled soldiers were always hospitably received and well cared for by Harry, the excellent major-domo of the establishment, and his worthy wife, Eliza [a married servant couple].

". . . For many years it has been Mr. Stephens's practice, during court week, to entertain all the lawyers in attendance from other counties. As he lived on the line of the railroad, every one who passed between Augusta and Atlanta, whether previously acquainted with him or not, felt entirely free to favor Mr. Stephens with a brief call,—a visit of a day or two, or a stay of several weeks, as they might feel inclined. Some came out of respect, some from curiosity, some to ask pecuniary assistance, and many from the feeling that his house was open to everybody. As for the people of Taliaferro County, there was not a man, woman, or child there who did not feel as much at home in Mr. Stephens's house as in their own, which they were free to enter at any time and stay as long as they pleased. So it can be easily surmised that, although his personal manner of living has always been of the simplest kind, his domestic expenses have been exceedingly heavy. In addition to the sums he has bestowed on the education of young men, as already mentioned, he has probably expended in charity a greater proportion of his income than has any other man of his part of the country.

"Rarely does a chance visitor call at Liberty Hall at dinnertime that he does not find other guests, some of whom were as little expected as himself. Mr. Johnston has often seen a plain countryman walk into Mr. Stephens's office, where the latter was writing, and after an exchange of greetings not a word has been spoken until dinner was announced. Immediately after dinner the guest has departed with as little ceremony as graced his entry; very frequently first asking and receiving an order on the village store for groceries, or a pair of shoes, or a frock for his wife. It may be thought that this practice does not tend to improve the independence and self-respect of the stalwart yeomen of Taliaferro; but they seem to feel that they stand in a different and closer relation to Mr. Stephens than to the rest of their more affluent neighbors.

John Quincy Adams

"Mr. Stephens, however, never allows himself to be incommoded by these visitations. If he is occupied, he welcomes his guests and then continues what he has in hand, leaving them to entertain themselves. His dinner-hour is never postponed; and whether his guests be few or many, they must content themselves with what is already prepared or can be got ready without delay."[665]

The story of how and why Confederate Vice President Stephens was released from a U.S. prison in October 1865 after only five months, is not generally known. Richard M. Johnston and William H. Browne record it here for posterity:

❦ "With regard to Mr. Stephens's release from Fort Warren . . . he was not aware until long after that it was largely due to the active intervention of Mr.

John W. Garrett. In the fall of 1865, Mr. W. Prescott Smith, Superintendent of Transportation of the Baltimore and Ohio Railroad, while on a tour to the White Mountains, stopped at Boston to visit Mr. Stephens. Greatly shocked at the condition to which confinement had reduced the prisoner, and the sufferings which it was evident would soon put an end to his life, Mr. Smith at once abandoned his proposed tour and hurried back to Baltimore to solicit the offices of Mr. Garrett with the [U.S.] Government. Mr. Garrett went to Washington the next morning, but his application was met by a stern refusal from Mr. [Edwin M.] Stanton, who declared, with bitterness, that he looked upon Mr. Stephens as more responsible than any other man in the South for the secession, because of his eminent abilities, and his refusal to exert them to prevent a rupture, which it was known that he did not approve, at a time when such exertions might have frustrated the whole design.

"Mr. Garrett replied that Mr. Stanton judged Mr. Stephen from the stand-point of the North; that he was himself fully convinced that Mr. Stephens had acted under as firm a conviction of duty and of patriotism as the Secretary himself; and that he had no doubt whatever that had Mr. Stanton been born and reared at the South and in the Southern political faith, his services on the side of the South would have been as ready, as eminent, and as conscientious as they had been on that of the North. He added that if Mr. Stephens, as was more than probable, should die from this totally unnecessary rigor, the reputation of those who were responsible for it would be sullied forever.

"The discussion was prolonged to some length, and the final result was the success of Mr. Garrett's intervention and the release of Mr. Stephens. Some years after, Mr. Garrett and Mr. Stephens happening to meet (at the house of Richard M. Johnston), the grateful remembrance of the one, and the natural gratification of the other, were very impressive to those who witnessed the meeting."[666]

In April 1869 the London Saturday Review *made the followings comments in a review of Stephens' first volume of* A Constitutional View of the Late War Between the States:
❦ "In justice to a brave, high-minded and most unfortunate people, and in due regard to historical truth and to the interests of political science, it is even now worth while to hear what a scholar, a man of deep political learning, of profound knowledge of constitutional history, of moderate opinions and temperate spirit, has to say in defense of principles which, however generally repudiated in 1866, were as generally entertained ten years before, and which the South deemed worth upholding with her whole wealth and her best blood. Mr. Stephens, if any one, may be expected to think and speak fairly and

Paul Jones Semmes

impartially on this subject. He was more consistent than any Northern opponent of secession; he is less embittered than any Southern secessionist. . . . "The opinions and arguments of such a man are entitled, *a priori*, to respectful attention; when they are so just, so clear, so well reasoned, so amply supported by authorities of the highest character and of every class as we find them in the volume before us, they cannot but assist us greatly in forming a true judgment upon the nature and merits of the controversy. . . . A sovereign can have no judge, and the Federal Constitution provided no means by which one State could bring another to justice for wrong-doing or non-fulfillment of engagements. In like manner there existed no legal mode whereby the Federal government could coerce a State which should exercise the right of sovereignty to redress its wrongs under the compact by renouncing the compact itself. A sovereign power is the judge of its own rights. Its subjects must obey it and defend it, right or wrong. It follows therefore from the sovereignty of the States that they were entitled legally to secede, if they chose, and that their citizens were bound to follow and to fight for the choice of the State. This was the view on which Stephens acted; and in its support he cites eminent authorities. . . . He calls Daniel Webster to testify that the systematic violation of the Constitution in the case of fugitive slaves was alone a sufficient vindication of the total repudiation by the South of a compact which the North observed only so far as she pleased. It is impossible, within our limits, to give a fair idea even of the outlines of such an argument; much more to convey a just impression of the lucidity, power of thought, vast and appropriate reading, and vigorous reasoning by which it is sustained. It would be difficult to name a more perfect masterpiece of constitutional reasoning and political disquisition; a work which might with greater advantage be placed in the hands of a young lawyer, who desired to see how those high questions, which are the common ground of the lawyer, the historian and the statesman, can be treated by one who combines the qualifications of all three. The book . . . may be confidently recommended as indispensable to every one who wishes really to understand either the Federal Constitution or the Civil War; and it will be ranked among the most valuable of those materials which the writers of this age are accumulating for the future historian of America."[667]

Of Stephens' work A Constitutional View, *William P. Trent wrote:*
❦ ". . . he undertook, at the suggestion of a Philadelphia publisher, to write a history of the war, which occupied him off and on for nearly four years, being completed by April, 1870. It is unquestionably the ablest exposition and defence of the Southern cause that has yet been made by any participant in the stirring events it describes, and it is written in an admirable temper. It is deficient just where Mr. Stephens's own statesmanship was deficient,—it argues constitutional questions from the point of view of the lawyer rather than from that of the historian, a procedure not without precedent in the North. It endeavors to fit a government to a theory, and it treats as rigid and stationary elements of a people's life that are peculiarly, subject to evolution and growth. It is a book that will be read with respect, in spite of its dialogue form, by every serious student of American history; and it will always be a monument to its author's fine qualities of heart and head."[668]

From an audience member attending one of Stephens' speeches:
❦ "There is nothing about him but lungs and brains!"[669]

After the publication of A Constitutional View, *Stephens' old nemesis Benjamin H. Hill, whom Stephens had challenged to a duel earlier in 1856, began attacking his fellow Georgian once again; this time as a "traitor" to the U.S. and a major contributor to both the cause and the continuance of Lincoln's War. Though Stephens had been the Confederacy's vice president, Hill had served as a Confederate Georgia state senator during the War and had been an ally of Jefferson Davis. Thus in the public eye, Hill's arguments carried nearly as much weight as Stephens'. The two wrote five lengthy rebuttals to one another. Stephens' appeared in the Augusta* Constitutionalist, *while Hill's were printed in the Atlanta* Constitution. *The following venomous attack on Stephens is an excerpt from one of Hill's letters, this one dated June 16, 1874:*
❦ "To what shall we liken him? We must not blaspheme the dead by hunting among them for his model. We will not insult the living by seeking among them for his rival. We cannot libel the innocent unborn by supposing that among them he could ever have an imitator. No! this defamer of Davis and eulogist of [Ulysses S.] Grant, this reckless accuser of despotism in the

Confederacy and ready apologist of usurpations by Radicalism; this pretentious oracle of State sovereignty, and supple persecutor of manacled Louisiana; this wicked maligner of others and worshiping adulator of himself; this lord of slanderers, king of demagogues, and hero of marplots must be left forever alone—unapproached and unapproachable—in the ghostly solitude of his own irreconcilable and anomalous self, serene, self-adored and infamous!"[670]

In July 1876 Richard M. Johnston paid a visit to "Liberty Hall," Stephens' Georgia home, and recorded the following impressions:

James Henry Hammond

❦ "In October of [1875, Mr. Stephens] . . . was stricken down with one of the most violent attacks of illness he had ever suffered from, and was unable to reach Washington during the first session of the Forty-fourth Congress. He was confined to his bed for nearly nine months, and his life was frequently despaired of. He, however, at last slowly improved; and in July, 1876, a short time after he had been able to leave his bed, [I] . . . made him a rather prolonged visit, when [I] . . . was more than ever struck with the peculiar domestic economy of Liberty Hall. This is probably the only mansion in the country where the domestic and social arrangements are entirely unaffected by the sickness or health of the master of the house. Visitors come and go, partake of his hospitality, make themselves at home, whether he be able to receive them in person or not. Almost every train that stops brings coming guests and bears away departing. Dinner is served at one [o'clock P.M.], and all who happen to be present take their places at the board. Later visitors take supper, and early ones breakfast; and as the night-train is sure to bring one or more who take what sleep the time allows, the breakfast-table always presents new faces.

"Mr. Stephens's own habit was to rise at nine, and after dressing, to be rolled in his easy-chair [wheel chair] out upon the piazza, where he usually called for a [card] game of whist,—an amusement which had become a habit with him, and helped to solace many an hour of suffering. After an hour or two he returned to bed and rested till dinner, when he rose and took the head of his table, this being the only meal he took in the dining-room. After dinner conversation and whist were in order, and at seven he went to bed.

"Crawfordville is situated on the Georgia Railroad, sixty-four miles from Augusta, and a hundred and seven from Atlanta, on the foot-hills of the great Alleghany ranges, and has an elevation of six hundred and eighteen feet above the sea. It is an unpretending village, with an air of faded respectability as of one who has seen better days. Liberty Hall is just beyond the village, in a skirt of native forest. Large oaks and hickories, interspersed with many fine transplanted trees and choice exotics, are scattered over an inclosure of about three acres, casting a delightful shade over a grassy lawn. The house is a spacious one, and furnished with elegant simplicity. At the rear, separated by a piazza, are the owner's study and library, the latter more richly stored than is usual among Southern country gentlemen. His law library contains about fifteen hundred volumes; his miscellaneous library about five thousand, collected during many years, at a cost of more than sixteen thousand dollars [about $300,000 in today's currency]."[671]

Mr. Johnston's comments on his visit with Stephens in July 1876 continue. In the following excerpt we see the tremendous respect and admiration the vice president's black neighbors had for him:

❧ "During the visit referred to an incident of more than common interest occurred. The colored Sunday-schools of Taliaferro and the adjacent counties assembled to celebrate the Fourth of July in a grove near Crawfordville. They had previously expressed a wish to march in procession to Liberty Hall, after the celebration and the dinner, and sing some of their songs to Mr. Stephens, if agreeable to him, to which he cordially assented. The scene which followed we give in the words of an eye-witness.

'At about half-past two in the afternoon we saw them coming, preceded by the brass band of the Tillage, and a goodly sight it was. Besides the eight or ten Taliaferro County schools, there were a number from Greene, Hancock, and Wilkes. Mr. Stephens was rolled in his [wheel] chair out into the long piazza as the vast crowds advanced up the lawn. As the various delegations arrived at the piazza they filed alternately to right and left, and pausing under the shade of the trees, each in turn sang a song, and then, wheeling, retired to the rear until the last delegation had sung. Then, all forming in mass, a young colored man standing upon the steps announced that all the schools would sing several pieces in chorus.

'Perhaps you have never heard a Georgia negro sing. At all events, I am sure that you have never heard three thousand of them sing in chorus as they did on that afternoon, partly to please the invalid statesman whom of all men they honor and love the most, and partly in their humble way for the worship of God. As they began, there was some danger lest in such a throng the time of the music might be not well preserved; but Mr. Gorham, the leader of the band, stood forward on the piazza, and marking the time with his cane, the chorus kept in even harmony to the end. Such a sight and such a hearing I might desire, but cannot expect to witness again. Men and women, young and old, boys and girls, and even some little children, lifted up their voices in that shady old grove, and sent them towards heaven in a flood of harmony in which not a discordant note was to be heard, in the midst of which the tears which we could not repress flowed from our eyes. The most of these schools had been taught Sunday-school music under the superintendence of their white pastors, and carried their music-books in their hands. The negro's voice is almost always true, and when, as in this case, it has had some training, it is wonderful to notice the harmony and compass which it can attain in numerous chorus. In such chorus these sang with all their heart and all their might on that afternoon. Their grand music,—I can find no fitter epithet,—their neat and orderly appearance, with their Sunday clothes and simple banners, not only gratified Mr. Stephens, but, as he afterwards said, enraptured him.

'When the whole chorus was over, the young man upon the steps, as the spokesman of the assembly, asked Mr. Stephens to address them. I have known him for many years, and have often heard him speak, but have never seen him under the influence of such intense feeling. He could not stand, but leaning forward in his chair, with his arms resting on the railing, spoke to the hushed crowd; and weak as he was, and even in that unfavorable position, his voice at times, under the inspiration of his feelings, rang out so that it could be heard at the village nearly half a mile distant. He told them how gratified he was to see the progress the colored people were making, especially in his neighborhood, amid the friendly relations of the two races: he advised them, cautioned them, encouraged them to persevere. He told them of the duties they owed to themselves, of the duty of educating their children that they might understand the position in which they were placed, the new responsibilities that rested on them, and the all-importance of a faithful and intelligent performance of duty. His heart seemed overflowing with kindness and benevolence, and he ceased only when he was too much exhausted to speak further.

'Several songs were then called for from separate schools, after which, as the sun was nearly set, they marched in file past, and each touched Mr. Stephens's feeble hand as they retired. Though greatly exhausted, he was reluctant to see them depart. That night, on his bed, he said that no celebration on that day had ever delighted him so much, and, if it had been God's will, he could almost have wished to die while listening to that music which of all he had ever heard was the most enrapturing. And then he spoke of the generally good condition of the negroes in that section, where many of them own snug little farms and other property, and between whom and their white neighbors the most friendly relations obtain. Though he said nothing of their attachment to him or his services to them, yet his strong feeling in the matter was very plain. It is delightful to see the many thousands of negroes in that section look up to him as their greatest and best earthly friend, and his influence on them has been most beneficent."[672]

Robert R. Livingston

From Louis Pendleton, in 1907:

❦ "As the kindly relationship between master and servant was as real as any other phase of the slavery regime, the evidence volunteered by Eliza Stephens, a typical, coal-black 'mammy' of the old South [who worked for Stephens throughout her entire life], is not without historical interest. She spoke of her former master no less affectionately than reverently and declared that he was the 'best' man in the world. 'Ef he ain't in heaven,' she said, ''tain't no use for anybody else to try to git dere.' She declared there was never a time when she was not ready to 'work her fingers off,' in order to win his praise of her industry. She stated that she had belonged to him ever since she was six years old, and during all the long period he had 'never said a cross word.' She delighted to talk of the 'big dinners' at 'Liberty Hall' in former times, which were of three kinds: those that the master allowed the servants to give their friends at intervals, without restriction as to cost; those of the barbecue variety for the white people of the countryside, for whom a whole beef, lambs, pigs and chickens were slaughtered; and those of a more private and social character in honor of General [Robert A.] Toombs, Governor [Herschel V.] Johnson and other distinguished persons, with delicate as well as sumptuous dishes, and a half-dozen wine glasses at the plate of each guest. The narrator was particular to state that her hero had never been known to 'say a cuss word,' or even to make an ill-natured remark, whatever the provocation. Heard in a period when the two races are continually drifting farther apart in sympathy, the fond reminiscences of this faithful old servitor were of the nature of echoes from an almost forgotten past."[673]

From Louis Pendleton, in 1907:
❧ "Unlike many politicians [Stephens] . . . had made no money at Washington, but the practice of his profession [law] during the two years following his retirement brought him twenty-two thousand dollars. 'A rule adopted by him on entering Congress in 1843,' declared his friend R. M. Johnston in 1878, 'was not to make a dollar in Washington beyond his salary. For all his services rendered to his constituents before the Departments, as well as the Supreme Court, when Congress was in session, receiving for them upward of three hundred thousand dollars, he would never accept a dollar, though compensation was often urged upon him. He never took a case into one of his State courts while he was in Congress; though during that period he often appeared, as an advocate, on trial of causes; but always refused to engage himself as such advocate, if that duty would conflict with his duties at Washington.

"In this way he made considerable sums, often as much as two thousand dollars at a time; all of which he devoted to charitable purposes, aiding in building churches and the education of young persons without means."[674]

From the Louisville (Kentucky) Journal, *1865:*
❧ "Stephens is the most brilliant man in the Southern states."[675]

From the Macon (Georgia) Telegraph, *September 6, 1865:*
❧ ". . . the whole people of Georgia look upon him with a feeling akin to idolatry."[676]

Of his elder brother Alexander, Linton Stephens once said:

❦ "As a judge of mankind in the aggregate, brother sometimes seems to me almost infallible. He can foresee what the multitude will do. But as to individuals, I do not know any one who can be so deceived and put upon."[677]

While working for the Atlanta Sun *in the early 1870s, Stephens often wrote in great detail about his own personal life in his editorials, earning himself the nickname the "amiable egotist." In late 1872 Stephens' lifelong friend Robert A. Toombs commented on Stephens' propensity for thoroughness, saying:*

❦ "Oh yes, that's the way with Alec—always posing before the public. He won't be satisfied until he corrects the proofs of his own obituary."[678]

In December 1872 Stephens announced himself a candidate for the U.S. Senate. Though defeated by former Confederate General John B. Gordon, he was elected to fill a sudden vacancy that had arisen. Thus began his ninth term as a Georgia state representative, this time in the 43rd Congress. New York's Commercial Advertiser *made the following comments on Stephens' appointment in February 1873:*

❦ "Alexander H. Stephens does not emulate the modesty of the rose. He positively refuses to 'pine upon the bush.' He is not only ready to be plucked but means to oblige somebody to pluck him. He feels that his dear Georgia cannot get along without him at Washington. . . . [We admit, however, that] this little irrepressible human steam engine, with a big brain and scarcely any body, is one of the most accomplished parliamentarians the world has ever seen. . . . [Now that he has graciously consented to return to Congress,] let him come back."[679]

In late 1873 Northern Liberals introduced a bill that would force social and political equality between the races. In 1884 Richard M. Johnston and William H. Browne commented on Stephens' reaction:

❦ "This bill Mr. Stephens strongly opposed in a speech delivered January 5th, 1874. He first explained that his opposition did not arise from an indisposition to concede full justice to every human being within the Federal jurisdiction, nor from any prejudice founded on race or previous servitude. While he had never held nor believed the manifestly false assertion that all men are equal, he held 'that all men have an equal right to justice, and stand, so far as governmental powers are concerned or exercised over them, perfectly equal before the law.' That the blacks should have full security in their persons and property, and that they should enjoy, as amply as the whites, the protection and redress afforded by the law, was a doctrine which he had publicly advocated shortly after the close of the war, and never ceased to hold; and that doctrine, when presented by him in an address, had been unanimously approved by the Georgia Legislature, showing the feelings and dispositions of the leading men of that State."[680]

In 1876 another Northern newspaper, this one unnamed, wrote the following about Stephens' time as a Washington politician:

❧ "A little way up the aisle sits a queer-looking bundle. An immense cloak, a high hat, and peering somewhere out of the middle a thin, pale, sad little face. This brain and eyes enrolled in countless thicknesses of flannel and broadcloth wrappings belong to Hon. Alexander H. Stephens, of Georgia. How anything so small and sick and sorrowful could get here all the way from Georgia is a wonder. If he were to draw his last breath any instant you would not be surprised. If he were laid out in his coffin he need not look any different, only then the fires would have gone out in those burning eyes. Set, as they are, in the wax-white face, they seem to burn and blaze. Still, on the countenance is stamped that pathos of long-continued suffering which goes to the heart. That he is here at all to offer the counsels of moderation and patriotism proves how invincible is the soul that dwells in his shrunken and aching frame.

John Adams

He took the modified oath in his chair, and, when he had taken it, his friends picked him up in it and carried him off as if he were a feather. So old Thaddeus Stevens used to be picked up and carried in and out when this same man, of the same name and an opposite lineage, was the Vice-President of the Southern

Confederacy. The old lion of Pennsylvania rests from the fight; and the great 'rebel' of Georgia, with the very shadow of death upon his face, lifts his failing voice in behalf of moderation and peace."[681]

In 1877 Richard M. Johnston wrote the following about the relationship between Linton and his elder brother:

❦ "It was always beautiful to me to observe the relations between him and his brother, Alexander. I suspect that no two brothers ever stood in the relation to each other of greater love and sympathy. While they were never partners in the law, yet they would never appear in court on opposing sides. Their love was such that each, I believe, could not endure the thought of attempting, or even wishing for things different or adverse among themselves. It was for sometime unfavorable to the growth of Linton's reputation, that the general public delayed to give him full credit for independence in his political opinions. The truth is, that their thorough intimacy and their mutual fondness had induced a similarity of thinking upon most subjects; and though living in different counties, they often, and indeed generally, would form instantaneously the same judgments upon questions that had newly arisen, and upon which they had not had time to confer. I have noticed, sometimes, the pleasure each has felt in such a case.

"The brothers sympathized always and entirely. The joy and the grief of one were the joy and the grief of the other. This was most especially the case with the elder brother [Alexander]. To Linton he had been both brother and father. He had educated him with almost unequaled care, and, I am sure, that his greatest happiness, aside from the consciousness of performing his own duties, consisted in seeing Linton successful and happy. Their love for each other was perfect in its kind. The death of Linton would have broken the heart of the survivor, but for his religious faith, and his sense of obligation to hold out to the last in the work which he had yet to do."[682]

Richard M. Johnston and William H. Browne recorded the following 1877 incident:

❦ "Not long after [Mr. Stephens] . . . had taken his seat [in the U.S. Congress] he was again prostrated by an attack of pneumonia (January 1st, 1877), and laid upon a bed from which few of his friends dared to hope that he would ever rise. He was himself convinced that his end was near, but gave an example of how tenacious vitality may be, even in the frailest bodies. For weeks together he took almost no food, never slept but under the influence of narcotics, and grew more and more emaciated, until it seemed almost incredible that a form so attenuated could retain life at all, and he himself wondered that he did not die. Once a report of his death was telegraphed all over the country, and most of the newspapers published obituary notices and short biographical sketches, which, afterwards, he found a sort of grim amusement in reading. All the houses in Crawfordville were draped with mourning. When the report was found to be false, the greatest joy prevailed; there were congratulations and handshakings, and the little town took holiday."[683]

On March 4, 1883, the day of Stephens' death, the Atlanta Constitution published the following article describing the Georgia governor's last moments:

❧ "About six o'clock last night it was discovered that Mr. Stephens was sinking very rapidly, and after consultation[,] Dr. Raines, Dr. Steiner, and Dr. Miller announced that his death was simply a matter of a few hours. He was still unconscious, and lingered along without any apparent suffering until when, with scarcely a quiver, he yielded up the fight that he had maintained so long and so bravely and against such fearful odds, and his soul winged its way to the judgment-bar of God.

William Henry Harrison

"Late yesterday it became known in certain circles of Atlanta that Governor Stephens's life had been despaired of, and that he would probably die during the night. The mansion was filled from that time forward with anxious inquirers as to his condition, but the extremity of his case was not generally known, and the news of his death which we print this morning will be read with surprise by thousands who had counted on his wonderful vitality to pull him through this last dread struggle.

'The Governor is dying!'

"This was the message that greeted all comers about ten o'clock. In the parlor, fronting the quiet group, was the Stephens historic chair, empty and desolate-looking. So long had he lived with it, so intimately had its life been interwoven with his, so completely had it pulsed and throbbed and quivered under the touch of his gentle fingers, and so faithfully had it responded to his slightest impulse and interpreted his innermost and unuttered thoughts, that it seemed to be part of him as it sat there so still and silent.

"As the rooms were filling gradually, the other parlor was lighted, and the whole lower floor was lit up just as it was when, a few months ago, many of the same persons who were then present had escorted Mr. Stephens, amid the applause and enthusiasm of a vast crowd, to his first night in the mansion. The callers made sad groups in the parlors, the library, or the hall, and talked in low tones. As one of the doctors came from the sick man he was at once surrounded by questioners. The steady response was, 'He is sinking rapidly and can live but a few moments.' Even after all hope had been abandoned by those who knew best, many clung to the idea that the Governor would still fight his way through the cloud that gathered about him.

"Dr. Miller and Steiner remained at Mr. Stephens's bedside almost constantly. In the bedroom were only the physicians and relatives of the Governor. No one was denied admission, and many friends paused in the door for a moment. The Governor was lying on the front part of the bed. He was very much emaciated, and his pallor was intense. He seemed to be in no pain whatever, but breathed heavily, with apparent effort. His eyes were half closed and wore a strained expression. His left hand was resting on his breast and his right hand lost beneath the cover.

"At about two o'clock in the morning it was evident that Mr. Stephens was much weaker and that a crisis was approaching. The doctors had prepared a strong mustard-plaster and put it on his wrist. They let it remain there for perhaps twenty minutes. When they removed it there was not the slightest sign of inflammation, showing that there was very little vitality left. At about half-past two his extremities became cold and clammy, assuming a purplish hue. Dr. Miller said, 'The end is not far off.'

"As the close drew near, Mr. Stephens was lying on his back, with his head turned slightly to the right. The husky rattle in his throat that had been plainly perceptible earlier in the night had ceased entirely. There was no more heavy breathing and not the slightest gasping. He was as quiet as a baby asleep in its mother's arms. Dr. Miller held his slender wrist anxiously. The tired pulse had almost ceased to beat. Only once in a while could the trained fingers detect a flickering throb as the ebbing tide wasted slowly away.

"At three o'clock Drs. Steiner and Haines, who had gone to sleep, were awakened. When Dr. Steiner reached his bedside Mr. Stephens was very much weaker. Two lady relatives, Mrs. John A. Stephens and Mrs. Aaron G. Grier, who had retired for a little sleep, entered the room and took their place by the bed. There were then present, besides those and the physicians. Colonel John A. Stephens, A. L. Kontz, C. W. Seidell, R. K. Paul, and Aleck Kent, the

Governor's faithful body-servant. The breathing grew fainter and fainter, but there was not the slightest disturbance on the pallid face. At length Dr. Steiner lifted the wrist and bent with intentness over the bed. He then drew back, and, putting on his glasses, looked into Governor Stephens's face and said, 'I'm afraid he is gone.'

"This was precisely at twenty-four minutes past three.

"After another earnest look he said, 'He is dead!'

"So gently had the golden cord been loosened that not even the physician, who stood with his hand upon the wrist, knew when the last link had slipped asunder.

"As one stood looking at the worn and wasted frame, rocked and tossed and strained for so many years, but now at peace at last, and thought of the bitter and persistent fight against pain and suffering now so softly ended, those quaint lines of Judge Logan E. Bleckley's came into mind,—

> 'How costly is life! at what heavy expense
> Do we temper the blood and nourish the sense!
> But death unto all is offered so cheap,
> It is but closing the eyes and ceasing to weep.'

"It is uncertain what were the last words uttered by the great statesman before his death. It seems to be agreed that his last clearly conscious conversation was with Dr. Steiner. Mr. Seidell says that Saturday afternoon he recognized Mr. John A. Stephens, his nephew. Mr. Stephens asked the Governor if he knew him, and he replied, 'Yes; it's John.' Dr. Raines says further, that after this occurrence, he was attending to some of his wants, and moving him in his bed, when he said, 'Doctor, you hurt me.'

"Dr. Raines says that those were the last words he ever uttered. This was purely an accidental exclamation. If this be true—and there is no report of words uttered after these—it is a strange fate that the last words wrested from Mr. Stephens's pallid and drawn lips should be an appeal against the physical agony with which his whole life had been racked. For more than half a century the spirit of pain had clouded his existence, freighted his every breath with suffering. And at last, when the shadows of death had gathered about his bedside, and the compassionate mercy of God seemed to have tempered the pangs of dissolution, his old enemy, relentless and unsparing, invaded even that presence, defied even that mercy, and inspired the last language his trembling lips should utter upon this earth."[684]

Of Stephens' final days and funeral, Richard M. Johnston and William H. Browne wrote:
🍂 "His last public appearance was at the Sesquicentennial celebration in

John Brown Gordon

Savannah on February 12th. This was the most imposing pageant that had ever been in the State, and drew thousands from far and near. The aged statesman, seated in his chair, reviewed the past, the humble beginnings of a great State. When he had spoken, his hearers crowded round to touch his withered hand in reverent affection. He enjoyed the scene greatly, but the exposure to inclement weather did fatal harm to one who was already much exhausted. On returning to Atlanta, he betook himself at once to his bed, evidently foreseeing that he should rise from it no more. The strange hold, apparently so slight, and yet so tenacious, that he had on life, that had held through seventy-one years of uninterrupted sickness, was loosened at last. He sank gently away; so quietly that the watchers by his bed did not notice his departure. His death occurred on March 4th, 1883.

"Rarely, if ever, has such a funeral been seen in this country. From seventy-five to eighty thousand persons were in attendance, of whom many thousands came to the city for that purpose alone. The funeral sermon was preached by the Rev. John Jones, and many of the leading orators of the South gave eloquent expression to their universal sorrow and sense of a great loss. Perhaps the most touching tribute was that of his life-long friend, General Toombs: 'I come only to bring my tears.' No similar death has called forth more general and sincere grief; for of all the men whom the South in this century has produced, he was the most widely known and beloved. Far-distant cities displayed the ensigns of mourning, with lowered flag and tolling bells, and the whole land lamented that a chief of the people had fallen."[685]

In 1897 William P. Trent wrote:

❦ "Stephens was poor, and fought his way to distinction by arguing before juries in a crowded courthouse, before excited voters and rival candidates on the hustings, and amid jarring factions in Congress during the two most tumultuous decades of our political history. For sheer pluck, and conscientious, successful use of native faculty, the world's history presents us with few characters, more worthy of our regard than Alexander H. Stephens."[686]

In 1904 Sherman Williams wrote:

❦ "Mr. Stephens labored hard in public and in private to prevent secession, but without success. Like most men of the South he held himself bound by the action of his state and reluctantly joined in the effort for disunion. It was not his nature to do anything in a half-hearted way, and when his state voted for secession he put forth his best efforts for the success of the cause to which he felt himself in honor bound.

"He was chosen vice president of the Confederacy and might have been its president had he felt physically able to bear the burden of that office. Of the result of that long and bitter contest this is no place to speak.

"After the close of the war Mr. Stephens again served in Congress, making a faithful and wise representative. He wrote a history of the Civil War. To the end his life was an active one. For a time he edited a newspaper at Atlanta. He opposed the election of [Horace] Greeley [in 1872], for which he was bitterly denounced by Democrats [Conservatives], North and South [who had endorsed Greeley due to his call to end Reconstruction and allow the South to once again govern herself]. In 1882 [Stephens] . . . was elected governor of

Georgia, but died before the close of his term of office. His funeral was attended by more than fifty thousand people. His memory was honored by the adjournment of courts and public councils and by the passage of resolutions throughout Georgia and in many towns and cities in other states.

"Alexander H. Stephens had faults, as who has not. He made some mistakes, as all mortals will. He seemed at times to be vacillating, but it must be said that no man ever knew him well who failed to love him. He struggled with infirmities that would have crushed most men. He was generous and forgiving. He was a benefactor to many, and never intentionally did harm to any one. His is a life that calls for much commendation and little reproof.

"A careful study of the life of Mr. Stephens will be in many ways profitable. We will come to know a really great and good man who won success in spite of many obstacles and be stimulated thereby. We will become better acquainted with an important period of our history and learn to understand better than some of us now do the feelings of the Southern people just before and during the Civil War."[687]

Of Stephens' death, Louis Pendleton wrote:
❦ "A great life, full of tragedy both public and private, yet also full of triumph and of usefulness, was ended. The Latin phrase, *Non sibi, sed alii* ['Not for themselves but for others'] on the tomb of Georgia's 'great commoner' at Crawfordville, is more than official eulogy. Though a sufferer in body and spirit throughout life, though the victim of ills which only through great courage and patience could be endured, he furnished innumerable proofs of an unselfish and high devotion to other than self—to friends, neighbors, to all in need, to his State, his section, the country and the public at large. His religion, which was simple and genuine, may be described in the single phrase, character is salvation. This was illustrated when, during his last illness, prayer and Bible reading at his bedside were proposed. He objected, not to these things in themselves, but to

John Hancock

them as suggesting a 'death-bed repentance,' explaining: 'I have made it the rule of my life to live each day as if it were to be my last. In the heat of politics I may have sometimes forgotten myself, but I am no better to-day on my death-bed than I have tried to be every day of my life, and I have no special preparations to make and no special pleas to offer.'

"The last rites were attended by all the dignity with which a great State could invest the observances in honor of its deceased chief magistrate. Many thousands of both races viewed the body as it lay in state in the capitol. The memorial was a notable gathering of statesmen and prominent citizens. Robert Toombs wept as he praised his life-long friend. He declared that Stephens always dared to follow his convictions, whatever the consequences, and recalled how he had said after the fall of the Confederacy: 'I am old and weak in bodily infirmity, but I have done my duty to God and my country, and I am ready for whatever fate may be assigned to me.' Of the many tributes of speakers at the many memorial gatherings in Southern cities, of the public estimate shown in the resolutions of State legislatures and of the Congress of the United States, it is unnecessary to speak here.

"Though not a source of strength to the warring Confederacy, Alexander H. Stephens served the South well before the great crisis, and after it his wisely directed efforts were no small factor among the forces that brought to an end the era of [Southern] passion and [Yankee] despotism. Of his wider usefulness, it may be said that the thanks of all American patriots are due to him as an untiring champion of Constitutional government and home rule within the States, as opposed to threatening encroachments of the Federal power. For these he wrought mightily when they were most imperiled, and the possible day when the republic of North America shall be merged into the all of empire except the name has been made more distant as a result of his efforts.

"The heritage of the American people is greatness, even though new 'world-power' responsibilities threaten the integrity of our early institutions, even though the individual liberty of the past be impaired by complex modern conditions of industrialism and finance. Stephens was ever and would be still an optimist, although to the end he was pursued by the fear that during the fifteen years of revolution from 1861 to 1876 the cause of Constitutional government in this country had received a blow from which it would never recover. It may be that the fathers of the Federated [Confederated] American republic would confess to similar fears for the future could they know of the present tendencies toward a greater extension of the Federal power at the expense of the States, as well as an expansion of the prerogatives of the Executive at the cost of the coordinate branches of the government, and that, moreover, the chief magistrate of the republic in our time [U.S. President

Varina Banks Howell Davis

Theodore Roosevelt] is also the protector of San Domingo, the suzerain of Cuba, the virtual supervisor of Latin-America, and the imperial overlord of Tutuila, Guam, Porto Rico, and the thousand islands of the Philippines."[688]

Lucious L. Knight gave this description of Stephens' final days:
❦ "[In the early months of 1883], immediately upon returning home [from a trip out of town] Mr. Stephens was taken violently ill. He was destined never to rise from the bed which he was now obliged to seek. However, it was not the visit to Savannah which caused or even hastened Mr. Stephens's death. The time fixed for his departure was at hand. The candle had slowly melted down to the socket and the hour hand had reached the fatal number on the dial-plate. But the spirit of the great statesman had so often hovered along the mysterious hedge-rows of life that in spite of the years which were now heavily multiplied upon his feeble shoulders it was not seriously thought that the time of the Great Commoner had come. Neither the people of Georgia who were so accustomed to reading bedside bulletins from Mr. Stephens in the morning newspaper prints, nor the old statesman himself, who was so accustomed to waging sick-room battles with the minions of disease, seemed to realize that death was imminent. But nevertheless the Grim Destroyer was encamped upon the executive lawn.

"Back into the cosy apartment at the extreme end of the hall on the left, which Mr. Stephens had selected as his bedroom on taking possession of his new official home in Atlanta, the pale invalid sufferer was again borne; nor was he destined to leave the embrasure of that room until his eyelids had closed in the deepening dusk of that mysterious sleep which had puzzled the weary Hamlet. One of the first official acts of Mr. Stephens three months before had been to order down the huge bedstead which had conjured up at once in his simple democratic mind the powdered wig and pampered flesh of that spoiled child of royalty Louis the XIV. In place of the sprawling claws of this 'flowery bed of ease' Mr. Stephens had substituted an unpretentious little single couch which looked as if it might have filled an humble corner in the cotter's highland home. It had always been the pet notion of the Great Commoner, more sentimental perhaps than scientific, that he could sleep better if he paralleled the course of the Mississippi river and slept with his head directed toward the arctic zone while his limbs meandered toward the equatorial belt. Amusing as it may seem, this whim controlled the legislation by which his domestic economy was governed; and he had caused his little cot to be pointed north and south in keeping with the precise bearings of the compass. In another corner of the room he had arranged for the reclining comforts of his colored bodyguard, whose tidy bedstead revealed no adverse discrimination, and whose familiar name, like his distinguished master's, was Aleck. It might be time well spent to pause upon the beautiful relations which existed between the faithful [black] bodyguard, whose ear was as keenly attuned as an Indian's to the softest accents of the night, and the invalid master, whose life had never known the sweet companionship which heaven had graciously vouchsafed to man, when age-long years ago the first lone hermit awoke from the most ravishing of dreams—minus a rib but plus a helpmeet—to find himself no more an Eden bachelor.

"But this apartment, under the new administration, had been devoted to affairs much more substantial than the airy fabrics of sleep. It was the workshop of Mr. Stephens. On account of the delicate health of the feeble old Governor the office at the State Capitol had been exchanged, except on occasions of urgent necessity, for the office at the executive mansion. Such was the arrangement which he had made at the start; and, besides purchasing a clock to arouse the inmates of the room betimes, he had also procured, apparently from Noah's ark, a row of files which he had placed against the walls for important documents and letters. And, indeed, it almost looked as if Robinson Crusoe, in addition to housing his man Friday, had also made arrangements for accommodating his pigeons.

"During the two weeks in which Mr. Stephens lingered after taking his bed for the last time there were frequent intervals in the midst of severe bodily suffering which he gave to official business. It was characteristic of the great man that the pains which racked his body unless accompanied by the severest pangs of the guillotine or the worst tortures of the Inquisition were never allowed to disturb his official obligations; and as long as he could rationally sign the name which he meant for Alexander H. Stephens, but which no one without the key could ever decipher, unless he had first mastered the ancient symbols of the Egyptian monuments, he continued to pen it to official documents. It was equally characteristic of the Great Commoner that the last service in which his feeble fingers were ever employed was an act of executive clemency. The altruism which ennobled the whole life of Mr. Stephens asserted itself in the most trivial things. Some one had sent him a box of oranges from Florida; and though he had passed the point where he any longer had relish for the fruit, he ordered the oranges to be parcelled out between the inmates of the house so that each could receive two.

"The cause of Mr. Stephens's death was an old malady superinduced by riding up from the [train] depot in a [horse-drawn] cab from which a pane of glass had been displaced, exposing him to the cold draft of an inclement February morning. The physical distress which followed bore so plainly the features of former attacks that Mr. Stephens was not at first alarmed; but when the customary remedies failed to give the usual relief he began to feel some uneasiness. However, it was not the trepidation which is felt by one who dreads the future which he finds himself obliged to face. Mr. Stephens had long ago put his house in order. He labored under none of the fears which are born of the darkness. Dr. Steiner was hastily summoned from Washington; but being detained at the death-bed of [former Confederate] Gen. Dudley M. DuBose, he could not respond at once. However, he hurried to Atlanta as soon as he could get release.

Thaddeus Stevens

"Mr. Stephens rallied somewhat after Dr. Steiner arrived. An invincible hope kept him busy down to the last moment, planning what he expected to do when he was well. It was the cheerful optimism characteristic of the invalid who has fought and won so many grim battles; but it was pathetic to the point of tears to watch the brave spirit as it still continued to struggle even after the pale flag had commenced to flutter above the wasted citadel. Often had the newspapers of the State told of the death of Mr. Stephens only to recall the premature announcement, but the sables of mourning were now to be donned upon authoritative tidings. Often had the grave yawned to receive the victim who was ever at the gates, but the tomb had been robbed for the last time, and the jealous portals were now to claim the coveted tenant.

"Among those who gathered about the sick-bedside to witness the last scene in the life which was now slowly ebbing were the two ladies of the household, Mrs. Stephens and Mrs. Grier, both near relatives; Dr. Steiner, the old family physician, who had so often attended the patient; Col. C. W. Seidell, his private secretary; Col. John A. Stephens, his nephew; Hon. John T. Henderson, Dr. H. V. M. Miller, Dr. Raines, Judge Hall, A. L. Kontz, E. C. Kontz, T. B. Bradley and R. K. Paul. Besides there were two servants. It was not until Saturday, March the third, that the condition of Mr. Stephens had become alarming. But he had now commenced to sink rapidly, and shortly before midnight Dr. Steiner had spoken the message: 'The Governor is dying.'

"Though it had to come it was none the less bitter to those who had so long waited upon the helpless sufferer; and not the least forlorn of the silent group was the faithful black bodyguard, poor Aleck, whose best friend was now telling him good-by. Dr. Miller, who had been devoted to Mr. Stephens for years, kept his hands almost constantly upon the feeble wrist in which so faint were the pulsations that the existence of life could hardly be detected; and neither Dr. Miller nor Dr. Steiner could tell the precise moment when the spark was extinguished. But the invalid had ceased to suffer. The great Democrat [Conservative] had died as simply as he had lived.

"One of the warmest admirers of Mr. Stephens in the sorrowful coterie about the sick bedside was Anton Kontz, and being then the superintendent of the Pullman Company, it was Mr. Kontz who had furnished the handsome Pullman coach which had brought Mr. Stephens from Crawfordville to Atlanta. Several invited guests had gone to escort the Governor-elect to the Capitol; and in the speech-making which preceded the departure from Crawfordville one of the orators had told him that he was to travel like a prince; but Mr. Stephens, without waiting for him to stop, had interrupted the speaker with the remark: 'There are no princes in Georgia. At least I am not one of them. I am only the servant of the people.'

"It is said by those who stood at the bedside that the last articulate utterance which ever fell from the lips of the Great Commoner was: 'Get ready, we are almost home.' Perhaps in the delirium of his dying moments the old Governor, weary of the cares of State in the busy capital, was hurrying back over the iron rails to Crawfordville, and, looming above the tree-tops on the distant hillside, he had caught the familiar turrets of old Liberty Hall. Perhaps it was the black face of his old bodyguard which framed itself in his dying thoughts as he spoke those simple words, 'Get ready, we are almost home.' But, even if this was all, those commonplace words addressed to an old negro whom he loved were not unworthy of the golden approaches to the palace of the King.

"With such an executive command still warm on the lips of the old Governor, it could not be said that death had really darkened the abode of power which had so lately opened amid the flare of tapers and the sparkle of gems to welcome the incoming occupant. An almost breathless hush pervaded the halls of the executive mansion. The tapers were out and the jewels flashed against sorrowful faces; but, in spite of the doleful symbols of an altered scene, it was far more appropriate to say that the old Governor had been once more inaugurated!

"All was at last over. The doctor was now dismissed. The crutch was laid aside for good. The roller-chair was no longer needed. At last after seventy years there had fluttered down through the Sabbath hush of the sick-bedroom an old, old prescription which had made the invalid well. His wish had come true at last. Those lips had been dashed at the fountain which the Spaniard sought in vain. Those limbs had waxed strong and youthful. Those heart-beats had commenced anew to keep perpetual step to music that never ceases. It is unseemly in the mute mourner who bends over the attenuated figure to keep back the tears; for the absent loved ones are always missed. But over the beautiful clay let the laurel instead of the cypress rest; for in the goblet of death, fresh from the vintages of yonder hills, Alexander H. Stephens has found the elixir of life."[689]

Notes

1. There are several reasons Stephens remained unmarried. 1) Suffering from lifelong "incurable melancholy," and regarding himself as a "helpless invalid," he did not want to be a burden to a wife. 2) Though he did show some romantic interest in women as a youth, some surmise that Stephens, a brainy religious man whose favorite occupations always seemed to be intellectual and spiritual in nature, was actually asexual, and simply preferred platonic love to any other. See Pendleton, p. 33.
2. Johnston and Browne, p. 46.
3. Johnston and Browne, pp. 54-55, 56-57.
4. Pendleton, pp. 33-34.
5. Johnston and Browne, pp. 72-73.
6. Johnston and Browne, p. 74.
7. Johnston and Browne, p. 74.
8. Johnston and Browne, p. 76.
9. Johnston and Browne, p. 76.
10. Johnston and Browne, p. 77.
11. Johnston and Browne, p. 77.
12. Johnston and Browne, p. 78.
13. Johnston and Browne, p. 79.
14. Johnston and Browne, p. 80.
15. Johnston and Browne, p. 80.
16. Johnston and Browne, pp. 80-81.
17. Johnston and Browne, pp. 81-82.
18. Johnston and Browne, p. 82.
19. Johnston and Browne, pp. 82-83.
20. Johnston and Browne, p. 83.
21. Johnston and Browne, p. 83.
22. Johnston and Browne, p. 83.
23. Johnston and Browne, p. 86.
24. Johnston and Browne, p. 86.
25. Johnston and Browne, pp. 86-87.
26. Johnston and Browne, p. 88.
27. Johnston and Browne, p. 89.
28. Johnston and Browne, pp. 90-91.
29. Johnston and Browne, p. 89.
30. Johnston and Browne, p. 95.
31. Johnston and Browne, p. 95.
32. Johnston and Browne, p. 98.
33. Johnston and Browne, p. 101.
34. Johnston and Browne, p. 101.
35. Johnston and Browne, pp. 102-103.
36. Johnston and Browne, p. 106.
37. Johnston and Browne, p. 106.
38. Johnston and Browne, p. 107.
39. Johnston and Browne, p. 129.
40. Johnston and Browne, pp. 129-130.
41. Pendleton, pp. 42-43.
42. Pendleton, p. 36.
43. Johnston and Browne, p. 142.
44. Johnston and Browne, p. 143.
45. Johnston and Browne, p. 144.
46. Johnston and Browne, p. 144.

47. Johnston and Browne, pp. 145-146.
48. Johnston and Browne, p. 148.
49. Johnston and Browne, pp. 148-149.
50. Johnston and Browne, p. 149.
51. Johnston and Browne, pp. 150-152.
52. Johnston and Browne, p. 152.
53. Johnston and Browne, p. 155.
54. Johnston and Browne, p. 155.
55. Johnston and Browne, p. 169.
56. Johnston and Browne, p. 170.
57. Johnston and Browne, pp. 170-171.
58. Johnston and Browne, p. 172.
59. Pendleton, pp. 74-75.
60. Johnston and Browne, pp. 183-184.
61. Seabrook, TTAHSR, p. 27.
62. Johnston and Browne, pp. 194-195.
63. Johnston and Browne, p. 195.
64. Johnston and Browne, p. 195.
65. Johnston and Browne, p. 196.
66. Johnston and Browne, p. 196.
67. Johnston and Browne, p. 197.
68. Johnston and Browne, p. 201.
69. Johnston and Browne, pp. 201-202.
70. Johnston and Browne, p. 202.
71. Johnston and Browne, p. 204.
72. Johnston and Browne, p. 217.
73. Johnston and Browne, p. 218.
74. Johnston and Browne, pp. 218-219.
75. Johnston and Browne, p. 222.
76. Johnston and Browne, p. 222.
77. Johnston and Browne, p. 222.
78. Johnston and Browne, pp. 222-223.
79. Johnston and Browne, p. 225.
80. Johnston and Browne, p. 235.
81. Johnston and Browne, p. 237.
82. Johnston and Browne, pp. 238-239.
83. Johnston and Browne, p. 243.
84. Johnston and Browne, pp. 244, 245.
85. Johnston and Browne, p. 250.
86. Johnston and Browne, p. 251.
87. Pendleton, p. 46.
88. Pendleton, p. 46.
89. Johnston and Browne, p. 252.
90. Johnston and Browne, p. 254.
91. Johnston and Browne, p. 254.
92. Johnston and Browne, p. 254.
93. Johnston and Browne, pp. 254-255.
94. Johnston and Browne, pp. 255-256.
95. Johnston and Browne, p. 258.
96. Johnston and Browne, p. 254.
97. Knight, p. 75.
98. Johnston and Browne, pp. 262-263.
99. Seabrook, TTAHSR, p. 29.
100. Johnston and Browne, p. 265.
101. Ross, pp. 14-15.
102. Johnston and Browne, pp. 268-269.
103. Pendleton, p. 144.

104. Johnston and Browne, p. 271.
105. Johnston and Browne, p. 272.
106. Johnston and Browne, p. 273.
107. Johnston and Browne, pp. 273-274.
108. Phillips, p. 345.
109. Johnston and Browne, p. 277.
110. Phillips, p. 346.
111. Johnston and Browne, p. 279.
112. Johnston and Browne, p. 284.
113. Johnston and Browne, pp. 284-286.
114. Johnston and Browne, p. 286.
115. Johnston and Browne, pp. 287-288.
116. Johnston and Browne, pp. 288-289.
117. Johnston and Browne, p. 291.
118. Johnston and Browne, pp. 291-292.
119. Johnston and Browne, p. 292.
120. Johnston and Browne, p. 292.
121. Johnston and Browne, p. 293.
122. Pendleton, p. 144.
123. Johnston and Browne, p. 294.
124. Johnston and Browne, pp. 295-296.
125. Johnston and Browne, p. 299.
126. Johnston and Browne, p. 300.
127. Johnston and Browne, p. 302.
128. Johnston and Browne, p. 307.
129. Johnston and Browne, p. 308.
130. Johnston and Browne, p. 308.
131. Johnston and Browne, p. 100.
132. Johnston and Browne, p. 314.
133. Johnston and Browne, pp. 315-316.
134. Johnston and Browne, p. 316.
135. Johnston and Browne, p. 324.
136. Johnston and Browne, pp. 324-325.
137. Johnston and Browne, pp. 325-326.
138. Johnston and Browne, p. 326.
139. Johnston and Browne, p. 327.
140. Johnston and Browne, pp. 328-329.
141. Johnston and Browne, p. 330.
142. Johnston and Browne, p. 330.
143. Johnston and Browne, p. 331.
144. Johnston and Browne, p. 332.
145. Johnston and Browne, p. 335.
146. Johnston and Browne, p. 336.
147. Johnston and Browne, p. 338.
148. Johnston and Browne, pp. 6-7.
149. Johnston and Browne, pp. 341-342.
150. Johnston and Browne, pp. 344-345.
151. Johnston and Browne, p. 343.
152. Johnston and Browne, p. 344.
153. Johnston and Browne, p. 350.
154. Johnston and Browne, p. 352.
155. Johnston and Browne, p. 355.
156. Johnston and Browne, p. 357.
157. Johnston and Browne, p. 365.
158. Johnston and Browne, pp. 365-366.
159. Johnston and Browne, p. 368.
160. Pendleton, pp. 167-168.

161. Johnston and Browne, pp. 369-370.
162. Seabrook, TTAHSR, pp. 776-778.
163. Johnston and Browne, pp. 374-376.
164. Johnston and Browne, p. 376.
165. Johnston and Browne, p. 376.
166. Johnston and Browne, pp. 376-377.
167. Johnston and Browne, p. 377.
168. Johnston and Browne, pp. 377-378.
169. Judson, p. 177.
170. Johnston and Browne, pp. 378-379.
171. Johnston and Browne, p. 384.
172. Johnston and Browne, p. 385.
173. Johnston and Browne, p. 385.
174. Johnston and Browne, p. 385.
175. Johnston and Browne, pp. 385-386.
176. Johnston and Browne, pp. 386-387.
177. Johnston and Browne, p. 387.
178. Johnston and Browne, p. 391.
179. Johnston and Browne, p. 391.
180. Johnston and Browne, p. 391.
181. Johnston and Browne, p. 391.
182. Johnston and Browne, p. 392.
183. Johnston and Browne, p. 392.
184. Johnston and Browne, p. 392.
185. Johnston and Browne, p. 393.
186. Johnston and Browne, p. 393.
187. Johnston and Browne, pp. 396-397.
188. Johnston and Browne, p. 397.
189. Johnston and Browne, p. 397.
190. Johnston and Browne, p. 397.
191. Johnston and Browne, pp. 398-399.
192. Johnston and Browne, p. 399.
193. Johnston and Browne, p. 401.
194. Johnston and Browne, p. 401.
195. Johnston and Browne, p. 401.
196. Johnston and Browne, p. 402.
197. Johnston and Browne, p. 402.
198. Johnston and Browne, pp. 402-403.
199. Johnston and Browne, pp. 404-405.
200. Johnston and Browne, pp. 405-406.
201. See Johnston and Browne, p. 406. Some modern studies suggest that there were 32,230 Rebels and 28,450 Yanks on the Manassas battlefield that day, July 21, 1861.
202. Johnston and Browne, pp. 406-407.
203. Johnston and Browne, p. 407.
204. Johnston and Browne, pp. 410-411.
205. Johnston and Browne, p. 413.
206. Johnston and Browne, pp. 413-414.
207. Johnston and Browne, pp. 414-415.
208. Johnston and Browne, p. 417.
209. Johnston and Browne, pp. 417-418.
210. Johnston and Browne, p. 418.
211. See Seabrook, EYWTACWW, pp. 191-195.
212. Johnston and Browne, pp. 418-420.
213. Johnston and Browne, p. 425.
214. Johnston and Browne, pp. 425-426.
215. Johnston and Browne, p. 426.
216. Johnston and Browne, p. 427.

217. Johnston and Browne, pp. 427-428.
218. Johnston and Browne, p. 428.
219. Johnston and Browne, pp. 431-432.
220. Johnston and Browne, p. 432.
221. Johnston and Browne, pp. 432-433.
222. Johnston and Browne, p. 435.
223. Johnston and Browne, pp. 435-436.
224. Johnston and Browne, p. 436.
225. Johnston and Browne, p. 437.
226. Johnston and Browne, pp. 437-438.
227. Johnston and Browne, p. 438.
228. Johnston and Browne, pp. 438-440.
229. Johnston and Browne, p. 440.
230. Johnston and Browne, pp. 431-432.
231. Johnston and Browne, p. 441.
232. Johnston and Browne, p. 442.
233. Johnston and Browne, pp. 442-443.
234. Johnston and Browne, p. 443.
235. Johnston and Browne, p. 443.
236. Johnston and Browne, p. 444.
237. Johnston and Browne, p. 444.
238. Johnston and Browne, p. 444.
239. Johnston and Browne, pp. 444-445.
240. Johnston and Browne, p. 445.
241. Johnston and Browne, p. 447.
242. Johnston and Browne, pp. 447-448.
243. Johnston and Browne, pp. 448-449.
244. Johnston and Browne, p. 69.
245. Johnston and Browne, pp. 35-40.
246. Williams, p. 112.
247. Johnston and Browne, p. 450.
248. Johnston and Browne, p. 450.
249. Johnston and Browne, pp. 450-451.
250. Johnston and Browne, pp. 452-453.
251. Johnston and Browne, p. 454.
252. Johnston and Browne, pp. 454-455.
253. Johnston and Browne, p. 455.
254. Johnston and Browne, p. 459.
255. Johnston and Browne, p. 460.
256. Johnston and Browne, pp. 462-463.
257. Johnston and Browne, pp. 463-464.
258. Johnston and Browne, pp. 465-467.
259. Johnston and Browne, pp. 467-468.
260. Johnston and Browne, p. 468.
261. Johnston and Browne, p. 469.
262. Johnston and Browne, pp. 470-471.
263. Johnston and Browne, p. 472.
264. Johnston and Browne, pp. 472-473.
265. Johnston and Browne, pp. 473-474.
266. Johnston and Browne, pp. 474-475.
267. Seabrook, TTAHSR, pp. 82-84.
268. Pendleton, p. 259.
269. Johnston and Browne, pp. 475-476.
270. Johnston and Browne, p. 476.
271. Johnston and Browne, p. 476.
272. Johnston and Browne, pp. 482-483.
273. Johnston and Browne, p. 483.

274. Johnston and Browne, pp. 483-484.
275. See Seabrook, TTAHSR, pp. 966-1001.
276. Johnston and Browne, pp. 484-485.
277. Johnston and Browne, pp. 486-487.
278. Johnston and Browne, p. 487.
279. Seabrook, TTAHSR, pp. 86-88.
280. Avary, pp. 527-529.
281. Avary, pp. 530-531.
282. Johnston and Browne, pp. 489-490.
283. Johnston and Browne, p. 490.
284. Johnston and Browne, p. 491.
285. Johnston and Browne, p. 491.
286. Johnston and Browne, p. 491.
287. Johnston and Browne, pp. 491-492.
288. Johnston and Browne, p. 492.
289. Phillips, pp. 680-681.
290. Seabrook, TTAHSR, p. 89.
291. Johnston and Browne, p. 493.
292. Stephens was not aware that the Vikings had arrived in North America 500 years before Columbus.
293. Stewart, pp. 29-34.
294. Stewart, pp. 37-43.
295. Johnston and Browne, pp. 494-495.
296. Johnston and Browne, pp. 495-496.
297. Johnston and Browne, p. 496.
298. Johnston and Browne, p. 496.
299. Johnston and Browne, p. 497.
300. Johnston and Browne, p. 497.
301. Johnston and Browne, p. 497.
302. Johnston and Browne, p. 498.
303. Johnston and Browne, p. 500.
304. Johnston and Browne, pp. 500-501.
305. Johnston and Browne, p. 501.
306. Johnston and Browne, p. 501.
307. Johnston and Browne, p. 501.
308. Johnston and Browne, p. 505.
309. Johnston and Browne, p. 511.
310. Johnston and Browne, pp. 512-513.
311. Johnston and Browne, pp. 513-514.
312. Johnston and Browne, p. 515.
313. Johnston and Browne, p. 516.
314. Johnston and Browne, p. 516.
315. Johnston and Browne, p. 517.
316. Johnston and Browne, p. 520.
317. Johnston and Browne, p. 535.
318. Johnston and Browne, p. 543.
319. Johnston and Browne, p. 543.
320. Johnston and Browne, p. 543.
321. Johnston and Browne, p. 544.
322. Johnston and Browne, p. 545.
323. Johnston and Browne, p. 547.
324. Johnston and Browne, p. 548.
325. Johnston and Browne, p. 548.
326. Johnston and Browne, p. 551.
327. Johnston and Browne, p. 552.
328. Johnston and Browne, pp. 552, 553.
329. Seabrook, TAHSR, p. 1014.
330. Seabrook, TAHSR, p. 73.

331. Seabrook, TAHSR, pp. 75-76.
332. Seabrook, TAHSR, pp. 79-80.
333. Seabrook, TAHSR, p. 80.
334. Seabrook, TAHSR, pp. 81-82.
335. Seabrook, TAHSR, p. 103.
336. Seabrook, TAHSR, p. 145.
337. Johnston and Browne, pp. 185-186.
338. Johnston and Browne, p. 187.
339. Johnston and Browne, pp. 187-188.
340. Johnston and Browne, pp. 188-189.
341. Johnston and Browne, pp. 190-192.
342. Johnston and Browne, pp. 230, 231.
343. Pendleton, p. 104.
344. Seabrook, TAHSR, p. 41.
345. Seabrook, TAHSR, pp. 64-65.
346. Seabrook, TAHSR, p. 72.
347. Seabrook, TAHSR, p. 76.
348. Seabrook, TAHSR, pp. 76-77.
349. Seabrook, TAHSR, p. 116.
350. Seabrook, TAHSR, pp. 117-118.
351. Seabrook, TAHSR, p. 145.
352. Seabrook, TAHSR, p. 184.
353. Seabrook, TAHSR, p. 637.
354. Seabrook, TAHSR, p. 649.
355. Seabrook, TAHSR, pp. 834-835.
356. Seabrook, TAHSR, p. 927.
357. Seabrook, TAHSR, p. 104.
358. Seabrook, TAHSR, p. 117.
359. Seabrook, TAHSR, p. 120.
360. Pendleton, pp. 92-94.
361. Pendleton, p. 96.
362. Johnston and Browne, pp. 247-248.
363. Seabrook, TAHSR, p. 144.
364. Seabrook, TAHSR, p. 145.
365. Pendleton, p. 145.
366. Seabrook, TAHSR, pp. 162-163.
367. Seabrook, TAHSR, pp. 45-46.
368. Seabrook, TAHSR, p. 788.
369. Seabrook, TAHSR, p. 793.
370. Seabrook, TAHSR, pp. 342-343.
371. Seabrook, TAHSR, p. 343.
372. Seabrook, TAHSR, p. 345.
373. Seabrook, TAHSR, p. 347.
374. Seabrook, TAHSR, p. 350.
375. Seabrook, TAHSR, p. 334.
376. Seabrook, TAHSR, p. 335.
377. Seabrook, TAHSR, p. 336.
378. Seabrook, TAHSR, pp. 95-96.
379. Seabrook, TAHSR, pp. 549-550.
380. Seabrook, TAHSR, pp. 575-576.
381. Seabrook, TAHSR, p. 578.
382. Seabrook, TAHSR, pp. 578-579.
383. Seabrook, TAHSR, pp. 579-580.
384. Seabrook, TAHSR, pp. 583-584.
385. Seabrook, TAHSR, p. 96.
386. Seabrook, TAHSR, p. 619.
387. Seabrook, TAHSR, p. 697.

388. Seabrook, TAHSR, p. 310.

389. Seabrook, TAHSR, pp. 186-187.

390. Seabrook, TAHSR, p. 213.

391. Seabrook, TAHSR, p. 574.

392. Seabrook, TAHSR, p. 870.

393. Seabrook, TAHSR, p. 929.

394. Seabrook, TAHSR, p. 1023.

395. Seabrook, TAHSR, p. 75.

396. Johnston and Browne, pp. 355-357.

397. Seabrook, TAHSR, pp. 77-78.

398. Seabrook, TAHSR, pp. 78-79.

399. Seabrook, TAHSR, p. 79.

400. Seabrook, TAHSR, p. 322.

401. Seabrook, TAHSR, pp. 322-323.

402. Seabrook, TAHSR, pp. 323-324.

403. Seabrook, TAHSR, pp. 327-328.

404. Seabrook, TAHSR, pp. 328-329.

405. Seabrook, TAHSR, p. 633.

406. Seabrook, TAHSR, pp. 734-735.

407. Seabrook, TAHSR, p. 772.

408. Seabrook, TAHSR, p. 1023.

409. Pendleton, p. 66.

410. Pendleton, pp. 154-155.

411. Pendleton, pp. 159-160.

412. Pendleton, pp. 160-161.

413. Seabrook, TAHSR, p. 795.

414. Pendleton, p. 162.

415. Seabrook, TAHSR, p. 797.

416. Trent, p. 198.

417. Seabrook, TAHSR, pp. 190-191.

418. Seabrook, TAHSR, pp. 191-192.

419. Seabrook, TAHSR, p. 192.

420. Seabrook, TAHSR, pp. 192-193.

421. Seabrook, TAHSR, p. 213.

422. Seabrook, TAHSR, p. 214.

423. Seabrook, TAHSR, pp. 74-75.

424. Seabrook, TAHSR, p. 77.

425. Seabrook, TAHSR, p. 581.

426. Seabrook, TAHSR, pp. 91-92.

427. Seabrook, TAHSR, pp. 92-93.

428. Seabrook, TAHSR, pp. 94-95.

429. Seabrook, TAHSR, pp. 324-325.

430. Seabrook, TAHSR, p. 325.

431. Seabrook, TAHSR, pp. 332-333.

432. Seabrook, TAHSR, p. 352.

433. Seabrook, TAHSR, p. 352.

434. Seabrook, TAHSR, pp. 352-353.

435. Seabrook, TAHSR, pp. 360, 362.

436. Seabrook, TAHSR, pp. 372, 373.

437. Seabrook, TAHSR, p. 376.

438. Seabrook, TAHSR, p. 384.

439. Seabrook, TAHSR, pp. 385-387.

440. Seabrook, TAHSR, pp. 393, 394.

441. Seabrook, TAHSR, p. 397.

442. Seabrook, TAHSR, p. 404.

443. Seabrook, TAHSR, pp. 404-405.

444. Seabrook, TAHSR, p. 407.

445. Seabrook, TAHSR, pp. 408-409.
446. Seabrook, TAHSR, p. 415.
447. Seabrook, TAHSR, pp. 416-417.
448. Seabrook, TAHSR, p. 438.
449. Seabrook, TAHSR, p. 451.
450. Seabrook, TAHSR, pp. 478-479.
451. Seabrook, TAHSR, p. 526.
452. Seabrook, TAHSR, p. 574.
453. Seabrook, TAHSR, pp. 585-586.
454. Seabrook, TAHSR, pp. 588-589.
455. Seabrook, TAHSR, p. 597.
456. Seabrook, TAHSR, pp. 610-611.
457. Seabrook, TAHSR, p. 611.
458. Seabrook, TAHSR, pp. 612-613.
459. Seabrook, TAHSR, pp. 310-311.
460. Stephens, TRR, pp. 188-195.
461. Seabrook, TAHSR, pp. 649-650.
462. Seabrook, TAHSR, p. 795.
463. Seabrook, TAHSR, p. 802.
464. Seabrook, TAHSR, pp. 837-838.
465. Seabrook, TAHSR, pp. 888-889.
466. Seabrook, TAHSR, p. 890.
467. Seabrook, TAHSR, p. 935.
468. Seabrook, TAHSR, pp. 937-938.
469. Seabrook, TAHSR, p. 1024.
470. Seabrook, TAHSR, p. 742.
471. Seabrook, TAHSR, pp. 766-767.
472. Seabrook, TAHSR, pp. 769-771.
473. Seabrook, TAHSR, p. 803.
474. Seabrook, TAHSR, pp. 920, 921.
475. Seabrook, TAHSR, p. 924.
476. Seabrook, TAHSR, p. 931.
477. Seabrook, TAHSR, p. 962.
478. Seabrook, TAHSR, p. 998.
479. Cleveland, pp. 157-159.
480. Johnston and Browne, pp. 394, 396.
481. Seabrook, TAHSR, pp. 194-195.
482. Seabrook, TAHSR, pp. 195-196.
483. Seabrook, TAHSR, p. 197.
484. Seabrook, EYWTACWW, pp. 83-85.
485. Seabrook, TAHSR, pp. 197-198.
486. Seabrook, TAHSR, pp. 198-199.
487. Seabrook, TAHSR, pp. 200-201.
488. Seabrook, TAHSR, pp. 201-202.
489. Seabrook, TAHSR, pp. 202-203.
490. Seabrook, TAHSR, pp. 203-204.
491. Seabrook, TAHSR, pp. 247-248.
492. Seabrook, TAHSR, pp. 604-605.
493. Seabrook, TAHSR, pp. 214-216.
494. Seabrook, TAHSR, p. 823.
495. Seabrook, TAHSR, p. 72.
496. Seabrook, TAHSR, pp. 72-73.
497. Johnston and Browne, pp. 423-424.
498. Seabrook, TAHSR, pp. 230-231.
499. Seabrook, TAHSR, pp. 231-233.
500. Seabrook, TAHSR, pp. 233-236.
501. Seabrook, TAHSR, p. 250.

502. Seabrook, TAHSR, pp. 250-251.
503. Seabrook, TAHSR, pp. 251-252.
504. Seabrook, TAHSR, p. 66.
505. Seabrook, TAHSR, pp. 83-84.
506. Seabrook, TAHSR, p. 826.
507. Seabrook, TAHSR, p. 827.
508. Seabrook, TAHSR, p. 833.
509. Seabrook, TAHSR, pp. 933-934.
510. Seabrook, TAHSR, pp. 936-937.
511. Seabrook, TAHSR, p. 121.
512. Pendleton, pp. 99-100.
513. Johnston and Browne, p. 271.
514. Johnston and Browne, p. 278.
515. Johnston and Browne, p. 279.
516. Johnston and Browne, p. 280.
517. Johnston and Browne, pp. 282-283.
518. Seabrook, TAHSR, pp. 147-148.
519. Seabrook, TAHSR, pp. 148-149.
520. Seabrook, TAHSR, pp. 150-151.
521. Seabrook, TAHSR, pp. 158-160.
522. Seabrook, TAHSR, pp. 160-161.
523. Seabrook, TAHSR, pp. 161-162.
524. Seabrook, TAHSR, p. 164.
525. Seabrook, TAHSR, p. 165.
526. Seabrook, TAHSR, p. 184.
527. Seabrook, TAHSR, p. 185.
528. Seabrook, TAHSR, pp. 217-219.
529. Seabrook, TAHSR, pp. 260-261.
530. Seabrook, TAHSR, pp. 261-264.
531. Seabrook, TAHSR, pp. 613-614.
532. Seabrook, TAHSR, pp. 614-615.
533. See Seabrook, EYWTACWW, pp. 69-108.
534. Seabrook, TAHSR, pp. 620-621.
535. Seabrook, TAHSR, pp. 621-622.
536. Seabrook, TAHSR, pp. 622-623.
537. Seabrook, TAHSR, pp. 623-624.
538. Seabrook, TAHSR, p. 624.
539. Seabrook, TAHSR, pp. 624-626.
540. Seabrook, TAHSR, pp. 626-627.
541. Seabrook, TAHSR, pp. 651-653.
542. Seabrook, TAHSR, p. 653.
543. Seabrook, TAHSR, pp. 654-656.
544. Seabrook, TAHSR, pp. 656-657.
545. Seabrook, TAHSR, pp. 660-661.
546. Seabrook, TAHSR, p. 665.
547. Seabrook, TAHSR, pp. 665-666.
548. Seabrook, TAHSR, pp. 666-667.
549. Seabrook, TAHSR, pp. 667-668.
550. Johnston and Browne, p. 515.
551. Seabrook, TAHSR, p. 778.
552. Seabrook, TAHSR, p. 784.
553. Seabrook, TAHSR, p. 785.
554. Seabrook, TAHSR, p. 785.
555. Seabrook, TAHSR, p. 785.
556. Johnston and Browne, p. 397.
557. Johnston and Browne, p. 437.
558. Seabrook, TAHSR, pp. 860-861.

559. Seabrook, TAHSR, p. 779.
560. Seabrook, TAHSR, p. 782.
561. Seabrook, TAHSR, p. 783.
562. Seabrook, TAHSR, pp. 870-871.
563. Seabrook, TAHSR, pp. 872-873, 874.
564. Seabrook, TAHSR, pp. 891, 892.
565. Seabrook, TAHSR, p. 894.
566. Seabrook, TAHSR, p. 950.
567. Seabrook, EYWTACWW, passim.
568. Seabrook, L, p. 647.
569. Seabrook, L, pp. 159, 166, 243, 320, 641, 650, 662, 680, 681.
570. Seabrook, ALSV, p. 254.
571. Seabrook, TUAL, p. 91.
572. Seabrook, TAHSR, pp. 988-989.
573. Seabrook, TAHSR, pp. 989-990.
574. Seabrook, TAHSR, p. 991. Lincoln's phrase is commonly translated as "Let 'em root, pig, or perish!"
575. Seabrook, TAHSR, p. 958.
576. Seabrook, TAHSR, p. 62.
577. Seabrook, TAHSR, p. 62.
578. Seabrook, TAHSR, p. 66.
579. Seabrook, TAHSR, pp. 627-628, 630.
580. Seabrook, TAHSR, p. 632.
581. Seabrook, TAHSR, pp. 206-208.
582. Seabrook, TAHSR, p. 208.
583. Seabrook, TAHSR, p. 210.
584. Seabrook, TAHSR, pp. 211-212.
585. Seabrook, TAHSR, pp. 227-228.
586. Seabrook, TAHSR, p. 229.
587. Seabrook, TAHSR, pp. 312-314.
588. Seabrook, TAHSR, pp. 316-317.
589. Seabrook, TAHSR, p. 329.
590. Seabrook, TAHSR, p. 838.
591. Seabrook, TAHSR, pp. 845-847.
592. Seabrook, TAHSR, p. 863.
593. Seabrook, TAHSR, p. 864.
594. Seabrook, TAHSR, p. 866.
595. Seabrook, TAHSR, p. 868.
596. Seabrook, TAHSR, p. 868.
597. Seabrook, TAHSR, pp. 869-870.
598. Seabrook, TAHSR, pp. 876, 877.
599. Seabrook, TAHSR, pp. 878-879.
600. Seabrook, TAHSR, pp. 916, 917.
601. Seabrook, TAHSR, p. 918.
602. Seabrook, TAHSR, p. 34.
603. Johnston and Browne, pp. 280-282.
604. Seabrook, TAHSR, pp. 297-298.
605. Seabrook, TAHSR, p. 298.
606. Seabrook, TAHSR, pp. 299-300.
607. Seabrook, TAHSR, pp. 300-301.
608. Seabrook, TAHSR, p. 907.
609. Seabrook, TAHSR, p. 928.
610. Seabrook, TAHSR, p. 1000.
611. Seabrook, TAHSR, p. 40.
612. Seabrook, TAHSR, pp. 216-217.
613. Seabrook, TAHSR, p. 907.
614. Seabrook, TAHSR, pp. 924-926.
615. Seabrook, TAHSR, pp. 268-269.

616. Seabrook, TAHSR, p. 87.

617. Seabrook, TAHSR, p. 87.

618. Seabrook, TAHSR, pp. 252-254.

619. Seabrook, TAHSR, pp. 254-255.

620. Seabrook, TAHSR, p. 255.

621. Seabrook, TAHSR, p. 255.

622. Seabrook, TAHSR, pp. 255-256.

623. Seabrook, TAHSR, p. 265.

624. Seabrook, TAHSR, pp. 266-267.

625. Seabrook, TAHSR, pp. 89-90.

626. Seabrook, TAHSR, pp. 681-682.

627. Seabrook, TAHSR, pp. 1014-1015.

628. Seabrook, TAHSR, p. 1019.

629. Seabrook, TAHSR, p. 1021.

630. Johnston and Browne, pp. 624-629.

631. Cleveland, pp. 225-226.

632. Seabrook, TAHSR, pp. 297-298.

633. Seabrook, TAHSR, p. 88.

634. Seabrook, TAHSR, pp. 88-89.

635. Seabrook, TAHSR, p. 89.

636. Seabrook, TAHSR, p. 97.

637. Seabrook, TAHSR, pp. 97-98.

638. Seabrook, TAHSR, pp. 1007-1009.

639. Seabrook, TAHSR, pp. 1009-1011.

640. Seabrook, TAHSR, pp. 1012-1013.

641. Seabrook, TAHSR, pp. 1013-1014.

642. Seabrook, TAHSR, p. 1015.

643. Seabrook, TAHSR, p. 1018.

644. Seabrook, TAHSR, p. 1022.

645. Seabrook, TAHSR, p. 1022.

646. Seabrook, TAHSR, p. 1025.

647. Seabrook, TAHSR, p. 301.

648. Johnston and Browne, pp. 522-527.

649. Johnston and Browne, p. 32.

650. Pendleton, p. 38.

651. Cleveland, pp. 52-53.

652. Johnston and Browne, pp. 136-137.

653. Knight, pp. 64-65.

654. Cleveland, p. 58.

655. Pendleton, p. 40.

656. Pendleton, p. 42.

657. Pendleton, p. 68.

658. Pendleton, p. 68.

659. Johnston and Browne, pp. 232-234.

660. Pendleton, pp. 68-69.

661. Pendleton, p. 70.

662. Johnston and Browne, p. 348.

663. Knight, p. 78.

664. Pendleton, pp. 70-71.

665. Johnston and Browne, pp. 453-454.

666. Johnston and Browne, pp. 544-545.

667. Pendleton, pp. 378-379.

668. Trent, pp. 250-251.

669. Pendleton, p. 72.

670. Pendleton, pp. 381-382.

671. Johnston and Browne, pp. 531-532.

672. Johnston and Browne, pp. 532-533.

673. Pendleton, pp. 100-101.
674. Pendleton, pp. 151-152.
675. Pendleton, p. 345.
676. Pendleton, p. 345.
677. Johnston and Browne, p. 555.
678. Pendleton, p. 384.
679. Pendleton, p. 386.
680. Johnston and Browne, pp. 521-522.
681. Johnston and Browne, p. 534.
682. Waddell, pp. 187-188.
683. Johnston and Browne, pp. 534-535.
684. Johnston and Browne, pp. 630-632.
685. Johnston and Browne, pp. 553-554.
686. Trent, p. 205.
687. Williams, pp. 118-119.
688. Pendleton, pp. 389-392.
689. Knight, pp. 84-90.

Bibliography

Avary, Myrta Lockett. *Recollections of Alexander H. Stephens: His Diary Kept When A Prisoner at Fort Warren, Boston Harbor, 1865*. New York, NY: Doubleday, Page and Co., 1910.

Beecher, Henry Ward. *Patriotic Addresses in America and England, From 1850 to 1885, on Slavery, the Civil War, and the Development of Civil Liberty in the United States*. New York, NY: Fords, Howard, and Hulbert, 1891.

Bennett, Lerone. *Forced into Glory: Abraham Lincoln's White Dream*. Chicago, IL: Johnson Publishing Co., 2000.

Cleveland, Henry. *Alexander H. Stephens, in Public and Private*. Philadelphia, PA: National Publishing Co., 1866.

Congressional Globe (pub.). *Speech of Hon. Alexander H. Stephens, of Georgia, on the Kansas Election*. Washington, D.C., 1856.

Davis, Jefferson. *The Rise and Fall of the Confederate Government*. 2 vols. New York, NY: D. Appleton and Co., 1881.

——. *A Short History of the Confederate States of America*. New York, NY: Belford, 1890.

Gideon, J. and G. S. (printers). *Speech of Mr. Stephens, of Georgia, on the War and Taxation*. N.p., 1848.

Herskovits, Melville J. *The Myth of the Negro Past*. 1941. Boston, MA: Beacon Press, 1958 ed.

Hill, Charles E. *Leading American Treaties*. New York, NY: Macmillan Co., 1922.

Johnson, Ludwell H. *North Against South: The American Iliad 1848-1877*. 1978. Columbia, SC: Foundation for American Education, 1993 ed.

Johnston, Richard Malcolm, and William Hand Browne. *Life of Alexander H. Stephens*. Philadelphia, PA: J. B. Lippincott and Co., 1884.

Judson, Levi Carroll. *A Biography of the Signers of the Declaration of Independence and of Washington and Patrick Henry*. Philadelphia, PA: J. Dobson, and Thomas, Cowperthwait and Co., 1839.

Katcher, Philip. *The Civil War Source Book*. 1992. New York, NY: Facts On File, 1995 ed.

ORA (full title: *The War of the Rebellion: A Compilation of the Official Records of the Union and Confederate Armies*. (Multiple volumes.) Washington, D.C.: Government Printing Office, 1880.

Owsley, Frank Lawrence. *King Cotton Diplomacy: Foreign Relations of the Confederate States of America*. 1931. Chicago, IL: University of Chicago Press, 1959 ed.

Pendleton, Louis. *Alexander H. Stephens*. Philadelphia, PA: George W. Jacobs and Co., 1907.

Phillips, Ulrich Bonnell (ed.). *The Correspondence of Robert Toombs, Alexander H. Stephens, and Howell Cobb* (from the "Annual Report of the American Historical Association for the Year 1911"). Vol. 2. Washington, D.C.: N.p., 1913.

Pollard, Edward A. *Southern History of the War*. 2 vols. in 1. New York, NY: Charles B.

Richardson, 1866.

——. *The Lost Cause*. 1867. Chicago, IL: E. B. Treat, 1890 ed.

——. *The Lost Cause Regained*. New York, NY: G. W. Carlton and Co., 1868.

——. *Life of Jefferson Davis, With a Secret History of the Southern Confederacy, Gathered "Behind the Scenes in Richmond."* Philadelphia, PA: National Publishing Co., 1869.

Rawle, William. *A View of the Constitution of the United States of America*. Philadelphia, PA: Philip H. Nicklin, 1829.

Ross, D. Barton. *A Souther Speaker: Containing Selections From the Orations, Addresses and Writings of the Best-Known Southern Orators, Southern Statesmen and Southern Authors*. New York, NY: Hinds, Noble and Eldredge, 1901.

Rutherford, Mildred Lewis. *A True Estimate of Abraham Lincoln and Vindication of the South*. N.p., n.d.

——. *Truths of History: A Historical Perspective of the Civil War From the Southern Viewpoint*. Confederate Reprint Co., 1920.

——. *The South Must Have Her Rightful Place In History*. Athens, GA, 1923.

Seabrook, Lochlainn. *Britannia Rules: Goddess-Worship in Ancient Anglo-Celtic Society - An Academic Look at the United Kingdom's Matricentric Spiritual Past*. 1999. Franklin, TN: Sea Raven Press, 2007 ed.

——. *The Caudills: An Etymological, Ethnological, and Genealogical Study - Exploring the Name and National Origins of a European-American Family*. 2003. Franklin, TN: Sea Raven Press, 2010 ed.

——. *Carnton Plantation Ghost Stories: True Tales of the Unexplained From Tennessee's Most Haunted Civil War House!* 2005. Franklin, TN: Sea Raven Press, 2010 ed.

——. *Nathan Bedford Forrest: Southern Hero, American Patriot: Honoring a Confederate Hero and the Old South*. 2007. Franklin, TN: Sea Raven Press, 2010 ed.

——. *Abraham Lincoln: The Southern View - Demythologizing America's Sixteenth President*. 2007. Franklin, TN: Sea Raven Press, 2013 ed.

——. *The McGavocks of Carnton Plantation: A Southern History - Celebrating One of Dixie's Most Noble Confederate Families and Their Tennessee Home*. 2008. Franklin, TN: Sea Raven Press, 2011 ed.

——. *A Rebel Born: A Defense of Nathan Bedford Forrest, Confederate General, American Legend*. Franklin, TN: Sea Raven Press, 2010.

——. *Everything You Were Taught About the Civil War is Wrong, Ask a Southerner!* 2010. Franklin, TN: Sea Raven Press, 2012 ed.

——. *The Quotable Jefferson Davis: Selections From the Writings and Speeches of the Confederacy's First President*. Franklin, TN: Sea Raven Press, 2011 Sesquicentennial Civil War Edition.

——. *The Quotable Robert E. Lee: Selections From the Writings and Speeches of the South's Most Beloved Civil War General*. Franklin, TN: Sea Raven Press, 2011 Sesquicentennial Civil War Edition.

——. *The Unquotable Abraham Lincoln: The President's Quotes They Don't Want You to Know!* Franklin, TN: Sea Raven Press, 2011 Sesquicentennial Civil War Edition.

——. *Lincolnology: The Real Abraham Lincoln Revealed in His Own Words - A Study of Lincoln's Suppressed, Misinterpreted, and Forgotten Writings and Speeches*. Franklin, TN: Sea Raven Press, 2011 Sesquicentennial Civil War Edition.

——. *The Old Rebel: Robert E. Lee As He Was Seen By His Contemporaries*. Franklin, TN: Sea Raven Press, 2012 Sesquicentennial Civil War Edition.

——. *The Quotable Stonewall Jackson: Selections From the Writings and Speeches of the South's Most Famous General*. Franklin, TN: Sea Raven Press, 2012 Sesquicentennial Civil War

Edition.

——. *Honest Jeff and Dishonest Abe: A Southern Children's Guide to the Civil War*. Franklin, TN: Sea Raven Press, 2012 Sesquicentennial Civil War Edition.

——. *Give 'Em Hell Boys! The Complete Military Correspondence of Nathan Bedford Forrest*. Franklin, TN: Sea Raven Press, 2012 Sesquicentennial Civil War Edition.

——. *The Constitution of the Confederate States of America Explained: A Clause-by-Clause Study of the South's Magna Carta*. Franklin, TN: Sea Raven Press, 2012 Sesquicentennial Civil War Edition.

——. *The Great Impersonator! 99 Reasons to Dislike Abraham Lincoln*. Franklin, TN: Sea Raven Press, 2012 Sesquicentennial Civil War Edition.

——. *Forrest! 99 Reasons to Love Nathan Bedford Forrest*. Franklin, TN: Sea Raven Press, 2012 Sesquicentennial Civil War Edition.

——. *The Quotable Nathan Bedford Forrest: Selections From the Writings and Speeches of the Confederacy's Most Brilliant Cavalryman*. Franklin, TN: Sea Raven Press, 2012 Sesquicentennial Civil War Edition.

——. *Encyclopedia of the Battle of Franklin: A Comprehensive Guide to the Conflict That Changed the Civil War*. Franklin, TN: Sea Raven Press, 2012 Sesquicentennial Civil War Edition.

——. *The Alexander H. Stephens Reader: Excerpts From the Works of a Confederate Founding Father*. Franklin, TN: Sea Raven Press, 2013 Sesquicentennial Civil War Edition.

——. *Saddle, Sword, and Gun: A Biography of Nathan Bedford Forrest For Teens*. Franklin, TN: Sea Raven Press, 2013 Sesquicentennial Civil War Edition.

Simpson, Lewis P. (ed.). *I'll Take My Stand: The South and the Agrarian Tradition*. 1930. Baton Rouge, LA: Louisiana State University Press, 1977 ed.

Stephens, Alexander Hamilton. *A Constitutional View of the Late War Between the States; Its Causes, Character, Conduct and Results—Vol. 1*. Philadelphia, PA: National Publishing Co., 1868.

——. *A Constitutional View of the Late War Between the States; Its Causes, Character, Conduct and Results—Vol. 2*. Philadelphia, PA: National Publishing Co., 1870.

——. *The Reviewers Reviewed*. New York, NY: D. Appleton and Co., 1872.

——. *A Compendium of the History of the United States: From the Earliest Settlements to 1872*. New York, NY: E. J. Hale and Son, 1874.

Stewart, James A. *Conservative Views: The Government of the United States, What Is It?* Atlanta, Georgia: Franklin Printing House, 1869.

Trent, William Peterfield. *Southern Statesmen of the Old Régime: Washington, Jefferson, Randolph, Calhoun, Stephens, Toombs, and Jefferson Davis*. New York, NY: Thomas Y. Crowell and Co., 1897.

Trimpi, Helen P. *Crimson Confederates: Harvard Men Who Fought for the South*. Knoxville, TN: University of Tennessee Press, 21010.

Waddell, James D. (ed.). *Biographical Sketch of Linton Stephens*. Atlanta, GA: Dodson and Scott, 1877.

Warner, Ezra J. *Generals in Gray: Lives of the Confederate Commanders*. 1959. Baton Rouge, LA: Louisiana State University Press, 1989 ed.

——. *Generals in Blue: Lives of the Union Commanders*. 1964. Baton Rouge, LA: Louisiana State University Press, 2006 ed.

Williams, Sherman. *Some Successful Americans*. Boston, MA: Ginn and Co., 1904.

𝕰pitaph

"The South is my home—my fatherland. There sleep the ashes of my sires; there are my hopes and prospects; with her my fortunes are cast; her fate is my fate, and her destiny my destiny."

Alexander Hamilton Stephens, 1845

~ Meet the Author ~

LOCHLAINN SEABROOK, winner of the Jefferson Davis Historical Gold Medal for his "masterpiece," *A Rebel Born: A Defense of Nathan Bedford Forrest*, is an unreconstructed Southern historian, award-winning author, Civil War scholar, and traditional Southern Agrarian of Scottish, English, Irish, Welsh, German, and Italian extraction. An encyclopedist, lexicographer, anthologist, musician, artist, graphic designer, genealogist, and photographer, as well as an award-winning poet, songwriter, and screenwriter, he has a thirty year background in historical nonfiction writing and is a member of the Sons of Confederate Veterans, the Civil War Trust, and the Grange.

Due to similarities in their writing styles, ideas, and literary works, Seabrook is referred to as the "American ROBERT GRAVES," after his cousin, the prolific English writer, historian, mythographer, poet, and author of the classic tomes *The White Goddess* and *The Greek Myths*.

The grandson of an Appalachian coal-mining family, Seabrook is a seventh-generation Kentuckian, co-chair of the Jent/Gent Family Committee (Kentucky), founder and director of the Blakeney Family Tree Project, and a board member of the Friends of Colonel Benjamin E. Caudill. Seabrook's literary works have been endorsed by leading authorities, museum curators, award-winning historians, bestselling authors, celebrities, noted scientists, TV show hosts, well respected educators, renown military artists, esteemed Southern organizations, and distinguished academicians from around the world.

(Illustration © Tracy Latham)

As a professional writer Seabrook has authored some thirty popular adult books specializing in the following topics: the American Civil War, pro-South studies, Confederate biographies, anthologies, and histories, genealogical monographs, theology, thealogy, Jesus and the Bible, self-help, healing, health, anthropology, ghost stories, the paranormal, family histories, military encyclopedias, etymological dictionaries, ufology, social issues, comparative analysis of the origins of Christmas, and cross-cultural studies of the family and marriage.

Seabrook's eight children's books include a Southern children's guide to the Civil War, a dictionary of religion and myth, a rewriting of the King Arthur legend (which reinstates the original pre-Christian motifs), two bedtime stories for preschoolers, a naturalist's guidebook to owls, a worldwide look at the family, and an examination of the Near-Death Experience.

Of blue-blooded Southern stock through his Kentucky, Tennessee, Virginia, West Virginia, and North Carolina ancestors, he is a direct descendant of European royalty via his 6th great-grandfather, the EARL OF OXFORD, after which London's famous Harley Street is named. Among his celebrated male Celtic ancestors is ROBERT THE BRUCE, King of Scotland, Seabrook's 22nd great-grandfather. The 21st great-grandson of EDWARD I "LONGSHANKS" PLANTAGENET), King of England, Seabrook is a thirteenth-generation Southerner through his descent from the colonists of Jamestown, Virginia (1607).

Seabrook is related to numerous Confederate icons and other 19th-Century luminaries, among them: ROBERT E. LEE, NATHAN BEDFORD FORREST, STONEWALL JACKSON, ALEXANDER H. STEPHENS, JESSE JAMES, JEB STUART, JOHN HUNT MORGAN, NATHANIEL F. CHEAIRS, EDMUND W. RUCKER, STATES RIGHTS GIST, RICHARD TAYLOR, JOHN S. MOSBY, JOHN B. WOMACK, PIERRE G. T. BEAUREGARD, JOHN BELL HOOD, GEORGE W. GORDON, THEODRICK "TOD" CARTER, ABRAM POINDEXTER MAURY, WILLIAM GILES HARDING, JOHN W. MCGAVOCK, JOHN LAWTON SEABROOK, and MARY CHESNUT.

(Photo © Lochlainn Seabrook)

A cousin The 2nd, 3rd, and 4th great-grandson of dozens of Confederate soldiers, one of his closest connections to the War for Southern Independence is through his 3rd great-grandfather, ELIAS JENT, SR., who fought for the Confederacy in the Thirteenth Cavalry Kentucky under Seabrook's 2nd cousin, Colonel BENJAMIN E. CAUDILL. The Thirteenth, also known as "Caudill's Army," fought in numerous conflicts, including the Battles of Saltville, Gladsville, Mill Cliff, Poor Fork, Whitesburg, and Leatherwood.

Born with music in his blood, Seabrook is an award-winning, multi-genre, BMI-Nashville songwriter and lyricist who has composed some 3,000 songs (250 albums), and whose original music has been heard on TV and radio worldwide. In 2012 his poignant ballad *That's My Girl*—recorded and produced by JOHN CARTER CASH (son of JOHNNY CASH and executive producer of the five-time Academy Award-winning film *Walk the Line*)—was selected for inclusion in the film *Cowgirls N' Angels*, starring BAILEE MADISON, JACKSON RATHBONE, and JAMES CROMWELL.

A musician, producer, multi-instrumentalist, and renown performer—whose keyboard work has been variously compared to pianists from HARGUS ROBBINS and VINCE GUARALDI to ELTON JOHN and LEONARD BERNSTEIN—Seabrook has opened for groups such as the EARL SCRUGGS REVIEW, TED NUGENT, and BOB SEGER, and has performed privately for such public figures as PRESIDENT RONALD REAGAN, BURT REYNOLDS, and SENATOR EDWARD W. BROOKE.

Seabrook's cousins in the entertainment business include: JOHNNY CASH, ELVIS PRESLEY, BILLY RAY and MILEY CYRUS, PATTY LOVELESS, TIM MCGRAW, LEE ANN WOMACK, DOLLY PARTON, REESE WITHERSPOON, PAT BOONE, NAOMI, WYNONNA, and ASHLEY JUDD, RICKY SKAGGS, the SUNSHINE SISTERS, TOM CRUISE, MARTHA CARSON, and CHET ATKINS.

Seabrook lives with his wife and family in historic Middle Tennessee, the heart of the Confederacy, where his conservative Southern ancestors fought valiantly against liberal Lincoln and the progressive North in defense of Jeffersonianism, constitutional government, and personal liberty.

❧ Meet the Cover Artist ❧

CHRISTOPHER ROMMEL is an award-winning Master Caricaturist and freelance illustrator who has been drawing ever since he was old enough to hold a pencil. He is the founder and owner of Exaggerated Entertainment, through which he serves as a party caricaturist for all types of events, including holiday parties, company picnics, birthdays, anniversaries, bar/bat mitzvahs, confirmations, wedding receptions, reunions, banquets, proms, student lock-ins, graduations, open houses, grand openings, trade shows, conventions, conferences, concerts, fund raisers, and boat cruises.

(Illustration © Chris Rommel)

A member of the International Society of Caricature Artists, Rommel won the organization's prestigious "Golden Nosey" award (the Oscar of the caricature industry) for Caricaturist of the Year in 2006. The recipient of numerous other awards for such likenesses as Donald Trump and Christopher Reeve, he is also a nationally published illustrator whose work has appeared in a variety of periodicals and publications, such as *Playboy*, *FHM*, *Flex*, *Exaggerated Features*, and Sea Raven Press.

Rommel launched his career as a professional caricature artist in 1998 when he applied for a summer job at Valleyfair Amusement Park in Shakopee, Minnesota. While employed there he came under the tutelage of renowned *MAD Magazine* artist Tom Richmond. His enrollment at the Academy of Art University in San Francisco, California, as well as two Wisconsin state universities, educated him in a variety of art concentrations. He earned a Bachelor of Fine Arts degree from the University of Wisconsin-Eau Claire in 1999.

Since then, Rommel has drawn some 50,000 live caricatures of people at amusement parks, state fairs, shopping malls, corporate events and private parties. Among his better known clients are Harley-Davidson, Applebee's, Bank of America, Pillsbury, Mars Chocolate, Wells Fargo, First Bank and Trust, Hormel Foods, Petco, Absolut Vodka, Boston Scientific, Walmart and The Home Depot.

Rommel currently resides in Eau Claire, Wisconsin, where he continues to develop both his craft and his well deserved reputation as one of America's premier artists.

ChrisRommel.com

If you enjoyed Mr. Seabrook's *The Quotable Alexander H. Stephens* you will enjoy his in-depth companion work:

THE ALEXANDER H. STEPHENS READER:
EXCERPTS FROM THE WORKS OF A CONFEDERATE FOUNDING FATHER

Available from Sea Raven Press and wherever fine books are sold.

CPSIA information can be obtained
at www.ICGtesting.com
Printed in the USA
BVOW08s1654061217
502054BV00001B/45/P